Introduction to Business and Professional Development

BUSN 1101

UNC Charlotte

| PEARSON COLLECTIONS |

2   16

Attention bookstores: For permission to return any unsold stock, contact us at pe-uscustomreturns@pearson.com

Pearson Learning Solutions, 501 Boylston Street, Suite 900, Boston, MA 02116

A Pearson Education Company
www.pearsoned.com

ISBN 10: 1323522492

ISBN 13: 9781323522493

Printed in the USA

Table of Contents

The U.S. Business Environment

From Chapter 1 of *Business Essentials*, Eleventh Edition. Ronald J. Ebert, Ricky W. Griffin. Copyright © 2017 by Pearson Education, Inc. All rights reserved.

The U.S. Business Environment

The best way to make money is to sell products that

consumers want or need. While this

sounds simple,

only a few strike gold.

After reading this chapter, you should be able to:

1 **Define** the nature of U.S. business, describe the external environments of business, and discuss how these environments affect the success or failure of organizations.

2 **Describe** the different types of global economic systems according to the means by which they control the factors of production.

3 **Show** how markets, demand, and supply affect resource distribution in the United States, identify the elements of private enterprise, and explain the various degrees of competition in the U.S. economic system.

4 **Explain** the importance of the economic environment to business and identify the factors used to evaluate the performance of an economic system.

What Goes Up ... Can also Come Down!

What did you pay for the last bottle of water or cup of coffee you bought? If you paid, say $1.50, you likely paid the same price the last time you bought one and will pay the next time as well. Although the price may eventually go up, increases generally happen only occasionally and then remain the same for a while. Now, how much did you pay for a gallon of gasoline the last time you filled your tank? How did that price compare to the time before? How about the time before that? Chances are, each time you fill up, the price is a little different—sometimes a few cents more, sometimes a few cents less. But sometimes the prices jump—or drop—substantially more than just a few cents. In the year 2008 alone, we saw the highest monthly average ever at $4.11 per gallon, followed by prices plummeting to only $1.75 per gallon by December of the same year. Prices peaked around $4.00 per gallon in 2011, but fell to $2.63 by the end of 2014.

Why have gasoline prices gone up and down so dramatically, and why do prices change from one day to the next? In general, gas prices fluctuate as a result of four forces: supply, demand, global trends, and uncertainty. In the past, gas prices generally increased only when the supply was reduced. But the circumstances underlying the increases from 2004 to 2012 were much more complex. In the early part of the past decade, U.S. gasoline producers were unable to supply enough for U.S. demand and much of the gasoline sold here was purchased on the world market. However, more recently, the United States has sharply increased their production capabilities and has even begun exporting gasoline to other countries. Second, demand for gasoline in the United States has continued to rise as a result of a growing population, the continued popularity of large gas-guzzling vehicles, and a strong demand for other petroleum-based products.

Another major piece of the puzzle has been a surging global economy that, until recently, caused a higher demand for oil and gasoline. China, in particular, has become a major consumer of petroleum, passing Japan in 2005 to trail only the United States in total consumption. The global recession that started in 2008, however, reduced demand in most industrialized countries. The recession, in fact, probably played a role in the dip in prices in 2009 just as the gradual recovery that started in 2010 helped spur higher prices once again. Political turmoil in the Middle East also played a major role. As the United States ramped up

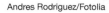
Andres Rodriguez/Fotolia

what's in it for me?

The forces that have caused oil prices to fluctuate wildly reflect both the opportunities and challenges you'll find in today's business world. All businesses are subject to the influences of economic forces. But these same economic forces also provide astute managers and entrepreneurs with opportunities for profits and growth. By understanding these economic forces and how they interact, you'll be better able to (1) appreciate how managers must contend with the challenges and opportunities resulting from economic forces from the standpoint of an employee and a manager or business owner, and (2) understand why prices fluctuate from the perspective of a consumer. You should have a deeper appreciation of the environment in which managers work and a better understanding of why the prices you pay for goods and services go up and down.

In this chapter, we'll first introduce the concepts of profit and loss and then describe the external environments of businesses. As we will see, the domestic business environment, the global business environment, and the technological, political-legal, sociocultural, and economic environments are also important. Next, we'll look at some basic elements of economic systems and describe the economics of market systems. We'll also introduce and discuss several indicators that are used to gauge the vitality of our domestic economic system.

production of gasoline, tapping into new sources, a sharp increase in supply resulted in steadily decreasing prices over the last half of 2014. By January 2015, a gallon of gasoline cost $2.21, down 34 percent from the same month in 2014.[1]

These price fluctuations have also led to a wide array of related consequences. Based on high prices for gasoline from 2011 through 2013, automobile manufacturers stepped up their commitment to making more fuel-efficient cars even as automobile sales plummeted during the recent recession. Refiners posted record profits. (In fact, some critics charged that the energy companies were guilty of price gouging.) Even local police officers were kept busy combating a surge in gasoline theft, yet another indication that gas was becoming an increasingly valuable commodity!

While surging oil and gas prices occupied the thoughts of consumers, government officials began to worry about the bigger picture. The surging global demand for gasoline has forced experts to face a stark reality—the global supply of petroleum will soon peak and then slowly begin to decline. Although no one can pinpoint when this will happen, virtually all the experts agree that it will happen well before the middle of this century.

So then what? The laws of supply and demand will continue to work, but perhaps in different ways. First, just because the supply of oil will decline doesn't mean that it will disappear immediately. Although there may be gradual reductions in supply, oil and gas will remain available for at least another century—but at prices that may make those of today seem like a bargain. New technology may also allow businesses to extract petroleum from locations that are not currently accessible, such as from the deepest areas under the oceans.

Second, and more significant, businesses everywhere will have market incentives to figure out how to replace today's dependence on oil and gas with non-petroleum alternatives. For instance, automobile manufacturers are already seeing increased demand for their hybrid products, which are cars and trucks that use a combination of gasoline and electrical power. Completely electric vehicles are also gaining ground, with virtually every major manufacturer, including Chevrolet, BMW, and Cadillac, having at least one commercially available completely electric car. In addition, firms that can produce alternative sources of energy will spring up, and those who find viable answers will prosper; companies that can figure out how to replace today's plastic products with new products that don't rely on petroleum will also find willing buyers.[2] (After studying the content in this chapter, you should be able to answer the set of discussion questions found at the end of the chapter.)

Business, Profit, and the External Environment

OBJECTIVE 1
Define

the nature of U.S. business, describe the external environments of business, and discuss how these environments affect the success or failure of organizations.

What do you think of when you hear the word *business*? Does it conjure up images of large, successful corporations, such as Apple and Google? Or of once-great but now struggling companies like Sears and Yahoo!? Do you think of multinational giants such as Toyota or Nestle? Are you reminded of smaller firms, such as your local supermarket or favorite chain restaurant? Or do you think of even smaller family-owned operations, such as your neighborhood pizzeria or the florist down the street?

Business and Profit

Business *organization that provides goods or services to earn profits*

Profits *difference between a business's revenues and its expenses*

All these organizations are **businesses**, organizations that provide goods or services that are then sold to earn profits. Indeed, the prospect of earning **profits**, the difference between a business's revenues and its expenses, is what encourages people to open and expand businesses. After all, profits are the rewards owners get for risking their money and time. The right to pursue profits distinguishes a business from those organizations—such as most universities, hospitals, and government agencies—that run in much the same way but that generally don't seek profits.[3]

Consumer Choice and Demand In a capitalistic system, such as that in the United States, businesses exist to earn profits for owners; within certain broad constraints, an owner is free to set up a new business, grow that business, sell it, or even shut it down. But consumers also have freedom of choice. In choosing how to pursue profits, businesses must take into account what consumers want or need. No matter how efficient a business is, it won't survive if there is no demand for its goods or services. Neither a snowblower shop in Florida nor a beach umbrella store in Alaska is likely to do well.

Opportunity and Enterprise If enterprising businesspeople can spot a promising opportunity and then develop a good plan for capitalizing on it, they can succeed. For example, although large retailers such as Circuit City and Linens-N-Things closed their doors in 2009, other firms profited from these closings by handling the inventory liquidations of those failed retailers. And as oil prices have dropped, gasoline producers like Chevron and Shell have seen their profits begin to decline. But food distributors like Sysco and delivery services such as UPS are seeing their expenses drop and hence their profits start to grow. In general, then, business opportunity involves goods or services that consumers need or want— especially if no one else is supplying them or if existing businesses are doing so inefficiently or incompletely.

The Benefits of Business So what are the benefits of businesses? Businesses produce most of the goods and services we consume, and they employ most working people. They create most innovations and provide a vast range of opportunities for new businesses, which serve as their suppliers. A healthy business climate also contributes to the quality of life and standard of living of people in a society. Business profits enhance the personal incomes of millions of owners and stockholders, and business taxes help to support governments at all levels. Many businesses support charities and provide community leadership. However, some businesses also harm the Earth's environment, and their decision makers sometimes resort to unacceptable practices for their own personal benefit.

We now turn our attention to the environment in which businesses operate. Understanding the environment provides a foundation for our subsequent discussions dealing with economic forces that play a major role in the success and failure of businesses everywhere.

The External Environments of Business

All businesses, regardless of their size, location, or mission, operate within a larger external environment. This **external environment** consists of everything outside an organization's boundaries that might affect it. (Businesses also have an *internal environment*, more commonly called *corporate culture*.) Not surprisingly, the external environment plays a major role in determining the success or failure of any organization. Managers must, therefore, have a complete and accurate understanding of their environment and then strive to operate and compete within it. Businesses can also influence their environments. Figure 1 shows the major dimensions and elements of the external environment as it affects businesses today. As you can see, these include the *domestic business environment*, the *global business environment*, the *technological environment*, the *political-legal environment*, the *sociocultural environment*, and the *economic environment*.

External Environment *everything outside an organization's boundaries that might affect it*

Domestic Business Environment The **domestic business environment** refers to the environment in which a firm conducts its operations and

Domestic Business Environment *the environment in which a firm conducts its operations and derives its revenues*

finding a better way

The B Team

As a general rule, we would say that the goal of every business is to achieve and maximize profits. The executives of the organization also have a responsibility to shareholders and investors to seek profits, making this their goal in decision making. On the other hand, many nonprofit organizations, such as the Red Cross, American Cancer Society, and the Appalachian Heritage Museum, work to serve the public good or solve social problems. B (or Benefit) Corporations fall in the space between the two.

B corporations are businesses—each is an organization that seeks to earn profits—but performance is measured not only by profits or growth in stock price but also by the organization's impact on society and the environment. Portland, Oregon-based EcoZoom is a B corporation that began in 2011 with a goal of generating a profit as well as concern for the health of their customers, economic development, and environmental awareness. Founder Ben West left his successful career in the transportation industry to earn an MBA. One of his professors was on the board of directors of Aprovecho, a nonprofit that designed cookstoves for use in developing countries. Although Aprovecho had developed great technology, they didn't know how to get the product to the market. This is where EcoZoom entered the story. EcoZoom manufactures the stoves in China and sells them in the United States for camping and other outdoor uses.[4] However, their primary market is developing countries, where existing stove technology had serious health impacts. Using traditional stoves, women and children were exposed to toxic smoke that made them more susceptible to acute illnesses such as pneumonia, lung cancer, and heart disease.[5]

EcoZoom produces several models of low-emissions cookstoves, each very energy efficient. Because the cookstoves

EcoZoom

reduce fuel use and cooking time, women have more time to spend with their families and on other tasks, such as maintaining their gardens. Their stoves can burn traditional biomass fuels, such as corncobs and cow dung, as well as wood and charcoal. The company also tries to impact the larger economic environment by selling their products through local distributors in countries such as Somalia, Kenya, and Rwanda. In the future, they hope to establish production facilities in these countries to expand their economic impact.[6] It may just be that EcoZoom, and other B corporations, have found a better way.

derives its revenues. In general, businesses seek to be close to their customers, to establish strong relationships with their suppliers, and to distinguish themselves from their competitors. Take Urban Outfitters, for example. The firm initially located its stores near urban college campuses; it now locates stores in other, often more upscale, areas as well. The company also has a strong network of suppliers and is itself a wholesale supplier to other retailers through its Free People division. It has established a clear identity for itself within the domestic business environment that enables it to compete effectively with such competitors as American Eagle and J. Crew.

Global Business Environment
the international forces that affect a business

Global Business Environment The **global business environment** refers to the international forces that affect a business. Factors affecting the global environment at a general level include international trade agreements, international economic conditions, political unrest, and so forth. For example, as political protests spread through much of the Middle East in 2013, oil prices began to surge and companies with operations in the region took emergency measures to protect their employees. But in 2014, a global oil surplus caused oil prices to plunge. At a more immediate level, any given business is likely to be affected by international market opportunities, suppliers, cultures, competitors, and currency values. For instance,

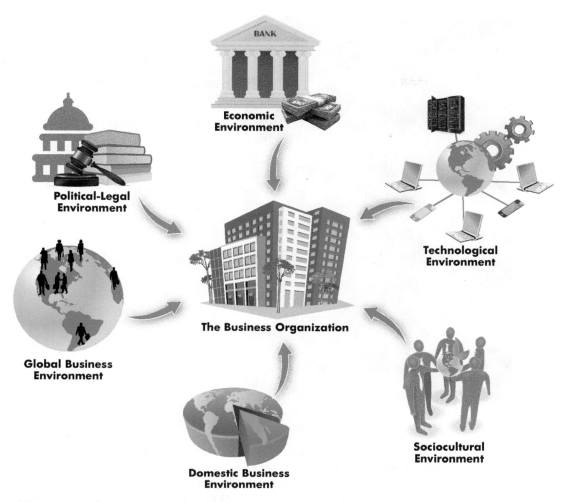

FIGURE 1 Dimensions of the External Environment

Urban Outfitters currently has stores in the United States, Canada, Belgium, France, Denmark, Germany, Ireland, Scotland, Sweden, and several others and ships to customers in 133 countries. But as it has expanded into other parts of the world, it has to contend with different languages, more diverse cultures, different forms of technology, different currencies, and many other factors. Complicating things further, many of its suppliers are foreign companies.

Technological Environment The **technological environment** generally includes all the ways by which firms create value for their constituents. Technology includes human knowledge, work methods, physical equipment, electronics and telecommunications, and various processing systems that are used to perform business activities. For instance, Urban Outfitters relies on a sophisticated information system that tracks sales and inventory levels to be highly responsive to its customers. The firm also enjoys considerable success with its e-commerce websites. Urban Outfitters has developed a strong market presence in Japan, for example, even though it has no traditional brick-and-mortar retail outlets in that country.

Political-Legal Environment The **political-legal environment** reflects the relationship between business and government, usually in the form of government regulation of business. This environment is important for several reasons. First, the legal system defines in part what an organization can and cannot do. For instance, Urban Outfitters is subject to a variety of political and legal forces, including

Technological Environment all the ways by which firms create value for their constituents

Political-Legal Environment the relationship between business and government

Urban Outfitters is affected by the external environment in many different ways. The domestic business environment, global business environment, technological environment, political-legal environment, sociocultural environment, and economic environment all interact to provide Urban Outfitters with both opportunities and challenges.

LE Robshaw/Alamy

product identification laws, employee hiring restrictions, and local zoning requirements. Likewise, various government agencies regulate important activities, such as advertising practices, safety and health considerations, and acceptable standards of business conduct. Pro- or anti-business sentiment in government and political stability are also important considerations, especially for international firms. For instance, shortly after President Barack Obama first took office, a number of new regulations were imposed on businesses. For instance, the president signed legislation that imposed new restrictions on lobbying and on political action committees.

Sociocultural Environment *Sociocultural Environment the customs, mores, values, and demographic characteristics of the society in which an organization functions*

Sociocultural Environment The **sociocultural environment** includes the customs, mores, values, and demographic characteristics of the society in which an organization functions. Sociocultural processes also determine the goods and services, as well as the standards of business conduct, that a society is likely to value and accept. For example, a few years ago, Urban Outfitters introduced a Monopoly-like game called *Ghettopoly*. The company received a lot of unfavorable publicity about the game, based on critics' charges that it made light of poverty and other social problems. In response, Urban Outfitters pulled it from shelves and discontinued its sale. But the firm continues to push the limits. For instance, in recent years, Urban Outfitters has been criticized for selling t-shirts with a pocket patch resembling the yellow stars Jews were forced to wear during the Nazi regime in Germany, for clothing items with a color option listed as Obama Black, and for a holiday catalog with numerous items containing words and images that some people saw as offensive.[7]

Economic Environment *Economic Environment relevant conditions that exist in the economic system in which a company operates*

Economic Environment The **economic environment** refers to relevant conditions that exist in the economic system in which a company operates. For example, if an economy is doing well enough that most people have jobs and wages are high, a growing company may find it necessary to pay even higher wages and offer more benefits to attract workers from other companies. But if many people in an economy are looking for jobs, a firm may be able to pay less and offer fewer benefits. Like many retailers, Urban Outfitters experienced some financial pressures during the recent recession but its revenues and profits are now healthy once again. The rest of this chapter is devoted to the economic environment.

Economic Systems

A U.S. business operates differently from a business in France or the People's Republic of China, and businesses in those countries differ from those in Japan or Brazil. A key factor in these differences is the economic system of a firm's *home country*, the nation in which it does most of its business. An **economic system** is a nation's system for allocating its resources among its citizens, both individuals and organizations.

Economic System *a nation's system for allocating its resources among its citizens*

Factors of Production

A basic difference between economic systems is the way in which a system manages its **factors of production**, the resources that a country's businesses use to produce goods and services. Economists have long focused on four factors of production: *labor, capital, entrepreneurs,* and *physical resources.* In addition to these traditional four factors, many economists now include *information resources.* Note that the concept of factors of production can also be applied to the resources that an individual organization *manages* to produce tangible goods and intangible services.

Factors of Production *resources used in the production of goods and services—labor, capital, entrepreneurs, physical resources, and information resources*

Labor People who work for businesses provide labor. **Labor**, sometimes called **human resources** or *human capital*, includes the physical and intellectual contributions people make while engaged in economic production. Starbucks, for example, employs more than 182,000 people.[8] The firm's workforce includes the baristas who prepare coffees for customers, store managers, regional managers, coffee tasters, quality control experts, coffee buyers, marketing experts, financial specialists, and other specialized workers and managers.

Labor (Human Resources) *physical and mental capabilities of people as they contribute to economic production*

Capital Obtaining and using labor and other resources requires **capital**, the financial resources needed to operate a business. You need capital to start a new business and then to keep it running and growing. For example, when Howard Schultz decided to buy the fledgling Starbucks coffee outfit back in 1987, he used personal savings and a loan to finance his acquisition. As Starbucks grew, he came to rely more on Starbucks's profits. Eventually, the firm sold stock to other investors to raise even more money. Starbucks continues to rely on a blend of current earnings and both short- and long-term debt to finance its operations and fuel its growth. Moreover, even when the firm decided to close several hundred coffee shops a few years ago, it employed capital to pay off leases and provide severance pay to employees who lost their jobs.

Capital *funds needed to create and operate a business enterprise*

Entrepreneurs An **entrepreneur** is a person who accepts the risks and opportunities entailed in creating and operating a new business. Three individuals founded Starbucks back in 1971 and planned to emphasize wholesale distribution of fresh coffee beans. However, they lacked the interest or the vision to see the retail potential for coffee. Schultz, however, was willing to accept the risks associated with retail growth and, after buying the company, he capitalized on the market opportunities for rapid growth. Had his original venture failed, Schultz would have lost most of his savings. Most economic systems encourage entrepreneurs, both to start new businesses and to make the decisions that allow them to create new jobs and make more profits for their owners.

Entrepreneur *individual who accepts the risks and opportunities involved in creating and operating a new business venture*

Physical Resources **Physical resources** are the tangible things that organizations use to conduct their business. They include natural resources and raw

Physical Resources *tangible items that organizations use in the conduct of their businesses*

Starbucks uses various factors of production, including (a) labor, such as this Starbucks barista; (b) entrepreneurs, such as CEO Howard Schultz; and (c) physical resources, including coffee beans.

materials, offices, storage and production facilities, parts and supplies, computers and peripherals, and a variety of other equipment. For example, Starbucks relies on coffee beans and other food products, the equipment it uses to make its coffee drinks, and paper products for packaging, as well as office equipment and storage facilities for running its business at the corporate level.

Information Resources *data and other information used by businesses*

Information Resources The production of tangible goods once dominated most economic systems. Today, **information resources**, data and other information used by businesses, play a major role. Information resources that businesses rely on include market forecasts, the specialized knowledge of people, and economic data. In turn, much of what businesses do with the information results either in the creation of new information or the repackaging of existing information for new users. For example, Starbucks uses various economic statistics to decide where to open new outlets. It also uses sophisticated forecasting models to predict the future prices of coffee beans. And consumer taste tests help the firm decide when to introduce new products.

Types of Economic Systems

Different types of economic systems view these factors of production differently. In some systems, for example (and in theory), the ownership of both the factors of production and the actual businesses is private; that is, ownership is held by entrepreneurs, individual investors, and other businesses. As discussed next, these are market economies. In other systems, though (and also in theory), the factors of production and all businesses are owned or controlled by the government. These are

entrepreneurship and new ventures

Open Sesame

You've likely heard the story of Ali Baba, the rags-to-riches tale of a woodcutter who finds a cave where a band of 40 thieves are storing their ill-gotten gains. To gain entrance to the cave, Ali Baba discovers that he must utter the secret password, "open sesame." Like Ali Baba, Jack Ma has discovered the key to entering the very lucrative Chinese market. China has an evolving planned economy, where there is government ownership of many of the factors of production, but some entrepreneurship is allowed. Jack Ma is an unlikely entrepreneur—he was once an English teacher at Hangzhou Electronics Technology College with no family or government connections. In 1999, Ma founded Alibaba, an online wholesale and retail network. By 2014, Alibaba's sales had grown to $300 billion. Today, Jack Ma is one of the richest men in the world—he has a net worth of over $20 billion and in 2015 Forbes ranked him as one of the 50 richest people in the world.[9]

Gan Jun/Imaginechina/AP Images

Just how has Alibaba grown into such an empire? Diversification and sensitivity to the market have been the keys. The empire began with Alibaba.com, a business-to-business platform that allowed even small businesses access to a network of sellers. Building upon this success, Ma launched Taobao and Tmall.com, retail sites targeting the burgeoning Chinese middle class. One of the keys to the success of these sites is Alipay, a financial services firm that provides safe transactions, accounting for as much as 80 percent of online sales. Through Alipay, money is held in escrow until quality of goods is confirmed. This protection has helped to overcome concerns about subpar goods and inadequate remedies through the Chinese legal system.[10]

Currently, more than 95 percent of Alibaba's sales are inside China, but Jack Ma sees international growth as essential. The initial target of expansion is Europe, where he sees a larger market for Chinese goods. But he also sees the potential for imports. According to Ma, "There will be [hundreds of millions of members of the] new middle classes in the next 10 to 15 years, and they need good products and services. Europe has the best quality, good health products and services.... Europe needs China, and China needs Europe." He has also targeted Japan, Korea, and India, although he's currently not particularly interested in entering the already crowded U.S. market.[11]

called *planned economies*. Note that we described these kinds of systems as being "in theory." Why? Because in reality, most systems fall between these extremes.

Economic systems also differ in the ways decisions are made about production and allocation. A **planned economy** relies on a centralized government to control all or most factors of production and to make all or most production and allocation decisions. In a **market economy**, individual producers and consumers control production and allocation by creating combinations of supply and demand. Let's look at each of these types of economic systems as well as mixed market economies in more detail.

Planned Economies There are two basic forms of planned economies: *communism* (discussed here) and *socialism* (discussed later as a form of mixed market economy). As envisioned by nineteenth-century German economist Karl Marx, **communism** is a system in which the government owns and operates all factors of production. Under such a system, the government would assign people to jobs; it would also own all business and control business decisions—what to make, how much to charge, and so forth. Marx proposed that individuals would contribute according to their abilities and receive benefits according to their needs. He also expected government ownership of production factors to be temporary; once society had matured, government would wither away, and workers would take direct ownership of the factors of production.

Planned Economy *economy that relies on a centralized government to control all or most factors of production and to make all or most production and allocation decisions*

Market Economy *economy in which individuals control production and allocation decisions through supply and demand*

Communism *political system in which the government owns and operates all factors of production*

The former Soviet Union and many Eastern European countries embraced communism until the end of the twentieth century. In the early 1990s, however, one country after another renounced communism as both an economic and a political system. Today, North Korea, Vietnam, Laos, Cuba, and the People's Republic of China are the only nations remaining that are controlled by communist parties. However, China in particular now functions much more like a mixed market economy (discussed later) than a pure communist-based economy.

Market Economies A **market** is a mechanism for exchange between the buyers and sellers of a particular good or service. (Like *capital*, the term *market* can have multiple meanings.) Market economies rely on capitalism and free enterprise to create an environment in which producers and consumers are free to sell and buy what they choose (within certain limits). As a result, items produced and prices paid are largely determined by supply and demand. The underlying premise of a market economy is to create shared value—in theory, at least, effective businesses benefit because they earn profits on what they sell, and customers also benefit by getting what they want for the best price available.[12]

To understand how a market economy works, consider what happens when you go to a fruit market to buy apples. One vendor is selling apples for $1 per pound; another is charging $1.50. Both vendors are free to charge what they want, and you are free to buy what you choose. If both vendors' apples are of the same quality, you will buy the cheaper ones. If the $1.50 apples are fresher and healthier looking, you may buy them instead. In short, both buyers and sellers enjoy freedom of choice; that is, the vendors are free to charge whatever price they choose for their apples, and the customer is free to decide whether to buy the $1 apples, the $1.50 apples, someone else's apples, or no apples at all.

Taken to a more general level of discussion, individuals in a market system are free to not only buy what they want but also to work where they want and to invest, save, or spend their money in whatever manner they choose. Likewise, businesses are free to decide what products to make, where to sell them, and what prices to charge. This process contrasts markedly with that of a planned economy, in which individuals may be told where they can and cannot work, companies may be told what they can and cannot make, and consumers may have little or no choice in what they purchase or how much they pay. The political basis of market processes is called **capitalism**, which allows the private ownership of the factors of production and encourages entrepreneurship by offering profits as an incentive. The economic basis of market processes is the operation of demand and supply, which we discuss in the next section.

Mixed Market Economies In reality, there are really no "pure" planned or "pure" market economies. Most countries rely on some form of **mixed market economy** that features characteristics of both planned and market economies. Even a market economy that strives to be as free and open as possible, such as the U.S. economy, restricts certain activities. Some products can't be sold legally, others can be sold only to people of a certain age, advertising must be truthful, and so forth. And the People's Republic of China, the world's most important planned economy, is increasingly allowing private ownership and entrepreneurship (although with government oversight). Indeed, it is probably more accurate today to describe China as a mixed market economy in a country controlled by the communist party.

When a government is making a change from a planned economy to a market economy, it usually begins to adopt market mechanisms through **privatization**, the process of converting government enterprises into privately owned companies. In Poland, for example, the national airline was sold to a group of private investors. In recent years, this practice has spread to many other countries as well. For example, the postal system in many countries is government owned and government managed. The Netherlands, however, privatized its TNT Post Group N.V., and it is among the world's most efficient post office operations. Canada has also privatized its air traffic control system. In each case, the new enterprise reduced its payroll,

Market *mechanism for exchange between buyers and sellers of a particular good or service*

Capitalism *system that sanctions the private ownership of the factors of production and encourages entrepreneurship by offering profits as an incentive*

Mixed Market Economy *economic system featuring characteristics of both planned and market economies*

Privatization *process of converting government enterprises into privately owned companies*

Many formerly planned economies have moved toward a more mixed economic model. For example, the People's Republic of China has used a planned economic model for decades but is now moving more toward a mixed market economy. Hong Kong, meanwhile, has been using the mixed market model for years. These signs on a busy Hong Kong street, for instance, are promoting a variety of goods and services provided by merchants along the street.

Geoff A Howard/Alamy

boosted efficiency and productivity, and quickly became profitable. More recently, the government of Iran has privatized numerous oil refineries and petrochemical plants that were previously state owned (although they have not revealed their productivity data).

In the partially planned system called **socialism**, the government owns and operates selected major industries. In such mixed market economies, the government may control banking, transportation, or industries producing basic goods such as oil and steel. Smaller businesses, such as clothing stores and restaurants, though, are privately owned. Many Western European countries, including England and France, allow free market operations in most economic areas but keep government control of others, such as health care. When the U.S. government took an ownership stake in General Motors and Chrysler as part of the recession-driven bailout in 2009, many critics of President Obama derisively called the decision an act of socialism.

Socialism *planned economic system in which the government owns and operates only selected major sources of production*

The Economics of Market Systems

Understanding the complex nature of the U.S. economic system is essential to understanding the environment in which U.S. businesses operate. In this section, we describe the workings of the U.S. market economy. Specifically, we examine the nature of *demand and supply, private enterprise*, and *degrees of competition*. We will then discuss private enterprise and forms of competition.

Demand and Supply in a Market Economy

A market economy consists of many different markets that function within that economy. As a consumer, for instance, the choices you have and the prices you pay for gas, food, clothing, and entertainment are all governed by different sets of market

OBJECTIVE 3
Show

how markets, demand, and supply affect resource distribution in the United States, identify the elements of private enterprise, and explain the various degrees of competition in the U.S. economic system.

forces. Businesses also have many different choices about buying and selling their products. Dell Computer, for instance, can purchase keyboards from literally hundreds of different manufacturers. In addition to deciding where to buy supplies, its managers also have to decide what inventory levels should be, at what prices they should sell their goods, and how they will distribute these goods. Similarly, online retailers can decide to use FedEx, UPS, or the U.S. Postal Service to deliver products bought by customers. Literally billions of exchanges take place every day between businesses and individuals; between businesses; and among individuals, businesses, and governments. Moreover, exchanges conducted in one area often affect exchanges elsewhere. For instance, when gas prices are high, this may also lead to prices going up for other products, ranging from food to clothing to delivery services. Why? Because each of these businesses relies heavily on gas to transport products.

The Laws of Demand and Supply

On all economic levels, decisions about what to buy and what to sell are determined primarily by the forces of demand and supply.[13] **Demand** is the willingness and ability of buyers to purchase a product (a good or a service). **Supply** is the willingness and ability of producers to offer a good or service for sale. Generally speaking, demand and supply follow basic laws:

- The **law of demand**: Buyers will purchase (demand) *more* of a product as its price *drops* and *less* of a product as its price *increases*.

- The **law of supply**: Producers will offer (supply) *more* of a product for sale as its price *rises* and *less* of a product as its price *drops*.

THE DEMAND AND SUPPLY SCHEDULE To appreciate these laws in action, consider the market for pizza in your town (or neighborhood). If everyone is willing to pay $25 for a pizza (a relatively high price), the town's only pizzeria will produce a large supply. But if everyone is willing to pay only $5 (a relatively low price), it will make fewer pizzas. Through careful analysis, we can determine how many pizzas will be sold at different prices. These results, called a **demand and supply schedule**, are obtained from marketing research, historical data, and other studies of the market. Properly applied, they reveal the relationships among different levels of demand and supply at different price levels.

DEMAND AND SUPPLY CURVES The demand and supply schedule can be used to construct demand and supply curves for pizza in your town. A **demand curve** shows how many products—in this case, pizzas—will be demanded (bought) at different prices. A **supply curve** shows how many pizzas will be supplied (baked or offered for sale) at different prices.

Figure 2 shows demand and supply curves for pizzas. As you can see, demand increases as price decreases; supply increases as price increases. When demand and supply curves are plotted on the same graph, the point at which they intersect is the **market price** (also called the **equilibrium price**), the price at which the quantity of goods demanded and the quantity of goods supplied are equal. In Figure 2, the equilibrium price for pizzas in our example is $10. At this point, the quantity of pizzas demanded and the quantity of pizzas supplied are the same: 1,000 pizzas per week.

SURPLUSES AND SHORTAGES What if the pizzeria decides to make some other number of pizzas? For example, what would happen if the owner tried to increase profits by making *more* pizzas to sell? Or what if the owner wanted to lower overhead, cut back on store hours, and *reduce* the number of pizzas offered for sale? In either case, the result would be an inefficient use of resources and lower profits. For instance, if the pizzeria supplies 1,200 pizzas and tries to sell them for $10 each, 200 pizzas will not be bought. Our demand schedule shows that only 1,000 pizzas will be demanded at this price. The pizzeria will therefore have a **surplus**, a situation in which the quantity supplied exceeds the quantity demanded. It will lose the money that it spent making those extra 200 pizzas.

Demand *the willingness and ability of buyers to purchase a good or service*

Supply *the willingness and ability of producers to offer a good or service for sale*

Law of Demand *principle that buyers will purchase (demand) more of a product as its price drops and less as its price increases*

Law of Supply *principle that producers will offer (supply) more of a product for sale as its price rises and less as its price drops*

Demand and Supply Schedule *assessment of the relationships among different levels of demand and supply at different price levels*

Demand Curve *graph showing how many units of a product will be demanded (bought) at different prices*

Supply Curve *graph showing how many units of a product will be supplied (offered for sale) at different prices*

Market price (equilibrium price) *profit-maximizing price at which the quantity of goods demanded and the quantity of goods supplied are equal*

Surplus *situation in which quantity supplied exceeds quantity demanded*

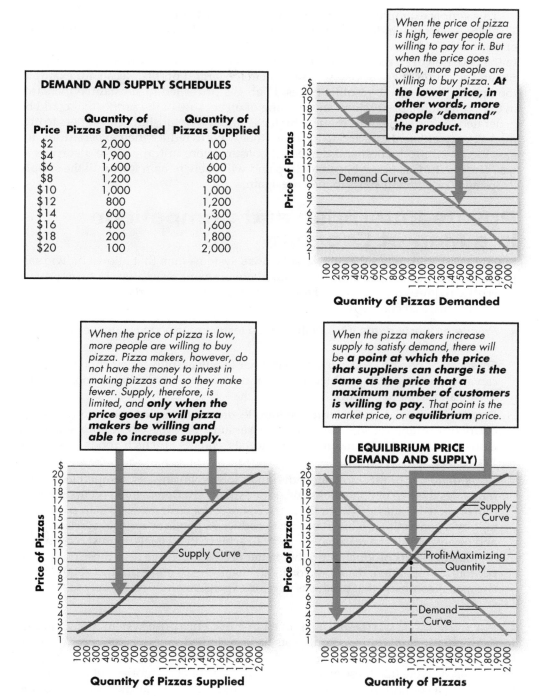

DEMAND AND SUPPLY SCHEDULES

Price	Quantity of Pizzas Demanded	Quantity of Pizzas Supplied
$2	2,000	100
$4	1,900	400
$6	1,600	600
$8	1,200	800
$10	1,000	1,000
$12	800	1,200
$14	600	1,300
$16	400	1,600
$18	200	1,800
$20	100	2,000

When the price of pizza is high, fewer people are willing to pay for it. But when the price goes down, more people are willing to buy pizza. **At the lower price, in other words, more people "demand" the product.**

Demand Curve

Quantity of Pizzas Demanded

When the price of pizza is low, more people are willing to buy pizza. Pizza makers, however, do not have the money to invest in making pizzas and so they make fewer. Supply, therefore, is limited, and **only when the price goes up will pizza makers be willing and able to increase supply.**

Supply Curve

Quantity of Pizzas Supplied

When the pizza makers increase supply to satisfy demand, there will be **a point at which the price that suppliers can charge is the same as the price that a maximum number of customers is willing to pay.** That point is the market price, or **equilibrium** price.

EQUILIBRIUM PRICE (DEMAND AND SUPPLY)

Supply Curve

Profit-Maximizing Quantity

Demand Curve

Quantity of Pizzas

FIGURE 2 Demand and Supply

Conversely, if the pizzeria supplies only 800 pizzas, a **shortage** will result, meaning the quantity demanded will be greater than the quantity supplied. The pizzeria will "lose" the extra profit that it could have made by producing 200 more pizzas. Even though consumers may pay more for pizzas because of the shortage, the pizzeria will still earn lower total profits than if it had made 1,000 pizzas. It will also risk angering customers who cannot buy pizzas and encourage other entrepreneurs to set up competing pizzerias to satisfy unmet demand. Businesses should seek the ideal combination of price charged and quantity supplied so as to maximize profits, maintain goodwill among customers, and discourage competition. This ideal combination is found at the equilibrium point.

Shortage *situation in which quantity demanded exceeds quantity supplied*

This simple example involves only one company, one product, and a few buyers. The U.S. economy—indeed, any market economy—is far more complex. Thousands of companies sell hundreds of thousands of products to millions of buyers every day. In the end, however, the result is much the same: Companies try to supply the quantity and selection of goods that will earn them the largest profits. Recall, for example, the opening case about gasoline prices. High gas prices led to substantial increases in the exploration, production, and refining of oil because of the profits that could be generated. At the same time, though, high gas prices were pushing consumers to buy more energy-efficient cars and to look for other ways to reduce their expenditures for gas. Increased production and decreased consumption, in turn, led to a surplus in gas. The result? Gas prices began to drop and will likely remain low until the supply drops and/or demand starts to increase again.

Private Enterprise and Competition in a Market Economy

Private Enterprise *economic system that allows individuals to pursue their own interests without undue governmental restriction*

Market economies rely on a **private enterprise** system—one that allows individuals to pursue their own interests with minimal government restriction. In turn, private enterprise requires the presence of four elements: private property rights, freedom of choice, profits, and competition.

1 *Private property rights.* Ownership of the resources used to create wealth is in the hands of individuals.
2 *Freedom of choice.* You can sell your labor to any employer you choose. You can also choose which products to buy, and producers can usually choose whom to hire and what to produce.
3 *Profits.* The lure of profits (and freedom) leads some people to abandon the security of working for someone else and to assume the risks of entrepreneurship. Anticipated profits also influence individuals' choices of which goods or services to produce.
4 *Competition.* If profits motivate individuals to start businesses, competition motivates them to operate those businesses efficiently. **Competition** occurs when two or more businesses vie for the same resources or customers. To gain an advantage over competitors, a business must produce its goods or services efficiently and be able to sell at a reasonable profit. To achieve these goals, it must convince customers that its products are either better or less expensive than those of its competitors. Competition, therefore, forces all businesses to make products better or cheaper. A company that produces inferior, expensive products is likely to fail.

Competition *vying among businesses for the same resources or customers*

Degrees of Competition Even in a free enterprise system, not all industries are equally competitive. Economists have identified four degrees of competition in a private enterprise system: *perfect competition, monopolistic competition, oligopoly,* and *monopoly*. Note that these are not always truly distinct categories but instead tend to fall along a continuum; perfect competition and monopoly anchor the ends of the continuum, with monopolistic competition and oligopoly falling in between. Table 1 summarizes the features of these four degrees of competition.

Perfect Competition *market or industry characterized by numerous small firms producing an identical product*

PERFECT COMPETITION For **perfect competition** to exist, two conditions must prevail: (1) all firms in an industry must be small, and (2) the number of firms in the industry must be large. Under these conditions, no single firm is powerful enough to influence the price of its product. Prices are, therefore, determined by such market forces as supply and demand.

In addition, these two conditions also reflect four principles:

1 The products of each firm are so similar that buyers view them as identical to those of other firms.
2 Both buyers and sellers know the prices that others are paying and receiving in the marketplace.

table 1 Degrees of Competition

Characteristic	Perfect Competition	Monopolistic Competition	Oligopoly	Monopoly
Example	Local farmer	Stationery store	Steel industry	Public utility
Number of competitors	Many	Many, but fewer than in perfect competition	Few	None
Ease of entry into industry	Relatively easy	Fairly easy	Difficult	Regulated by government
Similarity of goods or services offered by competing firms	Identical	Similar	Can be similar or different	No directly competing goods or services
Level of control over price by individual firms	None	Some	Some	Considerable

3 Because each firm is small, it is easy for firms to enter or leave the market.

4 Going prices are set exclusively by supply and demand and accepted by both sellers and buyers.

U.S. agriculture is a good example of perfect competition. The wheat produced on one farm is the same as that from another. Both producers and buyers are aware of prevailing market prices. It is relatively easy to start producing wheat and relatively easy to stop when it's no longer profitable.

MONOPOLISTIC COMPETITION In **monopolistic competition**, numerous sellers are trying to make their products at least seem to be different from those of competitors. Although many sellers are involved in monopolistic competition, there tend to be fewer than in pure competition. Differentiating strategies include brand names (Tide versus Cheer versus in-store house brands of detergent), design or styling (Diesel versus Lucky versus True Religion jeans), and advertising (Coke versus Pepsi versus Dr. Pepper). For example, in an effort to attract weight-conscious consumers, Kraft Foods promotes such differentiated products as low-fat Cool Whip, low-calorie Jell-O, and sugar-free Kool-Aid.

Monopolistic Competition market or industry characterized by numerous buyers and relatively numerous sellers trying to differentiate their products from those of competitors

Monopolistically competitive businesses may be large or small, but they can still enter or leave the market easily. For example, many small clothing stores compete successfully with large apparel retailers, such as Abercrombie & Fitch, Banana Republic, and J. Crew. A good case in point is bebe stores. The small clothing chain controls its own manufacturing facilities and can respond just as quickly as firms such as the Gap to changes in fashion tastes. Likewise, many single-store clothing businesses in college towns compete by developing their own T-shirt and baseball cap designs with copyrighted slogans and logos.

Product differentiation also gives sellers some control over prices. For instance, even though Target shirts may have similar styling and other features, Ralph Lauren Polo shirts can be priced with little regard for lower Target prices. But the large number of buyers relative to sellers applies potential limits to prices; although Polo might be able to sell shirts for $20 more than a comparable Target shirt, it could not sell as many shirts if they were priced at $200 more.

OLIGOPOLY When an industry has only a handful of sellers, an **oligopoly** exists. As a general rule, these sellers are quite large. The entry of new competitors is hard because large capital investment is needed. Thus, oligopolistic industries (automobile, airline, and steel industries) tend to stay that way. Only two companies make large commercial aircraft: Boeing (a U.S. company) and Airbus (a European consortium). Furthermore, as the trend toward globalization continues, most experts believe that oligopolies will become increasingly prevalent.

Oligopoly market or industry characterized by a handful of (generally large) sellers with the power to influence the prices of their products

Oligopolists have more control over their strategies than do monopolistically competitive firms, but the actions of one firm can significantly affect the sales of every other firm in the industry. For example, when one firm cuts prices or offers incentives to increase sales, the others usually protect sales by doing the same. Likewise, when one firm raises prices, others generally follow suit. Therefore, the prices of comparable products are usually similar. When an airline announces new fare discounts, others adopt the same strategy almost immediately. Just as quickly, when discounts end for one airline, they usually end for everyone else.

MONOPOLY A **monopoly** exists when an industry or market has only one producer (or else is so dominated by one producer that other firms cannot compete with it). A sole producer enjoys complete control over the prices of its products. Its only constraint is a decrease in consumer demand as a result of increased prices. In the United States, laws, such as the Sherman Antitrust Act (1890) and the Clayton Act (1914), forbid many monopolies and regulate prices charged by **natural monopolies**, industries in which one company can most efficiently supply all needed goods or services. Many electric companies are natural monopolies because they can supply all the power needed in a local area. Duplicate facilities—such as two power plants and two sets of power lines—would be wasteful.

Monopoly *market or industry in which there is only one producer that can therefore set the prices of its products*

Natural Monopoly *industry in which one company can most efficiently supply all needed goods or services*

the importance of the economic environment to business and identify the factors used to evaluate the performance of an economic system.

Economic Indicators *statistics that help assess the performance of an economy*

Economic Indicators

Because economic forces are so volatile and can be affected by so many things, the performance of a country's economic system varies over time. Sometimes it gains strength and brings new prosperity to its members (this describes the U.S. economy during the early years of the twenty-first century); other times, it weakens and damages fortunes (as was the case during 2009–2010). Clearly, then, knowing how an economy is performing is useful for business owners and investors alike. Most experts look to various **economic indicators**—statistics that show whether an economic system is strengthening, weakening, or remaining stable—to help assess the performance of an economy.

Economic Growth, Aggregate Output, and Standard of Living

At one time, about half the U.S. population was involved in producing the food that we needed. Today, less than 1 percent of the U.S. population claim farming as their occupation.[14] But agricultural efficiency has actually improved because the industry has devised better ways of producing products with more efficient technology. We can say that agricultural productivity has increased because we have been able to increase total output in the agricultural sector.

We can apply the same concepts to a nation's economic system, although the computations are more complex. Fundamentally, how do we know whether an economic system is growing or not? Experts call the pattern of short-term ups and downs (or, better, expansions and contractions) in an economy the **business cycle**. The primary measure of growth in the business cycle is **aggregate output**, the total quantity of goods and services produced by an economic system during a given period.[15]

To put it simply, an increase in aggregate output is growth (or economic growth). When output grows more quickly than the population, two things usually follow:

Business Cycle *short-term pattern of economic expansions and contractions*

Aggregate Output *the total quantity of goods and services produced by an economic system during a given period*

1 Output per capita—the quantity of goods and services per person—goes up.

2 The system provides more of the goods and services that people want.

When these two things occur, people living in an economic system benefit from a higher **standard of living**, which refers to the total quantity and quality of goods and services that they can purchase with the currency used in their economic system. To know how much your standard of living is improving, you need to know how much

Standard of Living *the total quantity and quality of goods and services people can purchase with the currency used in their economic system*

table 2 U.S. GDP and GDP per Capita

2013 GDP ($ Trillion)	2013 GDP: Real Growth Rate (%)	2013 GDP per Capita: Purchasing Power Parity
$16.77	1.8%	$53,042

GDP (gross domestic product)

your nation's economic system is growing (see Table 2).[16] For instance, although the U.S. economy reflects overall growth in most years, in 2009 the economy actually shrank by 2.6 percent due to the recession.

Gross Domestic Product
Gross domestic product (GDP) refers to the total value of all goods and services produced within a given period by a national economy through domestic factors of production. GDP is a measure of aggregate output. Generally speaking, if GDP is going up, aggregate output is going up; if aggregate output is going up, the nation is experiencing *economic growth*.

Sometimes, economists also measure **gross national product (GNP)**, which refers to the total value of all goods and services produced by a national economy within a given period regardless of where the factors of production are located. What, precisely, is the difference between GDP and GNP? Consider a General Motors automobile plant in Brazil. The profits earned by the factory are included in U.S. GNP—but not in GDP—because its output is not produced domestically (that is, in the United States). Conversely, those profits are included in Brazil's GDP—but not GNP—because they are produced domestically (that is, in Brazil). Calculations quickly become complex because of different factors of production. The labor, for example, will be mostly Brazilian but the capital mostly American. Thus, wages paid to Brazilian workers are part of Brazil's GNP even though profits are not.

REAL GROWTH RATE GDP and GNP usually differ by less than 1 percent, but economists argue that GDP is a more accurate indicator of domestic economic performance because it focuses only on domestic factors of production. With that in mind, let's look at the middle column in Table 2. Here, we find that the real growth rate of U.S. GDP—the growth rate of GDP *adjusted for inflation and changes in the value of the country's currency*—was 1.8 percent in 2013. But what does this number actually mean? Remember that *growth depends on output increasing at a faster rate than population*. The U.S. population is growing at a rate of 0.77 percent per year.[17] The *real growth rate* of the U.S. economic system, therefore, has been modest since 2011.

GDP PER CAPITA The number in the third column of Table 2 is a reflection of the standard of living: **GDP per capita** means GDP per individual person. We get this figure by dividing total GDP ($16.77 trillion) by total population, which happens to be a bit over about 322 million.[18] In a given period (usually calculated on an annual basis), the United States produces goods and services equal in value to $53,042 for every person in the country. Figure 3 shows both GDP and GDP per capita in the United States between 1950 and 2013. GDP per capita is a better measure than GDP itself of the economic well-being of the average person.

REAL GDP **Real GDP** means that GDP has been adjusted to account for changes in currency values and price changes. To understand why adjustments are necessary, assume that pizza is the only product in a hypothetical economy. In 2014, a pizza cost $10; in 2015, a pizza cost $11. In both years, exactly 1,000 pizzas were produced. In 2014, the local GDP was $10,000 ($10 × 1,000); in 2015, the local GDP was $11,000 ($11 × 1,000). Has the economy grown? No. Because 1,000 pizzas were produced in both years, *aggregate output* remained the same. The point is to not be misled into believing that an economy is doing better than it is. If it is not adjusted, local GDP for 2015 is **nominal GDP**—GDP measured in current dollars or with all components valued at current prices.[19]

PURCHASING POWER PARITY In the example, *current prices* would be 2015 prices. On the other hand, we calculate real GDP when we adjust GDP to account for changes in

Gross Domestic Product (GDP) *total value of all goods and services produced within a given period by a national economy through domestic factors of production*

Gross National Product (GNP) *total value of all goods and services produced by a national economy within a given period regardless of where the factors of production are located*

GDP per Capita *gross domestic product divided by total population*

Real GDP *GDP adjusted to account for changes in currency values and price changes*

Nominal GDP *GDP measured in current dollars or with all components valued at current prices*

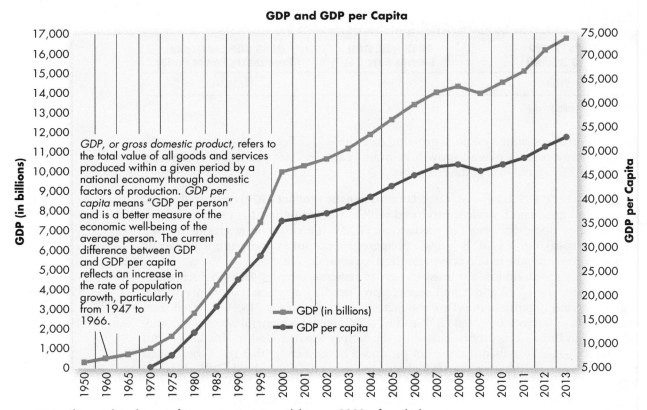

FIGURE 3 GDP and GDP per Capita

Sources: http://www.bea.gov/iTable/index_nipa.cfm and http://www.census.gov/popest/data/historical/index.html; http://bea.gov/national/index.htm#gdp; and http://data.worldbank.org/indicator/NY.GDP.PCAP.CD

Purchasing Power Parity *the principle that exchange rates are set so that the prices of similar products in different countries are about the same*

currency values and price changes. When we make this adjustment, we account for both GDP and **purchasing power parity**, the principle that exchange rates are set so that the prices of similar products in different countries are about the same. Purchasing power parity gives us a much better idea of *what people can actually buy with the financial resources allocated to them by their respective economic systems.* In other words, it gives us a better sense of standards of living across the globe. Figure 4 illustrates a popular approach to see how purchasing power parity works in relation to a Big Mac. For instance, the figure pegs the price of a Big Mac in the United States at $4.79. Based on currency exchange rates, a Big Mac would cost $7.54 in Switzerland and $6.30 in Norway. But the same burger would cost only $2.77 in China and $1.75 in India.

Productivity *a measure of economic growth that compares how much a system produces with the resources needed to produce it*

Productivity A major factor in the growth of an economic system is **productivity**, which is a measure of economic performance that compares how much a system produces with the resources needed to produce it. Let's say that it takes 1 U.S. worker and 1 U.S. dollar to make 10 soccer balls in an 8-hour workday. Let's also say that it takes 1.2 Mexican workers and the equivalent of 1.5 dollars in pesos, the currency of Mexico, to make 10 soccer balls in the same 8-hour workday. We can say that the U.S. soccer-ball industry is more productive than the Mexican soccer-ball industry. The two factors of production in this extremely simple case are labor and capital.

If more products are being produced with fewer factors of production, the prices of these products will likely go down. As a consumer, therefore, you would need less of your currency to purchase the same quantity of these products. In short, your standard of living—at least with regard to these products—has improved. If your entire economic system increases its productivity, then your overall standard

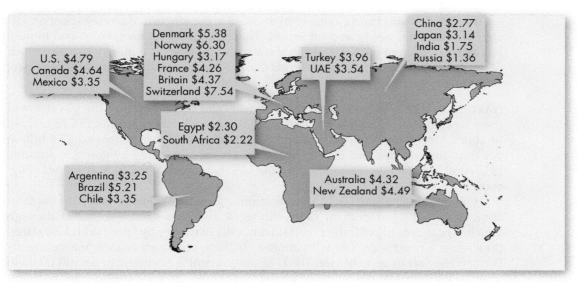

FIGURE 4 Price of a Big Mac in U.S. Currency in July 2013
Source: http://www.economist.com/content/big-mac-index

of living improves. In fact, standard of living improves *only* through increases in productivity.[20] Real growth in GDP reflects growth in productivity.

Productivity in the United States is generally increasing, and as a result, so are GDP and GDP per capita in most years (excluding the 2009 recession). Ultimately, increases in these measures of growth mean an improvement in the standard of living. However, things don't always proceed so smoothly. Several factors can inhibit the growth of an economic system, including *balance of trade* and the *national debt*.

BALANCE OF TRADE A country's **balance of trade** is the economic value of all the products that it exports minus the economic value of its imported products. The principle here is quite simple:

Balance of Trade *the economic value of all the products that a country exports minus the economic value of all the products it imports*

- A *positive* balance of trade results when a country exports (sells to other countries) more than it imports (buys from other countries).

- A *negative* balance of trade results when a country imports more than it exports.

A negative balance of trade is commonly called a *trade deficit*. In 2014, the U.S. trade deficit was about $727 billion. The United States is a *debtor nation* rather than a *creditor nation*. Recent trends in the U.S. balance of trade are shown in Figure 5.

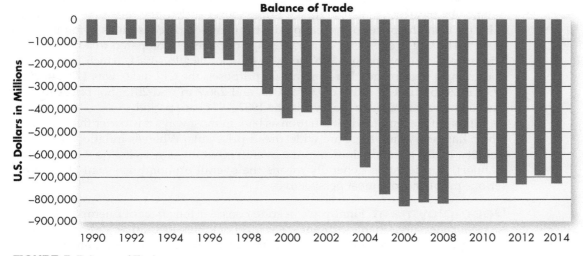

FIGURE 5 Balance of Trade
Source: http://www.census.gov/foreign-trade/balance/c0004.html#2008

Trade deficit affects economic growth because the amount of money spent on foreign products has not been paid in full. Therefore, it is, in effect, borrowed money, and borrowed money costs more in the form of interest. The money that flows out of the country to pay off the deficit can't be used to invest in productive enterprises, either at home or overseas.

National Debt *the amount of money the government owes its creditors*

NATIONAL DEBT Its **national debt** is the amount of money that the government owes its creditors. As of this writing, the U.S. national debt is around $18.15 trillion, or about $56,500 per U.S. citizen, and is increasing at a rate of around $2.4 billion per day. You can find out the national debt on any given day by going to any one of several Internet sources, including the U.S. National Debt Clock at www.brillig.com/debt_clock.

How does the national debt affect economic growth? Although taxes are the most obvious way the government raises money, it also sells *bonds*—securities through which it promises to pay buyers certain amounts of money by specified future dates. (In a sense, a bond is an IOU with interest.[21]) These bonds are attractive investments because they are extremely safe: The U.S. government is not going to default on them (that is, fail to make payments when due). Even so, they must also offer a decent return on the buyer's investment, and they do this by paying interest at a competitive rate. By selling bonds, therefore, the U.S. government competes with every other potential borrower for the available supply of loanable money. The more money the government borrows, the less money is available for the private borrowing and investment that increase productivity.

Economic Stability

Stability *condition in which the amount of money available in an economic system and the quantity of goods and services produced in it are growing at about the same rate*

Stability is a condition in which the amount of money available in an economic system and the quantity of goods and services produced in it are growing at about the same rate. A chief goal of an economic system, stability can be threatened by certain factors.

Inflation *occurs when widespread price increases occur throughout an economic system*

Inflation **Inflation** occurs when an economic system experiences widespread price increases. Instability results when the amount of money injected into an economy exceeds the increase in actual output, so people have more money to spend but the same quantity of products available to buy. As supply and demand principles tell us, when people compete with one another to buy available products, prices go up. These high prices will eventually bring the amount of money in the economy back down. However, these processes are imperfect—the additional money will not be distributed proportionately to all people, and price increases often continue beyond what is really necessary. As a result, purchasing power for many people declines.

Consumer Price Index *a measure of the prices of typical products purchased by consumers living in urban areas*

Keeping in mind that our definition of inflation is the occurrence of widespread price increases throughout an economic system, it stands to reason that we can measure inflation by measuring price increases. Price indexes such as the **consumer price index (CPI)** measure the prices of typical products purchased by consumers living in urban areas.[22] The CPI is expressed as a percentage of prices as compared to a base period. The current base period used to measure inflation is 1982–1984, which is set at 100 (indicating a percentage). For comparison purposes, the CPI index was 172.2 in 2000, 195.3 in 2005, 218.1 in 2010, 229.6 in 2012, and 236.7 in mid-2015. So, prices in 2010 reached more than double the level in the 1982–1984 base period.

Although we tend to view inflation as bad, in most ways it is better than *deflation*, which happens when there are widespread price cuts. Whereas inflation creates instability, it also generally indicates the overall economy is growing (just in an erratic manner). But deflation generally means the overall economy is shrinking, a more serious problem from most perspectives.

Unemployment *the level of joblessness among people actively seeking work in an economic system*

Unemployment Finally, we need to consider the effect of unemployment on economic stability. **Unemployment** is the level of joblessness among people actively seeking work in an economic system. When unemployment is low, there is a shortage of labor available for businesses to hire. As businesses compete with one another for the available supply of labor, they raise the wages they are willing to pay.

Then, because higher labor costs eat into profit margins, they raise the prices of their products. Although consumers have more money to inject into the economy, this increase is soon undone by higher prices, so purchasing power declines.

At least two problems are related to unemployment:

1　If wage rates get too high, businesses will respond by hiring fewer workers and unemployment will go up.

2　Businesses could raise prices to counter increased labor costs, but they won't be able to sell as many of their products at higher prices. Because of reduced sales, they will cut back on hiring and, once again, unemployment will go up.

What if the government tries to correct this situation by injecting more money into the economic system—say by cutting taxes or spending more money? Prices in general may go up because of increased consumer demand. Again, purchasing power declines and inflation may set in.[23] During the recession of 2009 and its aftermath, millions of workers lost their jobs as businesses such as Circuit City closed their doors, and others, such as General Motors and Kodak, cut thousands of jobs in an effort to stem losses. Indeed, in early 2010, unemployment in the United States reached a 25-year

managing in turbulent times

What Goes Around...

It seems like just yesterday. In 2005, the global economy was booming. In the United States, for example, business profits were soaring, jobs were plentiful, and home ownership was at an all-time high. The stock market reached unprecedented highs, pension plans were burgeoning, and new business opportunities were plentiful.

Fast-forward just four short years to 2009, and things looked a lot different. In the 16 months between October 2007 and February 2009, the S&P 500, a broad indicator of prices on the New York Stock exchange, fell by 50 percent, with average prices falling to 1997 levels! For investors, this meant that 12 years of gains had been wiped out in just over a year. Similarly, business profits were down, hundreds of thousands of jobs were lost, unemployment claims soared, and mortgage foreclosures were the order of the day. Unemployment, which had hovered around 5 percent of the workforce for years, suddenly doubled to 10 percent by mid-2009. Unemployed homeowners found it nearly impossible to keep up with mortgage payments, and foreclosure rates peaked in September 2010, only to fall steadily over the next several years.

How can we explain this pattern? Economists call it the *business cycle*. Historically, our economy has followed long periods of growth and prosperity with periods of cutbacks and retreats. And that's what started in 2008. During extended periods of prosperity, people sometimes start to act as though good times will last forever. They continue to bid up stock prices, for instance, far beyond rational value. They also take on too much debt, save too little money, and spend beyond their means. Businesses, too, start taking more risks, carrying larger inventories, expanding too quickly, and hiring too many people. But things have a way of correcting themselves, and

that's what happened when our economy went into recession beginning in 2008.

So what does the future hold? Although no one has a crystal ball, most experts agree that the economy is entering a period of prosperity. Indeed, by mid-2011, the stock market was inching back up, continued to slowly recover throughout 2012, and was at nearly triple the 2009 low by early 2015. As investors gained confidence in the economy because of strong earnings reports, the economy entered a period of expansion. By early 2015, unemployment had dropped below 6 percent, back to prerecession levels.[24] In the near future, it's likely that businesses will embark on ambitious hiring plans, the stock market will continue to soar, and business opportunities will again be plentiful. Managers should try to remember, of course, that even when the good times are rolling again, another correction will take place somewhere down the road.

high of 10.2 percent. By November 2011, as the economy was gradually pulling out of recession, unemployment had dropped to around 8.7 percent, and by November of 2012, official unemployment was 7.7 percent. By the end of 2014, it had dropped even further, to 5.6 percent.[25]

RECESSIONS AND DEPRESSIONS Unemployment is sometimes a symptom of a system-wide disorder in the economy. During a downturn in the business cycle, people in different sectors may lose their jobs at the same time. As a result, overall income and spending may drop. Feeling the pinch of reduced revenues, businesses may cut spending on the factors of production—including labor. Yet more people will be put out of work, and unemployment will only increase further. Unemployment that results from this vicious cycle is called *cyclical unemployment*.

If we look at the relationship between unemployment and economic stability, we are reminded that when prices get high enough, consumer demand for goods and services goes down. We are also reminded that when demand for products goes down, producers cut back on hiring and, not surprisingly, eventually start producing less. Consequently, aggregate output decreases. When we go through a period during which aggregate output declines, we have a recession. During a *recession*, producers need fewer employees—less labor—to produce products. Unemployment, therefore, goes up.

To determine whether an economy is going through a recession, we start by measuring aggregate output. Recall that this is the function of real GDP, which we find by making necessary adjustments to the total value of all goods and services produced within a given period by a national economy through domestic factors of production. A **recession** is more precisely defined as a period during which aggregate output, as measured by real GDP, declines. As noted previously, most economists agree that the U.S. economy went into recession in 2008; most also agree that we were gradually emerging from that recession in 2011. A prolonged and deep recession is a **depression**. The last major depression in the United States started in 1929 and lasted more than 10 years. Most economists believe that the 2008–2011 recession, although the worst in decades, was not really a depression. However, it has come to be popularly known as the Great Recession.

Managing the U.S. Economy

The government acts to manage the U.S. economic system through two sets of policies: fiscal and monetary. It manages the collection and spending of its revenues through **fiscal policies**. Tax rates, for example, can play an important role in fiscal policies helping to manage the economy. One key element of President Obama's presidential platform was an overhaul of the U.S. tax system. Among other things, he proposed cutting taxes for the middle class while simultaneously raising taxes for both higher-income people and businesses. For a variety of reasons, however, little ever gets accomplished in the area of comprehensive tax reform.

Monetary policies focus on controlling the size of the nation's money supply. Working primarily through the Federal Reserve System (the nation's central bank, often referred to simply as "the Fed"), the government can influence the ability and willingness of banks throughout the country to lend money. For example, to help combat the Great Recession, the government injected more money into the economy through various stimulus packages. On the one hand, officials hoped that these funds would stimulate business growth and the creation of new jobs. On the other hand, though, some experts feared that increasing the money supply might also lead to inflation.

Taken together, fiscal policy and monetary policy make up **stabilization policy**, government economic policy in which the goal is to smooth out fluctuations in output and unemployment and to stabilize prices. In effect, the Great Recession was a significant departure from stabilization as business valuations dropped and jobs were eliminated. The various government interventions, such as financial bailouts, represented strategies to restore economic stability.

Recession *a period during which aggregate output, as measured by GDP, declines*

Depression *a prolonged and deep recession*

Fiscal Policies *policies used by a government regarding how it collects and spends revenue*

Monetary Policies *policies used by a government to control the size of its money supply*

Stabilization Policy *government economic policy intended to smooth out fluctuations in output and unemployment and to stabilize prices*

summary of learning objectives

OBJECTIVE 1

Define the nature of U.S. business, describe the external environments of business, and discuss how these environments affect the success or failure of organizations.

A *business* is an organization that sells goods or services to earn profits. The prospect of earning *profits*, the difference between a business's revenues and expenses, encourages people to open and expand businesses. Businesses produce most of the goods and services that Americans consume and employ most working people. A healthy business environment supports innovation and contributes to the quality of life and standard of living of people in a society.

The *external environment* of business refers to everything outside its boundaries that might affect it. Both the *domestic* and the *global business environment* affect virtually all businesses. The domestic business environment is the environment in which a business conducts its operations and derives its revenues. The global business environment also refers to the international forces that affect a business, for example, international trade agreements, economic conditions, and political unrest.

The *technological, political-legal, sociocultural,* and *economic environments* are also important. The technological environment includes all of the ways by which firms create value for their constituents. Technology includes human knowledge, work methods, physical equipment, electronics, telecommunications, and various processing systems that are used to perform business functions. The political-legal environment reflects the relationship between business and government, usually in the form of government regulation of business. The sociocultural environment includes the customs, mores, values, and demographic characteristics of the society in which an organization functions. Sociocultural processes also determine the goods and services that a society is likely to value and accept. The economic environment refers to the relevant conditions that exist in the economic system in which an organization functions.

OBJECTIVE 2

Describe the different types of global economic systems according to the means by which they control the factors of production.

Economic systems differ in the ways in which they manage the five *factors of production* (1) *labor*, or *human resources*, (2) *capital*, (3) *entrepreneurship*, (4) *physical resources*, and (5) *information resources*. Labor, or human resources, includes the physical and intellectual contributions people make while engaged in business. Capital includes all financial resources needed to operate a business. Entrepreneurs are an essential factor of production. They are the people who accept the risks and opportunities associated with creating and operating businesses. Virtually every business will rely on physical resources, the tangible things organizations use to conduct their business. Physical resources include raw materials, storage and production facilities, computers, and equipment. Finally, information resources are essential to the success of a business enterprise. Information resources include data and other information used by business.

Economic systems can be differentiated based on the way that they allocate the factors of production. A *planned economy* relies on a centralized government to control factors of production and make decisions. Under *communism*, the government owns and operates all sources of production. In a *market economy*, individuals—producers and consumers—control production and allocation decisions through supply and demand. A *market* is a mechanism for exchange between the buyers and sellers of a particular product or service. Sellers can charge what they want, and customers can buy what they choose. The political basis of market processes is *capitalism*, which fosters private ownership of the factors of production and encourages entrepreneurship by offering profits as an incentive. Most countries rely on some form of *mixed market economy*—a system featuring characteristics of both planned and market economies. *Socialism* may be considered a planned economy or a mixed economy, with government ownership of selected industries but considerable private ownership, especially among small businesses.

OBJECTIVE 3

Show how markets, demand, and supply affect resource distribution in the United States, identify the elements of private enterprise, and explain the various degrees of competition in the U.S. economic system.

Decisions about what to buy and what to sell are determined by the forces of demand and supply. *Demand* is the willingness and ability of buyers to purchase a product or service. *Supply* is the willingness and ability of producers to offer a product or service for sale. A *demand and supply schedule* reveals the relationships among different levels of demand and supply at different price levels. The point at which the demand and supply curves intersect is called the market or equilibrium price. If a seller attempts to sell above the market price, he will have a surplus where the quantity supplied exceeds the demand at that price. Conversely, a shortage occurs when a product is sold below the equilibrium price and demand outstrips supply.

Market economies reflect the operation of a *private enterprise system*, a system that allows individuals to pursue their own interests without government restriction. Private enterprise requires the presence of four elements: (1) private property rights, (2) freedom of choice, (3) profits, and (4) competition. Economists have identified four degrees of competition in a private enterprise system: (1) *perfect competition*, (2) *monopolistic competition*, (3) *oligopoly*, and (4) *monopoly*. Perfect competition exists when all firms in an industry are small, there are many of them, and no single firm is powerful enough to influence prices. In monopolistic competition, numerous sellers try to differentiate their product from that of the other firms. An oligopoly exists when an industry has only a few sellers. It is usually quite difficult to enter the market in an oligopoly and the firms tend to be large. A monopoly exists when there is only one seller in a market. A firm operating in a monopoly has complete control over the price of its products.

OBJECTIVE 4

Explain the importance of the economic environment to business and identify the factors used to evaluate the performance of an economic system.

Economic indicators are statistics that show whether an economic system is strengthening, weakening, or remaining stable. The overall health of the economic environment—the economic system in which businesses operate—affects organizations. The two key goals of the U.S. system are *economic growth* and *economic stability*. Growth is assessed by *aggregate output, the total quantity of goods and services produced by an economic system*. Although gains in productivity can create growth, the *balance of trade* and the *national debt can inhibit growth*. While growth is an important goal, some countries may pursue economic stability. *Economic stability* means that the amount of money available in an economic system and the quantity of goods and services produced in it are growing at about the same rate. The two key threats to stability are *inflation* and *unemployment*. The government manages the economy through two sets of policies: *fiscal policies* (such as tax increases) and *monetary policies* that focus on controlling the size of the nation's money supply.

key terms

aggregate output	depression	gross national product (GNP)
balance of trade	domestic business environment	inflation
business	economic environment	information resources
business cycle	economic indicators	labor (human resources)
capital	economic system	law of demand
capitalism	entrepreneur	law of supply
communism	external environment	market
competition	factors of production	market economy
consumer price index (CPI)	fiscal policies	market price (equilibrium price)
demand	global business environment	mixed market economy
demand and supply schedule	gross domestic product (GDP)	monetary policies
demand curve	GDP per capita	monopolistic competition

monopoly
national debt
natural monopoly
nominal GDP
oligopoly
perfect competition
physical resources
planned economy
political-legal environment

private enterprise
privatization
productivity
profits
purchasing power parity
real GDP
recession
shortage
socialism

sociocultural environment
stability
stabilization policy
standard of living
supply
supply curve
surplus
technological environment
unemployment

MyBizLab

To complete the problems with the ✪, go to EOC Discussion Questions in the MyLab.

questions & exercises

QUESTIONS FOR REVIEW

✪ 1. What are the benefits of businesses? Can a business negatively affect society?

2. What are the factors of production? Is one factor more important than the others? If so, which one? Why?

3. What is a demand curve? A supply curve? At what point to they intersect?

✪ 4. Why is inflation both good and bad? How does the government try to control it?

QUESTIONS FOR ANALYSIS

✪ 5. Identify and describe at least three trends in the external environment that affect college enrollment. Explain how each trend affects colleges and universities.

6. Give an example of a situation in which a surplus of a product led to decreased prices. Similarly, give an example of a situation in which a shortage led to increased prices. What eventually happened in each case? Why?

7. Explain how current economic indicators, such as inflation and unemployment, affect you personally. Explain how they may affect you as a manager.

8. At first glance, it might seem as though the goals of economic growth and stability are inconsistent with one another. How can you reconcile this apparent inconsistency?

APPLICATION EXERCISES

9. Visit a local shopping mall or shopping area. List each store that you see and determine what degree of competition it faces in its immediate environment. For example, if only one store in the mall sells shoes, that store represents a "local" monopoly. Note businesses that have direct competitors (two jewelry stores) and show how they compete with one another.

10. Interview a business owner or senior manager. Ask this individual to describe for you the following things: (1) how demand and supply affect the business, (2) what essential factors of production are most central to the firm's operations, and (3) how fluctuations in economic indicators affect his or her business.

building a business: continuing team exercise

Build a team of three to five classmates. You will be working with this team throughout the semester to make decisions about the launch of a new product.

Assignment

Meet with your team members and develop specific responses to the following:

11. Have each team member work individually to identify at least three trends in the external environment that will create business opportunities. Come together as a group and create a master list of trends.

12. Which trend do you think creates the greatest opportunity for success? Why?

13. Identify a product, either a good or a service, that will take advantage of this opportunity. Although you will refine this throughout the semester, write a four- to six-sentence description of your product and how it will spark buyer interest.

14. Who is your competition for this product, either direct competition or substitute products?

team exercise

PAYING THE PRICE OF DOING E-BUSINESS

Background Information

Assume that you are the owner of a local gym and fitness studio. You've worked hard to build a loyal customer base and your facility is top-notch, with the latest equipment and a variety of classes for customers at all fitness levels. Within your area are three other gyms, each charging the same price—$40 per month for individuals, $70 per month for a couple, and $80 per month for families. However, you've become concerned because one of your competitors has just announced that they will be reducing membership costs by $10 per month for each of the three categories of memberships. Rumor has it that another facility plans to follow suit in the near future. You can't afford to get into a price war because you are just barely making a profit at your current price structure.

Team Activity

Assemble a group of four or five people. Each group should develop a general strategy for responding to competitors' price changes. Be sure to consider the following factors:

- How price changes affect the demand for your product
- The number of competitors selling the same or a similar product
- The methods you can use—other than price—to attract new customers and retain current customers

FOLLOW-UP QUESTIONS

15. What form of competition best characterizes this market?
16. Develop specific pricing strategies based on each of the following situations:
    - A month after dropping prices by $5 per month, one of your competitors returns to your current pricing.
    - Two of your competitors drop their prices even further, reducing membership costs by $8 per month. As a result, your business falls off by 25 percent.
    - One of the competitors has announced that it will keep its prices low, but it will charge members $2 per session for high-demand classes such as Pilates.
    - Each of the competitors that lowers the prices makes an adjustment, with reduced rates for families and couples, but they plan to return to $40 per month for single members.
    - All four providers (including you) have reduced their monthly fees. One goes out of business, and you know that another is in poor financial health.
17. Discuss the role that various inducements other than price might play in affecting demand and supply in this market.
18. Is it always in a company's best interest to feature the lowest prices?

exercising your ethics

GETTING CAUGHT OUT IN THE COLD

The Situation

You are the owner of a small company that provides home heating oil to residential and business customers in a rural Midwest county. The business has been in your family for several generations and you are a well-respected member of the community. Although the business had once provided a steady income for you and your family, increased energy efficiency and a move away from oil heat have cut your profits to almost nothing in recent years.

The Dilemma

After the retirement of your long-time marketing manager, you've hired a recent college graduate, Huma. Huma has analyzed your firm's financial position, as well as the most up-to-date demographic and market information. In the prior heating season, oil prices were quite high and your customers became accustomed to paying more than $4.00 per gallon. You've done your research, though, and know that it's very likely that the price that you must pay suppliers will be much lower this winter as a result of an increase in the supply of heating oil. While you're hoping to pass these cost savings onto your customers, Huma is recommending just the opposite. Huma proposes that you send out a "special offer" to your customers, allowing them to lock into a price of $3.80 per gallon for the upcoming heating season, in spite of the fact that you think that you could sell profitably at a much lower price. She believes that many of your customers will jump at the opportunity and you will be able to make a significant profit during the upcoming winter. On one hand, it would be nice to generate a large profit and rebuild your savings, but you're wondering if this is really the right thing to do.

QUESTIONS TO ADDRESS

19. What are the roles of supply and demand in this scenario?
20. What are the underlying ethical issues?
21. What would you do if you were actually faced with this situation?

cases

What Goes Up ... Can also Come Down!

At the beginning of this chapter, you read about how a variety of forces affect retail gasoline prices. Using the information presented in this chapter, you should now be able to answer these questions.

QUESTIONS FOR DISCUSSION

22. What has happened to gasoline prices since the beginning of 2015? You can find monthly average price data from the U.S. Energy Information Administration at www.eia.gov.

23. Explain how the concepts of the demand and supply of petroleum combine to determine market prices.

24. What economic indicators are most directly affected by energy prices?

25. Does the global energy situation increase or decrease your confidence in a capitalistic system based on private enterprise?

26. Should there be more government intervention in the exploration for and pricing of petroleum products? Why or why not?

Taking a Bite Out of Internet Radio

For more than a decade, Apple has been recognized as one of the most innovative companies in the world. In 2003, Apple revolutionized the music industry with the launch of the iTunes music store. Digital downloads quickly grew, as a result of iTunes and other sites, and now account for approximately 37 percent of music industry revenues. In 2007, Apple unveiled the iPhone—integrating smartphone technology with their popular iPod interface. However, in recent years, competitors like Samsung have cut into Apple's market dominance. Apple and Samsung were in a virtual dead heat, each with about 23 percent of the worldwide smartphone market in 2011, but Samsung soared above 30 percent in 2013 and Apple fell to below 15 percent. However, with the introduction of the iPhone 6, Apple has recaptured much of their lost market, mostly at the expense of Samsung.[26]

To Apple, it's clear that product innovation is the key to their long-term success. In June 2013, Apple announced its intention to roll out the iTunes Radio streaming service in the fall of the same year. The music industry is in a period of rapid change. The sale of CDs and LPs is declining and digital downloads are holding steady, but streaming radio is sharply increasing. In just three years, from 2011 to 2014, streaming radio services tripled from 9 percent to 27 percent of music industry revenues. Paid subscriptions soared from just 1.8 billion in 2011 to 7.7 billion in 2014.[27]

iTunes Radio has more than 200 stations and the ability, like competitor Pandora, for users to create custom stations to fit their personal musical tastes. The service also integrates with the Siri mobile assistant, allowing users to ask Siri, "Who plays this song?" The option is similar to something currently available through Shazam. A free ad-supported option is available for the iTunes Radio service, as well as a yearly ad-free option for $24.99.[28]

However, Apple has no shortage of competition in this venture, and they were late to enter the market. Market leader Pandora offers a free ad-supported version and a subscription service for $55 per year. In addition, Pandora is available for Android, BlackBerry, Kindle Fire, Nook, and Windows Phone, as well as the iPhone. Pandora is not the only competition. Spotify has more than 30 million licensed songs in its library, with Rdio edging them out slightly at 32 million. Apple's service, in comparison, is built on a library of 26 million songs and builds on the customer loyalty associated with the iTunes Store.[29]

Industry analysts, however, are unsure about Apple's venture into Internet radio. Ken Volkman, chief technical officer at SRV Network, concludes "They have a large and loyal customer base established and the capability to be competitive with advertising revenue rates, both providing great incentive for music publishers." Not everyone is convinced. Rocco Pendola, from the finance site The Street, told CNN, "iTunes Radio is a Pandora knockoff. It absolutely will not come close to Pandora in terms of functionality and user experience. It can't possibly do that. Pandora is a 13-year old company... Apple is just doing what everyone else has done—copying it."

While the future of iTunes Radio is uncertain, it is clear that the future of Internet radio is bright. Will Apple surge past its competitors or fade into the background? Only time will tell.

QUESTIONS FOR DISCUSSION

27. Identify the external environments of business that will affect the success or failure of Apple's iTunes Radio.

28. What factors will influence the demand for iTunes Radio?

29. In terms of degrees of competition, how would you describe the market for Internet radio? Do you think that this will change in the next five years? If so, how?

30. To customize your listening experience, Internet radio services collect data on your listening habits. Are you comfortable with this use of "big data"? Why or why not?

31. Do you think that Apple will be successful in this new venture? Do you think that it was a wise decision for them to enter the already crowded market?

MyBizLab

Go to the Assignments section of your MyLab to complete these writing exercises.

32. Describe the factors of production. How are the factors of production allocated in planned, market, and mixed economies? Characterize the allocation of the factors of production in the United States. Is the U.S. a planned, market, or mixed economy? Be sure to support your conclusion.

33. Stakeholders in businesses often look to economic indicators to determine the health of the economy. These indicators affect the way these stakeholders react to the current economic environment. Choose two economic indicators. Explain how each indicator is important to measuring the health of an economic system. Which of these do you think is more important to private enterprises versus public enterprises? Global enterprises versus domestic enterprises? Owners versus investors? Support your decision.

end notes

[1] U.S. Department of Energy. "Petroleum and Other Liquids." Independent Statistics and Analysis. Accessed April 13, 2015. http://www.eia.gov/dnav/pet/hist/LeafHandler.ashx?n=pet&s=emm_epm0_pte_nus_dpg&f=m.

[2] "If Unrest Spreads, Gas May Hit $5," *USA Today*, February 22, 2011, p. 1A; "Why the World Is One Storm Away from Energy Crisis," *Wall Street Journal*, September 24, 2005, A1, A2; "Higher and Higher—Again: Gasoline Prices Set a Record," *USA Today*, May 25, 2004, p. B1; "Who Wins and Loses When Gas Prices Skyrocket?" *Time*, May 8, 2006, p. 28; "Gas Prices Climbing Despite Hefty Supply," *USA Today*, February 2, 2011, pp. B1, B2; "Fear and Loathing in the Oil Markets," *Time*, March 14, 2011, p. 22; "Low Gas Prices of 2012 on Verge of Evaporating," *USA Today*, January 7, 2013, p. 3A.

[3] See Paul Heyne, Peter J. Boetke, and David L. Prychitko, *The Economic Way of Thinking*, 12th ed. (Upper Saddle River, NJ: Pearson, 2010), 171–176.

[4] Baker, Linda. 2012. "Cooking Clean." *Oregon Business Magazine* 35, no. 9: 9. Business Source Premier, EBSCOhost (accessed April 18, 2015).

[5] United Nations Foundation. "Health." Global Alliance for Clean Cookstoves. Accessed April 19, 2015. http://cleancookstoves.org/impact-areas/health/

[6] Roberts, Olivia Florio. "EcoZoom: a model for selling clean cookstoves in Africa." Christian Science Monitor, November 29, 2013. Accessed April 19, 2015. http://www.csmonitor.com/World/Making-a-difference/Change-Agent/2013/1129/EcoZoom-a-model-for-selling-clean-cookstoves-in-Africa

[7] See "Urban Outfitters Swears by Naughty Holiday Catalog," *USA Today*, December 12, 2012, p. 1B.

[8] *Hoover's Handbook of American Business*. 2014 (Austin: Hoover's, 2014), pp. 790–791.

[9] 2015. "The World's Fifty Richest." *Forbes 195*, No. 4:26–27. Business Source Premier, EBSCOhost (accessed April 13, 2015).

[10] Chen, Liyan. 2014. "Happy Singles Day! China's Anti-Valentine's Festival Is The World's Biggest E-Commerce Holiday." Forbes.Com 19. Business Source Premier, EBSCOhost (accessed April 14, 2015).

[11] 2015. "Jack Ma Wary Of Alibaba's Future." WWD: *Women's Wear Daily 209*, no. 42: 2–1. Business Source Premier, EBSCOhost (accessed April 14, 2015).

[12] Porter, Michael, and Kramer, Mark. "Creating Shared Value," *Harvard Business Review*, January–February 2011, pp. 62–77.

[13] See Karl E. Case and Ray C. Fair, *Principles of Economics*, 10th ed., updated (Upper Saddle River, NJ: Prentice Hall, 2011), 103–105.

[14] http://www.epa.gov/agriculture/ag101/demographics.html (January 10, 2015)

[15] Case and Fair, *Principles of Economics*, 432–433.

[16] https://www.cia.gov/library/publications/the-world-factbook/geos/us.html, accessed on January 2, 2015

[17] http://www.census.gov/popest/data/historical/2010s/vintage_2011/index.html, accessed on January 2, 2015

[18] http://www.census.gov/popest/data/historical/2010s/vintage_2011/index.html, accessed on January 2, 2015

[19] See Olivier Blanchard, *Macroeconomics*, 6th ed. (Upper Saddle River, NJ: Pearson, 2013), 24–26.

[20] See Jay Heizer and Barry Render, *Operations Management*, 11th ed. (Upper Saddle River, NJ: Prentice Hall, 2014).

[21] Heyne, Paul, Boetke, Peter J., and Prychitko, David L. *The Economic Way of Thinking*, 12th ed. (Upper Saddle River, NJ: Pearson, 2010), 491–493.

[22] Ayers, Ronald M., and Collinge, Robert A. *Economics: Explore and Apply*, (Upper Saddle River, NJ: Prentice Hall, 2004), 163–167.

[23] See Heyne, Boetke, and Prychitko, *The Economic Way of Thinking*, 403–409, 503–504.

[24] United States Department of Labor. "Labor Force Statistics from the Current Population Survey." Bureau of Labor Statistics. Accessed April 13, 2015. http://data.bls.gov/timeseries/LNS14000000

[25] http://www.ncsl.org/research/labor-and-employment/national-employment-monthly-update.aspx on January 3, 2015

[26] IDC. "Smartphone Vendors." IDC: Analyze the Future. Accessed April 13, 2015. http://www.idc.com/prodserv/smartphone-market-share.jsp

[27] Friedlander, Joshua P. "News and Notes on 2014 RIAA Music Industry Shipment and Revenue Statistics." RIAA. Accessed April 13, 2015. http://riaa.com/media/D1F4E3E8-D3E0-FCEE-BB55-FD8B35BC8785.pdf

[28] Blair, Nancy. "Apple's iTunes Radio Service: 3 Things to Know." *USA Today*. N.p. 11 June 2013. Web. 13 June 2013.

[29] Gross, Doug. "Apple Arrives (Late?) to Music Streaming with iTunes Radio." *CNN.com*. Cable News Network, 11 June 2013. Web. 13 June 2013.

glossary

Aggregate Output the total quantity of goods and services produced by an economic system during a given period.

Balance of Trade the economic value of all the products that a country exports minus the economic value of all the products it imports.

Business organization that provides goods or services to earn profits.

Business Cycle short-term pattern of economic expansions and contractions.

Capital funds needed to create and operate a business enterprise.

Capitalism system that sanctions the private ownership of the factors of production and encourages entrepreneurship by offering profits as an incentive.

Communism political system in which the government owns and operates all factors of production.

Competition vying among businesses for the same resources or customers.

Consumer Price Index (CPI) a measure of the prices of typical products purchased by consumers living in urban areas.

Demand the willingness and ability of buyers to purchase a good or service.

Demand and Supply Schedule assessment of the relationships among different levels of demand and supply at different price levels.

Demand Curve graph showing how many units of a product will be demanded (bought) at different prices.

Depression a prolonged and deep recession.

Domestic Business Environment the environment in which a firm conducts its operations and derives its revenues.

Economic Environment relevant conditions that exist in the economic system in which a company operates.

Economic Indicator a statistic that helps assess the performance of an economy.

Economic System a nation's system for allocating its resources among its citizens.

Entrepreneur business person who accepts both the risks and the opportunities involved in creating and operating a new business venture.

External Environment everything outside an organization's boundaries that might affect it.

Factors of Production resources used in the production of goods and services labor, capital, entrepreneurs, physical resources, and information resources.

Fiscal Policies policies used by a government regarding how it collects and spends revenue.

Global Business Environment the international forces that affect a business.

Gross Domestic Product (GDP) total value of all goods and services produced within a given period by a national economy through domestic factors of production.

GDP Per Capita gross domestic product divided by total population.

Gross National Product (GNP) total value of all goods and services produced by a national economy within a given period regardless of where the factors of production are located.

Inflation occurs when widespread price increases occur throughout an economic system.

Information Resources data and other information used by businesses.

Labor (Human Resources) physical and mental capabilities of people as they contribute to economic production.

Law of Demand principle that buyers will purchase (demand) more of a product as its price drops and less as its price increases.

Law of Supply principle that producers will offer (supply) more of a product for sale as its price rises and less as its price drops.

Market mechanism for exchange between buyers and sellers of a particular good or service.

Market Economy economy in which individuals control production and allocation decisions through supply and demand.

Market Price (Equilibrium Price) profit-maximizing price at which the quantity of goods demanded and the quantity of goods supplied are equal.

Mixed Market Economy economic system featuring characteristics of both planned and market economies.

Monetary Policies policies used by a government to control the size of its money supply.

Monopolistic Competition market or industry characterized by numerous buyers and relatively numerous sellers trying to differentiate their products from those of competitors.

Monopoly market or industry in which there is only one producer that can therefore set the prices of its products.

National Debt the amount of money the government owes its creditors.

Natural Monopoly industry in which one company can most efficiently supply all needed goods or services.

Nominal GDP GDP measured in current dollars or with all components valued at current prices.

Oligopoly market or industry characterized by a handful of (generally large) sellers with the power to influence the prices of their products.

Perfect Competition market or industry characterized by numerous small firms producing an identical product.

Physical Resources tangible items that organizations use in the conduct of their businesses.

Planned Economy economy that relies on a centralized government to control all or most factors of production and to make all or most production and allocation decisions.

Political-Legal Environment the relationship between business and government, usually in the form of government regulation of business.

Private Enterprise economic system that allows individuals to pursue their own interests without undue governmental restriction.

Privatization process of converting government enterprises into privately owned companies.

Productivity a measure of economic growth that compares how much a system produces with the resources needed to produce it.

Profits difference between a business's revenues and its expenses.

Purchasing Power Parity the principle that exchange rates are set so that the prices of similar products in different countries are about the same.

Real GDP GDP adjusted to account for changes in currency values and price changes.

Recession a period during which aggregate output, as measured by GDP, declines.

Shortage situation in which quantity demanded exceeds quantity supplied.

Socialism planned economic system in which the government owns and operates only selected major sources of production.

Sociocultural Environment the customs, mores, values, and demographic characteristics of the society in which an organization functions.

Stability condition in which the amount of money available in an economic system and the quantity of goods and services produced in it are growing at about the same rate.

Stabilization Policy government economic policy intended to smooth out fluctuations in output and unemployment and to stabilize prices.

Standard of Living the total quantity and quality of goods and services people can purchase with the currency used in their economic system.

Supply the willingness and ability of producers to offer a good or service for sale.

Supply Curve graph showing how many units of a product will be supplied (offered for sale) at different prices.

Surplus situation in which quantity supplied exceeds quantity demanded.

Technological Environment all the ways by which firms create value for their constituents.

Unemployment the level of joblessness among people actively seeking work in an economic system.

Entrepreneurship, New Ventures, and Business Ownership

From Chapter 3 of *Business Essentials*, Eleventh Edition. Ronald J. Ebert, Ricky W. Griffin. Copyright © 2017 by Pearson Education, Inc. All rights reserved.

Entrepreneurship, New Ventures, and Business Ownership

NETFLIX
.com

Martin E. Klimek/ZUMA Press, Inc./Alamy

36

What makes entrepreneurs tick? What drives

them to succeed even if they first fail?

The lessons they

offer pave the road to business victory.

After reading this chapter, you should be able to:

1   **Define** *small business*, discuss its importance to the U.S. economy, and explain popular areas of small business.

2   **Explain** entrepreneurship and describe some key characteristics of entrepreneurial personalities and activities.

3   **Describe** distinctive competence, the business plan, and the start-up decisions made by small businesses and identify sources of financial aid available to such enterprises.

4   **Discuss** the trends in small business start-ups and identify the main reasons for success and failure among small businesses.

5   **Explain** sole proprietorships, partnerships, and cooperatives and discuss the advantages and disadvantages of each.

6   **Describe** corporations, discuss their advantages and disadvantages, and identify different kinds of corporations; explain the basic issues involved in managing a corporation and discuss special issues related to corporate ownership.

It All Started
With a Late Fee

In the 1980s and 1990s, consumers who wanted to watch movies at home headed to their neighborhood movie rental store. Blockbuster was the clear leader in the market. Consumers were able to rent a movie for a flat fee of several dollars, but late fees were steep. In 1997, California entrepreneur Reed Hastings incurred a $40 late fee at Blockbuster. "It was six weeks late," he admits. "I had misplaced the cassette [and] I didn't want to tell my wife.... I was embarrassed about it." After locating the *Apollo* 13 movie that he had rented several weeks before, he dropped off the VHS cassette and paid the late fee on his way to the gym. As it turns out, his itinerary for the day was quite opportune: In the middle of his workout, he recalls, "I realized [the gym] had a much better business model. You could pay $30 or $40 a month and work out as little or as much as you wanted."

Thus, the idea for Netflix was born. But Hastings knew he needed to start slowly. So, when Netflix was launched in 1997, its only innovations involved the convenience of ordering movies over the Internet and receiving and returning them by mail; Netflix merely rented movies for $4 apiece plus $2 for postage (and, yes, it charged late fees). Basically, the customer base consisted of people who wanted to watch movies without having to leave the house. But Hastings and co-founder Marc Randolph quickly decided to test a subscription-based model, unlimited rentals by mail for a flat fee and, perhaps most important, no due dates (and thus no late fees). Current customers were first offered the opportunity to shift from their pay-per-rental plans to subscription plans on a free-trial basis and then given the chance to renew the subscription plan on a paid basis. "We knew it wouldn't be terrible," says Hastings, "but we didn't know if it would be great." In the first month, however, 80 percent of Netflix users who'd tried the no-cost subscription plan had renewed on a paid basis.

"Having unlimited due dates and no late fees," said Hastings back in 2003, "has worked in a powerful way and now seems obvious, but at that time, we had no idea if customers would even build and use an online queue." The "queue," as any Netflix user will tell you, is the list of movies that the customer wants to watch. Netflix maintains your queue, follows your online directions in keeping it up to date, and automatically sends you the next movie you want each time you send one back.

The essence of queuing—and of the Netflix business model—is clearly convenience. Although the ability to enhance customer convenience, even when combined with cost savings, often gives a company a competitive advantage in its industry, it doesn't always have the industry-wide effect that it's had in the case of Netflix. Not only did the Netflix subscriber model

Minerva Studio/Fotolia

what's in it
for me?

A recent Gallup poll suggests that almost half of the young people in the United States today are interested in entrepreneurship.[1] Even if you are not among that number, you will still be called on to interact with small businesses and entrepreneurs as a customer, as an investor, or as a client. You may also be trying to sell products or services to small businesses and entrepreneurs. One key to understanding entrepreneurship is to understand entrepreneurs themselves and what it takes for them to succeed. Reed Hastings displays many of the characteristics key to entrepreneurial success. Netflix also highlights some of the problems inherent in converting a great business idea into a profitable enterprise. If you ever aspire to start and run your own business, you can learn valuable lessons from the experiences of Hastings and his management team. As an investor, you should also be better prepared to assess the market potential for new and up-and-coming businesses. This chapter will discuss these and additional issues important for starting and owning a business, including the business plan, reasons for success and failure, and the advantages and disadvantages of different kinds of ownership. First, we'll start by defining a small business and identifying its importance in the U.S. economy.

improve the service provided by the industry in an unexpected way but ultimately it also weakened the competitive positions of companies already doing business in the industry—notably, Blockbuster. By 2010, Blockbuster had declared bankruptcy, and Dish Network acquired the company the following year. In the years since, all of Blockbuster's retail stores have been closed as well as its DVD rental-by-mail operation, although Dish Network still retains rights to the name. Investors who had purchased a share of Netflix stock in early 2009 for $36 found that their stock had grown to more than $440 by the beginning of 2015.

How had Hastings's upstart company managed to put itself in such an enviable position? For one thing, it got off to a fast start. In 1997, when DVDs were just being test-marketed in the United States, Hastings and Randolph decided that the new medium would eventually overtake videocassettes as the format of choice for both the home-movie industry and the home-movie renter. They were right, of course. By 2002, one in four U.S. households owned a DVD player, but the number today is close to 9 in 10. (In any case, it would have cost about $4 to mail a videocassette both ways, compared to the $0.78 that it costs to ship a DVD disc back and forth.)

More important, as the first company to rent movies by mail, Netflix was the first to establish a rental-by-mail customer base. At first, says Hastings, "people thought the idea was crazy. But it was precisely because it was a contrarian idea that [it] enabled us to get ahead of our competitors." As Netflix has continued to expand and nurture its subscriber base, it's also generated both brand recognition and brand loyalty. "Netflix has customer loyalty. It's a passion brand," explains Hastings, who hastens to add that keeping customers happy is crucial "because the more someone uses Netflix, the more likely they are to stay with us."

Today, Netflix continues to be at the forefront of innovation and has established a strong position in the emerging video-on-demand market. Netflix continues to innovate, developing original content such as the wildly popular *House of Cards* and *Orange Is the New Black*. (After studying this chapter, you should be able to respond to the set of discussion questions found at the end of the chapter.)

OBJECTIVE 1
Define

small business, discuss its importance to the U.S. economy, and explain popular areas of small business.

Small Business Administration (SBA) *government agency charged with assisting small businesses*

Small Business *independently owned business that has relatively little influence in its market*

What Is a Small Business?

The term *small business* is not easy to define. Locally owned-and-operated restaurants, dry cleaners, and hair salons are obviously small businesses, and giant corporations, such as Dell, Starbucks, Apple, Walmart, and Netflix, are clearly big businesses. Between these two extremes, though, fall thousands of companies that cannot be easily categorized.

The U.S. Department of Commerce has traditionally considered a business to be small if it has fewer than 500 employees. The U.S. **Small Business Administration (SBA)**, a government agency that assists small businesses, has different standards based on industry. For instance, a manufacturer is considered to be small if it has 1,500 or fewer employees. A wholesaling firm is small if it has between 100 and 500 employees. Other industries, though, such as services, retailing, and construction, are classified based on revenue. Because strict numerical terms sometimes lead to contradictory classifications, we will consider a **small business** to be one that is independent (that is, not part of a larger business) and that has relatively little influence in its market. A small neighborhood grocer would be small, assuming it is not part of a chain and that market forces largely set the prices it pays to wholesalers and that it can charge its customers. Dell Computer was a small business when founded by Michael Dell in 1984, but today it's one of the world's largest computer companies and is not small in any sense of the term. Hence, it can negotiate from a position of strength with its suppliers and can set its prices with less consideration for what other computer firms are charging.

The Importance of Small Business in the U.S. Economy

As Figure 1 shows, most U.S. businesses employ fewer than 100 people, and most U.S. workers are employed by small business. Moreover, this same pattern exists across most free-market economies.

Figure 1(a) shows that 89.29 percent of all businesses employ 20 or fewer people. Another 8.88 percent employ between 20 and 99 people, and 1.52 percent employ between 100 and 499. Only about .16 of 1 percent employ 1,000 or more people. Figure 1(b) also shows that 17.74 percent of all workers are employed by firms with fewer than 20 people, and 17.11 percent are employed by firms with between 20 and 99 people. Another 14.52 percent are employed by firms with between 100 and 499 people. So, around half of all workers are employed by firms with 500 or fewer employees and the other half work for larger organizations. We can measure the contribution of small business in terms of its impact on key aspects of the U.S. economic system, including *job creation, innovation*, and their *contributions to big business*.

Job Creation Small businesses—especially in certain industries—are an important source of new (and often well-paid) jobs. In recent years, small businesses have accounted for around 40 percent of all new jobs in high-technology sectors of the economy.[2] Jobs are created by companies of all sizes, all of which hire and lay off workers. Although small firms often hire at a faster rate, they also tend to cut jobs at a higher rate. They are generally the first to hire in times of economic recovery, and big firms are generally the last to lay off workers during downswings.

However, relative job growth among businesses of different sizes is not easy to determine. For one thing, when a successful small business starts adding employees

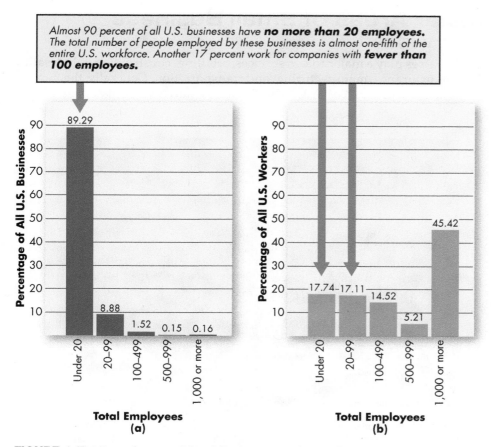

Almost 90 percent of all U.S. businesses have **no more than 20 employees.** The total number of people employed by these businesses is almost one-fifth of the entire U.S. workforce. Another 17 percent work for companies with **fewer than 100 employees.**

FIGURE 1 The Pervasiveness of Small Business in the United States
Source: Data from www.census.gov/

at a rapid clip, it may quickly cease being small. For example, Dell Computer had 1 employee in 1984 (Dell himself). But the payroll grew to 100 employees in 1986; 2,000 in 1992; more than 39,000 in 2004; 94,300 in 2010; and 111,300 in 2014. Although there was no precise point at which Dell turned from "small" into "large," some of the jobs it created could be counted in the small business sector and some in the large.

Innovation History reminds us that major innovations are as likely to come from small businesses (or individuals) as from big ones. Small firms and individuals invented the PC, the stainless-steel razor blade, the photocopier, and the jet engine and launched Facebook, Amazon, Starbucks, and eBay. Innovations are not always new products, though. Dell didn't invent the PC; he developed an innovative way to build it (buy finished components and then assemble them) and an innovative way to sell it (directly to consumers, first by telephone and now online). Similarly, Reed Hastings invented neither the DVD nor the DVD rental business, but he did introduce revolutionary new payment and delivery models. In general, small businesses produce 13 times as many patents per employee as large patenting firms.[3]

Contributions to Big Business Most of the products made by big businesses are sold to consumers by small ones. For example, most dealerships that sell Fords, Toyotas, and Volvos are independently operated. Even as more shoppers turn to online shopping, smaller businesses still play critical roles. For instance, most larger online retailers actually outsource the creation of their websites and the distribution of their products to other firms, many of them small or regional companies. Smaller businesses also provide data storage services for larger businesses. Moreover, small businesses provide big ones with many of their services and raw materials. Microsoft, for instance, relies on hundreds of small firms for most of its routine code-writing functions.

Popular Areas of Small Business Enterprise

Small businesses play a major role in services, retailing, construction, wholesaling, finance and insurance, manufacturing, and transportation. Generally, the more resources that are required, the harder a business is to start and the less likely it is that

New businesses often emerge in response to emerging opportunities. For instance, an increase in the number of working families with pets has created an opportunity for professional dog walkers. Most dog walkers, in turn, are individual entrepreneurs.

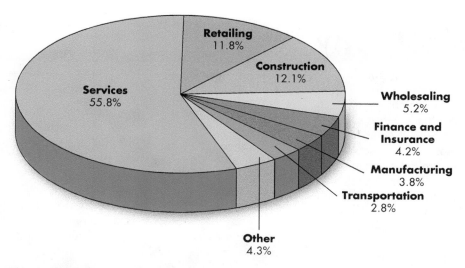

FIGURE 2 Small Business by Industry
Source: www.census.gov/econ/susb/

small firms dominate an industry. *Small* is a relative term. The criteria (number of employees and total annual sales) differ among industries and are often meaningful only when compared with truly large businesses. Figure 2 shows the distribution of all U.S. businesses employing fewer than 20 people across industry groups.

Services About 55.8 percent of businesses with fewer than 20 employees are involved in the service industry, which ranges from marriage counseling to computer software, from management consulting to professional dog walking. Partly because they require few resources (and hence don't cost as much to start), service providers are the fastest-growing segment of small business.

Retailing Retailers, which sell products made by other firms directly to consumers, account for about 11.8 percent of small businesses. Usually, people who start small retail businesses favor specialty shops, such as big men's clothing or gourmet coffees that let the owners focus limited resources on narrow or small market segments.

Construction About 12.1 percent of all U.S. businesses are involved in construction. Because many construction jobs are small local projects, such as a homeowner adding a garage or remodeling a room, local contractors are often best suited to handle them.

Wholesaling Small business owners often do well in wholesaling, which accounts for about 5.2 percent of businesses with fewer than 20 employees. Wholesalers buy products in bulk from manufacturers or other producers and store them in quantities and locations convenient for selling them to retailers.

Finance and Insurance Financial and insurance firms account for about 4.2 percent of small businesses. Most of these businesses, such as local State Farm Insurance offices, are affiliates of or agents for larger national firms. Small locally owned banks are also common in smaller communities and rural areas.

Manufacturing More than any other industry, manufacturing lends itself to big business, but it still accounts for about 3.8 percent of firms with fewer than 20 employees. Indeed, small manufacturers sometimes outperform big ones in such innovation-driven industries as electronics, equipment and machine parts, and computer software.

finding a better way

The Rise of Services

Manufacturing is a form of business that combines and transforms resources into tangible outcomes that are then sold to others. Goodyear is a manufacturer because it combines rubber and chemical compounds and uses blending equipment and molding machines to create tires. Broyhill is a manufacturer because it buys wood and metal components, pads, and fabric and then combines them into furniture. And Apple is a manufacturer because it uses electronic, metal, plastic, and composite components to build smartphones, computers, and other digital products.

Manufacturing was once the dominant technology in the United States. During the 1970s, though, manufacturing entered a long period of decline, primarily because of foreign competition. U.S. firms had grown lax and sluggish, and new foreign competitors came onto the scene with better equipment, much higher levels of efficiency, and employees willing to work for lower wages. For example, steel companies in Asia were able to produce high-quality steel for much lower prices than large U.S. steel companies such as Bethlehem Steel and U.S. Steel. Faced with a battle for survival, some companies disappeared, but many others underwent a long and difficult period of change by eliminating waste and transforming themselves into leaner, more efficient, and responsive entities. They reduced their workforces dramatically, closed antiquated or unnecessary plants, and modernized their remaining plants. Over the last decade or so, however, their efforts have started to pay dividends because U.S. manufacturing has regained a competitive position in many different industries. Although low wages continue to center a great deal of global manufacturing in Asia, once-strong manufacturers are once again thriving in the United States.

During the decline of the manufacturing sector, a tremendous growth in the service sector, often fueled by visionary entrepreneurs, kept the overall U.S. economy from declining at the same rate. A service organization is one that transforms resources into an intangible output and creates time or place utility for its customers. For example, Netflix provides video rentals through mail order and online delivery options. Facebook offers its members a venue for networking and interacting with others. And your local hairdresser cuts your hair. In 1947, the service sector was responsible for less than half of the U.S. gross national product (GNP). By 1975, however, this figure reached 65 percent, and by 2006, it had surpassed 75 percent. The service sector has been responsible for almost 90 percent of all new jobs created in the United States since 1990.

Moreover, employment in service occupations is expected to continue to represent a larger share of employment in the

Gemenacom/Shutterstock

U.S. economy. In 2002, 76.3 percent of U.S. workers were employed in the service sector and this grew to 79.9 percent in 2012. By 2022, it is expected that 80.9 percent of workers in this country will be employed in service jobs. Among all service jobs, it is expected that professional and business services and health care and social assistance will represent an increased share. Looking at the Bureau of Labor Statistics list of the fastest-growing occupations between 2012 and 2022, we see that almost all of these occupations are in the service sector, largely in the areas of professional and business services and health care and social assistance.

Managers have come to see that many of the tools, techniques, and methods that are used in a factory are also useful to a service firm. For example, managers of automobile plants and hair salons each have to decide how to design their facility, identify the best location for it, determine optimal capacity, make decisions about inventory storage, set procedures for purchasing raw materials, and set standards for productivity and quality. At the same time, though, service-based firms must hire and train employees based on a different skill set than is required by most manufacturers. For instance, consumers seldom come into contact with the Toyota employee who installs the seats in their car, so that person can be hired based on technical skills. But Toyota must also recruit people for sales and customer service jobs who not only know how to do a job but who can also effectively interface with a variety of consumers. In addition, most services are simultaneously produced and consumed, so traditional models of quality control need to be revisited. As the service economy grows, managers will need to learn more about how to effectively recruit, train, and reward employees in service jobs.[4]

Transportation About 2.8 percent of small companies are in transportation and related businesses, including many taxi and limousine companies, charter airplane services, and tour operators.

Other The remaining 4.3 percent or so of small businesses are in other industries, such as small research-and-development laboratories and independent media companies—start-up web channels, small-town newspapers, and radio broadcasters.

Entrepreneurship

OBJECTIVE 2
Explain
entrepreneurship and describe some key characteristics of entrepreneurial personalities and activities.

We noted previously that Dell Computer started as a one-person operation and grew into a giant corporation. Dell's growth was spurred by the imagination and skill of Michael Dell, the entrepreneur who founded the company. **Entrepreneurs** are people, like Dell, who assume the risk of business ownership.[5] **Entrepreneurship** is the process of seeking business opportunities under conditions of risk. However, not all entrepreneurs have the same goals.

Entrepreneur *businessperson who accepts both the risks and the opportunities involved in creating and operating a new business venture*

Entrepreneurship *the process of seeking businesses opportunities under conditions of risk*

Entrepreneurship Goals

People may decide to pursue entrepreneurship for a variety of reasons. Many entrepreneurs seek to launch a new business with the goal of independence—independence from working for someone else, coupled with some reasonable degree of financial security. Such entrepreneurs want to achieve a safe and secure financial future for themselves and their families but do not necessarily aspire to grow their business beyond their capacity to run it. Consider Jack Matz, a former corporate executive in Houston who lost his job when his firm merged with another. Rather than look for another management position, Matz opened a photocopying and custom printing business near a local university. His goal was to earn enough money to lead a comfortable life until he retires in 10 years. The term *small business* is most closely associated with these kinds of enterprises.

Other entrepreneurs, however, launch new businesses with the goal of growth and expansion—that is, to transform their venture into a large business. This was Dell's vision when he started his business; likewise, when Howard Schultz took over Starbucks, he also had plans to grow and develop the fledgling coffee company into a much larger enterprise. Terms such as *new ventures* and *start-ups* are often used to refer to these kinds of businesses.

In still other cases, the goals of an entrepreneur may not always be clear in the early stages of business development. For instance, one entrepreneur might launch a business with little or no expectation that it will have huge growth potential but then find that it can grow dramatically. Mark Zuckerberg, for example, had no idea that his Facebook firm would grow to its present size. Another entrepreneur might start out with ambitious growth plans but find that expected opportunities cannot be realized: Perhaps there is no large market or another firm established dominance over that market first.

Entrepreneurial Characteristics

Regardless of their goals, many successful entrepreneurs share certain characteristics. Among these characteristics are resourcefulness and a concern for good, often personal, customer relations. Most of them also have a strong desire to be their own bosses. Many express a need to "gain control over my life" or "build for the family" and believe that building successful businesses will help them do it. They can also deal with uncertainty and risk.

Yesterday's entrepreneur was often stereotyped as "the boss"—self-reliant, male, and able to make quick, firm decisions. Today's entrepreneur is seen more often as an open-minded leader who relies on networks, business plans, and consensus. Past and present entrepreneurs also have different views on such topics as how to succeed, how to automate business, and when to rely on experience in the trade or on basic business acumen.[6]

Consider Yoshiko Shinohara, who had lost her father by the age of 8, was divorced by the age of 28, and never received a college education. At the age of 70, she is Chairman and Director of Tempstaff, a Japanese temp agency that she started out of her one-room apartment more than 35 years ago. Fueled by Japan's need for temps during a period of stagnation in the 1990s and Shinohara's ambition, Tempstaff is now a $3.1 billion company with a high-rise headquarters in Tokyo.[7]

Among other things, Shinohara's story illustrates what is almost always a key element in entrepreneurship: risk. Interestingly, most successful entrepreneurs seldom see what they do as risky. Whereas others may focus on possibilities for failure and balk at gambling everything on a new venture, most entrepreneurs are so passionate about their ideas and plans that they see little or no likelihood of failure. For example, when Shinohara started Tempstaff, few Japanese businesses understood or had even heard of the temporary worker concept. But Shinohara felt that she "had nothing to lose anyway" and preferred taking that risk to ending up "serving tea or just being a clerical assistant."[8]

Starting and Operating a New Business

OBJECTIVE 3
Describe
distinctive competence, the business plan, and the start-up decisions made by small businesses and identify sources of financial aid available to such enterprises.

First the Internet and more recently social media have dramatically changed the rules for starting and operating a small business. Setting up is easier and faster than ever, there are more potential opportunities than at any other time, and the ability to gather and assess information is at an all-time high. Today, for example, many one-person retailers do most of their business—both buying and selling—on Internet auction sites, such as eBay.

Even so, would-be entrepreneurs must make the right start-up decisions. For instance, they need to have a clear vision of why their business will succeed. They must also decide how to get into business—should they buy an existing business or build from the ground up? They must know when to seek expert advice and where to find sources of financing. If, for example, a new firm needs financial backing from investors or a line of credit from vendors or distributors, the entrepreneur must have in place a comprehensive, well-crafted business plan. Creating a business plan, in turn, begins with understanding the potential firm's distinctive competences.

Understanding Distinctive Competencies

An organization's distinctive competencies are the aspects of business that the firm performs better than its competitors. The distinctive competencies of small business usually fall into three areas: (1) the ability to identify new niches in established markets, (2) the ability to identify new markets, and (3) the ability to move quickly to take advantage of new opportunities.

Established Market *one in which many firms compete according to relatively well-defined criteria*

Niche *a segment of a market that is not currently being exploited*

Identifying Niches in Established Markets
An **established market** is one in which many firms compete according to relatively well-defined criteria. For example, the video rental market was well established when Hastings decided to launch Netflix. Blockbuster was the dominant firm, but many independent video rental firms were also prospering. Retail outlets kept an inventory of video products available for rent. Customers drove or walked to the stores, paid a fee, and took a video home. They kept it for a defined period of time and then returned it to the store (with a late fee, if they kept it too long). A **niche** is simply a segment of a market that is not currently being exploited. In general, small entrepreneurial businesses are better at discovering these niches than are larger organizations. Large organizations usually have

so many resources committed to older, established business practices that they may be unaware of new opportunities. Entrepreneurs can see these opportunities and move quickly to take advantage of them. Hastings's decision to rent by mail allowed Netflix to exploit a niche.

Entrepreneurs Dave Gilboa and Neil Blumenthal founded Warby Parker, a business that sells prescription eyewear through the mail. The entrepreneurs realized that most consumers disliked the experience of going to an optical shop to try on glasses and then were irritated at the price of those glasses. So, Warby Parker offers lower-priced glasses with hip designs and a money-back guarantee. Astute marketing then allowed them to get a quick start with their niche business, selling more than 50,000 pairs of glasses and generating profits after only a single year of operation.[9] Warby Parker has now established itself as a leading eyewear retailer.

Identifying New Markets Successful entrepreneurs also excel at discovering whole new markets. Discovery can happen in at least two ways. First, an entrepreneur can transfer a product or service that is well established in one geographic market to a second market. This is what Marcel Bich did with ballpoint pens, which occupied a well-established market in Europe before Bich introduced them in the United States more than 50 years ago. Bich's company, Société Bic, eventually came to dominate the U.S. market.

Second, entrepreneurs can sometimes create entire industries. Entrepreneurial inventions of the dry paper copying process and the semiconductor have created vast new industries. Not only were the first companies to enter these markets successful (Xerox and National Semiconductor, respectively) but their entrepreneurial activity also spawned the development of hundreds of other companies and hundreds of thousands of jobs. Again, because entrepreneurs are not encumbered with a history of doing business in a particular way, they are usually better at discovering new markets than are larger, more mature organizations.

First-Mover Advantages A **first-mover advantage** is any advantage that comes to a firm because it exploits an opportunity before any other firm does. Sometimes large firms discover niches within existing markets or new markets at just about the same time as small entrepreneurial firms, but they cannot move as quickly as small companies to take advantage of these opportunities. Many of the "app" developers for smartphones exploit first-mover advantage.

There are numerous reasons for the difference. For example, many large organizations make decisions slowly because each of their many layers of hierarchy has to approve an action before it can be implemented. Also, large organizations may sometimes put a great deal of their assets at risk when they take advantage of new opportunities. Every time Boeing decides to build a new model of a commercial jet, it is making a decision that could literally bankrupt the company if it does not turn out well. The size of the risk may make large organizations cautious. The dollar value of the assets at risk in a small organization, in contrast, is quite small. Managers may be willing to "bet the company" when the value of the company is only $100,000. They might be unwilling to "bet the company" when the value of the company is $1 billion.

First-Mover Advantage any advantage that comes to a firm because it exploits an opportunity before any other firm does

Crafting a Business Plan

After the would-be entrepreneur has defined a potential distinctive competence and made the decision to proceed, the next step is formulating a **business plan** in which the entrepreneur describes his or her business strategy for the new venture and demonstrates how it will be implemented.[10] A real benefit of a business plan is the fact that in the act of preparing it, the would-be entrepreneur is forced to develop the business idea on paper and firm up his or her thinking about how to launch it before investing time and money in it. The idea of the business plan isn't new. What is new is the use of specialized business plans, mostly because creditors and investors demand them as tools for deciding whether to finance or invest.

Business Plan document in which the entrepreneur summarizes his or her business strategy for the proposed new venture and how that strategy will be implemented

Setting Goals and Objectives A business plan describes the match between the entrepreneur's abilities and experiences and the requirements for producing or marketing a particular product. It also defines strategies for production and marketing, legal elements and organization, and accounting and finance. In particular, a business plan should answer three questions: (1) What are the entrepreneur's goals and objectives? (2) What strategies will be used to obtain them? (3) How will these strategies be implemented?

Sales Forecasting Although a key element of any business plan is sales forecasts, plans must carefully build an argument for likely business success based on sound logic and research. Entrepreneurs, for example, can't forecast sales revenues without first researching markets. Simply asserting that the new venture will sell 100,000 units per month is not credible; the entrepreneur must demonstrate an understanding of the current market, of the strengths and weaknesses of existing firms, and of the means by which the new venture will compete. Without the sales forecast, no one can estimate the required size of a plant, store, or office or decide how much inventory to carry and how many employees to hire.

Financial Planning Financial planning refers to the entrepreneur's plan for turning all other activities into dollars. It generally includes a cash budget, an income statement, balance sheets, and a breakeven chart. The cash budget shows how much money you need before you open for business and how much you need to keep the business going before it starts earning a profit.

Starting the Small Business

A Chinese proverb says that a journey of a thousand miles begins with a single step. This is also true of a new business. The first step is the individual's commitment to becoming a business owner. In preparing a business plan, the entrepreneur must choose the industry and market in which he or she plans to compete. This choice means assessing not only industry conditions and trends but also one's own abilities and interests. Like big business managers, small business owners must understand the nature of the enterprises in which they are engaged.

Buying an Existing Business After an entrepreneur has forecast sales and completed the financial planning, then he or she must decide whether to buy an existing business or start from scratch. Many experts recommend the first approach because, quite simply, the odds are better: If it's successful, an existing business has already proven its ability to attract customers and generate profit. It has also established relationships with lenders, suppliers, and other stakeholders. Moreover, an existing track record gives potential buyers a much clearer picture of what to expect than any estimate of a start-up's prospects.

Ray Kroc bought McDonald's as an existing business, added entrepreneurial vision and business insight, and produced a multinational giant. Both Southwest Airlines and Starbucks were small but struggling operations when entrepreneurs took over and grew them into large businesses. About 35 percent of all new businesses that were started in the past decade were bought from someone else.

Franchising Most McDonald's, Subway, 7 Eleven, RE/Max, Holiday Inn, and Dunkin' Donuts outlets are franchises operating under licenses issued by parent companies to local owners. A **franchise** agreement involves two parties, a *franchisee* (the local owner) and a *franchiser* (the parent company).[11]

Franchisees benefit from the parent corporation's experience and expertise, and the franchiser may even supply financing. It may pick the store location, negotiate the lease, design the store, and purchase equipment. It may train the first set of employees and managers and issue standard policies and procedures. Once the business is open, the franchiser may offer savings by allowing the franchisee to purchase from

Franchise *arrangement in which a buyer (franchisee) purchases the right to sell the good or service of the seller (franchiser)*

a central location. Marketing strategy (especially advertising) may also be handled by the franchiser. In short, franchisees receive—that is, invest in—not only their own ready-made businesses but also expert help in running them.

Franchises have advantages for both sellers and buyers. Franchises can grow rapidly by using the investment money provided by franchisees. The franchisee gets to own a business and has access to big-business management skills. The franchisee does not have to build a business step by step, and because each franchise outlet is probably similar to other outlets, failure is less likely. Recent statistics show that franchising is on the upswing. For instance, franchise businesses added 247,000 jobs in 2014 and generated economic output of $889 billion. The franchise sector will contribute an estimated 3 percent of the U.S. GDP in 2015.[12]

Perhaps the most significant disadvantage in owning a franchise is the start-up cost. Franchise prices vary widely. The fee for a Fantastic Sam's hair salon is $185,000; however, the franchisee must also invest additional funds in building and outfitting the salon. A McDonald's franchise has an initial fee of at least $1 million, but again requires the additional funds to construct and outfit a restaurant; the costs generally run the total outlay to over $2 million. And professional sports teams (which are also franchises) can cost several hundred million dollars. Franchisees may also be obligated to contribute a percentage of sales to parent corporations. From the perspective of the parent company, some firms choose not to franchise to retain more control over quality and earn more profits for themselves. Starbucks, for instance, does not franchise its coffee shops. (Starbucks does have licensing agreements where other firms operate Starbucks kiosks and other niche outlets; it does not, though, franchise individual free-standing coffee shops to individuals.)

Starting from Scratch Despite the odds, some people seek the satisfaction that comes from planting an idea and growing it into a healthy business. There are also practical reasons to start from scratch. A new business doesn't suffer the ill effects of a prior owner's errors, and the start-up owner is free to choose lenders, equipment, inventories, locations, suppliers, and workers. Of all new businesses begun in the past decade, about 64 percent were started from scratch. Dell Computer, Walmart, Microsoft, Amazon, and Twitter are among today's most successful businesses that were started from scratch by an entrepreneur.

But as we have already noted, the risks of starting a business from scratch are greater than those of buying an existing firm. New business founders can only make projections about their prospects. Success or failure depends on identifying a genuine opportunity, such as a product for which many customers will pay well but which is currently unavailable. To find openings, entrepreneurs must study markets and answer the following questions:

- Who and where are my customers?

- How much will those customers pay for my product?

- How much of my product can I expect to sell?

- Who are my competitors?

- Why will customers buy my product rather than the product of my competitors?

Financing the Small Business

Although the choice of how to start a business is obviously important, it's meaningless unless you can get the money to finance your ideas. Among the more common sources for funding are family and friends, personal savings, lending institutions, investors, and governmental agencies. Lending institutions are more likely to help finance the purchase of an existing business because the risks are better understood. Individuals starting new businesses will probably have to rely on personal resources. One of the many causes of the 2008–2011 recession was a sharp reduction in the availability of credit, including funds to help start new businesses. This credit crunch, in turn, limited both new start-up funding and funding for existing businesses wanting to make new investments.

According to the National Federation of Independent Business, personal resources, not loans, are the most important sources of money. Including money borrowed from friends and relatives, personal resources account for more than two-thirds of all money invested in new small businesses, and one-half of that is used to purchase existing businesses. Getting money from banks, independent investors, and government loans requires extra effort. At a minimum, banks and private investors will want to review business plans, and government loans have strict eligibility guidelines.

Venture capital companies are groups of small investors seeking to make profits on companies with rapid growth potential. Most of these firms do not lend money. They invest it, supplying capital in return for partial ownership (like stocks, discussed later in this chapter). They may also demand representation on boards of directors. In some cases, managers need approval from the venture capital company before making major decisions. In most cases, venture capitalists do not provide money to start a new business; instead, once a business has been successfully launched and its growth potential established, they provide the funds to fuel expansion. Of all venture capital currently committed in the United States, about 30 percent comes from true venture capital firms. Steve Case, founder of AOL, operates a successful venture capital company. He looks to invest in new start-ups that have a great business idea, a passionate entrepreneur, and a solid and well-crafted business plan.[13]

Small business investment companies (SBICs) also invest in companies with potential for rapid growth. They are federally licensed to borrow money from the SBA and to invest it in or lend it to small businesses, and they are themselves investments for their shareholders. Past beneficiaries of SBIC capital include Apple Computer, Intel, and FedEx. The government also sponsors *minority enterprise small business investment companies (MESBICs)*. As the name suggests, MESBICs target minority-owned businesses.

SBA Financial Programs

Since its founding in 1953, the SBA has sponsored financing programs for small businesses that meet standards in size and independence. Eligible firms must be unable to get private financing at reasonable terms. The most common form of SBA financing, its *7(a) loans programs*, allows small businesses to borrow from commercial lenders and guarantees to repay up to 85 percent of loans of up to $150,000 and 75 percent of loans of more than $150,000.[14] The SBA's *special purpose loans* target businesses with specific needs, such as meeting international demands or implementing pollution-control measures. For loans under $50,000, the SBA offers the *micro loan program*. The *Certified Development Company (504) program* offers fixed interest rates on loans from nonprofit community-based lenders to boost local economies.[15]

The SBA also helps entrepreneurs improve their management skills. The Service Corps of Retired Executives (SCORE) is made up of retired executives who volunteer to help entrepreneurs start new businesses. The **Small Business Development Center (SBDC)** program consolidates information from various disciplines and institutions for use by new and existing small businesses.

Other Sources of Financing

Some entrepreneurs find financing from overseas investors. James Buck developed a new implantable heart device to treat certain heart conditions but could not find adequate funding to start his business. He ended up looking to investors in Asia and obtained $5 million from the government of Malaysia.[16]

The Internet has also opened doors to new financing options. For instance, Kabbage.com is an online company that provides cash advances to small business.[17]

Margin glossary terms:

Venture Capital Company *group of small investors who invest money in companies with rapid growth potential*

Small Business Investment Company (SBIC) *government-regulated investment company that borrows money from the SBA to invest in or lend to a small business*

Small Business Development Center (SBDC) *SBA program designed to consolidate information from various disciplines and make it available to small businesses*

Trends, Successes, and Failures in New Ventures

OBJECTIVE 4
Discuss
the trends in small business
start-ups and identify the main
reasons for success and failure
among small businesses.

For every Sam Walton, Mark Zuckerberg, Mary Kay Ash, or Bill Gates—entrepreneurs who transformed small businesses into big ones—there are many entrepreneurs who fail. Each year, generally between 610,000 and 835,000 new businesses are launched in the United States. On the other hand, between 605,000 and 805,000 businesses fail each year.[18] In 2014, for instance, approximately 668,000 new firms started operations and another 691,000 closed down. In this section, we look first at a few key trends in small business start-ups. Then we examine some of the reasons for success and failure in small business undertakings.

Trends in Small Business Start-Ups

As noted previously, thousands of new businesses are started in the United States every year. Several factors account for this trend, and in this section, we focus on five of them.

Emergence of E-commerce The most significant recent trend is the rapid emergence of e-commerce. Because the Internet provides fundamentally new ways of doing business, savvy entrepreneurs have created and expanded new businesses faster and easier than ever before. Such leading-edge firms as Google, Amazon, and eBay owe their existence to the Internet. Figure 3 underscores this point by summarizing the growth in e-commerce from 2003 through 2010.

Crossovers from Big Business More businesses are being started by people who have opted to leave big corporations and put their experience to work for themselves. In some cases, they see great new ideas that they want to develop. Others get burned out in the corporate world. Some have lost their jobs, only

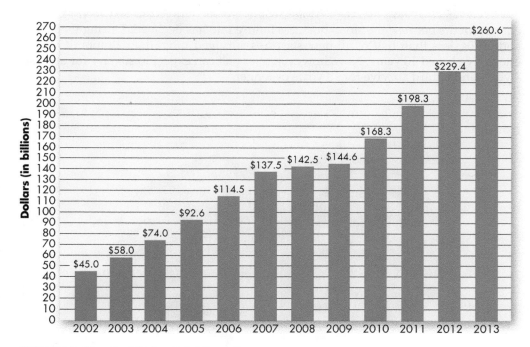

FIGURE 3 Growth of Online Retail Spending
Source: http://www.census.gov/retail/

to discover that working for themselves was a better idea anyway. John Chambers spent several years working at IBM and Wang Laboratories/GLOBAL before he decided to try his hand at entrepreneurship. After resigning from Wang in 1991, he signed on to help Cisco, then a small and struggling firm. Under his leadership and entrepreneurial guidance, Cisco has become one of the largest and most important technology companies in the world.

Opportunities for Minorities and Women

More small businesses are also being started by minorities and women.[19] The number of businesses owned by African Americans increased by 60 percent during the most recent five-year period for which data are available and now is about 2 million. The number of Hispanic-owned businesses has grown 44 percent and now is about 2.25 million. Ownership among Asians has increased 41 percent and among Pacific Islanders 35 percent.[20]

Almost 9.1 million businesses are also now owned by women, and they generate a combined $1.4 trillion in revenue a year and employ about 7.9 million workers.[21] Figure 4 shows some of the reasons women cite for starting their own businesses. Anne Beiler bought a small Amish-owned pretzel stand to support her family when her husband decided to become a no-fee marriage counselor. She worked long hours and continued to tinker with both her menu and pretzel recipes until things began to take off. Today, her firm is known as Auntie Anne's Soft Pretzels, has 1,200 locations, and generates over $400 million in annual revenues.[22]

Global Opportunities

Many entrepreneurs are also finding new opportunities in foreign markets. Doug Mellinger founded PRT Group, a software development company. One of Mellinger's biggest problems was finding trained programmers. There aren't enough U.S.-based programmers to go around, and foreign-born programmers face strict immigration quotas. So Mellinger set up shop on Barbados, a Caribbean island where the government helped him attract foreign programmers and did everything it could to make things easier. Today, PRT has customers and suppliers from dozens of nations.

Better Survival Rates

More people are encouraged to test their skills as entrepreneurs because the small business failure rate has declined. During the 1960s and 1970s, less than half of all new start-ups survived more than 18 months; only one in five lasted 10 years. Now, however, over half can expect to survive for at least 4 years and a third survive for 10 years or longer.[23]

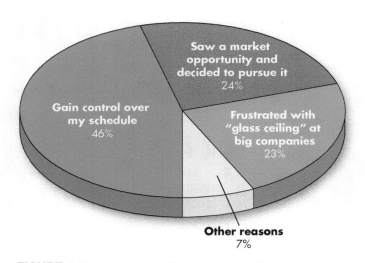

FIGURE 4 Reasons Women Give for Starting Businesses

managing in turbulent times

The Wide World of Risk

When a well-established individual or business needs a loan, they generally head to the bank. Armed with a credit score and a financial history, they are generally able to borrow money to grow their business. But what happens when someone needs just a little money to get started, but they lack any type of credit history or even a banking relationship? It's exactly this situation that has created the new world of micro-lending—very small loans made to individuals to start a new business. The challenge is particularly pronounced in developing nations, where budding entrepreneurs need just one or two hundred dollars to get their business off the ground. The concept of micro-lending has caught on, but lenders still look for some kind of data to determine who is the best candidate for even the smallest of loans. Shivani Siroya had a career that included working both as an investment banker and United Nations researcher. In April 2011, she founded Inventure, a California-based tech company that leverages mobile technology to create credit scores for unbanked individuals in India, Kenya, and South Africa.

To collect data that could be used for credit decisions on micro-loans, Inventure developed an application that can be downloaded to Android phones. The app monitors the length of users' phone calls and tracks their financial transactions. Using

Dan Monick/Corbis

a proprietary algorithm, Inventure evaluates over 10,000 indicators of responsibility. For example, applicants whose average phone calls were longer than four minutes were thought to have stronger relationships, making them a better credit risk. Using this and other more complex data, Inventure accepted half of its applicants, making small loans, often between $20 and $100, and charging just 5 percent interest. Even more impressive was the repayment rate of 85 percent in the company's first year of operation.[24]

Reasons for Failure

Unfortunately, even though survival rates have improved, almost half of all new businesses still will not enjoy long-term success. Why do some succeed and others fail? Although no set pattern has been established, four general factors contribute to failure:

1 *Managerial incompetence or inexperience.* Some entrepreneurs put too much faith in common sense, overestimate their own managerial skills, or believe that hard work alone ensures success. If managers don't have a sound business plan, don't know how to make basic business decisions, or don't understand basic management principles, they aren't likely to succeed in the long run.

2 *Neglect.* Some entrepreneurs try to launch ventures in their spare time, and others devote only limited time to new businesses. But starting a small business demands an overwhelming time commitment. If you aren't willing to put in the time and effort that a business requires, you aren't likely to survive.

3 *Weak control systems.* Effective control systems keep a business on track and alert managers to potential trouble. If your control systems don't signal impending problems, you may be in serious trouble before you spot more obvious difficulties. For instance, some businesses fail because they do a poor job of managing their credit collection policies. Anxious to grow, they may be too liberal in extending credit to their customers and then end up not being able to collect all the money that is owed to them.

4 *Insufficient capital.* Some entrepreneurs are overly optimistic about how soon they'll start earning profits. In most cases, it takes months or even years. Amazon

didn't earn a profit for 10 years but obviously still required capital to pay employees and to cover other expenses. Experts say you need enough capital to operate at least six months without earning a profit; some recommend enough to last a year.[25]

Reasons for Success

Four basic factors are also typically cited to explain small business success:

1 *Hard work, drive, and dedication.* Small business owners must be committed to succeeding and willing to spend the time and effort to make it happen. Tai Lee wanted to open a restaurant in College Station, Texas, but did not have sufficient capital. He partnered with a local investor and opened Veritas Wine and Bistro in 2009. In the early days, he typically spent 14 hours a day managing the restaurant, handling the cooking, and greeting customers. His wife also worked beside him, waiting on customers and taking reservations. This schedule persisted for over three years. Eventually, though, Veritas took off and became a big success. Today, Tai owns two restaurants and has a gourmet food truck that has received national acclaim.

2 *Market demand for the products or services being provided.* Careful analysis of market conditions can help small business owners assess the probable reception of their products. Attempts to expand restaurants specializing in baked potatoes, muffins, and gelato often struggle, but hamburger and pizza chains continue to expand. In the case of Veritas, College Station had relatively few fine dining options and that segment of the market was clearly underserved.

3 *Managerial competence.* Successful owners may acquire competence through training or experience or by drawing on the expertise of others. Few, however, succeed alone or straight out of college. Most spend time in successful companies or partner with others to bring expertise to a new business. Tai Lee studied both business and culinary arts before opening Veritas. He also sought advice from other successful entrepreneurs.

4 *Luck.* After Alan McKim started Clean Harbors, an environmental cleanup firm in New England, he struggled to keep his business afloat and was running low on capital. Before his funding was exhausted, though, the U.S. government committed $1.6 billion to toxic waste cleanup—McKim's specialty. He quickly landed several large government contracts and put his business on solid financial footing. Had the government fund not been created at just the right time, McKim might well have failed. Similarly, Netflix might not have succeeded if it had not started just as customers were shifting away from video cassettes to DVDs.

OBJECTIVE 5
Explain
sole proprietorships, partnerships, and cooperatives and discuss the advantages and disadvantages of each.

Noncorporate Business Ownership

Whether they intend to launch a small local business or a new venture projected to grow rapidly, all entrepreneurs must decide which form of legal ownership best suits their goals: *sole proprietorship, partnership,* or *corporation*. Because this choice affects a host of managerial and financial issues, few decisions are more critical. Entrepreneurs must consider their own preferences, their immediate and long-range needs, and the advantages and disadvantages of each form. Table 1 compares the most important differences among the three major ownership forms.

Sole Proprietorships

Sole Proprietorship *business owned and usually operated by one person who is responsible for all of its debts*

The **sole proprietorship** is owned and usually operated by one person. About 74 percent of all U.S. businesses are sole proprietorships; however, they account for only about 4 percent of total business revenues. Though usually small, they may be as large as steel mills or department stores.

table 1   Comparative Summary: Three Forms of Business Ownership

Business Form	Liability	Continuity	Management	Sources of Investment
Proprietorship	Personal, unlimited	Ends with death or decision of owner	Personal, unrestricted	Personal
General Partnership	Personal, unlimited	Ends with death or decision of any partner	Unrestricted or depends on partnership agreement	Personal by partner(s)
Corporation	Capital invested	As stated in charter, perpetual or for specified period of years	Under control of board of directors, which is selected by stockholders	Purchase of stock

Advantages of Sole Proprietorships Freedom may be the most important benefit of sole proprietorships. Because they own their businesses, sole proprietors answer to no one but themselves. Sole proprietorships are also easy to form. Sometimes, you can go into business simply by putting a sign on the door. The simplicity of legal setup procedures makes this form appealing to self-starters and independent spirits, as do low start-up costs.

Another attractive feature is the tax benefits extended to businesses that are likely to suffer losses in their early stages. Tax laws permit owners to treat sales revenues and operating expenses as part of their personal finances, paying taxes based on their personal tax rate. They can cut taxes by deducting business losses from income earned from personal sources other than the business.

Disadvantages of Sole Proprietorships A major drawback is **unlimited liability**; a sole proprietor is personally liable for all debts incurred by the business. If the company fails to generate enough cash, bills must be paid out of the owner's pocket. Another disadvantage is lack of continuity; a sole proprietorship legally dissolves when the owner dies. Although the business can be reorganized by a successor, executors or heirs must otherwise sell its assets.

Finally, a sole proprietorship depends on the resources of one person whose managerial and financial limitations may constrain the business. Sole proprietors often find it hard to borrow money to start up or expand. Many bankers fear that they won't be able to recover loans if owners become disabled or insolvent.

Unlimited Liability *legal principle holding owners responsible for paying off all debts of a business*

Partnerships

The most common type of partnership, the **general partnership**, is similar to a sole proprietorship but is owned by more than one person. Partners may invest equal or unequal sums of money. In most cases, partners share the profits equally or in proportion to their investment. In certain cases, though, the distribution of profits may be based on other things. A locally prominent athlete, for instance, may lend her or his name to the partnership and earn profits without actually investing funds. And sometimes one partner invests all of the funds needed for the business but plays no role in its management. This person is usually called a *silent partner*. Another partner might invest nothing but provide all the labor. In this case, the financial investor likely owns the entire business, and the labor partner owns nothing. But over time, and as specified in a contract, the labor partner gradually gains an ownership stake in the business (usually called *sweat equity*).

General Partnership *business with two or more owners who share in both the operation of the firm and the financial responsibility for its debts*

Advantages of Partnerships The most striking advantage of general partnerships is the ability to grow by adding new talent and money. Because banks prefer to make loans to enterprises that are not dependent on single individuals, partnerships find it easier to borrow money when compared to sole proprietorships. They can also invite new partners to join by investing money.

Like a sole proprietorship, a partnership can be organized by meeting only a few legal requirements. Even so, all partnerships must begin with an agreement of some kind. In all but two states, the Revised Uniform Limited Partnership Act requires the filing of specific information about the business and its partners. Partners may also agree to bind themselves in ways not specified by law. In any case, an agreement should answer questions such as the following:

- Who invested what sums?

- Who will receive what share of the profits?

- Who does what, and who reports to whom?

- How may the partnership be dissolved? In the event of dissolution, how will assets be distributed?

- How will surviving partners be protected from claims made by a deceased partner's heirs?

The partnership agreement is strictly a private document. No laws require partners to file agreements with any government agency. Nor are partnerships regarded as legal entities. In the eyes of the law, a partnership is just two or more people working together. Because partnerships have no independent legal standing, the Internal Revenue Service (IRS) taxes partners as individuals.

Disadvantages of Partnerships

For general partnerships as for sole proprietorships, unlimited liability is the greatest drawback. Each partner may be liable for all debts incurred by the partnership. If any partner incurs a business debt, all partners may be liable, even if some of them did not know about or agree to the new debt.

Partnerships also share with sole proprietorships the potential lack of continuity. When one partner dies or leaves, the original partnership dissolves, even if one or more of the other partners want it to continue. But dissolution need not mean a loss of sales revenues. Survivors may form a new partnership to retain the old firm's business.

A related disadvantage is difficulty in transferring ownership. No partner may sell out without the consent of the others. A partner who wants to retire or to transfer interest to a son or daughter must have the other partners' consent.

Alternatives to General Partnerships

Because of these disadvantages, general partnerships are among the least popular forms of business. Roughly 3.5 million U.S. partnerships generate only 15 percent of total sales revenues. To resolve some of the problems inherent in general partnerships, especially unlimited liability, some partners have tried alternative agreements. The **limited partnership** allows for **limited partners** who invest money but are liable for debts only to the extent of their investments. They cannot, however, take active roles in business operations. A limited partnership must have at least one **general (or active) partner**, mostly for liability purposes. This is usually the person who runs the business and is responsible for its survival and growth.

Under a **master limited partnership**, an organization sells shares (partnership interests) to investors on public markets such as the New York Stock Exchange. Investors are paid back from profits. The master partner retains at least 50 percent ownership and runs the business, and minority partners have no management voice. (The master partner differs from a general partner, who has no such ownership restriction.) The master partner must regularly provide minority partners with detailed operating and financial reports.

Cooperatives

Sometimes, groups of sole proprietorships or partnerships agree to work together for their common benefit by forming cooperatives. **Cooperatives** combine the freedom

Limited Partnership *type of partnership consisting of limited partners and a general (or managing) partner*

Limited Partner *partner who does not share in a firm's management and is liable for its debts only to the limits of said partner's investment*

General (or active) Partner *partner who actively manages a firm and who has unlimited liability for its debts*

Master Limited Partnership *form of ownership that sells shares to investors who receive profits and that pays taxes on income from profits*

Cooperatives *form of ownership in which a group of sole proprietorships or partnerships agree to work together for common benefits*

of sole proprietorships with the financial power of corporations. They give members greater production power, greater marketing power, or both. On the other hand, they are limited to serving the specific needs of their members. Although cooperatives make up only a minor segment of the U.S. economy, their role is still important in agriculture. Ocean Spray, the Florida Citrus Growers, Riceland, and Cabot Cheese are among the best-known cooperatives.

Corporations

OBJECTIVE 6
Describe
corporations, discuss their advantages and disadvantages, and identify different kinds of corporations; explain the basic issues involved in managing a corporation and discuss special issues related to corporate ownership.

There are about 6 million corporations in the United States. As you can see from Figure 5, they account for about 17 percent of all U.S. businesses but generate about 81 percent of all sales revenues.[26] Almost all large businesses use this form, and corporations dominate global business. As we will see, corporations need not be large; many small businesses also elect to operate as corporations.

According to the most recent data, Walmart, the world's largest corporation, posted annual revenue of over $477 billion, with total profits of more than $16 billion. Even "smaller" large corporations post huge sales figures. The New York Times Company, though five hundredth in size among U.S. corporations, posted a profit of $38 million on revenues of $1.6 billion. Given the size and influence of this form of ownership, we devote a great deal of attention to various aspects of corporations.

The Corporate Entity

When you think of corporations, you probably think of giant operations such as Walmart, Google, or Apple. The very word *corporation* inspires images of size and power. In reality, however, your corner newsstand has as much right to incorporate as a giant automaker. Moreover, the newsstand and Apple would share the characteristics of all **corporations**: legal status as separate entities, property rights and obligations, and indefinite life spans.

In 1819, the U.S. Supreme Court defined a corporation as "an artificial being, invisible, intangible, and existing only in contemplation of the law." The court

Corporation *business that is legally considered an entity separate from its owners and is liable for its own debts; owners' liability extends to the limits of their investments*

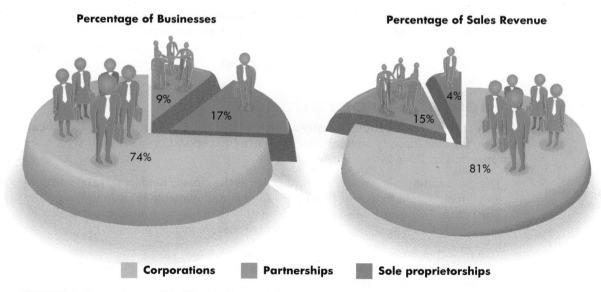

Percentage of Businesses

9%
17%
74%

Percentage of Sales Revenue

4%
15%
81%

■ **Corporations** ■ **Partnerships** ■ **Sole proprietorships**

FIGURE 5 Proportions of U.S. Firms in Terms of Organization Type and Sales Revenue
Sources: http://www.census.gov/compendia/statab/2012/tables/12s0744.pdf, http://www.irs.gov/pub/irssoi/08coccr.pdf, http://www.irs.gov/pub/irssoi/08pareturnsnap.pdf, http://www.irs.gov/pub/irssoi/10sumbulsolprop.pdf

defined the corporation as a legal person. Corporations may, therefore, perform the following activities:

- Sue and be sued
- Buy, hold, and sell property
- Make and sell products
- Commit crimes and be tried and punished for them

Limited Liability *legal principle holding investors liable for a firm's debts only to the limits of their personal investments in it*

Advantages of Incorporation The biggest advantage of corporations is **limited liability**; investor liability is limited to personal investment (through stock ownership, covered later) in the corporation. In the event of failure, the courts may seize and sell a corporation's assets but cannot touch the investors' personal possessions. If, for example, you invest $1,000 in stock in a corporation that ends up failing, you may lose your $1,000, but no more. In other words, your liability is limited to the $1,000 you invested.

Another advantage is continuity. Because it has a legal life independent of founders and owners, a corporation can, at least in theory, continue forever. Shares of stock may be sold or passed on to heirs, and most corporations also benefit from the continuity provided by professional management. Finally, corporations have advantages in raising money. By selling stock, they expand the number of investors and the amount of available funds. Continuity and legal status tend to make lenders more willing to grant loans.

Tender Offer *offer to buy shares made by a prospective buyer directly to a target corporation's shareholders, who then make individual decisions about whether to sell*

Double Taxation *situation in which taxes may be payable both by a corporation on its profits and by shareholders on dividend incomes*

Disadvantages of Incorporation Although a chief attraction is ease of transferring ownership, this same feature can create complications. For example, using a legal process called a **tender offer**, an offer to buy shares made by a prospective buyer directly to a corporation's shareholders, a corporation can be taken over against the will of its managers. Another disadvantage is start-up cost. Corporations are heavily regulated, and incorporation entails meeting the complex legal requirements of the state in which the firm is chartered.

The biggest disadvantage of incorporation, however, is **double taxation**. In addition to income taxes on company profits, stockholders also pay taxes on income returned by their investments in the corporation. Thus, the profits earned by corporations are taxed twice—once at the corporate level and then again at the ownership level. Because profits are treated as owners' personal income, sole proprietorships and partnerships are taxed only once.

The advantages and disadvantages of corporate ownership have inspired laws establishing different kinds of corporations. Most are intended to help businesses take advantage of the benefits of the corporate model without assuming all the disadvantages. We discuss these corporate forms next.

Types of Corporations

Closely Held (or Private) Corporation *corporation whose stock is held by only a few people and is not available for sale to the general public*

Publicly Held (or Public) Corporation *corporation whose stock is widely held and available for sale to the general public*

S Corporation *hybrid of a closely held corporation and a partnership, organized and operated like a corporation but treated as a partnership for tax purposes*

We can classify corporations as either *public* or *private*. But within these broad categories, we can identify several specific types of corporations, some of which are summarized in Table 2.

- The most common form of U.S. corporation is the **closely held (or private) corporation**. Stock is held by only a few people and is not available for sale to the public. The controlling group of stockholders may be a family, a management group, or even the firm's employees. Most smaller corporations fit this profile.

- When shares are publicly issued, the firm becomes a **publicly held (or public) corporation**. Stock is widely held and available for sale to the public. Many large businesses are of this type.

- The **S corporation** (more fully called the *Subchapter S corporation*) is a hybrid of a closely held corporation and a partnership. It is organized and operates like a corporation,

table 2 Types of Corporations

Type	Distinguishing Features	Examples
Closely Held	Stock held by only a few people Subject to corporate taxation	Blue Cross/Blue Shield MasterCard Primestar
Publicly Held	Stock widely held among many investors Subject to corporate taxation	Apple Starbucks Texas Instruments
Subchapter S	Organized much like a closely held corporation Subject to additional regulation Subject to partnership taxation	Minglewood Associates Entech Pest Systems Frontier Bank
Limited Liability	Organized much like a publicly held corporation Subject to additional regulation Subject to partnership taxation	Pacific Northwest Associates Global Ground Support Ritz Carlton
Professional	Subject to partnership taxation Limited business liability Unlimited professional liability	Norman Hui, DDS & Associates B & H Engineering Anderson, McCoy & Oria
Multinational	Spans national boundaries Subject to regulation in multiple countries	Toyota Nestlé General Electric

but it is treated like a partnership for tax purposes. To qualify, firms must meet stringent legal conditions. For instance, stockholders must be individual U.S. citizens.

● Another hybrid is the **limited liability corporation (LLC)**. Owners are taxed like partners, each paying personal taxes only. However, they also enjoy the benefits of limited liability accorded to publicly held corporations. LLCs have grown in popularity in recent years, partially because of IRS rulings that allow corporations, partnerships, and foreign investors to be partial owners.

Limited Liability Corporation (LLC) *hybrid of a publicly held corporation and a partnership in which owners are taxed as partners but enjoy the benefits of limited liability*

● **Professional corporations** are most likely composed of doctors, lawyers, accountants, or other professionals. Although the corporate structure means protection from unlimited financial liability, members are not immune from unlimited liability. Professional negligence by a member can entail personal liability on an individual's part.

Professional Corporation *form of ownership allowing professionals to take advantage of corporate benefits while granting them limited business liability and unlimited professional liability*

● As the term implies, the **multinational (or transnational) corporation** spans national boundaries. Stock may be traded on the exchanges of several countries, and managers are likely to be of different nationalities.

Multinational (or Transnational) Corporation *form of corporation spanning national boundaries*

Managing a Corporation

Creating any type of corporation can be complicated because of the various legal conditions that must be met. In addition, once the corporate entity comes into existence, it must be managed by people who understand the principles of **corporate governance**,

Corporate Governance *roles of shareholders, directors, and other managers in corporate decision making and accountability*

entrepreneurship and new ventures

More Than Just a Burger and Fries

In 2001, restauranteur Danny Meyer opened a hot dog cart in New York City's Madison Square Park. He hoped to attract more people to the area and provide additional opportunities for employees at his nearby restaurant. That little hot dog cart quickly grew into the fast-casual restaurant Shake Shack. According to Meyer, "We entertained a bunch of names for the kiosk (most of them pretty bad—like Custard's First Stand, Dog Run, and Madison Mixer) and ultimately settled on Shake Shack." The company website explains their niche: "This modern-day "roadside" burger stand serves up the most delicious burgers, hot dogs, frozen custard, shakes, beer, wine and more. An instant neighborhood fixture, Shake Shack welcomed people from all over the city, country, and world who gathered together to enjoy fresh, simple, high-quality versions of the classics in a majestic setting. The rest, as they say, is burger history." The company prides itself by using only Angus beef that has been vegetarian fed, humanely raised, and antibiotic-free.

From this single location, the restaurant grew. Meyer took on investors to fuel the expansion, including two limited partnerships, Green Equity Investors and Select Equity Group, and a private equity backer, Jonathan Sokoloff. Expansion was focused in several key U.S. locations: New York, Massachusetts, Chicago, and Washington, DC. The only restaurant west of the Mississippi is located in Las Vegas, Nevada. Internationally, the company had 13 locations by the beginning of 2015, including London, Moscow, and Dubai. The restaurants are so popular that people often line up for more than an hour in hopes of getting one of their famed burgers and crinkle-cut fries.

John Angelillo/UPI/Newscom

With an eye on expanding from the current 63 restaurants to 450 locations, the company had an initial public offering of stock in January 2015. At the time of the IPO, Danny Meyer owned 21 percent of the company's stock, with two limited partnerships, Green Equity Investors and Select Equity Group, owning 38.3 percent. Jonathan Sokoloff (a private equity backer) owned 26 percent. The company offered 5 million new shares of stock for sale at a price of $21 per share. Through this IPO, Shake Shack raised $105 million dollars to fuel expansion. The company hopes to open at least 10 new restaurants each year. Days after the IPO, the company's stock had more than doubled from its issue price and Meyer's stock alone was worth more than $340 million. Select Equity Group, one of the initial investors, sold their interest of more than 4 million shares just days after the IPO, realizing millions of dollars of return on their investment. And all of this started with a hot dog cart in the park.[27]

the roles of shareholders, directors, and other managers in corporate decision making and accountability. In this section, we discuss the principles of *stock ownership* and *stockholders' rights* and describe the role of *boards of directors*. We then examine some special issues related to corporate ownership.

Corporate governance is established by the firm's bylaws and usually involves three distinct bodies. **Stockholders (or shareholders)** are the owners of a corporation, investors who buy ownership shares in the form of stock. The *board of directors* is a group elected by stockholders to oversee corporate management. Corporate *officers* are top managers hired by the board to run the corporation on a day-to-day basis.

Stockholder (or Shareholder) *owner of shares of stock in a corporation*

Stock Ownership and Stockholders' Rights
Corporations sell shares, called *stock*, to investors who then become stockholders, or shareholders. Profits are distributed among stockholders in the form of *dividends*, and corporate managers serve at stockholders' discretion. In a closely held corporation, only a few people own stock. Shares of publicly held corporations are widely held.

Board of Directors *governing body of a corporation that reports to its shareholders and delegates power to run its day-to-day operations while remaining responsible for sustaining its assets*

Boards of Directors
The governing body of a corporation is its **board of directors**. Boards communicate with stockholders and other stakeholders through

such channels as an annual report, a summary of a firm's financial health. They also set policy on dividends, major spending, and executive compensation. They are legally responsible and accountable for corporate actions and are increasingly being held personally liable for them.

Officers Although board members oversee operations, most do not participate in day-to-day management. Rather, they hire a team of managers to run the firm. This team, called **officers**, is usually headed by the firm's **chief executive officer (CEO)**, who is responsible for overall performance. Other officers typically include a *president*, who is responsible for internal management, and *vice presidents*, who oversee various functional areas such as marketing and operations.

Officers *top management team of a corporation*

Special Issues in Corporate Ownership

In recent years, several issues have grown in importance in the area of corporate ownership, including *joint ventures and strategic alliances, employee stock ownership plans*, and *institutional ownership*. Other important issues in contemporary corporate ownership involve *mergers, acquisitions, divestitures*, and *spin-offs*.

Joint Ventures and Strategic Alliances

In a **strategic alliance**, two or more organizations collaborate on a project for mutual gain. When partners share ownership of what is essentially a new enterprise, it is called a **joint venture**. The number of strategic alliances has increased rapidly in recent years on both domestic and international fronts. For example, General Motors and Ford recently announced a new strategic alliance to jointly develop 10-speed transmissions for automobiles.[28] Ford also has joint ventures with Volkswagen (in South America) and Mazda (in Japan).

Strategic Alliance *strategy in which two or more organizations collaborate on a project for mutual gain*

Joint Venture *strategic alliance in which the collaboration involves joint ownership of the new venture*

Employee Stock Ownership Plans

An **employee stock ownership plan (ESOP)** allows employees to own a significant share of the corporation through trusts established on their behalf. Current estimates count about 11,500 ESOPs in the United States. The growth rate in new ESOPs has slowed a bit in recent years, but they still are an important part of corporate ownership patterns in the United States.

Employee Stock Ownership Plan (ESOP) *arrangement in which a corporation holds its own stock in trust for its employees, who gradually receive ownership of the stock and control its voting rights*

Institutional Ownership

Most individual investors don't own enough stock to exert influence on corporate managers. In recent years, however, more stock has been purchased by **institutional investors**. Because they control enormous resources, these investors—especially mutual and pension funds—can buy huge blocks of stock. The national teachers' retirement system (TIAA CREF) has assets of more than $400 billion, much of it invested in stocks. Institutional investors own almost 55 percent of all the stock issued in the United States.

Institutional investor *large investor, such as a mutual fund or a pension fund, that purchases large blocks of corporate stock*

Mergers, Acquisitions, Divestitures, and Spin-Offs

Another important set of issues includes mergers, acquisitions, divestitures, and spin-offs. Mergers and acquisitions involve the legal joining of two or more corporations. A divestiture occurs when a corporation sells a business operation to another corporation; with a spin-off, it creates a new operation.

MERGERS AND ACQUISITIONS (M&As) A **merger** occurs when two firms combine to create a new company. For example, United Airlines and Continental merged to create one of the world's largest airlines. The new airline bears the United name but retains the equipment design of Continental. Continental's CEO assumed control of the new company. The firm took more than two years to integrate their respective operations into a unified new firm. Even more recently, American Airlines and US Airlines announced that they, too, were merging and as of this writing are finalizing their integration plans.

Merger *the union of two corporations to form a new corporation*

In an **acquisition**, one firm buys another outright. Many deals that are loosely called mergers are really acquisitions. Why? Because one of the two firms will usually control

Acquisition *the purchase of one company by another*

the newly combined ownership. In general, when the two firms are roughly the same size, the combination is usually called a merger even if one firm is taking control of the other. When the acquiring firm is substantially larger than the acquired firm, the deal is really an acquisition. So-called M&As are an important form of corporate strategy. They let firms increase product lines, expand operations, go international, and create new enterprises. Halliburton Corporation recently acquired Boots and Coots, an oil-field firefighting business, and more recently announced plans to buy Baker Hughes.

DIVESTITURES AND SPIN-OFFS Sometimes, a corporation decides to sell a part of its existing business operations or set it up as a new and independent corporation. There may be several reasons for such a step. A firm might decide, for example, that it should focus more specifically on its core businesses, and thus it will sell off unrelated or underperforming businesses. Such a sale is called a **divestiture**. When a firm sells part of itself to raise capital, the strategy is known as a **spin-off**. A spin-off may also mean that a firm deems a business unit more valuable as a separate company. The Limited, for example, spun off three of its subsidiaries, Victoria's Secret, Bath & Body Works, and White Barn Candle Co., to create a new firm, Intimate Brands, which it then offered through an Initial Public Offering (IPO). The Limited retained 84 percent ownership of Intimate Brands while getting an infusion of new capital.

Divestiture *strategy whereby a firm sells one or more of its business units*

Spin-off *strategy of setting up one or more corporate units as new, independent corporations*

summary of learning objectives

OBJECTIVE 1

Define *small business*, discuss its importance to the U.S. economy, and explain popular areas of small business.

A *small business* is independently owned and managed and has relatively little influence in its market. Most U.S. businesses are small businesses and employ fewer than 20 people. Small businesses are vitally important to the economy because of (1) *job creation*, (2) *innovation*, and (3) *contributions to big business*. The most common types of small businesses are firms engaged in (1) *services*, (2) *retailing*, and (3) *construction*. Services comprise the largest sector, in part because most service businesses require relatively little capital to start. In contrast, there are relatively fewer small businesses who manufacture products because the start-up costs are often high.

OBJECTIVE 2

Explain entrepreneurship and describe some key characteristics of entrepreneurial personalities and activities.

Entrepreneurs are people who assume the risk of business ownership. Some entrepreneurs have a goal of independence and financial security, and others want to launch a new venture that can be grown into a large business. Most successful entrepreneurs are resourceful and concerned for customer relations. They have a strong desire to be their own bosses and can handle ambiguity and surprises. Today's entrepreneur is often an open-minded leader who relies on networks, business plans, and consensus and is just as likely to be female as male. Finally, although successful entrepreneurs understand the role of risk, they do not necessarily regard what they do as being risky.

OBJECTIVE 3

Describe distinctive competence, the business plan, and the start-up decisions made by small businesses and identify sources of financial aid available to such enterprises.

A new business must first understand its potential distinctive competence, such as the ability to identify a niche (or unmet need) in an established market. Another distinctive competence is the ability to serve a new unexploited market. Still another is the ability to move quickly to take advantage of new opportunities, often called "first-mover advantage."

After identifying a potential distinctive competence, the next step in entrepreneurship is developing a business plan. A *business plan* summarizes business strategy for the new venture and shows how it will be implemented. The key elements of a business plan are setting goals and objectives, sales forecasting, and financial planning. Business plans are increasingly important because creditors and investors demand them as tools for deciding whether to finance or invest.

Entrepreneurs must also decide whether to buy an existing business, operate a franchise, or start from scratch. Entrepreneurs who choose to buy an existing business have better chances for success compared to those who start from scratch because of existing relationships with vendors and customers. Franchises provide considerable support in setup and operation, but franchise costs can be high and severely cut into profits. Starting a business from scratch can be the most risky, yet rewarding, way to start a new business.

To start a new business, it is essential to have money to finance the operation. Common funding sources include personal funds, family and friends, savings, lenders, investors, and governmental agencies. Lending institutions are more likely to finance an existing business than a new business because the risks are better understood. *Venture capital companies* are groups of small investors seeking to make profits on companies with rapid growth potential. Most of these firms do not lend money but rather invest it, supplying capital in return for partial ownership. New businesses may also seek funding from small business investment companies (SBICs) as well as through Small Business Administration (SBA) programs.

Discuss the trends in small business start-ups and identify the main reasons for success and failure among small businesses.

Five trends have helped facilitate the growth in new businesses started in the United States every year. These trends are: (1) *the emergence of e-commerce,* (2) *crossovers from big business,* (3) *increased opportunities for minorities and women,* (4) *new opportunities in global enterprise,* and (5) *improved rates of survival among small businesses.*

However, more than half of all small businesses fail. Four basic factors contribute to most small business failure: (1) *managerial incompetence or inexperience,* (2) *neglect,* (3) *weak control systems,* and (4) *insufficient capital.* Likewise, four basic factors explain most small business success: (1) *hard work, drive, and dedication,* (2) *market demand for the products or services being provided,* (3) *managerial competence,* and (4) *luck.*

Explain sole proprietorships, partnerships, and cooperatives and discuss the advantages and disadvantages of each.

A *sole proprietorship* is a business that is owned by one person. The most significant advantage to organizing as a sole proprietorship is the freedom to make decisions. In addition, it is relatively easy to form and operate a sole proprietorship. There are tax benefits for new businesses that are likely to suffer losses in early stages because these losses can offset income from another business or job on the tax return of a sole proprietor. A major drawback is *unlimited liability*, which is the legal concept that makes the owners of a sole proprietorship personally responsible for all its debts. Another disadvantage is that a sole proprietorship lacks continuity; when the owner dies or leaves the business, it does not continue to exist. Finally, a sole proprietorship depends on the resources of a single individual.

A *general partnership* is a sole proprietorship multiplied by the number of partner owners. The biggest advantage is its ability to grow by adding new talent and money. Partners report their share of the partnership's income and it is taxed on their individual tax return. Like a sole proprietorship, *unlimited liability* is a drawback. Partnerships may lack continuity, and transferring ownership may be hard. No partner may sell out without the consent of the others. There are also special forms of partnerships, most notably limited partnerships and master limited partnerships.

Cooperatives combine the freedom of sole proprietorships with the financial power of corporations. A cooperative is a group of sole proprietorships or partnerships working together to gain greater production or marketing power.

Describe corporations, discuss their advantages and disadvantages, and identify different kinds of corporations; explain the basic issues involved in managing a corporation and discuss special issues related to corporate ownership.

All *corporations* share certain characteristics: legal status as separate entities, property rights and obligations, and indefinite life spans. They may sue and be sued; buy, hold, and sell property; make and sell products; and commit crimes and be tried and punished for them. The biggest advantage of incorporation is *limited liability*: Investor liability is limited to one's personal investments in the corporation. Another advantage is continuity; a corporation can last indefinitely and does not end with the death or withdrawal of an owner. Finally, corporations have advantages in raising money. By selling stock, they expand the number of investors and the amount of available funds. Continuity and the ability to sell stock tend to make lenders more willing to grant loans.

One disadvantage is that a corporation can be taken over against the will of its managers. Another disadvantage is start-up cost. Corporations are heavily regulated and must meet complex legal requirements in the states in which they're chartered. The greatest potential drawback to incorporation is *double taxation* of profits. Profits are taxed first at the level of the corporation and then taxed as dividends when distributed to the stockholders. Corporations may be either private or public. A private, or closely held, corporation has only a small number of owners and shares of stock are not available to the general public. Public corporations are able to sell their stock on the stock exchanges and have the ability to raise large amounts of capital. Special forms of ownership, such as S corporations, LLCs, and professional corporations, combine limited liability of a corporation with tax treatment of partnerships.

Corporations sell shares, called *stock*, to investors who then become *stockholders* (or shareholders) and the real owners. Profits are distributed among stockholders in the form of *dividends*, and managers serve at their discretion. The governing body of a corporation is its *board of directors*. Most board members do not participate in day-to-day management but rather hire a team of managers. This team, called *officers*, is usually headed by a *chief executive officer (CEO)* who is responsible for overall performance.

Several issues have grown in importance in the area of corporate ownership. In a *strategic alliance*, two or more organizations collaborate on a project for mutual gain. When partners share ownership of a new enterprise, the arrangement is called a *joint venture*. An *employee stock ownership plan (ESOP)* allows employees to own a significant share of the corporation through trusts established on their behalf. More stock is now being purchased by *institutional investors*. A *merger* occurs when two firms combine to create a new company, and in an *acquisition*, one firm buys another outright. A *divestiture* occurs when a corporation sells a part of its existing business operations or sets it up as a new and independent corporation. When a firm sells part of itself to raise capital, the strategy is known as a *spin-off*.

key terms

acquisition	general (or active) partner	publicly held (or public) corporation
board of directors	general partnership	S corporation
business plan	institutional investor	small business
chief executive officer (CEO)	joint venture	Small Business Administration
closely held (or private) corporation	limited liability	(SBA)
cooperative	limited liability corporation	Small Business Development Center
corporate governance	(LLC)	(SBDC)
corporation	limited partner	small business investment company
divestiture	limited partnership	(SBIC)
double taxation	master limited partnership	sole proprietorship
employee stock ownership plan (ESOP)	merger	spin-off
entrepreneur	multinational (or transnational)	stockholder (or shareholder)
entrepreneurship	corporation	strategic alliance
established market	niche	tender offer
first-mover advantage	officers	unlimited liability
franchise	professional corporation	venture capital company

MyBizLab

To complete the problems with the ✪, go to EOC Discussion Questions in the MyLab.

questions & exercises

QUESTIONS FOR REVIEW

✪ 1. Why are small businesses important to the U.S. economy?

2. Which industries are easiest for a small business to enter? Which are hardest? Why?

3. What are the primary reasons for new business failure and success?

4. What are the basic forms of noncorporate business ownership? What are the key advantages and disadvantages of each?

QUESTIONS FOR ANALYSIS

5. After considering the characteristics of entrepreneurs, do you think that you would be a good candidate to start your own business? Why or why not?

6. If you were going to open a new business, what type would it be? Why?

7. Would you prefer to buy an existing business or start from scratch? Why?

8. Why might a closely held corporation choose to remain private? Why might it choose to be publicly traded?

APPLICATION EXERCISES

9. Interview the owner/manager of a sole proprietorship or a general partnership. What characteristics of that business form led the owner to choose it? Does he or she ever contemplate changing the form of the business?

10. Although more than half of all small businesses don't survive five years, franchises have a much better track record. However, it can be difficult to buy a franchise. Research a popular food industry franchise, such as Panera Bread, Sonic, California Tortilla, or Subway, and detail the requirements for net worth and liquid cash for the franchisee as well as up-front and annual fees.

building a business: continuing team exercise

Assignment

Meet with your team members and discuss your new business venture within the context of this chapter. Develop specific responses to the following:

11. To what extent do each of you really want to be an entrepreneur?

12. For the specific business you are starting (in this exercise), does it make more sense to start from scratch, to buy an existing business, or to buy a franchise? Why?

13. How will you most likely finance your new venture?

14. What factors will most likely contribute to your success? What factors might cause your business to fail? Is there a way to minimize or eliminate these risk factors?

15. What form of ownership will your group use? What are the advantages and disadvantages of this approach?

team exercise

A TASTY IDEA

Background Information

Suppose that you and three friends from college would like to open a new restaurant. Collectively, you have almost 20 years of experience in the restaurant industry and, with lots of new houses in the area, you think that there's an opportunity to make a lot of money if you can offer interesting food at good prices. You've even identified a great location, but you realize that it's going to take a lot of money to get this business off the ground. As recent college graduates, you don't have a lot of money, so you're looking for the best source of funding. Realistically, you realize that you're going to need at least $100,000 to sustain operations until your business starts to return a profit.

Team Activity

STEP 1

Individually or in a group of two or three students, brainstorm a list of options for financing. You'll want to do some online research to find out more about some of the loan programs identified in the chapter.

STEP 2

For each of the funding options, develop a list of pros and cons. Be sure to consider all the implications of each form of financing, including interest rates, repayment options, and eligibility requirements.

FOLLOW-UP QUESTIONS

16. Before getting financing, what will be expected of you and your business partners?

17. Which source of financing would be best for you and your partners? Why?

18. What form of business ownership would be most appropriate for your new restaurant and why?

exercising your ethics

BREAKING UP IS HARD TO DO

The Situation

Connie and Mark began a 25-year friendship after finishing college and discovering their mutual interest in owning a business. Established as a general partnership, their home furnishings center is a successful business sustained for 20 years by a share-and-share-alike relationship. Start-up cash, daily responsibilities, and profits have all been shared equally. The partnership agreement was general and doesn't require specific work hours. The partners both average four days a week in the store except in particularly busy seasons. Shared goals and compatible personalities have led to a solid give-and-take relationship that helps them overcome business problems while maintaining a happy interpersonal relationship.

The division of work is a natural match and successful combination because of the partners' different but complementary interests. Mark is a natural salesman and has most of the face-to-face contact with customers; he also handles personnel matters (hiring and training employees). Connie manages the inventory, buys shipping supplies, keeps the books, and oversees the finances. Both partners share in decisions about advertising and promotions.

The Dilemma

Things began changing two years ago when Connie became less interested in the business and got more involved in other activities. Whereas Mark's enthusiasm remained high, Connie's time was increasingly consumed by travel, recreation, and community service activities. At first, she reduced her work commitment from four to three days a week. Although not physically present as many hours, she was attentive to e-mails and often worked from home ordering inventory and paying

bills. Then she indicated that she wanted to cut back further, to just two days. At first, the store continued to operate pretty well, but problems began to arise. With Connie spending less time managing the inventory, Mark found that they often had empty spaces on the showroom floor. Furthermore, Connie had less time to focus on their financial situation and suppliers starting complaining about late payments on invoices. While Connie feels that her contributions are still substantial, Mark feels that their 50/50 is no longer fair. Connie, on the other hand, believes that she's keeping up her end of the bargain and doesn't want to make any changes to the partnership agreement.

QUESTIONS TO ADDRESS

19. What are the reasons the business has been successful? How did each partner contribute to the success?
20. Looking ahead, what are the biggest risks to their venture?
21. Is it fair for Connie to work fewer hours than Mark? What changes could they make to create equity and fairness in their agreement?

cases

It All Started with a Late Fee

At the beginning of this chapter, you read about how the idea for Netflix came about and how the company chose their business model. Using the information presented in this chapter, you should now be able to answer the following questions:

QUESTIONS FOR DISCUSSION

22. What are some of the primary reasons Netflix has been successful?
23. Netflix is a corporation. Why do you think the firm uses this form of ownership?
24. What threats might derail Netflix's success? What steps might the firm take today to thwart those threats?
25. Suppose Reed Hastings asked you for advice on how to make Netflix better. What would you tell him?

Ice Cream Headache

If you have ever visited a Cold Stone Creamery, you are familiar with the seemingly endless list of ice creams and toppings, as well as prepared cakes and other confections. You may not be aware, however, that Cold Stone is a franchise sold by Kahala Brands, whose other franchisee opportunities include Blimpie's sandwich shops and Samurai Sam's Teriyaki Grills.[29] Cold Stone has approximately 1,400 locations in 20 countries. In case you are considering opening your own Cold Stone, you might be interested in the conditions of ownership. Those who wish to purchase a Cold Stone franchise must show that they are financially sound, with at least $125,000 of cash available and a $250,000 net worth. The up-front franchise fee is $27,000 and the franchise is good for a ten-year term. Cold Stone provides plenty of assistance in selecting a location and opening a store, but start-up costs are estimated to be over $250,000. The company estimates

that the average time to open a location is four to twelve months, which presents a real challenge for a new franchise owner. Once in operation, franchisees will pay a royalty fee of 6 percent of gross sales and an advertising fee of 3 percent of gross sales.[30]

Cold Stone's parent organization provides support in site selection, lease terms, and equipment selection. They provide 11 days of training at the company's headquarters and three additional days of training at the franchisee's location. Once the business is up and running, they provide continued support through newsletters and annual meetings, cooperative advertising arrangements, and a toll-free hotline. In 2015, Entreprenuer.com ranked Cold Stone Creamery #54 in its list of Top 500 franchise opportunities.[31]

Revenues for Cold Stone franchises have declined in recent years. In 2005, the typical location earned approximately $400,000 in revenues, but this number dipped to $352,000 in 2011. Tough economic times cut into discretionary spending, hurting the ice cream business. In 2012, a group of Cold Stone Creamery franchise owners threatened to file suit against the company, alleging that the company was not delivering on promised marketing campaigns. In addition, there was an ongoing dispute over revenue and interest from unused gift cards. Tensions between franchisors and franchisees are becoming increasingly common. Eric Stites, managing director of *Franchise Business Review*, reflects, "When franchises aren't making money, that's when you see them form associations and sue the franchiser." Franchises in the food industry seem to have been hurt especially hard. Although the initial investment is often close to $450,000, annual profits average only $88,382. Although a bowl of ice cream will brighten almost anyone's day, a Cold Stone Franchise may not be a sure thing.[32]

QUESTIONS FOR DISCUSSION

26. What would be the advantages of buying a Cold Stone Creamery franchise as opposed to starting a business from scratch?

27. What are the disadvantages of buying a Cold Stone Creamery franchise?

28. While franchise owners must have at least $125,000 of cash available, average start-up costs are more than double this amount. What are the most likely sources of funding for a franchise?

29. How would you research a franchise purchase before making the decision to invest?

30. Do you think that you would be interested in owning a Cold Stone Creamery franchise? Why or why not?

MyBizLab

Go to the Assignments section of your MyLab to complete these writing exercises.

31. Research suggests that certain characteristics are common for most entrepreneurs. Pick three and explain why they are important for an entrepreneurial mind-set. Compare and contrast how some might be more important than others given different situations. Are there situations where these characteristics might hinder successful entrepreneurship? Explain your answers.

32. What are the three primary forms of business ownership? Provide a description of each as well as the most significant advantages and disadvantages. When is each form most appropriate or desirable?

end notes

[1]"Oh, To Be Young, and An Entrepreneur," *USA Today*, February 8, 2013, p. 8B.

[2]See http://www.sba.gov

[3]See http://www.sba.gov/aboutsba

[4]*Employment Projections: 2012–2022 Summary*, U.S. Bureau of Labor Statistics, March 14, 2015.

[5]Byrne, John. "The 12 Greatest Entrepreneurs of Our Time," *Fortune*, April 9, 2012, pp. 68–86.

[6]"A New Generation Rewrites the Rules," *Wall Street Journal* (May 22, 2002), R4; See also Mark Henricks, "Up to the Challenge," *Entrepreneur* (February 2006), 64–67.

[7]"Special Report—Stars of Asia," *BusinessWeek* (July 12, 2004), p. 18; see also https://www.tempstaff.co.jp/english/corporate/, accessed on January 27, 2015.

[8]"Special Report—Stars of Asia," p. 18.

[9]"A Startup's New Prescription for Eyewear," *Business Week*, July 4–10, 2011, pp. 49–51.

[10]See Thomas Zimmerer and Norman Scarborough, *Essentials of Entrepreneurship and Small Business Management*, 5th ed. (Upper Saddle River, NJ: Prentice Hall, 2008).

[11]Combs, James, Ketchen, David, Shook, Christopher, and Jeremy Short. "Antecedents and Consequences of Franchising: Past Accomplishments and Future Challenges, *Journal of Management*, January 2011, pp. 99–126.

[12]See http://www.franchise.org/Franchise-News-Detail.aspx?id=63438, accessed on January 30, 2015.

[13]"Case Looks for Passion in Start-Ups," *USA Today*, March 26, 2013, p. 3B.

[14]See https://www.sba.gov/content/7a-loan-amounts-fees-interest-rates, accessed on January 28, 2015.

[15]http://www.census.gov/ces/dataproducts/bds/data_firm.html

[16]"To Fund a Startup, Go to Kuala Lumpur," *Bloomberg Businessweek*, February 25–March 3, 2012.

[17]"Small Businesses Go Alternative for Loans," *USA Today*, November 14, 2012, p. 1B. See also "Alternative Online Lenders Fill Funding Needs for Small Businesses," *Forbes*, September 23, 2014, accessed at forbes.com on January 20, 2015.

[18]http://www.census.gov/ces/dataproducts/bds/data_firm.html

[19]U.S. Census Bureau, "1997 Economic Census Surveys of Minority and Women Owned Business Enterprises," at http://www.census.gov/csd/mwb

[20]Hoy, Peter. "Minority and Women Owned Businesses Skyrocket," *Inc.* (May 1, 2006), pp. 20–24.

[21]Zimmerer and Scarborough, *Essentials of Entrepreneurship and Small Business Management*, 20; See also http://nawbo.org/section_103.cfm http://nawbo.org/pdfs/2014_State_of_Women-owned_Businesses.pdf, accessed on January 20, 2015.

[22]"Soft Pretzels out of Hard Times," *Fortune*, July 22, 2014, pp. 23–26.

[23]See U.S. Small Business Administration, "Frequently Asked Questions," at http://app1.sba.gov/faqs/faqIndex-All.cfm?areaid=24, accessed on February 20, 2011; see also https://www.sba.gov/sites/default/files/FAQ_March_2014_0.pdf, accessed on January 20, 2015.

[24]"Inventure." CrunchBase. Accessed March 22, 2015. De La Merced, Michael. "Shake Shack More Than Doubles Its I.P.O. Price in Market Debut." DealBook, January 30, 2015. Accessed March 22, 2015. http://dealbook.nytimes.com/2015/01/30/shake-shack-more-than-doubles-its-i-p-o-price-in-market-debut/?_r=2 Lidsky, David. "The World's 50 Most Innovative Companies

2015: Inventure." *Fast Company*. Accessed March 22, 2015. De La Merced, Michael. "Shake Shack More Than Doubles Its I.P.O. Price in Market Debut." DealBook, January 30, 2015. Accessed March 22, 2015. http://dealbook.nytimes.com/2015/01/30/shake-shack-more-than-doubles-its-i-p-o-price-in-market-debut/?_r=2 Zimmerer and Scarborough, *Essentials of Entrepreneurship and Small Business Management*.

[25]Ibid.

[26]Ibid.

[27]De La Merced, Michael. "Shake Shack More Than Doubles Its I.P.O. Price in Market Debut." *DealBook*, January 30, 2015. Accessed March 22, 2015. http://dealbook.nytimes.com/2015/01/30/shake-shack-more-than-doubles-its-i-p-o-price-in-market-debut/?_r=2: "Investor Overview." Shake Shack Inc. Accessed March 22, 2015. http://investor.shakeshack.com/investors-overview/overview/default.

aspx; Williams, Trey. "6 things to know about Shake Shack with IPO set to start trading." MarketWatch. Last modified January 30, 2015. Accessed March 22, 2015. http://www.marketwatch.com/story/6-things-to-know-about-shake-shack-ahead-of-its-ipo-2015-01-20

[28]"GM, Ford Team to Develop 10-Speed Transmissions," *USA Today*, April 16, 2013, p. 2B.

[29]"Benefits of Franchising." *Cold Stone Creamery*. Kahala Franchising, LLC, n.d. Web. 13 June 2013.

[30]"Cold Stone Creamery Franchise Information." *Entrepreneur.com*. Entrepreneur Media, Inc, n.d. Web. 13 June 2013.

[31]"Facts on Ownership." *Cold Stone Creamery*. Kahala Franchising, LLC, n.d. Web. 13 June 2013.

[32]Needleman, Sarah E. "Tough Times for Franchising." *Wall Street Journal*. Dow Jones Company, Inc., 9 Feb. 2012. Web. 13 June 2013.

glossary

Acquisition the purchase of one company by another.

Board of Directors governing body of a corporation that reports to its shareholders and delegates power to run its day-to-day operations while remaining responsible for sustaining its assets.

Business Plan document in which the entrepreneur summarizes his or her business strategy for the proposed new venture and how that strategy will be implemented.

Chief Executive Officer (CEO) top manager who is responsible for the overall performance of a corporation.

Closely Held (or Private) Corporation corporation whose stock is held by only a few people and is not available for sale to the general public.

Cooperative form of ownership in which a group of sole proprietorships or partnerships agree to work together for common benefits.

Corporate Governance roles of shareholders, directors, and other managers in corporate decision making and accountability.

Corporation business that is legally considered an entity separate from its owners and is liable for its own debts; owners' liability extends to the limits of their investments.

Divestiture strategy whereby a firm sells one or more of its business units.

Double Taxation situation in which taxes may be payable both by a corporation on its profits and by shareholders on dividend incomes.

Employee Stock Ownership Plan (ESOP) arrangement in which a corporation holds its own stock in trust for its employees, who gradually receive ownership of the stock and control its voting rights.

Entrepreneur business person who accepts both the risks and the opportunities involved in creating and operating a new business venture.

Entrepreneurship the process of seeking business opportunities under conditions of risk.

Established Market one in which many firms compete according to relatively well-defined criteria.

First-Mover Advantage any advantage that comes to a firm because it exploits an opportunity before any other firm does.

Franchise arrangement in which a buyer (franchisee) purchases the right to sell the good or service of the seller (franchiser).

General (or Active) Partner partner who actively manages a firm and who has unlimited liability for its debts.

General Partnership business with two or more owners who share in both the operation of the firm and the financial responsibility for its debts.

Institutional Investor large investor, such as a mutual fund or a pension fund, that purchases large blocks of corporate stock.

Joint Venture strategic alliance in which the collaboration involves joint ownership of the new venture.

Limited Liability legal principle holding investors liable for a firm's debts only to the limits of their personal investments in it.

Limited Liability Corporation (LLC) hybrid of a publicly held corporation and a partnership in which owners are taxed as partners but enjoy the benefits of limited liability.

Limited Partner partner who does not share in a firm's management and is liable for its debts only to the limits of said partner's investment.

Limited Partnership type of partnership consisting of limited partners and a general (or managing) partner.

Master Limited Partnership form of ownership that sells shares to investors who receive profits and that pays taxes on income from profits.

Merger the union of two corporations to form a new corporation.

Multinational (or Transnational) Corporation form of corporation spanning national boundaries.

Niche a segment of a market that is not currently being exploited.

Officers top management team of a corporation.

Professional Corporation form of ownership allowing professionals to take advantage of corporate benefits while granting them limited business liability and unlimited professional liability.

Publicly Held (or Public) Corporation corporation whose stock is widely held and available for sale to the general public.

S Corporation hybrid of a closely held corporation and a partnership, organized and operated like a corporation but treated as a partnership for tax purposes.

Small Business independently owned business that has relatively little influence in its market.

Small Business Administration (SBA) government agency charged with assisting small businesses.

Small Business Development Center (SBDC) SBA program designed to consolidate information from various disciplines and make it available to small businesses.

Small Business Investment Company (SBIC) government regulated investment company that borrows money from the SBA to invest in or lend to a small business.

Sole Proprietorship business owned and usually operated by one person who is responsible for all of its debts.

Spin Off strategy of setting up one or more corporate units as new, independent corporations.

Stockholder (or Shareholder) owner of shares of stock in a corporation.

Strategic Alliance arrangement (also called *joint venture*) in which a company finds a foreign partner to contribute approximately half of the resources needed to establish and operate a new business in the partner's country.

Tender Offer offer to buy shares made by a prospective buyer directly to a target corporation's shareholders, who then make individual decisions about whether to sell.

Unlimited Liability legal principle holding owners responsible for paying off all debts of a business.

Venture Capital Company group of small investors who invest money in companies with rapid growth potential.

Understanding the Global Context of Business

From Chapter 4 of *Business Essentials*, Eleventh Edition. Ronald J. Ebert, Ricky W. Griffin. Copyright © 2017 by Pearson Education, Inc.

No matter where in the world a firm does

business, management drives its success.

International

businesses create unique management

challenges in

markets scattered

around the globe.

After reading this chapter, you should be able to:

1   **Discuss** the rise of international business and describe the major world marketplaces, trade agreements, and alliances.

2   **Explain** how differences in import–export balances, exchange rates, and foreign competition determine the ways in which countries and businesses respond to the international environment.

3   **Discuss** the factors involved in deciding to do business internationally and in selecting the appropriate levels of international involvement and international organizational structure.

4   **Explain** the role and importance of the cultural environment in international business.

5   **Describe** some of the ways in which economic, legal, and political differences among nations affect international business.

The Door Opens

In December 2014, President Barack Obama made the historic announcement that he planned to normalize diplomatic relations with Cuba. While only Congress can put an end to the U.S. embargo on trade with Cuba, this announcement creates a number of opportunities for U.S. businesses. One of the most significant impacts will be the ability of U.S. citizens to travel to Cuba. In the past, travel to Cuba was limited to certain educational or humanitarian efforts. However, travel to Cuba now can be authorized under 12 broad categories, including athletic competitions and people-to-people programs, and travelers will not have to apply for any special licenses before they travel.

In Cuba's socialist economy, most hotels are partially or completely government owned and often lack the amenities desired by American travelers. In addition, hotel capacity is limited and no new hotels are under construction. However, many private homes are available for short-term stays and San Francisco Airbnb is stepping in to fill the void. Within weeks of the announcement, more than 1,000 Cuban listings appeared on the Airbnb site. For as little as $25 per night, travelers can arrange a stay in a private home in Cuba, soaking up the warm weather and Caribbean sunshine.[1]

In spite of the restoration of diplomatic relations and easing of travel restrictions, the embargo on Cuban exports remains. The U.S. embargo, which was first imposed in 1960 in response to the revolutionary communist government's appropriation of U.S. land holdings in the country, prevents "U.S. persons" and entities "owned or controlled" by "U.S. persons" from engaging in any transactions in which Cuba has an "interest of any nature whatsoever, direct or indirect." Cuba, therefore, has no access to the U.S. market, does without U.S. imports, and amasses substantial debts to other trading partners. But observers also point out that if the embargo were dropped, the effects might not be as dramatic as some people think. Why? The embargo doesn't really have much effect on Cuba or its people.

Cubans now buy ice cream and soft drinks from Swiss-based Nestlé, soap and shampoo from Anglo-Dutch Unilever, and cigarettes from Brazil's Souza Cruz. The fact that the United States is the world's largest market for rum did not deter French-owned Pernod-Ricard from building a new distillery in Cuba, and Britain's Imperial Tobacco expects to double sales when Americans can once again purchase premium hand-rolled Cuban cigars. Most of the directors of Canada's Sherritt International are barred from the United States by provisions of the embargo, but they apparently regard the ban as a small price to pay for future returns on a $1.5-billion investment in Cuba's nickel, oil, and gas industries. Cuba has also lifted restrictions on many products

Mocker_bat/Fotolia

what's in it for me?

As we will see in this chapter, global forces—business as well as political—affect each and every one of us on a daily basis. As you begin your business career, regardless of whether you see yourself living abroad, working for a big company, or starting your own business, the global economy will affect you in a variety of ways. Exchange rates for different currencies and global markets for buying and selling are all of major importance to everyone, regardless of their role or perspective. As a result, this chapter will better enable you to (1) understand how global forces affect you as a customer, (2) understand how globalization affects you as an employee, and (3) assess how global opportunities and challenges can affect you as a business owner and an investor. You will also gain insights into how wages and working conditions in different regions are linked to what we buy and the prices we pay.

This chapter explores the global context of business. We begin with an exploration of the major world marketplaces and trade agreements that affect international business. Next, we examine several factors that help determine how countries and businesses respond to international opportunities and challenges. We then direct our attention to some of the decisions managers must make if they intend to compete in international markets. Finally, we conclude with a discussion of some of the social, cultural, economic, legal, and political factors that affect international business.

once unavailable to Cuban consumers, such as computers, DVDs, and mobile phones, and sales of all these products will be a boon to Telecom Italia, which holds a 27 percent stake in the country's state-owned telecom operations.

Paul Katzeff, founder of Thanksgiving Coffee Company, a California producer of specialty coffees, regards the U.S. embargo as impractical (on the grounds that it hasn't achieved its goals) and immoral (on the grounds that it punishes Cuban people rather than their government). Katzeff is thinking the same thing that many U.S. businesspeople are undoubtedly thinking: When the embargo is dropped, there will be new business opportunities. As he sees it, Cuban coffee has a promising post-embargo future: Its potential is enormous because of the quality of the coffee beans. Although Katzeff's geopolitics may rankle some people, his business sense seems sound. At present, of course, he can't actually do business with Cuban coffee growers, but he has figured out a way to lay the groundwork. He has already established working relationships with coffee cooperatives, groups of individual growers who pool their crops to enter the export market and secure higher prices, in Latin America and Africa. His longer-term goal is to invest the same capital and acquired know-how in relationships with Cuban growers.

The director of Thanksgiving's Cuba project, Nick Hoskins, has already developed contacts in Cuba's coffee-growing regions, and Katzeff hopes to establish a *twinning agreement*, an exchange of people-to-people programs, with cooperatives in the coffee-growing province of Santiago de Cuba. In the meantime, though, Thanksgiving is willing to settle for a public relations program of transactions—monetary and otherwise—with U.S. coffee drinkers.[2] (After studying this chapter, you should be able to respond to the set of discussion questions found at the end of the chapter.)

OBJECTIVE 1
Discuss

the rise of international business and describe the major world marketplaces, trade agreements, and alliances.

Globalization *process by which the world economy is becoming a single interdependent system*

Import *product made or grown abroad but sold domestically*

Export *product made or grown domestically but shipped and sold abroad*

The Contemporary Global Economy

The total volume of world trade is immense—more than $19.3 trillion in merchandise is traded each year. Foreign investment in the United States exceeds $236 billion, and U.S. investment abroad is more than $300 billion.[3] As more firms engage in international business, the world economy is fast becoming an interdependent system through a process called **globalization**.

We often take for granted the diversity of products we can buy as a result of international trade. Your television, your shoes, and even your morning coffee or juice are probably **imports**, products made or grown abroad and sold domestically in the United States. At the same time, the success of many U.S. firms depends on **exports**, products made or grown here, such as machinery, electronic equipment, and grains, and shipped for sale abroad.

Firms such as McDonald's, Microsoft, Apple, and Starbucks have found international markets to be a fruitful area for growth. But firms sometime stumble when they try to expand abroad. Home Depot has closed most of the stores it opened in China, for example, because labor costs are so low there that few homeowners are interested in "do-it-yourself" projects. Similarly, Best Buy also closed its stores in China because consumers there tend to buy their electronics goods at lower prices from local or online merchants.[4]

The impact of globalization doesn't stop with firms looking to open locations abroad or having to close locations that fail. Small firms with no international operations (for example, an independent coffee shop) may still buy from international suppliers, and even individual contractors or self-employed people can be affected by fluctuations in exchange rates.

Indeed, international trade is becoming increasingly important to most nations and their businesses. Many countries that once followed strict policies to protect domestic business now encourage trade just as aggressively. They are opening borders

Some globalization protestors, like this man, fear that multinational companies will wipe out small domestic businesses like family farms.

to foreign businesses, offering incentives for domestic businesses to expand internationally, and making it easier for foreign firms to partner with local firms. Likewise, as more industries and markets become global, so, too, are the firms that compete in them.

Several forces have combined to spark and sustain globalization. For one thing, governments and businesses are more aware of the benefits of globalization to businesses and shareholders. These benefits include the potential for higher standards of living and improved business profitability. New technologies have made international travel, communication, and commerce faster and cheaper than ever before. Finally, there are competitive pressures: Sometimes a firm must expand into foreign markets simply to keep up with competitors.

Globalization is not without its detractors. Some critics charge that globalization allows businesses to exploit workers in less-developed countries and bypass domestic environmental and tax regulations. For example, businesses pay workers in Vietnam and Indonesia lower wages than their counterparts in the United States. Factories in China are not subject to the same environmental protection laws as are firms in Europe. And businesses that headquarter their corporate offices in the Cayman Islands pay lower taxes. Critics also charge that globalization leads to the loss of cultural heritages and often benefits the rich more than the poor. For instance, as the English language becomes increasingly widespread throughout the world, some local languages are simply disappearing. Similarly, local residents in Africa receive relatively little economic benefits when oil or precious minerals are discovered on their land; prosperous investors buy the rights from landowners, who often don't realize the value of these resources. As a result, many international gatherings of global economic leaders are marked by protests and demonstrations.

The Major World Marketplaces

Managers involved with international businesses need a solid understanding of the global economy, including the major world marketplaces. This section examines some fundamental economic distinctions among countries based on wealth and then looks at some of the world's major international marketplaces.

Distinctions Based on Wealth The World Bank, an agency of the United Nations, uses per-capita income, average income per person, to make distinctions among countries. Its current classification method consists of four different categories of countries:[5]

1 *High-income countries:* Those with annual per-capita income greater than $12,746

2 *Upper-middle-income countries:* Those with annual per-capita income of $12,746 or less but more than $3,595

3 *Lower-middle-income countries:* Those with annual per-capita income of $3,595 or lower but more than $905

4 *Low-income countries* (often called *developing countries*): Those with annual per-capita income of $905 or less

Geographic Clusters The world economy generally revolves around three major marketplaces: North America, Europe, and Pacific Asia. In general, these clusters include relatively more of the upper-middle- and high-income nations but relatively few low- and lower-middle-income countries.

NORTH AMERICA As the world's largest marketplace and most stable economy, the United States dominates the North American market. Canada also plays a major role in the international economy, and the United States and Canada are each other's largest trading partners.

Mexico has been a major manufacturing center, especially along the U.S. border, where cheap labor and low transportation costs have encouraged many firms from the United States and other countries to build factories. However, Mexico's role as a low-cost manufacturing center is in flux. Just a few years ago, many experts believed that the emergence of China as a low-cost manufacturing center would lead companies to begin to shift their production from Mexico to China.[6] (The escalating drug-related violence along the northern Mexican border also contributed to this shift.) But a recent reversal of this trend is discussed in the boxed feature *Finding a Better Way*.

EUROPE Europe is often regarded as two regions—Western and Eastern. Western Europe, dominated by Germany, the United Kingdom, and France, has long been a mature but fragmented marketplace. The transformation of this region via the European Union (discussed later in this chapter) into an integrated economic system has further increased its importance. E-commerce and technology have also become increasingly important in this region. There has been a surge in Internet start-ups in southeastern England, the Netherlands, and the Scandinavian countries; Ireland is now one of the world's largest exporters of software; Strasbourg, France, is a major center for biotech start-ups; Barcelona, Spain, has many flourishing software and Internet companies; and the Frankfurt region of Germany is dotted with software and biotech start-ups.

Eastern Europe, once primarily communist, has also gained in importance, both as a marketplace and as a producer. Such multinational corporations as Daewoo, Nestlé, General Motors, and ABB Asea Brown Boveri have all set up operations in Poland. Ford, General Motors, Suzuki, and Volkswagen have built new factories in Hungary. On the other hand, governmental instability, corruption, and uncertainty have hampered development in parts of Russia, Bulgaria, Albania, Romania, and other countries.

PACIFIC ASIA Pacific Asia is generally agreed to consist of Japan, China, Thailand, Malaysia, Singapore, Indonesia, South Korea, Taiwan, the Philippines, and Australia. Fueled by strong entries in the automobile, electronics, and banking industries, the economies of these countries grew rapidly in the 1970s and 1980s. After a currency crisis in the late 1990s that slowed growth in virtually every country of the region, Pacific Asia showed clear signs of revitalization until the global recession in 2009. As the global economy begins to regain its momentum, Pacific Asia is expected to again be on the forefront. This is especially true of Japan, which, led by firms such as Toyota, Toshiba, and Nippon Steel, dominates the region. South Korea (home to firms Samsung and Hyundai, among others), Taiwan (owner of Chinese Petroleum

finding a better way

Too Much of a Good Thing? China's Success Creates More Jobs in Mexico

In today's competitive global economy, businesses strive for every possible advantage. Many manufacturers, for example, locate their factories in countries that have an ample supply of low-cost skilled labor. During the 1980s and 1990s, the place to be was Mexico. Hundreds of factories were built just across the U.S.–Mexican border, and workers streamed to the region from other parts of Mexico for stable and well-paying jobs. But in the late 1990s, the world started to shift.

Mexican prosperity, fueled in part by its role as a center of manufacturing, led to increases in the cost-of-living, followed quickly by wage increases so workers could keep up. At about that same time, China began to emerge as an attractive manufacturing alternative. For instance, in 2003, wages in China were only one-third of the wages in Mexico. And there was certainly no shortage of workers eager to take steady jobs in factories making products for other countries. China's boom was Mexico's bust, as one company after another reduced or eliminated manufacturing there and moved to Asia.

In recent years, things have started to tilt back in Mexico's favor. Why? As China's economy has flourished, its labor costs have crept higher and higher, so it's less of a bargain than it used to be. Whereas Mexican wages were once three times higher than wages in China, Mexican wages today are approximately 20 percent less than those in China, according to research by Merrill Lynch.[7] When manufacturers factor in shipping costs (which have increased because of fuel prices), producing in Mexico may cost the same or less than in China.

vario images GmbH & Co.KG/Alamy

Time differences between the United States and China also can make it difficult to schedule videoconferences and telephone calls. Several companies have also been burned by China's lack of protection for industrial and intellectual property.

Mexico is making enormous gains in the automobile sector. Companies such as Nissan, Honda, Volkswagen, and Mazda have invested billions of dollars in Mexican production vehicles, with over 3 million vehicles produced in 2014. Eighty percent of these cars are exported to other countries, with the bulk being sent to the United States. Because of NAFTA, as well as other trade agreements, Mexico can export cars without tariffs to North and South America as well as Europe and Japan. According to Volkswagen's Vice President of Corporate Affairs in Mexico, "There's not another country in the world where you can do that."[8]

---

and the manufacturing home of many foreign firms), and Hong Kong (a major financial center) are also successful players in the international economy.

China, one of the world's most densely populated countries, has emerged as an important market and now boasts one of the world's largest economies. Although its per-capita income remains low, the sheer number of potential consumers makes it an important market. India, though not part of Pacific Asia, is also rapidly emerging as one of the globe's most important economies. As in North America and Europe, technology promises to play an increasingly important role in the future of this region. In some parts of Asia, however, poorly developed electronic infrastructures, slower adoption of computers and information technology, and a higher percentage of lower-income consumers hamper the emergence of technology firms.

Trade Agreements and Alliances

Various legal agreements have sparked international trade and shaped the global business environment. Virtually every nation has formal trade treaties with other nations. A *treaty* is a legal agreement that specifies areas in which nations will cooperate with one another. Among the most significant treaties is the *North American Free Trade Agreement*. The *European Union*, the *Association of Southeast Asian Nations*, and the *World Trade Organization*, all governed by treaties, are also instrumental in promoting international business activity.

North American Free Trade Agreement The **North American Free Trade Agreement (NAFTA)** removes most tariffs and other trade barriers among the United States, Canada, and Mexico and includes agreements on environmental issues and labor abuses.

Most observers agree that NAFTA is achieving its basic purpose—to create a more active and unified North American market. It has created several hundred thousand new jobs, although this number is smaller than NAFTA proponents had hoped. One thing is clear, though; the flood of U.S. jobs lost to Mexico predicted by NAFTA critics, especially labor unions, has not occurred.

The European Union The **European Union (EU)** includes most European nations, as shown in Figure 1. These nations have eliminated most quotas and set uniform tariff levels on products imported and exported within their group. In 1992, virtually all internal trade barriers went down, making the EU the largest free marketplace in the world. The adoption of a common currency, the *euro*, by most member nations further solidified the EU's position in the world economy.

North American Free Trade Agreement (NAFTA) *agreement to gradually eliminate tariffs and other trade barriers among the United States, Canada, and Mexico*

European Union (EU) *agreement among major European nations to eliminate or make uniform most trade barriers affecting group members*

FIGURE 1 The Nations of the European Union
Source: http://europa.eu/abc/maps/index_en.htm, accessed April 5, 2013.

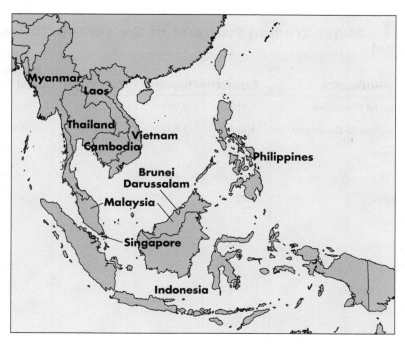

FIGURE 2 The Nations of the Association of Southeast Asian Nations (ASEAN)

The Association of Southeast Asian Nations

The **Association of Southeast Asian Nations (ASEAN)** was founded in 1967 as an organization for economic, political, social, and cultural cooperation. In 1995, Vietnam became the group's first communist member. Figure 2 shows a map of the ASEAN countries. Because of its relative size, the ASEAN does not have the same global economic significance as NAFTA and the EU.

Association of Southeast Asian Nations (ASEAN) organization for economic, political, social, and cultural cooperation among Southeast Asian nations

The World Trade Organization

The **General Agreement on Tariffs and Trade (GATT)** was signed in 1947. Its purpose was to reduce or eliminate trade barriers, such as tariffs and quotas. It did so by encouraging nations to protect domestic industries within agreed-on limits and to engage in multilateral negotiations. The GATT proved to be relatively successful. So, to further promote globalization, most of the world's countries joined to create the **World Trade Organization (WTO)**, which began on January 1, 1995. (The GATT is the actual treaty that governs the WTO.) The 160-member countries are required to open markets to international trade, and the WTO is empowered to pursue three goals:[9]

General Agreement on Tariffs and Trade (GATT) international trade agreement to encourage the multilateral reduction or elimination of trade barriers

World Trade Organization (WTO) organization through which member nations negotiate trading agreements and resolve disputes about trade policies and practices

1 Promote trade by encouraging members to adopt fair-trade practices.

2 Reduce trade barriers by promoting multilateral negotiations.

3 Establish fair procedures for resolving disputes among members.

International Trade

The global economy is essentially defined by international trade. International trade occurs when an exchange involving goods, services, and/or currency takes place across national boundaries. Although international trade has many advantages, it can also pose problems if a country's imports and exports don't maintain an acceptable balance. Table 1 lists the United States' 15 largest trading partners. However, the United States also does business with many more countries. For instance, in 2013, the United States exported $5.1 billion to Egypt, $2.4 billion to Kuwait, $3.0 billion to Poland, and $132.9 million to Zambia; imports from those same countries were $2.8

OBJECTIVE 2
Explain

how differences in import–export balances, exchange rates, and foreign competition determine the ways in which countries and businesses respond to the international environment.

table 1 Major Trading Partners of the United States
(In Millions)

Rank	Country	Exports	Imports	Total Trade	Percent of Total Trade
---	**Total, All Countries**	**1,489.6**	**2,149.0**	**3,638.6**	**100.0%**
---	**Total, Top 15 Countries**	**1,034.2**	**1,632.7**	**2,666.9**	**73.3%**
1	Canada	287.8	317.4	605.2	16.6%
2	China	111.8	426.1	537.9	14.8%
3	Mexico	221.4	270.3	491.7	13.5%
4	Japan	61.2	122.5	183.6	5.0%
5	Germany	45.7	113.1	158.7	4.4%
6	Korea, South	40.7	63.6	104.3	2.9%
7	United Kingdom	49.2	49.2	98.4	2.7%
8	France	28.7	43.1	71.7	2.0%
9	Brazil	39.3	27.5	66.8	1.8%
10	Taiwan	24.5	37.4	61.8	1.7%
11	India	19.7	41.8	61.4	1.7%
12	Saudi Arabia	16.4	44.1	60.5	1.7%
13	Netherlands	40.0	19.2	59.2	1.6%
14	Italy	15.6	38.5	54.0	1.5%
15	Belgium	32.2	19.2	51.5	1.4%

Source: www.census.gov/foreign-trade/statistics/highlights/top/top1411yr.html

billion, $12.2 billion, $4.2 billion, and $62 million, respectively. In deciding whether an overall balance exists between imports and exports, economists use two measures: *balance of trade* and *balance of payments*.

Balance of Trade

Balance of Trade *economic value of all products a country exports minus the economic value of all products it imports*

A country's **balance of trade** is the total economic value of all the products that it exports minus the economic value of all the products that it imports. A *positive balance of trade* results when a country exports (sells to other countries) more than it imports (buys from other countries). A *negative balance of trade* results when a country imports more than it exports.

Relatively small trade imbalances are common and are unimportant. Large imbalances, however, are another matter. The biggest concern about trade balances involves the flow of currency. When U.S. consumers and businesses buy foreign products, dollars flow from the United States to other countries; when U.S. businesses are selling to foreign consumers and businesses, dollars flow back into the United States. A large negative balance of trade means that many dollars are controlled by interests outside the United States.

Trade Deficit *situation in which a country's imports exceed its exports, creating a negative balance of trade*

Trade Surplus *situation in which a country's exports exceed its imports, creating a positive balance of trade*

A **trade deficit** occurs when a country's imports exceed its exports, when it has a negative balance of trade. When exports exceed imports, the nation enjoys a **trade surplus**. Several factors, such as general economic conditions and the effect of trade agreements, influence trade deficits and surpluses. For example, higher domestic costs, greater international competition, and continuing economic problems among some of its regional trading partners have slowed the tremendous growth in exports

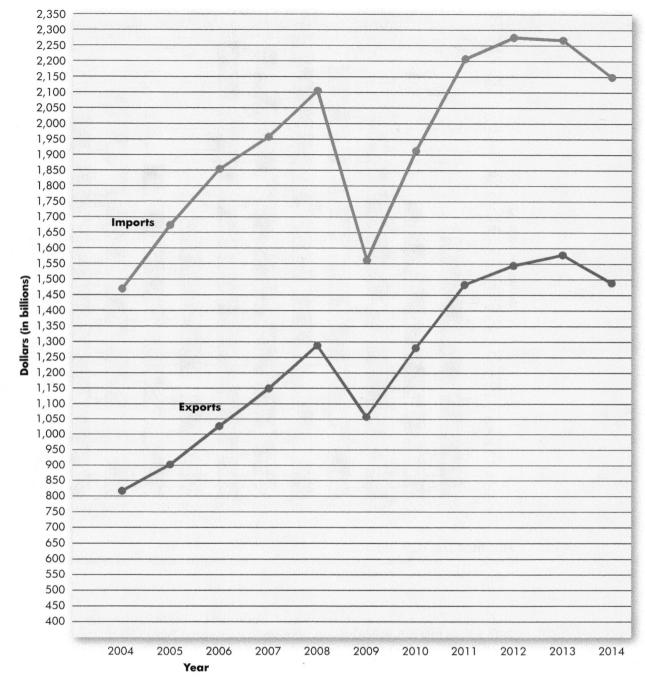

FIGURE 3 U.S. Imports and Exports
Source: http://www.census.gov/foreign-trade/balance/c0015.html#2014

that Japan once enjoyed. But rising prosperity in China and India has led to strong increases in both exports from and imports to those countries.

Figures 3 and 4 highlight two series of events: (1) recent trends in U.S. exports and imports and (2) the resulting trade deficit. As Figure 3 shows, both U.S. imports and U.S. exports, with minor variations, have been generally increasing—a trend that's projected to continue.

Trade deficits between 2001 and 2014 are shown in Figure 4. There was a deficit in each of these years because more money flowed out to pay for foreign imports than flowed in to pay for U.S. exports. For example, in 2008, the United States exported $1,287.4 billion in goods and services and imported $2,103.6 billion in goods

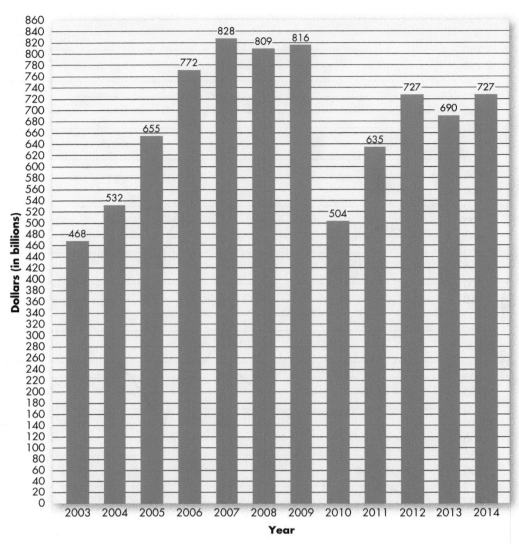

FIGURE 4 U.S. Trade Deficit
Source: U.S. Census Bureau: Foreign Trade Statistics, at http://www.census.gov/foreign-trade/statistics/highlights/annual.html, accessed 2015

and services. Because imports exceeded exports, the United States had a *trade deficit* of $816 billion (the difference between exports and imports). Note also that both exports and imports declined in 2008 and 2009 from the previous year. This was a result of the global economic slowdown.

Balance of Payments

The **balance of payments** refers to the flow of *money* into or out of a country. The money that a country pays for imports and receives for exports, its balance of trade, accounts for much of its balance of payments. Other financial exchanges are also factors. Money spent by tourists in a country, money spent by a country on foreign-aid programs, and money exchanged by buying and selling currency on international money markets affect the balance of payments.

For instance, suppose that the United States has a negative balance of trade of $1 million. Now, suppose that this year, U.S. citizens travel abroad as tourists and spend a total of $200,000 in other countries. This amount gets added to the balance of trade to form the balance of payments, which is now a negative $1.2 million dollars. Now, further suppose that tourists from other countries come to the United States and spend the equivalent of $300,000 while they are here. This has the effect of reducing the negative balance of payments to $900,000. Then, further suppose that the United States then sends $600,000 in aid to help the victims of a tsunami-ravaged country in Asia. Because this represents additional dollars leaving the United States, the balance of payments is now a negative $1.5 million. For many years, the United States enjoyed a positive balance of payments. Recently, however, the overall balance has become negative.

Exchange Rates

The balance of imports and exports between two countries is affected by the rate of exchange between their currencies. An **exchange rate** is the rate at which the currency of one nation can be exchanged for that of another. Suppose, for example, that the exchange rate between the U.S. dollar and the British pound was $2 to £1. This means that it costs £1 to "buy" $2 or $1 to "buy" £0.5. Stated differently, £1 and $2 have the same purchasing power, or £1 = $2.

At the end of World War II, the major nations of the world agreed to set *fixed exchange rates*. The value of any country's currency relative to that of another would remain constant. The goal was to allow the global economy to stabilize. Today, however, *floating exchange rates* are the norm, and the value of one country's currency relative to that of another varies with market conditions. For example, when many British citizens want to spend pounds to buy U.S. dollars (or goods), the value of the dollar relative to the pound increases. Demand for the dollar is high, and a currency is strong when demand for it is high. It's also strong when there's high demand for the goods manufactured with that currency. On a daily basis, exchange rates fluctuate very little. Significant variations usually occur over longer time spans. Highly regulated economic systems such as in China are among the few that still use fixed exchange rates. The Chinese government regulates the flow of currency—its own as well as all others—into and out of China and determines the precise rate of exchange within its borders.

Exchange-rate fluctuation can have an important impact on balance of trade. Suppose you want to buy some English tea for £10 per box. At an exchange rate of $2 to £1, a box will cost you $20 (£10 × 2 = 20). But what if the pound is weaker? At an exchange rate of, say, $1.25 to £1, the same box would cost you only $12.50 (£10 × 1.25 = 12.50). If the dollar is strong in relation to the pound, the prices of all U.S.-made products will rise in England, and the prices of all English-made products will fall in the United States. The English would buy fewer U.S. products, and Americans would be prompted to spend more on English-made products. The result would probably be a U.S. trade deficit with England.

One of the most significant developments in foreign exchange has been the introduction of the **euro**, the common currency of the EU. The euro was officially introduced in 2002 and has replaced other currencies, such as the German Deutsche Mark, the Italian lira, and the French franc. In the years since its debut, the euro has become one of the world's most important currencies. When it was first introduced, the euro's value was pegged as being equivalent to the dollar: €1 = $1. But because the dollar was relatively weak in the years that followed, its value eroded relative to that of the euro. At one point in the late 1990s, $1 was worth only about half a euro. In the aftermath of the Great Recession, though, the dollar has strengthened relative to the euro and the exchange in early 2015 was $1 = €0.90.

Companies with international operations must watch exchange-rate fluctuations closely because changes affect overseas demand for their products and can be a major factor in competition. In general, when the value of a country's currency rises—becomes stronger—companies based there find it harder to export products to foreign markets and easier for foreign companies to enter local markets. It also makes it more cost-efficient for domestic companies to move operations to lower-cost foreign sites. When the value of a currency declines—becomes weaker—the opposite occurs. As the value of a country's currency falls, its balance of trade usually improves because domestic companies should experience a boost in exports. There should also be less reason for foreign companies to ship products into the domestic market and less reason to establish operations in other countries.

Exchange Rate *rate at which the currency of one nation can be exchanged for the currency of another nation*

Euro *a common currency shared among most of the members of the EU (excluding Denmark, Sweden, and the United Kingdom)*

Forms of Competitive Advantage

Before we discuss the fundamental issues involved in international business management, we must consider one last factor: forms of *competitive advantage*. Because no country can produce everything that it needs, countries tend to export what they can produce better or less expensively than other countries and use the proceeds to import what they can't produce as effectively. This principle doesn't fully explain why nations export and import what they do. Such decisions hinge partly on the advantages that a particular country enjoys regarding its abilities to create or sell certain products and resources.[10] Economists traditionally focused on absolute and comparative advantage to explain international trade. But because this approach focuses narrowly on such factors as natural resources and labor costs, a more contemporary view of national competitive advantage has emerged.

Absolute Advantage *the ability to produce something more efficiently than any other country can*

Absolute Advantage An **absolute advantage** exists when a country can produce something that is cheaper or of higher quality than any other country. Saudi oil, Brazilian coffee beans, and Canadian timber come close (because these countries have such abundant supplies of these resources), but examples of true absolute advantage are rare. For example, many experts say that the vineyards of France produce the world's finest wines. But the burgeoning wine business in California demonstrates that producers there can also make good wines—wines that rival those from France but come in more varieties and at lower prices.

Comparative Advantage *the ability to produce some products more efficiently than others*

Comparative Advantage A country has a **comparative advantage** in goods that it can produce more efficiently or better than other nations. If businesses in a given country can make computers more efficiently than they can make automobiles, then that nation has a comparative advantage in computer manufacturing.

managing in turbulent times

The Ups and Downs of Globalization

In 2010, Toyota and other Japanese automakers found themselves in a very tough position. Several high-profile recalls had cut into Toyota's sales, and the exchange rate of yen for dollars made a bad situation worse. The yen was at a 15-year high against the dollar and a nine-year high versus the euro. Toyota made more than half of their cars in Japan, where costs were high, yet sold many overseas. Sales made in the United States and Europe converted to fewer yen, sharply cutting into Toyota's profit margins. As a result, Toyota began to expand production of both cars and their components to lower-cost countries as well as major markets.[11] Although Toyota's stock was selling above $130 per share in late 2006, five years later, Toyota's stock price had plummeted by half to less than $65 per share.

ITAR-TASS Photo Agency/Alamy

In the fiscal year that ended in March 2015, Toyota had its most profitable year ever and exchange rates, somewhat surprisingly, were a big part of their success. Their stock price soared to prices higher than the 2006 peak, selling at more than $140 per share. What changed in such a short time? After several years of record-breaking deflation, Japan's central bank began pumping money into the economy. While the additional capital has stimulated the Japanese economy, the value of the yen compared to the dollar and euro sharply declined. By early 2015, a dollar bought 50 percent more yen than it did just four years earlier. Even more concerning to U.S. automakers, the yen is now cheaper than it has been since the 1970s. Masahiro Akita, an industry analyst at Credit Suisse, explains, "For automakers, the key factors are volume, exchange rates, and fixed costs. If you can get all those things to go your way, you're in good shape. And Toyota has."[12]

In general, both absolute and comparative advantages translate into competitive advantage. Brazil, for instance, can produce and market coffee beans knowing full well that few other countries have the right mix of climate, terrain, and altitude to enter the coffee bean market. The United States has comparative advantages in the computer industry (because of technological sophistication) and in farming (because of large amounts of fertile land and a temperate climate). South Korea has a comparative advantage in electronics manufacturing because of efficient operations and cheap labor. As a result of each country's comparative advantage, U.S. firms export computers and grain to South Korea and import DVD players from South Korea. South Korea can produce food, and the United States can build DVD players, but each nation imports certain products because the other holds a comparative advantage in the relevant industry.

National Competitive Advantage In recent years, a theory of national competitive advantage has become a widely accepted model of why nations engage in international trade.[13] **National competitive advantage** derives from four conditions:

1 **Factor conditions** are the following factors of production—*labor, capital, entrepreneurs, physical resources*, and *information resources*.

2 **Demand conditions** reflect a large domestic consumer base that promotes strong demand for innovative products.

3 **Related and supporting industries** include strong local or regional suppliers or industrial customers.

4 **Strategies, structures, and rivalries** refer to firms and industries that stress cost reduction, product quality, higher productivity, and innovative products.

When all attributes of national competitive advantage exist, a nation is likely to be heavily involved in international business. Japan, for instance, has an abundance of natural resources and strong domestic demand for automobiles. Its carmakers have well-oiled supplier networks, and domestic firms have competed intensely with one another for decades. These circumstances explain why Japanese car companies such as Toyota and Honda are successful in foreign markets.

National Competitive Advantage *international competitive advantage stemming from a combination of factor conditions, demand conditions, related and supporting industries, and firm strategies, structures, and rivalries*

International Business Management

OBJECTIVE 3
Discuss
the factors involved in deciding to do business internationally and in selecting the appropriate levels of international involvement and international organizational structure.

Regardless of where a firm is located, its success depends largely on how well it's managed. International business is so challenging because basic management tasks—planning, organizing, directing, and controlling—are much more difficult when a firm operates in markets scattered around the globe.

Managing means making decisions. In this section, we examine the three basic decisions that a company must make when considering globalization. The first decision is whether to go international. Once that decision has been made, managers must decide on the level of international involvement and on the organizational structure that will best meet the firm's global needs.

Going International

As the world economy becomes increasingly globalized, more and more firms are expanding their international operations. U.S. firms are aggressively expanding abroad, and foreign companies such as BP and Nestlé continue to expand into foreign markets as well, including the U.S. market. This route, however, isn't appropriate for every company. If you buy and sell fresh fish, you'll probably find it more profitable to confine your activities to limited geographic areas because storage and transport costs may be too high to make international operations worthwhile. As Figure 5 shows, several factors affect the decision to go international.

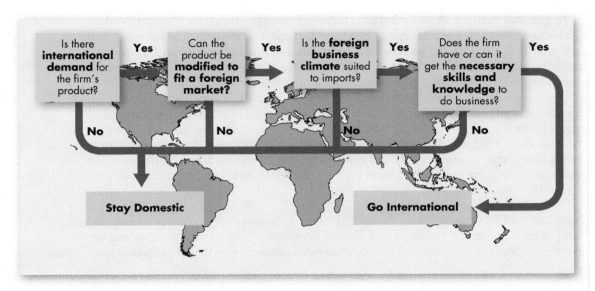

FIGURE 5 Going International

Gauging International Demand

In considering international expansion, a company must determine whether there is a demand for its products abroad. Products that are successful in one country may be useless in another. Even when there is demand, advertising may still need to be adjusted. For example, bicycles are largely used for recreation in the United States but are seen as basic transportation in China. Hence, a bicycle maker would need to use different marketing strategies in each of these countries. Market research or the prior market entry of competitors may indicate whether there's an international demand for a firm's products.

Adapting to Customer Needs

If its product is in demand, a firm must decide whether and how to adapt it to meet the special demands of foreign customers. For example, to satisfy local tastes, McDonald's sells wine in France, beer in Germany, gazpacho in Spain, and provides some vegetarian sandwiches in India. Likewise, consumer electronics companies have to be aware that different countries use different kinds of electric sockets and different levels of electric power. Therefore, regardless of demand, customer needs must still be considered.

Outsourcing and Offshoring

Outsourcing the practice of paying suppliers and distributors to perform certain business processes or to provide needed materials or services

Offshoring the practice of outsourcing to foreign countries

Outsourcing, the practice of paying suppliers and distributors to perform certain business processes or to provide needed materials or services, has become a popular option for going international. It has become so popular because (1) it helps firms focus on their core activities and avoid getting sidetracked on secondary activities, and (2) it reduces costs by locating certain business functions in areas where relevant costs are low.[14]

The practice of outsourcing to foreign countries is more specifically referred to as **offshoring**. Many companies today contract their manufacturing to low-cost factories in Asia. Similarly, many service call centers today are outsourced to businesses located in India. The Oscar-winning movie *Slumdog Millionaire* featured a young Indian man who worked for an international call center in Mumbai. In real life, DirecTV, Chase Bank Credit Card Services, and several home mortgage support businesses have established call centers in India and have enjoyed considerable success. On the other hand, though, the network of FTD florists opened a call center in India but subsequently closed it. As it turns out, many people who call to order flowers need more personal assistance—advice on type of flowers, colors of arrangements, and so forth—than can be provided by someone from a different culture on the other side of the world.

entrepreneurship and new ventures

A Better Coconut Water

Founded in 2009, Harmless Harvest is the manufacturer and distributor of a popular line of organic coconut water that is available in stores across the United States. Douglas Riboud and Justin Guilbert saw an opportunity with the sudden popularity of coconut water, but they were troubled by environmental and economic concerns. After extensive research, Riboud and Guilbert concluded that the best-tasting coconut water could be produced from a single species of coconut from Thailand, in spite of lower yields and more complex cultivation. Unlike other producers, their coconut water is pasteurized through high-pressure treatment rather than heat, creating a raw, better-tasting product. According to Riboud, "The most important thing for us is taste. And the best we can do, the hardest job you can do as a manufacturer who works in food, is not screw up the ingredient you had in the first place." [15]

Harmless Harvest has addressed environmental concerns by making sure that their product is organic. They made an early commitment to working with farmers to make sure that no harmful pesticides or synthetic fertilizers were used and worked to obtain organic certification. Although this process was time-consuming and costly, it assured Riboud and Guilbert that their entire supply chain was built upon their vision of sustainability.

Finally, Harmless Harvest has contributed to economic change in a number of ways. In 2013, they built a manufacturing facility in Thailand rather than importing coconuts to the

Hirun Wanthongsri/123RF

United States or outsourcing production. According to their website, "This location allows us to oversee vital steps in our production cycle and adds value to the area by developing employment opportunities for the surrounding communities." The company has also worked to obtain Fair for Life Social & Fair Trade Certification, further testament to their commitment to their cause. This certification attests to their commitment to paying fair prices for the coconuts that they purchase from local farmers and making sure that they work with companies that pay a living wage.[16]

Levels of International Involvement

After deciding to go international, a firm must determine the level of its involvement. Several levels are possible: a firm may act as an exporter or importer, organize as an international firm, or (like most of the world's largest industrial firms) operate as a multinational firm.

Exporters and Importers An **exporter** makes products in one country to distribute and sell in others. An **importer** buys products in foreign markets and brings them home for resale. Both conduct most of their business in their home nations. Both entail the lowest level of involvement in international operations, and both are good ways to learn the fine points of global business. Many large firms entered international business as exporters. General Electric and Coca Cola, among others, exported to Europe for several years before setting up production sites there. It is also useful to remember that most import/export transactions involve both activities. A bottle of French wine sold in New York, for instance, was exported by the French winery and imported by the U.S. wine distributor.

Exporter *firm that distributes and sells products to one or more foreign countries*

Importer *firm that buys products in foreign markets and then imports them for resale in its home country*

International Firms As exporters and importers gain experience and grow, many move to the next level of involvement. **International firms** conduct a meaningful amount of their business abroad and may even maintain overseas manufacturing facilities. An international firm may be large, but it's still basically a domestic company with international operations. Hershey, for instance, buys ingredients for its chocolates from several foreign suppliers and makes all of its

International Firm *firm that conducts a significant portion of its business in foreign countries*

products in the United States but has one plant in Mexico. Moreover, although it sells its products in approximately 70 other countries, it generates most of its revenues from its domestic market.[17]

Multinational Firm *firm that designs, produces, and markets products in many nations*

Multinational Firms Most **multinational firms**, firms that design, produce, and market products in many nations, such as ExxonMobil, Nestlé, Honda, and Ford, don't think of themselves as having domestic and international divisions. Headquarters locations are almost irrelevant, and planning and decision making are geared to international markets. The world's largest multinationals in 2014, based on sales, profits, and employees, are shown in Table 2.

We can't underestimate the economic impact of multinational firms. Consider just the impact of the 500 largest multinationals: In 2013, these 500 firms generated $31.1 trillion in revenues and nearly $2 trillion in owner profits.[18] They employed tens of millions of people, bought materials and equipment from literally thousands of other firms, and paid billions in taxes. Moreover, their products affected the lives of hundreds of millions of consumers, competitors, investors, and even protestors.

International Organization Structures

Different levels of international involvement entail different kinds of organizational structures. A structure that would help coordinate an exporter's activities would be inadequate for those of a multinational. In this section, we consider the spectrum of organizational strategies, including *independent agents, licensing arrangements, branch offices, strategic alliances,* and *foreign direct investment.*

Independent Agent *foreign individual or organization that agrees to represent an exporter's interests*

Independent Agents An **independent agent** is a foreign individual or organization that represents an exporter in foreign markets. Independent agents often act as sales representatives: They sell the exporter's products, collect payment, and make sure that customers are satisfied. They often represent several firms at once and usually don't specialize in a particular product or market. Peter So operates an

table 2 The World's Largest Non-U.S. Companies by Sales, Profits, and Number of Employees (2014)

Company	Sales ($millions)	Profits ($billions)	Employees
Royal Dutch Shell	459,599		
Sinopec	457,201		
China Nat'l Petro.	432,007		
BP	396,217		
State Grid	333,386		
Samsung			
Industrial and Commercial Bank of China		42.7	
Gazprom		35.7	
China Construction Bank		34.9	
Samsung		27.2	
Agricultural Bank of China		27.1	
G4S plc			618,000
Randstad Holding NV			595,730
Volkswagen			555,097
PetroChina Co. Ltd.			544,083

Source: http://www.usatoday.com/story/money/business/2014/10/25/24-7-wall-st-most-profitable-companies/17707869/ and http://www.usatoday.com/story/money/business/2014/08/24/24-7-wall-st-biggest-employers/14443001/

import–export office in Hong Kong. He and his staff of three handle imports from about 15 foreign companies into Hong Kong and about 10 Hong Kong firms that export products abroad.

Licensing Arrangements Companies seeking more involvement may opt for licensing arrangements. A **licensing arrangement** is a contract under which one firm allows another to use its brand name, operating procedures, or proprietary technology. Firms give foreign individuals or companies exclusive rights (called *licensing agreements*) to manufacture or market their products in that market. In return, the exporter receives a fee plus ongoing payments (royalties) that are calculated as a percentage of the license holder's sales. Franchising is a popular form of licensing. For example, McDonald's, Pizza Hut, and Hertz Car Rental have franchises around the world.

Branch Offices Instead of developing relationships with foreign agents or licensing companies, a firm may send its own managers to overseas branch offices, where the firm has more direct control than it does over agents or license holders. **Branch offices** also furnish a more visible public presence in foreign countries, and foreign customers tend to feel more secure when there's a local branch office. Halliburton, a Houston-based oil field supply and services company, opened a branch office in Dubai to more effectively establish relationships with customers in the Middle East.

Strategic Alliances In a **strategic alliance**, a company finds a partner in the country in which it wants to do business. Each party agrees to invest resources and capital into a new business or to cooperate in some mutually beneficial way. This new business, the alliance, is owned by the partners, who divide its profits. Such alliances are sometimes called *joint ventures*, but the term *strategic alliance* has arisen because such partnerships are playing increasingly important roles in the strategies of major companies. Ford and Russian automaker Sollers have a joint venture in Russia. Sollers manufactures Ford products in Russia and the two partners work together on marketing them.[19] In many countries, such as Mexico, India, and China, laws make alliances virtually the only way to do international business. Mexico, for example, requires that all foreign firms investing there have local partners. Likewise, local interests own the majority of both Disney theme parks in China; Disney is the minority owner but also collects management and licensing fees.

In addition to easing the way into new markets, alliances give firms greater control over foreign activities than agents and licensees. Alliances also allow firms to benefit from the knowledge and expertise of foreign partners. Microsoft, for example, relies heavily on alliances when it expands into new international markets. This approach has helped the firm learn the intricacies of doing business in China and India, two of the hardest emerging markets to crack.

Foreign Direct Investment **Foreign direct investment (FDI)** involves buying or establishing tangible assets in another country. Dell Computer, for example, has built assembly plants in Europe and China. Volkswagen has built a factory in Brazil, and Coca-Cola has built bottling plants in dozens of different countries. FedEx has a major distribution center in Paris. Each of these activities represents FDI by a firm in another country.

Understanding the Cultural Environment

A major factor in the success—or failure—of international business activity is having a deep understanding of the cultural environment and how it affects business. Disney's Hong Kong theme park struggled after it first opened, in large part because Disney made the mistake of minimizing all elements of Chinese culture in the park—essentially making it a generic miniature reproduction of the original

Licensing Arrangement *arrangement in which firms choose foreign individuals or organizations to manufacture or market their products in another country*

Branch Office *foreign office set up by an international or multinational firm*

Strategic Alliance *arrangement (also called joint venture) in which a company finds a foreign partner to contribute approximately half of the resources needed to establish and operate a new business in the partner's country*

Foreign Direct Investment (FDI) *arrangement in which a firm buys or establishes tangible assets in another country*

OBJECTIVE 4
Explain
the role and importance of the cultural environment in international business.

Disneyland in California. Disney also confused potential visitors with ads showing a father, mother, and two children walking hand-in-hand toward the theme park, overlooking China's laws that restrict many families to a single child. Only after a refurbishment to make the park more Chinese and a revised ad campaign did attendance begin to improve.[20] A country's culture includes all the values, symbols, beliefs, and language that guide behavior.

Values, Symbols, Beliefs, and Language

Cultural values and beliefs are often unspoken; they may even be taken for granted by those who live in a particular country. Cultural factors do not necessarily cause problems for managers when the cultures of two countries are similar. Difficulties can arise, however, when there is little overlap between the home culture of a manager and the culture of the country in which business is to be conducted. For example, most U.S. managers find the culture and traditions of England relatively familiar. The people of both countries speak the same language and share strong historical roots, and there is a history of strong commerce between the two countries. When U.S. managers begin operations in Japan or the Middle East, however, most of those commonalities disappear.

In Japanese, the word *hai* (pronounced "hi") means "yes." In conversation, however, this word is used much like people in the United States use "uh-huh"; it moves a conversation along or shows the person with whom you are talking that you are paying attention. So when does *hai* mean "yes" and when does it mean "uh-huh"? This turns out to be a relatively difficult question to answer. If a U.S. manager asks a Japanese manager if he agrees to some trade arrangement, the Japanese manager is likely to say, "Hai"—but this may mean "Yes, I agree," "Yes, I understand," or "Yes, I am listening." Some U.S. managers become frustrated in negotiations with the Japanese because they believe that the Japanese continue to raise issues that have already been settled (because the Japanese managers said "Yes"). What many of these managers fail to recognize is that "yes" does not always mean "yes" in Japan.

Cultural differences between countries can have a direct impact on business practice. For example, the religion of Islam teaches that people should not make a living by exploiting the misfortune of others; as a result, charging interest payments is seen as immoral. This also means that in Saudi Arabia there are few businesses that provide auto-towing services to take stalled cars to a garage for repair (because that would be capitalizing on misfortune), and in the Sudan, banks cannot pay or charge interest. Given these cultural and religious constraints, those two businesses—automobile towing and banking—do not seem to hold great promise for international managers in those particular countries!

Some cultural differences between countries can be even subtler and yet have a major impact on business activities. For example, in the United States, most managers clearly agree about the value of time. Most U.S. managers schedule their activities tightly and then try to adhere to their schedules. Other cultures do not put such a premium on time. In the Middle East, managers do not like to set appointments, and they rarely keep appointments set too far into the future. U.S. managers interacting with managers from the Middle East might misinterpret the late arrival of a potential business partner as a negotiation ploy or an insult, when it is rather a simple reflection of different views of time and its value.[21]

Language itself can be an important factor. Beyond the obvious and clear barriers posed by people who speak different languages, subtle differences in meaning can also play a major role. For example, Imperial Oil of Canada markets gasoline under the brand name Esso. When the firm tried to sell its gasoline in Japan, it learned that *esso* means "stalled car" in Japanese. Likewise, when Chevrolet first introduced a U.S. model called the Nova in Latin America, General Motors executives could not understand why the car sold poorly. They eventually learned, though, that, in Spanish, *no va* means "It doesn't go." The color green is used extensively in Muslim countries, but it signifies death in some other countries. The color associated with femininity in the United States is pink, but in many other countries, yellow is the most feminine color.

Employee Behavior Across Cultures

Managers in international business also have to understand that there are differences in what motivates people in different cultures. Although it's impossible to predict exactly how people from different cultures will react in the workplace, some insights have been developed from research on individual behaviors and attitudes across different cultures. This research, conducted by Geert Hofstede, identifies five important dimensions along which people seem to differ across cultures. These dimensions are illustrated in Figure 6.

The first dimension is **social orientation**. Social orientation is a person's beliefs about the relative importance of the individual versus groups to which that person belongs. The two extremes of social orientation are individualism and collectivism. *Individualism* is the cultural belief that the person comes first. Research suggests that people in the United States, the United Kingdom, Australia, Canada, New Zealand, and the Netherlands tend to be relatively individualistic. *Collectivism* is the belief that the group comes first. Research has found that people from Mexico, Greece, Hong Kong, Taiwan, Peru, Singapore, Colombia, and Pakistan tend to be relatively collectivistic in their values. In countries with higher levels of individualism, many workers may prefer reward systems that link pay with the performance of individual employees. In a more collectivistic culture, such a reward system may in fact be counterproductive.

A second important dimension is **power orientation**, the beliefs that people in a culture hold about the appropriateness of power and authority differences in

Social Orientation *a person's beliefs about the relative importance of the individual versus groups to which that person belongs*

Power Orientation *the beliefs that people in a culture hold about the appropriateness of power and authority differences in hierarchies such as business organizations*

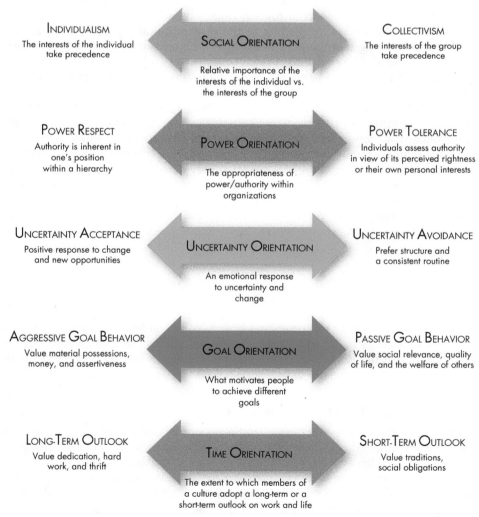

FIGURE 6 Hofstede's Five Dimensions of National Culture

hierarchies such as business organizations. Some cultures are characterized by *power respect*. This means that people tend to accept the power and authority of their superiors simply on the basis of their position in the hierarchy and to respect their right to hold that power. Research has found that people in France, Spain, Mexico, Japan, Brazil, Indonesia, and Singapore are relatively power accepting. In contrast, people in cultures with a *power tolerance* orientation attach much less significance to a person's position in the hierarchy. These individuals are more willing to question a decision or mandate from someone at a higher level or perhaps even refuse to accept it. Research suggests that people in the United States, Israel, Austria, Denmark, Ireland, Norway, Germany, and New Zealand tend to be more power tolerant.

Uncertainty Orientation *the feeling individuals have regarding uncertain and ambiguous situations*

The third basic dimension of individual differences is *uncertainty orientation*. **Uncertainty orientation** is the feeling individuals have regarding uncertain and ambiguous situations. People in cultures with *uncertainty acceptance* are stimulated by change and thrive on new opportunities. The research suggests that many people in the United States, Denmark, Sweden, Canada, Singapore, Hong Kong, and Australia are among those in this category. In contrast, people with *uncertainty avoidance* tendencies dislike and will avoid ambiguity whenever possible. The research found that many people in Israel, Austria, Japan, Italy, Columbia, France, Peru, and Germany tend to avoid uncertainty whenever possible.

Goal Orientation *the manner in which people are motivated to work toward different kinds of goals*

The fourth dimension of cultural values is goal orientation. In this context, **goal orientation** is the manner in which people are motivated to work toward different kinds of goals. One extreme on the goal orientation continuum is *aggressive goal behavior*. People who exhibit aggressive goal behaviors tend to place a high premium on material possessions, money, and assertiveness. On the other hand, people who adopt *passive goal behavior* place a higher value on social relationships, quality of life, and concern for others. According to the research, many people in Japan tend to exhibit relatively aggressive goal behaviors, whereas many people in Germany, Mexico, Italy, and the United States reflect moderately aggressive goal behaviors. People from the Netherlands and the Scandinavian countries of Norway, Sweden, Denmark, and Finland all tend to exhibit relatively passive goal behaviors.

Time Orientation *the extent to which members of a culture adopt a long-term versus a short-term outlook on work, life, and other elements of society*

A fifth dimension is called time orientation. **Time orientation** is the extent to which members of a culture adopt a long-term versus a short-term outlook on work, life, and other elements of society. Some cultures, such as Japan, Hong Kong, Taiwan, and South Korea, have a longer-term orientation. One implication of this orientation is that people from these cultures are willing to accept that they may have to work hard for many years before achieving their goals. Other cultures, such as Pakistan and West Africa, are more likely to have a short-term orientation. As a result, people from these cultures may prefer jobs that provide more immediate rewards. Research suggests that people in the United States and Germany tend to have an intermediate time orientation.[22]

OBJECTIVE 5
Barriers to International Trade

Describe
some of the ways in which economic, legal, and political differences among nations affect international business.

Whether a business is truly multinational or sells to only a few foreign markets, several factors will affect its international operations. Success in foreign markets will largely depend on the ways a business responds to *social and cultural forces* (as described previously) *and economic, legal*, and *political barriers* to international trade.

Economic Differences

Although cultural differences are often subtle, economic differences can be fairly pronounced. Moreover, in dealing with mixed-market economies like those of France and Sweden, firms must know when—and to what extent—the government is involved in a given industry. The French government, for instance, is heavily involved in all aspects of airplane design and manufacturing. The impact of economic differences can be even greater in planned economies such as those of China and Vietnam, where the government owns and operates many factors of production.

Legal and Political Differences

Governments can affect international business in many ways. They can set conditions for doing business within their borders and even prohibit doing business altogether. They can control the flow of capital and use tax legislation to discourage or encourage activity in a given industry. They can even confiscate the property of foreign-owned companies. In this section, we discuss some of the more common legal and political issues in international business: *quotas, tariffs,* and *subsidies; local content laws;* and *business practice laws.*

Quotas, Tariffs, and Subsidies

Even free market economies, such as the United States, have some quotas or tariffs, both of which affect prices and quantities of foreign-made products. A **quota** restricts the number of products of a certain type that can be imported and, by reducing supply, raises the prices of those imports. The United States has imposed quotas on ice cream and timber: Belgian ice-cream makers can't ship more than 922,315 kilograms to the United States each year, and Canada can ship no more than 14.7 billion board feet of softwood timber per year. Quotas are often determined by treaties. Better terms are often given to friendly trading partners, and quotas are typically adjusted to protect domestic producers.

Quota restriction on the number of products of a certain type that can be imported into a country

The ultimate quota is an **embargo**, a government order forbidding exportation or importation of a particular product—or even all products—from a specific country. Many nations control bacteria and disease by banning certain agricultural products. Since the days of the Cold War, the United States had an embargo against Cuba, and it wasn't until 2015 that this embargo started to be lifted. The United States also has embargoes against trade with Libya, Iran, and North Korea. When the United States imposes an embargo, it means that U.S. firms can't invest in these countries, and their products can't legally be sold in U.S. markets.

Embargo government order banning exportation or importation of a particular product or all products from a particular country

Tariffs are taxes on imported products. They raise the prices of imports by making consumers pay not only for the products but also for tariff fees. Tariffs take two forms: revenue and protectionist. Revenue tariffs are imposed to raise money for governments, but most tariffs, called protectionist tariffs, are meant to discourage particular imports. Did you know that firms that import ironing-board covers into the United States pay a 7 percent tariff on the price of the product? Firms that import women's athletic shoes pay a flat rate of $0.90 per pair plus 20 percent of the product price. Such figures are determined through a complicated process designed to put foreign and domestic firms on competitive footing (that is, to make the foreign goods cost about the same as the domestic goods).

Tariff tax levied on imported products

Quotas and tariffs are imposed for numerous reasons. The U.S. government aids domestic automakers by restricting the number of Japanese cars imported into this country. Because of national security concerns, we limit the export of technology (for example, computer and nuclear technology to China). The United States isn't the only country that uses tariffs and quotas. To protect domestic firms, Italy imposes high tariffs on electronic goods. As a result, Asian-made DVD players are very expensive in Italy.

A **subsidy** is a government payment to help a domestic business compete with foreign firms. They're actually indirect tariffs that lower the prices of domestic goods rather than raise the prices of foreign goods. For example, many European governments subsidize farmers to help them compete against U.S. grain imports.

Subsidy government payment to help a domestic business compete with foreign firms

The Protectionism Debate

In the United States, **protectionism**, the practice of protecting domestic business at the expense of free market competition, is controversial. Supporters argue that tariffs and quotas protect domestic firms and jobs as well as shelter new industries until they're able to compete internationally. They contend that we need such measures to counter steps taken by other nations. During the 2012 London Olympics, critics were outraged when it was discovered that Ralph Lauren, provider of official U.S. team uniforms, had outsourced the production of those uniforms to firms in China. These critics charged that the jobs of making the uniforms should have gone to U.S. workers. On the other hand, Ralph Lauren pointed out that the uniforms would have cost a lot more if they had been made in the United States. Other advocates justify protectionism in the name of

Protectionism practice of protecting domestic business against foreign competition

national security. A nation, they argue, must be able to produce efficiently the goods needed for survival in case of war.

Critics cite protectionism as a source of friction between nations. They also charge that it drives up prices by reducing competition. They maintain that although jobs in some industries would be lost as a result of free trade, jobs in other industries (for example, electronics and automobiles) would be created if all nations abandoned protectionist tactics.

Protectionism sometimes takes on almost comic proportions. Neither Europe nor the United States grows bananas, but both European and U.S. firms buy and sell bananas in foreign markets. Problems arose a few years ago when the EU put a quota on bananas imported from Latin America, a market dominated by two U.S. firms, Chiquita and Dole, to help firms based in current and former European colonies in the Caribbean. To retaliate, the United States imposed a 100 percent tariff on certain luxury products imported from Europe, including Louis Vuitton handbags, Scottish cashmere sweaters, and Parma ham.

Local Content Laws Many countries, including the United States, have **local content laws**, requirements that products sold in a country be at least partly made there. Firms seeking to do business in a country must either invest there directly or take on a domestic partner. In this way, some of the profits from doing business in a foreign country stay there rather than flow out to another nation. In some cases, the partnership arrangement is optional but wise. In Mexico, for instance, Radio Shack de México is a joint venture owned by Tandy Corporation (49 percent) and Mexico's Grupo Gigante (51 percent). This allows the retailer to promote a strong Mexican identity; it also makes it easier to address certain import regulations that are easier for Mexican than for U.S. firms. Both China and India currently require that when a foreign firm enters into a joint venture with a local firm, the local partner must have the controlling ownership stake.

Business Practice Laws Many businesses entering new markets encounter problems in complying with stringent regulations and bureaucratic obstacles. Such practices are affected by the **business practice laws** by which host countries govern business practices within their jurisdictions. As part of its entry strategy in Germany several years ago, Walmart had to buy existing retailers rather than open brand-new stores because, at the time, the German government was not issuing new licenses to sell food products. Walmart also was not allowed to follow its normal practice of refunding price differences on items sold for less by other stores because the practice is illegal in Germany. In addition, Walmart had to comply with business-hour restrictions: Stores can't open before 7:00 A.M., must close by 8:00 P.M. on weeknights and 4:00 P.M. on Saturday, and must remain closed on Sunday. After a few years, Walmart eventually decided its meager profits in Germany didn't warrant the effort it required to generate them and closed all of its stores there.

Sometimes, a legal—even an accepted—practice in one country is illegal in another. In some South American countries, for example, it is sometimes legal to bribe business and government officials. These bribe are generally called "expediting fees" or something similar. The existence of **cartels**, associations of producers that control supply and prices, also gives tremendous power to some nations, such as those belonging to the Organization of Petroleum Exporting Countries (OPEC). U.S. law forbids both bribery and cartels.

Finally, many (but not all) countries forbid **dumping**, selling a product abroad for less than the cost of production at home. U.S. antidumping legislation sets two conditions for determining whether dumping is being practiced:

1 Products are being priced at "less than fair value."
2 The result unfairly harms domestic industry.

Just a few years ago, the United States charged Japan and Brazil with dumping steel at prices 70 percent below normal value. To protect local manufacturers, the U.S. government imposed a significant tariff on steel imported from those countries.

Local Content Law *law requiring that products sold in a particular country be at least partly made there*

Business Practice Law *law or regulation governing business practices in given countries*

Cartel *association of producers whose purpose is to control supply and prices*

Dumping *practice of selling a product abroad for less than the cost of production*

summary of learning objectives

OBJECTIVE 1

Discuss the rise of international business and describe the major world marketplaces, trade agreements, and alliances.

Importing and exporting products from one country to another greatly increases the variety of products available to consumers and businesses. Several forces have combined to spark and sustain globalization. Governments and businesses have become aware of the potential for higher standards of living and increased profits. New technologies make international travel, communication, and commerce faster and less expensive. In addition, some companies expand into foreign markets just to keep up with their competitors.

North America, Europe, and Pacific Asia represent three geographic clusters that are the major marketplaces for international business activity. These major marketplaces include relatively more of the upper-middle-income and high-income nations but relatively few low-income and low-middle-income countries.

Trade treaties are legal agreements that specify how countries will work together to support international trade. The most significant treaties are (1) the *North American Free Trade Agreement (NAFTA)*, (2) the *European Union (EU)*, (3) the *Association of Southeast Asian Nations (ASEAN)*, and (4) the *General Agreement on Tariffs and Trade (GATT)*.

OBJECTIVE 2

Explain how differences in import–export balances, exchange rates, and foreign competition determine the ways in which countries and businesses respond to the international environment.

Economists use two measures to assess the balance between imports and exports. A nation's *balance of trade* is the total economic value of all products that it exports minus the total economic value of all products that it imports. When a country's imports exceed its exports, it has a *negative balance of trade* and it suffers a *trade deficit*. A *positive balance of trade* occurs when exports exceed imports, resulting in a *trade surplus*.

The *balance of payments* refers to the flow of money into or out of a country. Payments for imports and exports, money spent by tourists, funding from foreign-aid programs, and proceeds from currency transactions all contribute to the balance of payments.

Exchange rates, the rates at which one nation's currency can be exchanged for that of another, are a major influence on international trade. Most countries use *floating exchange rates*, in which the value of one currency relative to that of another varies with market conditions.

Countries *export* what they can produce better or less expensively than other countries and use the proceeds to *import* what they can't produce as effectively. Economists once focused on two forms of advantage to explain international trade: *absolute advantage* and *comparative advantage*. Today, the theory of *national competitive advantage* is a widely accepted model of why nations engage in international trade. According to this theory, comparative advantage derives from four conditions: (1) factor of production conditions, (2) demand conditions, (3) related and supporting industries, and (4) strategies, structures, and rivalries.

OBJECTIVE 3

Discuss the factors involved in deciding to do business internationally and in selecting the appropriate levels of international involvement and international organizational structure.

Several factors enter into the decision to go international. A company wishing to sell products in foreign markets should consider the following questions: (1) Is there a *demand* for its products abroad? (2) If so, must it *adapt* those products for international consumption? Companies may also go international through outsourcing and offshoring.

After deciding to go international, a firm must decide on its level of involvement. Several levels are possible: (1) *exporters and importers*, (2) *international firms*, and (3) *multinational firms*.

Different levels of involvement require different kinds of organizational structure. The spectrum of international organizational strategies includes the following: (1) *independent agents*, (2) *licensing arrangements*, (3) *branch offices*, (4) *strategic alliances* (or *joint ventures*), and (5) *foreign direct investment (FDI)*. Independent agents are foreign individuals or organizations that represent an exporter in foreign markets. Another option, licensing arrangements, represents a contract under which one firm allows another to use its brand name, operating procedures, or proprietary technology. Companies may also consider establishing a branch office by sending managers overseas to set up a physical presence. A strategic alliance occurs when a company seeking international expansion finds a partner in the country in which it wishes to do business. Finally, FDI is the practice of buying or establishing tangible assets in another country.

OBJECTIVE 4

Explain the role and importance of the cultural environment in international business.

A country's culture includes all the values, symbols, beliefs, and language that guide behavior. Cultural values and beliefs are often unspoken; they may even be taken for granted by those who live in a particular country. Cultural factors do not necessarily cause problems for managers when the cultures of two countries are similar. Difficulties can arise, however, when there is little overlap between the home culture of a manager and the culture of the country in which business is to be conducted. Cultural differences between countries can have a direct impact on business practice. Some cultural differences between countries, such as the meaning of time, can be even subtler and yet have a major impact on business activities. Language itself can be an important factor. Beyond the obvious and clear barriers posed by people who speak different languages, subtle differences in meaning can also play a major role.

Managers in international business also have to understand that there are differences in what motivates people in different cultures. Social orientation is a person's beliefs about the relative importance of the individual versus groups to which that person belongs. A second important dimension is power orientation, the beliefs that people in a culture hold about the appropriateness of power and authority differences in hierarchies, such as business organizations. Uncertainty orientation is the feeling individuals have regarding uncertain and ambiguous situations. Goal orientation is the manner in which people are motivated to work toward different kinds of goals. Time orientation is the extent to which members of a culture adopt a long-term versus a short-term outlook on work, life, and other elements of society.

OBJECTIVE 5

Describe some of the ways in which economic, legal, and political differences among nations affect international business.

Economic differences among nations can be fairly pronounced and can affect businesses in a variety of ways. Common legal and political issues in international business include *quotas*, *tariffs, subsidies, local content laws,* and *business practice laws*. Quotas restrict the number of certain products that can be imported into a country, and a tariff is a tax that a country imposes on imported products. Subsidies are government payments to domestic companies to help them better compete with international companies. Another legal strategy to support a nation's businesses is implementing local content laws that require that products sold in a country be at least partially made there. Business practice laws control business activities within their jurisdiction and create obstacles for businesses trying to enter new markets.

The term *protectionism* describes the practice of protecting domestic businesses at the expense of free market competition. Although some economists argue that legal strategies such as quotas, tariffs, and subsidies are necessary to protect domestic firms, others argue that protectionism ultimately hurts consumers because of the resulting higher prices.

A final obstacle to international business is that business practices that are legal in one country may not be legal in another. Bribery, the formation of cartels, and dumping are forbidden in the United States, but legal in other countries, which is challenging for U.S. companies trying to enter some foreign markets.

key terms

absolute advantage
Association of Southeast Asian Nations (ASEAN)
balance of payments
balance of trade
branch office
business practice law
cartel
comparative advantage
dumping
embargo
euro
European Union (EU)
exchange rate
export
exporter

foreign direct investment (FDI)
General Agreement on Tariffs and Trade (GATT)
globalization
goal orientation
import
importer
independent agent
international firm
licensing arrangement
local content law
multinational firm
national competitive advantage
North American Free Trade Agreement (NAFTA)
offshoring

outsourcing
power orientation
protectionism
quota
social orientation
strategic alliance
subsidy
tariff
time orientation
trade deficit
trade surplus
uncertainty orientation
World Trade Organization (WTO)

MyBizLab

To complete the problems with the ✪, go to EOC Discussion Questions in the MyLab.

questions & exercises

QUESTIONS FOR REVIEW

✪ 1. What are the advantages and disadvantages of globalization?

2. What are the three possible levels of involvement in international business? Give examples of each.

3. What are the elements of national competitive advantage?

4. Describe the five international organizational structures.

QUESTIONS FOR ANALYSIS

5. List all the major items in your bedroom, including furnishings, and identify the country in which each item was made. Develop a hypothesis about why each product was made in the United States or abroad.

6. Describe the United States in terms of the five cultural orientations.

✪ 7. Do you support protectionist tariffs for the United States? If so, in what instances and for what reasons? If not, why?

✪ 8. Do you think that a firm operating internationally is better advised to adopt a single standard of ethical conduct or to adapt to local conditions? Under what kinds of conditions might each approach be preferable?

APPLICATION EXERCISES

9. The World Bank uses per-capita income to make distinctions among countries. Use Web or database research to identify at least three countries in the following categories for last year: high-income countries, upper-middle-income countries, lower-middle-income countries, and lower-income countries. In addition, identify the source of the data that you used to draw these conclusions.

10. China is one of the fastest-growing markets in the world. Use Web or database research to uncover how to best describe China according to the five cultural dimensions. Cite the sources for your information.

building a business: continuing team exercise

Assignment

Meet with your team members and discuss your new business venture within the context of this chapter. Develop specific responses to the following:

11. Are you likely to acquire any of your materials, products, or services from abroad? Why or why not?

12. Are there likely to be any export opportunities for your products or services? Why or why not? If you are able to export your product, will it need to be adapted to sell in foreign markets?

13. To what extent, if any, will your new venture be affected by social and cultural differences, economic differences, and/or legal and political differences across cultures?

team exercise

WEIGHING THE TRADE-OFFS

The Situation

Able Systems is a software company specializing in technology solutions for the food industry, including supermarkets and restaurants. All of your customers are located in the United States and operate nearly 24 hours a day. You provide excellent phone support for customers who have an issue, but your expenses are increasing and you're looking for ways to contain costs.

The Dilemma

Able Systems has tried to stem escalating phone support costs by limiting the number of specialists working on each shift, but long wait times have angered customers. Because of the technical and problem-solving skills needed to provide remote support, hiring less-qualified employees is just not an option. You're looking at your competitors and you've noticed that many have offshored their operations—hiring employees in other countries to provide support. Because of a large number of English speakers and an adequate supply of applicants with the education needed for a support position, you are considering setting up a phone support center in Jamaica.

This solution is not without concerns. If you offshore your support operation, you will have to lay off most of the U.S. support employees. You're willing to provide outplacement services to make sure that they can find new jobs, but you're still concerned about the impact of layoffs on your remaining employees. A group of programmers who caught wind of this proposal have begun to wonder if their jobs are next. In addition, local elected officials are concerned about the impact of layoffs on the local economy. Your boss is pressuring you for a recommendation and you're weighing the pros and cons of both options.

TEAM ACTIVITY

14. Have each member of the team create a list of the pros and cons of offshoring the phone support. As you develop your list, be sure to consider all of the stakeholders in this decision—the company's executives, employees, customers, and community.

15. Gather your group together and reveal, in turn, each member's lists of pros. Narrow the list to the three or four most commonly cited and important advantages of offshoring phone support.

16. In similar fashion, have each member of the team read their list of disadvantages. Identify the most significant disadvantages based on your team's assessment.

17. Considering the interests of all stakeholders, what is the best option in this situation?

exercising your ethics

PAYING HEED TO FOREIGN PRACTICES

The Situation

Assume that you're an up-and-coming manager at a medium-sized manufacturing company. Your company is one of only a few companies making certain components for radiant floor-heating systems. The primary advantage of these systems is that they are energy efficient and can result in significantly lower heating costs. Although radiant floor heating is just catching on in the United States, there is a lot of potential in foreign markets where energy is expensive. You've been assigned to head up your company's new operations in a Latin American country. Because at least two of your competitors are also trying to enter this same market, your boss wants you to move as quickly as possible. You also sense that your success in this assignment will likely determine your future with the company.

You would like to build a production facility and have just completed meetings with local government officials. However, you're pessimistic about your ability to get things moving quickly. You've learned, for example, that it will take 10 months to get a building permit for a needed facility. Moreover, once the building's up, it will take another 6 months to get utilities. Finally, the phone company says that it may take up to 2 years to install the phone lines that you need for high-speed Internet access.

The Dilemma

Various officials have indicated that time frames could be considerably shortened if you were willing to pay special "fees." You realize that these fees are bribes, and you're well aware that the practice of paying such fees is both unethical and illegal in the United States. In this foreign country, however, it's not illegal and not even considered unethical. Moreover, if you don't pay and one of your competitors does, you'll be at a major competitive disadvantage. In any case, your boss isn't likely to understand the long lead times necessary to get the operation running. Fortunately, you have access to a source of funds that you could spend without the knowledge of anyone in the home office.

QUESTIONS TO ADDRESS

18. What are the key ethical issues in this situation?

19. What do you think most managers would do in this situation?

20. What would you do?

cases

The Door Opens

At the beginning of this chapter, you read about the historic changes to restrictions on travel to Cuba, as well as the continued embargo on U.S. exports to this island nation. Using the information presented in this chapter, you should now be able to respond to these questions.

QUESTIONS FOR DISCUSSION

21. How will opening Cuba to international travel affect the travel industry in the United States and other countries? What are the potential benefits of virtually open travel to Cuba to Cuban citizens as well as the Cuban government?

22. How have changes in the *structure of the global economy* affected the U.S. embargo, which has been in effect for around 50 years? More specifically, how can U.S. companies deal with changing *environmental challenges—economic, political and legal*, and *cultural*—in their relations not only with Cuba but also with other countries in Latin America?

23. How might U.S. businesses best prepare themselves for a possible elimination of the embargo?

Not My Cup of Tea

China is a country famous for tea. Over thousands of years, tea has been the beverage of choice in China. This, however, did not deter Starbucks from entering one of the fastest-growing consumer markets in the world. The first Starbucks opened in Taipei, Taiwan, in 1998 and the first mainland store was opened in Beijing in 1999. Since that time, they have expanded to over 1,500 stores in almost 90 cities.[23]

Starbucks analyzed the Chinese market and found that their brand was valued not only for their food and beverage offerings but also for the atmosphere of Starbucks stores. Chinese consumers enjoyed the opportunity to meet with friends and business partners in a comfortable location and appreciated the upbeat music and chic interiors. While kiosks have become popular in the United States, some Chinese Starbucks locations are as large as 3,800 square feet.

Starbucks has customized its product offerings, introducing the Green Tea Frappuccino® Blended Crème beverage in 2002 and Starbucks bottled Frappuccino® coffee drinks into Chinese markets in 2007. Not all Chinese consumers are fans of Starbucks coffee. Cheng Xiaochen, an English teacher who likes to meet students at Starbucks, exclaims, "It's a good place to meet people, but the coffee is so bitter it tastes like Chinese medicine." Responding to Mr. Cheng and others like him, the company offers mint hot chocolate and red bean frappuccinos. Food offerings have also been customized to the Chinese market, with Hainanese chicken sandwiches and rice wraps.[24]

Starbucks has also worked to enter the ready-to-drink market, teaming up with Chinese Company Tingyi Holding, a leader in ready-to-drink teas and instant noodles. Starbucks hopes to expand its sales of bottled beverages, which were available in approximately 6,000 retail locations in 2014. The ready-to-drink market is especially appealing because it is projected to grow at a rate of 20 percent over the next three years in the very large Chinese market. Through this partnership, Starbucks will provide "coffee expertise, brand development, and future product innovation," while Tingyi will manufacture and distribute the product.[25]

Starbucks acknowledges that employees are at the center of its success and makes a considerable investment in training, developing, and retaining these employees. However, Starbucks faced a challenge in an achievement-oriented Chinese culture, where parents aspire for their children to take jobs in traditionally successful fields such as financial services and banking. In response, Starbucks launched a family forum in 2012, which provided stories from managers who have worked their way up the career ladder with Starbucks.[26]

Starbucks has worked to extend every component of its corporate culture into its Chinese expansion. The company has a long-established tradition of community commitment, and they have brought this to China. Through a $5 million grant to the Starbucks China Education Project, the company aims to help students and teachers in rural China, increase access to clean drinking water, and provide relief from the 2008 Sichaun earthquake.[27] Starbucks has demonstrated that a long-term commitment and sensitivity to international market conditions are the keys to success.[28]

QUESTIONS FOR DISCUSSION

24. What motivates companies like Starbucks to expand into international markets with little perceived interest for their product?

25. How has Starbucks adapted to Chinese culture?

26. How will expansion in the ready-to-drink market help or hinder sales in their Starbucks stores?

27. China has a collectivist culture. How do you believe that this will affect managers in a Starbucks store?

28. If China wished to slow Starbucks' expansion, what legal barriers would be most helpful? How would these barriers affect Chinese consumers and businesses?

crafting a business plan

THE CONTEMPORARY BUSINESS ENVIRONMENT

Goal of the Exercise

The starting point for virtually every new business is a *business plan*. Business plans describe the business strategy for any new business and demonstrate how that strategy will be implemented. One benefit of a business plan is that in preparing it, would-be entrepreneurs must develop their idea on paper and firm up their thinking about how to launch their business before investing time and money in it. In this exercise, you'll get started on creating your own business plan.

Exercise Background

The starting point for any business plan is coming up with a "great idea." This might be a business that you've already considered setting up. If you don't have ideas for a business already, look around. What are some businesses with which you come into contact on a regular basis? Restaurants, childcare services, and specialty stores are a few examples you might consider. You may also wish to create a business that is connected with a talent or interest you have, such as crafts, cooking, or car repair. It's important that you create a company from "scratch" rather than use a company that already exists. You'll learn more if you use your own ideas.

Once you have your business idea, your next step is to create an "identity" for your business. This includes determining a name for your business and an idea of what your business will do. It also includes identifying the type of ownership your business will take. This part of the plan also briefly looks at who your ideal customers are as well as how your business will stand out from the crowd. This part of the plan also looks at how the business will interact with the community and demonstrate social responsibility. Finally, almost all business plans today include a perspective on the impact of global business.

Your Assignment

STEP 1

To complete this assignment, you need to answer the following questions:

29. What is the name of your business?
    Hint: When you think of the name of your business, make sure that it captures the spirit of the business you're creating.

30. What will your business do?
    Hint: Imagine that you are explaining your idea to a family member or a friend. Keep your description to 30 words or fewer.

31. What form of business ownership (sole proprietorship, partnership, or corporation) will your business take? Why did you choose this form?

32. Briefly describe your ideal customer. What are they like in terms of age, income level, and so on?

33. Why will customers choose to buy from your business instead of your competition?
    Hint: In this section, describe what will be unique about your business. For example, is the product special or will you offer the product at a lower price?

34. All businesses have to deal with ethical issues. One way to address these issues is to create a code of ethics. List three core principles your business will follow.

35. A business shows social responsibility by respecting all of its stakeholders. What steps will you take to create a socially responsible business?
    Hint: Consider what steps can you take to be a "good citizen" in the community? Consider also how you may need to be socially responsible toward your customers and, if applicable, investors, employees, and suppliers.

36. Will you sell your product in another country? If so, what countries and why? What challenges will you face?
    Hint: Consider how you will expand internationally (i.e., independent agent, licensing, etc.). Do you expect global competition for your product? What advantages will foreign competitors have?

MyBizLab

Go to the Assignments section of your MyLab to complete these writing exercises.

37. Some countries have more national competitive advantages than others. Based on the four conditions described to create national competitive advantage, what are some national competitive advantage opportunities in the United States? In China? In India? Provide examples of businesses utilizing these advantages. How can each of these countries benefit from the national competitive advantage of the other?

38. A company that wishes to expand internationally must choose the most appropriate organizational structure. Describe each of the options and when they are most appropriate.

end notes

[1] Sampson, Hannah. "U.S.-based Airbnb adding private Cuban homes to listings." Miami Herald, April 2, 2015. Accessed April 7, 2015. www.miamiherald.com/news/business/article17152853.html

[2] Merchants of Green Coffee, "About the Merchants," at www.merchantsofgreencoffee.com, accessed on April 5, 2013; "Cuban Organic Shade-Grown Coffee from Merchants of Green Coffee," *TreeHugger.com*, May 19, 2005, at www.treehugger.com, accessed on April 5, 2013; Thanksgiving Coffee Co., "End the Embargo on Cuba," at www.endtheembargo.com, accessed on April 5, 2013; Luxner, Larry. "Coffee with a Cause," *Tea & Coffee Trade Journal*, at www.teaandcoffee.net, accessed on April 5, 2013; Williams, Carol J. "Some Cuban Exiles Hope Obama Can Help," *Los Angeles Times*, November 10, 2008, at http://articles.latimes.com, accessed on April 5, 2013; Palmer, Doug. "Business Urges Obama to Loosen Cuba Embargo," December 4, 2008, *Reuters*, at www.reuters.com, accessed on April 5, 2013; "Cuba Embargo Benefits European, Canadian Firms," *Reuters*, March 20, 2008, at www.reuters.com, accessed on April 5, 2013; Katzeff, Paul. "Cooperatives," Thanksgiving Coffee Co., at www.thanksgivingcoffee.com, accessed on April 5, 2013.

[3] See http://stats.oecd.org/index.aspx?queryid=167 and www.bea.gov/international/di1usdbal.htm, accessed on January 31, 2015.

[4] "Best Buy, Home Depot Find China Market a Tough Sell," *USA Today*, February 23, 2011, p. 5B.

[5] Griffin, Ricky W., and Pustay, Michael W. *International Business: A Managerial Perspective*, 8th ed. (Upper Saddle River, NJ: Prentice Hall, 2015).

[6] Friedman, Thomas. *The World Is Flat* (New York: Farrar, Straus, and Giroux, 2005).

[7] Thomson Reuters. "Mexico hourly wages now lower than China's." Reuters. Accessed April 4, 2013. www.reuters.com/article/2013/04/04/economy-mexico-wages-idUSL2N0CR1TY20130404

[8] Muller, Joann. 2014. "America's Car Capital Will Soon Be … Mexico." *Forbes 194*, No. 3: 128-134. Business Source Premier, EBSCOhost (accessed April 6, 2015).

[9] World Trade Organization, at www.wto.org/English/thewto_e/whatis_e/tif_e/org6_e.htm, accessed on January 10, 2015.

[10] Griffin and Pustay, *International Business: A Managerial Perspective*; see also Steven Husted and Michael Melvin, *International Economics*, 5th ed. (Boston: Addison Wesley Longman, 2001), 54–61; and Karl E. Case and Ray C. Fair, *Principles of Economics*, 8th ed. (Upper Saddle River, NJ: Prentice Hall, 2007), 700–708.

[11] Tabuchi, Hiroko. "Toyota Feels Exchange-Rate Pinch as Rivals Gain." *New York Times*, September 2, 2010. Accessed April 6, 2015. www.nytimes.com/2010/09/03/business/global/03toyota.html

[12] Soble, Jonathan. "Toyota Profit Gets Lift From U.S. Market and Favorable Exchange Rates." *New York Times*, February 4, 2015. Accessed April 6, 2015. www.nytimes.com/2015/02/05/business/toyota-profit-gets-lift-from-favorable-exchange-rates.html?_r=0

[13] Porter, Michael. *The Competitive Advantage of Nations* (Boston: Addison-Wesley Longman, 2001), 54–61; see also Case and Fair, *Principles of Economics*, 669–677.

[14] Krajewski, Lee J., Malhotra, Manoj, and Ritzman, Larry P. *Operations Management: Processes and Value Chains*, 8th ed. (Upper Saddle River, NJ: Prentice Hall, 2007), 401–403.

[15] Peters, Adele. "Can This Startup Help Lead The Booming Coconut Water Industry to Sustainability?" *Fast Company*, February 19, 2015. Accessed April 7, 2015. www.fastcoexist.com/3042078/can-this-startup-help-lead-the-booming-coconut-water-industry-to-sustainability

[16] "Constructive Capitalism." Harmless Harvest. Accessed April 7, 2015. www.harmlessharvest.com/constructive-capitalism/

[17] *Hoover's Handbook of American Business 2014* (Austin, Texas: Hoover's Business Press, 2014), 432–433.

[18] http://money.cnn.com/magazines/fortune/global500/2012/full_list/index.html, accessed on January 12, 2015.

[19] "Ford, Russian Automaker Make Deal," *USA Today*, February 21, 2011, p. 1B.

[20] "Main Street, H.K.—Disney Localizes Mickey to Boost Its Hong Kong Theme Park," *Wall Street Journal*, January 23, 2008, pp. B1, B2.

[21] "What If There Weren't Any Clocks to Watch?" *Newsweek*, June 30, 1997, p. 14.

[22] Hofstede, Geert. *Culture's Consequences: International Differences in Work-Related Values* (Beverly Hills, CA: Sage, 1980); Hofstede, Geert. "The Business of International Business Is Culture," *International Business Review*, 1994, Vol. 3, No. 1, pp. 1–14.

[23] Flannery, Russell. 2015. "Starbucks Takes Aim At 'Massive' China Ready-To-Drink Market Through Pact With Tingyi." Forbes.Com 16. Business Source Premier, EBSCOhost (accessed April 6, 2015).

[24] Burkitt, Laurie. "Starbucks Plays to Local Chinese Tastes." *Wall Street Journal*. Dow Jones Company, Inc., 26 Nov. 2012. Web. 13 June 2013.

[25] Flannery, Russell. 2015. "Starbucks Takes Aim At 'Massive' China Ready-To-Drink Market Through Pact With Tingyi." *Forbes.Com* 16. *Business Source Premier*, EBSCOhost (accessed April 6, 2015).

[26] Peterson, Hayley. "5 Ways Starbucks Is Different In China." Business Insider, August 8, 2014. Accessed April 6, 2015. www.businessinsider.com/how-starbucks-is-different-in-china-2014-8

[27] "Greater China." *Starbucks.com*. Starbucks Corporation, n.d. Web. 13 June 2013.

[28] Wang, Helen H. "Five Things Starbucks Did to Get China Right." *Forbes*. Forbes.com, LLC, 10 Aug. 2012. Web. 13 June 2013.

glossary

Absolute Advantage the ability to produce something more efficiently than any other country can.

Association of Southeast Asian Nations (ASEAN) organization for economic, political, social, and cultural cooperation among Southeast Asian nations.

Balance of Payments flow of all money into or out of a country.

Balance of Trade the economic value of all the products that a country exports minus the economic value of all the products it imports.

Branch Office foreign office set up by an international or multinational firm.

Business Practice Law law or regulation governing business practices in given countries.

Cartel association of producers whose purpose is to control supply and prices.

Comparative Advantage the ability to produce some products more efficiently than others.

Dumping practice of selling a product abroad for less than the cost of production.

Embargo government order banning exportation or importation of a particular product or all products from a particular country.

Euro a common currency shared among most of the members of the EU (excluding Denmark, Sweden, and the United Kingdom).

European Union (EU) agreement among major European nations to eliminate or make uniform most trade barriers affecting group members.

Exchange Rate rate at which the currency of one nation can be exchanged for the currency of another nation.

Export product made or grown domestically but shipped and sold abroad.

Exporter firm that distributes and sells products to one or more foreign countries.

Foreign Direct Investment (FDI) arrangement in which a firm buys or establishes tangible assets in another country.

General Agreement on Tariffs and Trade (GATT) international trade agreement to encourage the multilateral reduction or elimination of trade barriers.

Globalization process by which the world economy is becoming a single interdependent system.

Goal Orientation the manner in which people are motivated to work toward different kinds of goals.

Import product made or grown abroad but sold domestically.

Importer firm that buys products in foreign markets and then imports them for resale in its home country.

Independent Agent foreign individual or organization that agrees to represent an exporter's interests.

International Firm firm that conducts a significant portion of its business in foreign countries.

Licensing Arrangement arrangement in which firms choose foreign individuals or organizations to manufacture or market their products in another country.

Local Content Law law requiring that products sold in a particular country be at least partly made there.

Multinational Firm firm that designs, produces, and markets products in many nations.

National Competitive Advantage international competitive advantage stemming from a combination of factor conditions, demand conditions, related and supporting industries, and firm strategies, structures, and rivalries.

North American Free Trade Agreement (NAFTA) agreement to gradually eliminate tariffs and other trade barriers among the United States, Canada, and Mexico.

Offshoring the practice of outsourcing to foreign countries.

Outsourcing the practice of paying suppliers and distributors to perform certain business processes or to provide needed materials or services.

Power Orientation the beliefs that people in a culture hold about the appropriateness of power and authority differences in hierarchies such as business organizations.

Protectionism practice of protecting domestic business against foreign competition.

Quota restriction on the number of products of a certain type that can be imported into a country.

Social Orientation a person's beliefs about the relative importance of the individual versus groups to which that person belongs.

Strategic Alliance arrangement (also called *joint venture*) in which a company finds a foreign partner to contribute approximately half of the resources needed to establish and operate a new business in the partner's country.

Subsidy government payment to help a domestic business compete with foreign firms.

Tariff tax levied on imported products.

Time Orientation the extent to which members of a culture adopt a long-term versus a short-term outlook on work, life, and other elements of society.

Trade Deficit situation in which a country's imports exceed its exports, creating a negative balance of trade.

Trade Surplus situation in which a country's exports exceed its imports, creating a positive balance of trade.

Uncertainty Orientation the feeling individuals have regarding uncertain and ambiguous situations.

World Trade Organization (WTO) organization through which member nations negotiate trading agreements and resolve disputes about trade policies and practices.

Managing the Business

From Chapter 5 of *Business Essentials*, Eleventh Edition. Ronald J. Ebert, Ricky W. Griffin. Copyright © 2017 by Pearson Education, Inc. All rights reserved.

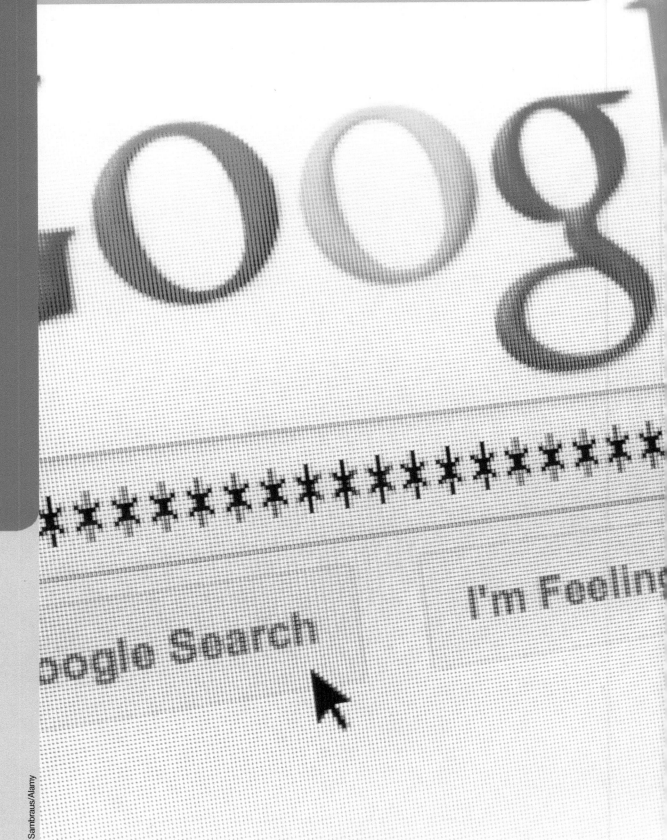

Science and statistics don't hold all the answers;

managers must rely on their gut—on

the basis of

intuition, experience, instinct, and

personal insight.

After reading this chapter, you should be able to:

1 **Describe** the nature of management and identify the four basic functions that constitute the management process.

2 **Identify** different types of managers likely to be found in an organization by level and area.

3 **Describe** the basic roles and skills required of managers.

4 **Explain** the importance of strategic management and effective goal setting in organizational success.

5 **Discuss** contingency planning and crisis management in today's business world.

6 **Describe** the development and explain the importance of corporate culture.

Google

✳✳✳✳✳✳✳✳✳✳✳✳✳✳✳✳✳✳✳✳✳✳✳✳✳✳✳

I'm Feeling Lucky

Search

Google Keeps
Growing

Sergey Brin and Larry Page met at Stanford University in 1995, when both were graduate students in computer science. At the time, Page was working on a software-development project designed to create an index of websites by scouring sites for key words and other linkages. Brin joined him on the project, and when they were satisfied that they'd developed something with commercial value, they tried to license the technology to other search companies. As luck would have it, they couldn't find a buyer and settled instead for procuring enough investment capital to keep refining and testing their product.

In 2000, Brin and Page ran across the description of a business model based on the concept of selling advertising in the form of sponsored links and search-specific ads. They adapted it to their own concept and went into business for themselves, eventually building Google into the world's largest search engine. Following an initial public offering (IPO) in 2004, the company's market capitalization rose steadily; it stood at more than $350 billion by the end of 2015, when Google controlled 75 percent of the U.S. search market (compared to Yahoo!'s 10.4 percent and Microsoft's 12.1 percent). Google, however, is much more than a mere search engine. Services include searches for news, shopping, local businesses, interactive maps, and discussion groups, as well as blogs, web-based e-mail and voice mail, and a digital photo-management system. You can access the results of any Google search from the Google website, from your own user's toolbar, from your Windows taskbar, and from wireless devices such as smartphones and tablets. Google estimates that 15 percent of searches conducted each day are new—never having been searched before.

How did two young computer scientists build this astoundingly successful company, and where will they take it in the future? Brin and Page remain in the forefront of Google's search for technological innovations. They believe in the power of mathematics and have developed unique algorithms for just about every form of activity in the firm. One of the most successful is an algorithm for auctioning advertising placements that ensures the highest-possible prices.

Brin and Page have also been remarkably successful in attracting talented and creative employees and providing them with a work environment and culture that foster the kind of productivity and innovation for which they were hired.

Finally, although the founders avoid formal strategic planning, they've managed to diversify extensively through acquisitions and key alliances. Typically, Google absorbs an acquired firm and then improves on its technology, thereby adding variety to its own online offerings. Recent acquisitions include YouTube, a leader

Se media/Fotolia

what's in it
for me?

Sergey Brin and Larry Page clearly are effective managers, and they understand what it takes to build a business and then keep it at the forefront of its industry. A **manager** is someone whose primary responsibility is to carry out the management process. In particular, a manager is someone who plans and makes decisions, organizes, leads, and controls human, financial, physical, and information resources. Today's managers face a variety of interesting and challenging situations. The average executive works more than 60 hours a week, has enormous demands placed on his or her time, and faces increased complexities posed by globalization, domestic competition, government regulation, shareholder pressure, and Internet-related uncertainties. The job is complicated even more by rapid changes (such as the recession of 2008–2011 and the recovery that really began to take hold in 2015), unexpected disruptions, exciting new opportunities, and both minor and major crises. The manager's job is unpredictable and fraught with challenges, but it is also filled with opportunities to make a difference. Good managers can propel an organization into unprecedented realms of success, whereas poor managers can devastate even the strongest of organizations.[4] After reading this chapter, you'll be better positioned to carry out various management responsibilities yourself. And from the perspective of a consumer or investor, you'll be able to more effectively assess and appreciate the quality of management in various companies.

In this chapter, we explore the importance of strategic management and effective goal setting to organizational success. We also examine the functions that constitute the management process and identify different types of managers likely to be found in an organization by level and area. Along the way, we look at basic management skills and roles and explain the importance of corporate culture.

in online video sharing; Postini, a leader in communications-security products; and Double Click, a leader in online advertising services. Strategic alliances include those with foreign online service providers that offer Google searches on their sites.

For the immediate future, at least, Google plans on following its basic proven recipe for success, competing head to head with financial-service providers for stock information and with iTunes for music and videos. Google plans to integrate online bill paying into the popular Gmail service. Users would receive their bill in their Gmail account and would be able to pay without going to another website. The new product, initially dubbed *Pony Express*, builds on existing payment systems such as Google Wallet.[1] Google is also working on Google Glass, as well as driverless cars, at Google X, the company's research and development lab.[2]

Nobody knows for sure what else is on the drawing board. In fact, outsiders—notably potential investors—often criticize Google for being a "black box" when they want a few more details on Google's long-range strategy. "We don't talk about our strategy," explains Page, "…. because it's strategic. I would rather have people think we're confused than let our competitors know what we're going to do." [3] (After studying this chapter, you should be able to answer a set of discussion questions found at the end of this chapter.)

OBJECTIVE 1
Describe

the nature of management and identify the four basic functions that constitute the management process.

The Management Process

All corporations depend on effective management. Whether they run a multibillion-dollar business such as Google or a small local fashion boutique, managers perform many of the same functions and have many of the same responsibilities. These include analyzing their competitive environments and planning, organizing, directing, and controlling day-to-day operations of their business. Ultimately, they are also responsible for the performance and effectiveness of the teams, divisions, or companies that they head.

Although our focus is on managers in business settings, remember that the principles of management apply to all kinds of organizations. Managers work in charities, churches, social organizations, educational institutions, and government agencies. The prime minister of Canada, curators at the Museum of Modern Art, the dean of your college, and the chief administrator of your local hospital are all managers. Remember, too, that managers bring to small organizations much the same kinds of skills—the ability to make decisions and respond to a variety of challenges—that they bring to large ones. Regardless of the nature and size of an organization, managers are among its most important resources.

Basic Management Functions

Management *process of planning, organizing, leading, and controlling an organization's resources to achieve its goals*

Management itself is the process of planning, organizing, leading, and controlling an organization's financial, physical, human, and information resources to achieve its goals. Managers oversee the use of all these resources in their respective firms. All aspects of a manager's job are interrelated. Any given manager is likely to be engaged in each of these activities during the course of any given day. Consider the management process at Google. Brin and Page must first create goals and plans that articulate what they want the company to accomplish. Then they rely on effective organization to help make those goals and plans reality. Brin and Page also pay close attention to the people who work for the company, and they keep a close eye on how well the company is performing. Each of these activities represents one of the four basic managerial functions: (1) setting goals is part of planning, (2) setting up the organization is part of organizing, (3) managing people is part of leading, and (4) monitoring performance is part of controlling.

Kristoffer Tripplaar/Alamy

Slaven Vlasic/Everett Collection/Alamy

dpa picture alliance/Alamy

Kenneth Chenault (CEO of American Express), Indra Nooyi (Chairman and CEO of PepsiCo), and Tim Cook (President and CEO of Apple) are all senior managers responsible for overseeing the planning, organizing, leading, and control functions in their businesses.

Planning Determining what the organization needs to do and how best to get it done requires *planning*. **Planning** has three main components. It begins when managers determine the firm's goals. Next, they develop a comprehensive *strategy* for achieving those goals. After a strategy is developed, they design *tactical and operational plans* for implementing the strategy. We discuss these three components in more detail later in this chapter. When Alan Mulally took over the ailing Ford Motor Company a few years ago, he walked into a business that had low cash reserves, an unpopular product line, a confusing strategy, and a culture that was so resistant to change that one insider said it was "calcified." His first agenda was to set performance goals for all of Ford's top executives and clarify the strategic direction that would guide Ford in the future. He also worked to ensure that strategic, tactical, and operational planning were all integrated and consistent with one another.[5] Planning is covered in more detail later in this chapter.

Planning *management process of determining what an organization needs to do and how best to get it done*

Organizing Managers must also organize people and resources. For example, some businesses prepare charts that diagram the various jobs within the company and how those jobs relate to one another. These *organization charts* help everyone understand roles and reporting relationships, key parts of the **organizing** function. Some businesses go so far as to post their organization chart on an office wall. But in most larger businesses, roles and reporting relationships, although important, may be too complex to draw as a simple box-and-line diagram. After Mulally clarified Ford's strategy, he then overhauled the company's bureaucratic structure to facilitate coordination across divisions and promote faster decision making.

Organizing *management process of determining how best to arrange an organization's resources and activities into a coherent structure*

Leading Managers have the power to give orders and demand results. Leading, however, involves more complex activities. When **leading**, a manager works to guide and motivate employees to meet the firm's objectives. Legendary management figures such as Walt Disney, Sam Walton (of Walmart), and Herb Kelleher (of Southwest Airlines) had the capacity to unite their employees in a clear and targeted manner and motivate them to work in the best interests of their employer. Their employees respected them, trusted them, and believed that by working together, both the firm and themselves as individuals would benefit. Mulally took several steps to change the leadership culture that existed at Ford. The firm had previously used a directive, top-down approach to management. But Mulally decentralized many activities so as to put the responsibility for making decisions in the hands of those best qualified to make them. He also clarified channels of communication and revamped the

Leading *management process of guiding and motivating employees to meet an organization's objectives*

incentive system used for senior managers. Leading involves a number of different processes and activities.

Controlling

Controlling is the process of monitoring a firm's performance to make sure that it is meeting its goals. All CEOs must pay close attention to costs and performance. Managers at United Airlines, for example, focus almost relentlessly on numerous indicators of performance that they can constantly measure and adjust. Everything from on-time arrivals to baggage-handling errors to the number of empty seats on an airplane to surveys of employee and customer satisfaction are regularly and routinely monitored. If on-time arrivals start to slip, managers focus on the problem and get it fixed. If customers complain too much about the food, catering managers figure out how to improve it. As a result, no single element of the firm's performance can slip too far before it's noticed and fixed. At Ford, Mulally installed a more rigorous financial reporting system so that he could better assess how various parts of the far-flung Ford empire were performing and get information he needed to make strategic decisions faster and easier than was the case when he first took over.

Figure 1 illustrates the control process that begins when management establishes standards, often for financial performance. If, for example, a company sets a goal of increasing its sales by 20 percent over the next 10 years, an appropriate standard to assess progress toward the 20-percent goal might be an increase of about 2 percent a year.

Managers then measure actual performance each year against standards. If the two amounts agree, the organization continues along its present course. If they vary significantly, however, one or the other needs adjustment. If sales have increased 2.1 percent by the end of the first year, things are probably fine. If sales have dropped 1 percent, some revision in plans may be needed. For example, managers can decide to lower the original goal or spend more money on advertising.

Control can also show where performance is running better than expected and can serve as a basis for providing rewards or reducing costs. For example, when Chevrolet introduced the Super Sport Roadster (a classic, late-1940s pickup-style vehicle with a two-seat roadster design), the firm thought it had a major hit on its

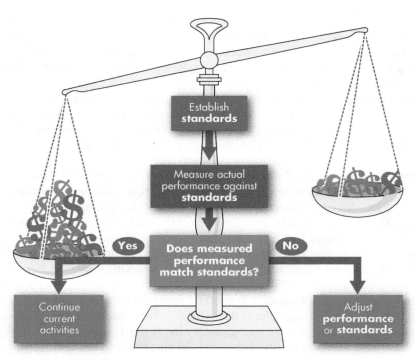

FIGURE 1 The Control Process

hands. But poor sales led to Chevrolet's decision to suspend production of the vehicle. On the other hand, Apple's iPad has been so successful that the firm has not been forced to discount or offer incentives for people to buy the device.

The Science and the Art of Management

Given the complexity inherent in the manager's job, one may ask whether management is more of a science or an art. In fact, effective management is a blend of both science and art. And successful executives recognize the importance of combining both the science and the art of management as they practice their craft.[6]

The Science of Management Many management problems and issues can be approached in ways that are rational, logical, objective, and systematic. Managers can gather data, facts, and objective information. They can use quantitative models and decision-making techniques to arrive at "correct" decisions. They need to take such a scientific approach to solving problems whenever possible, especially when they are dealing with relatively routine and straightforward issues. When Starbucks considers entering a new market, its managers look closely at a wide variety of objective details as they formulate their plans. Technical, diagnostic, and decision-making skills (which we will discuss later in the chapter) are especially important when approaching a management task or problem from a scientific perspective.

The Art of Management Even though managers may try to be scientific as often as possible, they must frequently make decisions and solve problems on the basis of intuition, experience, instinct, and personal insights. Relying heavily on conceptual, communication, interpersonal, and time-management skills, for example, a manager may have to decide among multiple courses of action that look equally attractive. And even "objective facts" may prove to be wrong. When Starbucks was planning its first store in New York City, market research clearly showed that New Yorkers preferred drip coffee to more exotic espresso-style coffees. After first installing more drip coffeemakers and fewer espresso makers than in their other stores, managers had to backtrack when New Yorkers lined up, clamoring for espresso. Starbucks now introduces a standard menu and layout in all its stores, regardless of presumed market differences, and then makes necessary adjustments later. Thus, managers must blend an element of intuition and personal insight with hard data and objective facts.[7]

Becoming a Manager

How does one acquire the skills necessary to blend the science and art of management and become a successful manager? Although there are as many variations as there are managers, the most common path involves a combination of education and experience.[8]

The Role of Education Many of you reading this chapter right now are doing so because you are enrolled in a management course at a college or university. You are already acquiring management skills in an educational setting. When you complete the course, you will have a foundation for developing your management skills in more advanced courses. A college degree has become almost a requirement for career advancement in business, and virtually all CEOs in the United States have a college degree. MBA degrees are also common among successful executives today. More and more foreign universities, especially in Europe, are also beginning to offer academic programs in management.

Even after obtaining a degree, most prospective managers have not seen the end of their management education. Many middle and top managers periodically return to campus to participate in executive or management development programs,

Education plays a vital role in becoming a manager. Prospective managers usually complete at least one degree in business, taking courses in finance, marketing, accounting, management, and other areas.

ranging in duration from a few days to several weeks. First-line managers also take advantage of extension and continuing education programs offered by institutions of higher education or through online media. A recent innovation in extended management education is the executive MBA program offered by many top business schools, in which middle and top managers with several years of experience complete an accelerated program of study on weekends.[9] Finally, many large companies have in-house training programs for furthering managers' education. Indeed, some firms have even created what are essentially corporate universities to provide the specialized education they feel is required for their managers for them to remain successful.[10] McDonald's and Shell Oil are among the leaders in in-house courses. Alongside formal education routes, there is also a distinct trend toward online educational development for managers.[11]

The primary advantage of education as a source of management skills is that, as a student, a person can follow a well-developed program of study, becoming familiar with current research and thinking on management. Many college students can devote full-time energy and attention to learning. On the negative side, management education is often general and meets the needs of a wide variety of students; specific know-how may be hard to obtain. Further, although many aspects of the manager's job can be discussed in a book, it is hard to appreciate and understand them until you have experienced them.

The Role of Experience Even if you were to memorize every word in every management book ever written, however, you could not then step into a top management position and immediately be effective. Why not? Management skills must also be learned through experience. Most managers advanced to their present positions from other jobs. Only by experiencing the day-to-day pressures a manager faces and by meeting a variety of managerial challenges can an individual develop insights into the real nature and character of managerial work.

For this reason, most large companies, and many smaller ones as well, have developed management-training programs for their prospective managers. People are hired from college campuses, from other organizations, or from the ranks of the organization's first-line managers and operating employees. These people are systematically assigned to a variety of jobs. Over time, the individual is exposed to most, if not all, of the major aspects of the organization. In this way, the manager learns by experience. The training programs at some companies, such as Procter &

Gamble, General Mills, and Shell Oil, are so good that other companies try to hire people who have graduated from them.[12] Even without formal training programs, managers can achieve success as they profit from varied experiences. For example, Kelleher was a practicing attorney before he took over at Southwest Airlines and led it to become one of the most successful and admired businesses in the United States. Of course, natural ability, drive, and self-motivation also play roles in acquiring experience and developing management skills.

The majority of effective managers learn their skills through a combination of education and experience. Some type of college degree, even if it is not in business administration, usually provides a foundation for a management career. The individual then gets his or her first job and subsequently progresses through a variety of management situations. During the manager's rise in the organization, occasional education "updates," such as management-development programs, may supplement on-the-job experience. Increasingly, managers also need to acquire international expertise as part of their personal development. As with general managerial skills, international expertise can be acquired through a combination of education and experience.[13]

Types of Managers

OBJECTIVE 2
Identify
different types of managers likely to be found in an organization by level and area.

Although all managers plan, organize, lead, and control, not all managers have the same degree of responsibility for these activities. It is helpful to classify managers according to levels and areas of responsibility.

Levels of Management

The three basic levels of management are *top, middle,* and *first-line* management. As summarized in Table 1, most firms have more middle managers than top managers and more first-line managers than middle managers. Both the power of managers and the complexity of their duties increase as they move up the ladder.

Top Managers Like Brin, Page, and Mulally, the fairly small number of executives who get the chance to guide the fortunes of most companies are top managers. Common titles for top managers include *president, vice president, treasurer, chief*

table 1 The Three Levels of Management

Level	Examples	Responsibilities
Top managers	President, vice president, treasurer, CEO, chief financial officer (CFO)	• Responsible for the overall performance and effectiveness of the firm • Set general policies, formulate strategies, and approve all significant decisions • Represent the company in dealings with other firms and with government bodies
Middle managers	Plant manager, operations manager, division manager, regional sales manager	• Responsible for implementing the strategies and working toward the goals set by top managers
First-line managers	Supervisor, office manager, project manager, group leader, sales manager	• Responsible for supervising the work of employees who report to them • Ensure employees understand and are properly trained in company policies and procedures

Top Manager *manager responsible for a firm's overall performance and effectiveness*

executive officer (CEO), and *chief financial officer (CFO)*. **Top managers** are responsible for the overall performance and effectiveness of the firm. They set general policies, formulate strategies, approve all significant decisions, and represent the company in dealings with other firms and with government bodies. Indra Nooyi, Chairperson and CEO of PepsiCo, is a top manager.

Middle Managers Just below the ranks of top managers is another group of managers who also occupy positions of considerable autonomy and importance and who are called middle managers. Titles such as *plant manager, operations manager*, and *division manager* designate middle-management slots. In general, **middle managers** are responsible for implementing the strategies and working toward the goals set by top managers.[14] For example, if top management decides to introduce a new product in 12 months or to cut costs by 5 percent in the next quarter, middle managers are primarily responsible for determining how to meet these goals. The manager of an American Express service center or a regional sales manager of Frito-Lay snack products (a division of PepsiCo) will likely be a middle manager.

Middle Manager *manager responsible for implementing the strategies and working toward the goals set by top managers*

First-Line Managers Those who hold such titles as *supervisor, office manager, project manager*, and *group leader* are **first-line managers**. Although they spend most of their time working with and supervising the employees who report to

First-Line Manager *manager responsible for supervising the work of employees*

entrepreneurship and new ventures

Building Your Core

While the strength of a company is often measured by the individuals at the top, Verne Harnish claims that middle management may be the key. Harnish is the CEO of Gazelles, Inc., an executive education firm whose tagline is "growing leaders—growing companies." Writing in *Forbes* magazine, he has five recommendations for companies that wish to grow:

Courtesy of Verne Harnish/Gazelles, Inc.

1 Draft Your Senior Team. Harnish sees a key role of top managers as mentoring and developing those who work for them. For example, at New York-based Kemp Technologies, each of the six members of the executive team mentors a few middle managers for one hour a month.

2 Cross-Train. Very often, top managers see their role as arbitrating complaints and disputes among middle managers. Harnish proposes that top managers empower middle managers to work together to resolve disagreements and solve problems. Not only does this encourage cross-functional decision-making but it also reduces the workload of senior managers.

3 Increase Flexibility. One of the key responsibilities of middle managers is to coach and guide those who report to them. According to Harnish, leadership is not a one-size-fits-all activity. He advocates use of the situational leadership theory.

4 Keep Them in the Ring. Middle managers also need to learn to effectively communicate with their peers. When

difficult issues arise, Harnish recommends using face-to-face or phone discussions over e-mails, which can quickly escalate. Albert Busch, CEO of Datacolor, believes that this strategy has paid off for his firm, stating, "Ninety percent of issues raised to me in the past no longer come to me."

5 Invest Early. At Kemp Technologies, leaders are identified early. The company, with 175 employees, has identified 20 high-potential individuals and has given them special assignments and training opportunities. This is especially important to companies during the growth phase, where there is an expectation that the management team will grow in the near future.[15]

them, first-line managers' activities are not limited to that arena. At a building site, for example, the project manager not only ensures that workers are carrying out construction as specified by the architect but also interacts extensively with materials suppliers, community officials, and middle- and upper-level managers at the home office. The supervisor of delivery drivers for Frito-Lay products in Kansas City would be considered a first-line manager.

Areas of Management

In any large company, top, middle, and first-line managers work in a variety of areas, including human resources, operations, marketing, information, and finance. For the most part, these areas correspond to the types of basic management skills described later in this chapter.

Human Resource Managers
Most companies have *human resource managers* who hire and train employees, evaluate performance, and determine compensation. At large firms, separate departments deal with recruiting and hiring, wage and salary levels, and labor relations. A smaller firm may have a single department—or a single person—responsible for all human resource activities.

Operations Managers
The term *operations* refers to the systems by which a firm produces goods and services. Among other duties, *operations managers* are responsible for production, inventory, and quality control. Manufacturing companies such as Texas Instruments, Ford, and Caterpillar have a strong need for operations managers at many levels. Such firms typically have a *vice president for operations* (top manager), *plant managers* (middle managers), and *production supervisors* (first-line managers). In recent years, sound operations management practices have become increasingly important to a variety of service organizations.

Marketing Managers
Marketing encompasses the development, pricing, promotion, and distribution of goods and services. *Marketing managers* are responsible for getting products from producers to consumers. Marketing is especially important for firms that manufacture consumer products, such as Nike, Coca-Cola, and Apple. Such firms often have large numbers of marketing managers at several levels. For example, a large consumer products firm is likely to have a *vice president for marketing* (top manager), several *regional marketing managers* (middle managers), and several *district sales managers* (first-line managers).

Information Managers
Occupying a fairly new managerial position in many firms, *information managers* design and implement systems to gather, organize, and distribute information. Huge increases in both the sheer volume of information and the ability to manage it have led to the emergence of this important function. Although still relatively few in number, the ranks of information managers are growing at all levels. Some firms have a top-management position for a *chief information officer (CIO)*. Middle managers help design information systems for divisions or plants. Computer systems managers within smaller businesses are usually first-line managers.

Financial Managers
Nearly every company has *financial managers* to plan and oversee its accounting functions and financial resources. Levels of financial management may include *CFO* or *vice president for finance* (top), a *division controller* (middle), and an *accounting supervisor* (first-line manager). Some financial institutions, such as Bank of America and Prudential, have even made effective financial

management the company's reason for being.

Other Managers Some firms also employ other specialized managers. Many companies, for example, have public relations managers. Chemical and pharmaceutical companies such as Monsanto and Merck have research and development managers. The range of possibilities is wide, and the areas of management are limited only by the needs and imagination of the firm.

Management Roles and Skills

Regardless of their levels or areas within an organization, all managers must play certain roles and exhibit certain skills if they are to be successful. The concept of a role, in this sense, is similar to the role an actor plays in a theatrical production. A person does certain things, meets certain needs, and has certain responsibilities in the organization. In the sections that follow, first we highlight the basic roles managers play and then discuss the skills they need to be effective.

Managerial Roles

Research offers a number of interesting insights into the nature of managerial roles.[16] Based on detailed observations of what executives do, it appears that many of their activities fall into 10 different roles. These roles, summarized in Table 2, fall into three basic categories: interpersonal, informational, and decisional.

Interpersonal Roles *A category of managerial roles, including figurehead, leader, and liaison.*

Interpersonal Roles Three **interpersonal roles** are inherent in the manager's job. First, the manager is often expected to serve as a *figurehead*—taking visitors to dinner, attending ribbon-cutting ceremonies, and the like. These activities are typically more ceremonial and symbolic than substantive. The manager is also expected to serve as a *leader*—hiring, training, and motivating employees. A manager who formally or informally shows subordinates how to do things and how to perform under pressure is leading. Finally, managers can have a *liaison* role. This role often involves serving as a coordinator or link among people, groups, or organizations. For example, companies in the computer industry may use liaisons to keep other companies informed about their plans. This enables Microsoft, for example, to create software for interfacing with new Hewlett-Packard printers at the same time those

table 2 Basic Managerial Roles

Category	Role	Sample Activities
Interpersonal	Figurehead	Attending ribbon-cutting ceremony for new plant
	Leader	Encouraging employees to improve productivity
	Liaison	Coordinating activities of two project groups
Informational	Monitor	Scanning industry reports to stay abreast of developments
	Disseminator	Sending memos outlining new organizational initiatives
	Spokesperson	Making a speech to discuss growth plans
Decisional	Entrepreneur	Developing new ideas and fostering innovation
	Disturbance handler	Resolving conflict between two subordinates
	Resource allocator	Reviewing and revising budget requests
	Negotiator	Reaching agreement with a key supplier or labor union

printers are being developed. And, at the same time, managers at Hewlett-Packard can incorporate new Microsoft features into the printers they introduce.

Informational Roles The three **informational roles** flow naturally from the interpersonal roles just discussed. The process of carrying out the interpersonal roles places the manager at a strategic point to gather and disseminate information. The first informational role is that of *monitor*, one who actively seeks information that may be of value. The manager questions subordinates, is receptive to unsolicited information, and attempts to be as well informed as possible. The manager is also a *disseminator* of information, transmitting relevant information back to others in the workplace. When the roles of monitor and disseminator are viewed together, the manager emerges as a vital link in the organization's chain of communication. The third informational role focuses on external communication. The *spokesperson* formally relays information to people outside the unit or outside the organization. For example, a plant manager at Union Carbide may transmit information to top-level managers so that they will be better informed about the plant's activities. The manager may also represent the organization before a chamber of commerce or consumer group. Although the roles of spokesperson and figurehead are similar, there is one basic difference between them. When a manager acts as a figurehead, the manager's presence as a symbol of the organization is what is of interest. In the spokesperson role, however, the manager carries information and communicates it to others in a formal sense.

Informational Roles *A category of managerial roles, including monitor, disseminator, and spokesperson.*

Decisional Roles The manager's informational roles typically lead to the **decisional roles**. The information acquired by the manager as a result of performing the informational roles has a major bearing on important decisions that he or she makes. There are four decisional roles. First, the manager has the role of *entrepreneur*, the voluntary initiator of change. A manager at 3M Company developed the idea for the Post-it Note but had to "sell" it to other skeptical managers inside the company. A second decisional role is initiated not by the manager but by some other individual or group. The manager responds to her role as *disturbance handler* by handling such problems as strikes, copyright infringements, or problems in public relations or corporate image.

The third decisional role is that of *resource allocator*. As resource allocator, the manager decides how resources are distributed and with whom he or she will work most closely. For example, a manager typically allocates the funds in the unit's operating

Decisional Roles *a category of managerial roles, including entrepreneur, disturbance handler, resource allocator, and negotiator*

Managers play a variety of important roles. One key interpersonal role is that of figurehead. These managers, for example, are cutting a ribbon symbolizing the opening of a new business.

budget among the unit's members and projects. A fourth decisional role is that of *negotiator*. In this role, the manager enters into negotiations with other groups or organizations as a representative of the company. For example, managers may negotiate a union contract, an agreement with a consultant, or a long-term relationship with a supplier. Negotiations may also be internal to the organization. The manager may, for instance, mediate a dispute between two subordinates or negotiate with another department for additional support.

Basic Management Skills

In addition to fulfilling numerous roles, managers also need a number of specific skills if they are to succeed. The most fundamental management skills are *technical, interpersonal, conceptual, diagnostic, communication, decision-making*, and *time-management* skills.[17] Global and technology skills are also becoming increasingly important.

Technical Skills The skills needed to perform specialized tasks are called **technical skills**. A programmer's ability to write code, an animator's ability to draw, and an accountant's ability to audit a company's records are all examples of technical skills. People develop technical skills through a combination of education and experience. Technical skills are especially important for first-line managers. Many of these managers spend considerable time helping employees solve work-related problems, training them in more efficient procedures, and monitoring performance.

Technical Skills *skills needed to perform specialized tasks*

Human Relations Skills Effective managers also generally have good **human relations skills**, skills that enable them to understand and get along with other people. A manager with poor human relations skills may have trouble getting along with subordinates, cause valuable employees to quit or transfer, and contribute to poor morale. Although human relations skills are important at all levels, they are probably most important for middle managers, who must often act as bridges between top managers, first-line managers, and managers from other areas of the organization. Managers should possess good communication skills. Many managers have found that being able both to understand others and to get others to understand them can go a long way toward maintaining good relations in an organization.

Human Relations Skills *skills in understanding and getting along with people*

Conceptual Skills **Conceptual skills** refer to a person's ability to think in the abstract, to diagnose and analyze different situations, and to see beyond the present situation. Conceptual skills help managers recognize new market opportunities and threats. They can also help managers analyze the probable outcomes of their decisions. The need for conceptual skills differs at various management levels. Top managers depend most on conceptual skills, first-line managers least. Although the purposes and everyday needs of various jobs differ, conceptual skills are needed in almost any job-related activity. In many ways, conceptual skills may be the most important ingredient in the success of executives in e-commerce businesses. For example, the ability to foresee how a particular business application will be affected by or can be translated to the Internet is clearly conceptual in nature.

Conceptual Skills *abilities to think in the abstract, diagnose and analyze different situations, and see beyond the present situation*

Decision-Making Skills **Decision-making skills** include the ability to effectively define a problem and to select the best course of action. These skills involve gathering facts, identifying solutions, evaluating alternatives, and implementing the chosen alternative. Periodically following up and evaluating the effectiveness of the choice are also part of the decision-making process. These skills allow some managers to identify effective strategies for their firm, such as Michael Dell's commitment to direct marketing as the firm's primary distribution model. But poor decision-making skills can also lead to failure and ruin. Indeed, poor decision making played a major role in the downfall of such U.S. business stalwarts as Montgomery Ward, Studebaker, Circuit City, and Enron.

Decision-Making Skills *skills in defining problems and selecting the best courses of action*

Time Management Skills

Time management skills are the productive use that managers make of their time. Suppose, for example, that a CEO is paid $2 million in base salary (this is not an especially large CEO salary, by the way!). Assuming that she works 50 hours a week and takes two weeks' vacation, our CEO earns $800 an hour—a little more than $13 per minute. Any amount of time that she wastes clearly represents a large cost to the firm and its stockholders. Most middle- and lower-level managers receive much smaller salaries than this, of course, but their time is still valuable, and poor use of it still translates into costs and wasted productivity.

To manage time effectively, managers must address four leading causes of wasted time:

1 *Paperwork.* Some managers spend too much time deciding what to do with letters and reports. Most documents of this sort are routine and can be handled quickly. Managers must learn to recognize those documents that require more attention.

2 *Telephone calls.* Experts estimate that managers get interrupted by the telephone every five minutes. To manage this time more effectively, they suggest having an assistant screen all calls and setting aside a certain block of time each day to return the important ones. Unfortunately, the explosive use of cell phones seems to be making this problem even worse for many managers.

3 *Meetings.* Many managers spend as much as four hours a day in meetings. To help keep this time productive, the person handling the meeting should specify a clear agenda, start on time, keep everyone focused on the agenda, and end on time.

4 *E-mail.* Increasingly, managers are relying heavily on e-mail and other forms of digital communication. Time is wasted when managers have to sort through spam and a variety of electronic folders, in-boxes, and archives.

Global Management Skills

Tomorrow's managers must equip themselves with the special tools, techniques, and skills needed to compete in a global environment—in other words, they need *global management skills*. They will need to understand foreign markets, cultural differences, and the motives and practices of foreign rivals. They also need to understand how to collaborate with others around the world on a real-time basis.

On a more practical level, businesses will need more managers who are capable of understanding international operations. In the past, most U.S. businesses hired local managers to run their operations in the various countries in which they operated. More recently, however, the trend has been to transfer U.S. managers to foreign locations. This practice helps firms transfer their corporate cultures to foreign operations. In addition, foreign assignments help managers become better prepared for international competition as they advance within the organization. The top management teams of large corporations today are also likely to include directors from other countries.

Management and Technology Skills

Another significant issue facing tomorrow's managers is technology, especially as it relates to communication. Managers have always had to deal with information. In today's world, however, the amount of information has reached staggering proportions. In the United States alone, people exchange hundreds of millions of e-mail messages every day. New forms of technology have added to a manager's ability to process information while simultaneously making it even more important to organize and interpret an ever-increasing wealth of input and to develop effective *technology skills*.

Technology has also begun to change the way the interaction of managers shapes corporate structures. Elaborate networks control the flow of a firm's lifeblood—information. This information no longer flows strictly up and down through hierarchies. It now flows to everyone simultaneously. As a result, decisions are made quicker, and more people are directly involved. With e-mail, videoconferencing, and other forms of communication, neither time nor distance—nor such corporate boundaries as departments and divisions—can prevent people from working more closely

Time Management Skills *skills associated with the productive use of time*

together. More than ever, bureaucracies are breaking down, and planning, decision making, and other activities are beginning to benefit from group building and teamwork.

Strategic Management: Setting Goals and Formulating Strategy

As we noted previously, planning is a critical part of the manager's job. Managers today are increasingly being called on to think and act strategically. **Strategic management** is the process of helping an organization maintain an effective alignment with its environment. For instance, if a firm's business environment is heading toward fiercer competition, the business may need to start cutting its costs and developing more products and services before the competition really starts to heat up. Likewise, if an industry is globalizing, a firm's managers may need to start entering new markets and developing international partnerships during the early stages of globalization rather than waiting for its full effects.

The starting point in effective strategic management is setting **goals**—objectives that a business hopes and plans to achieve. Every business needs goals. Remember, however, that deciding what it intends to do is only the first step for an organization. Managers must also make decisions about what actions will and will not achieve company goals. Decisions cannot be made on a problem-by-problem basis or merely to meet needs as they arise. In most companies, a broad program underlies those decisions. That program is called a **strategy**, which is a broad set of organizational plans for implementing the decisions made for achieving organizational goals. Let's begin by examining business goals more closely.

Setting Business Goals

Goals are performance targets, the means by which organizations and their managers measure success or failure at every level. Different organizations, of course, pursue different goals. And the goals of any given organization change over time. At AmEx, for example, CEO Kenneth Chenault is currently focusing on revenue growth, the firm's stock price, and digital technology. At Pepsi, CEO Indra Nooyi's goals include keeping abreast of changing consumer tastes and leveraging the firm's current products into new markets. And CEO Jeffrey Smisek's goals at United Airlines are to continue the smooth integration of Continental and United into one of the world's largest airlines.

Purposes of Goal Setting An organization functions systematically when it sets goals and plans accordingly. An organization commits its resources on all levels to achieve its goals. Specifically, we can identify four main purposes in organizational goal setting:

1 *Goal setting provides direction and guidance for managers at all levels.*
   If managers know precisely where the company is headed, there is less potential for error in the different units of the company. Starbucks, for example, has a goal of increasing capital spending by 10 percent, with all additional expenditures devoted to opening new stores. This goal clearly informs everyone in the firm that expansion into new territories is a high priority for the firm.

2 *Goal setting helps firms allocate resources.* Areas that are expected to grow will get first priority. The company allocates more resources to new projects with large sales potential than it allocates to mature products with established but stagnant sales potential. Thus, Starbucks is primarily emphasizing new store expansion, and its e-commerce initiatives are currently given a lower priority. "Our management team," says CEO Howard Schultz, "is 100 percent focused on growing our core business without distraction ... from any other initiative."

3 *Goal setting helps to define corporate culture.* For years, the goal at General Electric has been to push each of its divisions to first or second in its industry. The result is a competitive (and often stressful) environment and a corporate culture that rewards success and has little tolerance for failure. At the same time, however, GE's appliance business, medical technology, aircraft engine unit, and financial services business are each among the best in their respective industries. Eventually, the firm's CEO set an even higher companywide standard: to make the firm the most valuable one in the world.

4 *Goal setting helps managers assess performance.* If a unit sets a goal of increasing sales by 10 percent in a given year, managers in that unit who attain or exceed the goal can be rewarded. Units failing to reach the goal will also be compensated accordingly. GE has a long-standing reputation for evaluating managerial performance, richly rewarding those who excel—and getting rid of those who do not. Each year, the lower 10 percent of GE's managerial force are informed that either they make dramatic improvements in performance or consider alternative directions for their careers.

Kinds of Goals Goals differ from company to company, depending on the firm's purpose and mission. Every enterprise has a purpose, or a reason for being. Businesses seek profits, universities seek to discover and transmit new knowledge, and government agencies seek to set and enforce public policy. Many enterprises also have missions and **mission statements**, statements of how they will achieve their purposes in the environments in which they conduct their businesses.

Mission Statement *organization's statement of how it will achieve its purpose in the environment in which it conducts its business*

A company's mission is usually easy to identify, at least at a basic level. Starbucks sums up its mission succinctly: The firm intends to "establish Starbucks as the premier purveyor of the finest coffee in the world while maintaining our uncompromising principles while we grow." But businesses sometimes have to rethink their strategies and mission as the competitive environment changes. A few years ago, for example, Starbucks announced that Internet marketing and sales were going to become core business initiatives. Managers subsequently realized, however, that this initiative did not fit the firm as well as they first thought. As a result, they scaled back this effort and made a clear recommitment to their existing retail business. The demands of change force many companies to rethink their missions and revise their statements of what they are and what they do.

In addition to its mission, every firm also has *long-term, intermediate,* and *short-term goals*:

- **Long-term goals** relate to extended periods of time, typically five years or more. For example, AmEx might set a long-term goal of doubling the number of participating merchants during the next 10 years. Nikon might adopt a long-term goal of increasing its share of the digital camera market by 10 percent during the next eight years.

Long-Term Goal *goal set for an extended time, typically five years or more into the future*

- **Intermediate goals** are set for a period of one to five years. Companies usually set intermediate goals in several areas. For example, the marketing department's goal might be to increase sales by 3 percent in two years. The production department might want to reduce expenses by 6 percent in four years. Human resources might seek to cut turnover by 10 percent in two years. Finance might aim for a 3 percent increase in return on investment in three years.

Intermediate Goal *goal set for a period of one to five years into the future*

- **Short-term goals** are set for perhaps one year and are developed for several different areas. Increasing sales by 2 percent this year, cutting costs by 1 percent next quarter, and reducing turnover by 4 percent over the next six months are examples of short-term goals.

Short-Term Goal *goal set for the near future*

After a firm has set its goals, it then focuses attention on strategies to accomplish them.

Types of Strategy

As shown in Figure 2, the three types of strategy that are usually considered by a company are *corporate strategy, business* (or *competitive) strategy*, and *functional strategy*.

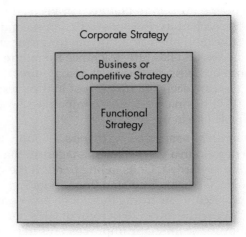

FIGURE 2 Hierarchy of Strategy
Source: Based on Thomas L. Wheelen and
J. David Hunger, *Strategic Management and
Business Policy*, 8th ed. (Upper Saddle River, NJ:
Prentice Hall, 2002), 14.

Corporate Strategy *strategy for determining the firm's overall attitude toward growth and the way it will manage its businesses or product lines*

Corporate Strategy

The purpose of **corporate strategy** is to determine what business or businesses a company will own and operate. Some corporations own and operate only a single business. The makers of WD-40, for example, concentrate solely on that brand. Other corporations own and operate many businesses. A company may decide to *grow* by increasing its activities or investment or to *retrench* by reducing them.

Sometimes a corporation buys and operates multiple businesses in compatible industries as part of its corporate strategy. For example, the restaurant chains operated by YUM! (KFC, Pizza Hut, and Taco Bell) are clearly related to one another. This strategy is called *related diversification*. However, if the businesses are not similar, the strategy is called *unrelated diversification*. Samsung, which owns electronics, construction, chemicals, catering, and hotel businesses, is following this approach. Under Kenneth Chenault, AmEx corporate strategy calls for strengthening operations through a principle of growth called *e-partnering*, buying shares of small companies that can provide technology that AmEx itself does not have.

Business (or Competitive) Strategy *strategy, at the business-unit or product-line level, focusing on improving a firm's competitive position*

Business (or Competitive) Strategy

When a corporation owns and operates multiple businesses, it must develop strategies for each one. **Business (or competitive) strategy**, then, takes place at the level of the business unit or product line and focuses on improving the company's competitive position. For example, at this level, AmEx makes decisions about how best to compete in an industry that includes Visa, MasterCard, and other credit card companies. In this respect, the company has committed heavily to expanding its product offerings and serving customers through new technology. Pepsi, meanwhile, has one strategy for its soft drink business as it competes with Coca-Cola, a different strategy for its sports drink division, and yet another strategy for its juice beverages division. It has still other strategies for its snack foods businesses.

Functional Strategy *strategy by which managers in specific areas decide how best to achieve corporate goals through productivity*

Functional Strategy

At the level of **functional strategy**, managers in specific areas such as marketing, finance, and operations decide how best to achieve corporate goals by performing their functional activities most effectively. At AmEx, for example, each business unit has considerable autonomy in deciding how to use the single website at which the company has located its entire range of services. Pepsi, meanwhile, develops functional strategies for marketing its beverage and snack foods products and operations strategies for distributing them. The real challenges—and opportunities—lie in successfully creating these strategies. Therefore, we now turn our attention to the basic steps in strategy formulation.

finding a better way

A New Model for Going Green

In 2009, Darin Budwig, a registered nurse in Glendale, California, wanted to do the "green" thing by going solar. Cost, however, was a problem: "I wanted to do the right thing for the environment," says Budwig, "but I really had to ask whether it was worth taking on $30,000 in debt." According to Lyndon Rive, CEO of SolarCity, a provider of solar-energy systems located in Foster City, California, the average cost is actually closer to $20,000, but he understands Budwig's reservations. "Even those who really want to make an environmental change," admits Rive, "can't part with $20,000.... The solution is just too costly for them."

That's why Rive revamped his strategy to make solar panels affordable for a much broader range of environmentally conscious consumers. He realized that he could put solar panels on people's roofs in much the same way that automakers put more expensive vehicles in their garages: by leasing them rather than selling them outright. Instead of borrowing $20,000, Budwig only had to put $1,000 down and agree to lease a SolarCity system for 15 years. At a cost of $73 a month, Budwig figured to save about $95 a month and recoup his $1,000 in less than a year. Too good to be true? "We hear that a lot," says Rive. "But we do save you money, and it doesn't cost you a cent to go solar." With leasing, he adds, "we can essentially make it so that everybody can now afford clean power." By introducing leasing, Rive also changed the control model being used by SolarCity to focus more on cash flow rather than revenue. Several years later, costs have fallen even further and the company offers monthly payments as low as $35 with no up-front installation costs.[18]

At the same time, however, Rive understands that price isn't the only consideration for potential customers like Budwig. "Widespread adoption," he admits, "will come if you can take away the complexity and hassle of installing solar." SolarCity thus made things easier for Budwig by lining up

ZUMA Press, Inc./Alamy

building permits, financing, and tax breaks. The company also streamlined costs by using innovative computer automation to custom-design Budwig's installation, which was based on satellite images of his rooftop. SolarCity even compiled utility-rate data to estimate Budwig's return on his solar investment. Again, Rive's new approach reflects a change to a more service-oriented strategy.

In just eight years, this small start-up has grown to employing more than 7,500 employees. SolarCity is the nation's largest installer of solar equipment, with more than 140,000 customers. Sales have skyrocketed and the stock price has soared, in spite of the fact that the company is not yet profitable due to large research and development investments. Interestingly, Lyndon Rive has some interesting entrepreneurial lineage. His great-grandmother was the first female chiropractor in South Africa, inspiring Rive to start selling homeopathic medicines while still in high school. In addition, Rive's mother and Elon Musk (founder of PayPal, SpaceX, and Tesla) are twins. In fact, Musk is a major investor in the company and the chairman of the company's board of directors. Building on a growing interest in clean, safe, renewable energy sources, SolarCity is poised for success.[19]

Formulating Strategy

Planning is often concerned with the nuts and bolts of setting goals, choosing tactics, and establishing schedules. In contrast, *strategy* tends to have a wider scope. By definition, it is a broad concept that describes an organization's intentions. Further, a strategy outlines how the business intends to meet its goals and includes the organization's responsiveness to new challenges and new needs. Because a well-formulated strategy is so vital to a business's success, most top managers devote substantial attention and creativity to this process. **Strategy formulation** involves the three basic steps summarized in Figure 3 and discussed next.

Step 1:   *Setting Strategic Goals* — **Strategic goals** are derived directly from a firm's mission statement. For example, Martin Winterkorn, CEO of Volkswagen, has clear strategic goals for the European carmaker. When he took over several years ago, Volkswagen was only marginally profitable, was

Strategy Formulation *creation of a broad program for defining and meeting an organization's goals*

Strategic Goal *goal derived directly from a firm's mission statement*

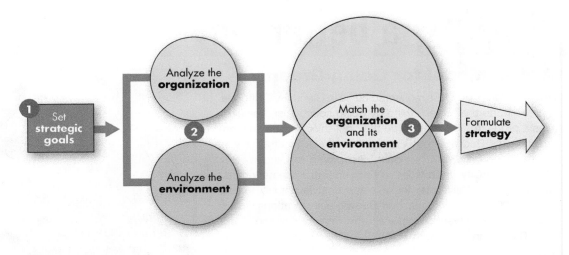

FIGURE 3 Strategy Formulation
Source: Adapted from Stephen P. Robbins and Mary Coulter, *Management*, 12th ed. (Upper Saddle River, NJ: Prentice Hall, 2014), 242.

SWOT Analysis *identification and analysis of organizational strengths and weaknesses and environmental opportunities and threats as part of strategy formulation*

Environmental Analysis *process of scanning the business environment for threats and opportunities*

Organizational Analysis *process of analyzing a firm's strengths and weaknesses*

regarded as an also-ran in the industry, and was thinking about pulling out of the U.S. market altogether because its sales were so poor. Over the next few years, however, Winterkorn totally revamped the firm, acquired Audi, Skoda, Scania, and Porsche, and is now making big profits. Volkswagen is also now a much more formidable force in the global automobile industry.

Step 2: *Analyzing the Organization and the Environment: SWOT Analysis*—After strategic goals have been established, managers usually attempt to assess both their organization and its environment. A common framework for this assessment is called a **SWOT analysis**. This process involves assessing organizational strengths and weaknesses (the S and W) and environmental opportunities and threats (the O and T). In formulating strategy, managers attempt to capitalize on organizational strengths and take advantage of environmental opportunities. During this same process, they may seek ways to overcome or offset organizational weaknesses and avoid or counter environmental threats. Scanning the business environment for threats and opportunities is often called **environmental analysis**. Changing consumer tastes and hostile takeover offers are threats, as are new government regulations that will limit a firm's opportunities. Even more important threats come from new products and new competitors. For example, online music services such as iTunes dramatically reduced consumer demand for CDs and CD players. Now, however, streaming music services like Spotify and SoundCloud have emerged as threats to iTunes. Likewise, the emergence of digital photography has dramatically weakened companies tied to print photography. Opportunities, meanwhile, are areas in which the firm can potentially expand, grow, or take advantage of existing strengths. For example, when Pepsi managers recognized the growing market potential for bottled water, they moved quickly to launch their Aquafina brand and to position it for rapid growth.

In addition to analyzing external factors by performing an environmental analysis, managers must also examine internal factors. The purpose of such an **organizational analysis** is to better understand a company's strengths and weaknesses. Strengths might include surplus cash, a dedicated workforce, an ample supply of managerial talent, technical expertise, or little competition. For example, Pepsi's strength in beverage distribution through its network of soft drink distributors was successfully extended to distribution of bottled water. A cash shortage, aging factories, a heavily unionized workforce, and a poor public image can all be important weaknesses.

Step 3: *Matching the Organization and Its Environment*—The final step in strategy formulation is matching environmental threats and opportunities against corporate strengths and weaknesses. This matching process is at the heart of strategy formulation. That is, a firm should attempt to leverage its strengths so as to capitalize on opportunities and counteract threats. It should also attempt to shield its weaknesses, or at least not allow them to derail other activities. For instance, knowing how to distribute consumer products (a strength) allows Pepsi to add new businesses and extend existing ones that use the same distribution models. But a firm that lacked a strong understanding of consumer product distribution would be foolish to add new products whose success relied heavily on efficient distribution.

Understanding strengths and weaknesses may also determine whether a firm typically takes risks or behaves more conservatively. Either approach can be successful. For example, Google's reputation as an innovator, its cadre of creative product designers and engineers, and strong cash reserves all allow the firm to constantly look for new product ideas and quickly test them in the market. On the other hand, Apple has many of the same strengths but because its products require longer design and manufacturing cycles, and in most cases more financial investment, the firm is more deliberate and systematic in rolling out new products.

A Hierarchy of Plans

The final step in formulating strategy is translating the strategy into more operational language. This process generally involves the creation of actual plans. Plans can be viewed on three levels: *strategic, tactical,* and *operational*. Managerial responsibilities are defined at each level. The levels constitute a hierarchy because implementing plans is practical only when there is a logical flow from one level to the next.

- **Strategic plans** reflect decisions about resource allocations, company priorities, and the steps needed to meet strategic goals. They are usually created by the firm's top management team but, as noted previously, often rely on input from others in the organization. So, the fundamental outcome of the strategic planning process is the creation of a strategic plan. General Electric's decision that viable businesses must rank first or second within their respective markets is a matter of strategic planning.

  > **Strategic Plan** *plan reflecting decisions about resource allocations, company priorities, and steps needed to meet strategic goals*

- **Tactical plans** are shorter-term plans for implementing specific aspects of the company's strategic plans. That is, after a strategic plan has been created, managers then develop shorter-term plans to guide decisions so they are consistent with the strategic plan. They typically involve upper and middle management. Dell's effort to extend its distribution expertise into the markets for televisions and other home electronics is an example of tactical planning.

  > **Tactical Plan** *generally short-term plan concerned with implementing specific aspects of a company's strategic plans*

- **Operational plans,** which are developed by mid-level and lower-level managers, set short-term targets for daily, weekly, or monthly performance. Starbucks, for instance, has operational plans dealing with how its stores must buy, store, and brew coffee.

  > **Operational Plan** *plan setting short-term targets for daily, weekly, or monthly performance*

Contingency Planning and Crisis Management

OBJECTIVE 5
Discuss
contingency planning and crisis management in today's business world.

Because business environments are often difficult to predict and because the unexpected can create major problems, most managers recognize that even the best-laid plans sometimes simply do not work out. For instance, when The Walt Disney

Company first announced plans to launch a cruise line replete with familiar Disney characters and themes, managers also began aggressively developing and marketing packages linking cruises with visits to Disney World in Florida. The inaugural sailing was sold out more than a year in advance, and the first year was booked solid six months before the ship was launched. Three months before the first sailing, however, the shipyard constructing Disney's first ship (the *Disney Magic*) notified the company that it was behind schedule and that delivery would be several weeks late. When similar problems befall other cruise lines, they can offer to rebook passengers on alternative itineraries. Because Disney had no other ship, it had no choice but to refund the money it had collected as prebooking deposits for its first 15 cruises.

The 20,000 displaced customers were offered big discounts if they rebooked on a later cruise. Many of them, however, could not rearrange their schedules and requested full refunds. Moreover, quite a few blamed Disney for the problem and expressed outrage at what they saw as poor planning by the entertainment giant. Fortunately for Disney, however, the *Disney Magic* was eventually launched and has now become popular and profitable. Because managers know such things can happen, they often develop alternative plans in case things go awry. Two common methods of dealing with the unknown and unforeseen are *contingency planning* and *crisis management*.

Contingency Planning

Contingency Planning *identifying aspects of a business or its environment that might entail changes in strategy*

Contingency planning seeks to identify in advance important aspects of a business or its market that might change. It also identifies the ways in which a company will respond to changes. Suppose, for example, that a company develops a plan to create a new division. It expects sales to increase at an annual rate of 10 percent for the next five years, and it develops a marketing strategy for maintaining that level. But suppose that sales have increased by only 5 percent by the end of the first year. Does the firm (1) abandon the venture, (2) invest more in advertising, or (3) wait to see what happens in the second year? Whichever choice the firm makes, its efforts will be more efficient if managers decide in advance what to do in case sales fall below planned levels.

Contingency planning helps them do exactly that. Disney learned from its mistake with its first ship; when the second ship was launched a year later, managers allowed for an extra two weeks between when the ship was supposed to be ready for sailing and its first scheduled cruise.

Crisis Management

Crisis Management *organization's methods for dealing with emergencies*

A crisis is an unexpected emergency requiring immediate response. **Crisis management** involves an organization's methods for dealing with emergencies. Seeing the consequences of poor crisis management after the California wildfires in 2010, the impact of Hurricane Sandy in 2012, and the Carnival cruise ship debacle in 2013 that left thousands of passengers floating in the Gulf of Mexico for days without power and toilet facilities, many firms today are working to create new and better crisis management plans and procedures. One of the most recent areas for crisis management is the growing threat of terrorism. Businesses are being challenged to consider how they might best respond if one of their facilities is bombed by terrorists or if an employee is taken hostage by a terrorist group.[20]

For example, both Reliant Energy and Duke Energy rely on computer trading centers where trading managers actively buy and sell energy-related commodities. If a terrorist attack or natural disaster were to strike their trading centers, they would essentially be out of business. Consequently, Reliant and Duke have created secondary trading centers at other locations. In the event of a shutdown at their main trading centers, these firms can quickly transfer virtually all their core trading activities to their secondary centers within 30 minutes or less.[21] However, many firms do not have comprehensive crisis management strategies. For example, as concerns grew about the outbreak of Ebola in 2015 and some officials warned of a possible pandemic, a survey found that only about 57 percent of U.S. businesses had plans in place to deal with a viral or bacterial pandemic.

managing in turbulent times

When Disaster Storms In

In late October 2012, tropical storm Sandy developed over the warm waters of the Caribbean. Over the next two weeks, the storm gained strength, became a hurricane, and crossed over Jamaica and Haiti, killing more than 50 people. As it approached the United States, it was downgraded to a Category 1 hurricane and few suspected that it would cause significant damage. However, as the storm approached the coast of New Jersey, it gained strength and size. A state of emergency was declared for much of the mid-Atlantic, including West Virginia, Maryland, Delaware, and Connecticut. By October 29, the impending storm prompted the New York Stock Exchange to suspend trading and government and business offices across the area closed. By the end of the following day, 7.9 million businesses and households were left without power across 15 states and the recovery effort began.[22]

While hurricanes are not an unusual occurrence, failure to plan for such events can have devastating effects on businesses. The storm surge from Sandy was much higher than expected and massive flooding resulted. The financial services firm Goldman Sachs planned for just such an event, stockpiling sandbags and installing back-up generators. While much of the rest of the area was without power and unable to continue operations, Goldman Sachs was able to ride out the storm with relatively minor impact.

On the other hand, ConEdison, the electric utility for New York City and Westchester County, had failed to properly plan for such as event. They had designed their electric production and distribution facilities to withstand a storm surge of 3.8

UN Collection/Alamy

meters, but Sandy's 4.3-meter storm surge devastated their network, leaving almost a million customers without power.

Sandy was just one of many natural disasters to test companies' emergency preparedness. In Japan, many companies prided themselves on their lean operations, having supplies arrive just-in-time for production. While a lean strategy can lower inventory carrying costs, it makes a company particularly vulnerable when disaster strikes. Even companies that were not directly affected by the 2011 tsunami found that they had to temporarily suspend operations because they were unable to get critically needed components from suppliers. In a business environment increasingly dependent upon outsourcing, planning for natural disasters becomes critically important.[23]

Management and the Corporate Culture

Every organization—big or small, more successful or less successful—has an unmistakable "feel" to it. Just as every individual has a unique personality, every company has a unique identity, or a **corporate culture**, the shared experiences, stories, beliefs, and norms that characterize an organization. This culture helps define the work and business climate that exists in an organization.

A strong corporate culture serves several purposes. For one thing, it directs employees' efforts and helps everyone work toward the same goals. Some cultures, for example, stress financial success to the extreme, whereas others focus more on quality of life. In addition, corporate culture helps newcomers learn accepted behaviors. If financial success is the key to a culture, newcomers quickly learn that they are expected to work long, hard hours, and that the "winner" is the one who brings in the most revenue. But if quality of life is more fundamental, newcomers learn that it's more acceptable to spend less time at work and that balancing work and nonwork is encouraged.

Building and Communicating Culture

Where does a business's culture come from? In some cases, it emanates from the days of an organization's founder. Firms such as Walt Disney, Hewlett-Packard, Walmart,

OBJECTIVE 6
Describe
the development and explain the importance of corporate culture.

Corporate Culture *the shared experiences, stories, beliefs, and norms that characterize an organization*

Sam Walton honed his craft as a retailer at Walton's five and dime.
He then used his experience to create a unique corporate culture when
he founded Walmart.

and JCPenney, for example, still bear the imprint of their founders. In other cases, an organization's culture is forged over a long period of time by a constant and focused business strategy. Pepsi, for example, has an achievement-oriented culture tied to its long-standing goal of catching its biggest competitor, Coca-Cola. Similarly, Google has a sort of "work hard, play hard" culture stemming from its constant emphasis on innovation and growth coupled with lavish benefits and high pay.

Corporate culture influences management philosophy, style, and behavior. Managers, therefore, must carefully consider the kind of culture they want for their organizations and then work to nourish that culture by communicating with everyone who works there.

To use a firm's culture to its advantage, managers must accomplish several tasks, all of which hinge on effective communication. First, managers themselves must have a clear understanding of the culture. Second, they must transmit the culture to others in the organization. Thus, training and orientation for newcomers in an organization often include information about the firm's culture. A clear and meaningful statement of the organization's mission is also a valuable communication tool. Finally, managers can maintain the culture by rewarding and promoting those who understand it and work toward maintaining it.

Changing Culture

Organizations must sometimes change their cultures. In such cases, they must also communicate the nature of the change to both employees and customers. According to the CEOs of several companies that have undergone radical change in the last decade or so, the process usually goes through three stages:

1   *At the highest level, analysis of the company's environment highlights extensive change as the most effective response to its problems.* This period is typically characterized by conflict and resistance.

2   *Top management begins to formulate a vision of a new company.* Whatever that vision, it must include renewed focus on the activities of competitors and the needs of customers.

3   *The firm sets up new systems for appraising and compensating employees who enforce the firm's new values.* The purpose is to give the new culture solid shape from within the firm.

Continental and United Airlines recently merged into a single, much larger airline. Top managers then developed a plan for creating one new unified corporate culture drawing from the best of the cultures at the two individual airlines. The entire process took more than three years.[24]

summary of learning objectives

Describe the nature of management and identify the four basic functions that constitute the management process.

Management is the process of planning, organizing, leading, and controlling of a firm's resources to achieve its goals. *Planning* is determining what the organization needs to do and how best to get it done. The process of arranging resources and activities into a coherent structure is called *organizing*. When *leading*, a manager guides and motivates employees to meet the firm's objectives. *Controlling* is the process of monitoring performance to make sure that a firm is meeting its goals.

Effective management is a blend of both science and art. Many management problems and issues can be approached in ways that are rational, logical, objective, and systematic. Managers can gather data, facts, and objective information and use quantitative models and decision-making techniques to arrive at "correct" decisions. But even though managers may try to be scientific as often as possible, they must frequently make decisions and solve problems on the basis of intuition, experience, instinct, and personal insights.

The most common path to becoming a successful manager involves a combination of education and experience. A college degree has become almost a requirement for career advancement in business, and virtually all CEOs in the United States have a college degree. Management skills must also be learned through experience. Most managers advanced to their present positions from other jobs. Only by experiencing the day-to-day pressures a manager faces and by meeting a variety of managerial challenges can an individual develop insights into the real nature and character of managerial work.

Identify different types of managers likely to be found in an organization by level and area.

The three levels of management are top, middle, and first-line. The few executives who are responsible for the overall performance of large companies are *top managers*. Just below top managers are *middle managers*, including plant, operations, and division managers, who implement strategies, policies, and decisions made by top managers. Supervisors and office managers are the *first-line managers* who work with and supervise the employees who report to them.

In any large company, most managers work in one of five areas. *Human resource managers* hire and train employees, evaluate performance, and determine compensation. *Operations managers* are responsible for production, inventory, and quality control. *Marketing managers* are responsible for getting products from producers to consumers. *Information managers* design and implement systems to gather, organize, and distribute information. Finally, *financial managers*, including the chief financial officer (top), division controllers (middle), and accounting supervisors (first-line), oversee accounting functions and financial resources.

Describe the basic roles and skills required of managers.

Most managerial activities fall into 10 different roles. These roles fall into three basic categories: interpersonal, informational, and decisional. Three interpersonal roles inherent in the manager's job are *figurehead, leader,* and *liaison*. The three informational roles are *monitor, disseminator,* and *spokesperson*. The four decisional roles are *entrepreneur, disturbance handler, resource allocator,* and *negotiator*.

Effective managers must develop a number of important skills. Traditionally, five managerial skills have been identified: technical skills, human relations skills, conceptual skills, decision-making skills, and time management skills. *Technical skills* are skills needed to perform specialized tasks, including a programmer's ability to write code or an animator's ability to draw. *Human relations skills* are skills in understanding and getting along with other people. *Conceptual skills* refer to the ability to think abstractly, diagnose and analyze different situations, and see beyond the present. *Decision-making skills* include the ability to define a problem and select the best course of action. *Time management skills* refer to the productive use of time, including managing e-mail, telephone calls, and meetings. In the twenty-first century, several new skills have become increasingly important to managers. *Global management skills* include understanding foreign markets, cultural differences, and the motives and practices of foreign rivals. *Technology management skills* include the ability to process, organize, and interpret an ever-increasing amount of information.

OBJECTIVE 4

Explain the importance of strategic management and effective goal setting in organizational success.

Strategic management is the process of helping an organization maintain an effective alignment with its environment. It starts with setting *goals*, objectives that a business hopes (and plans) to achieve. Goal setting is vitally important to the organization for several reasons. Goal setting provides direction and guidance for managers at all levels. Goal setting also helps firms to allocate resources and define corporate culture. Finally, goal setting is essential to managers who wish to assess performance. Most companies will create mission statements and long-term, intermediate, and short-term goals.

Strategy refers to a broad set of organizational plans for achieving organizational goals. The three types of strategy that are usually considered by a company are *corporate strategy*, *business* (or *competitive*) *strategy*, and *functional strategy*. Formulating strategy involves setting strategic goals, analyzing the organization and its environment, and then matching the organization to its environment. Most organizations have a hierarchy of strategic, tactical, and operational plans.

OBJECTIVE 5

Discuss contingency planning and crisis management in today's business world.

Companies often develop alternative plans in case things go awry. There are two common methods of dealing with the unforeseen, *contingency planning* and *crisis management*. Contingency planning is planning for change. It seeks to identify in advance important aspects of a business or its market that might change. It also identifies the ways in which a company will respond to changes. Crisis management involves an organization's methods for dealing with emergencies.

OBJECTIVE 6

Describe the development and explain the importance of corporate culture.

Every company has a unique identity called *corporate culture*: its shared experiences, stories, beliefs, and norms. It helps define the work and business climate of an organization. A strong corporate culture directs efforts and helps everyone work toward the same goals. Corporate culture can also help new employees learn acceptable behaviors. Managers must carefully consider the kind of culture they want for their organizations and then work to nourish that culture by communicating with everyone who works there. If an organization must change its culture, it must communicate the nature of the change to both employees and customers.

key terms

business (or competitive) strategy
conceptual skills
contingency planning
controlling
corporate culture
corporate strategy
crisis management
decisional roles
decision-making skills
environmental analysis
first-line manager
functional strategy
goal

human relations skills
informational roles
intermediate goal
interpersonal roles
leading
long-term goal
management
manager
middle manager
mission statement
operational plan
organizational analysis
organizing

planning
short-term goal
strategic goal
strategic management
strategic plan
strategy
strategy formulation
SWOT analysis
tactical plan
technical skills
time management skills
top manager

MyBizLab

To complete the problems with the ⭐, go to EOC Discussion Questions in the MyLab.

questions & exercises

QUESTIONS FOR REVIEW

1. Describe the roles and responsibilities of top, middle, and first-line managers.
2. What are the four main purposes of setting goals in an organization?
3. Identify and explain the three basic steps in strategy formulation.
⭐ 4. What is corporate culture? How is it formed? How is it sustained?

QUESTIONS FOR ANALYSIS

5. Relate the five basic management skills (technical, human relations, conceptual, decision-making, and time management) to the four activities in the management process (planning, organizing, leading, and controlling). For example, which skills are most important in leading?
⭐ 6. Identify managers by level and area at your school, college, or university.

⭐ 7. What specific types of contingency plans would a company need to develop in an area where hurricanes are common?
8. What differences might you expect to find in the corporate cultures of a 100-year-old manufacturing firm based in the Northeast and a 1-year-old e-commerce firm based in Silicon Valley?

APPLICATION EXERCISES

9. Interview a manager at any level of a local company. Inquire about the manager's education and work experience. Which management skills are most important for this manager's job?
10. Compare and contrast the corporate cultures of two companies that do business in your community. Give examples of the culture of each company.

building a business: continuing team exercise

Assignment

Meet with your team members and discuss your new business venture within the context of this chapter. Develop specific responses to the following:

11. What areas of management will be most important in your business? Will these change over time?
12. What basic management skills will be most important to your business? Will these change over time?

13. What are the specific business goals of your new venture?
14. For your venture, is there a difference between your corporate and business strategies?
15. Does your management team need to develop any contingency plans? Why or why not?
16. What sort of corporate culture do you want to create for your venture? What steps will you take to do so?

team exercise

DREAMS CAN COME TRUE

The Situation

Arturo Juarez has years of experience in the travel industry as a manager at a high-end hotel as well as sales director at a large travel agency. He is ready to start his own business, Dream Vacations, offering travel-planning services for individuals and families. His company will research destinations, hotels, and activities and help their customers make travel memories by providing top-notch service and creative solutions. To achieve this goal, Arturo is working to develop contracts with resorts in the Caribbean, South America, and the Mediterranean to get better pricing for his customers. He hopes that his business will grow at least 10 percent per year over the first five years through advertising and referrals. Initially, Arturo plans to operate out of office space in Atlanta, but his goal is to have offices in South Carolina, Alabama, and Tennessee within two years.

Team Activity

Arturo has asked for a team of students to provide him with assistance getting his company going. Form a group of three to five students to provide guidance to Arturo.

ACTION STEPS

17. Working with your group, develop a mission statement for Dream Vacations. Why is developing a mission statement important?
18. Considering Dream Vacations' mission statement and the information provided in the case, what are the company's long-term goals? How should Arturo measure these goals?
19. What intermediate goals will help Dream Vacations meet their long-term goals and realize their mission? What types of corrective action should Arturo take if the company fails to meet these goals?
20. Identify Dream Vacations' short-term goals. Are short-term goals more or less important than long-term goals?

exercising your ethics

TIME FOR THE AX?

The Situation

You are the sales manager for a well-established medical equipment company. You've been with the company a long time and, generally, you really enjoy your job. The company's new president is interested in proving herself and has set a goal of 10 percent sales growth per year. Each sales representative has a quota that they are expected to meet. Those who exceed their quota will receive a bonus, and those who fall short of their quota will be fired or placed on probation.

The Dilemma

Your sales staff have worked really hard over the past year to meet their new quotas. Six of the eight representatives met their quotas and received bonuses. However, two others have fallen below. Jane fell 2 percent short of her quota and you're not surprised. She's not hard working and often leaves work early to play golf. Bill, on the other hand, has been with the company a long time and is widely respected for his work ethic. However, he's struggling to care for his sick mother and fell 7 percent below his quota. You know that control is an important part of being a manager, but you're unsure what to do. The company president has asked to meet with you tomorrow to discuss the situation.

QUESTIONS TO ADDRESS

21. Which management functions are involved in setting goals and measuring performance?
22. What are the ethical issues in this situation?
23. What do you think most managers would do in this situation?
24. What would you do?

cases

Want to Know the Future? Just Google It ...

At the beginning of this chapter, you read about how Google's founders manage their employees and plan for the future. Using the information presented in this chapter, you should now be able to answer the following questions:

QUESTIONS FOR DISCUSSION

25. Describe examples of each of the management functions illustrated in this case.
26. Which management skills seem to be most exemplified in Sergey Brin and Larry Page?
27. What role have goals and strategy played in the success of Google?
28. How would you describe the corporate culture at Google?

When Old Is New and New Is Old

Late in 2011, JCPenney made a dramatic move, ousting CEO Myron Ullman and bringing in Ron Johnson. Johnson was perceived as a change agent who could reinvent the company as a new, hip place to shop, just as he had transformed the Apple Store from a run-of-the-mill mall store to an entertainment destination.[25] His vision was clear, stating, "In the United States, the department store has a chance to regain its status as the leader in style, the leader in excitement. It will be a period of true innovation for this company." Johnson proposed offering new products and interesting product lines, such as Martha Stewart and Joe Fresh, to lure in high-end customers. He also envisioned JCPenney as a destination, where shoppers would look forward to spending time browsing the store, similar to the excitement one often finds in an Apple Store.

Unfortunately for JCPenney, Johnson's new vision was a near complete failure. Penney's loyal customer base was unhappy with the new store and pricing strategies. The company failed to attract new customers and sales fell by 25 percent in one year. Even the major shareholder who championed Johnson's recruitment, Bill Ackman, realized that the company had made a new fatal error, lamenting, "One of the biggest mistakes was perhaps too much change too quickly without adequate testing on what the impact would be." Notre Dame marketing Professor Carol Phillips points out that the company failed to understand the buyer with its new value pricing, no sale strategy. "JCP's CEO Ron Johnson was … clueless about what makes shopping fun for women. It's the thrill of the hunt, not the buying." The new strategy was a mismatch with the company's existing managers, product lines, pricing strategies, and customer base. Sadly, the company moved too quickly without carefully analyzing the steps needed to implement the new vision. According to Virgin America CEO David Cush, "Don't destroy your old revenue model before you have proved your new revenue model. That's the box that JCPenney has put themselves in."[26]

In April 2013, JCPenney's board reinstated former CEO Ullman, whose number one priority was reconnecting with the company's former customer base. Matthew Boss, an analyst at JPMorgan Chase, reports, "He talked about having the right product, but more importantly having the price and the value perception, something that he believes was lost over the past year." This means returning to the company's prior pricing strategy of marking up prices, then offering heavy discounts and abundant coupons and other promotional offers. Ullman planned to begin a slow process of analyzing the company's environment and adjusting the company's strategy to increase sales and profitability.[27] Many were optimistic that Ullman would be able to restore Penney as a stronger, more diverse company. However, over the next two years, the stock price continued to tumble and investors became concerned.

Two years later, Ullman is stepping down, with Marvin Ellison stepping into the CEO position as of August 2015. Ellison joined the company as president in late 2014, with prior experience at both Home Depot and Target. Does Ellison have the secret to turning around JCPenney? Only time will tell.[28]

QUESTIONS FOR DISCUSSION

29. As CEOs, both Ullman and Johnson were involved in each of the four management functions. Briefly describe the types of decisions that the CEO of JCPenney must make as they relate to each of the four functions.

30. The text describes a variety of skills that are essential to management. Which two skills do you think will be most important for new CEO Ellison?

31. Do you think that Ron Johnson changed the mission of JCPenney or just implemented new strategies? Be sure to support your conclusion.

32. What do you think were Ron Johnson's biggest mistakes?

33. Do you think that Ellison will be successful in rescuing JCPenney, or is it too late?

MyBizLab

Go to the Assignments section of your MyLab to complete these writing exercises.

34. What is corporate culture and why is it important? How is corporate culture created? Is it possible to change an organization's culture? If so, how?

35. Managers can be found at nearly every level of an organization. As a manager moves up the corporate ladder, their responsibilities increase. If you were a manager in the manufacturing industry, how might your responsibilities differ if you were a top manager, middle manager, and first-line manager? Would your responsibilities differ in each of these positions if you were in a different industry? What management skills would be more important for each level of management?

end notes

[1] Adams, John. 2015. "Gmail Bill Pay a Bigger Threat to Banks Than Google Wallet." American Banker 180, no. F313: 1. Business Source Premier, EBSCOhost (accessed April 17, 2015).

[2] Banks, Tom. 2015. "Google Glass goes back to the drawing board." *Design Week* (Online Edition) 1. Business Source Premier, EBSCOhost (accessed April 17, 2015).

[3] Google, "Corporate Information," April 11, 2013, at http://www.google.com; "The Secret to Google's Success," *BusinessWeek*, March 6, 2008, http://www.businessweek.com; "In Search of the Real Google," *Time*, February 20, 2007, http://www.time.com; http://www.google.com/competition/howgooglesearchworks.html

[4] See "The Best (& Worst) Managers of the Year," *BusinessWeek*, January 22, 2014, pp. 50–72.

[5] "Ford's Savior?" *BusinessWeek*, March 16, 2009, pp. 31–34.

[6] Hamel, Gary, and Prahalad, C. K. "Competing for the Future," *Harvard Business Review*, July–August 1994, pp. 122–128; see also Joseph M. Hall and M. Eric Johnson, "When Should a Process Be Art, Not Science?" *Harvard Business Review*," March 2009, pp. 58–65.

[7] Waldroop, James, and Butler, Timothy. "The Executive as Coach," *Harvard Business Review*, November–December 1996, pp. 111–117.

[8] See Steven J. Armstrong and Anis Mahmud, "Experiential Learning and the Acquisition of Managerial Tacit Knowledge," *Academy of Management Learning & Education*, 2008, Vol. 7, No. 2, pp. 189–208.

[9] "The Executive MBA Your Way," *BusinessWeek*, October 18, 1999, pp. 88–92.

[10] "Despite Cutbacks, Firms Invest in Developing Leaders," *Wall Street Journal*, February 9, 2009, p. B4.

[11] "Turning B-School into E-School," *BusinessWeek*, October 18, 1999, p. 94.

[12] See "Reunion at P&G University," *Wall Street Journal,* June 7, 2000, pp. B1, B4, for a discussion of Procter & Gamble's training programs.

[13] For an interesting discussion of these issues, see Rakesh Khurana, "The Curse of the Superstar CEO," *Harvard Business Review*, September 2002, pp. 60–70.

[14] Raes, Anneloes, Heijltjes, Mrielle, Glunk, Ursula, and Row, Robert. "The Interface of the Top Management Team and Middle Managers: A Process Model," *Academy of Management Review*, January 2011, pp. 102–126.

[15] Harnish, Verne. 2015. "5 Ways to Strengthen Your Core." Fortune 171, no. 5: 34. Business Source Premier, EBSCOhost (accessed April 21, 2015).

[16] Mintzberg, Henry. *The Nature of Managerial Work* (Englewood Cliffs, NJ: 1973).

[17] See Robert L. Katz, "The Skills of an Effective Administrator," *Harvard Business Review*, September–October 1974, pp. 90–102, for a classic discussion of several of these skills. For a recent perspective, see J. Brian Atwater, Vijay R. Kannan, and Alan A. Stephens, "Cultivating Systemic Thinking in the Next Generation of Business Leaders," *Academy of Management Learning & Education*, 2008, Vol. 7, No. 1, pp. 9–25.

[18] Perrault, Michael. 2015. "SolarCity, Vivint Gear Up As Costs Fall." Investors Business Daily, March 05. A04. Business Source Premier, EBSCOhost (accessed April 17, 2015).

[19]Dumaine, Brian. 2014. "Mr. Sunshine." *Fortune* 170, no. 6: 96–104. Business Source Premier, EBSCOhost (accessed April 17, 2015).

[20] "Business World Must Be 'Watchful'," *USA Today*, January 24, 2015, p. 5T.

[21]Jones, Del. "Next Time," *USA Today* (October 4, 2005), 1B, 2B.

[22]CNN Library, ed. "Hurricane Sandy Fast Facts." CNN. Accessed April 21, 2015. http://www.cnn.com/2013/07/13/world/americas/hurricane-sandy-fast-facts/

[23]"Making it through the storm." *The Economist*, November 10, 2012. Accessed April 21, 2015. http://www.economist.com/news/business/21565975-hurricane-sandy-was-another-test-how-well-businesses-can-keep-going-when-disaster

[24]"Marriage at 30,000 Feet," *Bloomberg Businessweek*, February 6–February 12, 2012, pp. 36–40.

[25]Clifford, Stephanie. "J.C. Penney's New Plan Is to Reuse Its Old Plans." *New York Times*. N.p., 16 May 2013. Web. 17 June 2013.

[26]Denning, Steve. "J.C. Penney: Was Ron Johnson's Strategy Wrong?" *Forbes*, 09 Apr. 2013. Web. 17 June 2013.

[27]"Saving JCPenney: New CEO Ullman Plans Coupons, Discounts." *CNBC.com*. N.p., 10 Apr. 2013. Web. 17 June 2013.

[28]Wilson, Marianne. 2015. "Four Retailers to Watch in 2015." Chain Store Age 91, no. 1: 7. Business Source Premier, EBSCOhost (accessed April 17, 2015).

glossary

Business (or Competitive) Strategy strategy, at the business-unit or product-line level, focusing on improving a firm's competitive position.

Conceptual Skills abilities to think in the abstract, diagnose and analyze different situations, and see beyond the present situation.

Contingency Planning identifying aspects of a business or its environment that might entail changes in strategy.

Controlling management process of monitoring an organization's performance to ensure that it is meeting its goals.

Corporate Culture the shared experiences, stories, beliefs, and norms that characterize an organization.

Corporate Strategy strategy for determining the firm's overall attitude toward growth and the way it will manage its businesses or product lines.

Crisis Management organization's methods for dealing with emergencies.

Decision-Making Skills skills in defining problems and selecting the best courses of action.

Decisional Roles a category of managerial roles including entrepreneur, disturbance handler, resource allocator, and negotiator.

Environmental Analysis process of scanning the business environment for threats and opportunities.

First-Line Manager manager responsible for supervising the work of employees.

Functional Strategy strategy by which managers in specific areas decide how best to achieve corporate goals through productivity.

Goal objective that a business hopes and plans to achieve.

Human Relations Skills skills in understanding and getting along with people.

Intermediate Goal goal set for a period of one to five years into the future.

Leading management process of guiding and motivating employees to meet an organization's objectives.

Long-Term Goal goal set for an extended time, typically five years or more into the future.

Management process of planning, organizing, leading, and controlling an organization's resources to achieve its goals.

Middle Manager manager responsible for implementing the strategies and working toward the goals set by top managers.

Mission Statement organization's statement of how it will achieve its purpose in the environment in which it conducts its business.

Operational Plan plan setting short-term targets for daily, weekly, or monthly performance.

Organizational Analysis process of analyzing a firm's strengths and weaknesses.

Organizing management process of determining how best to arrange an organization's resources and activities into a coherent structure.

Planning management process of determining what an organization needs to do and how best to get it done.

Short-Term Goal goal set for the near future.

Strategic Goal goal derived directly from a firm's mission statement.

Strategic Management process of helping an organization maintain an effective alignment with its environment.

Strategic Plan plan reflecting decisions about resource allocations, company priorities, and steps needed to meet strategic goals.

Strategy broad set of organizational plans for implementing the decisions made for achieving organizational goals.

Strategy Formulation creation of a broad program for defining and meeting an organization's goals.

SWOT Analysis identification and analysis of organizational strengths and weaknesses and environmental opportunities and threats as part of strategy formulation.

Tactical Plan generally short-term plan concerned with implementing specific aspects of a company's strategic plans.

Technical Skills skills needed to perform specialized tasks.

Time Management Skills skills associated with the productive use of time.

Top Manager manager responsible for a firm's overall performance and effectiveness.

Operations Management and Quality

From Chapter 7 of *Business Essentials*, Eleventh Edition. Ronald J. Ebert, Ricky W. Griffin. Copyright © 2017 by Pearson Education, Inc. All rights reserved.

Operations Management and Quality

Ben Stansall/AFP/Getty Images/Newscom

There isn't a "perfect" way to produce a product or service; just be flexible. An **open mind and** the willingness to try new things drive efficient **operations** and lead to innovation.

After reading this chapter, you should be able to:

1 **Explain** the meaning of *operations* and discuss the growth in the services and goods sectors of the U.S. economy.

2 **Identify** the three kinds of utility created by operations and the characteristics that distinguish service operations from goods production.

3 **Explain** how companies with different business strategies are best served by having different operations capabilities.

4 **Identify** the major factors that are considered in operations planning.

5 **Discuss** the information contained in four kinds of operations schedules—the master operations schedule, detailed schedule, staff schedule, and project schedule.

6 **Discuss** the two key activities required for operations control.

7 **Identify** the activities and underlying objectives involved in total quality management.

8 **Explain** how a supply chain strategy differs from traditional strategies for coordinating operations among firms.

Passengers and Airlines:
Friends or Foes?[1]

Poor treatment by airlines has customers in an uproar because the many services that go into their flight experiences continue to deteriorate. Disturbances include everything from higher fares, inconvenient scheduling activities and discourteous airline personnel before getting to the airport, to unpleasant surprises at the airport such as overbooked flights, rude gate agents, additional baggage fees, long waits, and inaccurate information. Although airlines continue to eliminate onboard services, those that remain are available, increasingly, only with add-on fees. Because planes land late, departing passengers miss their connecting flights and are left stranded, often with little or no assistance from airline personnel. As to the customers' problems—the airlines don't seem to care.

As the list of service complaints grows, so too are the feelings of helplessness and frustration among customers. Little wonder, then, the number of passengers on U.S. airlines in 2009 dropped, with fewer flyers than any time since 2004, as poor economic conditions were aided by equally poor service quality in the airlines industry. With so many complaints, it is hardly a surprise that one 2011 poll shows that more U.S. passengers hold a negative, rather than positive view of airlines.

Why is all this happening? The airlines say they have to cut services and start charging for "extras" to stay profitable, or else go out of business. Although it's true for some in the industry, it should be noted that some airlines are "getting it right." Better-performing airlines are proving that good service quality need not be sacrificed to remain profitable. Among larger carriers, Southwest Airlines has demonstrated consistently that the two elements to airline success—high-quality service and profitability—go hand in hand. Southwest's service quality has attracted a loyal customer following. Passenger testimonials cite Southwest's refusal to charge extra for baggage, for booking flights on the phone, or for changing flights. They receive exceptionally high ratings for baggage handling (fewer lost bags), orderly boarding practices, and consistent on-time performance.[2] Southwest had the fewest number of consumer complaints for the most recent three consecutive years in the U.S. Department of Transportation's (DOT) official reports. They made the "2012 Customer Service Hall of Fame," ranking 10th among some 150 companies from 15 industries in *MSN Money*'s annual survey.[3] Along with quality, profitability continues to grow, while other airlines are operating at a loss. The company has been profitable for 42 consecutive years, all the more impressive with their emphasis not only on financial performance and productivity, but their social responsibility to their employees, customers, communities, and the environment.[4]

Airline quality ratings are well-documented, using measurements from airport operations records and from customer

Odua Images/Fotolia

what's in it for me?

Perhaps you are like the thousands of airline customers disrupted by inconvenience and mistreatment and have been disappointed or irritated in a good or service that you bought. Or, alternatively, you have been pleasantly surprised by a new product you purchased or smiled at excellent service. In either case you'll find it easy to relate to the topics in this chapter. We'll explore the numerous ways companies align their operations processes with their business plans, and discuss how these decisions contribute to a firm's ability to create a high-quality product. Gaining an appreciation for the many steps it takes to bring high-quality goods and services to market will help make you a smarter consumer and more effective employee. And if you're a manager, understanding that production activities are pliable and should be reoriented to better support new business strategies will help you redefine your company and its marketplace over time.

complaints on numerous service activities. At the DOT, for example, the Aviation Consumer Protection Division gathers data on flight delays, mishandled baggage, oversales (number of confirmed passengers denied boarding), and customer complaints (on cancellations, misconnections, delays, baggage, fares, ticketing mistakes, and rude or unhelpful employees). Airlines are ranked each month, from top (fewest complaints) to bottom on each service activity, and Southwest Airlines is at or near the top consistently.[5] Several other well-known brands, near the bottom, seem to have little interest in improving. Many passengers are left wondering, "Why don't more airlines adopt the Southwest model?" (After studying the content in this chapter you should be able to answer a set of discussion questions found at the end of the chapter.)

OBJECTIVE 1
Explain

the meaning of *operations* and discuss the growth in the services and goods sectors of the U.S. economy.

Service Operations (Service Production) *activities producing intangible and tangible products, such as entertainment, transportation, and education*

Goods Operations (Goods Production) *activities producing tangible products, such as radios, newspapers, buses, and textbooks*

Operations (Production) *activities involved in making products—goods and services—for customers*

What Does *Operations* Mean Today?

Although you're not always aware of it, as a customer you are constantly involved in business activities that provide goods and services to customers. You wake up to the sound of your favorite radio station, and on your bus ride to work or school, you are messaging on a smart phone. Your instructors, the bus driver, the messaging provider, and the morning radio announcer all work in **service operations** (or **service production**). They provide intangible and tangible service products, such as entertainment, transportation, education, and communications services. Firms that make only tangible products—radios, smart phones, buses, textbooks—are engaged in activities for **goods operations** (or **goods production**).

The term **operations** (or **production**) refers to all the activities involved in making products—goods and services—for customers. In modern societies, much of what we need or want, from health care to fast food, is produced by service operations. As a rule, managers in the service sector give more consideration to the human element in operations (as opposed to the equipment or technology involved), because success or failure depends often on provider-customer contact. As we saw with airlines in the opening story, employees who deal directly with customers affect customer feelings about the service. As we will see, a key difference between goods and services operations is the customer's involvement in service operations.

General Electric (GE) can be classified as both a goods producer (e.g., of the GE Wind Turbine) and a service provider (e.g., commercial finance).

Although companies are typically classified as either goods producers or service providers, the distinction is often blurred. Consider General Electric (GE). When you think of GE, you may first think of appliances and jet engines. However, GE is not just a goods producer. According to its annual report, GE's "growth engines"—its most vibrant business activities—are service operations, including insurance and real estate, consumer and commercial finance, investment, transportation services, and healthcare information, which account for more than 70 percent of the company's revenues.[6]

Growth in the Services and Goods Sectors

Historically, agriculture was the dominant sector in the early years of the United States. Thereafter, manufacturing grew, becoming the economic backbone from the nineteenth century into the mid-twentieth century. Services then began a rapid climb in economic importance in terms of both number of employees and percentage of gross domestic product (GDP)—the value of all goods and services produced by the economy, excluding foreign income. The outsourcing of U.S. manufacturing to other countries became a major concern in recent decades, so that by the year 2000, employment in the goods-producing sector (mining, construction, and manufacturing) was only about 20 percent of private sector employment versus 80 percent in services. Still, as recently as 2014 the United States remained the world's second largest exporter of manufactured goods, trailing only China and ahead of both Germany and Japan.

Of course, both goods and service industries are important, but as you can see from Figure 1, employment has risen significantly in the service sector and has leveled off at just 11 to 12 percent in goods-producing industries for years 2003 through 2014. Much of this growth comes from e-commerce, business services, health care, amusement and recreation, and education.

By 2011, the service sector's growth generated about 68 percent of private-sector national income. As Figure 2 shows, the service sector's greater percentage of GDP has hovered above 65 percent in recent years. At the same time, the smaller 11 percent of the workforce in goods-producing jobs produced 32 percent of national income.

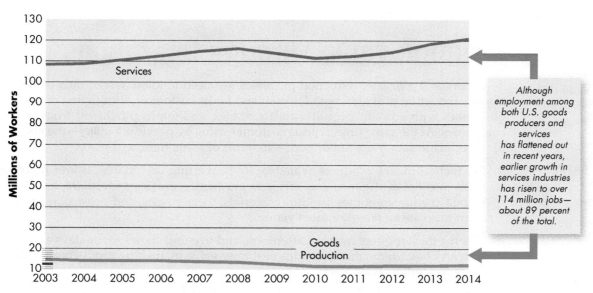

FIGURE 1 Employment in Goods and Services Sectors
Source: http://data.bls.gov/timeseries/CES0700000001?data_tool=XGtable http://www.data.bls.gov/cgi-bin/surveymost, accessed March 1, 2015.

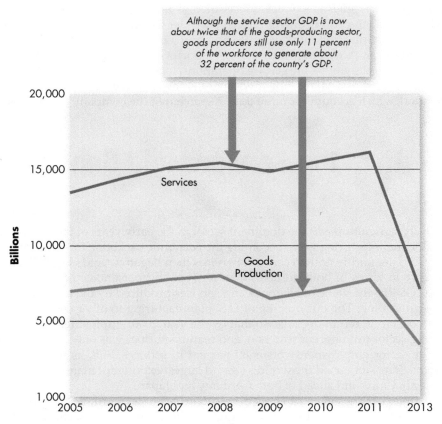

Although the service sector GDP is now about twice that of the goods-producing sector, goods producers still use only 11 percent of the workforce to generate about 32 percent of the country's GDP.

FIGURE 2 GDP from Goods and Services
Source: http://useconomy.about.com/od/grossdomesticproduct/f/GDP_Components.htm, accessed March 1, 2015.

Globally, U.S. manufacturing faces intense competition from other nations. A recent international survey of industrial executives ranks China as the most competitive manufacturing country, followed by Germany (second), the United States (third), Canada (seventh), and Japan (tenth).[7]

OBJECTIVE 2
Identify

the three kinds of utility created by operations and the characteristics that distinguish service operations from goods production.

Utility *product's ability to satisfy a human want or need*

Creating Value Through Operations

To understand a firm's production processes, we need to know what kinds of benefits its production provides, both for itself and for its customers. Production provides businesses with economic results: profits, wages, and goods purchased from other companies. At the same time, it adds customer value by providing **utility**—the ability of a product to satisfy a want or need—in terms of form, time, and place:

● Production makes products available: By converting raw materials and human skills into finished goods and services, production creates *form utility*, as when Regal Cinemas combines building materials, theater seats, and projection equipment to create an entertainment venue.

● When a theater offers midday, afternoon, and evening shows seven days a week, it creates *time utility*; that is, it adds customer value by making products available when consumers want them.

● When a theater offers a choice of 15 movies, all under one roof, at a popular location, it creates *place utility*: It makes products available where they are convenient for consumers.

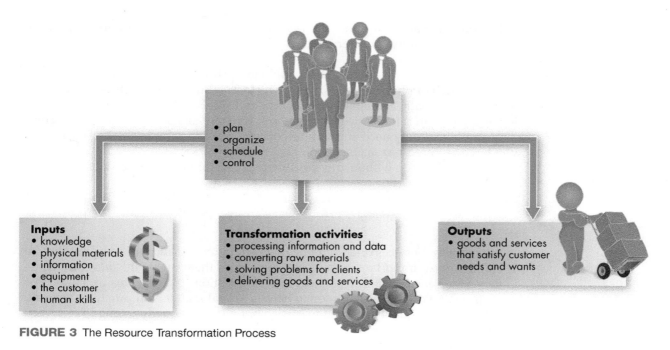

FIGURE 3 The Resource Transformation Process

Creating a product that customers value is no accident; it results from organized effort. **Operations (production) management** is the systematic direction and control of the activities that transform resources into finished services and goods that create value for and provide benefits to customers. In overseeing production, operations (production) managers are responsible for ensuring that operations activities create what customers want and need.

As Figure 3 shows, **Operations (Production) Managers** draw up plans to transform resources into products. First, they bring together basic resources: knowledge, physical materials, information, equipment, the customer, and human skills. Then, they put them to effective use in a facility where the service is provided or the physical good is produced. As demand for a product increases, operations managers schedule and control work to produce the required amount. Finally, they control costs, quality levels, inventory, and facilities and equipment. In some businesses, often in small startup firms such as sole proprietorships, the operations manager is one person. Typically, however, different employees work together to complete these different responsibilities.

Some operations managers work in service "factories," such as FedEx package-sorting depots, whereas others work in factories making smart phones; still others work in offices, restaurants, hospitals, and stores. Farmers are operations managers who create utility by transforming soil, seeds, fuel, and other inputs into soybeans, milk, and other outputs. They may hire crews of workers to plant and harvest, opt instead for automated machinery, or prefer some combination of workers and machinery. These types of decisions affect costs and determine the kinds of buildings and equipment farmers include in their operations and the quality and quantity of the goods they produce.

Differences between Service and Goods Manufacturing Operations

Both service and manufacturing operations transform raw materials into finished products. In service operations, however, the raw materials, or inputs, are not things like glass or steel. These service inputs are people who have either unsatisfied needs or possessions needing care or alteration. In service operations, finished products or outputs are people with needs met and possessions serviced.

There are several obvious differences between service and manufacturing operations. Four aspects of service operations can make service production more complicated than simple goods production: (1) interacting with customers, (2) the intangible

Operations (Production) Management *systematic direction and control of the activities that transform resources into finished products that create value for and provide benefits to customers*

Operations (Production) Managers *managers responsible for ensuring that operations activities create value and provide benefits to customers.*

and unstorable nature of some services, (3) the customer's presence in the process, and (4) service quality considerations.

Interacting with Customers Manufacturing operations emphasize outcomes in terms of physical goods, like a new jacket. But the products of most *service* operations are really combinations of goods and services—both making a pizza *and* delivering (serving) it. Service workers need different skills. For example, gas company employees may need strong interpersonal skills to calm frightened customers who have reported gas leaks. In contrast, factory workers who install gas pipes in manufactured homes without any customer contact don't need such skills.

Services Can Be Intangible and Unstorable Two prominent characteristics—*intangibility* and *unstorability*—set services apart from physical goods:

- *Intangibility.* Services often can't be touched, tasted, smelled, or seen, but they're still there. An important satisfier for customers, therefore, is the *intangible* value they receive in the form of pleasure, gratification, or a feeling of safety. For example, if you hire an attorney to handle a legal matter, you purchase not only the intangible quality of legal expertise but also the equally intangible reassurance that help is at hand.

- *Unstorability.* Many services, such as trash collection, transportation, child care, and house cleaning, can't be produced ahead of time and then stored for high-demand periods. If a service isn't used when available, it's usually wasted. Services, then, are typically characterized by a high degree of *unstorability*.

Customers' Presence in the Operations Process Because service operations transform customers or their possessions, the customer is often present in the operations process. To get a haircut, for example, most of us have to go to a hair salon. As participants in the operations process, customers can affect it. As a customer, you expect the salon to be conveniently located (place utility), to be open for business at convenient times (time utility), to provide safe and comfortable facilities, and to offer high-quality grooming (form utility) at reasonable prices (value for money spent). Accordingly, the manager sets hours of operation, available services, and an appropriate number of employees to meet her customer requirements. But what happens if a customer, scheduled for only a haircut, also asks for additional services, such as highlights or a shave when he or she arrives? In this case, the service provider must quickly adjust the service activities to provide customer satisfaction. High customer contact has the potential to affect the process significantly. The manufacturers who produce the salon's scissors, on the other hand, don't have to worry if a customer makes a last-minute change in demands.

Intangibles Count for Service Quality Consumers use different measures to judge services and goods because services include intangibles, not just physical objects. Most service managers know that quality of work and quality of service are not necessarily the same thing. Your car, for example, may have been flawlessly repaired (quality of work), but you'll probably be unhappy with the service if you're forced to pick it up a day later than promised because the work wasn't finished on time (quality of service).

Operations Processes

To better understand the diverse kinds of production in various firms and industries, it is helpful to classify production according to differences in operations processes. An **operations process** is a set of methods and technologies used to produce a good or a service. Banks, for example, use two processes—document shredding and data encryption—to protect confidential information. Automakers use precision painting methods (equipment and materials) to produce a glittering paint finish.

Operations Process *set of methods and technologies used to produce a good or a service*

Because service operations transform customers or their possessions, the customer is often present in the operations process. For example, customers who want their hair cut or colored must go in person to a hair salon in order to receive this service.

We can classify goods production into broad groupings, by asking whether its operations process has a "make-to-order" or a "make-to-stock" emphasis. We can classify services according to the extent of customer contact required.

Goods Production Processes: Make-to-Order versus Make-to-Stock Processes

Clothing, such as evening gowns, is available either off-the-shelf in department stores or custom-made at a designer or tailor shop. The designer or tailor's **make-to-order operations** respond to one-of-a-kind gown requirements, including unique patterns, materials, sizes, and shapes, depending on customers' characteristics. **Make-to-stock operations**, in contrast, produce standard gowns in large quantities to be stocked on store shelves or in displays for mass consumption. The production processes are quite different for the two settings, including procedures for designing gowns; planning for materials purchases; equipment and work methods for cutting, sewing, and assembling gowns; and employee skills for production.

Make-to-Order Operations *activities for one-of-a-kind or custom-made production*

Make-to-Stock Operations *activities for producing standardized products for mass consumption*

Service Production Processes: Extent of Customer Contact

In classifying services, we may ask whether we can provide a service without the customers' being present in the production system. In answering this question, we classify services according to *extent of customer contact*.

LOW-CONTACT SYSTEMS Consider the postal delivery operations at your local U.S. post office. Postal employees gather mail from mailboxes, sort it, and send it on its delivery journey to addressees. This operation is a **low-contact system**: Customers are not in contact with the post office while the service is performed. They can receive the service—mail sent and mail received—without setting foot in the processing center. Gas and electric companies, auto repair shops, and lawn-care services are other examples of low-contact systems.

Low-Contact System *level of customer contact in which the customer need not be part of the system to receive the service*

HIGH-CONTACT SYSTEMS Think about your local public transit system. The service is transportation; when you purchase transportation, you board a bus or train. For example, the Bay Area Rapid Transit (BART) system, which connects San Francisco with outlying suburbs is, like all public transit systems, a **high-contact system**: To receive the service, the customer must be part of the system. Thus, managers must worry about the cleanliness of trains, safety of passengers, and the usability of its ticket kiosks. By contrast, a firm that ships coal is less concerned with the appearance of its trains since no paying passengers are riding on them. A coal-shipping firm is a low-contact system.

High-Contact System *level of customer contact in which the customer is part of the system during service delivery*

Business Strategy as the Driver of Operations

OBJECTIVE 3
Explain

how companies with different business strategies are best served by having different operations capabilities.

There is no one standard way for doing production, either for services or for goods. Rather, it is a flexible activity that can be molded into many shapes to give quite different operations capabilities for different purposes. How, then, do companies go about selecting the kind of production that is best for them? They aim to adopt the kind of production that achieves the firm's larger business strategy in the most efficient way possible.

The Many Faces of Production Operations

Consider the four firms listed in Table 1. Two are in goods production (Toyota and 3M), and the other two (Save-a-Lot and FedEx) are in services. These successful companies have contrasting business strategies and, as we shall see, they have chosen different operations capabilities. Each company has identified a business strategy that it uses for attracting customers in its industry. More than 40 years ago, Toyota chose *quality* as the strategy for competing in selling autos. Save-A-Lot grocery stores, in contrast to others in the grocery industry, offer customers *lower prices*. The *flexibility* strategy at 3M emphasizes new product development in an ever-changing line of products for home and office. FedEx captures the overnight delivery market by emphasizing delivery *dependability*.

Business Strategy Determines Operations Capabilities

Successful firms design their operations to support the company's business strategy.[8] In other words, managers adjust production operations to support the firms' target markets. Because our four firms use different business strategies, we should expect to see differences in their operations, too. The top-priority **operations capability (production capability)**—the special ability that production does especially well to outperform the competition—is listed for each firm in Table 2, along with key operations characteristics for implementing that capability. Each company's operations capability matches up with its business strategy so that the firm's activities—from top to bottom—are focused in a particular direction.

For example, because Toyota's top priority focuses on quality, its operations, the resource inputs for production, the transformation activities, and the outputs from production are devoted first and foremost to that characteristic. Its car designs and production processes emphasize appearance, reliable performance, and desirable features at a reasonable price. All production processes, equipment, and training are designed

Operations Capability (Production Capability) *special ability that production does especially well to outperform the competition*

table 1 Business Strategies that Win Customers for Four Companies

Company	Strategy for Attracting Customers	What the Company Does to Implement Its Strategy
Toyota	Quality	Cars perform reliably, have an appealing fit and finish, and consistently meet or exceed customer expectations at a competitive price
Save-A-Lot	Low price	Foods and everyday items offered at savings up to 40 percent less than conventional food chains
3M	Flexibility	Innovation, with more than 55,000 products in a constantly changing line of convenience items for home and office
FedEx	Dependability	Every delivery is fast and on time, as promised

table 2 Operations Capabilities and Characteristics for Four Companies

Operations Capability	Key Operations Characteristics
Quality (Toyota)	• High-quality standards for materials suppliers • Just-in-time materials flow for lean manufacturing • Specialized, automated equipment for consistent product buildup • Operations personnel are experts on continuous improvement of product, work methods, and materials
Low Cost (Save-A-Lot)	• Avoids excessive overhead and costly inventory (no floral departments, sushi bars, or banks that drive up costs) • Limited assortment of products, staples, in one size only for low-cost restocking, lower inventories, and less paperwork • Many locations; small stores—less than half the size of conventional grocery stores—for low construction and maintenance costs • Reduces labor and shelving costs by receiving and selling merchandise out of custom shipping cartons
Flexibility (3M)	• Maintains some excess (expensive) production capacity available for fast startup on new products • Adaptable equipment and facilities for production changeovers from old to new products • Hires operations personnel who thrive on change • Many medium- to small-sized manufacturing facilities in diverse locations, which enhances creativity
Dependability (FedEx)	• Customer automation: uses electronic and online communications tools with customers to shorten shipping time • Wireless information system for package scanning by courier, updating of package movement, and package tracking by customer • Maintains a company air force, global weather forecasting center, and ground transportation for pickup and delivery, with backup vehicles for emergencies • The 25 automated regional distribution hubs process 3.5 million packages per day for next-day deliveries

to build better cars. The entire culture supports a quality emphasis among employees, suppliers, and dealerships. Had Toyota instead chosen to compete as the low-price car in the industry, as some successful car companies do, then a cost-minimization focus would have been appropriate, giving Toyota's operations an altogether different form. Toyota's operations support its chosen business strategy, and did it successfully until quality problems arose in 2008. Soon thereafter, the commitment to quality intensified. By 2012, Toyota had regained its position as the world's top-selling auto maker. Before the 2008 downturn, the company had more than 35 consecutive years of increasing sales for which quality was the foundation for greatness.

Expanding into Additional Capabilities Finally, it should be noted that excellent firms learn, over time, how to achieve more than just one competence. The firms in Table 1 eventually became excellent in several capabilities. Aside from dependability, FedEx is also noted for world-class service quality and cost containment. Regarding quality, FedEx was honored in the "2014 Customer Service Hall of Fame," ranking 8th for service quality among 150 companies in *MSN Money's* annual survey. To reduce costs, the company eliminates jobs that become unnecessary with advances in technology, sells off its older inefficient airplanes, and reduces the number of flights by re-routing its air and ground fleets.

Identify

the major factors that are
considered in operations
planning.

Operations Planning

Let's turn now to a discussion of production activities and resources that are considered in every business organization. Like all good managers, we start with planning. Managers from many departments contribute to decisions about operations. As Figure 4 shows, however, no matter how many decision makers are involved, the process is a logical sequence of decisions.

The business plan and forecasts developed by top managers provide guidance for long-term operations plans. Covering a two- to five-year period, the operations plan anticipates the number of plants or service facilities and the amount of labor, equipment, transportation, and storage needed to meet future demand for new and existing products. The planning activities fall into five categories: *capacity*, *location*, *layout*, *quality*, and *methods planning*.

Capacity Planning

Capacity *amount of a product that a company can produce under normal conditions*

The amount of a product that a company can produce under normal conditions is its **capacity**. A firm's capacity depends on how many people it employs and the number and size of its facilities. A supermarket's capacity for customer checkouts, for instance, depends on its number of checkout stations. A typical store has excess capacity—more cash registers than it needs—on an average day, but on Saturday morning or during the three days before Thanksgiving, they'll all be running at full capacity.

Long-range capacity planning considers both current and future requirements. If capacity is too small for demand, the company must turn away customers, a situation that cuts into profits and alienates both customers and salespeople. If capacity greatly exceeds demand, the firm is wasting money by maintaining facilities that are too large, keeping excess machinery online, or employing too many workers.

The stakes are high in capacity decisions: While expanding fast enough to meet future demand and to protect market share from competitors, managers must also

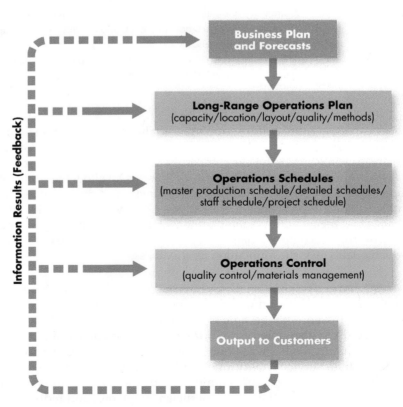

FIGURE 4 Operations Planning and Control

entrepreneurship and new ventures

Nothing Like a Home-Cooked Meal

It wasn't that long ago that families sat down at the dinner table every night for a home-cooked meal. Restaurant dining was reserved for special occasions and even prepared meals were the exception. Well, those days are long gone. Today, many families eat out or bring home take out several nights a week. And singles and couples without children are even more likely to do so. Stephanie Allen, a caterer from Washington state, was surprised to find herself in exactly this situation. Allen and a friend started to get together one Saturday a month to prepare a bunch of freezable meals that they could heat up with little preparation. Word of their strategy spread and Allen, along with partner Tina Kuna, started Dream Dinners in 2002. The company quickly expanded in the Seattle area and became a franchise the following year. A little more than 10 years late, they have 86 locations in 25 states.

Interested? Well, having a healthy, nutritious, and tasty dinner is easier than you think. Each location establishes a list of monthly menu options catering to a wide variety of palates. For example, you can chose between making herb crusted flank steak, sweet cider bbq chicken, pizza burger sliders on pretzel buns, soy glazed salmon, Rio Grande chicken fajitas, or terracotta chicken with pita and hummus. All the shopping is done ahead of time by Dream Dinners, with special attention to price and quality. Ingredients have been chopped and sliced, and laminated recipe cards tell would-be chefs how to assemble a

Monkey Business/Fotolia

tasty meal in a zippered bag or foil pan. Depending upon the store location, there may be one or more work stations with ingredients, and patrons move around the workstation selecting the items on their recipe cards in the prescribed quantities. When you're all done, just load your meals into a cooler and head home to put them in the freezer, where they will wait until you are ready for a delicious home-cooked meal. The cost of a meal varies based on the ingredients, but an average meal is about $5 per person, far less than a restaurant meal, and right in your own kitchen.[9]

consider the costs of expanding. When markets are growing, greater capacity is desirable. In troubled times, however, existing capacity may be too large and too expensive to maintain, requiring a reduction in size.

Location Planning

Because location affects production costs and flexibility, sound location planning is crucial for factories, offices, and stores. Depending on its site, a company may be able to produce low-cost products, or it may find itself at a cost disadvantage relative to its competitors.

Consider the reasons why Slovakia has become known as "Detroit East." Even during the worldwide slowdown in car sales resulting from the Great Recession, Slovakia's auto production held constant. And during the 2012 Euro-zone economic crisis it produced more cars per capita—including Volkswagen SUVs, Peugeot Citroens, and Kias—than most other Euro-zone countries. Its auto factories remain well-positioned to increase volume as the worldwide economy improves. The central European country is an ideal place to produce cars. It has a good railroad system and nearby access to the Danube River, meaning economical transportation for incoming materials and outgoing cars once auto factories are in operation. The area also has skilled, hard-working laborers, and wages lower than those of surrounding countries.[10]

In contrast to manufacturing, consumer services concentrate on being located near customers. Thus, fast-food restaurants, such as Taco Bell and McDonald's, are located near areas with high traffic, such as college campuses, hospital cafeterias, and shopping malls. At retail giant Walmart, managers of the company's huge distribution centers regard Walmart outlets as their customers. To ensure that truckloads of merchandise flow quickly to stores, distribution centers are located near the hundreds of Walmart stores that they supply, not near the companies that supply them.

Layout Planning

Layout is the physical location or floor plan for service centers, machinery, equipment, customers, and supplies. It determines whether a company can respond efficiently to demand for more and different products or whether it finds itself unable to match competitors' speed and convenience. Among the many layout possibilities, three well-known alternatives—*(1) process layouts (or custom-products layouts), (2) product layouts (or same-steps layouts),* and *(3) fixed-position layouts*—are presented here to illustrate how different layouts serve different purposes for operations.

Process Layout (Custom-Product Layout) *physical arrangement of production activities that groups equipment and people according to function*

Process Layouts In a **process layout** (also called **custom-product layout**), which is well suited to *make-to-order shops* (or *job shops*) specializing in custom work, equipment and people are grouped according to function. FedEx Office stores (formerly Kinko's Copy Centers), for example, use custom-products layouts to accommodate a variety of custom jobs. Specific activities or processes, such as photocopying, faxing, computing, binding, and laminating, are performed in separate, specialized areas of the store. Walk-in customers—local individuals and small-business clients—move from area-to-area using the self-service they need.

The main advantage of process layouts is flexibility—at any time, the shop can process individual customer orders, each requiring different kinds of work. Depending on its work requirements, a client being served or a job being processed may flow through three activity areas, another through just one area, and still others through four or more work zones. Figure 5 shows the process layout of a service provider—a medical clinic. The path taken through the facility reflects the unique treatments for one patient's visit. Goods producers such as machine shops, woodworking and print shops, dry cleaning stores, as well as health clinics and physical fitness studios are among the many facilities using custom-products layouts.

Product Layout (Same-Steps Layout) *physical arrangement of production steps designed to make one type of product in a fixed sequence of activities according to its production requirements*

Assembly Line Layout *a same-steps layout in which a product moves step by step through a plant on conveyor belts or other equipment until it is completed*

Product Layouts A **product layout** (also called a **same-steps layout** or **assembly line layout**) is set up to provide one type of service or make one type of product in a fixed sequence of production steps. All units go through the same set of steps.

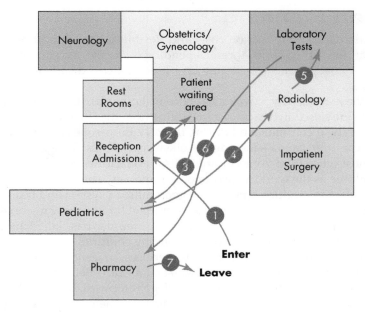

Example patient flow for one customer

FIGURE 5 Process Layout for a Service Provider—a Medical Clinic

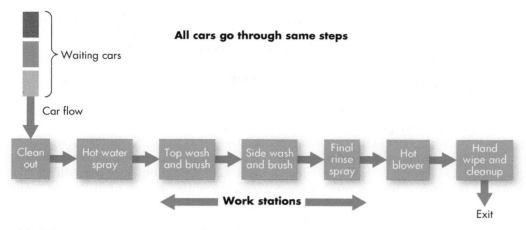

FIGURE 6 Product Layout for a Service—Automated Car Wash

It is efficient for large-volume make-to-stock operations that mass-produce many units of a product quickly: A partially finished product moves step by step through the plant on conveyor belts or other equipment, often in a straight line, as it passes through each stage until the product is completed. Automobile, food-processing, and television-assembly plants use same-steps layouts, as do mail-processing facilities, such as UPS or FedEx.

Figure 6 shows a product layout at a service provider—an automatic car wash. Figure 7 is a goods-producer assembling parts needed to make storm windows. Same-steps layouts are efficient because the work skill is built into the equipment, allowing unskilled labor to perform simple tasks. But they are often inflexible, especially where they use specialized equipment that's hard to rearrange for new applications.

Fixed Position Layouts A **fixed-position layout** is often used when size, shape, or other factors make it difficult to move the service to another production facility. In fixed-position layouts the product or client remains at one location; equipment, materials, and human skills are moved to that location, as needed, to perform the service or to build the product. While recovering at home from a knee replacement, for example, physical rehabilitation specialists come to the patient's home for rehab services. When home plumbing goes bad or the roof leaks, repair services are brought to that home—at its fixed position—where the services are performed. Such layouts are used for building huge ships that can't be moved, for constructing buildings, and for agricultural operations—plowing, fertilizing, and harvesting—at farm sites.

Fixed-Position Layout labor, equipment, materials, and other resources are brought to the geographic location where all production work is done

Quality Planning

Every operations plan includes activities for ensuring that products meet the firm's and customers' quality standards. The American Society for Quality defines

Same assembly steps for all frames

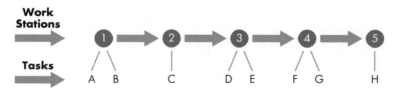

Work Stations

Tasks

A B   C   D E   F G   H

A: Assemble window frame
B: Install frame latch
C: Install rubber molding
D: Insert frame screws

E: Cover frame screws
F: Install frame handle
G: Install glass pane
H: Pack window unit

FIGURE 7 Product Layout for Goods Production—Storm Window Assembly

Quality *combination of "characteristics of a product or service that bear on its ability to satisfy stated or implied needs"*

quality as a subjective term, the combination of "characteristics of a product or service that bear on its ability to satisfy stated or implied needs."[11] Such characteristics may include a reasonable price and dependability in delivering the benefits it promises.

Planning for quality begins when products are being designed. As we will see later, product design is a marketing responsibility, but it involves operations managers, too. Early in the process, goals are established for both performance and consistency. **Performance** refers to how well the product does what it is supposed to do. For loyal buyers of Godiva premium chocolates, performance includes such sensory delights as aroma, flavor, color, and texture. "Truly fine chocolates," observes master chocolatier Thierry Muret, "are always fresh, contain high-quality ingredients like cocoa beans and butter…and feature unusual textures and natural flavors." The recipe was designed to provide these features. Superior performance helps Godiva remain one of the world's top brands.[12]

Performance *dimension of quality that refers to how well a product does what it is supposed to do*

In addition to performance, quality also includes **consistency**, the sameness of product quality from unit to unit. Business travelers using Courtyard by Marriott, for example, enjoy high consistency with each overnight stay, which is one reason Courtyard by Marriott is among the best-selling brands in the lodging industry. Courtyard by Marriot achieved this status by maintaining the same features at all of Marriott's more than 967 Courtyard hotels in 38 countries. Designed for business travelers, most guest rooms include a Courtyard Suite with high-speed Internet access, meeting space, and access to an exercise room, restaurant and lounge, swimming pool, and 24-hour access to food. The layout of the suites is identical at many locations, the rooms are always clean, and check-in/checkout procedures are identical so that lodgers know what to expect with each overnight stay. This consistency is achieved by monitoring for uniformity of materials and supplies, encouraging conscientious work, training employees, and maintaining equipment.

Consistency *dimension of quality that refers to sameness of product quality from unit to unit*

In addition to product design, quality planning includes employees deciding what constitutes a high-quality product—for both goods and services—and determining how to measure these quality characteristics.

Methods Planning

In designing operations systems, managers must identify each production step and the specific methods for performing it. They can then reduce waste and inefficiency by examining procedures on a step-by-step basis by using an approach called *methods improvement*.

Improving Process Flows Improvements for operations begin by documenting current production practices. A detailed description, often using a diagram called a *process flowchart*, is helpful in organizing and recording information. The flowchart identifies the sequence of production activities, movements of materials, and work performed at each stage of the process. It can then be analyzed to isolate wasteful activities, sources of delay, and other inefficiencies in both goods and services operations. The final step is implementing improvements.

Improving Customer Service Consider, for example, the traditional checkout method at hotels. The process flowchart in Figure 8 shows five stages of customer activities. Hotel checkout can be time consuming for customers standing in line to pay. They become impatient and annoyed, especially during popular checkout times when lines are long. Other hotel tasks are disrupted, too, as managers are forced to reassign employees to the front desk to assist with surging checkout lines. Hotel managers developed an improved checkout method that avoids wasting time in line for customers and reduces interruptions of other staff duties as well. It saves time by eliminating steps 1, 2, 3A, and 5. On the morning of departure customers find a copy of charges delivered under their room door. Or, they can scan their bills on television in the privacy of their rooms any time before departure. If the bill is correct, no further checkout is required, and the hotel submits the charges against the credit card that the customer submitted during check-in.

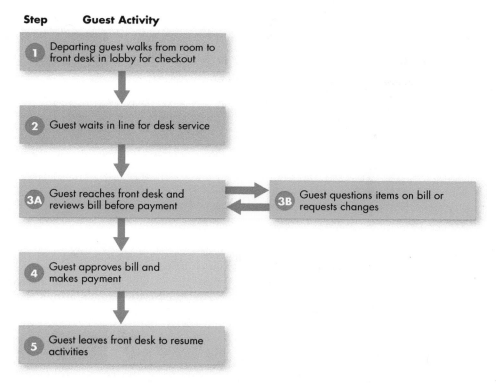

Step   Guest Activity

1. Departing guest walks from room to front desk in lobby for checkout

2. Guest waits in line for desk service

3A. Guest reaches front desk and reviews bill before payment

3B. Guest questions items on bill or requests changes

4. Guest approves bill and makes payment

5. Guest leaves front desk to resume activities

FIGURE 8 Flowchart of Traditional Guest Checkout

Operations Scheduling

OBJECTIVE 5
Discuss
the information contained in four kinds of operations schedules—the master operations schedule, detailed schedule, staff schedule, and project schedule.

Continuing with the flow of activities in Figure 4, once managers and their teams have determined the operations plans, they then develop timetables for implementing the plans. This aspect of operations, called *operations scheduling*, identifies times when specific activities will occur. In this section we consider four general kinds of schedules. (1) The *master schedule* is "the game plan" for deciding the volume of upcoming activities for months ahead. (2) *Detailed schedules* show day-to-day activities that will occur in production. (3) *Staff schedules* identify who and how many employees will be working, and when. (4) Finally, *project schedules* provide coordination for completing large-scale projects.

The Master Operations Schedule

Scheduling of operation occurs at different levels. First, a top-level **master operations schedule** shows which services or products will be produced and when, in upcoming time periods. Logan Aluminum, for example, makes coils of aluminum that it supplies to customer companies that use it to make beverage cans. Logan's master schedule, with a format like the partial schedule shown in Figure 9, covers production for 60 weeks in which more than 300,000 tons will be produced. For various types of coils (products), the master schedule specifies how many tons will

Master Operations Schedule
schedule showing which products will be produced, and when, in upcoming time periods

Coil # (Product)	8/4/14	8/11/14	8/18/14	...	11/3/14	11/10/14
TC016	1,500	2,500			2,100	600
TC032	900		2,700		3,000	
TR020	300		2,600			1,600

FIGURE 9 Example of Partial Master Operations Schedule

	Quarter/Year							
	1/2014	2/2014	3/2014	4/2014	1/2015	2/2015	3/2015	4/2015
Number of Stores	17	17	18	19	20	20	21	22
Staffing Level (no. of Employees)	1,360	1,360	1,530	1,615	1,700	1,700	1,653	1,827
Fresh Vegetables (tons)	204	204	192	228	240	240	230	260
Canned Goods (case loads)	73,950	77,350	80,100	80,100	83,000	84,500	88,600	90,200
Fresh Meats Etc.	–	–	–	–	–	–	–	–
–								
–								
–								

(left vertical label: KEY RESOURCES)

FIGURE 10 Food Retailer's Partial Operations Schedule

be produced each week, helping managers determine the kinds of materials, equipment, and other resources that will be needed for each upcoming week.

The master schedule for a service provider, such as a regional food retailer, may begin with the planned number of retail stores to be operating in each quarter of the coming two years. Then, key resources needed in each quarter to provide customer services for all stores are identified (estimated). Figure 10 shows an example of such a partial master schedule. It provides information for planning on how many people the company will have to hire and train, planning for purchases of food products and the financing needed for those purchases, and planning for construction requirements of new stores.

Detailed Schedules

Detailed Schedule *schedule showing daily work assignments with start and stop times for assigned jobs*

Although the master production schedule is the backbone for overall scheduling, additional information comes from **detailed schedules**, schedules showing daily work assignments with start and stop times for assigned jobs at each work station. Logan's production employees need to know the locations of all coils in the plant and their various stages of completion. Managers must assign start and stop times, and employees need scheduled work assignments daily, not just weekly. Detailed short-term schedules allow managers to use customer orders and information about equipment status to update sizes and the variety of coils to be made each day.

Staff Schedules and Computer-Based Scheduling

Staff Schedule *assigned working times in upcoming days for each employee on each work shift*

Scheduling is useful for employee staffing in service companies, too, including restaurants, hotels, and transportation and landscaping companies. **Staff schedules**, in general, specify assigned working times in upcoming days—perhaps for as many as 30 days or more—for each employee on each work shift. Staff schedules consider employees' needs and the company's efficiency and costs, including the ebbs and flows of demand for production.

Computer-based scheduling, using tools such as the *ABS Visual Staff Scheduler® PRO* (VSS Pro) software, can easily handle multishift activities for many employees—both part-time and full-time. It accommodates vacation times, holiday adjustments, and daily adjustments in staffing for unplanned absences and changes in production schedules.

Project Scheduling

Special projects, such as new business construction or redesigning a product, require close coordination and precise timing among many activities. In these cases, project management is facilitated by project scheduling tools, including Gantt charts and PERT.

The Gantt Graphical Method
Named after its developer, Henry Gantt, a **Gantt chart** breaks down large projects into steps to be performed and specifies the time required to perform each one. The project manager lists all activities needed to complete the work, estimates the time required for each step, records the progress on the chart, and checks the progress against the time scale on the chart to keep the project moving on schedule. If work is ahead of schedule, some employees may be shifted to another project. If it's behind schedule, workers may be added or completion delayed.

Gantt Chart *production schedule that breaks down large projects into steps to be performed and specifies the time required to perform each step*

Figure 11 shows a Gantt chart for the renovation of a college classroom. It shows progress to date and schedules for remaining work and that some steps can be performed at the same time (e.g., step D can be performed during the same time as steps C and E), but others cannot (e.g., step A must be completed before any of the others can begin). Step E is behind schedule; it should have been completed before the current date.

Project Scheduling with PERT Charts
The *Program Evaluation and Review Technique (PERT)* provides even more information for controlling the progress of large projects. Along with times required to perform the activities, the layout of the **PERT chart** uses arrows to show the necessary *sequence* among activities, from start to finish, for completing the project. It also identifies the *critical path*, the most time-consuming set of activities, for completing the project.

PERT Chart *production schedule specifying the sequence of activities, time requirements, and critical path for performing the steps in a project*

Figure 12 shows a PERT chart for renovating the college classroom. The project's nine activities and the times required to complete them are identified. Each activity

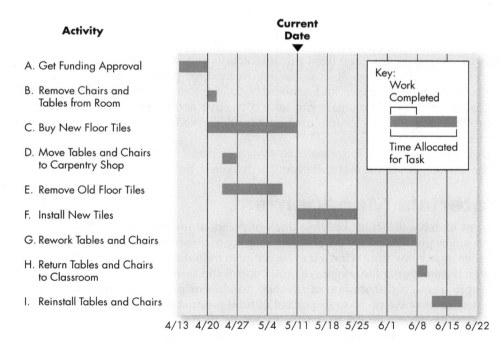

FIGURE 11 Gantt Chart

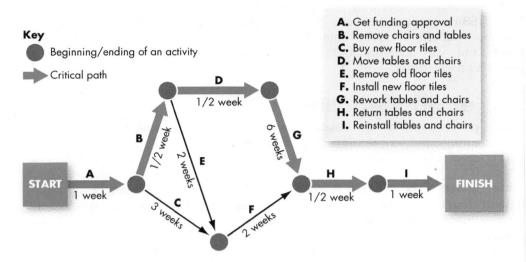

Key

● Beginning/ending of an activity

➔ Critical path

A. Get funding approval
B. Remove chairs and tables
C. Buy new floor tiles
D. Move tables and chairs
E. Remove old floor tiles
F. Install new floor tiles
G. Rework tables and chairs
H. Return tables and chairs
I. Reinstall tables and chairs

FIGURE 12 PERT Chart

is represented by an arrow. The arrows are positioned to show the required sequence for performing the activities. For example, chairs and tables can't be returned to the classroom (H) until after they've been reworked (G) and after new floor tiles are installed (F). Accordingly, the diagram shows arrows for G and F coming before activity H. Similarly, funding approval (A) has to occur before anything else can get started.

The critical path is informative because it reveals the most time-consuming path for project completion, and for most projects, speed of completion is vital. The critical path for classroom renovation consists of activities A, B, D, G, H, and I, requiring 9.5 weeks. It's critical because a delay in completing any of those activities will cause corresponding lateness beyond the planned completion time (9.5 weeks after startup). Project managers will watch those activities and, if potential delays arise, take special action—by reassigning workers and equipment—to speed up late activities and stay on schedule.

Operations Control

OBJECTIVE 6
Discuss
the two key activities required for operations control.

Operations Control *process of monitoring production performance by comparing results with plans and taking corrective action when needed*

Follow-Up *operations control activity for ensuring that production decisions are being implemented*

Once long-range plans have been put into action and schedules have been drawn up, **operations control** requires managers to monitor performance by comparing results with detailed plans and schedules. If employees do not meet schedules or quality standards, managers can take corrective action. **Follow-up**, checking to ensure that production decisions are being implemented, is a key and ongoing facet of operations.

Operations control includes *materials management* and *quality control*. Both activities ensure that schedules are met and products delivered, both in quantity and in quality.

Materials Management

Materials Management *process of planning, organizing, and controlling the flow of materials from sources of supply through distribution of finished goods*

Some of us have difficulty keeping track of personal items now and then—clothes, books, smart phones, and so on. Imagine keeping track of thousands, or even millions, of things at any one time. That's the challenge in **materials management**, the process by which managers plan, organize, and control the flow of materials from sources of supply through distribution of finished goods. For manufacturing firms, typical materials costs make up 50 to 75 percent of total product costs.

Materials Management Activities for Physical Goods Once a product has been designed, successful materials flows depend on five activities.

From selecting suppliers on through the distribution of finished goods, materials managers engage in the following areas that compose materials management:

- **Supplier selection** is the process of finding and choosing suppliers of services and materials. This step includes evaluating potential suppliers, negotiating terms of service, and maintaining positive buyer–seller relationships.

- **Purchasing** (sometimes called *procurement*) is the acquisition of all the raw materials and services that a company needs to produce its products. Most large firms have purchasing departments to buy proper services and materials in the amounts needed.

- **Transportation** is the means of transporting resources to the producer and finished goods to customers.

- **Warehousing** is the storage of both incoming materials for production and finished goods for distribution to customers.

- **Inventory control** includes the receiving, storing, handling, and counting of all raw materials, partly finished goods, and finished goods. It ensures that enough materials inventories are available to meet production schedules, while at the same time avoiding expensive excess inventories.

Lean Production Systems

Managers must take timing into consideration when managing materials, as well. Pioneered by Toyota, **lean production systems** are designed for smooth production flows that avoid inefficiencies, eliminate unnecessary inventories, and continuously improve production processes. **Just-in-time (JIT) production**, a type of lean system, brings together all needed materials at the precise moment they are required for each production stage, not before, thus creating fast and efficient responses to customer orders. All resources flow continuously—from arrival as raw materials to final assembly and shipment of finished products.

JIT production reduces the number of goods in process (goods not yet finished) to practically nothing. It minimizes inventory costs, reduces storage space requirements for inventories, and saves money by replacing stop-and-go production with smooth movement. Once smooth flow is the norm, disruptions are more visible and employees can resolve them more quickly. Finding and eliminating disruptions by the continuous improvement of production is a major objective of JIT production.

Inventory Management Is Crucial for Producing Services

For many service firms, too, the materials stakes are high. UPS delivers 20 million packages every day and promises that all of them will arrive on schedule. It keeps this promise by tracking the locations, schedules, and on-time performance of 625 aircraft and 93,361 vehicles. However, the most important "inventory" used for many high-contact services is not physical goods but exists in the form of information about service product offerings, clients, their interests, needs, activities, and even their plans for interactions with other clients.

Consider, as an example, the *inventories of information* at Collette Vacations where the *management of information* is a vital activity. Collette offers three product lines, Classic Touring, Explorations (for smaller groups), and Family Vacations, that collectively offer more than 150 escorted tours on seven continents including more than 50 countries. Each tour (the product), designed by a professional tour planner, includes a complete itinerary, duration, advanced arrangements for accommodations, and pricing. Vacationers select from among land tours, river cruises, and rail journeys that include sightseeing, meals, entertainment, and accommodations to experience new places, people history, and culture.

As a tour begins, one of the company's more than 100 Professional Tour Managers interacts face-to-face with clients as friend and guide for the entire duration, often 8-to-14 days, while handling all day-to-day details—confirming meals availabilities, ensuring hotel room accommodations, arranging local transportation, helping with sight-seeing selections, providing knowledge of local culture, assisting each tourist with any questions or problems, and handling emergencies.

Supplier Selection process of finding and choosing suppliers from whom to buy

Purchasing acquisition of the materials and services that a firm needs to produce its products

Transportation activities in transporting resources to the producer and finished goods to customers

Warehousing storage of incoming materials for production and finished goods for distribution to customers

Inventory Control process of receiving, storing, handling, and counting of all raw materials, partly finished goods, and finished goods

Lean Production System production system designed for smooth production flows that avoid inefficiencies, eliminate unnecessary inventories, and continuously improve production processes

Just-in-Time (JIT) Production type of lean production system that brings together all materials at the precise time they are required at each production stage

Quality control means taking action to ensure that operations produce products that meet specific quality standards. These quality control inspectors are checking finished goods before shipment to make sure they meet or surpass the standards set by their customers.

As you can see, these many activities create vast amounts of information—the *inventory of information*—that must be accurate and accessible for success with current tours and clients, and for all the thousands of clients booked on hundreds of future tours. It is also vital for contacting many thousands of potential customers with advance information about tours that will be offered a year or two in the future.[13]

Quality Control

Quality Control *action of ensuring that operations produce products that meet specific quality standards*

Quality control is taking action to ensure that operations produce goods or services that meet specific quality standards. Consider, for example, service operations in which customer satisfaction depends largely on the employees who provide the service. By monitoring services, managers and other employees can detect mistakes and make corrections. First, however, managers or other personnel must establish specific standards and measurements. At a bank, for example, quality control for teller services might require supervisors to observe employees periodically and evaluate their work according to a checklist. Managers would either review the results with employees and either confirm proper performance or indicate changes for bringing performance up to standards.

The high quality of customer-employee interactions is no accident in firms that monitor customer encounters and provide training for employee skills development. Many managers realize that without employees trained in customer-relationship skills, quality suffers, and businesses, such as airlines—as we saw in our opening story—and hotels, can lose customers to better-prepared competitors.

Quality Improvement and Total Quality Management

OBJECTIVE 7
Identify
the activities and underlying objectives involved in total quality management.

It is not enough to *control* quality by inspecting products and monitoring service operations as they occur, as when a supervisor listens in on a catalog sales service representative's customer calls. Businesses must also consider *building* quality into goods and services in the first place. Hospitals, such as St. Luke's Hospital of Kansas City, for example, use employee teams to design quality-assured treatment programs and patient-care procedures. Learning from past problems of staff and patients, teams

managing in turbulent times

Leaner Operations Are Restoring the U.S. Auto Industry

Recent signs of recovery for the U.S. auto industry stem from more than financial bailouts. General Motors and Chrysler, suffering grave financial losses in 2008, needed to demonstrate that they can survive and repay the bridge loans received from the U.S. Department of the Treasury. Under the guise of restructuring or reorganization, the steps automakers have taken can be summarized in just two words: *leaner operations*. GM, Chrysler, and Ford are adopting business strategies that Japanese producers have been using (and have mastered) for three decades to simplify production and capture a greater market share.[14]

A reduction in product offerings is the foundation for leaner operations: A smaller number of makes, models, and options such as colors, engine sizes, trims, etc. simplifies product design, production, and distribution. Fewer options and models also lead to lower costs, higher quality, and better customer service. Because it's easier to design fewer products, design and engineering requirements are vastly lowered. Designers strive for commonality of component parts so that all models use the same parts (e.g., all use the same door handles) rather than having separate designs for each model. Parts reductions simplify the supply chain, as well. Fewer suppliers are needed, communications are easier and faster, and closer relationships with suppliers provide faster supplier responses on short notice.

Design simplification is a blessing for assembly operations, too, because fewer production steps are required, and when quality problems arise, they are easier to find and are quickly corrected. Because fewer components require less inventory space and equipment, smaller factories, which are less costly and easier to maintain, become possible. Production scheduling is simpler, as are materials movements during production, so there is less work stoppage and fewer mistakes,

Keith Dannemiller/Alamy

product quality improves, and on-time deliveries to customers increase.

The company's distribution network is simplified, too, when some of its auto brands are eliminated. GM has downsized to just four core brands—Buick, Cadillac, Chevrolet, and GMC—after ending the Oldsmobile, Pontiac, Saturn, Hummer, and Saab brands under the GM label.[15] Chrysler's roster includes just three major brands: Chrysler, Jeep, and Dodge. Ford has discontinued its Mercury brand. Fewer brands means some auto dealerships are no longer needed, which lowered distribution costs. With speedier product designs and production operations, newer products get into the marketplace more quickly than those of competitors, and customer service improves. When the benefits of lower costs, higher quality, and lower prices are added together, it becomes apparent that lean production systems offer significant competitive advantages. Implementing these benefits, and doing so quickly, at GM, Chrysler, and Ford continues to be a massive challenge for survival in turbulent times.[16]

continuously redesign treatments, work methods, and procedures to eliminate the sources of quality problems, rather than allowing existing conditions to continue. That is, they insist that every job be done correctly without error ("do it right the first time"), rather than relying on inspection to catch mistakes and make corrections after they occur. To compete on a global scale, U.S. companies continue to emphasize a quality orientation. All employees, not just managers, participate in quality efforts, and firms have embraced new methods to measure progress and to identify areas for improvement. In many organizations, quality improvement has become a way of life.

The Quality-Productivity Connection

It's no secret that *quality* and *productivity* are watchwords in today's competitive environment. Companies are not only measuring productivity and insisting on improvements; they also are requiring that quality bring greater satisfaction to customers, improve sales, and boost profits.

Productivity *the amount of output produced compared with the amount of resources used to produce that output*

Productivity is a measure of economic performance: It compares how much we produce with the resources we use to produce it. The formula is fairly simple. The more services and goods we can produce while using fewer resources, the more productivity grows and the more everyone—the economy, businesses, and workers—benefits. At the national level, the most common measure is called *labor productivity*, because it uses the amount of labor worked as the resource to compare against the benefits, the country's GDP, resulting from using that resource:

$$\text{Labor productivity of a country} = \frac{\text{GDP for the year}}{\text{Total number of labor hours worked for the year}}$$

This equation illustrates the general idea of productivity. We prefer the focus on labor, rather than on other resources (such as capital or energy), because most countries keep accurate records on employment and hours worked. Thus, national labor productivity can be used for measuring year-to-year changes and to compare productivities with other countries. For 2014, for example, U.S. labor productivity was $64.12 of output per hour worked by the nation's labor force. By comparison, Norway was $86.61, Ireland was $71.31, and Belgium was $60.17. In contrast, the Republic of Korea was $26.83, lowest among the 20 measured countries.[17]

However, focusing on just the amount of output is a mistake because productivity refers to both the *quantity and quality* of what we produce. When resources are used more efficiently, the quantity of output is certainly greater. But experience has shown businesses that unless the resulting products are of satisfactory quality, consumers will reject them. And when consumers don't buy what is produced, GDP suffers and productivity falls. Producing quality, then, means creating fitness for use—offering features that customers want.

Managing for Quality

Total Quality Management (TQM) *all activities involved in getting high-quality goods and services into the marketplace*

Total quality management (TQM) includes all the activities necessary for getting high-quality goods and services into the marketplace. TQM begins with leadership and a desire for continuously improving both processes and products. It must consider all aspects of a business, including customers, suppliers, and employees. To marshal the interests of all these stakeholders, TQM first evaluates the costs of poor quality. TQM then identifies the sources causing unsatisfactory quality, assigns responsibility for corrections, and ensures that those who are responsible take steps for improving quality.

The Cost of Poor Quality As seen prominently in the popular press, Toyota recalled more than 24 million cars in 2009–2013, costing the world's then-number-one automaker billions of dollars and a severe blemish to its high-quality image. Problems ranging from sticking gas pedals to stalling engines and malfunctioning fuel pumps were dangerous and costly not only to Toyota, but also to many consumers.

As with goods producers, service providers and customers suffer financial distress from poor-quality service products. The banking industry is a current example. As a backbone of the U.S. financial system, banks and their customers are still suffering because of bad financial products, most notably home mortgage loans. Lenders during "good times" began relaxing (or even ignoring altogether) traditional lending standards for determining whether borrowers were creditworthy. Lenders in some cases intentionally overstated property values so customers could borrow more money than the property justified. Borrowers were sometimes encouraged to overstate (falsify) their incomes and were not required to present evidence of income or even employment. Some borrowers, unaware of the terms of their loan agreements, were surprised after an initial time lapse when a much higher interest rate (and monthly payment) suddenly kicked in. Unable to meet their payments, borrowers had to abandon their homes. Meanwhile, banks were left holding foreclosed properties, unpaid (defaulted) loans, and no cash. With shortages of bank funds threatening to shut down the entire financial system, the entire nation felt the widespread costs of poor quality—loss of equity by homeowners from foreclosures, a weakened economy, high unemployment, and loss of retirement funds in peoples' savings accounts.

Quality Ownership: Taking Responsibility for Quality To ensure high-quality goods and services, many firms assign responsibility for some aspects of TQM to specific departments or positions. These specialists and experts may be called in to assist with quality-related problems in any department, and they keep everyone informed about the latest developments in quality-related equipment and methods. They also monitor quality-control activities to identify areas for improvement.

The backbone of TQM, however, and its biggest challenge, is motivating all employees and the company's suppliers to achieve quality goals. Leaders of the quality movement use various methods and resources to foster a quality focus, such as training, verbal encouragement, teamwork, and tying compensation to work quality. When those efforts succeed, employees and suppliers will ultimately accept **quality ownership**, the idea that quality belongs to each person who creates it while performing a job.

With TQM, everyone—purchasers, engineers, janitors, marketers, machinists, suppliers, and others—must focus on quality. At Saint Luke's Hospital of Kansas City, for example, every employee receives the hospital's "balanced scorecard" showing whether the hospital is meeting its goals: fast patient recovery for specific illnesses, 94 percent or better patient-satisfaction rating, every room cleaned when a patient is gone to X-ray, and the hospital's return on investment being good enough to get a good bond rating in the financial markets. Quarterly scores show the achievement level reached for each goal. Every employee can recite where the hospital is excelling and where it needs improvement. In recognition of its employees' dedication to quality performance, Saint Luke's received the Malcolm Baldrige National Quality Award, the prestigious U.S. award for excellence in quality, and is a three-time winner of the Missouri Quality Award.[18]

> **Quality Ownership** *principle of total quality management that holds that quality belongs to each person who creates it while performing a job*

Tools for Total Quality Management

Hundreds of tools have proven useful for quality improvement, ranging from statistical analysis of product data, to satisfaction surveys of customers, to **competitive product analysis**, a process by which a company analyzes a competitor's products to identify desirable improvements. Using competitive analysis, for example, Toshiba might take apart a Xerox copier and test each component. The results would help managers decide which Toshiba product features are satisfactory, which features should be upgraded, and which operations processes need improvement. In this section, we survey five of the most commonly used tools for TQM: (1) *value-added analysis*, (2) *quality improvement teams*, (3) *getting closer to the customer*, (4) *the ISO series*, and (5) *business process reengineering*.

> **Competitive Product Analysis** *process by which a company analyzes a competitor's products to identify desirable improvements*

Value-Added Analysis **Value-added analysis** refers to the evaluation of all work activities, materials flows, and paperwork to determine the value that they add for customers. It often reveals wasteful or unnecessary activities that can be eliminated without jeopardizing customer service. The basic tenet is so important that Tootsie Roll Industries, the venerable candy company, employs it as a corporate principle: "We run a trim operation and continually strive to eliminate waste, minimize cost, and implement performance improvements."[19]

> **Value-added Analysis** *process of evaluating all work activities, materials flows, and paperwork to determine the value that they add for customers*

Quality Improvement Teams Companies throughout the world have adopted **quality improvement teams**, which are patterned after the successful Japanese concept of *quality circles*, collaborative groups of employees from various work areas who meet regularly to define, analyze, and solve common production problems. The teams' goal is to improve both their own work methods and the products they make. Quality improvement teams organize their own work, select leaders, and address problems in the workplace. For years, Motorola has sponsored

> **Quality Improvement Team** *total quality management tool in which collaborative groups of employees from various work areas work together to improve quality by solving common shared production problems*

companywide team competitions to emphasize the value of the team approach, to recognize outstanding team performance, and to reaffirm the team's role in the company's continuous-improvement culture.

Getting Closer to the Customer Successful businesses take steps to know what their customers want in the products they consume. On the other hand, struggling companies have often lost sight of customers as the driving force behind all business activity. Such companies waste resources by designing products that customers do not want. Sometimes, they ignore customer reactions to existing products, an example of which is the outpouring of complaints about airline services that go unanswered (see this chapter's opening case). Or companies fail to keep up with changing customer preferences. BlackBerry mobile devices, for example, fell behind competing products because they did not offer customers the features that Samsung, Motorola, and Apple provided.

Successful firms take steps to know what their customers want in the products they consume. Caterpillar's (CAT) financial services department, for example, received the Malcolm Baldrige National Quality Award for high ratings by its customers (that is, dealers and buyers of Caterpillar equipment). Buying and financing equipment from Cat Financial became easier as CAT moved its services increasingly online. Customers now have 24/7 access to information on how much they owe on equipment costing anywhere from $30,000 to $2 million, and they can make payments around the clock, too. In the past, the 60,000 customers had to phone a Cat representative, who was often unavailable, resulting in delays and wasted time. The improved online system is testimony to Cat Financial's dedication in knowing what customers want, and then providing it.[20]

IDENTIFYING CUSTOMERS—INTERNAL AND EXTERNAL Improvement projects are undertaken for both external and internal customers. Internal suppliers and internal customers exist wherever one employee or activity relies on others. For example, marketing managers rely on internal accounting information—costs for materials, supplies, and wages—to plan marketing activities for coming months. The marketing manager is a customer of the firm's accountants, the information user relies on the information supplier. Accountants in a TQM environment recognize this supplier–customer connection and take steps to improve information for marketing.

The ISO Series Perhaps you've driven past companies proudly displaying large banners announcing, "This Facility Is ISO Certified." The ISO (pronounced ICE-oh) label is a mark of quality achievement that is respected throughout the world and, in some countries, it's a requirement for doing business.

ISO 9000 ISO 9000 is a certification program attesting that a factory, a laboratory, or an office has met the rigorous quality management requirements set by the International Organization for Standardization (ISO). Today, more than 170 countries have adopted ISO 9000 as a national standard. Over 1 million certificates have been issued to organizations worldwide meeting the ISO standards.

The standards of *ISO 9000* allow firms to show that they follow documented procedures for testing products, training workers, keeping records, and fixing defects. It allows international companies to determine (or be assured of) quality of product (or the business) when shipping for, from, and to suppliers across borders. To become certified, companies must document the procedures followed by workers during every stage of production. The purpose is to ensure that a company's processes can create products exactly the same today as it did yesterday and as it will tomorrow.

ISO 14000 The **ISO 14000** program certifies improvements in environmental performance by requiring a firm to develop an *environmental management system*: a plan documenting how the company has acted to improve its performance in using resources (such as raw materials) and in managing pollution. A company must not only identify hazardous wastes that it expects to create, but it must also stipulate plans for treatment and disposal.

ISO 9000 program certifying that a factory, laboratory, or office has met the quality management standards set by the International Organization for Standardization

ISO 14000 certification program attesting to the fact that a factory, laboratory, or office has improved its environmental performance

Business Process Reengineering Every business consists of processes, activities that it performs regularly and routinely in conducting business, such as receiving and storing materials from suppliers, billing patients for medical treatment, filing insurance claims for auto accidents, and filling customer orders from Internet sales. Any business process can increase customer satisfaction by performing it well. By the same token, any business process can disappoint customers when it's poorly managed.

Business process reengineering focuses on improving a business process—rethinking each of its steps by starting from scratch. *Reengineering* is the fundamental rethinking and radical redesign of business processes to achieve dramatic improvements as measured by cost, quality, service, and speed. The discussion of CAT's changeover to an online system for customers is an example. CAT reengineered the whole payments and financing process by improving equipment, retraining employees, and connecting customers to CAT's databases. As the example illustrates, redesign is guided by a desire to improve operations and thereby provide higher-value services for customers.

> **Business Process Reengineering** *rethinking and radical redesign of business processes to improve performance, quality, and productivity*

Adding Value Through Supply Chains

> **OBJECTIVE 8**
> **Explain**
> how a supply chain strategy differs from traditional strategies for coordinating operations among firms.

The term *supply chain* refers to the group of companies and stream of activities that work together to create a product. A **supply chain** (or **value chain**) for any product is the flow of information, materials, and services that starts with raw-materials suppliers and continues adding value through other stages in the network of firms until the product reaches the end customer.

Figure 13 shows the chain of activities for supplying baked goods to consumers. Each stage adds value for the final customer. This bakery example begins with raw materials (grain harvested from the farm). It also includes storage and transportation activities, factory operations for baking and wrapping, and distribution to retailers. Each stage depends on the others for success in getting freshly baked goods to consumers. However, a failure by any link can spell disaster for the entire chain.

> **Supply Chain (Value Chain)** *flow of information, materials, and services that starts with raw-materials suppliers and continues adding value through other stages in the network of firms until the product reaches the end customer*

The Supply Chain Strategy

Traditional strategies assume that companies are managed as individual firms rather than as members of a coordinated supply system. Supply chain strategy is based on the idea that members of the chain will gain competitive advantage by working as a coordinated unit. Although each company looks out for its own interests, it works

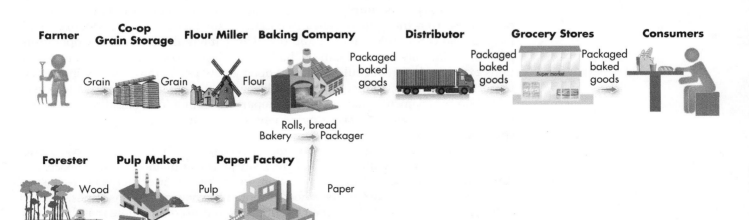

FIGURE 13 Supply Chain for Baked Goods

closely with suppliers and customers throughout the chain. Everyone focuses on the entire chain of relationships rather than on just the next stage in the chain.

A traditionally managed bakery, for example, would focus simply on getting production inputs from flour millers and paper suppliers, and then on supplying baked goods to distributors. Unfortunately, this approach limits the chain's performance and doesn't allow for possible improvements when activities are more carefully coordinated. Proper management and better coordination among supply chain activities can provide fresher baked goods at lower prices.

Supply Chain Management (SCM)
principle of looking at the supply chain as a whole to improve the overall flow through the system

Supply Chain Management

Supply chain management (SCM) looks at the chain as a whole to improve the overall flow through a system composed of companies working together. Because customers ultimately get better value, supply chain management gains competitive advantage for each of the chain's members.

An innovative supply chain strategy was the heart of Michael Dell's vision when he established Dell Inc. Dell's concept improves performance by sharing information among chain members. Dell's long-term production plans and up-to-the-minute sales data are available to suppliers via the Internet. The process starts when customer orders are automatically translated into updated production schedules in the factory. These schedules are used not only by operations managers at Dell but also by such parts suppliers as Sony, which adjust their own production and shipping activities to better meet Dell's production needs. In turn, parts suppliers' updated schedules are transmitted to their materials suppliers, and so on up the chain. As Dell's requirements change, suppliers up and down the chain synchronize their schedules to produce only the right materials and parts. As a result, Dell's prices are low and turnaround time for shipping PCs to customers is reduced to a matter of hours instead of days.

Reengineering Supply Chains for Better Results

Process improvements and reengineering often are applied in supply chains to lower costs, speed up service, and coordinate flows of information and material. Because the smoother flow of accurate information along the chain reduces unwanted inventories and transportation, avoids delays, and cuts supply times, materials move faster to business customers and individual consumers. SCM offers faster deliveries and lower costs than customers could get if each member acted only according to its own operations requirements.

Outsourcing and Global Supply Chains

Outsourcing *replacing internal processes by paying suppliers and distributors to perform business processes or to provide needed materials or services*

Outsourcing is the strategy of paying suppliers and distributors to perform certain business processes or to provide needed materials or services. The decision to outsource expands supply chains. The movement of manufacturing and service operations from the United States to countries such as China, Mexico, and India has reduced U.S. employment in traditional jobs. It has also created new operations jobs for SCM. Maytag, for example, had to develop its own internal global operations expertise before it could decide to open a new refrigerator factory in Mexico, import refrigerators from South Korea's Daewoo, and get laundry appliances from South Korea's Samsung Electronics. In departing from a long-standing practice of domestic production, Maytag adopted new supply chain skills for evaluating prospective outsourcing partners.

Skills for coordinating Maytag's domestic activities with those of its cross-border partners didn't end with the initial decision to get appliances from Mexico and Korea. Maytag personnel in their Newton, Iowa, headquarters have near-constant interaction with their partners on a host of continuing new operations issues. Product redesigns are transferred from the United States and used at remote manufacturing sites. Arrangements for cross-border materials flows require compliance with each country's commerce regulations. Production and global transportation scheduling

finding a better way

Too Good to Waste

In 2013, the Food and Agriculture Organization of the United Nations released a report on the impact of food waste. Among its more disturbing findings were that approximately one-third of all food produced is wasted or lost. According to FAO Director-General Jose Graziano da Silva, "We simply cannot allow one-third of all the food we produce to go to waste or be lost because of inappropriate practices, when 870 million people go hungry every day." According to this study, food waste occurs along the supply chain, with fifty-four percent occurring during production, post-harvest handling, and storage. However, there are some differences among low-income countries and their middle- and high-income counterparts. "Downstream" waste, at the retail or consumer level, is much higher in developed economies, creating additional opportunities for consumer education in these areas.

Nathaniel Noir/Alamy

In addition to the human impacts of food wastage, there are dire environmental consequences. For example, meat wastage has the most severe environmental consequences as the land use and carbon footprint associated with meat production is much higher. Unused grain and cereal products, such as rice, impact both land use and methane emissions (which are particularly high in rice production). On the other hand, the impact of fruit waste tends to be primarily associated with excess water consumption. Given the increasing scarcity of water supplies, this concern is not easily dismissed.

The key to minimizing food waste falls in supply chain management. Beginning with the producer, it is essential that predictive analytics are employed to balance production with downstream demand for the product. Even with better modeling, food surpluses will continue to occur, but they could be better managed. Rather than disposing of excess food in the supply chain, intermediaries need to be more diligent about finding alternative uses, whether it is donating it to food programs or diverting it for livestock feed. Consumers must also be educated about the importance of planning their food spending to avoid over-purchasing as well as the actual meaning of "best-before-dates," which often lead retailers and consumers to discard healthy and nutritious foods because they fail to meet certain aesthetic standards. Each member of the supply chain, from producer to consumer, has a role in reducing food waste, becoming better stewards of our planet and resources.[21]

are coordinated with U.S. market demand so that outsourced products arrive in the right amounts and on time without tarnishing Maytag's reputation for high quality. Although manufacturing operations are located remotely, they are closely integrated with the firm's home-base activities. That tightness of integration demands on-site operations expertise on both sides of the outsourcing equation. Global communication technologies are essential. The result for outsourcers is a greater need of operations skills for integration among dispersed facilities.

summary of learning objectives

Explain the meaning of *operations* and discuss the growth in the services and goods sectors of the U.S. economy.

Operations (or *production*) refers to all the activities involved in making products—goods and services—for customers. In modern societies, much of what we need or want is produced by service operations, where success or failure depends on provider-customer contact. Many companies, such as General Electric, provide both goods and services. Employment has risen significantly in the service sector over the past 10 years. However, the 11 percent of the U.S. workforce employed in producing goods generate 32 percent of national income.

Production or operations adds customer value by providing *utility*—the ability of a product to satisfy a want or need—in terms of form, time, and place: (1) *Form utility*: By turning raw materials and human skills into finished goods and services, production adds customer value by making products available. (2) *Time utility*: Production provides customer value by making products available when customers want them. (3) *Place utility*: Production adds customer value by making products available where they are convenient for customers.

Operations management is the systematic direction and control of the activities that transform resources into finished goods and services that create value for and provide benefits to customers. Through their operations processes—using resources that include knowledge, physical materials, information, equipment, the customer, and human skills—firms provide benefits for themselves and for their customers.

Identify the three kinds of utility created by operations and the characteristics that distinguish service operations from goods production.

Although the creation of both goods and services involves resources, transformations, and finished products, service operations differ from goods manufacturing in several important ways. In service production, the raw materials are not things such as glass or steel, but rather people who choose among sellers because they have unsatisfied needs or possessions in need of care or alteration. Therefore, whereas services are typically performed, goods are physically produced. In addition, services are largely *intangible* and more *unstorable* than most physical goods. It is difficult, as an example, to store a supply (an inventory) of childcare services. If the services are not consumed when available, they are lost forever.

Service businesses, therefore, focus explicitly on the intangibility and unstorable nature of their products. Because services are intangible, for instance, providers work to ensure that customers receive value in the form of pleasure, satisfaction, or a feeling of safety. Often they also focus on both the transformation process and the final product (such as making the loan interview a pleasant experience as well as providing the loan itself). As part of the transformation process, service providers typically focus on *customer-provider contact*. This requires service workers who, because they interact with customers, possess different skills than workers producing physical goods.

An *operations process* is a set of methods and technologies used to produce a good or service. Goods production can be classified as *make-to-order* or *make-to-stock*. Make-to-order operations respond to specific customer specifications, and make-to-stock operations produce standardized goods for mass consumption.

Service operations can be classified according to the extent of customer contact. In a *low-contact system*, customers have a limited presence as the service is performed. Low-contact systems include mail and package delivery, auto repair, lawn care services, and gas and electric providers. On the other hand, in a *high-contact system*, the customer is present as the service is delivered. Examples of high-contact systems include airlines and hair salons.

OBJECTIVE 3

Explain how companies with different business strategies are best served by having different operations capabilities.

Production is a flexible activity that can be molded into many shapes to give different operations capabilities (production capabilities) for different purposes. Its design is best driven from above by the firm's larger business strategy. When firms adopt different strategies for winning customers in specific target markets, they should also adjust their *operations capabilities*—what production must do especially well—to match the chosen strategy. That is, different target markets have different desires or expectations for the products—services and goods—that they seek. Accordingly, operations managers must clarify and understand their target market's most-preferred product characteristic from among the following: Do they want low-cost products? Highest quality products? Dependability of product performance? A wide variety of offerings rather than just a few? To meet any chosen strategy, then, they adopt an operations capability that is geared toward meeting the target customers' needs. The operations capability that is appropriate for a low-cost strategy, for example, is different than the kind of competence that is best for a dependability strategy. Accordingly, the operations characteristics, such as number and size of production facilities, employee skills, kinds of equipment, and its operations activities, will be different, resulting in different operations capabilities to better support their different purposes.

OBJECTIVE 4

Identify the major factors that are considered in operations planning.

Operations planning includes five major considerations: (1) *Capacity planning* considers current and future capacity requirements for meeting anticipated customer demand. The amount of a product that a company can produce under normal conditions is its *capacity*, and it depends on how many people it employs and the number and sizes of its facilities. (2) *Location planning* is crucial because a firm's location affects costs of production, ease of transportation, access to skilled workers, and convenient accessibility for customers. (3) *Layout planning* determines the physical location of service teams, machinery, equipment, and facilities and affects how efficiently a company can respond to customer demand. A *process (custom-products) layout* is effective for make-to-order production specializing in custom designed services or goods. A *product (same-steps) layout*, such as an assembly line, is often used for large-volume, make-to-stock production of services or goods. A *fixed-position layout* is necessary when, because of size, shape, or any other reason, the service to be provided cannot be moved to another facility. Instead, the product or client remains at one location; equipment, materials, and human skills are moved to that location, as needed, to perform the service or to build the product. (4) *Quality planning* begins when products are being designed and extends into production operations for ensuring that the desired performance and consistency are built into products. Quality is defined as the combination of "characteristics of a product or service that bear on its ability to satisfy stated or implied needs." Quality planning involves setting goals for both *performance* and *consistency*. (5) *Methods planning* considers each production step and the specific methods for performing it for producing services and goods. The purpose is to reduce waste and inefficiency by methods improvement procedures.

OBJECTIVE 5

Discuss the information contained in four kinds of operations schedules—the master operations schedule, detailed schedule, staff schedule, and project schedule.

Operations scheduling identifies times when specific operations activities will occur. The *master schedule*, the top-level schedule for upcoming production, shows how many of which products (services or goods) will be produced in each time period, in weeks or months ahead, to meet upcoming customer demand. Thereafter, the schedule shows how many units of each major resource—materials, employees, equipment—will be required. By identifying these future resource requirements, managers can develop plans for acquiring the resources on time for upcoming time periods.

Detailed schedules take a shorter-range perspective by specifying daily work assignments with start and stop times for assigned jobs at each workstation. Detailed schedules allow managers and other employees to make last-minute adjustments so that resources are available and matched to meet immediate customer service requirements.

Staff schedules identify who and how many employees will be working and their assigned working times on each work shift for the upcoming month or months. Staff scheduling considers the needs of employees as well as the company's goals of maximizing efficiency and controlling costs.

Finally, *project schedules* provide information for completing large-scale projects using project scheduling tools, such as Gantt and *PERT charts. A Gantt chart* breaks down special large projects into the sequence of steps to be performed and specifies the time required to perform each. Gantt charts help managers to assess if work is ahead or behind schedule so that adjustments can be made. PERT charts show the necessary sequence among activities, and identify the critical path—the most time-consuming set of activities for completing the project.

OBJECTIVE 6

Discuss the two key activities required for operations control.

Materials management and quality control are two key activities of operations control. Once plans and schedules have been drawn up, operations control requires managers to monitor performance by comparing results against those plans and schedules. If schedules or quality standards are not met, managers take corrective action. Follow-up—checking to ensure that decisions are being implemented—is an essential facet of operations control. Materials management—including supplier selection, purchasing, transportation, warehousing, and inventory control—facilitates the flow of materials. Materials management is the process by which managers plan, organize, and control the flow of materials and services from sources of supply through distribution of finished products to customers. For producing and delivering physical goods, it may use lean production systems, such as just-in-time operations, for smooth production flows that avoid inefficiencies, comply with schedules, eliminate unnecessary inventories, and continuously improve production processes. For high-contact services, such as tourism and vacation services, inventory exists in the form of information about service offerings, facilities arrangements, clients, client interests, activities schedules, and plans for interactions among and with clients. Quality control means taking action to ensure that operations produce goods and services that meet specific quality standards. By monitoring products and services, managers and other employees can detect mistakes, identify potential quality failures, and make corrections to avoid poor quality. Both materials management and quality control are essential to ensure that schedules are met and products delivered, both in quality and quantity.

OBJECTIVE 7

Identify the activities and underlying objectives involved in total quality management.

Successful companies focus on productivity, which measures both the quantity and quality of the products produced or delivered. Productivity compares the level of production with the amount of resources used to produce it. *Total quality management (TQM)* is a customer-driven culture for offering products with characteristics that customers want. It includes all the activities necessary for getting customer-satisfying goods and services into the marketplace and, internally, getting every job to give better service to internal customers (other departments) within the organization. TQM begins with leadership and a desire for continuously improving both processes and products. It considers all aspects of a business, including customers, suppliers, and employees. The TQM culture fosters an attitude of *quality ownership* among employees and suppliers, the idea that quality belongs to each person who creates it while performing a job, so that quality improvement becomes a continuous way of life. It identifies the *costs of poor quality*, including all forms of financial distress resulting from poor-quality products, and uses cost-of-poor-quality information as a guide for process improvement to prevent such costs in the future.

Numerous quality-improvement tools can then be used to gain those improvements and reduce those costs. Some process improvement tools of TQM include competitive product analysis, value-added analysis, the use of quality improvement teams, business process reengineering, and "getting closer to the customer" to gain valid information of what customers really want, so that improved products more closely meet customer desires.

ISO 9000 is a certification program attesting that a factory, laboratory, or office has met the rigorous quality management requirements set by the International Organization for Standardization. Similarly, *ISO 14000* certifies improvements in environmental performance. Finally, business process reengineering focuses on the radical redesign of business processes to achieve improvements in cost, quality, service, and speed.

OBJECTIVE 8

Explain how a supply chain strategy differs from traditional strategies for coordinating operations among firms.

The supply chain strategy is based on the idea that members of the *supply chain*, the stream of all activities and companies that add value in creating a product, will gain competitive advantage by working together as a coordinated unit. The supply chain for any product, be it a service or a physical good, is the flow of information, materials, and services that starts with raw-materials suppliers and continues adding value through other stages in the network of firms until the product reaches the end customer. In contrast, traditional strategies assume that companies are managed as individual firms, each acting in its own interest. By managing the chain as a whole—using *supply chain management*—companies can more closely coordinate activities throughout the chain. Because accurate information is shared between companies along the chain, they can reduce unwanted materials and transportation, avoid delays in deliveries to cut supply times, quickly add service centers to meet upsurges in demand, and move materials faster through the chain. By sharing information across all stages in the chain, overall costs and inventories can be reduced, quality can be improved, and overall flow through the system improves, thus providing customers higher value from faster deliveries and lower costs.

Outsourcing, the strategy of paying suppliers and distributors to perform certain business processes or to provide needed materials or services, expands supply chains. The prevalence of outsourcing has created new operations jobs in supply chain management.

key terms

assembly line layout	make-to-order operations	purchasing
business process reengineering	make-to-stock operations	quality
capacity	master operations schedule	quality control
competitive product analysis	materials management	quality improvement team
consistency	operations capability (production	quality ownership
detailed schedule	capability)	service operations (service
fixed-position layout	operations control	production)
follow-up	operations process	staff schedule
Gantt chart	operations (production)	supplier selection
goods operations (goods production)	operations (production) management	supply chain management
high-contact system	operations (production) managers	(SCM)
inventory control	outsourcing	supply chain (value chain)
ISO 9000	process layout (custom-product layout)	total quality management (TQM)
ISO 14000	product layout (same-steps layout)	transportation
just-in-time (JIT) production	productivity	utility
lean production system	performance	value-added analysis
low-contact system	PERT chart	warehousing

MyBizLab

To complete the problems with the ✪, go to EOC Discussion Questions in the MyLab.

questions & exercises

QUESTIONS FOR REVIEW

1. Describe the three forms of utility created through production.
2. What are the major differences between goods-production operations and service operations?
✪ 3. What are the major differences between high-contact and low-contact service systems?
4. What are the five major categories of operations planning?

QUESTIONS FOR ANALYSIS

✪ 5. Although we typically use these terms with goods production, is your college a make-to-order or make-to-stock operation? Be sure to support your conclusion.
6. What type of business strategy is used at Disney theme parks? What specific operations activities are most important?
7. Develop a list of internal customers and internal suppliers for some business that you use frequently (or where you work), such as a cafeteria, a dormitory or hotel, or a movie theater. Identify areas for potential quality improvement in these internal customer–supplier activity relationships.
✪ 8. If you were a member of a quality improvement team at your college, what would be five specific high-impact recommendations that you would support?

APPLICATION EXERCISES

9. Think of an everyday activity, either personal or professional, that you would like to streamline for faster performance or more convenience. It could be something like gassing up your car, going to work or school, enrolling in classes at school, or any other activity that involves several stages with which you are familiar. Describe how you would use methods planning as described in the chapter to improve the activity. Draw a process flowchart that shows the stages in the activity you chose, and then tell how you would use it.
10. Interview the manager of a local service business, such as a restaurant or hair salon. Identify the major decisions involved in planning that business's service operations.

building a business: continuing team exercise

Assignment

Meet with your team members to consider your new business venture and how it relates to the operations management and quality topics in this chapter. Develop specific responses to the following:

11. In what ways is your business connected with service operations? Identify the ways it is connected with goods production. Which of these, service operations or goods production, is more important to your business? Why?
12. Explain what must be done to ensure that your operations capabilities are consistent with your business strategy.
13. Discuss how your team is going to identify the key operations characteristics that best provide support for accomplishing your business strategy. Based on the discussion, what are the key characteristics that seem to be most prominent at this stage of development of your business?
14. Analyze the planned production activities for your business to determine the operations processes for which total quality management will be important.
15. In what ways, if any, will supply chains be of concern for your business? Explain.

team exercise

CALCULATING THE COST OF CONSCIENCE

The Situation

Product quality and cost affect every firm's reputation and profitability, as well as the satisfaction of customers. As director of quality for a major appliance manufacturer, Ruth was reporting to the executive committee on the results of a program for correcting problems with a newly redesigned compressor (the motor that cools the refrigerator) that the company had recently begun using in its refrigerators. Following several customer complaints, the quality lab had determined that some of the new compressor units ran more loudly than expected, although they still effectively cooled the units.

The Decision

Faced with this information, Ruth has been asked to recommend a strategy for the company. One corrective option was simply waiting until customers complained and responding to each complaint if and when it occurred. Fixing noisy units could be expensive, but the company wishes to maintain its high-quality image.

Ruth, however, decided that this approach was inconsistent with the company's policy of being the high-quality leader in the industry. Insisting on a proactive, "pro-quality" approach, Ruth suggests a program for contacting all customers who had purchased refrigerators containing the new compressor. Unfortunately, the "quality-and-customers-first" policy will be expensive. Service representatives nationwide will have to phone every customer, make appointments for home visits, and replace original compressors with a newer model. Because replacement time is only 30 minutes, customers will hardly be inconvenienced, and food will stay refrigerated without interruption.

Others have even suggested that the company require consumers to pay a part of the cost of repairing the noisy compressor because the compressors still meet all expectations with respect to cooling, and this is the primary function of the refrigerator. Advocates of this position argue that the new compressors will extend the life of the refrigerator and customers will benefit.

FOLLOW-UP QUESTIONS

16. If you were a customer, what would you hope that the company would do? Would your answer be different if you were an investor or stockholder?
17. How might Ruth's boss, the Vice President for Operations, view the situation differently than Ruth?
18. Which is the best of the three options in the short-term? What about in the long-term?
19. How could the company have avoided this situation?

exercising your ethics

PROMISES, PROMISES

The Situation

Unfortunately, false promises are not uncommon when managers feel pressure to pump up profits. Many operations managers no doubt recall times when excited marketing managers asked for unrealistic commitments from production to get a new customer contract. This exercise will introduce you to some ethical considerations pertaining to such promises and commitments.

The Dilemma

You are an operations manager for a factory that makes replacement car mufflers and tailpipes. Your products are distributed throughout the country to muffler-repair shops that install them on used vehicles. After several years of modest but steady growth, your company recently suffered a downturn and shut down 5 percent of the factory's production capacity. Two supervisors and 70 production workers were laid off.

After returning from lunch, you get a phone call from the general manager of King Kong Mufflers, one of the nation's top three muffler-repair chains, who says the following:

I suppose you know that we're about to sign a contract for your firm to supply us with replacement parts in large volumes, *beginning two months from now. Your sales manager assures me that you can reliably meet my needs, and I just want to confirm that promise with you before I sign the contract.*

This is the first you've heard about this contract. While your potential customer is talking, you realize that meeting his needs will require a 20-percent increase in your current production capacity. Two months, however, isn't enough time to add more equipment, acquire tools, hire and train workers, and contract for supplies. An increase this large might even require a bigger building (which would take considerably more than two months to arrange). On the other hand, you also know how much your firm needs the business. The caller waits in silence while you gather your thoughts.

QUESTIONS TO ADDRESS

20. What are the underlying ethical issues in this situation?
21. From an ethical standpoint, what is an appropriate response to the customer's question? What steps should you take in responding to it? Explain.
22. What would you say on the phone at this time to this customer?

cases

Passenger and Airlines; Friends, or Foes?

At the beginning of this chapter you read about the experiences of airline passengers and their reactions, both negative and positive, to the quality of services received. Using the information presented in this chapter you should now be able to answer these questions.

QUESTIONS FOR DISCUSSION

23. How would you define *quality* and how is quality measured in the airline industry? Are some measurements more useful than others? Explain.

24. Some *service activities*, such as weather delayed departures, are not under total control by airlines, but are affected by outside factors. Among all service activities that affect quality for customers, identify three or more that are totally controlled by airlines, and three or more that airlines cannot totally control. Should both sets of activities be included in the airlines' quality ratings? Explain.

25. Describe how *process flowcharts* may be helpful for methods improvement in airline service operations. What kinds of information would you hope to gain from the flowcharts?

26. Identify a major U.S. airline that has received *poor quality ratings*. Who are its customers, and what are the basic causes that led to declining quality?

27. U.S. airplane passengers must choose between two controversial security-screening procedures: full-body image detection or probing pat-downs. How might these procedures affect customers' *perceptions of airlines' services*? What actions would you recommend be considered by airlines to overcome negative perceptions?

Telecommuting Boosts Quality and Productivity ... Or Does It?

Early in 2013, Yahoo! CEO Marissa Mayer made the controversial decision to ban employees from working exclusively at home. Her action seems to run in the face of a years-long trend in the opposite direction by her company and other businesses across many industries. The question, then, that faces many organizations (and employees) is the following: Is telecommuting really beneficial? And if so, who reaps those benefits? Certainly today's information technologies provide telecommuting possibilities on a larger scale than ever before. Yahoo, like many other firms, has an internal Virtual Private Network, into which thousands of employees can log in at remote locations for conducting company business. Mayer's decision suggests that disadvantages outweigh advantages for her company at the present time.[22]

Included among the key questions at Yahoo and other companies is the following: "What happens with employee productivity and quality?" More and more U.S. employees are working remotely than ever before, and the trend is increasing. In 2010, for example, some 13.4 million were working at home one day or more per week. Previously, in 1997, that number was just 9.2 million. Because those numbers are growing, the future stakes for businesses and employees will depend even more on decisions about home-based versus office-based employment.[23]

Advocates for telecommuting cite its benefits. A Stanford study indicates a 13-percent productivity increase for call center employees working at home. It also cites greater work satisfaction and less employee turnover. Other studies report home-based employees work up to seven hours longer in their workweek than do those working at the office, have greater productivity, and less absenteeism. At-home employees note that they don't get distracted by co-workers, they avoid unnecessary commute time, take breaks when they prefer, and have a better quality of life, among other benefits.[24]

Critics, in contrast, note telecommuting's downside. Some people simply don't like to work alone. Others are not as productive working alone because better ideas and problem solutions are more forthcoming through face-to-face interactions and being physically nearby for work-related discussions. Also cited are advantages of separating home and workplace, avoiding the many distractions at home, and claims that telecommuting is widely abused. Employers report that having at least some scheduled on-site work time, even if not full-time, provides better performance including problem solutions for customer service.

Mayer concluded that Yahoo's quality and productivity were at unacceptable levels because of too many employees working exclusively at home. She is reported to favor working at the office, citing benefits of gaining information and ideas from meeting new people, from spontaneous conversations in the hallways, and quick accessibility to other face-to-face interactions for solving problems. "Speed and quality are often sacrificed when we work from home." Accordingly, Mayer suspected that Yahoo's telecommuting may be less productive than it should be. Rather than relying on mere suspicions, she wanted some factual basis, preferably backed up by data. So, she turned to Yahoo's Virtual Private Network and looked at the data files showing frequencies of employees' log-ins. She concluded that they were not checking in enough, thus indicating too much inactivity and too little productivity.[25]

Does face-to-face contact among employees really affect quality and productivity? A study of workers in call-center teams at Bank of America found that, yes, it does matter. Productivity was found to be greatest for workers in close-knit teams where workers mingled more frequently, rather than when working alone. Collaboration and spontaneous information sharing seemed to enhance productivity. But what about in other jobs where workers face different kinds of tasks, some more complex and others much simpler? Does either the office setting or the telecommuting setting, in general, always provide more promise for better productivity and quality? The answer is more likely to be situational rather than "one size fits all."[26]

QUESTIONS FOR DISCUSSION

28. How would you define *quality* for Yahoo's situation in this case? Explain why.

29. To figure out if Yahoo's telecommuting is less productive than it should have been, Mayer looked at the log of Yahoo's Virtual Private Network to see how frequently employees checked in. What do you think of this as a measure of productivity and quality? What other measure(s) would you suggest instead of the one she used?

30. Go to Yahoo's career website (https://careers.yahoo.com) and look at the kinds of jobs available at Yahoo. From these, identify two job descriptions that you recommend as appropriate for telecommuting. Identify two others that are appropriate for office-based employment. Explain the reasons for your recommendations.

31. Consider businesses such as hotels, television broadcasting, or others that provide services products to consumers. Suppose you want to improve the quality of such a service (choose one or two services). To do so, suppose you are considering allowing telecommuting by some employees, but requiring others to be office-based employees. Identify two kinds of work suitable for telecommuting, and two kinds for office-only jobs. Explain your reasoning.

32. In general, how would you measure a service-provider's quality and productivity? Recommend specific measures that will enable you to track changes in quality and productivity with the passage of time.

crafting a business plan

THE BUSINESS OF MANAGING

Goal of the Exercise

The first part of a business plan project is to formulate a basic identity for your business. The next part of the business plan project asks you to think about the goals of your business, some internal and external factors affecting the business, as well as the organizational structure of the business.

Exercise Background

Every business sets goals. In this part of the plan, you'll define some of the goals for your business.

This part of the business plan also asks you to perform a basic SWOT analysis for your business. A SWOT analysis looks at the business's *strengths, weaknesses, opportunities*, and *threats*. The strengths and weaknesses are internal factors—things that the business can control. The opportunities and threats are generally external factors that affect the business:

Sociocultural forces	Will changes in population or culture help your business or hurt it?
Economic forces	Will changes in the economy help your business or hurt it?
Technological forces	Will changes in technology help your business or hurt it?
Competitive forces	Does your business face much competition or very little?
Political-legal forces	Will changes in laws help your business or hurt it?

Each of these forces will affect different businesses in different ways, and some of these may not apply to your business at all.

This part of the business plan also asks you to determine how the business is to be run. Part of this will require you to create an organizational chart to get you thinking about the different tasks needed for a successful business. You'll also examine various factors relating to operating your business.

Your Assignment

For the purposes of this assignment, you need to answer the following questions:

33. Provide a brief mission statement for your business.

Hint: Be sure to include the name of your business, how you will stand out from your competition, and why a customer will buy from you.

34. Consider the goals for your business. What are three of your business goals for the first year? What are two intermediate to long-term goals?

Hint: Be as specific and realistic as possible with the goals you set. For example, if you plan on selling a service, how many customers do you want by the end of the first year, and how much do you want each customer to spend?

35. Perform a basic SWOT analysis for your business, listing its main strengths, weaknesses, opportunities, and threats.

Hint: We explained previously what factors you should consider in your basic SWOT analysis. Look around at your world, talk to classmates, or talk to your instructor for other ideas in performing your SWOT analysis.

36. Who will manage the business? Think about how many *levels* of management as well as what *kinds* of managers your business needs.

37. Show how the "team" fits together by creating a simple organizational chart for your business. Your chart should indicate who will work for each manager as well as each person's job title.

    Hint: As you create your organizational chart, consider the different tasks involved in the business. Whom will each person report to?

38. Create a floor plan of the business. What does it look like when you walk through the door?

    Hint: When sketching your floor plan, consider where equipment, supplies, and furniture will be located.

39. Explain what types of raw materials and supplies you will need to run your business. How will you produce your good or service? What equipment do you need? What hours will you operate?

    Hint: Refer to the discussion of operations in this chapter for information to get you started.

40. What steps will you take to ensure that the quality of the product or service stays at a high level? Who will be responsible for maintaining quality standards?

    Hint: Refer to the discussion of quality improvement and TQM in this chapter for information to get you started.

MyBizLab

Go to the Assignments section of your MyLab to complete these writing exercises.

41. What is operations management? Define the term "utility" and describe how operations creates various forms of utility, providing an example of each. How is operations management more complex when providing services?

42. Successful business leaders say that any business's success depends on the matchup (or compatibility) between its operations capabilities and its overall business strategy. That is, major competitive weaknesses exist when operations capabilities are not consistent with or conflict with company strategy. In contrast, successful companies ensure that operations are designed to support overall strategy. Compare and contrast two companies that have chosen different strategies for attracting customers, as follows: (a) Describe the differences in their strategies. (b) Identify and describe key operations capabilities and characteristics for each company. (c) Explain for each company how its operations characteristics either support its strategy, or how those characteristics do not support its overall strategy.

end notes

[1]"Number of Airline Passengers Declines 11.8 Percent," *Credit Unions Online*, May 15, 2009, at http://www.creditunionsonline.com/news/2009/Number-of-Airline-Passengers-Declines-11.8-Percent.html; Charisse Jones, "U.S. Airlines Flew Fewer Passengers in 2009," *USATODAY.com*, March 12, 2010, at http://www.usatoday.com/travel/flights/2010-03-12-airtravel12_ST_N.htm; Gary Stoller, "Extra Fees Add to Travelers' Distain for Bigger Airlines," *USATODAY.com*, April 15, 2010, at http://travel.usatoday.com/flights/2010-09-15-airline-complaints15_ST2_N.htm.

[2]Gary Stoller, "Extra Fees Add to Travelers' Disdain for Bigger Airlines," *USATODAY.com*, April 15, 2010, at http://travel.usatoday.com/flights/2010-09-15-airlinecomplaints15_ST2_N.htm.

[3]Karen Aho, "2012 Customer service Hall of fame," *MSN Money*, July 9, 2012, at http://money.msn.com/investing/2012-customer-service-hall-of-fame-1;Valaer

Murray, "Most-Complained-About Airlines," *Travel And Leisure.com*, June 2010, at http://www.travelandleisure.com/articles/most-complained-about-airlines/1; "Air Travel Consumer Report," *Office of Aviation Enforcement and Proceedings: U.S. Department of Transportation*, November 9, 2010, at http://airconsumer.dot.gov/reports/index.htm.

[4] *"Corporate Fact Sheet." Southwest Airlines Co.* Accessed April 28, 2015. http://www.swamedia.com/channels/Corporate-Fact-Sheet/pages/ corporate-fact-sheet.

[5] "Air Travel Consumer Report," *Office of Aviation Enforcement and Proceedings: U.S. Department of Transportation*, April 2015, at http://www.dot.gov/sites/dot.gov/files/docs/2015AprilATCR1.pdf.

[6] General Electric Company, *Annual Report for Year Ended Dec. 31, 2014, FORM 10-K*, (U.S. Securities and Exchange Commission, March 2, 2015).

[7] 2013 Global Manufacturing Competitiveness Index, Deloitte Touche Tohmatsu Limited, at http://www.deloitte.com/assets/Dcom-Gloal/Local%20Assets/Documents/Manufacturing/dttl_2013%20Global%20Manufacturing%20Competitiveness%20Index_11_15_12.pdf, accessed on March 1, 2013.

[8] Alex Hill and Terry Hill, *Manufacturing Operations Strategy*, 4th edition (Basingstoke, UK: Palgrave Macmillan, 2015); James A. Fitzsimmons, Mona J. Fitzsimmons, *Service Management: Operations Strategy, Information Technology*, 8th edition (Boston: Irwin McGraw-Hill, 2015).

[9] Stein, Joel. 2008. "Outsourcing Home Cooking." Time 171, no. 6: 61. Business Source Premier, EBSCOhost (accessed April 29, 2015).

[10] Martin Santa, "Slowing Car Production Prompts Slovak Industrial Output Decline," *Reuters.com*, February 8, 2013, at http://www.reuters.com/article/2013/02/08/slovakia-economy-idUSL5N0B85G120130208; Jack Ewing, "The Auto Slump Hits Slovakia," *SPIEGEL ONLINE*, June 19, 2009 at http://www.spiegel.de/international/business/0,1518,druck-631388,00.html; Gail Edmondson, Willam Boston, Andrea Zammert, "Detroit East," *BusinessWeek*, July 25, 2005, at http://www.businessweek.com/print/magazine/content/05_30/b3944003.htm?chan=gl/.

[11] American Society for Quality, "ASQ Glossary of Terms," at asq.org/glossary/q.html, accessed on February 25, 2013.

[12] "How We Make Chocolate," at http://www.godiva.com/experience-godiva/HowWeMakeChocolate_Rich Article,default,pg.html, accessed on February 25, 2013.

[13] "About Collette" and "Ways to Tour," *Collette Vacations* at www.collettevacations.com, accessed July 24, 2013.

[14] Cable, Josh. "GM, Ford and Chrysler Strive to Become The Lean Three." Industry Week, November 15, 2009. Accessed April 30, 2015. http://www.industryweek.com/articles/gm_ford_and_chrysler_strive_to_become_the_lean_three_20441.aspx.

[15] Valdes-Dapena, Peter. "GM to pull the plug on Pontiac." CNN Money. Last modified April 27, 2009. Accessed April 30, 2015. http://money.cnn.com/2009/04/24/ autos/pontiac_obit/.

[16] Muaddi, Nadeem. "Ford to Discontinue Mercury Brand." U.S. News and World Report, May 28, 2010. Accessed April 30, 2015. http://usnews.rankingsandreviews.com/cars-trucks/daily-news/100528-Ford-to-Discontinue-Mercury-Brand/.

[17] "International Comparisons of GDP per Capita and per Hour, 1960-2014," *U.S. Bureau of Labor Statistics*, at http://www.bls.gov/ilc/intl_gdp_capita_gdp_hour.htm#table03, accessed on March 1, 2013.

[18] "Missouri Quality Award: Fifth Win for Saint Luke's, Second Time as a Health System," November 2010, at https://www.saintlukeshealthsystem.org/article/missouri-quality-award; Del Jones, "Baldrige Award Honors Record 7 Quality Winners," *USA Today*, November 26, 2003, 6B.

[19] Tootsie Roll Industries, Inc., *Annual Report 2014* (Chicago: 2015), p. 1.

[20] Del Jones, "Baldrige Award Honors Record 7 Quality Winners," *USA Today*, November 26, 2003, 6B.

[21] "Corporate Fact Sheet." Southwest Airlines Co. Accessed April 28, 2015. http://www.swamedia.com/channels/Corporate-Fact-Sheet/pages/corporate-fact-sheet. Food and Agriculture Organization of the United Nations. "Food waste harms climate, water, land and biodiversity – new FAO report." News release. Accessed April 30, 2015. http://www.fao.org/news/story/en/item/196220/icode/.

[22] Nicholas Carlson, "How Marissa Mayer Figured Out Work-At-Home Yahoos Were Slacking Off," *Business Insider*, March 2, 2013 at http://www.businessinsider.com/how-marissa-mayer-figured-out-work-at-home-yahoos-were-slacking-off-2013-3.

[23] Neil Shah, "More Americans Working Remotely," *Wall Street Journal*, March 3, 2013, A3.

[24] Leanne Italie, "Yahoo Ban Turns Spotlight on Telecommuting," *Fort Worth Star Telegram*, March 9, 2013 at http://www.star-telegram.com/2013/03/09/4671879/yahoo-ban-turns-spotlight-on-telecommuting.html.

[25] "Yahoo CEO Marissa Mayer Demands Telecommuters Report to Office," *Huffington Post Business*, February 23, 2013 at http://www.huffingtonpost.com/2013/02/23/yahoo-working-remote_n_2750698.html.

[26] Rachel Emma Silverman, "Tracking Sensors Invade the Workplace," *Wall Street Journal*, March 7, 2013, B1–B2.

glossary

Assembly Line Layout a same-steps layout in which a product moves step by step through a plant on conveyor belts or other equipment until it is completed.

Business Process Reengineering rethinking and radical re-design of business processes to improve performance, quality, and productivity.

Capacity competence required of individuals entering into a binding contract.

Competitive Product Analysis process by which a company analyzes a competitor's products to identify desirable improvements.

Consistency dimension of quality that refers to sameness of product quality from unit to unit.

Detailed Schedule schedule showing daily work assignments with start and stop times for assigned jobs.

Fixed-Position Layout labor, equipment, materials, and other resources are brought to the geographic location where all production work is done.

Follow-Up operations control activity for ensuring that production decisions are being implemented.

Gantt Chart production schedule that breaks down large projects into steps to be performed and specifies the time required to perform each step.

Goods Operations (Goods Production) activities producing tangible products, such as radios, newspapers, buses, and textbooks.

High-Contact System level of customer contact in which the customer is part of the system during service delivery.

Inventory Control process of receiving, storing, handling, and counting of all raw materials, partly finished goods, and finished goods.

ISO 9000 program certifying that a factory, laboratory, or office has met the quality management standards set by the International Organization for Standardization.

ISO 14000 certification program attesting to the fact that a factory, laboratory, or office has improved its environmental performance.

Just-in-Time (JIT) Production type of lean production system that brings together all materials at the precise time they are required at each production stage.

Lean Production System production system designed for smooth production flows that avoid inefficiencies, eliminate unnecessary inventories, and continuously improve production processes.

Low-Contact System level of customer contact in which the customer need not be part of the system to receive the service.

Make-To-Order Operations activities for one-of-a-kind or custom-made production.

Make-To-Stock Operations activities for producing standardized products for mass consumption.

Master Operations Schedule schedule showing which products will be produced, and when, in upcoming time periods.

Materials Management process of planning, organizing, and controlling the flow of materials from sources of supply through distribution of finished goods.

Operations Capability (Production Capability) special ability that production does especially well to outperform the competition.

Operations Control process of monitoring production performance by comparing results with plans and taking corrective action when needed.

Operations Process set of methods and technologies used to produce a good or a service.

Operations (Production) Management systematic direction and control of the activities that transform resources into finished products that create value for and provide benefits to customers.

Operations (Production) Managers managers responsible for ensuring that operations activities create value and provide benefits to customers.

Outsourcing the practice of paying suppliers and distributors to perform certain business processes or to provide needed materials or services.

Performance dimension of quality that refers to how well a product does what it is supposed to do.

PERT Chart production schedule specifying the sequence of activities, time requirements, and critical paths for performing the steps in a project.

Process Layout (Custom-Product Layout) physical arrangement of production activities that groups equipment and people according to function.

Product Layout (Same-Steps Layout) physical arrangement of production steps designed to make one type of product in a fixed sequence of activities according to its production requirements.

Productivity a measure of economic growth that compares how much a system produces with the resources needed to produce it.

Purchasing acquisition of the materials and services that a firm needs to produce its products.

Quality combination of "characteristics of a product or service that bear on its ability to satisfy stated or implied needs."

Quality Control action of ensuring that operations produce products that meet specific quality standards.

Quality Improvement Team total quality management tool in which collaborative groups of employees from various work areas work together to improve quality by solving common shared production problems.

Quality Ownership principle of total quality management that holds that quality belongs to each person who creates it while performing a job.

Service Operations (Service Production) activities producing intangible and tangible products, such as entertainment, transportation, and education.

Staff Schedule assigned working times in upcoming days for each employee on each work shift.

Supplier Selection process of finding and choosing suppliers from whom to buy.

Supply Chain Management (SCM) principle of looking at the supply chain as a whole to improve the overall flow through the system.

Supply Chain (Value Chain) flow of information, materials, and services that starts with raw-materials suppliers and continues adding value through other stages in the network of firms until the product reaches the end customer.

Total Quality Management (TQM) all activities involved in getting high-quality goods and services into the marketplace.

Transportation activities in transporting resources to the producer and finished goods to customers.

Value-Added Analysis process of evaluating all work activities, materials flows, and paperwork to determine the value that they add for customers.

Warehousing storage of incoming materials for production and finished goods for distribution to customers.

Human Resource Management and Labor Relations

From Chapter 10 of *Business Essentials*, Eleventh Edition. Ronald J. Ebert, Ricky W. Griffin. Copyright © 2017 by Pearson Education, Inc.
All rights reserved.

Human Resource Management and Labor Relations

Effective human resource management is an organization's lifeblood. Putting people **first is the best** strategy a firm can have.

After reading this chapter, you should be able to:

1 **Define** *human resource management*, discuss its strategic significance, and explain how managers plan for their organization's human resource needs.

2 **Discuss** the legal context of human resource management and identify contemporary legal issues.

3 **Identify** the steps in staffing a company and discuss ways in which organizations recruit and select new employees.

4 **Describe** the main components of a compensation and benefits system.

5 **Describe** how managers develop the workforce in their organization through training and performance appraisal.

6 **Discuss** workforce diversity, the management of knowledge workers, and the use of a contingent workforce as important changes in the contemporary workplace.

7 **Explain** why workers organize into labor unions and describe the collective bargaining process.

A Unique Partnership
Drives Wegmans

If you're looking for the best Parmesan cheese for your chicken parmigiana recipe, you might try Wegmans, especially if you happen to live in the vicinity of Pittsford, New York. Cheese department manager Carol Kent will be happy to recommend the best brand because her job calls for knowing cheese as well as managing some 20 subordinates. Kent is a knowledgeable employee, and Wegmans sees that as a key asset. Specifically, Wegmans believes that its employees are more knowledgeable than are the employees of its competitors.

Wegmans Food Markets, a family-owned East Coast chain with more than 80 stores in six states, prides itself on its commitment to customers, and it shows. It ranks at the top of the latest *Consumer Reports* survey of the best national and regional grocery stores. But commitment to customers is only half of Wegmans' overall strategy, which calls for reaching its customers through its employees. "How do we differentiate ourselves?" asks CEO Danny Wegman, who then proceeds to answer his own question: "If we can sell products that require knowledge in terms of how you use them, that's our strategy. Anything that requires knowledge and service gives us a reason to be." That's the logic behind one of Kent's recent assignments—one that she understandably regards as a perk. Wegmans sent her to Italy to conduct a personal study of Italian cheese. "We sat with the families" that make the cheeses, she recalls, "broke bread with them. It helped me understand that we're not just selling a piece of cheese. We're selling a tradition, a quality."

Kent and the employees in her department also enjoy the best benefits package in the industry, including affordable high-quality health insurance. And that includes part-timers, who make up about two-thirds of the company's workforce of more than 44,000. In part, the strategy of extending benefits to this large segment of the labor force is intended to make sure that stores have enough good workers for crucial peak periods, but there's no denying that the costs of employee-friendly policies can mount up. At 15 to 17 percent of sales, for example, Wegmans' labor costs are well above the 12 percent figure for most supermarkets. But according to one company HR executive, holding down labor costs isn't necessarily a strategic priority: "We would have stopped offering free health insurance [to part-timers] a long time ago," she admits, "if we tried to justify the costs."

Besides, employee turnover at Wegmans is about 6 percent—a mere fraction of an industry average that hovers around 19 percent (and can approach 100 percent for part-timers). And this is an industry in which total turnover costs have been known to outstrip total annual profits by 40 percent. Wegmans

Kurhan/Fotolia

what's in it for me?

Do you—or will you in the future—work for someone else as an employee? Do you—or will you in the future—own a business and have employees who work for you? In either case, human resource management is a critical activity for you to understand. Effectively managing human resources is the lifeblood of organizations. A firm that takes this activity seriously and approaches it from a strategic perspective has a much better chance for success than does a firm that simply goes through the motions. By understanding the material in this chapter, you'll be better able to understand (1) the importance of properly managing human resources in a unit or business you own or supervise and (2) why and how your employer provides the working arrangements that most directly affect you.

We start this chapter by explaining how managers plan for their organization's human resource needs. We'll also discuss ways in which organizations select, develop, and

187

appraise employee performance and examine the main components of a compensation system. Along the way, we'll look at some key legal issues involved in hiring, compensating, and managing workers in today's workplace and discuss workforce diversity. Finally, we'll explain why workers organize into labor unions and describe the collective bargaining process. Let's get started with some basic concepts of human resource management.

employees tend to be knowledgeable because about 20 percent of them have been with the company for at least ten years, and many have logged at least a quarter century. Says one 19-year-old college student who works at an upstate-New York Wegmans while pursuing a career as a high school history teacher, "I love this place. If teaching doesn't work out, I would so totally work at Wegmans." Edward McLaughlin, who directs the Food Industry Management Program at Cornell University, understands this sort of attitude: "When you're a 16-year-old kid, the last thing you want to do is wear a geeky shirt and work for a supermarket," but at Wegmans, he explains, "it's a badge of honor. You're not a geeky cashier. You're part of the social fabric."

Wegmans recently placed seventh in *Fortune* magazine's annual list of "100 Best Companies to Work For"—a list that they've been on every year since 1998. "It says that we're doing something right," says a company spokesperson, "and that there's no better way to take care of our customers than to be a great place for our employees to work." In addition to its healthcare package, Wegmans has been cited for such perks as fitness center discounts, compressed workweeks, telecommuting, and domestic-partner benefits (which extend to same-sex partners).

Finally, under the company's Employee Scholarship Program, full-time workers can receive up to $2,200 a year for four years and part-timers up to $1,500. Since its inception in 1984, the program has handed out $100 million in scholarships to more than 32,000 employees. Like most Wegman policies, this one combines employee outreach with long-term corporate strategy: "This program has made a real difference in the lives of many young people," says president Colleen Wegman, who adds that it's also "one of the reasons we've been able to attract the best and the brightest to work at Wegmans."

Granted, Wegmans, which has remained in family hands since its founding in 1915, has an advantage in being as generous with its resources as its family of top executives wants to be. It doesn't have to do everything with quarterly profits in mind, and the firm likes to point out that taking care of its employees is a long-standing priority. Profit sharing and fully funded medical coverage were introduced in 1950 by Robert Wegman, son and nephew of brothers Walter and John, who opened the firm's original flagship store in Rochester, New York, in 1930. Why did Robert Wegman make such generous gestures to his employees way back then? "Because," he says simply, "I was no different from them."[1] (After studying the content of this chapter, you should be able to answer the set of discussion questions found at the end of the chapter.)

The Foundations of Human Resource Management

OBJECTIVE 1
Define

human resource management, discuss its strategic significance, and explain how managers plan for their organization's human resource needs.

Human Resource Management (HRM) *set of organizational activities directed at attracting, developing, and maintaining an effective workforce*

Human Resources (HR) *the people comprising an organization's workforce*

Human resource management (HRM) is the set of organizational activities directed at attracting, developing, and maintaining an effective workforce. In recent years, experts have come to appreciate the strategic importance of HRM as well as the need for systematic human resource planning.

The Strategic Importance of HRM

Human resources (HR) are the people comprising an organization's workforce. Human resources are critical for effective organizational functioning. HRM (or "personnel," as it is sometimes called) was once relegated to second-class status in many organizations, but its importance has grown dramatically in the last two decades. Its new importance stems from increased legal complexities, the recognition that HR are a valuable means for improving productivity, and the awareness of the costs associated with poor HRM.[2] For example, during the last ten years, Microsoft has announced two different large-scale layoffs (one numbering 5,000 and the other 14,000 employees), mostly individuals working in software development. At the same time, though, the firm has continued to expand and hire highly talented people for jobs related to Internet search and network integration, important growth areas for the company. This careful and systematic approach, reducing employees in areas where they are no longer needed and adding new talent to key growth areas, reflects a strategic approach to HRM.

Indeed, managers now realize that the effectiveness of their HR function has a substantial impact on the bottom-line performance of the firm. Poor HR planning can result in spurts of hiring followed by layoffs, which are costly in terms of unemployment compensation payments, training expenses, and morale. Haphazard compensation systems do not attract, keep, and motivate good employees, and outmoded recruitment practices can expose the firm to expensive and embarrassing discrimination lawsuits. Consequently, the chief HR executive of most large businesses is a vice president directly accountable to the CEO, and many firms are developing strategic HR plans and integrating those plans with other strategic planning activities.[3]

Even organizations with as few as 200 employees usually have a HR manager and a HR department charged with overseeing these activities. Responsibility for HR activities, however, is shared between the HR department and line managers. The HR department may recruit and initially screen candidates, but the final selection is usually made by managers in the department where the new employee will work. Similarly, although the HR department may establish performance appraisal policies and procedures, the actual evaluation and coaching of employees are done by their immediate superiors.

The growing awareness of the strategic significance of HRM has even led to new terminology to reflect a firm's commitment to people. **Human capital** reflects the organization's investment in attracting, retaining, and motivating an effective workforce. Hence, just as the phrase *financial capital* is an indicator of a firm's financial resources and reserves, so, too, does *human capital* serve as a tangible indicator of the value of the people who comprise an organization.[4] Similarly, some managers today talk about talent management. **Talent management** reflects the view that the people in an organization represent a portfolio of valuable talents that can be effectively managed and tapped in ways best targeted to organizational success.

Human Capital *reflects the organization's investment in attracting, retaining, and motivating an effective workforce*

Talent Management *the view that the people in an organization represent a portfolio of valuable talents that can be effectively managed and tapped in ways best targeted to organizational success*

HR Planning

As you can see in Figure 1, the starting point in attracting qualified HR is planning. Specifically, HR planning involves job analysis and forecasting the demand for, and supply of, labor.

Job Analysis **Job analysis** is a systematic analysis of jobs within an organization; most firms have trained experts who handle these analyses. A job analysis results in two things:

Job Analysis *systematic analysis of jobs within an organization*

- The **job description** lists the duties and responsibilities of a job; its working conditions; and the tools, materials, equipment, and information used to perform it.

- The **job specification** lists the skills, abilities, and other credentials and qualifications needed to perform the job effectively.

Job Description *description of the duties and responsibilities of a job, its working conditions, and the tools, materials, equipment, and information used to perform it*

Job analysis information is used in many HRM activities. For instance, knowing about job content and job requirements is necessary to develop appropriate selection methods, create job-relevant performance appraisal systems, and set equitable compensation rates.

Job Specification *description of the skills, abilities, and other credentials and qualifications required by a job*

Forecasting HR Demand and Supply After managers comprehend the jobs to be performed within an organization, they can start planning for the organization's future HR needs. The manager starts by assessing trends in past HR usage, future organizational plans, and general economic trends.

FIGURE 1 The HR Planning Process

Forecasting the supply of labor is really two tasks:

1 Forecasting *internal supply*, the number and type of employees who will be in the firm at some future date

2 Forecasting *external supply*, the number and type of people who will be available for hiring from the labor market at large

REPLACEMENT CHARTS At higher levels of an organization, managers plan for specific people and positions. The technique most commonly used is the **replacement chart**, which lists each important managerial position, who occupies it, how long that person will probably stay in it before moving on, and who is now qualified or soon will be qualified to move into it. (In most firms today, this information is computerized.) This technique allows ample time to plan developmental experiences for people identified as potential successors for critical managerial jobs. Halliburton, for instance, has a detailed replacement system that the firm calls its Executive Succession System (ESS). When a manager has his or her performance reviewed each year, notations are placed in the system about the person's readiness for promotion, potential positions for promotion, and what development activities are needed to prepare the individual for promotion. Other managers throughout the firm can access the system whenever they have positions available.

SKILLS INVENTORIES To facilitate both planning and identifying people for transfer or promotion, some organizations also have **employee information systems (skills inventories)** that contain information on each employee's education, skills, work experience, and career aspirations. Such a system can quickly locate every employee who is qualified to fill a position. Again, although these systems were once handled with charts and files, they are almost always in electronic form today.

Forecasting the external supply of labor is a different problem altogether. Planners must rely on information from outside sources, such as state employment commissions, government reports, and figures supplied by colleges on the numbers of students in major fields.

Matching HR Supply and Demand After comparing future demand and internal supply, managers can make plans to manage predicted shortfalls or overstaffing. If a shortfall is predicted, new employees can be hired, present employees can be retrained and transferred into understaffed areas, individuals approaching

Replacement Chart *list of each management position, who occupies it, how long that person will likely stay in the job, and who is qualified as a replacement*

Employee Information System (Skills Inventory) *computerized system containing information on each employee's education, skills, work experiences, and career aspirations*

retirement can be convinced to stay on, or labor-saving or productivity-enhancing systems can be installed. If overstaffing is expected to be a problem, the main options are transferring the extra employees, not replacing individuals who quit, encouraging early retirement, and laying off workers. During the recent Great Recession, many firms found it necessary to reduce the size of their workforces through layoffs. Others accomplished the same thing by reducing the number of hours their employees worked.

The Legal Context of HRM

OBJECTIVE 2
Discuss
the legal context of human resource management and identify contemporary legal issues.

A number of laws regulate various aspects of employee–employer relations, especially in the areas of equal employment opportunity, compensation and benefits, labor relations, and occupational safety and health. Several major ones are summarized in Table 1.

Equal Employment Opportunity

Title VII of the Civil Rights Act of 1964 forbids discrimination in all areas of the employment relationship, such as hiring, opportunities for advancement, compensation increases, layoffs, and terminations against members of certain protected classes

Title VII of the Civil Rights Act of 1964 forbids discrimination in all areas of the employment relationship

table 1 Major Laws and Regulations Affecting Human Resource Management

Equal Employment Opportunity

Title VII of the Civil Rights Act of 1964 (as amended by the Equal Employment Opportunity Act of 1972). Forbids discrimination in all areas of the employment relationship.

Age Discrimination in Employment Act. Outlaws discrimination against people older than 40 years.

Various executive orders, especially Executive Order 11246 in 1965. Requires employers with government contracts to engage in affirmative action.

Pregnancy Discrimination Act. Specifically outlaws discrimination on the basis of pregnancy.

Vietnam Era Veterans Readjustment Assistance Act. Extends affirmative action mandate to military veterans who served during the Vietnam War.

Americans with Disabilities Act. Specifically outlaws discrimination against disabled persons.

Civil Rights Act of 1991. Makes it easier for employees to sue an organization for discrimination but limits punitive damage awards if they win.

Compensation and Benefits

Fair Labor Standards Act. Establishes minimum wage and mandated overtime pay for work in excess of 40 hours per week.

Equal Pay Act of 1963. Requires that men and women be paid the same amount for doing the same job.

Employee Retirement Income Security Act (ERISA) of 1974. Regulates how organizations manage their pension funds.

Family and Medical Leave Act (FMLA) of 1993. Requires employers to provide up to 12 weeks of unpaid leave for family and medical emergencies.

Labor Relations

National Labor Relations Act. Spells out procedures by which employees can establish labor unions and requires organizations to bargain collectively with legally formed unions; also known as the *Wagner Act.*

Labor-Management Relations Act. Limits union power and specifies management rights during a union-organizing campaign; also known as the *Taft-Hartley Act.*

Health and Safety

Occupational Safety and Health Act (OSHA) of 1970. Mandates the provision of safe working conditions.

based on factors such as race, color, gender, religious beliefs, or national origin. The intent of Title VII is to ensure that employment decisions are made on the basis of an individual's qualifications rather than on the basis of personal biases. The law has reduced direct forms of discrimination (refusing to promote African Americans into management, failing to hire men as flight attendants, refusing to hire women as construction workers) as well as indirect forms of discrimination (using employment tests that Caucasians pass at a higher rate than do African Americans). Note, however, that managers are free to base employment decisions on such job-related factors as qualifications, performance, seniority, and so forth. For example, an organization can certainly hire a male job applicant instead of a female applicant if he is more qualified (i.e., has more education and/or experience related to the job). However, he cannot be hired simply because of his gender.

Employment requirements such as test scores and other qualifications are legally defined as having an adverse impact on minorities and women when such individuals meet or pass the requirement at a rate less than 80 percent of the rate of majority group members. Criteria that have an **adverse impact** on protected groups can be used only when there is solid evidence that they effectively identify individuals who are better able than others to do the job. The **Equal Employment Opportunity Commission (EEOC)** is charged with enforcing Title VII as well as several other employment-related laws.

The **Age Discrimination in Employment Act**, passed in 1967, amended in 1978 and 1986, is an attempt to prevent organizations from discriminating against older workers. In its current form, it outlaws discrimination against people older than 40 years. Both the Age Discrimination in Employment Act and Title VII require passive nondiscrimination, or **equal employment opportunity**. Employers are not required to seek out and hire minorities, but they must treat all who apply fairly.

Several executive orders, however, require that employers holding government contracts engage in **affirmative action**, intentionally seeking and hiring employees from groups that are underrepresented in the organization. These organizations must have a written **affirmative action plan** that spells out employment goals for underused groups and how those goals will be met. These employers are also required to act affirmatively in hiring Vietnam-era veterans (as a result of the Vietnam Era Veterans Readjustment Assistance Act) and qualified disabled individuals. Finally, the Pregnancy Discrimination Act forbids discrimination against women who are pregnant.

In 1990, Congress passed the **Americans with Disabilities Act**, which forbids discrimination on the basis of disabilities and requires employers to provide reasonable accommodations for disabled employees.

More recently, the **Civil Rights Act of 1991** amended the original Civil Rights Act as well as other related laws by making it easier to bring discrimination lawsuits while simultaneously limiting the amount of punitive damages that can be awarded in those lawsuits.

Compensation and Benefits

Laws also regulate compensation and benefits. The **Fair Labor Standards Act**, passed in 1938 and amended frequently since then, sets a minimum wage and requires the payment of overtime rates for work in excess of 40 hours per week. Salaried professional, executive, and administrative employees are exempt from the minimum hourly wage and overtime provisions. The **Equal Pay Act of 1963** requires that men and women be paid the same amount for doing the same job. Attempts to circumvent the law by having different job titles and pay rates for men and women who perform the same work are also illegal. Basing an employee's pay on seniority or performance is legal, however, even if it means that a man and woman are paid different amounts for doing the same job.

The provision of benefits is also regulated in some ways by state and federal laws. Certain benefits are mandatory, such as workers' compensation insurance for employees who are injured on the job. Employers who provide a pension plan

Adverse Impact *when minorities and women meet or pass the requirement for a job at a rate less than 80 percent of the rate of majority group members*

Equal Employment Opportunity Commission (EEOC) *federal agency enforcing several discrimination-related laws*

Age Discrimination in Employment Act *outlaws discrimination against people older than 40 years*

Equal Employment Opportunity *legally mandated nondiscrimination in employment on the basis of race, creed, sex, or national origin*

Affirmative Action *intentionally seeking and hiring employees from groups that are underrepresented in the organization*

Affirmative Action Plan *written statement of how the organization intends to actively recruit, hire, and develop members of relevant protected classes*

Americans with Disabilities Act *forbids discrimination on the basis of disabilities and requires employers to provide reasonable accommodations for disabled employees*

Civil Rights Act of 1991 *amended the original Civil Rights Act*

Fair Labor Standards Act *sets a minimum wage and requires the payment of overtime rates for work in excess of 40 hours per week*

Equal Pay Act of 1963 *requires that men and women be paid the same amount for doing the same job*

for their employees are regulated by the **Employee Retirement Income Security Act (ERISA) of 1974**. The purpose of this act is to help ensure the financial security of pension funds by regulating how they can be invested. The **Family and Medical Leave Act (FMLA) of 1993** requires employers to provide up to 12 weeks of unpaid leave for family and medical emergencies.

In the last few years, some large employers, most notably Walmart, have come under fire because they do not provide health care for all of their employees. In response to this, the state of Maryland passed a law, informally called the "Walmart bill," that requires employers with more than 10,000 workers to spend at least 8 percent of their payrolls on health care or else pay a comparable amount into a general fund for uninsured workers. Walmart appealed this rule and the case is still pending; meanwhile, several other states are considering the passage of similar laws.[5]

> **Employee Retirement Income Security Act (ERISA) of 1974** *ensures the financial security of pension funds by regulating how they can be invested*

> **Family and Medical Leave Act (FMLA) of 1993** *requires employers to provide up to 12 weeks of unpaid leave for family and medical emergencies*

Labor Relations

Union activities and management's behavior toward unions constitute another heavily regulated area. The **National Labor Relations Act** (also known as the **Wagner Act**), passed in 1935, sets up a procedure for employees to vote on whether to have a union. If they vote for a union, management is required to bargain collectively with the union. The **National Labor Relations Board (NLRB)** was established by the Wagner Act to enforce its provisions. Following a series of severe strikes in 1946, the **Labor-Management Relations Act** (also known as the **Taft-Hartley Act**) was passed in 1947 to limit union power. The law increases management's rights during an organizing campaign. The Taft-Hartley Act also contains the National Emergency Strike provision, which allows the president of the United States to prevent or end a strike that endangers national security. Taken together, these laws balance union and management power. Employees can be represented by a legally created and managed union, but the business can make non-employee-related business decisions without interference.

> **National Labor Relations Act** (*also known as the* **Wagner Act**) *sets up a procedure for employees to vote on whether to have a union*

> **National Labor Relations Board (NLRB)** *established by the Wagner Act to enforce its provisions*

> **Labor-Management Relations Act** (*also known as the* **Taft-Hartley Act**) *passed to limit union power*

Health and Safety

The **Occupational Safety and Health Act (OSHA) of 1970** directly mandates the provision of safe working conditions. It requires that employers (1) provide a place of employment that is free from hazards that may cause death or serious physical harm and (2) obey the safety and health standards established by the Department of Labor. Safety standards are intended to prevent accidents, whereas occupational health standards are concerned with preventing occupational disease. For example, standards limit the concentration of cotton dust in the air because this contaminant has been associated with lung disease in textile workers. The standards are enforced by OSHA inspections, which are conducted when an employee files a complaint of unsafe conditions or when a serious accident occurs.

> **Occupational Safety and Health Act (OSHA) of 1970** *federal law setting and enforcing guidelines for protecting workers from unsafe conditions and potential health hazards in the workplace*

Spot inspections of plants in especially hazardous industries such as mining and chemicals are also made. Employers who fail to meet OSHA standards may be fined. A Miami-based company, Lead Enterprises Inc., was cited by OSHA as knowingly failing to protect employees from lead exposure despite knowing the potential hazards (brain damage, kidney disease, and reproductive system damage). The company, which produces various lead products, including fish tackles and lead diving weights, was cited for 32 safety and health violations after multiple inspections and fined more than $307,000 in penalties.[6] More recently, a massive explosion at a fertilizer plant in the town of West, Texas, in 2013 may have been partially caused by unsafe work practices. Moreover, preliminary evidence suggested that OSHA inspectors had also missed some warning signs of a potential disaster at the plant.

Other Legal Issues

In addition to these established areas of HR legal regulation, several emerging legal issues will likely become more important in the future. These include employee safety and health, various emerging areas of discrimination law, employee rights, and employment at will.

AIDS in the Workplace Although AIDS is considered a disability under the Americans with Disabilities Act of 1990, the AIDS situation itself is severe enough that it warrants special attention. Employers cannot legally require an HIV test or any other medical examination as a condition for making an offer of employment. Organizations must accommodate or make a good-faith effort to accommodate individuals with HIV, maintain the confidentiality of all medical records, and try to educate coworkers about AIDS.

Sexual Harassment **Sexual harassment** is defined by the EEOC as unwelcome sexual advances in the work environment. If the conduct is indeed unwelcome and occurs with sufficient frequency to create an abusive work environment, the employer is responsible for changing the environment by warning, reprimanding, or firing the harasser. The courts have defined two types of sexual harassment:

> **Sexual Harassment** *making unwelcome sexual advances in the workplace*

1. In cases of **quid pro quo harassment**, the harasser offers to exchange something of value for sexual favors. A male supervisor, for example, might tell or suggest to a female subordinate that he will recommend her for promotion or give her a raise in exchange for sexual favors.

> **Quid Pro Quo Harassment** *form of sexual harassment in which sexual favors are requested in return for job-related benefits*

2. The creation of a **hostile work environment** is a more subtle form of sexual harassment. A group of male employees who continually make off-color jokes and lewd comments and perhaps decorate the work environment with inappropriate photographs may create a hostile work environment for a female colleague, who may become uncomfortable working in that environment.

> **Hostile Work Environment** *form of sexual harassment deriving from off-color jokes, lewd comments, and so forth*

In recent years, the concept of harassment has been expanded to encompass unwelcome or inappropriate behaviors regarding ethnicity, religion, and age.

Employment at Will The concept of **employment at will** holds that both employer and employee have the mutual right to terminate an employment relationship at any time for any reason, with or without advance notice to the other. Over the last two decades, however, terminated employees have challenged the employment-at-will doctrine by filing lawsuits against former employers on the grounds of wrongful discharge.

> **Employment at will** *principle, increasingly modified by legislation and judicial decision, that organizations should be able to retain or dismiss employees at their discretion*

In the last several years, such suits have put limits on employment-at-will provisions in certain circumstances. In the past, for example, organizations were guilty of firing employees who filed workers' compensation claims or took "excessive" time off to serve on jury duty. More recently, however, the courts have ruled that employees may not be fired for exercising rights protected by law.

The Patriot Act In response to the terrorist attacks of September 11, 2001, the U.S. government passed legislation that increases its powers to investigate and prosecute suspected terrorists. This legislation, known as the **Patriot Act**, has several key implications for HRM. For instance, certain "restricted" individuals (including ex-convicts and aliens from countries deemed by the State Department to have "repeatedly provided support for acts of international terrorism") are ineligible to work with potentially dangerous biological agents. More controversial are sections granting government investigators access to previously confidential personal and financial records.

> **Patriot Act** *legislation that increased U.S. government's power to investigate and prosecute suspected terrorists*

OBJECTIVE 3
Identify
the steps in staffing a company and discuss ways in which organizations recruit and select new employees.

Staffing the Organization

When managers have determined that new employees are needed and understand the legal context in which they operate, they must then turn their attention to recruiting and hiring the right mix of people. This involves two processes: (1) acquiring new employees from outside the company and (2) promoting current employees from within. Both external and internal staffing, however, start with effective *recruiting*.

Recruiting Employees

Recruiting is the process of attracting qualified persons to apply for the jobs that are open.

Internal Recruiting **Internal recruiting** means considering present employees as candidates for openings. Promotion from within can help build morale and keep high-quality employees from leaving. For higher-level positions, a skills inventory system may be used to identify internal candidates, or managers may be asked to recommend individuals to be considered.

External Recruiting **External recruiting** involves attracting people outside the organization to apply for jobs. External recruiting methods include posting jobs on the company website or other job sites, such as Monster.com; holding campus interviews for potential college recruits; using employment agencies or executive search firms to scout for potential talent; seeking referrals by present employees; advertising in print publications; and hiring "walk-ins" (unsolicited applicants).

The organization must also keep in mind that recruiting decisions often go both ways—the organization is recruiting an employee, but the prospective employee is also selecting a job.[7] For instance, when unemployment is low (meaning fewer people are seeking work), businesses may have to work harder to attract new employees. But when unemployment is higher (meaning more people are looking for work), organizations may find it easier to recruit prospective employees without having to resort to expensive hiring incentives. But even if a firm can take its pick of the best potential employees, it still should put its best foot forward, treat all applicants with dignity, and strive for a good person–job fit. Hiring the wrong employee can cost the company about half of a low-skilled worker's annual wages or three to five times upper-level employees' annual wages. Therefore, hiring the "wrong" employee for $50,000 per year could cost the company at least $25,000. These costs stem from training, counseling, low productivity, termination, and recruiting and hiring a replacement.

One generally successful method for facilitating a good person–job fit is the so-called **realistic job preview (RJP)**. As the term suggests, the RJP involves providing the applicant with a real picture of what performing the job that the organization is trying to fill would be like.[7] For example, it would not make sense for a firm to tell an applicant that the job is exciting and challenging when in fact it is routine and straightforward, yet some managers do this to hire the best people. The likely outcome is a dissatisfied employee who will quickly start looking for a better job. If the company is more realistic about a job, though, the person hired will be more likely to remain in the job for a longer period of time.

Selecting Employees

Once the recruiting process has attracted a pool of applicants, the next step is to select someone to hire. The intent of the selection process is to gather from applicants the information that will predict job success and then to hire the candidates likely to be most successful.

Application Forms The first step in selection is usually asking the candidate to fill out an application. An application form is an efficient method of gathering information about the applicant's previous work history, educational background, and other job-related demographic data. Application forms are seldom used for upper-level jobs; candidates for such positions usually provide the same information on their résumé. Most applications for larger firms are now prepared online and submitted at the firm's website.

Tests Employers sometimes ask candidates to take tests during the selection process. Tests of ability, skill, aptitude, or knowledge relevant to a particular job are usually the best predictors of job success, although tests of general intelligence or

Recruiting *process of attracting qualified persons to apply for jobs an organization is seeking to fill*

Internal Recruiting *considering present employees as candidates for openings*

External Recruiting *attracting persons outside the organization to apply for jobs*

Realistic Job Preview (RJP) *providing the applicant with a real picture of what it would be like performing the job the organization is trying to fill*

personality are occasionally useful as well. Some companies use a test of the "Big Five" personality dimensions (or other personality measures) to predict success.

Interviews *Interviews* are a popular selection device, although they are actually often a poor predictor of job success. For example, biases inherent in the way people perceive and judge others when they first meet affect subsequent evaluations. Interview validity can be improved by training interviewers to be aware of potential biases and by tightening the structure of the interview. In a structured interview, questions are written in advance, and all interviewers follow the same question list with each candidate. Structured interviews tend to be used for jobs that are relatively routine, such as some administrative assistant positions, data entry jobs, and college admissions processing positions. For interviewing managerial or professional candidates, a somewhat less structured approach can be used. Although question areas and information-gathering objectives are still planned in advance, specific questions vary with the candidates' backgrounds. Sometimes, companies are looking for especially creative employees and may try to learn more about the individual's creativity during an interview.

Other Techniques Organizations also use other selection techniques that vary with circumstances. Polygraph tests, once popular, are declining in popularity. On the other hand, organizations occasionally require applicants to take physical exams (being careful that their practices are consistent with the Americans with Disabilities Act). More organizations are using drug tests, especially in situations in which drug-related performance problems could create serious safety hazards. For example, potential employees who may be handling hazardous chemicals or medical waste or engaging in public transportation activities like driving busses are likely to be drug tested. Some organizations also run credit checks on prospective employees. Reference checks with previous employers are also used, but they have been shown to have limited value because individuals are likely to only provide the names of references that will give them positive recommendations. Even worse, some applicants literally make up references.[8]

OBJECTIVE 4
Describe
the main components of a compensation and benefits system.

Compensation and Benefits

Compensation System *total package of rewards that organizations provide to individuals in return for their labor*

People who work for a business expect to be paid, and most workers today also expect certain benefits from their employers. Indeed, a major factor in retaining skilled workers is a company's **compensation system**, the total package of rewards that it offers employees in return for their labor. Finding the right combination of compensation elements is always complicated by the need to make employees feel valued, while holding down company costs.

Wages and Salaries

Wages *compensation in the form of money paid for time worked*

Salary *compensation in the form of money paid for discharging the responsibilities of a job*

Wages and salaries are the dollar amounts paid to employees for their labor. **Wages** are paid for time worked. For example, if your job pays you $10 an hour, that is your wage. A **salary**, on the other hand, is paid for performing a job. A salaried executive earning $100,000 per year is paid to achieve results even if that means working 5 hours one day and 15 the next. Salaries are usually expressed as an amount paid per month or year.

In setting wage and salary levels, a company may start by looking at its competitors. Firms must also decide how their internal wage and salary levels will compare for different jobs. Although two employees may do exactly the same job, the employee with more experience may earn more.

The Great Recession of 2008–2011 prompted some firms to reduce the wages and salaries they were paying to lower costs. For example, Hewlett-Packard reduced the salaries of all but its top performers by amounts ranging from 2.5 to 20 percent.

CareerBuilder.com reduced all employee pay but also began giving all employees Friday afternoons off.

Incentive Programs

Studies have shown that beyond a certain point, more money will not produce better performance. Money motivates employees only if it is tied directly to performance. The most common method of establishing this link is the use of **incentive programs**, special pay programs designed to motivate high performance. Some programs are available to individuals, whereas others are distributed on a companywide basis.

A sales bonus is a typical incentive. Employees receive a **bonus**, special payments above their salaries, when they sell a certain number or certain dollar amount of goods for the year. Employees who fail to reach this goal earn no bonuses. **Merit salary systems** link pay raises to performance levels in nonsales jobs.

Executives commonly receive stock options as incentives. Halliburton CEO David Lesar, for example, can buy several thousand shares of company stock each year at a predetermined price. If his managerial talent leads to higher profits and stock prices, he can buy the stock at a price lower than the market value for which, in theory, he is largely responsible. He is then free to sell the stock at market price, keeping the profits for himself.

Another popular incentive plan is called **pay for performance (or variable pay)**. In essence, middle managers are rewarded for especially productive output with earnings that significantly exceed the cost of bonuses. The number of variable pay programs in the United States has been growing consistently for the last decade, and most experts predict that they will continue to grow in popularity. Many firms say that variable pay is a better motivator than merit raises because the range between generous and mediocre merit raises is usually quite small.

Companywide Incentives Some incentive programs apply to all the employees in a firm. Under **profit-sharing plans**, for example, profits earned above a certain level are distributed to employees. Also, **gainsharing plans** distribute bonuses to employees when a company's costs are reduced through greater work efficiency. **Pay-for-knowledge plans** pay workers to learn new skills and to become proficient at different jobs.

Benefits Programs

Benefits, compensation other than wages and salaries and other incentives offered by a firm to its workers, account for an increasing percentage of most compensation budgets. Most companies are required by law to pay tax for Social Security retirement benefits and provide **workers' compensation insurance**, insurance for compensating workers injured on the job. Most businesses also provide health, life, and disability insurance for their workers, as well as paid time off for vacations and holidays. Many also allow employees to use payroll deductions to buy stock at discounted prices. Counseling services for employees with alcohol, drug, or emotional problems are also becoming more common, as are on-site child-care centers. Some companies even provide reduced membership fees at gyms and health clubs, as well as insurance or other protection for identity theft.[9]

Retirement Plans Retirement plans (or pension plans) constitute another important—and sometimes controversial—benefit that is available to many employees. Most company-sponsored retirement plans are set up to pay pensions to workers when they retire. In some cases, the company contributes all the money to the pension fund. In others, both the company and employees make contributions. In recent years, some companies have run into problems because they have not set aside enough money to cover the retirement funds they have agreed to provide. Both FedEx and Goodyear, for instance, recently announced that they were freezing their pension programs to transition workers to riskier 401(k)s, in which payroll deductions

Incentive Program *special compensation program designed to motivate high performance*

Bonus *individual performance incentive in the form of a special payment made over and above the employee's salary*

Merit Salary System *individual incentive linking compensation to performance in nonsales jobs*

Pay for Performance (Variable Pay) *individual incentive that rewards a manager for especially productive output*

Profit-Sharing Plan *incentive plan for distributing bonuses to employees when company profits rise above a certain level*

Gainsharing Plan *incentive plan that rewards groups for productivity improvements*

Pay-for-Knowledge Plan *incentive plan to encourage employees to learn new skills or become proficient at different jobs*

Benefits *compensation other than wages and salaries*

Workers' Compensation Insurance *legally required insurance for compensating workers injured on the job*

finding a better way

Holding True at Nucor Steel

For the most part, the watchwords in U.S. business during the 2008–2011 recession were cutting payroll, reducing headcount, and eliminating jobs. But Nucor, the country's largest steelmaker, didn't lay off a single employee. Hit by a 50 percent plunge in output that had begun in September 2008, the U.S. steel industry had laid off some 10,000 workers by January 2009, and the United Steelworkers union was expecting the number to double before the recession came to an end. As of the end of 2010, however, Nucor had refused to follow suit. In fact, the company has not laid off a single employee because of lack of work in more than 30 years.

As far as top management is concerned, the company's ability to weather the recent economic crisis was based on several factors—most important, the firm's employees and culture. What's that culture like? It originated in the 1960s as the result of policies established by Ken Iverson, who brought a radical perspective on how to manage a company's HR to the job of CEO. Iverson figured that workers would be much more productive if an employer went out of its way to share authority with them, respect what they accomplished, and compensate them as handsomely as possible. Today, the basics of the company's HR model are summed up in its "Employee Relations Principles":

1 Management is obligated to manage Nucor in such a way that employees will have the opportunity to earn according to their productivity.

2 Employees should feel confident that if they do their jobs properly, they will have a job tomorrow.

3 Employees have the right to be treated fairly and must believe that they will be.

4 Employees must have an avenue of appeal when they believe they are being treated unfairly.

H. Mark Weidman Photography/Alamy

are invested in stocks and other nonguaranteed funds.[10] This trend increased during the Great Recession of 2008–2011. For example, 16 major U.S. employers stopped contributing to employee retirement accounts, and several more followed suit in 2010. Among these were Anheuser-Busch, Wells-Fargo, General Motors, AT&T, General Electric, and Saks.

Containing the Costs of Benefits As the range of benefits has increased, so has concern about containing the costs of these benefits. Many companies are experimenting with cost-cutting plans while still attracting and retaining valuable employees. One approach is the **cafeteria benefits plan**. A certain dollar amount of benefits per employee is set aside so that each employee can choose from a variety of alternatives.

Another area of increasing concern is healthcare costs. Medical expenses have increased insurance premiums, which have increased the cost to employers of maintaining benefits plans. Many employers are looking for new ways to cut those costs.

Cafeteria Benefits Plan *benefit plan that sets limits on benefits per employee, each of whom may choose from a variety of alternative benefits*

The Iverson approach is based on motivation, and the key to that approach is a highly original pay system. Step 1, which calls for base pay below the industry average, probably doesn't seem like a promising start, but the Nucor compensation plan is designed to get better as the results of the work get better. If a shift, for example, can turn out a defect-free batch of steel, every worker is entitled to a bonus that's paid weekly and that can potentially triple his or her take-home pay. In addition, there are one-time annual bonuses and profit-sharing payouts. In 2005, for instance, Nucor had an especially good year; it shipped more steel than any other U.S. producer, and net income hit $1.3 billion, up from $311 million in 2000. The average steelworker took home $79,000 in base pay and weekly bonuses, plus a $2,000 year-end bonus and an average of $18,000 in profit-sharing money.

The system, however, cuts both ways. Take that defect-free batch of steel, for example. If there's a problem with a batch, workers on the shift obviously don't get any weekly bonus. And that's if they catch the problem before the batch leaves the plant. If it reaches the customer, they may *lose* up to three times what they would have received as a bonus. "In average-to-bad years," adds HR vice president James M. Coblin, "we earn less than our peers in other companies. That's supposed to teach us that we don't want to be average or bad. We want to be good." During fiscal 2009, total pay at Nucor was down by about 40 percent.

Everybody in the company, from janitors to the CEO, is covered by some form of incentive plan tied to various goals and targets. Nucor's profit-sharing plan guarantees that the company will contribute 10 percent of all earnings before taxes to the plan. In addition, there are incentives at the level of the work group for production employees and at the departmental and divisional levels for managers.

The company has an unusually flat organizational structure—another Iverson innovation. There are just four layers of personnel between a janitor and senior management: general managers, department managers, line supervisors, and hourly personnel. Most operating decisions are made at the divisional level or lower, and the company is known for its tolerance of honest mistakes made in the line of decision-making duty. The Nucor website points out that workers are allowed to fail if that failure comes as a result of logical initiative and idea sharing. That is, if a worker approaches a problem in a logical manner and makes a sound decision that is defensible but turns out to be wrong, he or she is not punished. The reasoning behind this approach is that it promotes creativity and initiative.

The Nucor system works not only because employees share financial risks and benefits but also because, in sharing risks and benefits, they're a lot like owners. And people who think like owners are a lot more likely to take the initiative when decisions have to be made or problems solved. What's more, Nucor has found that teamwork is a good incubator for initiative as well as idea sharing. John J. Ferriola, who managed the Nucor mill in Hickman, Arkansas, before becoming CEO, remembers an afternoon in March 2006 when the electrical grid at his facility went down. His electricians got on the phone to three other company electricians, one in Alabama and two in North Carolina, who dropped what they were doing and went straight to Arkansas. Working 20-hour shifts, the joint team had the plant up and running again in three days (as opposed to an anticipated full week). There was nothing in it (at least financially) for the visiting electricians, but they knew that maintenance personnel get no bonuses when equipment in their facility isn't operating. "At Nucor," says one frontline supervisor, "we're not 'you guys' and 'us guys.' It's all of us guys. Wherever the bottleneck is, we go there, and everyone works on it."

One increasingly popular approach is for organizations to create their own networks of healthcare providers. These providers agree to charge lower fees for services rendered to employees of member organizations. In return, they enjoy established relationships with large employers and, thus, more clients and patients. Insurers also charge less to cover the employees of network members because they make lower reimbursement payments.

Developing the Workforce

OBJECTIVE 5
Describe
how managers develop the workforce in their organization through training and performance appraisal.

After a company has hired new employees, it must acquaint them with the firm and their new jobs. Managers also take steps to train and develop employees and to further develop necessary job skills. In addition, every firm has some system for performance appraisal and feedback.

Training and Development

In HRM, **training** usually refers to teaching operational or technical employees how to do the job for which they were hired. **Development** refers to teaching managers and professionals the skills needed for both present and future jobs.[11] Most organizations provide regular training and development programs for managers and employees. For example, IBM spends more than $750 million annually on programs and has a vice president in charge of employee education. U.S. businesses spend more than $70 billion annually on training and development programs away from the workplace (in 2010, the figure was $52.8 billion).[12] Over $130 billion is spent annually worldwide. And these figures do not include wages and benefits paid to employees while they are participating in such programs.

Assessing Training Needs The first step in developing a training plan is to determine what needs exist. For example, if employees do not know how to operate the machinery necessary to do their job, a training program on how to operate the machinery is clearly needed. On the other hand, when a group of office workers is performing poorly, training may not be the answer. The problem could be motivation, aging equipment, poor supervision, inefficient work design, or a deficiency of skills and knowledge. Only the last could be remedied by training. As training programs are being developed, the manager should set specific and measurable goals specifying what participants are to learn. Managers should also plan to evaluate the training program after employees complete it.

Common Training Methods Many different training and development methods are available. Selection of methods depends on many considerations, but perhaps the most important is training content. When the training content is factual material (such as company rules or explanations of how to fill out forms), assigned reading, programmed learning, and lecture methods work well. When the content is interpersonal relations or group decision making, however, firms must use a method that allows interpersonal contact, such as role-playing or case discussion groups. When employees must learn a physical skill, methods allowing practice and the actual use of tools and materials are needed, as in **on-the-job training** or **vestibule training**. (Vestibule training enables participants to focus on safety, learning, and feedback rather than on productivity.)

Web-based and other electronic media-based training are especially popular today. Such methods allow a mix of training content, are relatively easy to update and revise, let participants use a variable schedule, and lower travel costs.[13] On the other hand, they are limited in their capacity to simulate real activities and facilitate face-to-face interaction. Xerox, Massachusetts Mutual Life Insurance, and Ford have all reported tremendous success with these methods. In addition, most training programs rely on a mix of methods. Boeing, for example, sends managers to an intensive two-week training seminar involving tests, simulations, role-playing exercises, and flight-simulation exercises.[14]

Finally, some larger businesses have started creating their own self-contained training facility, often called a *corporate university*. McDonald's was among the first to start this practice with its so-called Hamburger University in Illinois. All management trainees for the firm attend training programs there to learn exactly how long to grill a burger, how to maintain good customer service, and so on. The cult hamburger chain In-N-Out Burger also has a similar training venue it calls In-N-Out University. Other firms that use this approach include Shell Oil and General Electric.[15]

Evaluation of Training Training and development programs should always be evaluated. Typical evaluation approaches include measuring one or more relevant criteria (such as attitudes or performance) before and after the training, and determining whether the criteria changed. Evaluation measures collected at the end of training are easy to get, but actual performance measures collected when the trainee is on the job are more important. Trainees may say that they enjoyed the training and learned a lot, but the true test is whether their job performance improves after their training.

Performance Appraisal

Once employees are trained and settled into their jobs, one of management's next concerns is performance appraisal.[16] **Performance appraisal** is a formal assessment of how well employees are doing their jobs. Employees' performance should be evaluated regularly for many reasons. One reason is that performance appraisal may be necessary for validating selection devices or assessing the impact of training programs. A second, administrative reason is to aid in making decisions about pay raises, promotions, and training. Still another reason is to provide feedback to employees to help them improve their present performance and plan their future careers.[17]

Because performance evaluations often help determine wages and promotions, they must be fair and nondiscriminatory. In the case of appraisals, managers use content validation to show that the appraisal system accurately measures performance on important job elements and does not measure traits or behavior that are irrelevant to job performance.

Performance Appraisal *evaluation of an employee's job performance to determine the degree to which the employee is performing effectively*

Common Appraisal Methods

Common Appraisal Methods Two basic categories of appraisal methods commonly used in organizations are objective methods and judgmental methods. Objective measures of performance include actual output (number of units produced), scrap rate, dollar volume of sales, and number of claims processed. Objective performance measures may be contaminated by "opportunity bias" if some persons have a better chance to perform than others. For example, a sales representative selling snowblowers in Michigan has a greater opportunity than does a colleague selling the same product in Alabama. Fortunately, adjusting raw performance figures for the effect of opportunity bias and thereby arriving at figures that accurately represent each individual's performance is often possible.

Judgmental methods, including ranking and rating techniques, are the most common way to measure performance. Ranking compares employees directly with one another and orders them from best to worst. Ranking has a number of drawbacks. Ranking is difficult for large groups because the individuals in the middle of the distribution may be hard to distinguish from one another accurately. Comparisons of people in different work groups are also difficult. For example, an employee ranked third in a strong group may be more valuable than an employee ranked first in a weak group. Another criticism of ranking is that the manager must rank people on the basis of overall performance, even though each person likely has both strengths and weaknesses. Furthermore, rankings do not provide useful information for feedback. To be told that one is ranked third is not nearly as helpful as to be told that the quality of one's work is outstanding, its quantity is satisfactory, one's punctuality could use improvement, or one's paperwork is seriously deficient.

Rating differs from ranking in that it compares each employee with a fixed standard rather than with other employees. A rating scale provides the standard. Figure 2 gives examples of three graphic rating scales for a bank teller. Each consists of a performance dimension to be rated (punctuality, congeniality, and accuracy), followed by a scale on which to make the rating. In constructing graphic rating scales, performance dimensions that are relevant to job performance must be selected. In particular, they should focus on job behaviors and results rather than on personality traits or attitudes.

Errors in Performance Appraisal

Errors in Performance Appraisal Errors or biases can occur in any kind of rating or ranking system.[18] One common problem is *recency error*, the tendency to base judgments on the subordinate's most recent performance because it is most easily recalled. Often a rating or ranking is intended to evaluate performance over an entire time period, such as six months or a year, so the recency

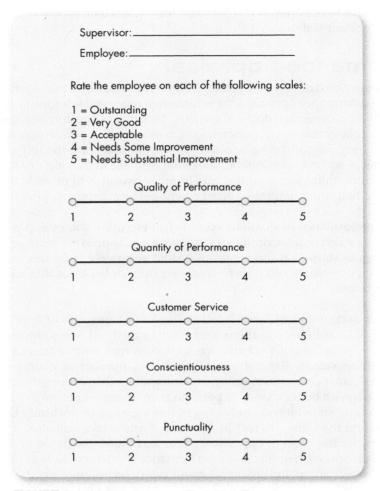

FIGURE 2 Sample Performance Evaluation Form

error does introduce error into the judgment. Other errors include overuse of one part of the scale—being too lenient, being too severe, or giving everyone a rating of "average."

Halo error is allowing the assessment of an employee on one dimension to "spread" to ratings of that employee on other dimensions. For instance, if an employee is outstanding on quality of output, a rater might tend to give her or him higher marks than deserved on other dimensions. Errors can also occur because of race, sex, or age discrimination, intentionally or unintentionally. The best way to offset these errors is to ensure that a valid rating system is developed at the outset and then to train managers in how to use it.

One interesting innovation in performance appraisal used in some organizations today is called **360-degree feedback**, in which managers are evaluated by everyone around them—their boss, their peers, and their subordinates. Such a complete and thorough approach provides people with a far richer array of information about their performance than does a conventional appraisal given by just the boss. Of course, such a system also takes considerable time and must be handled so as not to breed fear and mistrust in the workplace.[19]

Performance Feedback The last step in most performance appraisal systems is giving feedback to subordinates about their performance. This is usually done in a private meeting between the person being evaluated and his or her boss. The discussion should generally be focused on the facts: the assessed level of performance,

360-Degree Feedback *performance appraisal technique in which managers are evaluated by everyone around them—their boss, their peers, and their subordinates*

entrepreneurship and new ventures

Time to Go

Dan Yoo had everything going for him. He graduated cum laude from Georgetown University in 1999 with a degree in management and finance. After working for Merrill Lynch for a year, he moved onto Epoch Partners, a "technology-enabled" investment bank. Within a year, his dream job was gone. The company was acquired by Goldman Sachs and he and several recently hired employees were out of a job. In the years since, he's worked in a series of high-profile positions in the financial services and technology sectors. Most recently, he left his job as Vice President for Business Operations and Business Analytics at LinkedIn to become COO at NerdWallet, a San Francisco-based provider of customized financial advice and analysis.

Beginning with his unfortunate experience at Epoch partners, Yoo understands the importance of compassion in every interaction with employees. While very few people go into business because they look forward to conducting performance appraisals and even firing employees, strong human relations skills are essential for an entrepreneur. In an article in *Entreprenuer* magazine, Yoo offers advice on how to fire employees with compassion, whether as a result of poor performance or cost-cutting decisions.

- The first step in firing an employee begins on the day that the employee is hired. Employee behavior must be shaped, and supervisors cannot afford to overlook had behavior. In the start-up world, one weak performer can make a big difference, so it's important to let employees know where they stand. Yoo explains, "Just as there's a need for decisive action if it's not working out, there needs to be an aggressive onboarding and feedback loop to communicate problems quickly and give an opportunity for corrective action before swinging the axe."

- In the event that you must fire an employee, it's important to plan the discussion in advance, with your goal being to leave the termination meeting on the best terms possible. This is where empathy plays a big role — understanding the situation from the perspective of the terminated employee.

- It's important to be brief and direct because dragging out bad news doesn't really soften the blow. But it's also important to allow the employee to share their perspective and feel that they have been heard. Although it's unlikely to change your decision, it creates the opportunity for the manager to learn and the employee to feel valued.

- Finally, if it's possible, this is the time to be generous. Losing a job is so much more than money, but you can help ease the transition through extended health insurance benefits or outplacement services. When Yoo was fired from Epoch Partners, he and the other fired employees were able to collect their bonuses as well as vest their interests in the company's profit-sharing plan. While there was no legal obligation for the company to do so, it helped them part on good terms.[20]

how and why that assessment was made, and how it can be improved in the future. Feedback interviews are not easy to conduct. Many managers are uncomfortable with the task, especially if feedback is negative and subordinates are disappointed by what they hear. Properly training managers, however, can help them conduct more effective feedback interviews.[21]

Some firms use an aggressive approach to terminating people who do not meet expectations. General Electric actually implemented a system whereby each year the bottom 10 percent of its workforce is terminated and replaced with new employees. Company executives claim that this approach, although stressful for all employees, helps it to continuously upgrade its workforce. Other firms have started using this same approach. However, both Ford and Goodyear recently agreed to abandon similar approaches in response to age discrimination lawsuits.[22]

New Challenges in the Changing Workplace

OBJECTIVE 6
Discuss

workforce diversity, the management of knowledge workers, and the use of a contingent workforce as important changes in the contemporary workplace.

Workforce Diversity *the range of workers' attitudes, values, beliefs, and behaviors that differ by gender, race, age, ethnicity, physical ability, and other relevant characteristics*

In addition to the challenges we have already considered, HR managers face several new challenges reflecting the changing economic and social environments of business.

Managing Workforce Diversity

One extremely important set of HR challenges centers on **workforce diversity**, the range of workers' attitudes, values, beliefs, and behaviors that differ by gender, race, age, ethnicity, physical ability, and other relevant characteristics. In the past, organizations tended to work toward homogenizing their workforces, getting everyone to think and behave in similar ways. Partly as a result of affirmative action efforts, however, many U.S. organizations are now creating more diverse workforces than ever before.

Figure 3 projects the racial and ethnic composition of the U.S. workforce through 2050. The picture is clearly one of increasing diversity. The number of Caucasian Americans as a percentage of the total workforce is declining steadily, offset by increases in every other racial group. Most striking are the growing numbers

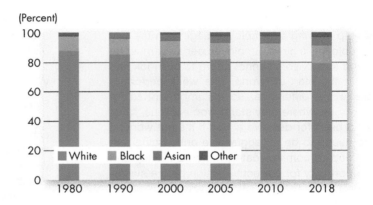

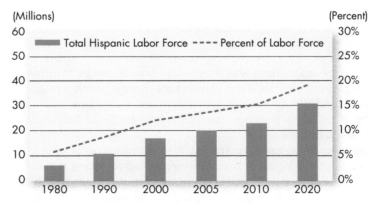

FIGURE 3 Distribution of the labor force by race 1990–2050
Source: http://www.dol.gov/asp/media/reports/workforce2007/ADW2007_Full_Text.pdf (p. 38). U.S. Department of Labor, "America's Dynamic Workforce," (August 2007), p. 38, at http://www.dol.gov/asp/media/reports/workforce2007/ADW2007_Full_Text.pdf.

of people of Hispanic origin (who may be members of any racial group). By 2050, the U.S. Department of Labor estimates that nearly a quarter of the workforce will be Hispanic.

Today, organizations are recognizing that diversity can be a competitive advantage. For example, by hiring the best people available from every single group rather than hiring from just one or a few groups, a firm can develop a higher-quality labor force. Similarly, a diverse workforce can bring a wider array of information to bear on problems and can provide insights on marketing products to a wider range of consumers.

Managing Knowledge Workers

Traditionally, employees added value to organizations because of what they did or because of their experience. In the information age, however, employees who add value because of what they know are usually called **knowledge workers**. Knowledge workers, which include computer scientists, engineers, physical scientists, and game developers, typically require extensive and highly specialized training. Once they are on the job, retraining and training updates are critical to prevent their skills from becoming obsolete. It has been suggested, for example, that the half-life of a technical education in engineering is about three years.

Knowledge Workers *employees who are of value because of the knowledge they possess*

A firm's failure to update the skills of its knowledge workers not only results in the loss of competitive advantage but it also increases the likelihood that those workers will go to other firms that are more committed to updating their skills. Hence, HR managers must ensure that the proper training is prepared to enable knowledge workers to stay current while also making sure they are compensated at market rates.

A major part of this challenge is recruiting new knowledge workers on a regular basis. Given both the high demand for knowledge workers and their relative short supply, firms often resort to extreme measures to recruit the best and brightest. For example, Google, Facebook, and Zynga often compete head-to-head for programmers and software engineers. To help recruit knowledge workers, these firms offer such lavish perks as free massages, laundry services, gourmet meals and snacks, and premium coffee.[23]

Contingent and Temporary Workers

A final contemporary HR issue of note involves the growing use of contingent and temporary workers. Many employers use contingent and temporary workers to increase their flexibility and, in most cases, lower their costs.

Trends in Contingent and Temporary Employment A **contingent worker** is a person who works for an organization on something other than a permanent or full-time basis. Categories of contingent workers include independent contractors, on-call workers, temporary employees (usually hired through outside agencies), and contract and leased employees. Another category is part-time workers. In recent years, there has been an explosion in the use of such workers by organizations. For instance, in 2015, almost 19 percent of employed U.S. workers fell into one of these categories, up from 10 percent in 2008.

Contingent Worker *employee hired on something other than a full-time basis to supplement an organization's permanent workforce*

Managing Contingent and Temporary Workers One key to managing contingent workers effectively is careful planning and analysis. Rather than having to call in workers sporadically, and with no prior notice, organizations try to bring in specified numbers of workers for well-defined periods of time. For instance, most retailers hire temporary seasonal employees for the Christmas holiday shopping period. Based on their past experience, they generally know how many people they need to hire and when they need to hire them. Firms should also be able to document the labor-cost savings of using contingent workers.

A second key is recognizing what can and cannot be achieved by using contingent and temporary workers. For instance, these workers may lack the firm-specific

managing in turbulent times

Temp or Perm?

Shortly after being denied tenure as a professor, Diana Bloom found herself desperate to work. She longed to stay home with her young son, but she needed to support her family. She made the unexpected decision to turn to Craigslist, an online network that posts free classified ads, and offered her services as a tutor, editor, and translator. Almost 15 years later, she's made a living patching together temporary and part-time work. Temp work is also appealing, she says, because "I'm not very outgoing, and getting my foot in the door to companies would have been hard." Of course, there's a downside, too. Temp work rarely offers benefits such as health insurance, sick days, or paid vacations.

Craigslist works in the other direction, too, with employers posting openings for jobs both permanent and temporary. Another New Yorker, Simone Sneed, scours the Craigslist "Gigs" section for jobs that last for perhaps a day, often for just a few hours. Whether as a backup singer or a grants writer, she's turned the strategy of patching together "gigs" into a convenient way to supplement the income from her full-time job. "I'll use the extra money to pay off my school loan," she says. "Every little bit helps."

During the most recent recession, both employers and employees began to look at part-time and temporary work differently. Employers found that they could often get by without hiring a full-time, permanent employee. And employees found that they had lots of options and variety if they expanded their job search to part-time and temporary positions. However, if you're employed short term or part-time, the Bureau of Labor Statistics (BLS) classifies you as "underemployed." Naturally, most people who are "underemployed" are, by definition, "overqualified." In fact, they often have years of professional experience but are willing to take jobs that don't call for their levels of training or experience.

Interestingly, for a lot of people, the adjustment to new labor-market conditions isn't necessarily as traumatic as you might think. A 2011 survey conducted by the temporary staffing agency Kelly Services found that as many as 26 percent of employed American adults regard themselves as "free agents" when it comes to the type of job that they're willing to take (up from 19 percent in 2006). Of all those polled, only 10 percent said that they're doing temporary work because they've

Andrey Popov/Shutterstock

been laid off from permanent jobs; 90 percent said that they're doing it because they like the variety and flexibility that temping affords them.

In fact, temping offers several advantages. It can, for example, provide income during career transitions, and it's a good way to exercise a little control over the balance between your work and personal life. In 1995, for example, when she was seven months pregnant with her first child, veteran retail manager Stacey Schick accepted a two-week data entry job with the Orange County (New York) Association of Realtors. "I didn't know how to turn on a computer," she remembers, but "they needed bodies." Now the mother of two, Schick is still with the Association as its education coordinator. "I would never have considered it," she says, if a job in her field had come up, but the job she landed in has turned out to be a much better fit with her lifestyle: "It's afforded me the opportunity to have a family and be able to have time with them."

The path taken by Schick is called "temp-to-perm," and it offers employers several advantages as well. Companies that are hesitant to make commitments to untested employees can "try before they buy"; they get a chance to see employees in action before finalizing hiring decisions. Because there are no fees to pay when an employee goes from temp to perm, trying out temps is also cheaper than paying an agency outright to find a hire. The big savings, of course, come from benefits, which can amount to one-third of the total cost of compensating a permanent position.[24]

knowledge to perform as effectively as a permanent employee would perform. They are also less committed to the organization and less likely to engage in organizational citizenship behaviors.

Finally, managers must make decisions about how to integrate contingent workers into the organization. These decisions may be as simple as whether to invite contingent workers to the holiday party, or they may be more complicated, such as whether to grant contingent workers access to such employee benefits as counseling services and child care.

Dealing with Organized Labor

OBJECTIVE 7
Explain
why workers organize into labor unions and describe the collective bargaining process.

A **labor union** is a group of individuals working together to achieve shared job-related goals, such as higher pay, shorter working hours, more job security, greater benefits, or better working conditions. **Labor relations** refers to the process of dealing with employees who are represented by a union.

Labor Union group of individuals working together to achieve shared job-related goals, such as higher pay, shorter working hours, more job security, greater benefits, or better working conditions

Labor Relations process of dealing with employees who are represented by a union

Unionism Today

In the years immediately following World War II and continuing through the mid-1960s, most unions routinely won certification elections. In recent years, however, labor unions have been winning certification only about half the time.[25] As a result, although millions of workers still belong to unions, union membership as a percentage of the total workforce has steadily declined. In 2007, only 12.1 percent of U.S. workers belonged to a labor union, down from 20.1 percent in 1983, when the U.S. Department of Labor first began compiling data.[26] As the recession of 2008–2011 began to increase fears about unemployment and wage cuts, union membership began to increase again, albeit only slightly. By 2010, it had dropped again, falling below prerecession levels. In 2014, union membership was 11.1 percent. These trends are shown in Figure 4.

The Future of Unions Even though several of its members withdrew from the parent organization in 2005, the American Federation of Labor and Congress of Industrial Organizations (AFL-CIO), as well as independent major unions such as the Teamsters and the National Education Association (NEA), still play a major role in U.S. business. Unions in the traditional strongholds of goods-producing industries continue to wield considerable power as well. The United Auto Workers (UAW) was for decades one of the largest unions in the United States. But it, too, seems to be entering a period of decline. The traumas experienced by the U.S. auto industry in 2008–2009, for instance, required the UAW to make many major concessions to help Ford, DaimlerChrysler, and General Motors survive. In addition, auto plant closures will dramatically reduce the number of auto jobs in the years to come.

Another issue affecting the future of unionism is the geographic shift in the U.S. economy. For the most part, unionism in the United States started in the North and Midwest regions and in cities such as Detroit, Pittsburgh, Cleveland, St. Louis, and Chicago. But over the past several decades, there has been a pronounced shift as

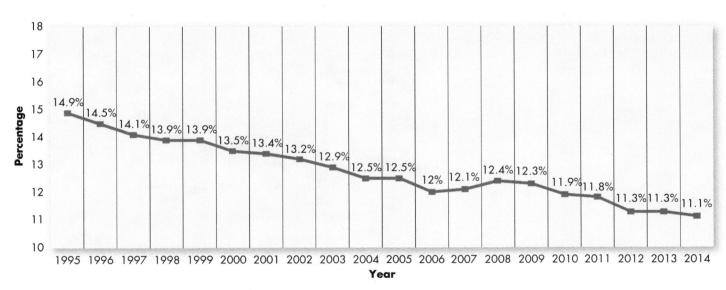

FIGURE 4 Percentage of Workers Who Belong to Unions: 1995–2010

Sources: U.S. Department of Labor, Bureau of Labor Statistics, www.aflcio.org/joinaunion/why/uniondifference/uniondiff11.cfm.

businesses have moved their operations to the South and Southwest, areas that do not have a strong union heritage. For instance, Nucor Steel, profiled in Finding a Better Way, locates its facilities in smaller communities in the southern United States in part because it knows these workers are not prone to unionization.

Collective Bargaining

Collective Bargaining *process by which labor and management negotiate conditions of employment for union-represented workers*

The power of unions comes from collective action, forcing management to listen to the demands of all workers rather than to just the few who speak out. **Collective bargaining** is the process by which labor and management negotiate conditions of employment for union-represented workers and draft a labor contract.

Reaching Agreement on Contract Terms
The collective bargaining process begins when the union is recognized as the exclusive negotiator for its members and union leaders meet with management representatives to agree on a contract. By law, both parties must sit down at the bargaining table and negotiate in good faith. Figure 5 shows what is called the "bargaining zone." For instance, in theory, employers want to pay as little as possible; they will generally pay more than the minimum, but there is also some upper limit beyond which they will not pay. Likewise, unions want the highest pay possible but expect to get less. But they, too, have a limit beyond which they will not go.

For example, suppose the bargaining issue is pay increases. The employer may initially propose a pay increase of 2 percent but (secretly) be willing to offer up to 6 percent. However, under no circumstances can it afford to pay more than 8 percent. The union, meanwhile, may initially demand a 10 percent increase but (secretly) be willing to accept as little as 4 percent. Assuming each party negotiates in good faith and is willing to make concessions to the other, the real bargaining zone falls between the union minimum (4 percent) and the employer maximum (6 percent). The real outcome will then depend on such things as other items being negotiated and the skills of the respective negotiators.

Sometimes, this process goes quite smoothly. At other times, the two sides cannot agree. For instance, the preceding example should result in an agreement because the union minimum and the employer maximum provide a bargaining zone. But if the union demands no less than 8 percent and the employer is unwilling to give more than a 4 percent increase, there is no bargaining zone. Resolving the impasse depends in part on the nature of the contract issues, the willingness of each side to use certain tactics, such as strikes, and the prospects for mediation or arbitration.

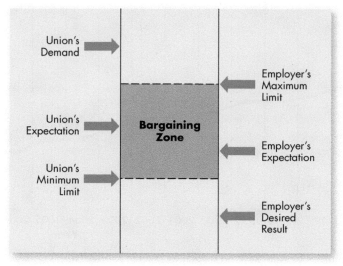

FIGURE 5 The Bargaining Zone

Contract Issues The labor contract itself can address an array of different issues. Issues that are typically most important to union negotiators include *compensation, benefits*, and *job security*. Certain management rights, such as control over hiring policies and work assignments, are also negotiated in most bargaining agreements. Other possible issues might include such specific details as working hours, overtime policies, rest period arrangements, differential pay plans for shift employees, the use of temporary workers, grievance procedures, and allowable union activities (dues collection, union bulletin boards, and so forth).

COMPENSATION Compensation includes both current and future wages. One common tool for securing wage increases is a **cost-of-living adjustment (COLA)**. Most COLA clauses tie future raises to the *Consumer Price Index (CPI)*, a government statistic that reflects changes in consumer purchasing power. Almost half of all labor contracts today include COLA clauses.

A union might be uncomfortable with a long-term contract based solely on COLA wage increases. One solution is a **wage reopener clause**, which allows wage rates to be renegotiated at preset times during the life of the contract.

Cost-of-Living Adjustment (COLA) *labor contract clause tying future raises to changes in consumer purchasing power*

Wage Reopener Clause *clause allowing wage rates to be renegotiated during the life of a labor contract*

BENEFITS Employee benefits are also an important component in most labor contracts. Unions typically want employers to pay all or most of the costs of insurance for employees. Other benefits commonly addressed during negotiations include retirement benefits, paid holidays, and working conditions. Because of surging healthcare costs, employee health insurance premiums have become a major point of contention in recent years. For example, many employees have much larger co-pays today when they visit their doctor than was the case a few years ago. (A *co-pay* is the dollar amount a patient pays to the doctor; insurance then pays the remainder.)

JOB SECURITY Job security also remains an important agenda item in many bargaining sessions today. In some cases, a contract may dictate that if the workforce is reduced, seniority will be used to determine which employees keep their jobs. Unions are setting their sights on preserving jobs for workers in the United States in the face of business efforts to outsource production in some sectors to countries where labor costs are cheaper. For example, the AFL-CIO has been an outspoken opponent of efforts to normalize trade relations with China, fearing that more businesses might be tempted to move jobs there to take advantage of lower wage levels.

When Bargaining Fails An impasse occurs when, after a series of bargaining sessions, management and labor have failed to agree on a new contract or a contract to replace an agreement that is about to expire. Although it is generally agreed that both parties suffer when an impasse is reached and some action by one part against the other is taken, each side can use several tactics to support its cause until the impasse is resolved.

UNION TACTICS Historically, one of the most common union tactics has been the **strike**, which occurs when employees temporarily walk off the job and refuse to work. The number of major strikes in the United States has steadily declined over the past few decades. From 1960 to 1980, for example, an average of 281 strikes occurred per year. In the 1980s, there was an average of 83 major strikes per year; in the 1990s, this figure fell to an average of 35 per year. Between 2000 and 2009, there was an average of 20 major strikes per year.[27] There were 19 major strikes in 2012.[28]

Strike *labor action in which employees temporarily walk off the job and refuse to work*

To support a strike, a union faced with an impasse has recourse to additional legal activities:

- In **picketing**, workers march at the entrance to the employer's facility with signs explaining their reasons for striking.

- A **boycott** occurs when union members agree not to buy the products of a targeted employer. Workers may also urge consumers to boycott the firm's products.

Picketing *labor action in which workers publicize their grievances at the entrance to an employer's facility*

Boycott *labor action in which workers refuse to buy the products of a targeted employer*

Work Slowdown *labor action in which workers perform jobs at a slower than normal pace*

● Another alternative to striking is a **work slowdown**. Instead of striking, workers perform their jobs at a much slower pace than normal. A variation is the *sickout*, during which large numbers of workers call in sick.

MANAGEMENT TACTICS Like workers, management can respond forcefully to an impasse with the following:

Lockout *management tactic whereby workers are denied access to the employer's workplace*

● **Lockouts** occur when employers deny employees access to the workplace. Lockouts are illegal if they are used as offensive weapons to give management a bargaining advantage. However, they are legal if management has a legitimate business need (for instance, avoiding a buildup of perishable inventory). When the National Football League failed to reach a new contract agreement with its players association in 2011, the league owners imposed a lockout until an agreement was reached. More recently, the Toronto Zoo locked out its employees in 2013 over a labor dispute, as did the St. Paul Chamber Orchestra.[29, 30, 31, 32, 33]

Strikebreaker *worker hired as a permanent or temporary replacement for a striking employee*

● A firm can also hire temporary or permanent replacements called **strikebreakers**. However, the law forbids the permanent replacement of workers who strike because of unfair practices. In some cases, an employer can obtain legal injunctions that either prohibit workers from striking or prohibit a union from interfering with its efforts to use replacement workers.

Mediation and Arbitration Rather than wield these often unpleasant weapons against one another, labor and management can agree to call in a third party to help resolve the dispute:

Mediation *method of resolving a labor dispute in which a third party suggests, but does not impose, a settlement*

In **mediation**, the neutral third party (the mediator) can suggest, but cannot impose, a settlement on the other parties.

Arbitration *method of resolving a labor dispute in which both parties agree to submit to the judgment of a neutral party*

In **arbitration**, the neutral third party (the arbitrator) dictates a settlement between the two sides, which have agreed to submit to outside judgment. In some disputes, such as those between the government and public employees, arbitration is compulsory, or required by law.

Managing an organization's HR is both a complex and important undertaking. Most businesses can buy the same equipment and use the same technology as their competitors. But differences in employee talent and motivation are not easily copied. Consequently, most well-managed companies today recognize the value provided by their employees and strive to ensure that the HR function is managed as efficiently and effectively as possible.

summary of learning objectives

Define *human resource management,* **discuss its strategic significance, and explain how managers plan for their organization's human resource needs.**

Human resource management (*HRM*) is the set of organizational activities directed at attracting, developing, and maintaining an effective workforce. Human resources (HR) are critical for effective organizational functioning. HRM was once relegated to second-class status in many organizations, but its importance has grown dramatically in the last two decades. Its new importance stems from increased legal complexities, the recognition that HR are a valuable means for improving productivity, and the awareness today of the costs associated with poor HRM. *Human capital* reflects the organization's investment in attracting, retaining, and motivating an effective workforce. Hence, just as the phrase *financial capital* is an indicator of a firm's financial resources and reserves, so, too, does human capital serve as a tangible indicator of the value of the people who comprise an organization.

Job analysis is a systematic analysis of jobs within an organization resulting in two things: a *job description* and a *job specification*. A job description lists the duties and responsibilities of a job, whereas a job specification identifies the skills, abilities, and qualifications needed to perform the job. Managers must plan for future HR needs by assessing past trends, future plans, and general economic trends. Forecasting labor supply is really two tasks: (1) *forecasting internal supply* and (2) *forecasting external supply*. To analyze internal supply, HR managers often develop *employee information systems* (or skills inventories). The next step in HR planning is matching HR supply and demand.

Discuss **the legal context of human resource management and identify contemporary legal issues.**

A number of laws regulate various aspects of employee–employer relations, especially in the areas of equal employment opportunity, compensation and benefits, labor relations, and occupational safety and health. *Title VII of the Civil Rights Act of 1964* forbids discrimination in all areas of the employment relationship such as hiring, opportunities for advancement, compensation increases, layoffs, and terminations against members of certain protected classes based on factors such as race, color, gender, religious beliefs, or national origin. In addition to enforcing rules against overt discrimination, the *Equal Employment Opportunity Commission (EEOC)* is also charged with evaluating employment requirements that have *adverse impact*. Several other laws have expanded the scope of antidiscrimination law. The *Age Discrimination in Employment Act*, passed in 1967, amended in 1978, and amended again in 1986, is an attempt to prevent organizations from discriminating against older workers. The *Pregnancy Discrimination Act* forbids discrimination against women who are pregnant. The *Americans with Disabilities Act* forbids discrimination on the basis of disabilities and requires employers to provide reasonable accommodations for disabled employees. The *Civil Rights Act of 1991* amended the original Civil Rights Act as well as other related laws by both making it easier to bring discrimination lawsuits while simultaneously limiting the amount of punitive damages that can be awarded in those lawsuits.

Affirmative action was created through executive order and requires government contractors to make proactive attempts to recruit, hire, and promote employees from groups that are underrepresented in the organization.

The *Fair Labor Standards Act*, passed in 1938 and amended frequently since then, sets a minimum wage and requires the payment of overtime rates for work in excess of 40 hours per week. The *Equal Pay Act of 1963* requires that men and women be paid the same amount for doing the same job. Employers who provide a pension plan for their employees are regulated by the *Employee Retirement Income Security Act (ERISA) of 1974*. The *Family and Medical Leave Act (FMLA) of 1993* requires employers to provide up to 12 weeks of unpaid leave for family and medical emergencies.

The *National Labor Relations Act* (also known as the Wagner Act), passed in 1935, sets up a procedure for employees to vote on whether to have a union. The *Labor-Management Relations Act* (also known as the Taft-Hartley Act) was passed in 1947 to limit union power. Taken together, these laws balance union and management power. Employees can be represented by a legally created and managed union, but the business can make non-employee-related business decisions without interference.

The *Occupational Safety and Health Act (OSHA) of 1970* directly mandates the provision of safe working conditions. Under the Americans with Disabilities Act of 1990, AIDS is considered a disability and employers cannot require an HIV test or any other medical examination as a condition of employment. Sexual harassment, both quid pro quo harassment and a hostile work environment, is forbidden under antidiscrimination law as well.

In general, employees work under the legal concept of *employment at will*, which gives both the employee and the employer the right to terminate an employment relationship at any time. However, this concept has been tested in the courts and limited in scope by a variety of legislative provisions.

OBJECTIVE 3

Identify the steps in staffing a company and discuss ways in which organizations recruit and select new employees.

Staffing an organization means recruiting and hiring the right mix of people. *Recruiting* is the process of attracting qualified persons to apply for open jobs, either from within the organization or from outside the organization. To help prospective employees understand the job, some employers offer a *realistic job preview (RJP)*.

The next step is the *selection process*, gathering information that will predict applicants' job success and then hiring candidates. Common selection techniques include application forms; tests of ability, aptitude, or knowledge; and interviews.

OBJECTIVE 4

Describe the main components of a compensation and benefits system.

A company's compensation system is the financial rewards given by the organization to its employees in exchange for their work. *Wages* are the hourly compensation paid to operating employees. *Salary* refers to compensation paid for total contributions, as opposed to pay based on hours worked. A good compensation system can help attract qualified applicants, retain present employees, and stimulate high performance at a cost reasonable for one's industry and geographic area.

Companies may also try to link compensation to performance through *incentive programs*. Individual incentive programs include *bonuses, merit salary systems*, and *variable pay*. Companywide incentives include *profit sharing, gainsharing*, and *pay-for-knowledge plans*.

Benefits are things of value other than wages that the organization provides to its workers. Most employers are required to pay into Social Security on behalf of employees and to maintain workers compensation insurance, protecting employees injured on the job. Many companies also provide health, life, and disability insurance. Other types of benefits include employee stock ownership plans, counseling services, on-site child care, and reduced-fee memberships at gyms and health clubs. Many companies provide retirement plans for their employees, although many are funded entirely by employee contributions. Companies that offer *cafeteria benefit plans* set aside a certain dollar amount per employee for benefits, allowing the employee to select the benefits most important to their individual situation.

OBJECTIVE 5

Describe how managers develop the workforce in their organization through training and performance appraisal.

In HRM, *training* usually refers to teaching operational or technical employees how to do the job for which they were hired. *Development* refers to teaching managers and professionals the skills needed for both present and future jobs. Most organizations provide regular training and development programs for managers and employees. The first step in developing a training plan is to determine what needs exist. Many different training and development methods are available—assigned reading, programmed learning, lecture, role-playing, case discussion groups, on-the-job training, vestibule training, web-based training, and other electronic media-based training. Training and development programs should always be evaluated for effectiveness.

Once employees are trained and settled into their jobs, one of management's next concerns is performance appraisal. *Performance appraisal* is a formal assessment of how well employees are doing their jobs. Because performance evaluations often help determine wages and promotions, they must be fair and nondiscriminatory. Two basic categories of appraisal methods commonly used in organizations are objective methods and judgmental methods. Objective measures of performance include actual output (number of units produced), scrap rate, dollar volume of sales, and number of claims processed. Judgmental methods, including ranking and rating techniques, are the most common way to measure performance. Ranking compares employees directly with one another and orders them from best to worst. Rating differs from ranking in that it compares each employee with a fixed standard rather than with other employees, with a rating scale providing the standard. Errors or biases can occur in any kind of rating or ranking system. One common problem is recency error—the tendency to base judgments on the subordinate's most recent performance because it is most easily recalled. Halo error is allowing the assessment of an employee on one dimension to "spread" to ratings of that employee on other dimensions. The last step in most performance appraisal systems is giving feedback to subordinates about their performance, usually done in a private meeting between the person being evaluated and his or her boss.

OBJECTIVE 6

Discuss workforce diversity, the management of knowledge workers, and the use of a contingent workforce as important changes in the contemporary workplace.

Workforce diversity refers to the range of workers' attitudes, values, beliefs, and behaviors that differ by gender, race, age, ethnicity, physical ability, and other relevant characteristics. In the past, organizations tended to work toward homogenizing their workforces; however, many organizations are now realizing that diversity can be a competitive advantage.

Employees who add value because of what they know are usually called *knowledge workers*, and managing them skillfully helps determine which firms will be successful in the future. *Contingent workers*, including independent contractors, on-call workers, temporary employees, contract and leased employees, and part-time employees, work for organizations on something other than a permanent or full-time basis. Organizations must understand when it is appropriate to use contingent workers and how to integrate them into the organization.

OBJECTIVE 7

Explain why workers organize into labor unions and describe the collective bargaining process.

Labor relations is the process of dealing with employees who are represented by a union. A *labor union* is a group of individuals working together to achieve shared job-related goals, such as higher pay, shorter working hours, more job security, greater benefits, or better working conditions. At one time, almost a third of the entire U.S. labor force belonged to a labor union, with the largest membership following World War II into the mid-1960s. Union membership fell from 20.1 percent of the workforce in 1983 to only 12.1 percent of the workforce in 2007.

The intent of *collective bargaining* is to agree on a labor contract between management and the union that is satisfactory to both parties. The contract contains agreements about such issues as wages, work hours, job security, promotion, layoffs, discipline, benefits, methods of allocating overtime, vacations, rest periods, and the grievance procedure. Sometimes, the process of collective bargaining goes quite smoothly and management and the union agree to the terms of a new contract. However, when bargaining fails, the union has the option to go on *strike, picket* the organization, organize a *boycott*, or implement a *work slowdown*. Management has options as well; they may *lock out* employees until an agreement has been reached or hire *strikebreakers*. Rather than wielding these weapons, labor and management can agree to call in a third party, either a *mediator* or *arbitrator*, to help resolve the dispute.

key terms

360-degree feedback	external recruiting	Occupational Safety and Health Act
adverse impact	Fair Labor Standards Act	(OSHA) of 1970
affirmative action	Family and Medical Leave Act (FMLA)	on-the-job training
affirmative action plan	of 1993	Patriot Act
Age Discrimination in Employment Act	gainsharing plan	pay for performance (or variable pay)
Americans with Disabilities Act	hostile work environment	pay-for-knowledge plan
arbitration	human capital	performance appraisal
benefits	human resources	picketing
bonus	human resource management (HRM)	profit-sharing plan
boycott	incentive program	quid pro quo harassment
cafeteria benefits plan	internal recruiting	realistic job preview (RJP)
Civil Rights Act of 1991	job analysis	recruiting
collective bargaining	job description	replacement chart
compensation system	job specification	salary
contingent worker	knowledge workers	sexual harassment
cost-of-living adjustment (COLA)	labor relations	strike
development	labor union	strikebreaker
employee information system (skills	Labor-Management Relations Act	talent management
inventory)	(Taft-Hartley Act)	Title VII of the Civil Rights Act of 1964
employment at will	lockout	training
Employment Retirement Income	mediation	vestibule training
Security Act (ERISA) of 1974	merit salary system	wage reopener clause
equal employment opportunity	National Labor Relations Act (Wagner	wages
Equal Employment Opportunity	Act)	work slowdown
Commission (EEOC)	National Labor Relations Board	workers' compensation insurance
Equal Pay Act of 1963	(NLRB)	workforce diversity

MyBizLab

To complete the problems with the ✪, go to EOC Discussion Questions in the MyLab.

questions & exercises

QUESTIONS FOR REVIEW

1. What are the advantages and disadvantages of internal and external recruiting? Under what circumstances is each more appropriate?

2. Why is the formal training of workers so important to most employers? Why don't employers simply let people learn about their jobs as they perform them?

✪ 3. What different forms of compensation do firms typically use to attract and keep productive workers?

4. What is a knowledge worker? What strategies do companies use to retain knowledge workers?

QUESTIONS FOR ANALYSIS

✪ 5. What are your views on drug testing in the workplace? What would you do if your employer asked you to submit to a drug test?

6. Workers at Ford, GM, and Chrysler are represented by the UAW. However, the UAW has been much less successful in its attempts to unionize U.S. workers employed at Toyota, Nissan, and Honda plants in the United States. Why do you think this is so?

7. What are the advantages and challenges of having a diverse workforce?

✪ 8. How much will benefit considerations affect your choice of an employer after graduation? What types of benefits would be most and least appealing to you and why?

APPLICATION EXERCISES

9. Go online and search for at least three companies that are considered great places to work. Describe the compensation, benefits, and perks at each of these companies. Of the three, which is most appealing to you and why?

10. Interview the HR manager at a local company about their hiring processes. Describe how they recruit employees to apply for jobs, the steps in the selection process, and their orientation program for new employees.

building a business: continuing team exercise

Assignment

Meet with your team members to consider your new business venture and how it relates to the concepts of HRM discussed in this chapter. Develop specific responses to the following:

11. As your new venture grows, you will need to hire employees. How will you recruit people to apply for jobs within your organization?
12. Ideally, you will be able to select from many applicants for jobs within your company. How will you select the best employee from the pool of applicants?

13. How will employees be compensated in your company? How do you think that this compensation system will reflect your company's mission and goals?
14. What types of benefits will you offer to employees? Understanding the high cost of benefits, how have you selected these benefits?
15. Describe your system for performance appraisal and training. How will you reward good employees? When you have weak employees, how will you change their behavior?

team exercise

HANDLING THE LAYOFFS

The Situation

You are the vice president of a moderate-sized company that is going through tough times after losing a major contract. As a result, the company is asking each manager to eliminate 10 percent of the staff in their department. One of your newer managers has come to you for advice. He is new to his position and has little experience to draw from. Of his seven employees, he is being asked to identify one to lay off. The members of the manager's team are as follows:

- Tony Jones: white male, 10 years with the company; average performer who reportedly drinks a lot after work
- Amanda Wiggens: white female; ambitious; 3 years with company; above-average performer; puts in extra time at work; is known to be abrasive when dealing with others
- Jorge Gonzalez: Latino, 20 years with the company; average performer; was laid off before but then called back when business picked up
- Dorothy Henderson: white female, 25 years with company, below-average performer, has filed five sexual harassment complaints in last 10 years
- Wanda Jackson: African-American female, 8 years with company; outstanding performer; is rumored to be looking for another job
- Jerry Loudder: white male, single parent, 5 years with company; average performer

- Martha Strawser: white female, 6 years with company; excellent performer but spotty attendance, is putting husband through college

Team Activity

Assemble a group of four students. Your group has agreed to provide the manager with a recommendation.

ACTION STEPS

16. As a group, discuss the underlying legal and ethical issues in this situation. What laws must be considered before making this decision?
17. Working individually, develop a recommendation about who should be laid off.
18. Have each team member discuss their recommendation with the group, justifying their decision on the basis of both the ethical and legal considerations.
19. Finally, develop a group recommendation about the order in which employees should be laid off.
20. Now that you have decided which employee to lay off, develop a set of recommendations on how layoffs should be handled. Be sure to consider how to communicate your decision to the employee being laid off as well as those who remain.

exercising your ethics

OPERATING TACTICALLY

The Situation

Assume that you work as a manager for a medium-sized, non-union company that is facing its most serious union-organizing campaign in years. Your boss, who is determined to keep the union, has just given you a list of things to do to thwart the efforts of the organizers. For example, he has suggested each of the following tactics:

- Whenever you learn about a scheduled union meeting, you should schedule a "worker appreciation" event at the same

time. He wants you to offer free pizza and to give cash prizes that winners must be present to receive.
- He wants you to look at the most recent performance evaluations of the key union organizers and to terminate the one with the lowest overall evaluation based on the "need to lower costs."
- He wants you to make an announcement that the firm is seriously considering such new benefits as on-site child care, flexible work schedules, telecommuting options, and exercise facilities. Although you know that the firm is indeed looking into these benefits, you also know that,

ultimately, your boss will provide far less lavish benefits than he wants you to suggest.

The Dilemma

When you questioned the ethics—and even the legality—of these tactics, your boss responded by saying, "Look, all's fair in love and war, and this is war." He went on to explain that he was seriously concerned that a union victory might actually shut down the company's domestic operations altogether, forcing it to move all of its production capacities to lower-cost foreign plants. He concluded by saying that he was really looking out for the employees, even if he had to play hardball to help

them. You easily see through his hypocrisy, but you also recognize some potential truth in his warning: If the union wins, jobs may actually be lost.

QUESTIONS TO ADDRESS

21. What are the ethical issues in this situation?
22. What are the basic arguments for and against extreme measures to fight unionization efforts?
23. What do you think most managers would do in this situation? What would you do?

cases

A Unique Partnership Drives Wegmans

At the beginning of this chapter, you read about Wegmans and its approach to human resource management. Using the information presented in this chapter, you should now be able to respond to these questions.

QUESTIONS FOR DISCUSSION

24. If you were an HR executive at Wegmans, would you focus more on *internal recruiting* or on *external recruiting*? Would your strategy for higher-level positions differ from your strategy for lower-level positions? How would current economic conditions influence your strategy?
25. As an HR executive at Wegmans, you need to hire a group of new employees as part of your management-trainee program—people who will be put on a track leading, ultimately, to positions as store managers. Briefly outline your program for developing these employees.
26. If you were an employee at Wegmans, how would you expect your annual performance appraisal to be conducted? Given the company's customer-relations strategy, which appraisal methods do you think would be most appropriate?

A Really Great Place to Work

Every year, *Fortune* magazine publishes a list of great places to work. Many of these are household names—Google, Wegmans, and The Container Store—well known for their pay, benefits, and perks. But you might not be as familiar with SAS Institute, which has been at the top of the list for years. A private tech company headquartered in Cary, North Carolina, SAS has a unique approach to compensation, benefits, and work/life balance. The company, which has more than 6,000 employees in the United States and twice that many worldwide, pays its employees well. This is important—as a company that helps businesses turn raw data into useful information, their employees are at the core of their success. However, unlike many other companies in the tech industry, SAS places a very high value on work/life balance. SAS has a companywide standard that employees don't work more than 37.5 hours per week. Of course, there are

times when employees need to put in extra hours, but they are encouraged to take time off soon afterward to recharge. And, while you're at work, you'll enjoy a private office (no cubicles or shared work spaces) and you'll be able to take advantage of the on-site hair and nail salons, shoe and jewelry repair shops, and dry-cleaning and tailoring services. Many services are provided for free on-site, such as tax preparation and a health clinic and pharmacy. They even offer a seasonal farmers market, right at their Cary headquarters.

SAS Institute is an ideal employer for those with families. Employees' children are welcomed at work, both at the subsidized on-site daycare center as well as in the cafeteria, which includes kid-friendly items such as octopus-shaped hot dogs on their menu. Employees with school-aged children are encouraged to bring their kids to work with them on the occasional teacher workdays, making the balancing act of parenting and working a little easier. In a recent survey, one employee put it this way, "SAS has provisions to support you at whatever stage of life you are in—child care for your newborn to preschooler, resources for dealing with your teenager and college planning, help with your elderly parent. More importantly, a real sense of community is built when people work together for so long."

Founder and CEO Jim Goodnight believes that it's essential that employees feel trusted and valued. By almost every metric, this has paid off. In the software industry, turnover tends to be about 20 percent per year, as employees hop from one job to the next in hopes of higher pay or better working conditions. This is not the case at SAS, where turnover is just about 4 percent. In a recent survey, more than 95 percent of employees rated SAS as an employer with great challenges, great atmosphere, great rewards, and even great bosses.

QUESTIONS FOR DISCUSSION

27. After reading about SAS Institute, what would appeal to you most about working there?
28. What trade-offs is SAS making to offer the benefits and culture described?
29. What types of policies and benefits do you believe are most supportive of work/life balance?
30. What challenges might you face as a manager working in this environment? How could you overcome these challenges?

crafting a business plan

PEOPLE IN ORGANIZATIONS

Goal of the Exercise

Consider that your business has an identity and you've described the factors that will affect your business and how you will operate it. This part of the business plan project asks you to think about your employees, the jobs they will be performing, and the ways in which you can lead and motivate them.

Exercise Background

In this part of the business plan exercise, you'll take the different job titles you created in the organizational chart and give thought to the *skills* that employees will need to bring to the job *before* they begin. You'll also consider *training* you'll need to provide *after* they are hired, as well as how you'll compensate your employees. This part of the plan of the business plan also asks you to consider how you'll lead your employees and keep them happy and motivated.

Your Assignment

For the purposes of this assignment, you need to answer the following questions:

31. What do you see as the "corporate culture" of your business? What types of employee behaviors, such as organizational citizenship, will you expect?

    Hint: Will your business demand a casual environment or a more professional environment?

32. What is your philosophy on leadership? How will you manage your employees day to day?

33. Briefly create a job description for each team member.

    Hint: As you learned in this chapter, a job description lists the duties and responsibilities of a job; its working conditions; and the tools, materials, equipment, and information used to perform it. Imagine your business on a typical day. Who is working and what are each person's responsibilities?

34. Next, create a job specification for each job, listing the skills, other credentials, and qualifications needed to perform the job effectively.

    Hint: As you write your job specifications, consider what you would write if you were composing an ad for the position. What would the new employee need to bring to the job to qualify for the position?

35. What sort of training, if any, will your employees need once they are hired? How will you provide this training?

    Hint: Refer to the discussion of training in this chapter. Will you offer your employees on-the-job training? Off-the-job training? Vestibule training?

36. A major factor in retaining skilled workers is a company's compensation system—the total package of rewards it offers employees in return for their labor. Part of this compensation system includes wages or salaries. What wages or salaries will you offer for each job? Why did you decide on that pay rate?

    Hint: Refer to the discussion in this chapter for more information on forms of compensation. You may also want to check out sites such as www.salary.com, which includes a salary wizard you can use to determine how much people with different job titles are making in your area and across the United States.

37. As you learned in this chapter, incentive programs are special programs designed to motivate high performance. What incentives will you use to motivate your workforce?

    Hint: Be creative and look beyond a simple answer, such as giving pay increases. Ask yourself: Who are my employees and what is important to them? Refer to the discussion in this chapter for more information on the types of incentives you may want to consider.

MyBizLab

Go to the Assignments section of your MyLab to complete these writing exercises.

38. In many organizations, there are experts who are responsible for job analysis and recruiting. Explain why job analysis should be conducted before recruitment. Assume your organization owns thirty-five casual dining restaurants across the Midwest. It's been many years since the company has looked at its job descriptions for managers. However, due to a recent vacancy, you've been asked to conduct job analysis for the general manager position for each restaurant. Write a job description and job specification for this position. If you were in charge of recruiting, where might you look to find someone to fulfill this position internally and externally?

39. In 2011, following the retirement of the NASA Space Shuttle Program, Boeing announced layoffs in the Space Exploration program. Boeing offered the 510 employees being laid off an option during the 60-day period of advance notice. The first option was that the employee could stay until the day of termination, during which time Boeing would search for a job opening in another of their programs, but potentially in a different location. If the employee chose this option, it was possible that Boeing would not find them a position and they would still be terminated. The second option was the employee could forego Boeing's career transition services and search for a job in a different company. If the employee chose this option, Boeing would not attempt to relocate them. The employee had to inform Boeing in advance of their choice. Write an essay in which you answer the following questions: (a) Do you agree with this type of layoff? Why or why not? (b) What are the advantages and disadvantages of using this type of termination in mass layoffs? (c) What are some alternatives that Boeing could have pursued?

end notes

[1] *HR Magazine*, "Nothing Partial About These Benefits," vol. 48, No. 8 by Elayne Robertson Demby, August 1,2003, see http://www.shrm.org/Publications/hrmagazine/EditorialContent/Pages/0803demby.aspx;; "The Wegmans Way," by Matthew Boyle, January 24, 2005, *Fortune Magazine*, see: http://money.cnn.com/magazines/fortune/fortune_archive/2005/01/24/8234048/; Jon Springer, "Danny Wegman," *Supermarket News*, July 14, 2009, at http://supermarketnews.com, accessed on April 15, 2013; Prospero, Michael A. "Employee Innovator: Wegmans," *Fast Company*, October 2004, at www.fastcompany.com, accessed on April 15, 2011, see http://www.fastcompany.com/51347/employee-innovator-wegmans; Mitchell, Dan. "Wegmans Price War Against Itself," *The Big Money*, November 2, 2009, at www.thebigmoney.com, accessed on April 15, 2013; "100 Best Companies to Work For," *Fortune*, 2011, at http://money.cnn.com, accessed on April 15, 2013; Business Civic Leadership Center, "Wegmans," *2009 Corporate Citizenship Awards* (U.S. Chamber of Commerce, 2009), at www.bclc.uschamber.com, accessed on April 15, 2013; "In 2010, Wegmans Announces Largest Group of Employee Scholarship Recipients Yet," press release, June 16, 2010, at www.wegmans.com, accessed on April 15, 2013, from http://www.wholefoodsmarket.com/mission-values/core-values/declaration-interdependence

[2] Wright, Patrick, and McMahan, Gary. "Strategic Human Resources Management: A Review of the Literature," *Journal of Management*, June 1992, pp. 280–319; see also Peter Cappelli, "Talent Management for the Twenty-First Century," *Harvard Business Review*, March 2008, pp. 74–84; and Edward E. Lawler III, "Making Human Capital a Source of Competitive Advantage," *Organizational Dynamics*, January–March 2009, pp. 1–7.

[3] Lado, Augustine, and Wilson, Mary. "Human Resource Systems and Sustained Competitive Advantage: A Competency-Based Perspective," *Academy of Management Review*, 1994, Vol. 19, No. 4, pp. 699–727.

[4] Lepak, David, and Snell, Scott. "Examining the Human Resource Architecture: The Relationships among Human Capital, Employment, and Human Resource Configurations," *Journal of Management*, 2002, Vol. 28, No. 4, pp. 517–543. See also Wayne F. Cascio and Herman Aguinis, "Staffing Twenty-First Century Organizations," in James P. Walsh and Arthur P. Brief, *The Academy of Management Annals*, Vol. 2 (London: Routledge, 2008), pp. 133–166.

[5] "Maryland First to OK "Wal-Mart Bill,'" *USA Today*, January 13, 2006, p. 1B.

[6] "OSHA Claims Company Knowingly Overexposed Workers to Lead," *Advanced Safety and Health*, January 21, 2011, pp. 35–41.

[7] Breaugh, James A., and Starke, Mary. "Research on Employee Recruiting: So Many Studies, So Many Remaining Questions," *Journal of Management*, 2000, Vol. 26, No. 3, pp. 405–434.

[8] "Employee Relations Principles," NUCOR Corporation; "Pain, but No Layoffs at Nucor," *BusinessWeek*, March 26, 2009, at www.businessweek.com, accessed on March 25, 2011; John Byrnes with Michael Arndt, "The Art of Motivation," *BusinessWeek*, May 1, 2006, at www.businessweek.com, accessed on March 26, 2011; "About Us," Nucor website, at www.nucor.com, accessed on April 2, 2011; "Nucor Reports Record Results for 2008,"

Reuters, January 27, 2009, at www.reuters.com, accessed on April 2, 2011; Mayer, Kathy. "Nucor Steel: Pioneering Mill in Crawfordsville Celebrates 20 Years and 30 Million Tons," *AllBusiness*, September 1, 2008, at www.allbusiness.com, accessed on April 3, 2011.

[9]"Some Employers Offer ID Theft Coverage," *USA Today*, September 12, 2005, p. 1B.

[10]"FedEx, Goodyear Make Big Pension Plan Changes," *Workforce Management* (March 1, 2007), at http://www.workforce.com/section/00/article/24/77/95.html

[11]Brown, Kenneth B., and Sitzmann, Traci. "Training and Employee Development for Improved Performance," in Zedeck, Sheldon (ed.), *Handbook of Industrial and Organizational Psychology*, Vol. 2: *Selecting and Developing Members for the Organization* (Washington, DC: American Psychological Association), pp. 469–504.

[12]"2010 Training Industry Report," *Training Magazine*, November 19, 2010, pp. 65–88.

[13]DeRouin, Renee, Fritzsche, Barbara, and Salas, Eduardo. "E-Learning in Organizations," *Journal of Management*, 2005, Vol. 31, No. 6, pp. 920–940. See Fred Luthans, James B. Avey, and Jaime L. Patera, "Experimental Analysis of a Web-Based Training Intervention to Develop Positive Psychological Capital," *Academy of Management Learning & Education*, 2008, Vol. 7, No. 2, pp. 209–221 for a recent illustration.

[14]"'Boeing U': Flying by the Book," *USA Today*, October 6, 1997, pp. 1B, 2B. See also "Is Your Airline Pilot Ready for Surprises?" *Time*, October 14, 2002, p. 72.

[15]"The Secret Sauce at In-N-Out Burger," *BusinessWeek*, April 20, 2009, pp. 68–69; "Despite Cutbacks, Firms Invest in Developing Leaders," *Wall Street Journal*, February 9, 2009, p. B4.

[16]Wildman, Jessica L., Bedwell, Wendy L., Salas, Eduardo, and Smith-Jentsch, Kimberly A. "Performance Measurement at Work: A Multilevel Perspective," in Zedeck, Sheldon (ed.), *Handbook of Industrial and Organizational Psychology*, Vol. 1: *Building and Developing the Organization* (Washington, DC: American Psychological Association, 2010), pp. 303–341.

[17]See Paul Levy and Jane Williams, "The Social Context of Performance Appraisal: A Review and Framework for the Future," *Journal of Management*, 2004, Vol. 30, No. 6, pp. 881–905.

[18]See Michael Hammer, "The 7 Deadly Sins of Performance Measurement (and How to Avoid Them)," *MIT Sloan Management Review*, Spring 2007, pp. 19–30.

[19]See Angelo S. DeNisi and Avraham N. Kluger, "Feedback Effectiveness: Can 360-Degree Appraisals Be Improved?" *Academy of Management Executive*, 2000, Vol. 14, No. 1, pp. 129–139.

[20]Yoo, Dan. "How to Fire Employees With Compassion," *Entrepreneur*, at www.entrepreneur.com, accessed May 19, 2015.

[21]Nathan, Barry R., Mohrman, Allan, and Milliman, John. "Interpersonal Relations as a Context for the Effects of Appraisal Interviews on Performance and Satisfaction:

A Longitudinal Study," *Academy of Management Journal*, June 1991, pp. 352–369.

[22]"Goodyear to Stop Labeling 10 percent of Its Workers as Worst," *USA Today*, September 12, 2002, p. 1B.

[23]"Welcome to Silicon Valley: Perksville, USA," *USA Today*, July 5, 2012, p. 1A.

[24]"For Some, a Patchwork of Jobs Pays the Bills," *Boston.com*, March 27, 2009, at www.boston.com, accessed on April 15, 2013; Kridel, Kristin. "Overqualified Applying for Temporary Work," *Spokesman.com*, March 4, 2009, at www.spokesman.com, accessed on April 15, 2013; Fisher, Anne. "Be a Manager and a Temp?" *CNNMoney.com*, March 16, 2009, at www.cmfassociates.com, accessed on April 15, 2013; Patel, Sital. "Skill Level of Temp Workers Rises amid Recession," *Fox Business*, February 27, 2009, at www.jobs-work-employment.com, accessed on April 15, 2013; U.S. Bureau of Labor Statistics (BLS); *The New York Times*, March 12, 2006, A Way to Try a Job on for Size Before Making a Commitment, by Mohn, Tanya; see: http://www.nytimes.com/2006/03/12/jobs/12jmar.html?pagewanted=print; "Table 12. Private Industry, by Industry Group and Full-Time and Part-Time Status," news release, December 2010, at www.bls.gov, accessed on April 15, 2013.

[25]http://www.bls.gov/opub/cwc/cb20100628ar01p1.htm

[26]U.S. Department of Labor, Bureau of Labor Statistics, at http://www.bls.gov/news.release/union2.nr0.htm, accessed on March 22, 2011.

[27]U.S. Department of Labor, Bureau of Labor Statistics, at http://www.bls.gov/news.release/pdf/wkstp.pdf, accessed on March 22, 2011.

[28]http://www.bls.gov/news.release/pdf/wkstp.pdf

[29]Brenoff, Ann. "8 Reasons Why Employees Never Want To Leave This Amazing Company." Huffington Post, November 18, 2013. Accessed May 19, 2015. http://www.huffingtonpost.com/2013/11/18/best-places-to-work_n_4240370.html. Great Place to Work Guides LLC. "SAS." Great Place to Work. Accessed May 19, 2015. http://us.greatrated.com/sas. http://www.thestar.com/news/gta/2013/04/09/zoo_lockout_could_threaten_panda_opening_union_says.html; http://www.twincities.com/allheadlines/ci_22978302/spco-lockout-appears-stalled.

[30]"Benefits." Wegmans.com. N.p., n.d. Web. 29 June 2013, wegmans.com.

[31]"Education." Wegmans.com. N.p., n.d. Web. 29 June 2013, wegmans.com.

[32]Walters, Candace. "Taking a Closer Look at Benefits: The Wegmans Way." *HR Works, Inc.* June 10, 2011. http://www.hrworks-inc.com/topics-in-hr/articles/3-benefits-administration-articles/350-taking-a-closer-look-at-benefits-the-wegmans-way, accessed on June 29, 2013.

[33]"Wegmans Food Markets." *CNNMoney*. Cable News Network, at http://money.cnn.com/magazines/fortune/best companies/2011/snapshots/3.html, accessed on June 29, 2013.

glossary

360-Degree Feedback performance appraisal technique in which managers are evaluated by everyone around them—their boss, their peers, and their subordinates.

Adverse Impact when minorities and women meet or pass the requirement for a job at a rate less than 80 percent of the rate of majority group members.

Affirmative Action intentionally seeking and hiring employees from groups that are underrepresented in the organization.

Affirmative Action Plan written statement of how the organization intends to actively recruit, hire, and develop members of relevant protected classes.

Age Discrimination in Employment Act outlaws discrimination against people older than 40 years.

Americans With Disabilities Act forbids discrimination on the basis of disabilities and requires employers to provide reasonable accommodations for disabled employees.

Arbitration method of resolving a labor dispute in which both parties agree to submit to the judgment of a neutral party.

Benefits compensation other than wages and salaries.

Bonus individual performance incentive in the form of a special payment made over and above the employee's salary.

Boycott labor action in which workers refuse to buy the products of a targeted employer.

Cafeteria Benefits Plan benefit plan that sets limits on benefits per employee, each of whom may choose from a variety of alternative benefits.

Civil Rights Act of 1991 amended the original Civil Rights Act.

Collective Bargaining the process by which union leaders and managers negotiate common terms and conditions of employment for the workers represented by unions.

Compensation System total package of rewards that organizations provide to individuals in return for their labor.

Contingent Worker employee hired on something other than a full-time basis to supplement an organization's permanent workforce.

Cost-of-Living Adjustment (COLA) labor contract clause tying future raises to changes in consumer purchasing power.

Development usually refers to teaching managers and professionals the skills needed for both present and future jobs.

Employee Information System (Skills Inventory) computerized system containing information on each employee's education, skills, work experiences, and career aspirations.

Employment at Will principle, increasingly modified by legislation and judicial decision, that organizations should be able to retain or dismiss employees at their discretion.

Employee Retirement Income Security Act (ERISA) of 1974 ensures the financial security of pension funds by regulating how they can be invested.

Equal Employment Opportunity legally mandated nondiscrimination in employment on the basis of race, creed, sex, or national origin.

Equal Employment Opportunity Commission (EEOC) federal agency enforcing several discrimination-related laws.

Equal Pay Act of 1963 requires that men and women be paid the same amount for doing the same job.

External Recruiting attracting persons outside the organization to apply for jobs.

Fair Labor Standards Act sets a minimum wage and requires the payment of overtime rates for work in excess of 40 hours per week.

Family and Medical Leave Act (FMLA) of 1993 requires employers to provide up to 12 weeks of unpaid leave for family and medical emergencies.

Gainsharing Plan incentive plan that rewards groups for productivity improvements.

Hostile Work Environment form of sexual harassment deriving from off-color jokes, lewd comments, and so forth.

Human Capital reflects the organization's investment in attracting, retaining, and motivating an effective workforce.

Human Resource Management (HRM) set of organizational activities directed at attracting, developing, and maintaining an effective workforce.

Incentive Program special compensation program designed to motivate high performance.

Internal Recruiting considering present employees as candidates for openings.

Job Analysis systematic analysis of jobs within an organization.

Job Description description of the duties and responsibilities of a job, its working conditions, and the tools, materials, equipment, and information used to perform it.

Job Specification description of the skills, abilities, and other credentials and qualifications required by a job.

Knowledge Workers employees who are of value because of the knowledge they possess.

Labor Relations process of dealing with employees who are represented by a union.

Labor Union group of individuals working together to achieve shared job-related goals, such as higher pay, shorter working hours, more job security, greater benefits, or better working conditions.

Labor-Management Relations Act (also known as the *Taft-Hartley Act*) passed to limit union power.

Lockout management tactic whereby workers are denied access to the employer's workplace.

Mediation a neutral third party (the mediator) can advise, but cannot impose a settlement on the other parties.

Merit Salary System individual incentive linking compensation to performance in nonsales jobs.

National Labor Relations Act (or Wagner Act) act that put labor unions on a more equal footing with management in terms of the rights of employees to organize and bargain.

National Labor Relations Board (NLRB) established by the Wagner Act to administer its provisions.

Occupational Safety and Health Act (OSHA) of 1970 federal law setting and enforcing guidelines for protecting workers from unsafe conditions and potential health hazards in the workplace.

On-the-Job Training training, sometimes informal, conducted while an employee is at work.

Patriot Act legislation that increased U.S. government's power to investigate and prosecute suspected terrorists.

Pay-for-Knowledge Plan incentive plan to encourage employees to learn new skills or become proficient at different jobs.

Performance Appraisal evaluation of an employee's job performance to determine the degree to which the employee is performing effectively.

Picketing labor action in which workers publicize their grievances at the entrance to an employer's facility.

Profit-Sharing Plan incentive plan for distributing bonuses to employees when company profits rise above a certain level.

Quid Pro Quo Harassment form of sexual harassment in which sexual favors are requested in return for job-related benefits.

Realistic Job Preview (RJP) providing the applicant with a real picture of what performing the job that the organization is trying to fill would be like.

Recruiting process of attracting qualified persons to apply for jobs an organization is seeking to fill.

Replacement Chart list of each management position, who occupies it, how long that person will likely stay in the job, and who is qualified as a replacement.

Salary compensation in the form of money paid for discharging the responsibilities of a job.

Sexual Harassment making unwelcome sexual advances in the workplace.

Strike labor action in which employees temporarily walk off the job and refuse to work.

Strikebreaker worker hired as a permanent or temporary replacement for a striking employee.

Title VII of the Civil Rights Act of 1964 forbids discrimination in all areas of the employment relationship.

Training usually refers to teaching operational or technical employees how to do the job for which they were hired.

Vestibule Training off-the-job training conducted in a simulated environment.

Wages compensation in the form of money paid for time worked.

Work Slowdown labor action in which workers perform jobs at a slower than normal pace.

Workers Compensation Insurance legally required insurance for compensating workers injured on the job.

Workforce Diversity the range of workers' attitudes, values, beliefs, and behaviors that differ by gender, race, age, ethnicity, physical ability, and other relevant characteristics.

Marketing Processes and Consumer Behavior

From Chapter 11 of *Business Essentials*, Eleventh Edition. Ronald J. Ebert, Ricky W. Griffin. Copyright © 2017 by Pearson Education, Inc.

Marketing Processes and Consumer Behavior

As consumers, we are the forces that drive marketing.

But those same marketing campaigns push

us in directions

without us even knowing it.

After reading this chapter, you should be able to:

1 **Explain** the concept of marketing and identify the five forces that constitute the external marketing environment.

2 **Explain** the purpose of a marketing plan and identify its main components.

3 **Explain** market segmentation and how it is used in target marketing.

4 **Discuss** the purpose of marketing research and compare the four marketing research methods.

5 **Describe** the consumer buying process and the key factors that influence that process.

6 **Discuss** the four categories of organizational markets and the characteristics of business-to-business (B2B) buying behavior.

7 **Discuss** the marketing mix as it applies to small business.

Building a Brand With
Social Media

Perhaps you are one of the more than 7 million people who subscribe to Michelle Phan's YouTube Channel. Or maybe you know someone who has purchased products from her L'Oreal product line.

Even if you've never heard the name Michelle Phan, you'll find that she has an interesting story that highlights the importance of believing in yourself, identifying a target market, and building a brand.

While taking a college class, Phan was given the opportunity to use a MacBook Pro. Excited about the new technology, Phan started a blog about her life. Well, not exactly. The blog depicted the life that she dreamed of, one with money and a fantastic family, a life that was much more exciting and glamorous than her real-life experience. Phan's childhood was difficult. She grew up in Florida in a community with few Asian children, she was subject to ridicule, and she felt out of place because of her Vietnamese heritage. To make things worse, her father had gambling issues and the family moved from home to home. Eventually, her father left and her mother remarried, only to have that relationship end. By the age of 17, Phan was working as a hostess at a restaurant to supplement her mom's meager pay as a nail technician, just to put a roof over their heads; they couldn't even afford much furniture. It was the chance of a lifetime when Phan's extended family found the resources to send her to the Ringling College of Art and Design, where she received that MacBook Pro.

However, her blog was just the start. Several subscribers to her blog asked her to post a tutorial about how she did her makeup, so Phan created a short video tutorial about creating a "natural" look. She had expected that the audience for the video would be just the few people who read her blog, but she had 40,000 views in the first week. So, she created more videos on how to create different looks, from dark and stormy to soft hues appropriate for church. Phan established herself as an authority on beauty and she shared her expertise. "You need interesting content that entertains or informs—preferably both. You want people to look forward to your posts and come back for more. People want to follow you. They want to hear your words and see your vision." Her lack of money to buy makeup didn't limit her ability to create new videos—she scoured the bargain bins at stores, picking up many items for less than a dollar. Eventually, she was able to generate advertising revenue from her YouTube channel, allowing her to quit her job as a waitress.

Within four years, Phan had become a brand. The name Michelle Phan conveyed an image and position in the market. Google offered her $1 million to create 20 hours of content, and she began creating video content for high-end cosmetics line Lancome. A year later, L'Oreal offered Phan her

Auremar/Fotolia

what's in it for me?

Businesses must adapt to their environment in many different ways. One common approach is to apply marketing basics in an innovative way to appeal to the forces of the external marketing environment. This chapter discusses these basics along with the marketing plan and components of the marketing mix, as well as target marketing and market segmentation. It also explores key factors that influence consumer and organizational buying processes. By grasping the marketing methods and ideas in this chapter, you will not only be better prepared as a marketing professional but you also will become a more informed consumer.

own makeup line. At that moment, Phan realized she had made it—she called her mother and told her she'd just done her last pedicure. And she meant it.

Phan has expanded her presence in the market by creating Ipsy, a beauty sample service and community. Subscribers pay $10 a month to sample products selected especially for them and are able to view video content to optimize their experience. Phan is also a co-founder of Shift Music Group, a music publishing company, and is creating a premium lifestyle network called ICON, partnering with Endemol USA. While not yet 30, Phan has established herself as a powerhouse in the beauty and life-style industry. She carefully monitors trends in her environment and quickly spots new opportunities. At the same time, she's kept a keen eye on her target market and understands the consumer buying process.

While many might perceive YouTube as a difficult path to a successful career, Phan believes just the opposite. She explains, "You're in control of how people perceive you and see you. I can't say the same for traditional media because you have other people who are editing you—producers and other people who have the final say. Your YouTube channel is your own show. I think it's a wonderful platform for anyone who wants to have stronger creative control over their content, their message, their vision, and their branding."[1] (After studying the content in this chapter, you should be able to answer a set of discussion questions found at the end of the chapter.)

OBJECTIVE 1
Explain

the concept of marketing and identify the five forces that constitute the external marketing environment.

What Is Marketing?

As consumers, we are influenced by the marketing activities of people like Michelle Phan and companies like L'Oreal and Google that want us to buy their products rather than those of their competitors. Being consumers makes us the essential ingredients in the marketing process. Every day, we express needs for such essentials as food, clothing, and shelter and wants for such nonessentials as entertainment and leisure activities. Our needs and wants are major forces that drive marketing.

What comes to mind when you think of marketing? Most of us think of marketing as advertisements for detergents and soft drinks. Marketing, however, encompasses a much wider range of activities. The American Marketing Association defines **marketing** as "activities, a set of institutions, and processes for creating, communicating, delivering, and exchanging offerings that have value for customers, clients, partners, and society at large."[2] To see this definition in action, we'll continue this chapter by looking at some marketing basics, including the ways marketers build relationships with customers. We'll then examine forces that constitute the external marketing environment, followed by marketing strategy, the marketing plan, and the components of the marketing mix. We'll then discuss market segmentation and how it is used in target marketing. Next, we'll examine marketing research, followed by a look at key factors that influence the buying processes of consumers and industrial buyers. Finally, we'll consider the marketing mix for small business and then go beyond domestic borders to explore the international marketing mix.

Marketing *activities, a set of institutions, and processes for creating, communicating, delivering, and exchanging offerings that have value for customers, clients, partners, and society at large.*

Delivering Value

What attracts buyers to one product instead of another? Although our desires for the many available goods and services may be unbounded, limited financial resources force most of us to be selective. Accordingly, customers usually try to buy products that offer the best value when it comes to meeting their needs and wants.

Value *relative comparison of a product's benefits versus its costs*

Value and Benefits The **value** of a product compares its benefits with its costs. Benefits include not only the functions of the product but also the emotional satisfaction associated with owning, experiencing, or possessing it. But every product has costs, including sales price, the expenditure of the buyer's time, and even the emotional costs of making a purchase decision. A satisfied customer perceives the benefits derived from the purchase to be greater than its costs. Thus, the simple but important ratio for value is derived as follows:

$$\text{Value} = \frac{\text{Benefits}}{\text{Costs}}$$

The marketing strategies of leading firms focus on increasing value for customers. Marketing resources are deployed to add benefits and decrease costs of products to provide greater value. To satisfy customers, a company may do the following:

- Develop an entirely new product that performs better (provides greater performance benefits) than existing products.

- Keep a store open longer hours during a busy season (adding the benefit of greater shopping convenience).

- Offer price reductions (the benefit of lower costs).

- Offer information that explains how a product can be used in new ways (the benefit of new uses at no added cost).

Value and Utility To understand how marketing creates value for customers, we need to know the kind of benefits that buyers get from a firm's goods or services. Those benefits provide customers with **utility**, the ability of a product to satisfy a human want or need. Think about the competitive marketing efforts for Microsoft's Xbox series and those for Sony's competing PlayStation game consoles. In both companies, marketing strives to provide four kinds of utility in the following ways:

Utility *ability of a product to satisfy a human want or need*

1 **Form utility**. Marketing has a voice in designing products with features that customers want. Microsoft's Xbox One features kineet technology (voice- and motion-detecting software) and can record a video of your game. Sony's newest PlayStation 4 (PS 4) touts a controller with a six-axis sensor.

Form Utility *providing products with features that customers want*

2 **Time utility**. Marketing creates a time utility by providing products *when* customers will want them. Both Sony and Microsoft create Internet buzzes and rumors among gamers by hinting at upcoming release dates without mentioning specifics.

Time Utility *providing products when customers will want them*

3 **Place utility**. Marketing creates a place utility by making products easily accessible—by making products available *where* customers will want them. Xbox One and PS 4 are available online at Amazon.com and at many brick-and-mortar retailers such as Best Buy and Target.

Place Utility *providing products where customers will want them*

4 **Possession utility**. Marketing creates a possession utility by transferring product ownership to customers by setting selling prices, setting terms for customer credit payments, if needed, and providing ownership documents. Hints about prices from both companies have fueled rumors: Xbox One sells for around $350, while the PS 4 runs about $400.

Possession Utility *transferring product ownership to customers by setting selling prices, setting terms for customer credit payments, and providing ownership documents*

As you can imagine, marketing responsibilities at Microsoft and Sony are extremely challenging in such a competitive arena, and the stakes are high. Because they determine product features, and the timing, place, and terms of sale that provide utility and add value for customers, marketers must understand customers' wants and needs. In today's fast-moving industries, those wants and needs must be determined quickly.

Goods, Services, and Ideas

The marketing of tangible goods is obvious in everyday life. It applies to two types of customers: those who buy consumer goods and those who buy industrial goods. In a department store, an employee may ask if you'd like to try a new cologne. A pharmaceutical company proclaims the virtues of its new cold medicine. Your local auto dealer offers an economy car at an economy price. These products are all

Consumer Goods *physical products purchased by consumers for personal use*

Industrial Goods *physical products purchased by companies to produce other products*

Services *products having non-physical features, such as information, expertise, or an activity that can be purchased*

consumer goods, tangible goods that you, the consumer, may buy for personal use. Firms that sell goods to consumers for personal consumption are engaged in consumer marketing, also known as business-to-consumer (B2C) marketing.

Marketing also applies to **industrial goods**, physical items used by companies to produce other products. Surgical instruments and bulldozers are industrial goods, as are components and raw materials such as integrated circuits, steel, coffee beans, and plastic. Firms that sell goods to other companies are engaged in industrial marketing, also known as business-to-business (B2B) marketing.

But marketing techniques are also applied to **services**, products with intangible (nonphysical) features, such as professional advice, timely information for decisions, or arrangements for a vacation. Service marketing, the application of marketing for services, continues to be a major growth area in the United States. Insurance companies, airlines, public accountants, and health clinics all engage in service marketing, both to individuals (consumer markets) and to other companies (industrial markets). Thus, the terms *consumer marketing* and *industrial marketing* include services as well as goods.

Finally, marketers also promote ideas, such as "inspirational values" as seen in "Encouragement, Pass It On," on YouTube and in the popular television commercials. Ads in theaters warn us against copyright infringement and piracy. Other marketing campaigns may stress the advantages of avoiding fast foods, texting while driving, or quitting smoking, or they may promote a political party or candidate.

Relationship Marketing and Customer Relationship Management

Relationship Marketing *marketing strategy that emphasizes building lasting relationships with customers and suppliers*

Although marketing often focuses on single transactions for products, services, or ideas, marketers also take a longer-term perspective. Thus, **relationship marketing** is a type of marketing that emphasizes building lasting relationships with customers and suppliers. Stronger relationships, including stronger economic and social ties, can result in greater long-term satisfaction, customer loyalty, and customer retention.[3] Michelle Phan has used relationship marketing very successfully. Similarly, Starbucks's Card Rewards attracts return customers with free coffee refills and other extras. Commercial banks also offer economic incentives to encourage longer-lasting relationships. Longtime customers who purchase a certain number of the bank's products (for example, checking accounts, savings accounts, and loans) accumulate credits toward free or reduced-price products or services, such as free investment advice.

Customer Relationship Management (CRM) *organized methods that a firm uses to build better information connections with clients, so that stronger company-client relationships are developed*

Like many other marketing areas, the ways that marketers go about building relationships with customers have changed dramatically. **Customer relationship management (CRM)** is an organized method that an enterprise uses to build better information connections with clients, so that managers can develop stronger enterprise–client relationships.

The power of Internet communications coupled with the ability to gather and assemble information on customer preferences allows marketers to better predict what clients will want and buy. Viking River Cruises communicates with booked vacationers months in advance of departures, including e-mails with menus and recipes from countries that vacationers will be visiting. Viking also encourages social networking among booked passengers to establish prevoyage friendships, which can lead to faster face-to-face acquaintanceships once they board the riverboat.

Data Warehousing *the collection, storage, and retrieval of data in electronic files*

Data Mining *the application of electronic technologies for searching, sifting, and reorganizing pools of data to uncover useful information*

The compiling and storage of customers' data, known as **data warehousing**, provides the raw materials from which marketers can extract information that enables them to find new clients and identify their best customers. Marketers can then inform these priority clients about upcoming new products and postpurchase service reminders. **Data mining** automates the massive analysis of data by using computers to sift, sort, and search for previously undiscovered clues about what customers look at and react to and how they might be influenced. Marketers use these tools to get a clearer picture of how knowing a client's preferences can satisfy those particular needs, thereby building closer, stronger relationships with customers.[4]

Toronto-based Fairmont Resort Hotels, for example, first used data mining to re-build its customer-relations package by finding out what kinds of vacations their customers prefer and then placed ads where they were more likely to reach those customers. When data mining revealed the worldwide destinations of Fairmont customers, it helped determine Fairmont's decision to buy their customers' number-one preference, the Savoy in London.[5] Fairmont's enhanced CRM has attracted new guests and strengthened relationships and loyalty among existing clients through Web-based promotions and incentives. Using profiles of guest information, Fairmont identifies target traveler segments and supplies travelers with personalized price discounts and special hotel services.[6]

The Marketing Environment

Marketing plans and strategies are not determined unilaterally by any business—rather, they are strongly influenced by powerful outside forces. As you see in Figure 1, every marketing program must recognize the factors in a company's *external environment*, which is everything outside an organization's boundaries that might affect it. In this section, we'll discuss how these external forces affect the marketing environment in particular.

Political-Legal Environment

The **political-legal environment**, both global and domestic, has profound effects on marketing. For example, environmental legislation has determined the destinies of entire industries. The political push for alternative energy sources is creating new markets and products for emerging companies such as India's Suzlon Energy Limited (large wind turbines), wind-powered electric generators by Germany's Nordex AG, and wind farms and power plants by Spain's Gamesa Corporation. Marketing managers try to maintain favorable political and legal environments in several ways. To gain public support for products and activities, marketers use ad campaigns to raise public awareness of important issues. Companies contribute to political candidates and frequently support the activities of political action committees (PACs) maintained by their respective industries.

Political-Legal Environment *the relationship between business and government, usually in the form of government regulation of business*

Sociocultural Environment

The **sociocultural environment** also impacts marketing. Changing social values force companies to develop and promote new products, such as poultry and meat without antibiotics and growth hormones, for both individual consumers and industrial customers. Just a few years ago, organic

Sociocultural Environment *the customs, mores, values, and demographic characteristics of the society in which an organization functions*

FIGURE 1 The External Marketing Environment

foods were available only in specialty food stores such as Whole Foods. Today, in response to a growing demand for healthy foods, Target's Archer Farms product line brings affordable organic food to a much larger audience. Grocers like Kroger and HEB also have set aside large areas in their stores where consumers can find organic and/or natural products. In addition, new industrial products reflect changing social values: A growing number of wellness programs are available to companies for improving employees' health. Quest Diagnostics, for example, a B2B company, supplies a "Blueprint for Wellness" service that assesses employee healthcare risks in client companies and recommends programs for reducing those risks. This and other trends reflect the values, beliefs, and ideas that shape society. In similar fashion, businesses strive to distance themselves from people and products that are potentially offensive. For instance, when Donald Trump announced his bid for the presidency in 2015, he made several controversial remarks about illegal immigrants from Mexico. In quick response, NBC dropped plans to televise the Miss Universe pageant owned by Trump and Macy's discontinued its line of Trump-endorsed menswear.

Technological Environment *all the ways by which firms create value for their constituents*

Technological Environment
The **technological environment** creates new goods and services. New products make existing products obsolete, and many products change our values and lifestyles. In turn, lifestyle changes often stimulate new products not directly related to the new technologies themselves. Mobile devices, the availability of a vast array of apps, and social media, for example, facilitate business communication just as prepackaged meals provide convenience for busy household cooks. Both kinds of products also free up time for recreation and leisure.

Economic Environment *relevant conditions that exist in the economic system in which a company operates*

Economic Environment
Because economic conditions determine spending patterns by consumers, businesses, and governments, the **economic environment** influences marketing plans for product offerings, pricing, and promotional strategies. Marketers are concerned with such economic variables as inflation, interest rates, and recession. Thus, they monitor the general business cycle to anticipate trends in consumer and business spending.

Competitive Environment *the competitive system in which businesses compete*

Competitive Environment
In a **competitive environment**, marketers must convince buyers that they should purchase one company's products rather than another's. Because both consumers and commercial buyers have limited resources, every

John Locher/AP Images

Marketing strategies are strongly influenced by powerful outside forces. For example, new technologies create new products, such as the cell phone "gas station" shown here. These recharging stations enable customers to recharge their mobile devices just as they would refuel their cars. The screens at the stations also provide marketers with a new way to display ads to waiting customers.

managing in turbulent times

Feeling the Pressure for "Green"

Today's marketers are struggling with pressures from several outside forces: Changes in the political–legal, sociocultural, technological, and economic environments are changing the competitive landscape. Industries ranging from automobiles to energy to housing are grappling with a common environmental theme: *going green*. For example, public sentiment turned decidedly toward alternatives to gas-guzzling cars. Home buyers also want energy-efficient heating and cooling, such as geothermal heat, in their homes. Environmentalists are pushing for alternative energy sources, notably wind and solar power, to replace fossil fuels. Local utilities are offering incentives for construction using environmentally sensitive building designs to conserve energy. Purchases of tiny houses are growing. Solar-powered wells are replacing mechanical windmills on farms. In Washington, DC, the Barack Obama administration and Congress continue their struggle to create more jobs and reduce the national debt while also meeting commitments for a cleaner environment using energy-saving technologies.

David Koscheck/Shutterstock

These outside pressures present challenges for all areas of marketing—from identifying the new target markets to designing new products for those markets and, in some cases, finding technologies to make those products. Success depends on coordinating the various marketing activities and making them compatible with one another. Marketers need to present a convincing rationale for a product's pricing and demonstrate how the product provides the benefits sought by the target markets. Distribution methods, how companies deliver products and after-services to customers, have to match up with promises in the promotional message so that, together, the marketing activities provide a persuasive package that delivers the desired value and benefits. Further, this integrated marketing strategy must be coordinated with financial management and production operations to provide timely customer satisfaction.

The marketing blueprint for Toyota's Prius automobile used an integrated marketing mix for meeting the challenge of *going green*. While developing the fuel-efficient hybrid technology, Toyota identified niche target markets of users in some 40 countries and determined a price range compatible with the company's performance reliability and quality reputation. Promotion in the U.S. market started two years before the car was released so customers could view and purchase a Prius. In one prelaunch promotion, Toyota teamed up with the Sierra Club and lent the Prius to environmentally sensitive Hollywood superstars to provide exposure and allow car testing in the target market. The main ad campaign to general audiences emphasized that consumers can still have speed and comfort along with environmental friendliness. And preorders were delivered on time to buyers. As a result, the Prius became the most successful hybrid automobile in the United States and the rest of the world.

High fuel prices, as well as concern for the environment, were a major factor in the popularity of the Prius and other hybrid vehicles. However, falling fuel prices in 2014 affected the types of vehicles that consumers purchased. Sales of SUVs and trucks rose 10 percent in 2014 and sales of hybrid and electric vehicles slowed. With lower fuel prices, it could take five years or more to recover the additional cost associated with a hybrid from the fuel savings. However, as dealers find that they have excess inventory in hybrid cars, they have begun to cut prices, making the economic argument more compelling.

It's important to note that there's more to the story than fuel savings. Consumers are increasingly committed to lower emissions and a smaller carbon footprint. Interestingly, many hybrid owners consider their choice of a vehicle as an extension of their social identity. By September 2014, Prius dominated the market—accounting for more than half of all sales and seven times higher sales than the second-place vehicle, the Honda Civic. One explanation for this phenomenon relates directly to the buyer's social identity. Unlike the Civic, which is also available in a standard fuel option, the Prius is a hybrid-only model. Its distinctive appearance brands the owner as environmentally conscious, reinforcing the self-image of the owner.[7]

dollar spent on one product is no longer available for other purchases. Each marketing program, therefore, seeks to make its product the most attractive. Expressed in business terms, a failed program loses the buyer's dollar forever (or at least until it is time for the next purchase decision).

To promote products effectively, marketers must first understand which of three types of competition they face:

Substitute Product *product that is dissimilar from those of competitors, but that can fulfill the same need*

1 **Substitute products** may not look alike or they may seem different from one another, but they can fulfill the same need. For example, your cholesterol level may be controlled with either of two competing products: a physical fitness program or a drug regimen. The fitness program and the drugs compete as substitute products. Similarly, online video streaming services like Netflix provide substitute products for conventional television programming.

Brand Competition *competitive marketing that appeals to consumer perceptions of benefits of products offered by particular companies*

2 **Brand competition** occurs between similar products and is based on buyers' perceptions of the benefits of products offered by particular companies. For Internet searches, do you turn to Google, Bing, or Yahoo!? Brand competition is based on users' perceptions of the benefits offered by each product.

International Competition *competitive marketing of domestic products against foreign products*

3 **International competition** matches the products of domestic marketers against those of foreign competitors. The intensity of international competition has been heightened by the formation of alliances, such as the European Union and the North American Free Trade Agreement (NAFTA). The U.S. Air Force recently opened bidding to foreign manufacturers for three new planes to replace the existing Presidential Air Force One fleet (made by Boeing). If Europe's Airbus had won the contract, it would have been the first time a U.S. president has flown in a non-U.S.-made Air Force One.[8] Instead, however, Airbus withdrew from bidding, leaving Boeing the sole competitor. However, Airbus remains as a formidable competitor of Boeing in today's commercial aircraft industry.

Having identified the kind of competition, marketers can then develop a plan for attracting more customers.

OBJECTIVE 2
Explain
the purpose of a marketing plan and identify its main components.

Developing the Marketing Plan

A marketing manager at a major home appliance manufacturing company explains the concept of *developing the marketing plan* by using the analogy of planning for a trip as follows:

- "First, you decide where you want to go and what you want to happen when you get there. Why take this trip and not others, instead?"
  [Identify the *objective* or *goal* to be achieved.]

- "At some stage, you decide when the trip will happen and how you'll get to the destination."
  [*Plan* for *when* it will happen, and for the *paths* (or *routes*) that will be taken to get there.]

- "Every trip requires resources, so you identify those resource requirements and compare them against resources that are available."
  [*Evaluate resource* requirements and availabilities.]

- "If available resources are too expensive, then you adjust the trip so it becomes affordable."
  [*Adjust plans* as needed to become *realistic* and *feasible*.]

- "During and after the trip, you assess the successes (what went right) and the drawbacks (what went wrong) and remember them so you can make the next trip even better."
  [Keep notes and data about what happened because *learning* from this experience increases the chances for *greater success on the next*.]

As you will see, our discussion of the marketing plan contains many of the preceding elements. The **marketing plan** identifies the marketing objectives stating what marketing will accomplish in the future. It contains a strategy that identifies the specific activities and resources that will be used to meet the needs and desires of customers in the firm's chosen target markets, so as to accomplish the marketing objectives.

First and foremost, marketing plans are future-oriented, showing what will be happening with marketing's upcoming activities. Every well-founded marketing plan, as shown in Figure 2, begins with objectives or goals that set the stage for everything that follows. **Marketing objectives**, the goals the marketing plan intends to accomplish, are the foundation that guides all the detailed activities in the plan. The marketing objectives themselves, however, exist solely to support the company's overall business mission (at the top in Figure 2) and typically focus on maintaining or enhancing the organization's future competitive position in its chosen markets. Hypothetically, Starbucks's overall business mission could aim at being the world's leading retailer of specialty coffee. Two supporting marketing objectives, then, could be (1) a 5 percent increase in its worldwide market share by, say, 2018, and (2) be the leading retailer (in dollar sales) of specialty coffee in China by 2020.

Marketing Plan detailed strategy for focusing marketing efforts on consumers' needs and wants

Marketing Objectives the things marketing intends to accomplish in its marketing plan

Marketing Strategy: Planning the Marketing Mix

The marketing team can develop a strategy once they have clarified the marketing objectives. Specifically, **marketing strategy** identifies the planned marketing programs, all the marketing activities that a business will use to achieve its marketing goals, and when those activities will occur. If planned activities are not affordable, then marketers need to adjust the activities or goals until realistic plans emerge. Finally,

Marketing Strategy all the marketing programs and activities that will be used to achieve the marketing goals

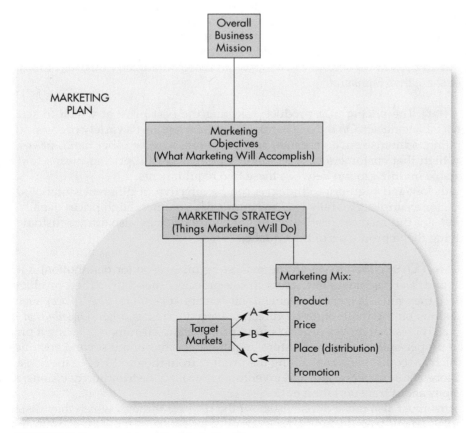

FIGURE 2 Components of the Marketing Plan

because marketing planning is an ongoing process—not just a one-time endeavor—it can be improved through experience by learning from past triumphs and mistakes.

Marketing managers are the people responsible for planning, organizing, leading, and controlling the organization's marketing resources toward supporting and accomplishing the organization's overall mission. To meet these responsibilities, marketing managers rely on mapping out a clear strategy for planning and implementing all the activities that result in the transfer of goods or services to customers. As you can see in Figure 2, the marketing strategy focuses on the needs and wants of customers in the company's chosen target markets. Marketing strategy also includes four basic components (often called the *Four Ps*) of the **marketing mix**—*product, pricing, place*, and *promotion*—that marketing managers use to satisfy customers in target markets. The specific activities for each of the Four Ps are designed differently to best meet the needs of each target market.

Marketing Manager *manager who plans and implements the marketing activities that result in the transfer of products from producer to consumer*

Marketing Mix *combination of product, pricing, promotion, and place (distribution) strategies used to market products*

Product *good, service, or idea that is marketed to fill consumers' needs and wants*

Product Differentiation *creation of a product feature or product image that differs enough from existing products to attract customers*

Product

Marketing begins with a **product**, a good, a service, or an idea designed to fill a customer's need or want. Producers often promote particular features of products to distinguish them in the marketplace. **Product differentiation** is the creation of a feature or image that makes a product differ enough from existing products to attract customers. For example, in the years since Apple introduced the first iPhone, a succession of newer models evolved with faster, more powerful, and increasingly consumer-friendlier innovations. The iPhone's industry-leading features have attracted an enormous customer following that contributes substantially to Apple's booming financial success. The design for the iPhone 6, for example, offers more new features than previous models to keep on top in the increasingly competitive smartphone market. The phone is thinner and lighter, has a new Retina HD display, improved camera, and faster operating system.[9]

Meanwhile, Samsung surged onto the scene with its competitive Galaxy series, most recently the Galaxy S5, with equally attractive, distinct features. Compared with previous Galaxy models, the Galaxy S5 has a more powerful, removable battery, faster download and upload speeds, the popular Android operating system, and numerous additional features. The phone is also dustproof and water-resistant.[10]

So far, Samsung's smartphone features are attracting more customers, holding almost a 30 percent share of worldwide smartphone sales at the end of 2014, versus around 20 percent for second-place Apple. In the U.S. market, however, Apple has a larger share than Samsung.

Pricing *process of determining the best price at which to sell a product*

Pricing

The **pricing** of a product, selecting the best price at which to sell it, is often a balancing act. On the one hand, prices must support a variety of costs, such as operating, administrative, research, and marketing. On the other hand, prices can't be so high that customers turn to competitors. Successful pricing means finding a profitable middle ground between these two requirements.

Both low-and high-price strategies can be effective in different situations. Low prices, for example, generally lead to larger sales volumes. High prices usually limit market size but increase profits per unit. High prices may also attract customers by implying that a product is of high quality.

Place (or Distribution) *part of the marketing mix concerned with getting products from producers to consumers*

Place (Distribution)

In the marketing mix, **place (or distribution)** refers to *where* and *how* customers get access to the products they buy. When products are created, they must become available to customers at some *location* (*place*) such as a retail store, on the Internet, or by direct delivery to the customer. *Distribution* is the set of activities that moves products from producers to customers. Placing a product in the proper outlet, like a retail store, requires decisions about several activities, all of which are concerned with getting the product from the producer to the consumer. Decisions about warehousing and inventory control are distribution decisions, as are decisions about transportation options.

Firms must also make decisions about the *channels* through which they distribute products. Many manufacturers, for example, sell goods to other companies that, in

Rolex has had sustained success as a result of its well-conceived marketing mix. The Swiss company focuses exclusively on high-quality watches (product), sells them for thousands of dollars (price), uses an exclusive network of quality retailers (distribution), and advertises them in interesting ways (promotion).

Weng lei/Imaginechina/AP Images

turn, distribute them to retailers. Others sell directly to major retailers, such as Target and Sears. Still others sell directly to final consumers.

Promotion The most visible component of the marketing mix is no doubt **promotion**, which is a set of techniques for communicating information about products. The most important promotional tools include advertising, personal selling, sales promotions, publicity/public relations, and direct or interactive marketing. In this chapter, we briefly describe four of the most important promotional tools.

ADVERTISING **Advertising** is any form of paid nonpersonal communication used by an identified sponsor to persuade or inform potential buyers about a product. For example, financial advisory companies that provide investment and securities products reach their customer audience by advertising in *Fortune* magazine and on the *Bloomberg* television network.

PERSONAL SELLING Many products (such as insurance, custom-designed clothing, and real estate) are best promoted through **personal selling**, person-to person sales. Industrial goods and services rely significantly on personal selling. When companies buy from other companies, purchasing agents and others who need technical and detailed information are often referred to the selling company's sales representatives.

SALES PROMOTIONS Historically, relatively inexpensive items have often been marketed through **sales promotions**, which involve one-time direct inducements to buyers. Premiums (usually free gifts), coupons, and package inserts are all sales promotions meant to tempt consumers to buy products. More recently, however, these promotions have expanded into B2B sales and to sales of larger items to consumers through Internet deals at sources such as Groupon.

PUBLIC RELATIONS **Public relations** includes all communication efforts directed at building goodwill. It seeks to build favorable attitudes in the minds of the public

Promotion *aspect of the marketing mix concerned with the most effective techniques for communicating information about products*

Advertising *any form of paid nonpersonal communication used by an identified sponsor to persuade or inform potential buyers about a product*

Personal Selling *person-to person sales*

Sales Promotion *direct inducements such as premiums, coupons, and package inserts to tempt consumers to buy products*

Public Relations *communication efforts directed at building goodwill and favorable attitudes in the minds of the public toward the organization and its products*

Urban Outfitters is a successful—but sometimes controversial—retailer. The company offers low-priced and unique products targeted at young, urban-oriented consumers. But the firm has also had some public relations problems due in part to some of its more offbeat products.

toward the organization and its products. The Ronald McDonald House Charities, and its association with McDonald's Corporation, is a well-known example of public relations.

Blending It All Together: Integrated Strategy An **integrated marketing strategy** ensures that the Four Ps blend together so that they are compatible with one another and with the company's nonmarketing activities. As an example, Toyota has become the world's largest automaker. Its nearly 30-year auto superiority, even with its massive product recalls a few years ago, stems from a coherent marketing mix that is tightly integrated with its production strategy. Offering a relatively small number of different models, Toyota targets auto customers that want high quality, excellent performance reliability, and moderate prices (a good value for the price). With a smaller number of different models than U.S. automakers, fewer components and parts are needed, purchasing costs are lower, and less factory space is required for inventory and assembly in Toyota's lean production system. Lean production's assembly simplicity yields higher quality, the factory's cost savings lead to lower product prices, and speedy production gives shorter delivery times in Toyota's distribution system. Taken together, this integrated strategy is completed when Toyota's advertising communicates its message of industry-high customer satisfaction.[11]

Integrated Marketing Strategy *strategy that blends together the Four Ps of marketing to ensure their compatibility with one another and with the company's nonmarketing activities*

Marketing Strategy: Target Marketing and Market Segmentation

OBJECTIVE 3
Explain
market segmentation and how it is used in target marketing.

Target Market *the particular group of people or organizations on which a firm's marketing efforts are focused*

Market Segmentation *process of dividing a market into categories of customer types, or "segments" having similar wants and needs and who can be expected to show interest in the same products*

Marketers have long known that products cannot be all things to all people. The emergence of the marketing concept and the recognition of customers' needs and wants led marketers to think in terms of **target markets**—the particular groups of people or organizations on which a firm's marketing efforts are focused. Selecting target markets is usually the first step in the marketing strategy.

Target marketing requires **market segmentation**, dividing a market into categories of customer types or "segments" having similar wants and needs and who can be expected to show interest in the same products. Once they have identified segments, companies may adopt a variety of strategies. Some firms market products by targeting more than one segment. General Motors, for example, once offered automobiles with various features and at various price levels. GM's past strategy was to provide an automobile for nearly every segment of the market. The financial crisis, however, forced GM's changeover to fewer target markets and associated brands by closing Saturn, phasing out Pontiac, and selling or shutting down Hummer and Saab.

In contrast, some businesses have always focused on a narrower range of products, such as Ferrari's high-priced sports cars, aiming at just one segment. Note that

238

segmentation is a strategy for analyzing consumers, not products. Once marketers identify a target segment, they can begin marketing products for that segment. The process of fixing, adapting, and communicating the nature of the product itself is called **product positioning**.

Product Positioning *process of fixing, adapting, and communicating the nature of a product*

Identifying Market Segments

By definition, members of a market segment must share some common traits that affect their purchasing decisions. In identifying consumer segments, researchers look at several different influences on consumer behavior. Five of the most important variables are discussed next.

Geographic Segmentation

Many buying decisions are affected by the places people call home. Urban residents don't need agricultural equipment, and sailboats sell better along the coasts than on the Great Plains. **Geographic variables** are the geographic units, from countries to neighborhoods, that researchers consider in a strategy of **geographic segmentation**. McDonald's restaurants in Germany, in contrast to those in the United States, offer beer on the menu. Pharmacies in Jackson Hole, Wyoming, sell firearms that are forbidden in Chicago. Starbucks is currently focusing on the growing geographic segment in China.

Geographic Variables *geographic units that may be considered in developing a segmentation strategy*

Geographic Segmentation *geographic units, from countries to neighborhoods, that may be considered in identifying different market segments in a segmentation strategy*

Demographic Segmentation

Demographic segmentation is a strategy used to separate consumers by demographic variables. **Demographic variables** describe populations by identifying traits, such as age, income, gender, ethnic background, marital status, race, religion, and social class, as detailed in Table 1. Depending on the marketer's purpose, a demographic segment can be a single classification (for example, ages 20–34) or a combination of categories (ages 20–34, married without children, earning $25,000–$44,999 a year).

Demographic Segmentation *a segmentation strategy that uses demographic characteristics to identify different market segments*

Demographic Variables *characteristics of populations that may be considered in developing a segmentation strategy*

For example, Hot Topic started as a California-based chain specializing in clothes, accessories, and jewelry designed to appeal to Generation Y and Millennials, a demographic consisting of U.S. consumers born between the 1980s and 1990s. The theme was pop culture music because it was the biggest influence on the demographic's fashion tastes. More recently, Hot Topic has become a national retail chain for clothing, accessories, and entertainment products relating to today's pop culture.

table 1 Examples of Demographic Variables

Age	Under 5, 5–11, 12–19, 20–34, 35–49, 50–64, 65+
Education	Grade school or less, some high school, graduated high school, some college, college degree, advanced degree
Family Life Cycle	Young single, young married without children, young married with children, older married with children under 18, older married without children under 18, older single, other
Family Size	1, 2–3, 4–5, 6+
Income	Less than $15,000, $15,000–$24,999, $25,000–$50,000, $50,000–$100,000, $100,000–$200,000, more than $200,000
Nationality	African, American, Asian, British, Eastern European, French, German, Irish, Italian, Latin American, Middle Eastern, Scandinavian
Race	American Indian, Asian, African American, Caucasian
Religion	Buddhist, Catholic, Hindu, Jewish, Muslim, Protestant
Gender	Male, female

Geo-Demographic Segmentation

As the name implies, **geo-demographic segmentation** is a combination strategy. **Geo-demographic variables** are a combination of geographic and demographic traits and are becoming the most common segmentation tools. An example would be Female Young Urban Professionals, well-educated 25- to 54-year-olds with high-paying professional jobs living in the "downtown" zip codes of major cities. Chico's targets many women in this segment, offering stylish travel clothing well suited to the needs of this subset in the larger population. Segmentation is more effective because the greater number of variables defines the market more precisely.

Psychographic Segmentation

Markets can also be separated into a **psychographic segmentation** according to such **psychographic variables** as lifestyles, interests, personalities, and attitudes. For example, Burberry, promoted as "The Iconic British Luxury Brand" whose raincoats have been a symbol of British tradition since 1856, has repositioned itself as a global luxury brand, like Gucci and Louis Vuitton. The strategy calls for attracting a different type of customer—the top-of-the-line, fashion-conscious individual—who enjoys the prestige of shopping at stores like Neiman Marcus and Bergdorf Goodman. Psychographics are particularly important to marketers because, unlike demographics and geographics, they can be changed by marketing efforts. With the onset of global interdependence and open communications, marketing today is changing some traditional lifestyles and attitudes in nations around the globe. Polish companies, for example, have overcome consumer resistance by promoting the safety and desirability of using credit cards rather than depending on solely using cash.[12]

Behavioral Segmentation

Behavioral segmentation uses **behavioral variables** to market items, including such areas as heavy users (buy in bulk, the key to Sam's and Costco); situation buyers (Halloween is now the second-largest "holiday" in terms of spending); or specific purpose (All Free is a detergent for people who have skin reactions to additives in other detergents).

Marketing Research

Marketing decisions are seldom perfect, yet the consequences of a firm's choices of marketing mix and segmentation strategy can be long lasting. Effective decisions must be customer focused and based on timely information about marketplace trends. **Marketing research**, the study of what customers need and want and how best to meet those needs and wants, is a powerful tool for gaining decision-making information.

The relationship of research to the overall marketing process is shown in Figure 3. Ultimately, its role is to increase competitiveness by clarifying the interactions among a firm's stakeholders (including customers), marketing variables, environmental factors, and marketing decisions. Researchers use several methods to obtain, interpret, and apply information about customers. They determine the kinds of information needed for decisions on marketing strategy, goal setting, and target-market selection. In doing so, they may conduct studies on customer responses to proposed changes in the marketing mix. One researcher, for example, might study response to an experimental paint formula (new product). Another might explore the response to a price reduction (new price) on condominiums. Still a third might check responses to a proposed advertising campaign (new promotion). Marketers also try to learn whether customers will more likely purchase a product in a specialty shop or on the Internet (new place).

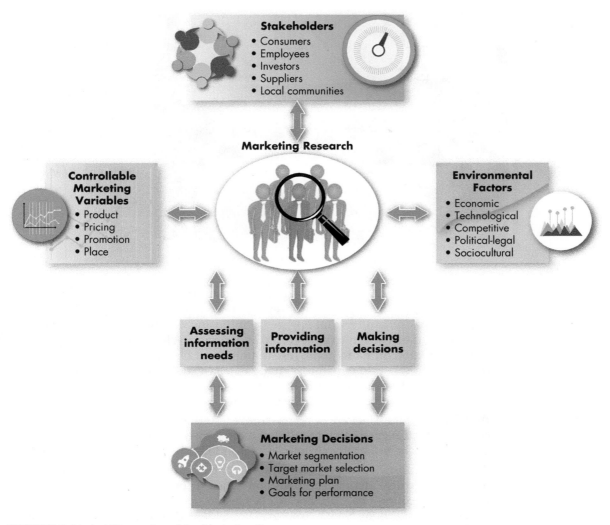

FIGURE 3 Market Research and the Marketing Process

The importance of selling products in international markets has expanded the role of marketing research. For example, when a company decides to sell goods or services globally, it must decide whether to standardize products or to specialize by offering different versions for each market. Accordingly, market research's orientation has become increasingly globalized.

The Research Process

Market research can occur at almost any point in a product's life cycle. Typically, however, it's used in developing new or altered products. Following are the five steps in performing market research:

1 **Study the current situation.** What is the need and what is being done to meet it? In the mid-1980s, Coca-Cola was alarmed by its declining market share. The company decided to undertake a now-famous market study to identify ways to recover its market position.

2 **Select a research method.** In choosing from a wide range of methods, marketers must consider the effectiveness and costs of different options. Coca-Cola's information suggested that the taste of Coke was the main source of the problem. Researchers decided to use taste tests for consumer opinions on a "New Coke" that was sweeter than original Coke.

Most companies undertake marketing research before launching new products. But even strong marketing research may prove to be inaccurate. For instance, when Google launched Google Glass in 2014 it anticipated huge demand. But slow sales caused the firm to stop distribution in early 2015.

Secondary Data *data that are already available from previous research*

3 ***Collect data.*** We distinguish here two types of research data. **Secondary data** are already available from previous research. The *Statistical Abstract of the United States* offers data on geographic and demographic variables. Secondary data can save time, effort, and money. When secondary sources are unavailable or inadequate, researchers must obtain **primary data**, new data from newly performed research. In Coca-Cola's study, primary data were collected from some 200,000 tasters who compared the New Coke versus the taste of the original Coke and Pepsi.

Primary Data *new data that are collected from newly performed research*

4 ***Analyze the data.*** Data are of no use until organized into information. Analysis of data in the Coke research found that more than one-half of the tasters rated New Coke to be tastier than original Coke and Pepsi.

5 ***Prepare a report.*** This report should sum up the study's methodology and findings. It should also identify solutions and, where appropriate, make recommendations on a course of action. Coca-Cola's resulting recommendation—to replace original Coke with the New Coke—was implemented. The decision was a costly disaster that eventually resulted in restoring original Coke under a new name—Classic Coke—and then withdrawing New Coke from the market. Research flaws had biased the results: (1) test tasters were not told that if New Coke was launched, then original Coke would no longer be available, and (2) consumers' long-standing attachment to the original Coke brand would be lost when the product was withdrawn from the market.[13]

This Coca-Cola example was a costly learning experience, illustrating that even the most successful companies encounter occasional marketing mistakes. Although Coke's market research ultimately led them down the wrong path, many others, including Marriott Hotels and Resorts, Samsung Electronics, and Procter & Gamble personal care products, have conducted market research campaigns that led to increased market share and a better understanding of their markets.

Research Methods

The success of a research study often depends on the method a research team uses. Consider the following four basic methods of market research:

Observation *research method that obtains data by watching and recording consumer behavior*

1 **Observation** involves watching and recording consumer behavior. Today, information technology systems, including live camera feeds and computer recordings, allow marketers to observe consumer preferences rapidly and with great accuracy. Electronic scanners and data files at brick-and-mortar stores, along with data storage of television viewing, phone transactions, and website activity allow marketers to see each consumer's purchasing history—what products and brands that person prefers over a set period of time.

finding a better way

The Truth about Your Online Customer Service

As more and more retail purchases are being made online, the number of online merchandisers has exploded. You are probably pretty familiar with the stores in your area and the quality of service that they provide, but this is often not true for online sales. With thousands of sites from which to choose, it can be difficult for consumers to decide where to buy. Many retail sites feature comments from prior customers, but there is always a concern that these comments have been posted by the company itself. So, how good are a company's online customer services, especially when compared to its online competitors? StellaService Inc. answered that question by providing a better way to measure online service, enabling it to become a market winner for online shoppers and retailers alike.

Following its start-up in 2010, StellaService spent two years gathering data on customer satisfaction provided by thousands of online retailers, including such giants as Amazon.com and LLBean.com. Armed with results, co-founders Jordy Leister and John Ernsberger were able to raise $22 million in venture capital to expand their ability to develop powerful analytics. StellaService measures satisfaction in four service areas—phone support, e-mail support, delivery, returns and refunds—for each retailer. Each area includes from 9 to as many as 25 different measurements. Phone support, for example, considers speed of answering the call and respondent's knowledge of the product, among its nine measurements. Delivery measurements include delivery time and product accuracy. By combining the various measurements, consumers can find summary scores for each of the four service areas. Results provide rankings of competitors, from top to bottom, showing where each retailer currently stands relative to competitors in each of the four areas of service. In the category of Sporting Goods, for example, Stella's monthly report might show Phone Support rankings among such firms as BassPro.com, Cabelas.com, DicksSportingGoods.com, and so forth, along with rankings on Delivery, E-mail Support, and Returns and Refunds. Rankings allow period-to-period tracking, revealing trends for improvements (or erosions) in each of the areas across time for each company.

With these measurements, StellaServices hopes to better inform the consumer public on the range of customer service they can expect from online retailers. Knowing that success

Courtesy of STELLAService, Inc., http://www.stellaservice.com

hinges on the validity and believability of their methods, Stella uses an independent third-party rating system; "secret shoppers" (trained employees) use strict and controlled measurement methods as they engage online retailers via e-mails, phone calls, and live chats to purchase, await deliveries, or make returns for refunds. As added assurance for validity, Stella maintains a "Customer Service Measurement Process Audit" detailing its measurements, procedures for gathering and processing data, with specific steps to assure accuracy and validity. In 2012, KPMG, a Big Four auditing and CPA firm, stated in its Independent Auditing Report that, in its opinion, StellaService's methodologies are complying with Stella's stated policies.

It's not only consumers who are interested in the level of service that companies provide. KPMG's report was an important piece of marketing associated with the move to offering subscription services to retailers, which began in 2013. Subscribers, for the first time, can receive measured data showing their standing, along with competitors, on phone support, e-mail support, delivery, and returns and refunds. This service allows retailers to base decisions on objective and independent information about their online customer service.

Based on StellaService's ratings, shoppers can expect "elite" service from well-known retailers such as Nordstrom and Zappos. On average, e-mails from customers were handled within three to six hours and calls to customer service are answered in fewer than 90 seconds. High ratings may encourage customers to purchase from an online retailer, while low ratings may encourage consumers to consider more than low prices when making a purchase decision. In addition, data collected by StellaService helps companies identify where they excel as well as opportunities for improvement.[14]

---

2 Sometimes, marketers must go a step further and ask questions. One way to get useful information is by taking **surveys**, a method of collecting data in which the researcher interacts with people to gather facts, attitudes, or opinions, either by mailing or e-mailing questionnaires, by telephone calls, or by conducting face-to-face interviews. United Parcel Service (UPS) surveyed customers to find out how to improve service. Clients wanted more interaction with drivers

Survey *research method of collecting consumer data using questionnaires, telephone calls, and face-to-face interviews*

because they can offer practical advice on shipping. As a result, UPS added extra drivers, providing them with more time with customers. Most surveys today are conducted online.

3 In a **focus group**, participants are gathered in one place, presented with an issue, and asked to discuss it. The researcher takes notes and makes video recordings but provides only a minimal amount of structure. This technique allows researchers to explore issues too complex for questionnaires and can produce creative solutions.

4 **Experimentation** compares the responses of the same or similar people under different circumstances. For example, a firm trying to decide whether to include walnuts in a new candy bar probably wouldn't learn much by asking people what they thought of the idea. But if it asked some people to try bars with nuts and some without, the responses could be helpful.

Focus Group *research method using a group of people from a larger population who are asked their attitudes, opinions, and beliefs about a product in an open discussion*

Experimentation *research method using a sample of potential consumers to obtain reactions to test versions of new products or variations of existing products*

OBJECTIVE 5
Describe

the consumer buying process and the key factors that influence that process.

Consumer Behavior *study of the decision process by which people buy and consume products*

Understanding Consumer Behavior

Although marketing managers can tell us what features people want in a new refrigerator, they cannot tell us why they buy particular refrigerators. What desires are consumers fulfilling? Is there a psychological or sociological explanation for why they purchase one product and not another? These questions and many others are addressed in the study of **consumer behavior**, the decision process by which people buy and consume products.

Influences on Consumer Behavior

To understand consumer behavior, marketers draw heavily on such fields as psychology and sociology. The result is a focus on four major influences on consumer behavior: (1) *psychological*, (2) *personal*, (3) *social*, and (3) *cultural*. By identifying which influences are most active in certain circumstances, marketers try to explain consumer choices and predict future buying behavior.

Psychological Influences *include an individual's motivations, perceptions, ability to learn, and attitudes that marketers use to study buying behavior*

Personal Influences *include lifestyle, personality, and economic status that marketers use to study buying behavior*

Social Influences *include family, opinion leaders (people whose opinions are sought by others), and such reference groups as friends, coworkers, and professional associates that marketers use to study buying behavior*

Cultural Influences *include culture, subculture, and social class influences that marketers use to study buying behavior*

Brand Loyalty *pattern of repeated consumer purchasing based on satisfaction with a product's performance*

Psychological influences include an individual's motivations, perceptions, ability to learn, and attitudes.

Personal influences include lifestyle, personality, and economic status.

Social influences include family, opinion leaders (people whose opinions are sought by others), and such reference groups as friends, coworkers, and professional associates.

Cultural influences include culture (the way of living that distinguishes one large group from another), subculture (smaller groups with shared values), and social class (the cultural ranking of groups according to such criteria as background, occupation, and income).

Although these factors can have a strong impact on a consumer's choices, their effect on actual purchases is sometimes weak or negligible. Some consumers, for example, exhibit high **brand loyalty**; they regularly purchase products, such as McDonald's foods, because they are satisfied with their performance. Such people are less subject to influence and stick with preferred brands.[15] On the other hand, the clothes you wear, the social network you choose, and the way you decorate your room often reflect social and psychological influences on your consumer behavior.

The Consumer Buying Process

Students of consumer behavior have constructed various models to help show how consumers decide to buy products. Figure 4 presents one such model. At the core of this and similar models is an awareness of the many influences that

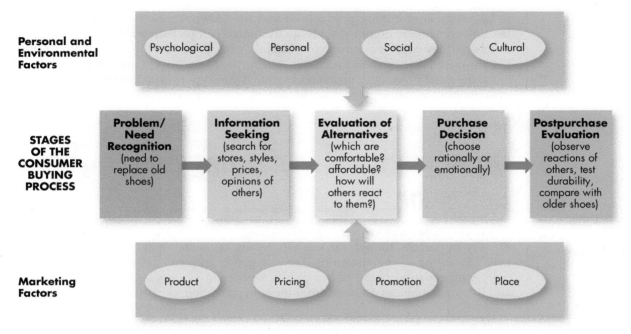

FIGURE 4 The Consumer Buying Process

lead to consumption. Ultimately, marketers use this information to develop marketing plans.

Problem or Need Recognition

This process begins when the consumer recognizes a problem or need. Need recognition also occurs when you have a chance to change your buying habits. When you obtain your first job after graduation, your new income may enable you to buy things that were once too expensive for you. You may find that you need professional clothing, apartment furnishings, and a car. Bank of America and Citibank cater to such shifts in needs when they market credit cards to college students.

Information Seeking

Having recognized a need, consumers often seek information. The search is not always extensive, but before making major purchases, most people seek information from personal sources, public sources, and experiences. Before joining a gym, you may read about your area gyms on yelp.com or you may visit several gyms in your neighborhood. From this information search, consumers develop an **evoked set (or consideration set)**, which is the group of products they will consider buying.

Evoked Set (Consideration Set) *group of products consumers will consider buying as a result of information search*

Evaluation of Alternatives

If someone is in the market for skis, they probably have some idea of who makes skis and how they differ. By analyzing product attributes (price, prestige, quality) of the consideration set, consumers compare products before deciding which one best meets their needs.

Purchase Decision

Ultimately, consumers make purchase decisions. "Buy" decisions are based on rational motives, emotional motives, or both. **Rational motives** involve the logical evaluation of product attributes: cost, quality, and usefulness. **Emotional motives** involve nonobjective factors and include sociability, imitation of others, and aesthetics. For example, you might buy the same brand of jeans as your friends to feel accepted in a certain group, not because your friends happen to have the good sense to prefer durable, reasonably priced jeans.

Rational Motives *reasons for purchasing a product that are based on a logical evaluation of product attributes*

Emotional Motives *reasons for purchasing a product that are based on nonobjective factors*

Postpurchase Evaluation

Marketing does not stop with the sale of a product; what happens after the sale is also important. Marketers want consumers to be happy after buying products so that they are more likely to buy them again. Because consumers do not want to go through a complex decision process for every purchase, they often repurchase products they have used and liked. Not all consumers are satisfied with their purchases, of course. These buyers are not likely to purchase the same product(s) again and are much more apt to broadcast their experiences than are satisfied customers.

Organizational Marketing and Buying Behavior

OBJECTIVE 6
Discuss
the four categories of organizational markets and the characteristics of business-to-business (B2B) buying behavior.

In the consumer market, buying and selling transactions are visible to the public. Equally important, though far less visible, are organizational (or commercial) markets. Marketing to organizations that buy goods and services used in creating and delivering consumer products or public services involves various kinds of markets and buying behaviors different from those in consumer markets.

Business Marketing

Business marketing involves organizational or commercial markets that fall into four B2B categories: (1) services companies, (2) industrial, (4) reseller, and (4) government and institutional markets. Taken together, the B2B markets do more than $25 trillion in business annually—more than two times the amount of business conducted in the U.S. consumer market.[16]

Services Companies Market *firms engaged in the business of providing services to the purchasing public*

Services Market The **services companies market** encompasses the many firms that provide services to the purchasing public. Imagine, for example, the materials and supplies Disney World needs to provide exceptional experiences for visitors. Similar needs exist to operate United Airlines, MTV, and the accounting firm Ernst & Young. Everything from veterinary clinics to hospitality services providers to healthcare centers and nursery schools buy resources needed to provide services to customers.

Industrial Market *organizational market consisting of firms that buy goods that are either converted into products or used during production*

Industrial Market The **industrial market** includes businesses that buy goods to be converted into other products or that are used up during production. It includes farmers, manufacturers, and some retailers. For example, clock-making company Seth Thomas buys electronics, metal components, plastic, and glass from other companies to make clocks for the consumer market. The company also buys office supplies, tools, and factory equipment—items never seen by clock buyers—that are used during production.

Reseller Market *organizational market consisting of intermediaries that buy and resell finished goods*

Reseller Market Before products reach consumers, they pass through a **reseller market** consisting of intermediaries, including wholesalers and retailers, that buy and resell finished goods. For example, as a leading distributor of parts and accessories for the pleasure boat market, Coast Distribution System buys lights, steering wheels, and propellers and resells them to marinas and boat-repair shops.

Institutional Market *organizational market consisting of such nongovernmental buyers of goods and services as hospitals, churches, museums, and charitable organizations*

Government and Institutional Market In addition to federal and state governments, there are over 89,000 local governments in the United States. In 2014, state and local governments spent $3.1 trillion for durable goods, nondurables, services, and construction.[17] The **institutional market** consists of nongovernmental organizations, such as hospitals, churches, museums, and charities, that also use supplies and equipment as well as legal, accounting, and transportation services.

B2B Buying Behavior

In some respects, organizational buying behavior bears little resemblance to consumer buying practices. Differences include the buyers' purchasing skills and an emphasis on buyer–seller relationships.

Differences in Buyers Unlike most consumers, organizational buyers purchase in large quantities and are professional, specialized, and well informed. Additional characteristics of B2B buyers include the following:

- Industrial buyers usually *buy in bulk or large quantities*. Because of this fact, and with so much money at stake, buyers are often experts about the products they buy. On a regular basis, B2B buyers study competing products and alternative suppliers by attending trade shows, by networking with others electronically, by reading trade literature, and by conducting technical discussions with sellers' representatives.

- As professionals, B2B buyers *are trained in methods for negotiating purchase terms*. Once buyer–seller agreements have been reached, they also arrange formal contracts.

- As a rule, industrial buyers *are company specialists in a line of items and are often experts about the products they buy*. As one of several buyers for a large bakery, for example, you may specialize in food ingredients. Another buyer may specialize in baking equipment, whereas a third may buy office equipment and supplies.

Differences in the Buyer–Seller Relationship Consumer–seller relationships are often impersonal, short-lived, one-time interactions. In contrast, B2B situations often *involve frequent and enduring buyer–seller relationships*. The development of a long-term relationship provides each party with access to the technical strengths of the other as well as the security of knowing what future business to expect. Thus, a buyer and a supplier may form a design team to create products to benefit both parties. Accordingly, industrial sellers emphasize personal selling by trained representatives who understand the needs of each customer.

Social Media and Marketing

Social networking as used by marketers today refers to communications that flow among people and organizations interacting through an online platform that facilitates building social relations among its users. **Social networking media** are the websites or access channels, such as Facebook, Twitter, LinkedIn, and YouTube, to which millions of consumers go for information and discussions before making their purchase decisions.

Viral Marketing and Social Networking **Viral marketing** is a form of marketing that relies on social networking and the Internet to spread information like a "virus" from person to person. The marketing purpose may be to increase brand awareness, to promote new product ideas, or to foster excitement for stimulating sales. Messages about new cars, sports events, and numerous other goods and services flow via networks among potential customers who pass the information on to others. Using various social network formats—games, contests, chat rooms, blogs, and bulletin boards—marketers encourage potential customers to try out products and tell other people about them. For example, as Disney plans to launch new movies featuring characters from the *Star Wars* mythology and the Marvel universe, it often releases brief sample footage months—or even years—in advance. The hope is that viewers will like what they see and help build anticipation for the new movie well before it actually opens in theaters. Marketers, including such giants as Bank of America, McDonald's, eBay, and Cisco, are using **corporate blogs** increasingly for public relations, branding, and otherwise spreading messages that stimulate chat about products to target markets.[18]

Social Networking *network of communications that flow among people and organizations interacting through an online platform*

Social Networking Media *websites or access channels, such as Facebook, Twitter, LinkedIn, and YouTube, to which consumers go for information and discussions*

Viral Marketing *type of marketing that relies on the Internet to spread information like a "virus" from person to person about products and ideas*

Corporate Blogs *comments and opinions published on the Web by or for an organization to promote its activities*

Web-Driven Revenue with Social Networking Although many major consumer companies have their own Facebook page, small businesses also use social media channels to increase revenues by networking with customers in target markets. A2L Consulting, for example, offers services to law firms, such as jury consulting, pretrial services, courtroom technologies, and litigation graphics, among other litigation services. The company uses multiple social networks, including Google+, YouTube, Pinterest, LinkedIn, and Twitter to increase Web-driven revenue. With 12,000 website visits each month, A2L derives considerable revenue from Web traffic. Company representatives credited LinkedIn, from among the social-media networks used by A2L, as the most effective for connecting with this B2B target market.[19] LinkedIn itself now has 332 million users and adds two new members every second.

How effective can it be? Viral marketing and social networking can lead to consumer awareness faster and with wider reach than traditional media messages—and at a lower cost. Success of the movie *Avatar* is credited to 20th Century Fox's use of prerelease viral tactics for stimulating public awareness of the blockbuster movie. And A2L, the supplier of litigation services to law firms, credits social networking for increasing the firm's revenues. It works for two reasons. First, people rely on the Internet for information that they used to get from newspapers, magazines, and television. Equally important, however, is the interactive element; the customer becomes a participant in the process of spreading the word by forwarding information to and seeking information from other network users.

The continuing growth of social media is changing marketing practices of businesses and consumer behavior, too. Facebook has become the Internet's most-used social media site, with about 1.4 billion active users each month and more than 890 million users each day. Although Facebook is the leader, Twitter is another fast-growing network, ranking number two in size with more than 288 million active users and handling about 500 million tweets each day. These numbers reflect not only the huge size of the social media industry but also the enormous population of participants that influence and persuade one another to explore new ideas and products, thus becoming both consumers and sellers. The industry's growth is attributed especially to (1) increasing numbers of mobile device users, (2) more participants in the older-than-55 demographic who are using Twitter, and (3) greater global reach to more potential users. As companies gain experience, they are using social media in new ways. In addition to advertising promotions, Kellogg Company uses social media for consumer research and to get new product ideas. Procter & Gamble has learned that viral exposure on Facebook can generate more sales than TV advertising. eBay finds that its sellers and buyers use social media to guide other buyers and sellers to eBay's website. For students of marketing, the social media trend has two clear implications: (1) as consumers using social media, you will receive a growing number of tempting product exposures, and (2) as a user of social media who becomes familiar with its applications and technical operations, you will find a growing number of career opportunities in social media positions.[20]

The International Marketing Mix

Marketing internationally means mounting a strategy to support global business operations. Foreign customers differ from domestic buyers in language, customs, business practices, and consumer behavior. If they go global, marketers must reconsider each element of the marketing mix: product, pricing, place, and promotion.

International Products Some products can be sold abroad with virtually no changes. Coca-Cola and Marlboro are the same in Peoria, Illinois, and Paris, France. In other cases, U.S. firms have had to create products with built-in flexibility, like an electric shaver that is adaptable to either 120- or 230-volt outlets, so travelers can use it in both U.S. and European electrical outlets. Frequently, however, domestic products require a major redesign for buyers in foreign markets. To sell computers in Japan, for example, Apple had to develop a Japanese-language operating system.

International Pricing When pricing for international markets, marketers must consider the higher costs of transporting and selling products abroad. For example, because of the higher costs of buildings, rent, equipment, and imported meat, as well as differences in exchange rates, a McDonald's Big Mac that costs $4.80 in the United States has a price tag of $7.76 in Norway.

International Distribution In some industries, including consumer products and industrial equipment, delays in starting new international distribution networks can be costly, so companies with existing distribution systems often enjoy an advantage. Many companies have avoided time delays by buying existing businesses with already-established distribution and marketing networks. Procter & Gamble, for example, bought Revlon's Max Factor and Betrix cosmetics, both of which have distribution and marketing networks in foreign markets. Many times, distribution methods used in the United States don't fit in international markets. For example, in Europe, Breathe Right Nasal Strips are identified as "medicinal" and must be sold in pharmacies.

International Promotion Occasionally, a good ad campaign is a good campaign just about anywhere. Quite often, however, U.S. promotional tactics do not succeed in other countries. Many Europeans believe that a product must be inherently shoddy if a company resorts to any advertising, particularly the U.S. hard-sell variety.

International marketers are ever more aware of cultural differences that can cause negative reactions to improperly advertised products. Some Europeans, for example, are offended by TV commercials that show weapons or violence. On the other hand, some European advertising is more provocative and sexually explicit than would be accepted in some countries. Meanwhile, cigarette commercials that are banned from U.S. television thrive in many Asian and European markets. Managers must carefully match product promotions to local customs and cultural values to successfully promote sales and avoid offending customers.

Before creating an international ad like this Chinese advertisement for Coca-Cola, it is crucial to research what disparities, such as meaning of words, traditions, and taboos, exist between different societies. For example, German manufacturers of backpacks label them as "body bags," not terribly enticing to the U.S. consumer. Can you guess why Gerber baby food is not sold in France? The French translation of Gerber is "to vomit"! Effective marketing does not just involve knowledge of culture abroad, but also requires a general sensitivity to social trends and language.

Indranil Kishor/Photoshot

Because of the need to adjust the marketing mix, success in international markets is hard won. But whether a firm markets in domestic or international markets, the basic principles of marketing still apply; only their implementation changes.

Small Business and the Marketing Mix

Many of today's largest firms were yesterday's small businesses. Behind the success of many small firms lies a skillful application of the marketing concept and an understanding of each element in the marketing mix.

Small-Business Products

Some new products and firms are doomed at the start because few customers want or need what they have to offer. Many fail to estimate realistic market potential, and some offer new products before they have clear pictures of their target segments. In contrast, a thorough understanding of what customers want has paid off for many small firms. Take, for example, the case of Little Earth Productions, Inc., a company that makes fashion accessories, such as handbags. Originally, the company merely considered how consumers would use its handbags. But after examining shopping habits, Little Earth Productions redesigned for better in-store display. Because stores can give handbags better visibility by hanging them instead of placing them on floors or low countertops, Little Earth Productions added small handles specifically for that purpose, resulting in increased sales. More recently, Little Earth has been concentrating on accessories for sports fans such as logoed purses, headbands, wallets, and hair accessories.

Small-Business Pricing

Haphazard pricing can sink a firm with a good product. Small-business pricing errors usually result from a failure to estimate operating expenses accurately. The founder of Nomie Baby, makers of spill-proof removable car seat covers for infants, started by setting prices too low. Considering only manufacturing and materials costs, other costs—shipping, storage, designing—were mistakenly ignored and not covered by the original selling price. Thereafter, when start-up prices were increased to cover all costs, sales fortunately did not diminish. Owners, for fear of pricing too high, often tend to underprice, resulting in financial crisis. Failing businesses have often been heard to say, "I didn't realize how much it costs to run the business!" Sometimes, however, firms discover their prices are too low, even when they cover all costs. A computer error at Headsets.com once caused cost-only prices rather than retail prices to be posted for the company's products on the Internet. The CEO was surprised that the erroneous low prices did not create a surge in sales. Instead, steady consumer response indicated that the firm's products were not as price-sensitive as believed, so the company raised original prices once, by 8 percent. Revenue rose as sales continued with little or no change from previous levels.[21] When small businesses set prices by carefully assessing costs and understanding their competitive market, many earn satisfactory profits.

Small-Business Distribution

The ability of many small businesses to attract and retain customers depends partly on the choice of location, especially for new service businesses.

In distribution, as in other aspects of the marketing mix, however, smaller companies may have advantages over larger competitors. A smaller company may be able to address customers' needs more quickly and efficiently with an added personal

entrepreneurship and new ventures

Farming Your Niche

By all accounts, seven acres would be a very small farm. But, Rick Crofford, who is employed full-time as an environmental manager for the Virginia Department of Transportation, has a bustling farming operation on the seven acres of former corn-fields that surround his Virginia home. His first foray into farm-ing was blueberries—he has nearly 200 blueberry bushes that produce 10 to 15 pints of fruit each year. However, the blueber-ries are labor intensive during harvesting and he's had to install fencing to keep out the deer. He's expanded his berry opera-tion to include 250 strawberry plants, as well, and three kinds of raspberries. Crofford has stretched his operation into other crops, including fingerling potatoes. A plot less than an acre yielded 1,000 pounds of four varieties, which average about $2 per pound. Garlic, hot peppers, and broccoli are all grown on the farm with the help of his four children and occasional tem-porary help. He's funneled all the profits into a college savings plan for his kids.

zigzagmtart/Fotolia

Not far away, Francis Ngoh grows mushrooms and other crops on his 39-acre farm. The West African native came to the United States to earn a degree in engineering at the University of Maryland. Although he held several corporate positions over the years, he has now focused his attention full-time on farm-ing. His main crop is shitake mushrooms, harvesting 3,000 to 4,000 pounds per year, but he also grows asparagus, leeks, garlic, peppers, and greens. Although not yet a certified or-ganic producer, Ngoh has embraced these standards and uses no chemicals. He's also catering to the local Muslim mar-ket with his livestock operation. He slaughters lambs on site according to Islamic tradition, with demand especially high on holy days.

Crofford and Ngoh have been supported in their efforts by finding the right distribution networks, as well as support from the Virginia Cooperative Extension Service. Crofford works ex-tensively with produce wholesaler The Fresh Link. Co-founder Mollie Visosky helps local producers understand the needs of high-end restaurants in the DC area, explaining, "We get

together with the chefs in January to find out what produce they will want during the next growing season. Then we try to match our growers with crops that they can grow best and make a nice profit." On the other hand, Ngoh has been able to sell his mushrooms and other vegetables to Whole Foods stores as well as a number of other local buyers.

Both Crofford and Ngoh have worked with Jim Haskins from the Virginia Cooperative Extension Service, a program operated jointly by agents from Virginia State University and Virginia Tech. Haskins explains, "I try to identify small produc-ers in our area and give them the technical support to be more successful." This support was key to Mr. Crofford's decision to plan fingerling potatoes, which have a much higher yield than traditional Irish potatoes. Grant funding also helped both farm-ers, providing them with free plants and seeds to get started. In fact, these two have become so successful that Haskins uses them to promote niche farming in the Fauquier County area. And it's likely that this symbiotic relationship is one of the keys to success. Haskins explains, "One of our goals is to increase farm income for small producers. Not only do we need to sus-tain the farm but we also need to sustain the farmer."[22]

touch. Everex Systems, Inc. of Fremont, California, designs and sells computers to wholesalers and dealers through a system that the company calls *zero response time*. Because Everex Systems is small and flexible, phone orders can be reviewed every two hours and factory assembly adjusted to match demand.

Small-Business Promotion

Successful small businesses plan for promotional expenses as part of start-up costs. Some hold down costs by using less expensive promotional methods, like publicity in local newspapers and online messaging. Other small businesses identify them-selves and their products with associated groups, organizations, and events. Thus, a crafts gallery might partner with a local art league to organize public showings of their combined products.

summary of learning objectives

OBJECTIVE 1

Explain the concept of marketing and identify the five forces that constitute the external marketing environment.

Marketing is responsible for creating, communicating, and delivering value and satisfaction to customers. With limited financial resources, customers buy products that offer the best value, measured by the relationship between benefits and costs. Marketers must understand customers' wants and needs because they determine product features, and the timing, place, and terms of sale that provide utility and add value for customers. A product may be a tangible good, a service, or even an idea. In addition, products may be classified as either consumer products or industrial products when they are marketed to businesses or nonprofit organizations. Although marketing often focuses on single transactions for products, services, or ideas, marketers also take a longer-term perspective by managing customer relationships to benefit the organization and its stakeholders. Customer *relationship marketing* emphasizes building lasting relationships with customers and suppliers. Stronger relationships, including stronger economic and social ties, can result in greater long-term satisfaction, customer loyalty, and customer retention.

Five outside factors make up a company's external environment and influence its marketing programs: (1) the *political and legal environment* includes laws and regulations that may define or constrain business activities, (2) the *sociocultural environment* involves peoples' values, beliefs, and ideas that affect marketing decisions, (3) the *technological environment* includes new technologies that affect existing and new products, (4) the *economic environment* consists of conditions such as inflation, recession, and interest rates that influence organizational and individual spending patterns, and (5) the *competitive environment* is that in which marketers must persuade buyers to purchase their products rather than their competitors'.

OBJECTIVE 2

Explain the purpose of a marketing plan and identify its main components.

A *marketing plan* is a statement of all the future marketing activities and resources that will be used to meet the desires and needs of customers so that the firm's overall business mission will be accomplished. It begins with objectives or goals setting the stage for everything that follows. *Marketing objectives*—the things marketing intends to accomplish—are the foundation that guides all of the detailed activities in the marketing plan. The marketing objectives focus on maintaining or enhancing the organization's future competitive position in its chosen markets. A marketing strategy can be developed once the marketing objectives have been clarified. *Marketing strategy* identifies the planned marketing programs, including all the marketing activities that will be used for achieving the marketing goals, when those activities will occur, and the contents of its programs. If planned activities are not affordable—requiring more resources than are available—then activities, programs, or goals are adjusted until realistic plans emerge.

Marketing strategy includes four basic components (often called the "Four Ps") of the *marketing mix*—product, pricing, place (distribution), and promotion—that marketing managers use to satisfy customers in target markets. The specific activities for each of the Four Ps are designed differently to best meet the needs of each target market. Marketing begins with a *product*, a good, service, or idea designed to fill a customer's need or want. Conceiving and developing new products is a constant challenge for marketers who must always consider changing technology, consumer wants and needs, and economic conditions. Producers often promote particular features of products to distinguish them in the marketplace. *Product differentiation* is the creation of a feature or image that makes a product differ enough from existing products to attract consumers. The *pricing* of a product is often a balancing act. Prices must be high enough to support a variety of operating, administrative, research, and marketing costs, but low enough that consumers don't turn to competitors. In the marketing mix, *place* (or distribution) refers to where and how consumers get access to the products they buy. The most visible component of the marketing mix is *promotion*, a set of techniques for communicating information about products. The most important promotional tools include advertising, personal selling, sales promotions, publicity/public relations, and direct or interactive marketing.

Explain market segmentation and how it is used in target marketing.

Marketers think in terms of *target markets*—particular groups of people or organizations on which a firm's marketing efforts are focused. Target marketing requires *market segmentation*—dividing a market into categories of customer types or "segments," such as age, geographic location, or level of income. Members of a market segment have similar wants and needs and share some common traits that influence purchasing decisions. Once they identify segments, companies adopt a variety of strategies for attracting customers in one or more of the chosen target segments. The following are five variables that are often used for segmentation: (1) *Geographic variables* are the geographical units that may be considered in developing a segmentation strategy. (2) *Demographic variables* describe populations by identifying such traits as age, income, gender, ethnic background, and marital status. (3) *Geo-demographic variables* combine demographic variables with geographic variables, such as an age category coupled with urban areas. (4) *Psychographic variables* include lifestyles, interests, and attitudes. (5) *Behavioral variables* include categories of behavioral patterns such as online consumers or large-volume buyers. Marketers search for segments showing promise for generating new sales if marketing efforts by other companies have overlooked or misjudged the segment's market potential. Such competitive weaknesses present marketing opportunities for other companies to enter into those segments. Desirable segments with market potential then become candidate target markets and, once chosen, they become part of the marketing strategy where its companion marketing mix is developed.

Discuss the purpose of marketing research and compare the four marketing research methods.

Effective marketing decisions should be customer based and focused on timely information about trends in the marketplace. *Marketing research* is a tool for gaining such information; it is the study of what customers want and how best to meet those needs. Researchers use several methods to obtain, interpret, and apply information about customers. They determine the kinds of information needed for marketing strategy, goal setting, target-market selection, and developing new or altered products for specific market segments. Marketing research's orientation has become increasingly globalized because of the increasing importance of selling products internationally.

Research success depends on which of four basic research methods is used: (1) *Observation* means watching and recording consumer preferences and behavior. By using live camera feeds, computer tracking, and other electronic technologies, marketers observe and record consumer preferences rapidly and with great accuracy. (2) The heart of any *survey* is a questionnaire on which participants record responses. Surveys can get responses to specific questions quickly and at relatively lower cost. (3) In a *focus group*, people are gathered in one place, presented with an issue or topic, and asked to discuss it. The researcher takes notes, makes video recordings, and encourages open discussion by providing only a minimal amount of structure for the group's discussion. This technique allows researchers to explore issues too complex for questionnaires; it can produce creative ideas and solutions. (4) *Experimentation* compares the responses and behaviors of the same or similar people under different conditions that are of interest to the researcher. Experimentation can be relatively expensive because of costs of obtaining the experimental setting, securing participants, paying participants, and paying those who administer the experiment.

Describe the consumer buying process and the key factors that influence that process.

In the study of *consumer behavior*, marketers evaluate the decision process by which people buy and consume products. There are four major influences on consumer behavior. (1) *Psychological influences* include an individual's motivations, perceptions, ability to learn, and attitudes. (2) *Personal influences* include lifestyle, personality, and economic status. (3) *Social influences* include family, opinion leaders, and reference groups such as friends, coworkers, and professional associates. (4) *Cultural influences* include culture, subculture, and social class. At times, these influences have a significant impact on buying decisions, although consumers demonstrate high *brand loyalty* at times, regularly purchasing the same products.

Observers of consumer behavior have constructed various models to help marketers understand how consumers decide to purchase products. One model considers five influences that lead to consumption: (1) *Problem or need recognition*: The buying process begins when the consumer recognizes a problem or need. (2) *Information seeking*: Having recognized a need, consumers seek information. The information search leads to an evoked set (or consideration set)—a group of products they will consider buying. (3) *Evaluation of alternatives*: By analyzing product attributes (price, prestige, quality) of the consideration set, consumers compare products to decide which product best meets their needs. (4) *Purchase decision*: "Buy" decisions are based on rational motives, emotional motives, or both. *Rational motives* involve the logical evaluation of product attributes, such as cost, quality, and usefulness. *Emotional motives* involve nonobjective factors and include sociability, imitation of others, and aesthetics. (5) *Postpurchase evaluations*: Consumers continue to form opinions after their purchase. Marketers want consumers to be happy after the consumption of products so that they are more likely to buy them again.

OBJECTIVE 6

Discuss the four categories of organizational markets and the characteristics of business-to-business (B2B) buying behavior.

The various organizational markets exhibit different buying behaviors from those in consumer markets. Business marketing involves organizational or commercial markets that fall into four B2B categories. (1) The *services companies market* encompasses the many firms that provide services to the purchasing public. Every service company, from pet care to hospitality services to health care and nursery schools, airlines, and more, buys resources needed to provide services to customers. (2) The *industrial market* consists of businesses that buy goods to be converted into other products or that are used during production. It includes farmers, manufacturers, and some retailers. (3) Before some products reach consumers, they pass through a *reseller market* consisting of intermediaries—wholesalers and retailers—that buy finished goods and resell them. (4) The *government and institutional market* includes federal, state, and local governments and nongovernmental buyers—hospitals, churches, museums, and charities—that purchase goods and services needed for serving their clients. Taken together, these four organizational markets do more than two times the business annually than do the U.S. consumer markets.

Unlike most consumers, organizational buyers purchase in large quantities and are professional, specialized, and well informed. As professionals, they are trained in methods for negotiating purchase terms. Once buyer–seller agreements have been reached, they also arrange formal contracts. In contrast with consumer–seller relationships that are often one-time interactions, B2B situations involve frequent and enduring buyer–seller relationships that provide each party, buyer and seller, with access to the technical strengths of the other. Thus, a buyer and a supplier may form a design team to create products to benefit both parties. Accordingly, industrial sellers emphasize personal selling by trained representatives who understand the needs of each customer.

OBJECTIVE 7

Discuss the marketing mix as it applies to small business.

Each element in the marketing mix can determine success or failure for any *small business*. Many *products* are failures because consumers don't need what they have to offer. A realistic market potential requires getting a clearer picture of what target segments want. Small-business *pricing* errors usually result from a failure to estimate start-up costs and operating expenses accurately. In addition to facilities construction or rental costs, shipping, storage, wages, taxes, utilities, and materials costs also must be considered. By carefully assessing costs, and by learning what customers are willing to pay, prices can be set to earn satisfactory profits. Perhaps the most crucial aspect of *place*, or distribution, is location, especially for services businesses, because locational convenience determines the ability to attract customers. Although *promotion* can be expensive and is essential for small businesses, costs can be reduced by using less expensive promotional methods. Local newspaper articles, online messaging, and television programming cover business events, thus providing free public exposure.

key terms

advertising	geo-demographic variables	product positioning
behavioral segmentation	industrial goods	promotion
behavioral variables	industrial market	psychographic segmentation
brand competition	institutional market	psychographic variables
brand loyalty	integrated marketing strategy	psychological influences
competitive environment	international competition	public relations
consumer behavior	market segmentation	rational motives
consumer goods	marketing	relationship marketing
corporate blogs	marketing manager	reseller market
cultural influences	marketing mix	sales promotion
customer relationship management	marketing objectives	secondary data
(CRM)	marketing plan	services
data mining	marketing research	services companies market
data warehousing	marketing strategy	social influences
demographic segmentation	observation	social networking
demographic variables	personal influences	social networking media
economic environment	personal selling	sociocultural environment
emotional motives	place (distribution)	substitute product
evoked set (or consideration set)	place utility	surveys
experimentation	political–legal environment	target market
focus group	possession utility	technological environment
form utility	pricing	time utility
geographic segmentation	primary data	utility
geographic variables	product	value
geo-demographic segmentation	product differentiation	viral marketing

MyBizLab

To complete the problems with the ✪, go to EOC Discussion Questions in the MyLab.

questions & exercises

QUESTIONS FOR REVIEW

1. What are the five forces in the external marketing environment?

2. How is the concept of the value package useful in marketing to consumers and industrial customers?

3. What is market segmentation and how is it used in target marketing?

✪ 4. How does the buying behavior of consumers differ from buyers in organizational markets?

QUESTIONS FOR ANALYSIS

5. Select an everyday product (personal fitness training, CDs, dog food, cell phones, or shoes, for example). Show how different versions of your product are aimed toward different market segments. Explain how the marketing mix differs for each segment.

✪ 6. Use the five-step model of rational decision making to describe the process of selecting a college. Does this model reflect the way that you made a decision about attending college? Why or why not?

7. Imagine being the marketing manager for a large U.S. hotel chain. How might the company have to adapt its marketing mix to move into foreign markets in South and Central America?

8. Choose an existing product that could benefit from viral marketing. Once you have identified the product, describe how you would use viral marketing to increase demand for the product.

APPLICATION EXERCISES

9. Identify a company with a product that interests you. Consider ways the company could use customer relationship management (CRM) to strengthen relationships with its target market. Specifically, explain your recommendations on how the company can use each of the four basic components of the marketing mix in its CRM efforts.

10. The U.S. Census collects an enormous amount of secondary data that is useful in marketing research. Go to the American Fact Finder home page at http://factfinder2.census.gov and collect data about people living in your zip code. Compare your zip code to your state as a whole in terms of factors such as age, race, household size, marital status, and educational attainment. Based on your data, what types of retail establishments would be specially appropriate to your area?

building a business: continuing team exercise

Assignment

Meet with your team members to consider your new business venture and how it relates to the marketing processes and consumer behavior topics in this chapter. Develop specific responses to the following:

11. Develop a "Statement of Marketing Objectives" for your company. Justify those marketing objectives by explaining how they contribute to the overall business mission of the company.

12. Identify the target market(s) for your business. Who are your customers? Describe the characteristics of customers in your target market(s).

13. Discuss how your team is going to identify the existing competitors in your chosen market. Based on the discussion, what are the key elements of your marketing plans that will give you a competitive edge over those competitors?

14. Consider, again, the customers in your target market(s). Are they individual consumers, organizations, or a mix of both consumers and organizations? Describe in detail the buying process(es) you expect them to use for purchasing your product(s). Discuss whether the customer buying process should or should not be a concern for your company.

15. Develop a preliminary design of the marketing mix for your target market(s).

team exercise

HOME AWAY FROM HOME

Green Hills College is a rapidly growing private college located in the Midwestern United States. Many of their students live on campus in dorms, but their growing enrollment has pushed a large percentage of the students off campus. A longtime resident of the community, Oliver Douglas, has decided to develop his farmland into student housing but is unsure exactly what type of housing is most appropriate.

Although he's been a farmer most of his life, Oliver Douglas realizes that the best use of his property is to develop it into student housing. He has made contacts in the county zoning office and has been assured that they are willing to rezone his property for student housing, given the importance of the college to the local economy. Oliver has done his research and has realized that he has several options. He can build dorm-style housing, apartments, townhouses, or even detached homes for students. Each has its pros and cons.

TEAM ACTIVITY

16. As a group, describe the characteristics, wants, and needs of the target market.

17. In addition to students, who else will have an influence on housing decisions?

18. Assign one team member to each of the four housing options: dorm-style housing, apartments, townhouses, and detached homes. Have each group member identify the pros and cons of the type of housing they have been assigned.

19. Have each group member share the advantages and disadvantages of the option they have been assigned.

20. Considering all the options, which housing option do you think makes most sense? Come to a group consensus and describe your reasoning.

21. Address each element of the marketing mix and describe how it will appeal to the target market.

exercising your ethics

WEIGHING THE ODDS

The Situation

You are the quality control manager for a major dietary supplement company. Because your products are sold over the counter as nutritional supplements rather than as medications, the supplements are not regulated by the Food and Drug Administration. Researchers have worked for years to develop a weight-loss product that is safe and effective. Several years ago, researchers identified a naturally occurring compound that was effective in appetite suppression. Your company has done several years of testing and you have found that 85 percent of people using the supplement were able to lose at least 20 pounds in the first year of use. In addition, those who continued to take the supplement were able to maintain their weight loss for an additional year. Company executives believe that this drug can bring billions of dollars in revenues in the first year of sales. Obesity has become an epidemic in the United States and much of the developed world and people who are obese are at a significantly greater risk of stroke, heart attack, and diabetes.

The Dilemma

You are reviewing the results of the clinical trials and are pleased to see that the product is effective. Just as you are ready to recommend that the company introduce the product to the market, you uncover some upsetting information. A small group of people who took the supplement during testing, actually less than 1 percent, developed a rare neurological disorder. It's not clear that the supplement is the cause of the disorder, but it was not observed in the control group that took a placebo. Because the risk is so small, the marketing manager is recommending that the company go ahead with introducing the supplement and monitor to see if consumers report a similar side effect. Commercialization of this product could make your company profitable and could potentially save thousands of lives by helping consumers lose weight, but you are unsure if this is the right thing to do.

QUESTIONS TO ADDRESS

22. How would you characterize the particular ethical issues in this situation?
23. From an ethical standpoint, what are the obligations of the quality control manager and the marketing manager regarding the introduction of the product in this situation?
24. If you were the quality control manager, how would you handle this matter?

cases

Building a Brand with Social Media

At the beginning of this chapter, you read about Michelle Phan and how she expanded a blog into a beauty and lifestyle empire. Using the information presented in this chapter, you should now be able to answer the following questions.

QUESTIONS FOR DISCUSSION

25. What forces in the external environment have created opportunities or challenges for Michelle Phan? Explain.
26. Who is Michelle Phan's target market?
27. Describe the consumer buying process for someone purchasing cosmetic products. Where would videos and a service like Ipsy fit into this process?
28. Go the website for Phan's beauty line with L'Oreal, www.emcosmetics.com. How does the product line appeal to Phan's target market?

Where Has All the Middle Gone?

Procter & Gamble (P&G), the iconic marketer of seemingly endless lines of household products since 1837, is confronted now with a puzzling marketing dilemma: "What's happening to the middle class in the United States? The number of mid-range shoppers is shrinking." With its lineup of popular brands such as Folgers, Clairol, Charmin, and Gillette, it is estimated that 98 percent of U.S. households are using at least one P&G product, a position that has grown largely by targeting middle-class consumers. Although its products are sold in more than 180 countries, U.S. consumers provide more than 35 percent of P&G sales and nearly 60 percent of annual profits.

The problem facing P&G is the shrinkage of middle-class purchasing power, a change that began with the 2008 recession and continues today. Many once-well-off middle-class families are pinched with rising prices for gasoline, food, education, and health care but little or no wage increases. The nation's economic condition, as a result, has been dubbed by Citigroup as the "Consumer Hourglass Theory." Advocates of the theory assert that purchasing power has shifted away from the once-massive middle and is concentrated now at the bottom and top. That's where consumer action is now, at the high-end market and the low-end market, and it will increase even more in those areas.[23]

On top of changing economics, preferences also are changing among consumers. Generation Y and Z buyers have been raised on premium brands. Rather than getting their clothes at bargain retailers, younger adults spent their teenage years in clothes from Hollister and Abercrombie & Fitch. As adults, they show a preference for premium brands, even when their incomes are solidly middle class. Will middle-class shrinkage continue, or is it a passing blip that will recover in the near future? Based on P&G's research, Melanie Healey, group president for P&G's North America business, expects middle-class downsizing will be a continuing trend. Accordingly, P&G and other companies are rethinking their target markets. Aiming at the high-end segment in 2009, the company introduced its more expensive Olay Pro-X skin-care product. Previously, P&G introduced Gain, the bargain-priced laundry detergent, which is aimed at the growing lower portion of the previous middle-class market following a dip in sales of the mid-priced Tide brand. Near the beginning of the recession, P&G's lower-priced Luvs diapers gained market share from the higher-priced Pampers brand. Following a path similar to that of P&G, H. J. Heinz has developed more food products for the lower-priced markets. Meanwhile, retailers focusing on lower-income consumers, such as Dollar General, are attracting customers from higher-priced Walmart and Target.[24]

Refocusing from the mainstream middle onto high- and low-end consumers is a new marketing experience at P&G. They have increased market research on lower-income households, often using face-to-face interviews to gain in-depth understanding of these consumers. So far, the low-end and the high-end segments each are generally smaller than the former massive middle-class market, which means P&G is splitting its marketing efforts, rather than having just a single larger thrust. As one company official noted, historically they have been good at doing things on a larger scale, but now they are learning how to deal with

smaller sales volumes for products in each of two segments. New product development is affected, too, because the high-end segment often involves fewer products with attractive extra features that will sell profitably at higher prices. P&G is betting that the Hourglass Theory has set the course for the company's future.

QUESTIONS FOR DISCUSSION

29. How would you best describe P&G's marketing strategy for the situation presented in this case? Explain why.
30. What elements of P&G's external marketing environment, if any, are influencing the company's marketing strategy? Explain your reasoning.
31. Why do you suppose P&G's marketing research includes face-to-face interviews for the situation described in this case? Would other forms of marketing research also be useful in this situation? Explain your reasoning.
32. Explain the roles of target marketing and market segmentation as they apply in this case.
33. In what ways are the components of P&G's marketing mix being affected by the situation described in this case? Give examples to illustrate.

MyBizLab

Go to the Assignments section of your MyLab to complete these writing exercises.

34. Marketing in every business must consider the firm's external environment and the environmental forces (or "marketing environments") that affect marketing decisions, successes, and failures. Recall and consider the major elements in the "marketing environment." Write an essay explaining how a firm's marketing strategy must consider each of those elements in the "marketing environment." In your discussion, give examples of how each element enters into the development of marketing strategy.
35. Describe the steps in the consumer buying process for someone purchasing a new automobile. What are the major influences on the consumer buying process? Explain how each might affect the decision made.

end notes

[1] Castillo, Michelle. 2014. "YouTube's Leading Ladies." *Adweek* 55, no. 41: 18–21. Business Source Premier, EBSCOhost (accessed May 29, 2015). "YouTube Makeup Guru Michelle Phan on Becoming a Beauty Superstar: 'My Only Goal Was to Help My Family.'" *Glamour*, September 2013. www.glamour.com/lipstick/2013/09/michelle-phan-youtube-beauty-glamour-october-2013. Stone, Madeline. "YouTube Superstar Michelle Phan Shares Her Tips for Building a Social Media Brand." *Business Insider*, November 2014. Accessed May 29, 2015. www.businessinsider.com/social-media-tips-from-youtube-star-michelle-phan-2014-11

[2] American Marketing Association, "Definition of Marketing," at www.marketingpower.com/aboutama/pages/definitionofmarketing.aspx, accessed on March 18, 2013.

[3] Kotler, Philip, and Armstrong, Gary. *Principles of Marketing*, 12th ed. (Upper Saddle River, NJ: Prentice Hall, 2008), 7.

[4] "CRM (customer relationship management)," *TechTarget.com*, at http://searchcrm.techtarget.com/definition/CRM, accessed on December 8, 2010; "Customer Relationship Management," *Wikipedia*, at http://en.wikipedia.org/wiki/Customer_relationship_management, accessed on December 8, 2010.

[5] Khanna, Poonam. "Hotel Chain Gets Personal with Customers," *Computing Canada*, April 8, 2005, p. 18.

[6] "Fairmont Hotels & Resorts: Website Development and Enhanced CRM," *accenture*, at www.accenture.com/Global/Services/By_Industry/Travel/Client_Successes/FairmontCrm.htm, accessed on December 8, 2010.

[7] "Tiny House Purchases See Big Growth," *Columbia Daily Tribune*, December 4, 2010, p. 11; "Solar Wells Displace Windmills on Range," *Columbia Daily Tribune*, July 22, 2010, p. 8B; McCarthy, Shawn, and Keenan, Greg. "Ottawa Demands Lower Auto Worker Costs," *The Globe and Mail*, January 19, 2009, at http://v1business.theglobeandmail.com/servlet/story/RTGAM.20090119.wrautos19/BNStory/Business; Edmondson, Gail, Rowley, Ian, Lakshman,

Nandini, Welch, David, and Roberts, Dexter. "The Race to Build Really Cheap Cars," *BusinessWeek*, April 23, 2007, at www.businessweek.com/magazine/content/07_17/b4031064.htm; McClatchy Newspapers (Las Vegas), "Downsizing to 'Right-Sizing,'" *Columbia Daily Tribune: Saturday Business*, January 31, 2009, p. 10; Henry, Jim. "Prius Hybrid Aimed Small, Stood Tall," *Automotive News*, October 29, 2007, p. 150 (3 pages) at www.autonews.com/apps/pbcs.dll/article?AID=/20071029/ANA06/710290326/1078&Profile=1078#; Luce, Burrelles. "Hitting the Right Note: Best Practices for Corporate Social Responsibility (CSR) Marketing," *E-Newsletter*, July 2007, at http://luceonline.us/newsletter/default_july07.php; "Are Green Cars Still Worth the Money?" *Consumer Reports* 80, no. 4: 16. *Business Source Premier*, EBSCO*host* (accessed May 20, 2015); Champniss, Guy, Wilson, Hugh N., and Macdonald, Emma K. 2015. "Why Your Customers' Social Identities Matter." *Harvard Business Review* 93 no. 1/2: 88–96. *Business Source Premier*, EBSCO*host* (accessed May 20, 2015).

[8]McClatchy Newspapers, "Airbus to Be Allowed to Bid to Replace Air Force One," *Columbia Daily Tribune*, January 25, 2009, p. 4D.

[9]Stern, Joanna. "iPhone 5: The Best 5 New Features," *ABC News*, September 13, 2012, at http://abcnews.go.com/Technology/iphone-top-features/story?id=17228259#

[10]Barton, Seth. "Samsung Galaxy s4 Release Date, Price & Specs Unveiled," *Expert Reviews*, March 17, 2013, at http://www.expertreviews.co.uk/smartphones/1298554/samsung-galaxy-s4-release-date-price-specs-unveiled

[11]Schifferes, Steve. "The Triumph of Lean Production," *BBC News*, February 27, 2007, at http://news.bbc.co.uk/2/hi/business/6346315stm

[12]"Financial Cards in Poland," Euromonitor International, (May 2008), at http://www.euromonitor.com/Consumer_Finance_in_Poland

[13]Smith, Scott. "Coca-Cola Lost Millions Because of This Market Research Mistake," Qualtrics (Qualtrics Blog), January 21, 2013, at www.qualtrics.com/blog/coca-cola-market-research/

[14]"A World with Better Customer Service—Helping Consumers Find It, and Helping Businesses Achieve It," *StellaService*, at www.stellaservice.com/, accessed on March 25, 2013; Dana Mattioli, "Data Firm Attracts Funding," *Wall Street Journal*, February 28, 2013, p. B5; Davis, Don. "StellaService Raises $15 Million and Starts Charging for its e-Retail Data," *Internet Retailer*, February 28, 2013, at www.internetretailer.com/2013/02/28/stellaservice-raises-15-million-and-starts-charging-data; "Say Goodbye to Fake Reviews." *Inc.* 36, no. 3: 108–110. *Business Source Premier,* EBSCO*host* (accessed May 20, 2015).

[15]"2008 Brand Keys Customer Loyalty Engagement Index." (March 18, 2008), at www.brandkeys.com/awards/cli08.cfm

[16]"Lists and Structure of Governments," *United States Census Bureau, U.S. Department of Commerce,* at www.census.gov/govs/go, accessed on March 18, 2013.

[17]"Lists and Structure of Governments."

[18]Strauss, Judy, El-Ansary, Adel, and Frost, Raymond. *E-Marketing,* 5th ed. (Upper Saddle River, NJ: Prentice Hall, 2007); "Ten Corporate Blogs Worth Reading," February 19, 2009, at www.blogtrepreneuer.com/2009/02/19/ten-corporate-blogs-worth-reading/

[19]Maltby, Emily, and Ovide, Shira. "Which Social Media Work?" *Wall Street Journal*, January 31, 2013, p. B8; "A2L Consulting Offers Its Complex Civil Litigation E-Book as a Free Download to Litigators and Litigation Support Professionals," *A2L Consulting*, January 15, 2013, at www.marketwire.com/press-release/a2l-consulting-offers-its-complex-civil-litigation-e-book-as-free-download-litigators-1745621.htm

[20]Protalinski, Emil. "Facebook Passes 1.11 Billion Monthly Active Users, 751 Million Mobile Users, and 665 Mission Daily Users," *TNW: The Next Web*, May 1, 2013, at http://thenextweb.com/facebook/2013/05/01/facebook-passes-1-11-billion-monthly-active-users-751-million-mobile-users-and-665-million-daily-users/; Edwards, Jim. "Meet the 30 Biggest Social Media Advertisers of 2012 [Ranked]," *Business Insider*, September 27, 2012, at www.businessinsider.com/the-30-biggest-social-media-advertisers-of-2012-2012-9?op=1; McCue, T. J. "Twitter Ranked Fastest Growing Social Media Platform in the World," *Forbes*, January 29, 2013, at www.forbes.com/sites/tjmccue/2013/01/29/twitter-ranked-fastest-growing-social-platform-in-the-world/

[21]Zimmerman, Eilene. "Real-Life Lessons in the Delicate Art of Setting Prices," *New York Times*, April 20, 2011, at www.nytimes.com/2011/04/21/business/smallbusiness/21sbiz.html?pagewanted=all&_r=0

[22]Lyne, David. "Small Plots Produce Nice Profits for Niche Farmers." *Fauquier Now* (Warrenton, VA), September 23, 2012. Accessed May 26, 2015. www.fauquiernow.com/index.php/fauquier_news/article/small-plots-produce-nice-profits-for-niche-farmers

[23]Bhatnagar, Roshni. "Why Citi's Consumer Hourglass Theory Matters," *Northwestern Business Review*, January 3, 2012 at http://northwesternbusinessreview.org/why-citis-consumer-hourglass-theory-matters/

[24]Byron, Ellen. "As Middle Class Shrinks, P&G Aims High and Low," *Wall Street Journal*, September 12, 2011, pp. A1, A16; Groth, Aimee. "The Consumer Hourglass Theory: This Is Why P&G, Saks, and Heinz Are Ignoring the Middle Class," *Business Insider*, September 24, 2011 at www.businessinsider.com/hourglass-consumer-theory-pg-citigroup-2011-9

glossary

Advertising any form of paid nonpersonal communication used by an identified sponsor to persuade or inform potential buyers about a product.

Behavioral Segmentation a segmentation strategy that uses behavioral variables to identify different market segments.

Behavioral Variables behavioral patterns displayed by groups of consumers and that are used in developing a segmentation strategy.

Brand Competition competitive marketing that appeals to consumer perceptions of benefits of products offered by particular companies.

Brand Loyalty pattern of repeated consumer purchasing based on satisfaction with a product's performance.

Competitive Environment the competitive system in which businesses compete.

Consumer Behavior study of the decision process by which people buy and consume products.

Consumer Goods physical products purchased by consumers for personal use.

Corporate Blogs comments and opinions published on the Web by or for an organization to promote its activities.

Cultural Influences include culture, subculture, and social class influences that marketers use to study buying behavior.

Customer Relationship Management (CRM) organized methods that a firm uses to build better information connections with clients, so that stronger company-client relationships are developed.

Data Mining the application of electronic technologies for searching, sifting, and reorganizing pools of data to uncover useful information.

Data Warehousing the collection, storage, and retrieval of data in electronic files.

Demographic Segmentation a segmentation strategy that uses demographic characteristics to identify different market segments.

Demographic Variables characteristics of populations that may be considered in developing a segmentation strategy.

Economic Environment relevant conditions that exist in the economic system in which a company operates.

Emotional Motives reasons for purchasing a product that are based on nonobjective factors.

Evoked Set (or Consideration Set) group of products consumers will consider buying as a result of information search.

Experimentation research method using a sample of potential consumers to obtain reactions to test versions of new products or variations of existing products.

Focus Group research method using a group of people from a larger population who are asked their attitudes, opinions, and beliefs about a product in an open discussion.

Form Utility providing products with features that customers want.

Geo-Demographic Segmentation using a combination of geographic and demographic traits for identifying different market segments in a segmentation strategy.

Geo-Demographic Variables combination of geographic and demographic traits used in developing a segmentation strategy.

Geographic Variables geographic units that may be considered in developing a segmentation strategy.

Geographic Segmentation geographic units, from countries to neighborhoods, that may be considered in identifying different market segments in a segmentation strategy.

Industrial Goods physical products purchased by companies to produce other products.

Industrial Market organizational market consisting of firms that buy goods that are either converted into products or used during production.

Institutional Market organizational market consisting of such nongovernmental buyers of goods and services as hospitals, churches, museums, and charitable organizations.

Integrated Marketing Strategy strategy that blends together the Four Ps of marketing to ensure their compatibility with one another and with the company's nonmarketing activities as well.

International Competition competitive marketing of domestic products against foreign products.

Market Segmentation process of dividing a market into categories of customer types, or "segments" having similar wants and needs and who can be expected to show interest in the same products.

Marketing activities, a set of institutions, and processes for creating, communicating, delivering, and exchanging offerings that have value for customers, clients, partners, and society at large.

Marketing Manager manager who plans and implements the marketing activities that result in the transfer of products from producer to consumer.

Marketing Mix combination of product, pricing, promotion, and place (distribution) strategies used to market products.

Marketing Objectives the things marketing intends to accomplish in its marketing plan.

Marketing Plan detailed strategy for focusing marketing efforts on consumer's needs and wants.

Marketing Research the study of what customers need and want and how best to meet those needs and wants.

Marketing Strategy all the marketing programs and activities that will be used to achieve the marketing goals.

Observation research method that obtains data by watching and recording consumer behavior.

Personal Influences include lifestyle, personality, and economic status that marketers use to study buying behavior.

Personal Selling promotional tool in which a salesperson communicates one-on-one with potential customers.

Place (Distribution) part of the marketing mix concerned with getting products from producers to consumers.

Place Utility providing products where customers will want them.

Political-Legal Environment the relationship between business and government, usually in the form of government regulation of business.

Possession Utility transferring product ownership to customers by setting selling prices, setting terms for customer credit payments, and providing ownership documents.

Pricing process of determining the best price at which to sell a product.

Primary Data new data that are collected from newly performed research.

Product good, service, or idea that is marketed to fill consumers' needs and wants.

Product Differentiation creation of a product feature or product image that differs enough from existing products to attract customers.

Product Positioning process of fixing, adapting, and communicating the nature of a product.

Promotion aspect of the marketing mix concerned with the most effective techniques for communicating information about and selling a product.

Psychographic Segmentation a segmentation strategy that uses psychographic characteristics to identify different market segments.

Psychographic Variables consumer characteristics, such as lifestyles, opinions, interests, and attitudes, that may be considered in developing a segmentation strategy.

Psychological Influences include an individual's motivations, perceptions, ability to learn, and attitudes that marketers use to study buying behavior.

Public Relations communication efforts directed at building goodwill and favorable attitudes in the minds of the public toward the organization and its products.

Rational Motives reasons for purchasing a product that are based on a logical evaluation of product attributes.

Relationship Marketing marketing strategy that emphasizes building lasting relationships with customers and suppliers.

Sales Promotion direct inducements such as premiums, coupons, and package inserts to tempt consumers to buy products.

Secondary Data data that are already available from previous research.

Services products having nonphysical features, such as information, expertise, or an activity that can be purchased.

Services Companies Market firms engaged in the business of providing services to the purchasing public.

Social Influences include family, opinion leaders (people whose opinions are sought by others), and such reference groups as friends, co-workers, and professional associates that marketers use to study buying behavior.

Social Networking network of communications that flow among people and organizations interacting through an online platform.

Social Networking Media websites or access channels, such as Facebook, Twitter, LinkedIn, and YouTube, to which consumers go for information and discussions.

Sociocultural Environment the customs, mores, values, and demographic characteristics of the society in which an organization functions.

Substitute Product product that is dissimilar from those of competitors, but that can fulfill the same need.

Survey research method of collecting consumer data using questionnaires, telephone calls, and face-to-face interviews.

Target Market the particular group of people or organizations on which a firm's marketing efforts are focused.

Technological Environment all the ways by which firms create value for their constituents.

Time Utility providing products when customers will want them.

Utility product's ability to satisfy a human want or need.

Value relative comparison of a product's benefits versus its costs.

Viral Marketing type of marketing that relies on the Internet to spread information like a "virus" from person to person about products and ideas.

Information Technology (IT) for Business

From Chapter 14 of *Business Essentials*, Eleventh Edition. Ronald J. Ebert, Ricky W. Griffin. Copyright © 2017 by Pearson Education, Inc.

Engineers alone do not design new products.

Customers, marketers, financiers, production

managers, and

purchasing employees use technology to

collaborate in

ways that seemed impossible in the past.

After reading this chapter, you should be able to:

1   **Discuss** the impacts information technology (IT) has had on the business world.

2   **Identify** the IT resources businesses have at their disposal and how these resources are used.

3   **Describe** the role of information systems, the different types of information systems, and how businesses use such systems.

4   **Identify** the threats and risks information technology poses on businesses.

5   **Describe** the ways in which businesses protect themselves from the threats and risks information technology poses.

Reported Web Forgery!

This web site at firstbanks.direct-upd... ...y and has been blocked base... ...d to trick

Think Before
You Click

"Start a 'work-at-home' job as an 'international sales representative' or a 'shipping manager,' with excellent pay. Simply open a new bank account in your name, accept money transfers into the account, then forward the money to our customers at locations around the globe." For out-of-work computer users, this e-mail message can be quite appealing. In reality, the victim is tricked into becoming a "mule" in a money-laundering racket. The new "employee" provides anonymous racketeers a safe way to launder stolen or otherwise illegal money. As Internet money transfers arrive, the mule relays them (illegally) to a global network of recipient racketeers.

Clearly, the Internet creates infinite opportunities to research careers, search for jobs, and build a network. But the very nature of the Internet creates risks as well as opportunities. Perhaps you've posted a resume on a website such as LinkedIn or monster.com. Well, cybercriminals, as well as legitimate employers, may be after you. In an-all-too common scam, criminals posing as employers contact individuals who have posted their resumes online. They conduct an interview, often electronically, and make the job hunter the offer of a great job. All that's left is collecting a little information, such as the person's Social Security number. Unfortunately, there's really no company and no job, but your Social Security number, as well as other personal information can be used to apply for credit cards that will never get paid. Before you share information like your Social Security number, be sure to know who is at the other end of an e-mail. Do some research and make sure that the company is legitimate and that the person with whom you are exchanging e-mails is really an employee.

In one popular work-at-home scam, the unsuspecting victim (the new online "employee") cashes checks sent from the "employer" in a foreign country and gets to keep 10 percent of the cash as a payment for service. The remaining 90 percent is sent via Western Union back to the employer. Because the checks are bogus, they bounce, and the victim must repay the full amounts to the bank. Alerting the public to another scam, SC Johnson, the company that makes household products such as Raid, Windex, and Pledge furniture cleaner, warns of phony online job offers for work-at-home customer service jobs falsely using the Johnson name. The scammers say the job pays trainees $20 an hour initially, advancing to $25 after training, but employees must first buy some training software—which, of course, they pay for but never receive.

To protect yourself from cybercriminals when looking for a job, there are a couple of red flags that should alert you that something is not quite right. These cybercriminals are not

Andres Rodriguez/Fotolia

what's in it
for me?

Protecting against cyber-attacks is an extreme example of the way the Internet and related technologies are reshaping the business landscape. But even the most traditional businesses must change with the times, whether those times are defined by paper and pencil, telephone and fax machine, or digital language translators and smartphones and smartwatches. Indeed, it may seem like the times are changing more rapidly with each passing year, and it is in this context that our discussion of the various kinds of information technology, their functions, and the benefits and risks associated with each assumes particular importance. By understanding the material in this chapter, you'll have a clearer picture of how technology is used by and affects business, and how you can use it to your best advantage—as an employee, investor, manager, or a business owner.

human resource professionals, so you may notice spelling or grammatical errors in e-mails. While mistakes can happen, this is a potential red flag that the communication is not legitimate. Similarly, if an offer seems too good to be true, it probably is. If you're offered a job, but required to pay money up front, there's a good chance that the offer is not legit. Finally, offers that are very time pressured are more likely to be fraudulent. Criminals don't want you to take the time to think through a bad deal and will encourage you to "act now" before this offer goes away.

Obviously, it's not just job-hunters who face risks. Text messages saying victims' credit cards have been deactivated lure bank customers into relaying account information to an unknown sender. Internet-based phone users receive fake caller IDs of real hospitals, government agencies, banks, and other businesses in a now-popular form of telephone phishing that talks victims into revealing personal information. Perhaps most impressive, cyber thieves are using marketing techniques—most notably "targeting"—to reach specific audiences. Also known as "spear phishing," with targeting, scammers do research to identify wealthy individuals, families, and professional money managers. Victims receive friendly sounding e-mails and social networking contacts containing contaminated attachments that, once opened, infect their computers, exposing bank account and other identity information to scammers. Although computer security devices—spam filters, data encryption, firewalls, and anti-virus software—catch a vast number of intrusions, the threat remains.[1]

Organizations, too, are victims of cyber invasions: Security consultants say that global cyber-attacks originating in China, and known as Night Dragon, have invaded computers of oil companies, stealing information on competitive bidding, financing, and operations practices. Some governments, to save money, are actively scamming others, using hackers to steal technology secrets for leading-edge military equipment, including defense systems of other countries. Organizations of all kinds are finding cyber security more difficult as more and more employees use their personal phones and computers for conducting business. Organizational information, then, is more widely dispersed and increasingly susceptible to intrusion via mobile-phone malware, virus-contaminated applications, and links containing spyware sent from text messages.[2] (After studying the content in this chapter, you should be able to answer a set of discussion questions found at the end of the chapter.)

Information Technology Impacts: A Driver of Changes for Business

OBJECTIVE 1
Discuss

the impacts information technology (IT) has had on the business world.

Information Technology (IT) *various appliances and devices for creating, storing, exchanging, and using information in diverse modes, including visual images, voice, multimedia, and business data*

The effect of **information technology (IT)** on business has been immeasurable. In fact, IT, the various appliances and devices for creating, storing, exchanging, and using information in diverse modes, including visual images, voice, multimedia, and business data, has altered the structure of business organizations, radically changing the way employees and customers interact. We see ads all the time for the latest cell phones, iPads, laptops, PDAs, tablets, and smartphones, and most of us connect daily to the Internet. E-mail has become a staple in business, and even such traditionally "low-tech" businesses as nail salons and garbage collection companies are dependent on the Internet, computers, and networks. As consumers, we interact with databases of IT networks every time we withdraw money from an ATM, order food at McDonald's, or check on the status of a package at UPS.com. Technology and its effects are evident everywhere.

E-commerce *use of the Internet and other electronic means for retailing and business-to-business transactions*

E-commerce (short for *electronic commerce*), the use of the Internet and other electronic means for retailing and business-to-business transactions, has created new market relationships around the globe. In this section, we'll look at how businesses are using IT to bolster productivity, improve operations and processes, create new opportunities, and communicate and work in ways not possible before.

Creating Portable Offices: Providing Remote Access to Instant Information

IT appliances such as Samsung mobile phones and Apple iPhones, along with IBM wireless Internet access and PC-style office applications, save businesses time and travel expenses by enabling employees, customers, and suppliers to communicate from any location. IT's mobile messaging capabilities mean that a geographic separation between the workplace and headquarters is more common. Employees no longer work only at the office or the factory, nor are all of a company's operations performed at one place; employees take the office with them. When using such devices, off-site employees have continuous access to information, instead of being forced to be at a desk to access their files and the Internet. Client project folders, e-mail, and voice messaging are accessible from any location. Such benefits currently attract 46 million enthusiastic subscribers worldwide to BlackBerry® smartphones and another 91 million users of Blackberry's messenger service.[3]

Looking to the future, a possible next step for office portability is Google's "Project Glass." This is a head-mounted, Internet-connected information display that may someday be blended into peoples' everyday eyeglasses. Using Google's *Android* system, it will respond to voice commands for rapid visual access to the Internet's vast ocean of digital information, all while on the move.[4]

Enabling Better Service by Coordinating Remote Deliveries

With access to the Internet, company activities may be geographically scattered but still remain coordinated through a networked system that provides better service for customers. Many businesses, for example, coordinate activities from one centralized location, but their deliveries flow from several remote locations, often at lower cost. When you order furniture—for example, a chair, a sofa, a table, and two lamps—from an Internet storefront, the chair may come from a warehouse in Philadelphia and the lamps from a manufacturer in California; the sofa and table may be shipped direct from different suppliers in North Carolina. Beginning with the customer's order, activities are coordinated through the company's network, as if the whole order were being processed at one place. This avoids the expensive in-between step of first shipping all the items to a central location.

Creating Leaner, More Efficient Organizations

Networks and technology are also leading to leaner companies with fewer employees and simpler structures. Because networks enable firms to maintain information linkages among both employees and customers, more work and customer satisfaction can be accomplished with fewer people. Bank customers connect into a 24-hour information system and monitor their accounts without employee assistance. Instructions that once were given to assembly workers by supervisors are now delivered to workstations electronically. IT communications provide better use of employee skills and greater efficiencies from physical resources. For example, truck drivers used to return to a shipping terminal to receive instructions from supervisors on reloading freight for the next delivery. Today, one dispatcher using IT has replaced several supervisors. Instructions to the fleet arrive on electronic screens in trucks on the road so drivers know in advance the next delivery schedule, and satellite navigation services, such as SiriusXM NavTraffic, alert drivers of traffic incidents ahead so they can reroute to avoid delivery delays.[5]

White House Photo/Alamy

Barack Obama's Blackberry uses an encrypted system for secure messaging with advisors and colleagues.

Enabling Increased Collaboration

Collaboration among internal units and with outside firms is greater when firms use collaboration (collaborative) software and other IT communications devices, which we'll discuss later in this chapter. Companies are learning that complex problems can be better solved through IT-supported collaboration, either with formal teams or spontaneous interaction among people and departments. The design of new products, for example, was once an engineering responsibility. Now it is a shared activity using information from customers, along with people in marketing, finance, production, engineering, and purchasing, who collectively determine the best design. For example, the design of Boeing's 787 Dreamliner aircraft is the result of collaboration, not just among engineers but also with passengers (who wanted electric outlets to recharge personal electronic devices), cabin crews (who wanted more bathrooms and wider aisles), and air-traffic controllers (who wanted larger, safer air brakes). Although the 787 suffered from some initial design flaws, solutions involved a worldwide network of technical collaboration among Boeing engineers, suppliers, customers, and NASA.[6]

This Boeing aircraft was the result of collaboration among Boeing engineers, suppliers, and customers.

dutchpilot22/Fotolia

Enabling Global Exchange

The global reach of IT enables business collaboration on a scale that was once unheard of. Consider Lockheed Martin's contract for designing and supplying thousands of Joint Strike Fighters in different versions for the United States, Britain, Italy, Denmark, Canada, and Norway. Lockheed can't do the job alone—over the project's 20-year life, more than 1,500 firms will supply everything from radar systems to engines to bolts. In just the start-up phase, Lockheed collaborated with Britain's BAE Systems along with more than 70 U.S. and 18 international subcontractors at some 190 locations, including an Australian manufacturer of aviation communications and a Turkish electronics supplier. In all, 40,000 remote computers are collaborating on the project using Lockheed's Internet-based system. Web collaboration on a massive scale is essential for coordinating design, testing, and construction while avoiding delays, holding down costs, and maintaining quality.[7]

Improving Management Processes

IT has also changed the nature of the management process. The activities and methods of today's manager differ significantly from those that were common just a few years ago. At one time, upper-level managers didn't concern themselves with all of the detailed information filtering upward from the workplace because it was expensive to gather, the collection and recording process was cumbersome, and information quickly became out of date. Workplace management was delegated to middle and first-line managers.

With electronic processing in digital databases, specialized software, and interactive networks, however, instantaneous information is accessible and useful to all levels of management. For example, consider *enterprise resource planning (ERP)*, which is an information system for organizing and managing a firm's activities across product lines, departments, and geographic locations. The ERP stores real-time information on work status and upcoming transactions and notifies employees when action is required if certain schedules are to be met. It coordinates internal operations with activities of outside suppliers and notifies customers of upcoming deliveries and billings. Consequently, more managers use it routinely for planning and controlling companywide operations. Today, a manager at Hershey Foods, for example, uses ERP to check on the current status of any customer order for Kisses or strawberry Twizzlers, inspect productivity statistics for each workstation, and analyze the delivery performance on any shipment. Managers can better coordinate companywide performance. They can identify departments that are working well together and those that are lagging behind schedule and creating bottlenecks.

Providing Flexibility for Customization

IT advances also create new manufacturing and service capabilities that enable businesses to offer customers greater variety, customizable options, and faster delivery cycles. Whether it's an iPhone app or a Rawlings baseball glove, today's design-it-yourself world is possible through fast, flexible manufacturing using IT networks. At Ponoko.com, you can design and make just about anything, from electronics to furniture. Buyers and materials suppliers, meeting electronically, have rapidly generated thousands of product designs online. The designs can be altered to suit each buyer's tastes. Similarly, at San Francisco–based Timbuk2's website, you can "build your own" custom messenger bag at different price levels with your choice of size, fabric, color combination, accessories, liner material, strap, and even left- or right-hand access.[8] This principle of **mass customization** allows companies to produce in large volumes, and IT allows each item to feature the unique options the customer prefers. With IT, the old standardized assembly line has become quickly adaptable because workers have instantaneous access to assembly instructions for all the product options, and equipment can be changed quickly for each customer's order.

Mass Customization *principle in which companies produce in large volumes, but each item features the unique options the customer prefers*

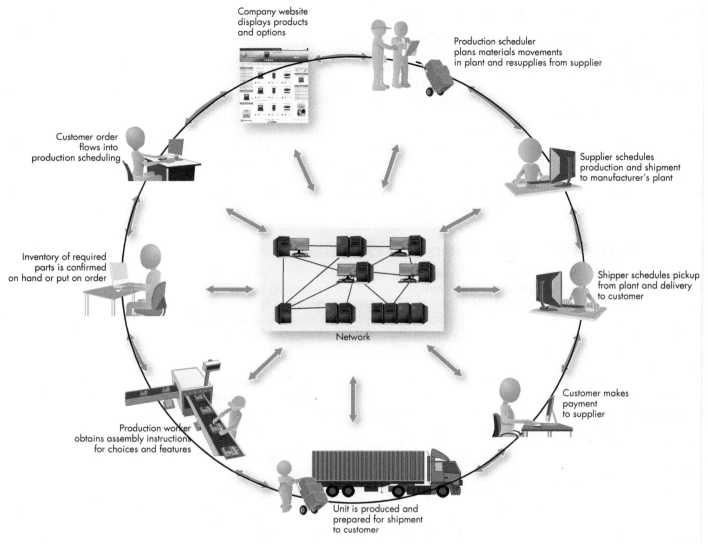

Company website displays products and options

Production scheduler plans materials movements in plant and resupplies from supplier

Customer order flows into production scheduling

Supplier schedules production and shipment to manufacturer's plant

Inventory of required parts is confirmed on hand or put on order

Shipper schedules pickup from plant and delivery to customer

Network

Customer makes payment to supplier

Production worker obtains assembly instructions for choices and features

Unit is produced and prepared for shipment to customer

FIGURE 1 Networking for Mass Customization of a Physical Product

As shown in Figure 1, flexible production and speedy delivery depend on an integrated network of information to coordinate all the activities among customers, manufacturers, suppliers, and shippers.

Service industries, too, including health care, banking, and recreation, are emphasizing greater flexibility for meeting customers' needs. Personalized pet care at HappyPetCare.net, for example, relies on IT for scheduling customized activities—dog walking, pet boarding, pet sitting, house-sitting, pet taxis, and other services. In tourism, at OceaniaCruises.com, passengers have flexibility for selecting personalized onboard services for meals, recreation and entertainment activities, educational classes, and spa treatments. They also customize your air travel schedules along with personalized pre- and post-cruise land programs.

Providing New Business Opportunities

Not only is IT improving existing businesses, it also is creating entirely new businesses where none existed before. For big businesses, this means developing new products, offering new services, and reaching new clients. Only a few years ago, today's multibillion-dollar behemoth known as Google was a fledgling search engine. That company boasts not just a search engine but hundreds of services, including virtual maps, YouTube video, Twitter accounts, Facebook pages, instant messaging, Gmail (Google's e-mail service), and online voicemail and software services such as photo editing and document creation.

IT-based industries, including computer backup and identity-theft protection, offer valuable services for individuals and business customers. Online backup protects against data loss resulting from hard-drive crashes, fire, flood, and other causes. Carbonite.com and Backblaze.com, for example, provide automatic continuous backup so clients can recover lost data quickly. For guarding against identity theft, firms such as LifeLock.com and IdentityGuard.com protect personal information by alerting clients to various information-theft risks and sending advice on steps for avoiding identity theft.

The IT landscape has also presented home-based businesses with new e-business opportunities. Consider Richard Smith. His love for stamp collecting began at age seven. Now, some 50 years after saving that first stamp, he's turned his hobby into a profitable eBay business. Each day begins at the PC in his home office, scanning eBay's listings for items available and items wanted by sellers and buyers around the world. With more than 6,000 sales transactions to date, Richard maintains a perfect customer rating and has earned more than $4,000 on each of several eBay transactions. Today, thousands of online marketplaces allow entrepreneurs to sell directly to consumers, bypassing conventional retail outlets, and enable business-to-business (B2B) selling and trading with access to a worldwide customer base. To assist start-up businesses, eBay's services network is a ready-made online business model, not just an auction market. Services range from credit financing to protection from fraud and misrepresentation, information security, international currency exchanges, and postsales management. These features enable users to complete sales transactions, deliver merchandise, and get new merchandise for future resale, all from the comfort of their own homes. Many eBay users, like Richard Smith, have carved profitable new careers with the help of these systems.

Improving the World and Our Lives

Can advancements in IT really make the world a better place? Developments in smartphones, social networking, home entertainment, automobile safety, and other applications have certainly brought enjoyment and convenience to the everyday lives of millions of people around the globe. Extending technology beyond previous-model cell phones and PCs, new technologies provide access to endless

After this capsule is swallowed, the camera inside it can transmit almost 50,000 images during its eight-hour journey through the digestive tract.

REX/Newscom

choices of *apps* (shorthand for *application software*), allowing each user to "build it your way," depending on what you want your device to do and how and where you'll be using it. Apps for computers and smartphones include *programs* for learning languages, music, work, games, traveling, art, and almost any other area of interest. Just two years after its opening, Apple's App Store had supplied more than 40 billion app downloads worldwide to users of Macs, iPhones, iPads, and iPod Touches.

Social networking, a valuable service for individuals and organizations, is made possible by IT. The many forms of social media—blogs, chats, and networks such as LinkedIn, Twitter, and Facebook—are no longer just playthings for gossips and hobbyists. They're also active tools for getting a job. With the economic meltdown, millions of job seekers turned to online networking—tapping leads from friends, colleagues, and acquaintances—for contacts with companies that may be hiring. Peers and recruiters are networking using electronic discussion forums and bulletin boards at websites of professional associations and trade groups, technical schools, and alumni organizations. Some social sites provide occupation-specific career coaching and job tips: Scientists are connecting with Epernicus, top managers use Meet the Boss, and graduate students are connecting with Graduate Junction.[9]

Organizations, too, including hospitals and medical equipment companies, are embracing IT advancements to provide better services. For example, when treating combat injuries, surgeons at Walter Reed National Military Medical Center in Bethesda, Maryland, rely on high-tech imaging systems that convert two-dimensional photographs of their patients' anatomies into three-dimensional (3D) physical models for presurgical planning. These 3D mockups of shoulders, femurs, and facial bones give doctors the opportunity to see and feel the anatomy as it will be seen in the operating room, before they even use their scalpels. Meanwhile, pill-sized cameras that patients swallow are providing doctors with images of the insides of the human body, helping them make better diagnoses for such ailments as ulcers and cancer.[10]

IT Building Blocks: Business Resources

OBJECTIVE 2
Identify
the IT resources businesses have at their disposal and how these resources are used.

Businesses today have a wide variety of IT resources at their disposal. In addition to the Internet and e-mail, these include communications technologies, networks, hardware devices, and software, as shown at technology media sites such as Techweb.com.

The Internet and Other Communication Resources

Internet *gigantic system of interconnected computer networks linked together by voice, electronic, and wireless technologies*

Hypertext Transfer Protocol (HTTP) *communications protocol used for the World Wide Web, in which related pieces of information on separate Web pages are connected using hyperlinks*

World Wide Web *branch of the Internet consisting of interlinked hypertext documents, or Web pages*

The **Internet** is a gigantic global system of interconnected computer networks belonging to millions of collaborating organizations and agencies—government, business, academic, and public—linked together by voice, electronic, and wireless technologies.[11] Computers within the networks are connected by various communications protocols, or standardized coding systems, such as the **hypertext transfer protocol (HTTP)**, which is used for the **World Wide Web**, a branch of the Internet consisting of interlinked hypertext documents, or Web pages. Other protocols serve a variety of purposes, such as sending and receiving e-mail. The World Wide Web and its protocols provide the common language that allows information sharing on the Internet. For thousands of businesses, the Internet has replaced the telephone, fax machine, and standard mail as the primary communications tool. The Internet has also spawned a number of other business communications technologies, including *intranets, extranets, electronic conferencing,* and *VSAT satellite communications.*

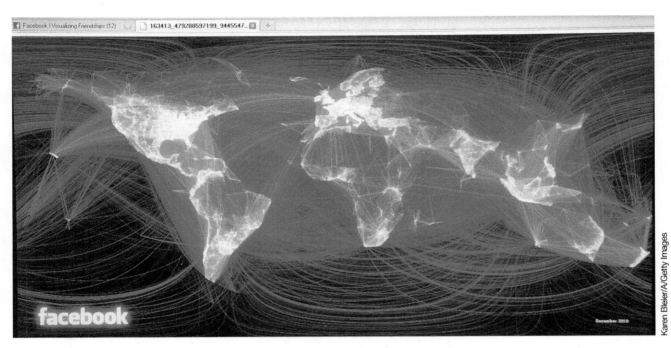

In this map of the Internet, from The Opte Project, each line represents a connection between computers or other network devices.

Intranets Many companies have extended Internet technology by maintaining internal websites linked throughout the firm. These private networks, or **intranets**, are accessible only to employees (and others who may be granted access) and may contain confidential information on benefits programs, a learning library, production management tools, or product design resources. The Ford Motor Company's intranet is accessible to 200,000 people daily at workstations in Asia, Europe, and the United States. In addition to Ford employees, the intranet is accessible to Ford dealers and suppliers around the world. Sharing information on engineering, distribution, and marketing has reduced the lead time for getting new models into production and has shortened customer delivery times.[12]

Intranet organization's private network of internally linked websites accessible only to employees

Extranets **Extranets** allow outsiders limited access to a firm's internal information network. The most common application allows buyers to enter a system to see which products are available for sale and delivery, thus providing convenient product availability information. Industrial suppliers are often linked into customers' information networks so that they can see planned production schedules and prepare supplies for customers' upcoming operations. The extranet at Chaparral Steel Company, for example, lets customers shop electronically through its storage yards and gives them electronic access to Chaparral's planned inventory of industrial steel products. Service industries, too, allow customers access to supplies of available services. For example, tour providers such as Tauck, Globus, and Viking River Cruises rely on major airlines such as Delta to provide flights for tour customers. Tour companies, by connecting into Delta's future flight schedules, reserve blocks of flight seats to accommodate tourists.

Extranet system that allows outsiders limited access to a firm's internal information network

Electronic Conferencing **Electronic conferencing** allows groups of people to communicate simultaneously from various locations via e-mail, phone, or video, thereby eliminating travel time and providing immediate contact. One form, called *data conferencing*, allows people in remote locations to work simultaneously on one document. *Video conferencing* allows participants to see one another on video screens while the conference is in progress. For example, Lockheed Martin's Joint Strike Fighter project, discussed previously, uses Internet collaboration systems with both voice and

Electronic Conferencing IT that allows groups of people to communicate simultaneously from various locations via e-mail, phone, or video

video capabilities. Although separated by oceans, partners can communicate as if they were in the same room for redesigning components and production schedules. Electronic conferencing is attractive to many businesses because it eliminates travel and saves money.

VSAT Satellite Communications Another Internet technology businesses use to communicate is **VSAT satellite communications**. VSAT (short for *very small aperture terminal*) systems have a transmitter-receiver (*transceiver*) that sits outdoors with a direct line of sight to a satellite. The hub, a ground-station computer at the company's headquarters, sends signals to and receives signals from the satellite, exchanging voice, video, and data transmissions. An advantage of VSAT is privacy. A company that operates its own VSAT system has total control over communications among its facilities, no matter their location, without dependence on other companies. A firm might use VSAT to exchange sales and inventory information, advertising messages, and visual presentations between headquarters and store managers at remote sites. For example, stores in Minneapolis, London, and Boston might communicate with headquarters in New York, sending and receiving information via a satellite, as shown in Figure 2.

Networks: System Architecture

A **computer network** is a group of two or more computers linked together, either hardwired or wirelessly, to share data or resources, such as a printer. The most common type of network used in businesses is a **client-server network**. In client-server networks, *clients* are usually the laptop or desktop computers through

---

VSAT Satellite Communications *network of geographically dispersed transmitter-receivers (transceivers) that send signals to and receive signals from a satellite, exchanging voice, video, and data transmissions*

Computer Network *group of two or more computers linked together by some form of cabling or by wireless technology to share data or resources, such as a printer*

Client-Server Network *common business network in which clients make requests for information or resources and servers provide the services*

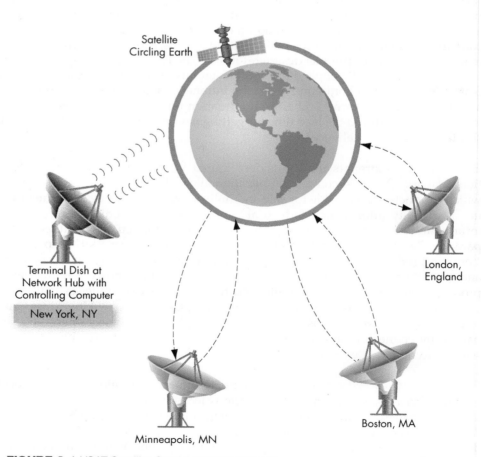

Satellite Circling Earth

Terminal Dish at Network Hub with Controlling Computer
New York, NY

London, England

Minneapolis, MN

Boston, MA

FIGURE 2 A VSAT Satellite Communication Network

which users make requests for information or resources. *Servers* are the computers that provide the services shared by users. In big organizations, servers are usually assigned a specific task. For example, in a local university or college network, an *application server* stores the word-processing, spreadsheet, and other programs used by all computers connected to the network. A *print server* controls the printers, stores printing requests from client computers, and routes jobs as the printers become available. An *e-mail server* handles all incoming and outgoing e-mail. With a client-server system, users can share resources and Internet connections—and avoid costly duplication.

Cloud computing modifies traditional networks by adding an externally located component—the "cloud"—that replaces the functions previously performed by application servers. With a cloud, information resources are retrieved via the Internet from a remote storage service, instead of relying on network-connected user-shared servers for storing data and software packages in client-server systems. Data and software resources are accessible through Internet-based devices, including laptops, desktops, tablets, mobile phones, and other devices with access to the Web. The cloud enhances user flexibility, especially for employees working remotely because users can access e-mails and data files from any online location, rather than from one particular location.

Amazon's Simple Storage Service (S3) is an example of a *public* cloud that rents Internet storage space where users can store any amount of data and retrieve it at anytime from anywhere on the Web. S3 services have become cost savers for companies by eliminating the need for buying, installing, and maintaining in-house server computers, many of which have excessive unused storage capacity "just in case it's needed in the future." S3 allows you to store and manage your application data, search files online, upgrade software quickly, and then download and share data. In contrast with public clouds, *private* cloud services such as JustCloud and ZipCloud provide an added layer of security by surrounding the user-company's storage with a firewall to ensure against intrusion. Private clouds provide added flexibility for creating customized data storage, automated data integration, and integrated software applications to better meet users' needs. Networks can be classified according to geographic scope and means of connection (either wired or wireless).

Wide Area Networks (WANs) Computers that are linked over long distances—statewide or even nationwide—through long-distance telephone wires, microwave signals, or satellite communications make up what are called **wide area networks (WANs)**. Firms can lease lines from communications vendors or maintain private WANs. Walmart, for example, depends heavily on a private satellite network that links thousands of U.S. and international retail stores to its Bentonville, Arkansas, headquarters.

Wide Area Network (WAN) *computers that are linked over long distances through telephone lines, microwave signals, or satellite communications*

Local Area Networks (LANs) In **local area networks (LANs)**, computers are linked in a smaller area such as an office or a building, using telephone wires, fiber-optic, or coaxial cables. For example, a LAN unites hundreds of operators who enter call-in orders at TV's Home Shopping Network facility. The arrangement requires only one computer system with one database and one software system.

Local Area Network (LAN) *computers that are linked in a small area, such as all of a firm's computers within a single building*

Wireless Networks Wireless networks use airborne electronic signals to link network computers and devices. Like wired networks, wireless networks can reach across long distances or exist within a single building or small area. For example, smartphone systems allow users to send and receive transmissions on the **wireless wide area networks (WWANs)** of hundreds of service providers service providers—such as Cellular One (United States), T-Mobile (United Kingdom and United States), and Vodafone Italia (Italy)—in more than 90 countries throughout the world. A *firewall* provides privacy protection. We'll discuss firewalls in more detail later in the chapter.

Wireless Wide Area Network (WWAN) *network that uses airborne electronic signals instead of wires to link computers and electronic devices over long distances*

Wi-Fi *technology using a wireless local area network*

Wireless Local Area Network (Wireless LAN or WLAN) *local area network with wireless access points for PC users*

Wi-Fi You probably use—or have at least heard of "hotspots"—millions of locations worldwide, such as coffee shops, hotels, airports, and cities, that provide wireless Internet connections for people on the go. Each hotspot, or **Wi-Fi** (a play on the audio recording term *Hi-Fi*) access point, uses its own small network, called a **wireless local area network (wireless LAN or WLAN)**. Although wireless service is free at some hotspots, others charge a fee—a daily or hourly rate—for the convenience of Wi-Fi service.

The benefit of Wi-Fi is that its millions of users are not tethered to a wire for accessing the Internet. Employees can wait for a delayed plane in the airport and still be connected to the Internet through their wireless-enabled laptops or other devices. However, as with every technology, Wi-Fi has limitations, including a short range of distance. This means that your laptop's Internet connection can be severed if you move farther than about 300 feet from the hotspot. In addition, thick walls, construction beams, and other obstacles can interfere with the signals sent out by the network. So, although a city may have hundreds of hotspots, your laptop must remain near one to stay connected. *WiMAX* (*Worldwide Interoperability for Microwave Access*), the next step in wireless advancements, improves this distance limitation with its wireless range of up to 30 miles.

"Super Wi-Fi" Network *a powerful Wi-Fi network with extensive reach and strong signals that flow freely through physical objects such as walls*

Proposing a bolder approach for the future, the U.S. Federal Communications Commission in 2013 announced a proposed multiyear project for nationwide **"super Wi-Fi" networks** to be developed by the federal government. More powerful than today's networks, the super Wi-Fi would have farther reach, stretching across major metropolitan areas and covering much of the rural countryside as well. Super Wi-Fi's stronger signals will flow more freely, without obstruction, through concrete walls, steel beams, forests, and hills. The proposal would enable users to surf the Internet and make mobile phone calls without paying a monthly cell phone bill or Internet bill.[13] Scientists have also encouraged the government to use the bandwidth from old television frequencies to support super Wi-Fi.

Airlines, too, are expanding Wi-Fi service beyond just domestic flights by providing satellite-based Internet service on long-haul international flights. Japan Airlines offers Wi-Fi on routes between New York and Tokyo, in addition to flights between Tokyo and Los Angeles, Chicago, and Jakarta, Indonesia. Other airlines gearing up for Wi-Fi on long-haul flights include Air France, Delta, and United. Meanwhile, Qantas—the Australian airline—discontinued its trial program because of passenger disinterest in international Wi-Fi service.

Hardware and Software

Hardware *physical components of a computer network, such as keyboards, monitors, system units, and printers*

Any computer network or system needs **hardware**, the physical components, such as keyboards, monitors, system units, and printers. In addition to the laptops and desktop computers, *handheld computers* and mobile devices are also used often in businesses. For example, Target employees roam the store aisles using handheld devices to identify, count, and order items; track deliveries; and update backup stock at distribution centers to keep store shelves replenished with merchandise.

Software *programs that tell the computer how to function, what resources to use, how to use them, and application programs for specific activities*

The other essential in any computer system is **software**: programs that tell the computer how to function. Software includes *system software*, such as Microsoft Windows 8 for PCs, which tells the computer's hardware how to interact with the software, what resources to use, and how to use them. It also includes *application software* (apps) such as Microsoft Live Messenger and Photo Gallery, which are programs that meet the needs of specific users. Some application programs are used to address such common, long-standing needs as database management and inventory control, whereas others have been developed for a variety of specialized tasks ranging from mapping the oceans' depths to analyzing the anatomical structure of the human body. For example, IBM's Visualization Data Explorer software uses data from field samples to model the underground structure of an oil field. The imagery in the photo presented earlier in the chapter, for example, provides engineers with better information on oil location and reduces the risk of their hitting less productive holes.

entrepreneurship and new ventures

Speaking Loud and Clear: A New Voice Technology

IT users for years have sought a natural-sounding voice interface to enhance IT systems with vocal output, beyond traditional print or visual output. Vocal technologies, however, were less than effective until 2005, when Matthew Aylett and Nick Wright formed CereProc (short for Cerebral Processing) in Edinburgh, Scotland.[14] From the outset, the firm has been dedicated to creating better synthetic voices with character and emotion that stimulate listeners with natural-sounding messages. Before CereProc, these lofty goals were prohibitive. Speech experts couldn't create text-to-voice software that sounds realistically conversational, varying tone-of-voice and providing various vocal inflections for different situations. Previous software couldn't adapt incoming text (from word processing or from text messages) into natural voice formats. To attack these challenges, CereProc brought together a team of leading speech experts. It also partnered with leading universities and research programs in speech science technology and in developing new applications and markets for voice output.

The company's main product is CereVoice, an advanced text-to-voice technology available on mobile devices, PCs, servers, and headsets, and that has applications in most any company's products for better synthetic voices. Any computer's existing voice system can be replaced with more natural-sounding speech in a choice of accents, including Southern British English, Scottish, and American, that can be sampled with live voice demos at the firm's website.[15] Potential applications are endless—kitchen appliances, alarm systems, traffic controllers, automobile appliances, radio broadcasting, telephone messaging, and movies, to name a few. Although consumers may not see the CereVoice label, they will be hearing its various voices often in their everyday lives.

CereProc's Voice Creation service can create a synthesized imitation of a person's voice, including its tones and inflections. That's how noted film critic, the late Roger Ebert, got his voice back, four years after losing the ability to speak following cancer-related surgery. CereProc's voice engineers used recordings of Ebert's voice from 40 years of past television broadcasts, capturing individual sounds and identifying various voice characteristics. With meticulous care, specialists

C.M. Wiggins/AB5 WENN Photos/Newscom

then pieced them back together into software that mimicked the Pulitzer-Prize–winner's earlier voice. Ebert typed his comments into a computer that, in turn, converted the text into words that were spoken in his voice. This first-of-its-kind application made a memorable public appearance on the *Oprah* show, as Roger enthusiastically demonstrated his voice coming from the computer.[16] Beyond its technical success, this project vividly displays a compassionate side in CereProc's business.

While CereProc has clearly established a niche in the market, many other companies are working on similar technology. Since the introduction of Siri, Apple has used technology supplied by Nuance Communications for voice recognition. However, realizing that voice recognition has gone from being a gimmick to an essential technology, Apple is assembling an in-house team, headquartered in Cambridge, Massachusetts, to develop enhanced capabilities in this area. In June 2015, Apple announced that Siri now outperformed Google Now and Microsoft Cortana, with just a 5 percent error rate. Compare this to the 8 percent error rate proudly touted by Google just weeks earlier. Clearly, we are seeing that the future is now; voice recognition and voice creation have entered the mainstream of IT capabilities.[17]

Finally, *groupware*, software that connects group members for e-mail distribution, electronic meetings, message storing, appointments and schedules, and group writing, allows people to collaborate from their own desktop PCs, even if they're remotely located. It is especially useful when people work together regularly and rely heavily on information sharing. Groupware systems include IBM Lotus software and Novell GroupWise.

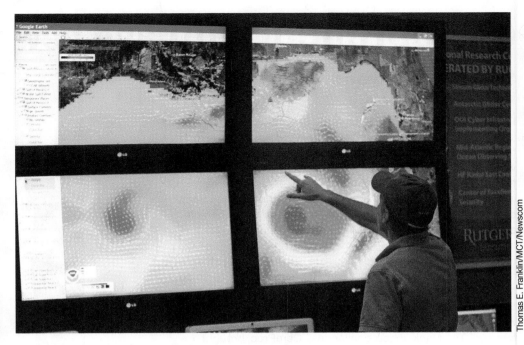

3-D computer modeling software gives engineers a better idea of where oil might be located.

Thomas E. Franklin/MCT/Newscom

Information Systems: Harnessing The Competitive Power of It

OBJECTIVE 3
Describe
the role of information systems, the different types of information systems, and how businesses use such systems.

Information System (IS) *system that uses IT resources to convert data into information and to collect, process, and transmit that information for use in decision making*

Data *raw facts and figures that, by themselves, may not have much meaning*

Information *meaningful, useful interpretation of data*

Business today relies on information management in ways that no one could foresee a decade ago. Managers now treat IT as a basic organizational resource for conducting daily business. At major firms, every activity—designing services, ensuring product delivery and cash flow, and evaluating personnel—is linked to *information systems*. An **information system (IS)** uses IT resources that enable managers to take **data**, raw facts and figures that, by themselves, may not have much meaning, and turn those data into **information**, the meaningful, useful interpretation of data. Information systems also enable managers to collect, process, and transmit that information for use in decision making.

Walmart is well known for its strategic use of information systems. The nerve center for company operations is a centralized IS in Bentonville, Arkansas. The IS drives costs down and raises efficiency because the same methods and systems are applied for all 11,000-plus stores in 27 countries. Data on the billions of sales transactions—time, date, and place—flow to Bentonville. The IS tracks millions of stock-keeping units (SKUs) weekly, enforces uniform reordering and delivery procedures on its more than 100,000 suppliers, including 20,000 in China, and regulates the flow of merchandise through its distribution centers and stores.

Beyond the firm's daily operations, information systems are also crucial in planning. Managers routinely use the IS to decide on products and markets for the next 5 to 10 years. The company's vast database enables marketing managers to analyze customer demographics for better marketing, and it is also used for financial planning, materials handling, and electronic funds transfers with suppliers and customers.

Information Systems Managers *managers who are responsible for the systems used for gathering, organizing, and distributing information*

Walmart, like most businesses, regards its information as a private resource, an asset that's planned, developed, and protected. Therefore, it's not surprising that they have **information systems managers** who are responsible for the systems used for gathering, organizing, and distributing information, just as they have production, marketing, and finance managers. These managers use many of the IT resources we discussed previously—the Internet, communications technologies, networks, hardware, and software—to sift through information and apply it to their jobs.

Leveraging Information Resources: Data Warehousing and Data Mining

Almost everything you do leaves a trail of information about you. Your preferences in movie rentals, television viewing, Internet sites, and groceries; the destinations of your phone calls, your credit card charges, your financial status; personal information about age, gender, marital status, and even your health are just a few of the items about each of us that are stored in scattered databases. The behavior patterns of millions of users can be traced by analyzing files of information gathered over time from their Internet usage and in-store purchases.

The collection, storage, and retrieval of such data in electronic files is called **data warehousing**. For managers, the data warehouse can be a gold mine of information about their business. Indeed, Kroger Co., the Ohio-based grocery chain, collects data on customer shopping habits to find ways to gain greater customer loyalty. As part owner of a data-mining firm, Kroger accumulates information from its shopper cards, analyzes the data to uncover shopping patterns, and sends money-saving coupons to regular customers for the specific products they usually buy. Kroger's precision targeting pays off, especially in a sluggish economy. With a rate of coupon usage up to as much as 50 times the industry average, it's a money saver for Kroger customers and boosts the company's sales, too.[18] To help put this in context, coupons from Kroger's quarterly mailers, uniquely customized for each customer, have a 70 percent redemption rate within six weeks of delivery.

Data Warehousing *the collection, storage, and retrieval of data in electronic files*

Data Mining After collecting information, managers use **data mining**, the application of statistics and electronic technologies for searching, sifting, and reorganizing pools of data to uncover useful information. Data mining helps managers plan for new products, set prices, and identify trends and shopping patterns. By analyzing what consumers actually do, businesses can determine what subsequent purchases they are likely to make and then send them tailor-made ads. The *Washington Post*, for example, uses data-mining software to analyze census data and target households likely to respond to sales efforts.[19]

Data Mining *the application of electronic technologies for searching, sifting, and reorganizing pools of data to uncover useful information*

Frank van Delft/Cultura/Getty Images

Retailers such as Wal-Mart and Sam's Club rely on data warehousing and mining to keep shelves stocked with in-demand merchandise.

managing in turbulent times

Better Care, Lower Costs

Imagine that you are an emergency room doctor and a patient has just come in complaining of chest pains. You know that this could be serious—a heart attack, stroke, or aortic dissection—or perhaps something less dire, such as acid reflux or bruised or broken ribs. You have only minutes to make a quick assessment and connect the patient with the right resources. In addition to the physical exam, the patient's electronic medical record may provide key information to make a quick and accurate diagnosis and treatment plan. Perhaps the patient has had a prior admission for heart-related conditions, or they have been prescribed medication for high blood pressure. This information might point the ER team in the direction of quickly ordering tests to identify if a heart attack or other heart-related condition is occurring. On the other hand, if the patient has recently been in a car accident, physicians may try to rule out broken ribs before ordering expensive, and possibly invasive, heart-related testing. "The opportunity to integrate the data coming out of the electronic medical record into health-care delivery is very exciting," according to Allen Kamer, Chief Commercial Officer for Analytics at Optum, a leader in health-care IT services. On their website, they state their mission as follows: "We help deliver better outcomes for hospitals, doctors, pharmacies, health plans, governments, employers, and the millions of lives they touch."

The move to electronic health records is relatively recent, with many doctors and hospitals just moving to an IT solution in the past five years. As more data is collected into electronic health records, a wealth of predictive analytics is beginning to

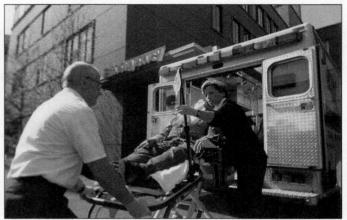

Keith Brofsky/Getty Images

emerge. In the past, much of established practice came out of clinical trials with small samples of patients. However, with larger sample sizes, essentially 100 percent of all patients, health professionals can make better decisions, not only when the patient becomes ill but also before this ever happens. Data from the healthcare record allows insurance companies to proactively advise their members about their health risks and provide recommendations about lifestyle changes and preventive testing and procedures. These interventions have resulted in reduced hospital admissions for some of the most serious and expensive conditions, such as COPD and heart disease. Clearly, the use of healthcare analytics is a win-win—better patient care at lower costs.[20]

Information Linkages with Suppliers The top priority for Walmart's IS—improving in-stock reliability—requires integration of Walmart and suppliers' activities with store sales. That's why Procter & Gamble (P&G), Johnson & Johnson, and other suppliers connect into Walmart's information system to observe up-to-the-minute sales data on individual items, by store. They can use the system's computer-based tools—spreadsheets, sales forecasting, and weather information—to forecast sales demand and plan delivery schedules. Coordinated planning avoids excessive inventories, speeds up deliveries, and holds down costs throughout the supply chain while keeping shelves stocked for retail customers.

Types of Information Systems

Employees have a variety of responsibilities and decision-making needs, and a firm's IS may actually be a set of several systems that share information while serving different levels of the organization, different departments, or different operations. Because they work on different kinds of problems, managers and their employees have access to the specialized information systems that satisfy their different information needs.

In addition to different types of users, each business *function*—marketing, human resources, accounting, production, or finance—has special information needs, as do groups working on major projects. Each user group and department, therefore, may need a special IS.

DM7/Shutterstock

The 3-D computer model of this dinosaur is constructed from digital scans of fossilized tissue.

Information Systems for Knowledge Workers

Knowledge workers are employees for whom information and knowledge are the raw materials of their work, such as engineers, scientists, and IT specialists who rely on IT to design new products or create new processes. These workers require **knowledge information systems**, which provide resources to create, store, use, and transmit new knowledge for useful applications—for instance, databases to organize and retrieve information, and computational power for data analysis.

Specialized support systems have also increased the productivity of knowledge workers. **Computer-aided design (CAD)** helps knowledge workers—and now ordinary people, too, as we saw with consumers designing customized products earlier in this chapter—design products ranging from cell phones to jewelry to auto parts by simulating them and displaying them in 3D graphics. In a more advanced version, known as *rapid prototyping*, the CAD system electronically transfers instructions to a computer-controlled machine that quickly builds a prototype—a physical model—of the newly designed product, such as a toy, an artificial limb for the disabled, or a solar panel. The older method—making handcrafted prototypes from wood, plastic, or clay—is replaced with faster, cheaper prototyping.

CAD is helping archaeological scientists uncover secrets hidden in fossils using 3D computer models of skeletons, organs, and tissues constructed with digital data from computed tomography (CT) scans of dinosaur fossils. From these models, scientists have learned, for example, that the giant apatosaurus's neck curved downward, instead of high in the air as once thought. By seeing how the animals' bones fit together with cartilage, ligaments, and vertebrae, scientists are discovering more about how these prehistoric creatures interacted with their environment.[21]

In a direct offshoot of computer-aided design, **computer-aided manufacturing (CAM)** uses computers to design and control the equipment needed in a manufacturing process. For example, CAM systems can produce digital instructions to control all the machines and robots on a production line, say, as an example, in making jewelry boxes. CAM-guided machines cut the materials, move them through the stages of production, and then assemble each stylish box without human physical involvement in production activities. CAD and CAM coupled together (CAD/CAM) are useful to engineers in a manufacturing environment for designing and testing new products and then designing the machines and tools to manufacture the new product.

Knowledge Information System *information system that supports knowledge workers by providing resources to create, store, use, and transmit new knowledge for useful applications*

Computer-Aided Design (CAD) *IS with software that helps knowledge workers design products by simulating them and displaying them in three-dimensional graphics*

Computer-Aided Manufacturing (CAM) *IS that uses computers to design and control equipment in a manufacturing process*

Information Systems for Managers Each manager's information activities and IS needs vary according to his or her functional area (accounting or human resources and so forth) and management level. The following are some popular information systems used by managers for different purposes.

MANAGEMENT INFORMATION SYSTEMS **Management information systems (MIS)** support managers by providing reports, schedules, plans, and budgets that can then be used for making both short- and long-term decisions. For example, at Walsworth Publishing Company, managers rely on detailed information—current customer orders, staffing schedules, employee attendance, production schedules, equipment status, and materials availability—for moment-to-moment decisions during the day. They require similar information to plan such midrange activities as personnel training, materials movements, and cash flows. They also need to anticipate the status of the jobs and projects assigned to their departments. Many MIS—cash flow, sales, production scheduling, and shipping—are indispensable for helping managers complete these tasks.

> **Management Information System (MIS)** *computer system that supports managers by providing information— reports, schedules, plans, and budgets—that can be used for making decisions*

For longer-range decisions involving business strategy, Walsworth managers need information to analyze trends in the publishing industry and overall company performance. They need both external and internal information, current and future, to compare current performance data to data from previous years and to analyze consumer trends and economic forecasts.

DECISION SUPPORT SYSTEMS Managers who face a particular kind of decision repeatedly can get assistance from **decision support systems (DSS)**, interactive systems that create virtual business models and test them with different data to see how they respond. When faced with decisions on plant capacity, for example, Walsworth managers can use a capacity DSS. The manager inputs data on anticipated sales, working capital, and customer-delivery requirements. The data flow into the DSS processor, which then simulates the plant's performance under the proposed data conditions. A proposal to increase facility capacity by, say, 10 percent could be simulated to find costs of operation, percent of customer order fulfillments, and other performance measures that would result with the expanded capacity. After experimenting with various data conditions, the DSS makes recommendations on the best levels of plant capacity—those that result in best performance—for each future time period.

> **Decision Support System (DSS)** *interactive system that creates virtual business models for a particular kind of decision and tests them with different data to see how they respond*

OBJECTIVE 4
Identify
the threats and risks information technology poses on businesses.

IT Risks and Threats

As with other technologies throughout history, IT continues to attract abusers set on doing mischief, with severity ranging from mere nuisance to outright destruction. Eager IT users everywhere are finding that even social networking and cell phones have a "dark side"—privacy invasion. Facebook postings of personal information about users have been intercepted and misused by intruders. Beacon, the former data-gathering service, caused a public uproar when it published peoples' online purchases publicly on their Facebook newsfeeds. And with cellular technology, some features of Bluetooth connections allow savvy intruders to read a victim's text messages, listen in on live conversations, and even view unwary users' photos.[22]

Businesses, too, are troubled with IT's dark side. Hackers break into computers, stealing personal information and company secrets, and launch attacks on other computers. Meanwhile, the ease of information sharing on the Internet has proven costly for companies who are having an increasingly difficult time protecting their intellectual property, and viruses that crash computers have cost companies many billions annually. In this section, we'll look at these and other IT risks. In the next section, we'll discuss ways in which businesses are protecting themselves from these risks.

Hackers

The term *breaking and entering* no longer refers merely to physical intrusion. Today, it applies to IT intrusions as well. **Hackers** are cybercriminals who gain unauthorized access to a computer or network, either to steal information, money, or property or to tamper with data. Twitter reported that hackers may have intercepted information—names, passwords, e-mail addresses—of some 250,000 of the social media's users. With different motives than the Twitter intruders, Chinese-based hackers, including the Chinese government, are suspected of continuing cyber-attacks into the computer systems of several newspapers, including *The New York Times*, *The Washington Post*, and *The Wall Street Journal*. China-based intruders have been accused of a multiyear campaign to illegally gain corporate secrets and confidential information that can be used to frighten critics from writing unfavorable articles, accusations that the Chinese government has denied.[23]

Another common hacker activity is to launch *denial of service (DoS) attacks*. DoS attacks flood networks or websites with bogus requests for information and resources, thereby overloading and shutting the networks or websites down, preventing legitimate users from accessing them.

Wireless mooching is a profitable industry for cybercriminals. In just five minutes, a *St. Petersburg Times* (Florida) reporter using a laptop found six unprotected wireless networks that were wide open to outside users.[24] Once inside an unsecured wireless network, hackers can use it to conduct illegal business, such as child pornography or money laundering. When police officers try to track down these criminals, they're long gone, leaving the innocent but naïve network host potentially exposed to criminal prosecution.

As we saw in this chapter's opening case, hackers, such as the Night Dragon, often break into company networks to steal company or trade secrets. But it's not just hackers who are doing the stealing. Because the chances of getting caught seem slim, home users continue, illegally, to download unpaid-for movies, music, and other resources from file-swapping networks. A recent study shows that sound piracy costs the United States $12.5 billion and 71,060 jobs annually. However, these losses also showcase what can happen to businesses that fail to adapt to changes in technology. Until recent years, the recording industry was reluctant to embrace the Internet as a path for distribution, preferring to prosecute pirates rather than offer them legal online alternatives. On the other hand, Apple has benefitted immensely from its online (download) distribution models, enabling it to become the world's most popular music vendor.[25]

Hacker *cybercriminal who gains unauthorized access to a computer or network, either to steal information, money, or property or to tamper with data*

Identity Theft

Once inside a computer network, hackers are able to commit **identity theft**, the unauthorized stealing of personal information (such as Social Security number and address) to get loans, credit cards, or other monetary benefits by impersonating the victim. Recent studies suggest that as many as 16.6 million victims fall prey to identify theft each year; identity theft is among the fastest-growing crimes in the United States.

Clever crooks get information on unsuspecting victims by digging in trash, stealing mail, or using *phishing* or *pharming* schemes to lure Internet users to bogus websites. For instance, a cybercriminal might send a PayPal user an e-mail notifying him or her of a billing problem with his or her account. When the customer clicks on the PayPal Billing Center link, he or she is transferred to a spoofed (falsified) Web page, modeled after PayPal's. The customer then submits the requested information—credit card number, Social Security number, and PIN—into the hands of the thief. The accounts are soon empty.

Identity Theft *unauthorized use of personal information (such as Social Security number and address) to get loans, credit cards, or other monetary benefits by impersonating the victim*

Intellectual Property Theft

Nearly every company faces the dilemma of protecting product plans, new inventions, industrial processes, and other **intellectual property**, something produced by the intellect or mind that has commercial value. Its ownership and right to its use

Intellectual Property *something produced by the intellect or mind that has commercial value*

may be protected by patent, copyright, trademark, and other means. But crooks may be able to steal information about intellectual property and create unauthorized duplications.

Computer Viruses, Worms, and Trojan Horses

Another IT risk facing businesses is rogue programmers who disrupt IT operations by contaminating and destroying software, hardware, or data files. *Viruses, worms*, and *Trojan horses* are three kinds of malicious programs that, once installed, can shut down any computer system. A *computer virus* exists in a file that attaches itself to a program and migrates from computer to computer as a shared program or as an e-mail attachment. It does not infect the system unless the user opens the contaminated file, and users typically are unaware they are spreading the virus by file sharing. It can, for example, quickly copy itself over and over again, using up all available memory and effectively shutting down the computer.

Worms are a particular kind of virus that travel from computer to computer within networked computer systems, without your needing to open any software to spread the contaminated file. In a matter of days, the notorious Blaster worm infected some 400,000 computer networks, destroying files and even allowing outsiders to take over computers remotely. The worm replicates itself rapidly, sending out thousands of copies to other computers in the network. Traveling through Internet connections and e-mail address books in the network's computers, it absorbs system memory and shuts down network servers, Web servers, and individual computers.

Unlike viruses, a *Trojan horse* does not replicate itself. Instead, it most often comes into the computer, at your request, masquerading as a harmless, legitimate software product or data file. Once installed, the damage begins. For instance, it may simply redesign desktop icons or, more maliciously, delete files and destroy information.

Spyware

As if forced intrusion isn't bad enough, Internet users unwittingly invite spies—masquerading as a friendly file available as a giveaway or shared among individual users on their PCs. This so-called **spyware** is downloaded by users who are lured by "free" software. Once installed, it "crawls" around to monitor the host's computer activities, gathering e-mail addresses, credit card numbers, passwords, and other inside information that it transmits back to someone outside the host system. Spyware authors assemble incoming stolen information to create their own "intellectual property" that they then sell to other parties to use for marketing and advertising purposes or for identity theft.[26]

Spyware *program unknowingly downloaded by users that monitors their computer activities, gathering e-mail addresses, credit card numbers, and other information that it transmits to someone outside the host system*

Spam

Spam, junk e-mail sent to a mailing list or a newsgroup (an online discussion group), is a greater nuisance than postal junk mail because the Internet is open to the public, e-mail costs are negligible, and massive mailing lists are accessible through file sharing or by theft. Spam operators send unwanted messages ranging from explicit pornography to hate mail to advertisements, and even destructive computer viruses. In addition to wasting users' time, spam also consumes a network's bandwidth, thereby reducing the amount of data that can be transmitted in a fixed amount of time for useful purposes. U.S. industry experts estimate spam's annual damage in lost time and productivity at between $20 and $50 billion in the United States alone and that it could be as high as $575 billion globally.[27]

Spam *junk e-mail sent to a mailing list or a newsgroup*

Although spammers sometimes gain significant incomes, they also risk anti-spanning prosecution that can be extremely costly. The judge in a lawsuit against Sanford Wallace, who proclaimed himself the "Spam King," issued a judgment for

$711 million against Wallace, one of the largest fines ever in an anti-spamming case. He was accused of sending 27 million spam mailings to Facebook, using phishing to get passwords from thousands of Facebook users, and then entering their accounts to post fraudulent information. He now faces criminal charges of electronic mail fraud, damage to protected computers, and criminal contempt.[28]

IT Protection Measures

Security measures against intrusion and viruses are a constant challenge. Most systems guard against unauthorized access by requiring users to have protected passwords. Other measures include firewalls, special software, and encryption.

Preventing Unauthorized Access: Firewalls

Firewalls are security systems with special software or hardware devices designed to keep computers safe from hackers. A firewall is located where two networks—for example, the Internet and a company's internal network—meet. It contains two components for filtering incoming data:

Firewall *security system with special software or hardware devices designed to keep computers safe from hackers*

- The company's *security policy*—Access rules that identify every type of data that the company doesn't want to pass through the firewall

- A *router*—A table of available routes or paths; a "traffic switch" that determines which route or path on the network to send each piece of data after it is tested against the security policy

Only the information that meets the conditions of the user's security policy is routed through the firewall and permitted to flow between the two networks. Data that fail the access test are blocked and cannot flow between the two networks.

Preventing Identity Theft

Although foolproof prevention is impossible, steps can be taken to avoid being victimized. A visit to the Identity Theft Resource Center (www.idtheftcenter.org) is a valuable first step to get information on everything from scam alerts to victim issues to legislation such as the Fair and Accurate Credit Transactions Act (FACTA). FACTA strengthens identity-theft protections by specifying how organizations must destroy information instead of dropping it in a dumpster. When a company disposes of documents that contain credit or Social Security information, they must be shredded, pulverized, or burned, and all electronic records (in computers and databases) must be permanently removed to keep them out of the hands of intruders.[29]

Preventing Infectious Intrusions: Anti-Virus Software

Combating viruses, worms, Trojan horses, and any other infectious software (collectively known as *malware*) has become a major industry for systems designers and software developers. Installation of any of hundreds of **anti-virus software** products protects systems by searching incoming e-mail and data files for "signatures" of known viruses and virus-like characteristics. Contaminated files are discarded or placed in quarantine for safekeeping. Many viruses take advantage of weaknesses in operating systems, such as Microsoft Windows, to spread and propagate. Network administrators must make sure that the computers on their systems are using the most up-to-date operating system that includes the latest security protection.

Anti-Virus Software *product that protects systems by searching incoming e-mails and data files for "signatures" of known viruses and virus-like characteristics*

Protecting Electronic Communications: Encryption Software

Security for electronic communications is another concern for businesses. Unprotected e-mail can be intercepted, diverted to unintended computers, and opened, revealing the contents to intruders. Protective software is available to guard against those intrusions, adding a layer of security by encoding e-mails so that only intended recipients can open them. An **encryption system** works by scrambling an e-mail message so that it looks like garbled nonsense to anyone who doesn't possess the "key," another part of the software that decodes encrypted e-mails.

Encryption System *software that assigns an e-mail message to a unique code number (digital fingerprint) for each computer so only that computer, not others, can open and read the message*

Avoiding Spam and Spyware

To help their employees avoid privacy invasion and to improve productivity, businesses often install anti-spyware and spam-filtering software on their systems. Although dozens of anti-spyware products provide protection—software such as Webroot Spy Sweeper and Microsoft Windows Defender—they can be continually updated to keep pace with new spyware techniques.

finding a better way

The Emerging Market for Cyber Insurance

If you are lucky enough to own a car, you probably have automobile insurance. Most states require drivers to be insured at a minimum level. In the event of an accident, automobile insurance may cover the direct costs to the vehicles involved, as well as medical bills and lost wages, in some cases. An insurance policy is a formal agreement to pay the policyholder a specified amount in the event of certain losses. Insurance is available for almost any type of loss. Increasingly, businesses are turning to cyber insurance to protect themselves against losses associated with data breaches.

In recent years, hardly a month goes by without a high-profile data breach. Whether it's Target, T.J. Maxx, Heartland, or the U.S. government, data breaches result in millions of dollars in expenses. On top of the enormous damage to the organization's reputation, there are serious impacts on their bottom line as expenses pile up. In one of the more famous data breaches in recent years, Sony Pictures was hacked in November 2014. Hackers gained access to virtually everything stored on the company's network, including internal e-mails, personal information about employees, and unreleased movies. However, in spite of all the bad press, there was a silver lining to the cloud—Sony had purchased cyber insurance, which is expected to offset much of the cost, according to a statement by Sony CEO Michael Lynton.

Cyber insurance can cover a wide range of costs that result from data theft, data loss, computer malfunction, and malware. Companies can recover a wide range of costs, including fines and lost income, as well as public relations expenses associated with crisis management. While cyber insurance is just a small part of the general business insurance market, accounting for just 2 to 4 percent, the Sony breach has taught

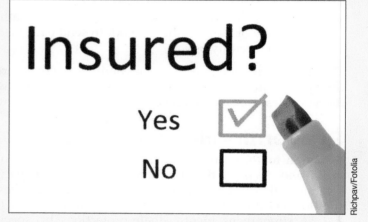

Richpav/Fotolia

businesses around the globe that it is an important element of IT risk management.

There are, however, limitations. Cyber insurance cannot replace good security procedures. Although many of the costs may be reimbursed, it's very likely that the company's reputation may be damaged for some time. In addition, a data breach or loss can result in a loss in momentum on important projects because talent and energy are redirected to the immediate crisis. As with other types of insurance, it's important for IT and risk managers to look at the fine print to see exactly what is and isn't covered. Rates for cyber insurance are based on a variety of factors, but they will reflect the confidence or lack of confidence of the insurance company in the insured company's data security practices. In fact, according to Rick Dakin, CEO of Coalfire, a company specializing in security audits, companies providing cyber insurance may actually require the insured to contract for an independent security audit as a condition of insurance.[30]

The federal CAN-SPAM Act of 2003 requires the Federal Trade Commission to shield the public from falsified header information, sexually explicit e-mails that are not so labeled, Internet spoofing (using trickery to make a message appear as if it came from a trusted source), and hijacking of computers through worms or Trojan horses. Although it cannot be prevented entirely, spam is abated by many Internet service providers (ISPs) that ban the spamming of ISP subscribers. In a now-classic punishment, an ISP in Iowa was awarded $1 billion in a lawsuit against 300 spammers that jammed the ISP system with an astounding 10 million e-mails a day. Anti-spam groups, too, promote the public's awareness of known spammers. The Spamhaus Project (www.spamhaus.org), for example, maintains a list of "The 10 Worst Spammers," career spammers that are responsible for most of the world's spam traffic.

Ethical Concerns in IT

It is apparent that IT developments and usage are progressing faster than society's appreciation for the potential consequences, including new ethical concerns. Along with IT's many benefits, its usage is creating previously unanticipated problems for which solutions are needed, yet they don't exist. Ease of access to computers, mobile devices, and the Internet, together with messaging capabilities and social networking, promote widespread public exposure about people's private lives, including personal information about how they think and feel. Just how this information should be used, by whom, under what conditions, and with what restrictions, if any, are issues teeming with ethical considerations. Several real-life episodes with ethical implications are shown in Table 1. See if you can identify significant ethical issues among the episodes in the table.

table 1 Areas for Ethical Concerns in Information Technology and Its Uses

- In a now-classic case of cyberbullying, a 13-year-old girl hanged herself after being taunted by a hoax message on her MySpace page.
- Secret webcasts of other people's behavior have resulted in embarrassment and even death: A university student, leaving a final message on his Facebook page, jumped from a bridge to his death after other students covertly webcast his sexual activities with another student.
- IT is used increasingly for sending out cries for help. Many college students have posted public messages requesting physical and emotional support. Others, having read those messages, are unsure if they should respond, or not.
- Employers and employees struggle about the extent of personal use of the company's IT. Many employees admit they use social networking and personal e-mailing at work, but should they? Many companies say, "No," adding that employees should know that the company has access to all e-mails sent, received, and stored on its IT system.
- States are forming database pools, sharing information to check on suspicious prescription drug activities. Data are gathered on purchases at pharmacies, physicians' prescriptions, and police records to identify drug abuse by individuals and companies within states and are being shared across state lines.
- The Department of Homeland Security abandoned one of its major data-mining tools for combating terrorism after questions about its compliance with privacy rules. It was discovered that DHS had tested the data-mining program using information about real people, without ensuring the privacy of that information.
- To save money, IT users retrieve and share intellectual property—movies, articles, books, music, industrial information—with others, ignoring copyright, trademark, and patent protections. Written content is often taken from the Internet, inserted into the user's written work, and represented as the user's own original creation without citing its true source.
- Job seekers are being asked to answer unexpected questions by interviewers: "What is your Facebook username and password?" Some applicants are responding, "No, that's a terrible privacy invasion." Others are revealing the requested information to interviewers.

summary of learning objectives

OBJECTIVE 1

Discuss the impacts information technology has had on the business world.

The growth of IT—the various appliances and devices for creating, storing, exchanging, and using information in diverse modes, including visual images, voice, multimedia, and business data—has changed the very structure of business organizations. Its adoption provides new modes of communication, including portable offices using mobile messaging capabilities, resulting in the geographic separation of the workplace from headquarters for many employees. With access to the Internet, company activities may be geographically scattered but still remain coordinated through a networked system that provides better service for customers. Networks and technology are also leading to leaner companies with fewer employees and simpler structures. Because networks enable firms to maintain information linkages among employees and customers, more work and customer satisfaction can be accomplished with fewer people. IT also contributes to greater flexibility in serving customers and enables closer coordination with suppliers. Company activities may be geographically scattered but remain coordinated through a network system that provides better service for customers. Many businesses coordinate activities from one centralized location, but their deliveries flow from several remote locations, often at lower cost. IT's global reach facilitates project collaboration with remote business partners and the formation of new market relationships around the globe. Just as electronic collaboration has changed the way employees interact with each other, IT networks have created new manufacturing flexibility for mass customization, and Internet access has brought new opportunities for small businesses.

OBJECTIVE 2

Identify the IT resources businesses have at their disposal and how these resources are used.

The Internet and the World Wide Web serve computers with information and provide communication flows among networks around the world. For many businesses, the Internet has replaced the telephone, fax machine, and standard mail as the primary communications tool. To support internal communications, many companies maintain internal websites—*intranets*—accessible only to employees. Some firms give limited network access to outsiders via *extranets* allowing access to private information among businesses, customers, and suppliers for better planning and coordination of their activities. Electronic conferencing allows simultaneous communication globally among groups from various locations, saving travel time, time for information exchanges, and expenses. *VSAT satellite networks* provide private remote communications for voice, video, and data transmissions.

   Computer networks, including wide area networks and local area networks, enable the sharing of information, hardware, software, and other resources over wired or wireless connections. *Wi-Fi* provides wireless Internet connections through laptops or other devices at "hotspots" or local access points. All computer networks or systems need hardware, the physical components such as keyboards, monitors, and printers. In addition, all systems require *software*, programs that tell the computer how to function. *Application software* includes programs to meet specific user needs, such as groupware with voice and video connections for remote collaboration.

OBJECTIVE 3

Describe the role of information systems, the different types of information systems, and how businesses use such systems.

An *information system (IS)* uses IT resources that enable users to create, process, and transmit information for use in decision making. An IS often includes *data warehousing*, a vast collection, storage, and retrieval system, which provides the data resources needed for creating information. The IS also includes *data mining* capabilities, the application of technologies for searching, sifting, and reorganizing data, to uncover useful information for planning new products, setting prices, and identifying trends.

The IS often is a set of several systems that share information while serving different levels of an organization, different departments, or different operations. *Knowledge information systems* support knowledge workers—engineers, scientists, and other specialists—by providing resources to create, store, use, and transmit new knowledge they use for specialty applications. Knowledge systems include *computer-aided design (CAD)*, software systems that receive engineering data and convert it into three-dimensional displays for rapid development of new products. *Computer-aided manufacturing (CAM)* uses computers to design and control the equipment needed in a manufacturing process. *Management information systems (MIS)* support managers by providing reports, schedules, plans, and budgets that can then be used for making decisions at all levels, ranging from detailed daily activities to long-range business strategies. The many uses of information systems include experimenting with *decision support systems (DSS)*, interactive systems that create business models and test them with different data to see how the models respond under diverse business conditions, to test the effectiveness of potential decisions.

Identify the threats and risks information technology poses on businesses.

IT has attracted abusers that do mischief, with severity ranging from mere nuisance to outright destruction, costing companies millions of dollars. Everything from Facebook postings to Bluetooth usage to private computer systems is subject to break-ins and destruction. *Hackers* break into computers, steal personal information and company secrets, tamper with data, and launch attacks on other computers. *Wireless moochers* use victims' networks for illegal activities, exposing the host to criminal prosecution. Once inside a computer network, hackers are able to commit *identity theft*, the unauthorized stealing of personal information to get loans, credit cards, or other monetary benefits by impersonating the victim. Even the ease of information sharing on the Internet poses a threat. It has proven costly for companies who are having a difficult time protecting their *intellectual property*, such as software products, movies, and music. Hackers break into company networks to steal anything of commercial value, including trade secrets, new inventions, and other valuable information that is protected by patent, copyright, or trademark. Another IT risk businesses face is system shutdown and destruction of software, hardware, or data files by *viruses, worms*, and *Trojan horses* that can shut down a computer system or otherwise disrupt IT operations by contaminating and destroying software, hardware, or data files. After invading a victim's computer, *spyware* gathers inside information and transmits it to outside spies. Masquerading as a friendly file available as a giveaway or shared among individual users on PCs and mobile devices, spyware is downloaded by unsuspecting users. Once installed, it monitors the host's electronic activities, gathers personal information, and transmits stolen information to an outside system. *Spam*, junk e-mail sent to a mailing list or news group, is costly in terms of lost time and productivity by overloading the network's capacity with massive mailings of unwanted messages.

Describe the ways in which businesses protect themselves from the threats and risks information technology poses.

Most systems guard against unauthorized access by requiring users to have protected passwords. In addition, many firms rely on *firewalls*, security systems with special software or hardware devices that intercept would-be intruders, so that only messages that meet the conditions of the company's security policy are permitted to flow through the network. Firms can protect against identity theft by using assistance from advisory sources, such as the Identity Theft Resource Center, and by implementing the identity-theft protection provisions of the federal FACTA rule for maintaining and destroying personal information records. To combat infectious intrusions by viruses, worms, and Trojan horses, *anti-virus software* products search incoming e-mail and data files for "signatures" of known viruses and virus-like characteristics.

Contaminated files are discarded or placed in quarantine for safekeeping. Additional intrusion protection is available by installing *anti-spyware* and *spam filtering software. Encryption* adds security by encoding, which is scrambling messages so they look like garbled nonsense to anyone who doesn't possess the key, so that the message can be read only by intended recipients. The federal *CAN-SPAM Act* requires the Federal Trade Commission to shield the public from falsified header information, sexually explicit e-mails that are not so labeled, Internet spoofing (using trickery to make a message appear as if it came from a trusted source), and hijacking of computers through worms or Trojan horses. Although it cannot be prevented entirely, *spam* is abated by many Internet service providers (ISPs) that ban the spamming of ISP subscribers.

key terms

anti-virus software
client-server network
computer-aided design (CAD)
computer-aided manufacturing
(CAM)
computer network
data
data mining
data warehousing
decision support system (DSS)
e-commerce
electronic conferencing
encryption system
extranet

firewall
hacker
hardware
hypertext transfer protocol (HTTP)
identity theft
information
information system (IS)
information systems managers
information technology (IT)
intellectual property
Internet
intranet
knowledge information system
local area network (LAN)

management information system
(MIS)
mass customization
software
spam
spyware
"super Wi-Fi" network
VSAT satellite communications
wide area network (WAN)
Wi-Fi
wireless local area network (wireless
LAN or WLAN)
wireless wide area network (WWAN)
World Wide Web

MyBizLab

To complete the problems with the ✪, go to EOC Discussion Questions in the MyLab.

questions & exercises

QUESTIONS FOR REVIEW

1. Compare and contrast an intranet with an extranet.
✪ 2. How can electronic conferencing increase a company's productivity and efficiency?
3. What are the advantages and risks of cloud computing?
4. Why should companies be concerned about hackers?
5. What is *intellectual property*? Provide at least three examples.

QUESTIONS FOR ANALYSIS

6. Describe how a company might use data warehousing and data mining in its information system to better plan for new products.
✪ 7. How could an airline use data mining to make better business decisions?
✪ 8. How do your bank, employer, and e-mail provider protect your personal information from unauthorized use?

APPLICATION EXERCISES

9. Consider your daily activities—as a consumer, student, parent, friend, homeowner or renter, car driver, employee, and so forth—and think about the ways that you are involved with IT systems. Make a list of your recent IT encounters and then recall instances in those encounters that you revealed personal information that could be used to steal your identity. Are some encounters on your list riskier than others? Why or why not?

10. After reading the first section of this chapter, consider how IT has changed the business of higher education. Identify at least three functions, services, or activities that would not have been available 25 years ago. How do you think that colleges and universities will change in the future because of advances in IT?

building a business: continuing team exercise

Assignment

Meet with your team members to consider your new business venture and how it relates to the information technology topics in this chapter. Develop specific responses to the following:

11. In what ways do you expect IT will enable collaboration among your employees? Identify examples of occasions where IT will be useful for providing remote access between employees, and remote access between employees and company data files.

12. In what ways will IT be used for collaboration with external stakeholders, such as customers, suppliers, and other constituents? What types of remote interactions do you expect, and what kinds of IT equipment and installations will be needed for those interactions? Discuss how your team is going to identify the IT equipment requirements at this stage of development of your business.

13. At what stage of your company's development will you begin planning for its information system(s), if any?

Discuss the technical skills and information-management skills necessary for determining the kind(s) of information system(s) needed for your company's first two years of operation.

14. Based on your findings for Question 14-13, where will your company get the skills and resources for IS development and implementation? Have you included the anticipated costs for developing the information systems in your financial plan for year one, or will you do so? Explain why, or why not.

15. What measures, if any, will you take for protecting against intrusions into your company's IT system? What actions will be taken to prevent unauthorized access to information of customers, suppliers, and other external constituents? What security measures will be taken to protect non-IT information? Explain.

team exercise

NEW AGE HELP DESK

The Situation

You are a member of the technical support team for a rapidly growing start-up that provides data analysis and business consulting to private schools and daycare centers. The company began several years ago when four recent college graduates spotted an unfilled niche in the market and combined their business and technical skills to meet the need. The company quickly grew, adding more than 80 employees in just five years. While all of the employees are located in the Washington, DC, area, most of them work from home at least one day a week. Initially, there was no technical support team at the company. An informal network of experts made decisions about which computers to buy, the software they purchased, and their high-speed Internet in the office, and employees depended on friends, family members, or coworkers if they had trouble with their hardware or software. However, the company's rapid growth has strained this informal network and the partners have decided to hire several IT professionals for a technical support department, with the challenge being that many employees will be working remotely. As the members of this department, you have been asked to make recommendations about a variety of issues.

QUESTIONS FOR DISCUSSION:

16. Many of the company's employees work from home. What benefits can the company and employee expect from allowing employees to do so? Are there some jobs where working from home is not appropriate?

17. The company has not had a consistent policy about the technology for those working from home. Should the company provide employees with a computer to use in their home office, or is this a responsibility of the employee? What are the benefits and costs of each?

18. How will you provide technical support to employees working from home? Would this be easier if the company provided the employee with a computer? Why or why not?

19. Are there additional data security risks with employees working from home? Describe the potential risks or concerns and how they might be addressed.

20. Briefly outline the policies, procedures, and guidelines that your department should propose in your first year on the job.

exercising your ethics

TO READ OR NOT TO READ

The Situation

Companies are able to monitor the ways that their employees use the company e-mail system as well as track a history of an employee's Internet use while using company resources. This

exercise illustrates how ethical issues may arise in tracking employee use of digital assets.

The Dilemma

You have recently been promoted to the position of a first-line manager at a local bio-technology company. This is a dream job and you are delighted to have been recognized for your hard work. As you are being oriented to your new job, the human resource (HR) manager explains that the company maintains logs of employee e-mails and tracks all Internet usage on company computers. You were surprised that you had not been informed about this when you were hired, but the HR director has assured you that this is completely legal. The company is concerned that employees may be wasting time on YouTube and other websites while at work, so they believe that there is a business purpose to this program. You will be expected to scan e-mail logs to make sure that employees are not sharing confidential information or trade secrets as well as monitor computer activities.

QUESTIONS TO ADDRESS

21. Given the factors in this situation, what, if any, ethical issues exist?
22. Do you think that the company is wise to monitor employees in this manner? Why or why not?
23. If you discovered that an employee was spending a lot of time on non-work–related searches, how would you address the issue with the employee?

cases

Think Before You Click

At the beginning of this chapter, you read about illicit activities of IT pirates and their methods for preying on victims, including both organizations and individuals around the globe. You saw that pirating aims to steal money and other resources by luring vulnerable potential victims with seemingly attractive offers of personal gain. Using the information presented in this chapter, you should now be able to answer the following questions.

QUESTIONS FOR DISCUSSION

24. Think about recent spam e-mails and text messages that you have received. What kinds of information were the intruders seeking?
25. Were you able to identify the e-mails and messages as "scams" before opening them, or did you discover their real contents after you opened them? What might have alerted you to the risks?
26. In what ways might the "opened" message from a scammer be harmful to you? To your IT devices and systems?
27. What steps can you take (or have you taken) to protect against such intrusions? What costs would be involved for gaining that protection?
28. Consider the various IT systems you use daily. What kinds of protection do they have to protect against invasion by cyber pirates?

Information Technology for Better Health Care

Going wireless to monitor a heart patient at home, a child's condition in an emergency department, an accident victim in an ambulance, and a patient's critical condition in a hospital room took a giant step forward after the Federal Communications Commission (FCC) authorized the use of Medical Body Area Network (MBAN) devices in 2012. MBAN is a wireless data system that transmits patients' conditions continuously so that changes can be detected quickly, and more serious problems can be detected before they fully develop. Small, lightweight, low-power sensors—much like Band-Aids in appearance—are attached to the patient's body to monitor vital signs that are transmitted over short distances to nearby "receiver devices" that, in turn, relay data over longer distances to nurse stations, physicians' offices, and other staff locations for real-time noninvasive continuous observation. The FCC, which controls the allocation and use of U.S. wireless frequencies, has established a unique wireless spectrum that gives MBAN devices a protected transmission frequency. Accordingly, the wireless medical devices do not have to use Wi-Fi networks, with their risks of interference from the devices of many other Wi-Fi users. MBAN's uncontaminated transmissions provide more information faster, enabling better health care at lower cost, than is possible with onsite continuous observation by nurses, healthcare technicians, and physicians.

Although wireless monitoring is noninvasive, an emerging surgical technique uses snake robots (snake-bots) that slither through patients' bodies while assisting in surgeries on hearts, prostates, and other body organs. Surgeons at New York Presbyterian Hospital, Columbia University Medical Center, and Cornell University Medical Center, among other facilities, have been using robots as tools for years in thousands of surgeries. Snake-bots armed with miniature cameras, forceps, sensors, and scissors enable surgeons to see more and do more than previously possible. Instead of opening the chest cavity for heart surgery, a small incision provides an entry for the tiny snake that crawls to the location in need of repair. The surgeon, as if shrunken and placed inside the patient's heart, controls the snake's movements and activities while repairing the heart valve. The snake's small size is less damaging to the patient, enabling faster recovery than traditional surgery. Developers believe that, as the snakes become much smaller, the snake technology will eventually make intricate surgeries faster and easier, thus reducing costs.

Snake-bots are but one example of a broader class of robotic-assisted surgery. The Da Vinci Surgical System, for example, became the first robotic system approved by the U.S. Food and Drug Administration for use in a variety of surgical applications, including vaginal and hysterectomy repair, prostate cancer, and mitral valve (heart) repair. The Da Vinci System is used in more than 45,000 operations each year at more than 800 hospitals in Europe and the Americas. The system's three components are: (1) a 3D vision system, (2) a surgeon's workstation that translates hand movements into movements of surgical instruments, and (3) a patient-side station with robotic arms controlled by the surgeon. The robotic station's surgical actions are totally under the surgeon's control. Most intriguing, perhaps, is that the surgeon does not need to be at the patient's surgical platform, so long as assisting professionals are nearby. This makes it possible for a surgeon in New York to remotely perform mitral valve repair on a patient in Germany or elsewhere.[31]

QUESTIONS FOR DISCUSSION

29. In what ways are the IT developments for health care presented in this case changing the activities, services, and organizational practices of hospitals and clinics? Explain your responses and give examples.

30. In what ways are healthcare customers being affected by the IT developments presented in this case? Are all of these effects positive, or might some be negative? Explain your response.

31. How might doctors and hospitals change their marketing strategies as a result of these innovations?

32. Suppose you are in charge of security for a hospital using the IT systems discussed in this case. Identify the kinds of IT risks and threats that should be expected. Beyond your own ideas, be sure to indicate other sources you would consult to help identify the risks and threats.

33. What protection measures can be taken to reduce the risks of intrusions and threats for the hospital's IT systems (for the systems discussed in this case)? Describe how you would determine the costs for implementing those protection measures.

MyBizLab

Go to the Assignments section of your MyLab to complete these writing exercises.

34. How has information technology changed the way that organizations do business? In what ways has IT helped companies become more efficient and effective? What challenges are created by advances in IT?

35. Some of the risks with IT include intrusions and abuses by outsiders and the damages that can result from those activities. Organizations are continuously seeking ways to protect against those risks. (a) Why do companies try to protect against those risks? (b) Choose four major kinds of IT risks and explain the dangers they pose. (c) Identify and describe protection measures for guarding IT systems against cyber abuses.

end notes

[1] McQueen, M. P. "Cyber-Scams on the Uptick in Downturn," *The Wall Street Journal*, January 29, 2009, pp. D1, D4; Joseph De Avila, "Beware of Facebook 'Friends' Who May Trash Your Laptop," *The Wall Street Journal*, January 29, 2009, pp. D1, D4; Acohido, Byron, and Swartz, Jon. "Data Scams Have Kicked into High Gear as Markets Tumble," *USAToday*, January 28, 2009, at www.usatoday.com/tech/news/computersecurity/2009-01-28-hackers-data-scams_N.htm; Wragge, Chris. "FBI Warns of High-Tech Cyber ID Theft," *wcbstv.com*, April 8, 2009, at http://wcbstv.com/local/cyber.criminals.fbi.2.980245.html; Robertson, Jordan. "Bad Economy Helps Web Scammers Recruit 'Mules'," *ABC News*, December 9, 2008, at http://abcnews.go.com/print?id=6422327. All sources accessed on May 10, 2015.

[2] "Hackers in China Blamed for Cyber-Attacks," *Columbia Daily Tribune*, February 10, 2011, p. 5B, and at www.columbiatribune.com/news/2011/feb/10/hackers-in-china-blamed-for-cyber-attacks/?news; Milbourn, Mary Ann. "Beware of Fake Job Offers," *The Orange County Register*, October 12, 2010, at http://economy.ocregister.com/2010/10/12/beware-of-fake-job-offers/42194/; Eppstein, Richard. "Scammers Pop Up During Economic Downturns," *Toledo Biz Insider*, March 4, 2010, at www.toledoblade.com/article/20100304/BUSINESS11/100309863/-1/BUSINESS; Warman, Matt. "Viruses on Smart-Phones: Security's New Frontier," *The Telegraph*, February 8, 2011, at www.telegraph.co.uk/technology/news/8311214/Viruses-on-smartphones-securitys-new-frontier.html. Accessed on May 10, 2015.

[3] Goldstein, Phil. "RIM Unveils BlackBerry Z10 and Q10, but Pushes U.S. Launch to March," *FierceWireless*, January 30, 2013, at http://fiercewireless.com/story/rim-unveils-blackberry-z10-and-q10-pushes-us-launch-march/2013-01-30. Accessed on May 10, 2015.

[4] Stern, Joanna. "Google's Project Glass is Ready, but for Developers' Eyes Only," January 16, 2013, at http://abcnews.go.com/blogs/technology/2013/01/googles-glass-is-ready-but-for-developers-eyes-only/. Accessed on May 10, 2015.

[5] See www.siriusxm.com/navtraffic/

[6] "Appropriator Asks NASA to Help Boeing Fix Dreamliner Problems," January 13, 2013, at http://fattah.house.gov/latest-news/appropriator-asks-nasa-to-help-boeing-fix-dreamliner-problems/. Accessed on May 10, 2015.

[7] "Lockheed Martin Aeronautics: Siemens' PLM Software," *Siemens*, at www.plm.automation.siemans.com/en_us/about-us/success/case_s, accessed on June 16, 2009, and May 10, 2015.

[8] Northrup, Laura. "Timbuk2 Really, Really Wants You to Be Happy with Their Bags," *The Consumerist*, June 5, 2009, at www.consumerist.com/2009/06/timbuk2really-really-wants-you-to-be-happy-with-their-bags.html. Accessed on May 10, 2015.

[9] LaGesse, David. "How to Turn Social Networking into a Job Offer," *U.S. News & World Report*, May 11, 2009, at www.usnews.com/money/careers/articles/2009/05/11/how-to-turn-social-networking-into-a-job-offer.html. Accessed on May 10, 2015.

[10]3D Systems, "3D Systems Helps Walter Reed Army Medical Center Rebuild Lives," at www.3dsystems.com/appsolutions/casestudies/walter_reed.asp, accessed on June 15, 2009; Hickey, Hannah. "Camera in a Pill Offers Cheaper, Easier Window on Your Insides," UWNews.org (January 24, 2008), at http://uwnews.org/article.asp?articleid=39292. Accessed on May 10, 2015; see also www.wrnmmc.capmed.mil/SitePages/home.aspx

[11]See www.internetworldstats.com/stats.htm. Accessed on May 10, 2015.

[12]"BAN AMRO Mortgage Group Offers One Fee to Ford Motor Company Employees," *Mortgage Mag*, February 14, 2005, at www.mortgagemag.com/n/502_003.htm; "An Intranet's Life Cycle," *morebusiness.com* (June 16, 1999), at www.morebusiness.com/getting_started/website/d928247851.brc; Ahmed, Sally. "Ford Motor Company—Case Study," *Ezine Articles*, August 18, 2008, at http://ezinearticles.com/?Ford-Motor-Company—Case-Study&id=1420478. Accessed on May 10, 2015.

[13]"Companies Take Sides on Super Wi-Fi," *Columbia Daily Tribune*, February 4, 2013, p. 6B.

[14]Brizius, Glen. "CereProc: An Example of a Technology Finally Fulfilling Its Potential," *Associated Content in Technology*, March 16, 2010, at www.associatedcontent.com/article/2786052/cereproc_an_example_of_a_technology.html?cat=5. Accessed on May 10, 2015.

[15]www.cereproc.com/en/products

[16]Sheppard, Alyson. "Giving Roger Ebert a New Voice: Q&A With CereProc," *Popular Mechanics*, March 8, 2010, at www.popularmechanics.com/science/health/prosthetics/rogerebertvoicetech; Millar, Hayley. "New Voice for Film Critic," *BBC News*, March 3, 2010, at http://news.bbc.co.uk/2/hi/uk_news/scotland/edinburgh_and_east/8547645.stm. Accessed on May 10, 2015.

[17]Novet, Jordan. "Apple claims Siri's speech recognition tech is more accurate than Google's," *VentureBeat*, June 8, 2015, at http://venturebeat.com/2015/06/08/apple-claims-siris-speech-recognition-tech-is-more-accurate-than-googles/

[18]"Kroger Tailors Ads to Its Customers," *Columbia Daily Tribune*, January 12, 2009, 7B; Pichler, Josh. "dunnhumby: Retailer's Secret Weapon," *Cincinnati.com*, January 31, 2013, at news.cincinnati.com/article/20130130/BIZ/301190100/dunnhumby-Retailers-secret-weapon?nclick_check=1. Accessed on May 10, 2015.

[19]"Data Mining Examples & Testimonials," at www.data-mining-software.com/data_mining_examples.htm, accessed February 24, 2011; Angwin, Julia, and Valentino-DeVries, Jennifer. "New Tracking Frontier: Your License Plates," *Wall Street Journal*, September 29–30, 2012, pp. A1, A13; Troianovski, Anton. "New Wi-Fi Pitch: Tracker," *Wall Street Journal*, June 19, 2012, p. B5. Accessed on May 10, 2015.

[20]Freedman, Lisa. "All Eyes on Predictive Analytics." *Business Week* no. 4423: S1–S4. *Business Source Premier*, EBSCOhost (accessed June 9, 2015).

[21]Marchant, Jo. "Virtual Fossils Reveal How Ancient Creatures Lived," *NewScientist*, May 27, 2009, at www.newscientist.com/article/mg20227103.500-virtual-fossils-reveal-how-ancient-creatures-lived.html. Accessed on May 10, 2015.

[22]Warman, Matt. "Viruses on Smartphones: Security's New Frontier," *The Telegraph*, February 8, 2011, at www.telegraph.co.uk/technology/news/8311214/

Viruses-on-smartphones-securitys-new-frontier.html; Cheng, Jacqui. "Canadian Group: Facebook 'A Minefield of Privacy Invasion'" May 30, 2008, at http://arstechnica.com/tech-policy/news/2008/05/canadian-group-files-complaint-over-facebook-privacy.ars; "Cell Phones a Much Bigger Privacy Risk Than Facebook," *Fox News*, February 20, 2009, at www.foxnews.com/printer_friendly_story/0,3566,497544,00.html. Accessed on May 10, 2015.

[23]Gorman, Siobhan, Barrett, Devlin, and Yadron, Danny. "China Hackers Hit U.S. Media," *Wall Street Journal*, February 1, 2013, pp. B1, B2; "Hackers Hit Twitter, Washington Post," *Columbia Daily Tribune*, February 4, 2013, p. 6B. Accessed on May 10, 2015.

[24]Leary, Alex. "Wi-Fi Cloaks a New Breed of Intruder," *St. Petersburg Times*, July 4, 2005, at www.sptimes.com/2005/07/04/State/Wi_Fi_cloaks_a_new_br.shtml. Accessed on May 10, 2015.

[25]Melanson, Donald. "Apple: 16 Billion iTunes Songs Downloaded, 300 Million iPods Sold," *Engadget*, October 4, 2011, at www.engadget.com/2011/10/04/apple-16-billion-itunes-songs-downloaded-300-million-ipods-sol/; Burgess, Christopher, and Power, Richard. "How to Avoid Intellectual Property Theft," *CIO*, July 10, 2006, at www.cio.com/article/22837; "For Students Doing Reports," *RIAA*, at www.riaa.com/faq.php, accessed on February 4, 2013; Sisario, Ben. "AC/DC Joins iTunes, as Spotify Emerges as Music's New Disrupter," *New York Times*, November 19, 2012, at mediadecoder.blogs.nytimes.com/2012/11/19/acdc-joins-itunes-as-spotify-emerges-as-musics-new-disrupter/. Accessed on May 10, 2015.

[26]See www.webopedia.com/TERM/S/spyware.html.

[27]Norman, Donald A. "Got Spam?" *MAPI: Manufacturers Alliance for Productivity and Innovation*, October 24, 2012, at www.mapi.net/blog/2012/10/got-spam. Accessed on May 10, 2015.

[28]"'Spam King' Faces Federal Fraud Charges," *Columbia Daily Tribune*, January 21, 2013, accessed at www.columbiatribune.com/wire/spam-king-faces-federal-fraud-charges/article_042ac575-7820-5bb4-bb17-3e425f2f24c0.html#.URE7hPKmFcI. Accessed on May 10, 2015.

[29]Carlson, Brad. "Organizations Face New Records-Destruction Rule," *Idaho Business Review*, July 25, 2005, at www.idahobusiness.net/archive.htm/2005/07/25/Organizations-face-new-recordsdestruction-rule. Accessed on May 10, 2015.

[30]Vijayan, Jaikumar. "5 Things You Should Know About Cyber Insurance." *Computerworld Digital Magazine*. 1 no. 11: 27–32. *Business Source Premier*, EBSCOhost (accessed June 9, 2015).

[31]Linebaugh, Kate. "Medical Devices in Hospitals to Go Wireless," *Wall Street Journal*, May 24, 2012, p. B8; "Tiny Snake Robots Aid Surgery," *Columbia Daily Tribune*, May 30, 2012, p. A2; Sandham, John. ""Robotic Assisted Surgery," *EBME Electrical and Biomedical Engineering*, December 2008, at www.ebme.co.uk/arts/robotic, accessed on May 11, 2013; iMedicalApps Team and Primosch, Robert D. "FCC Opens New Chapter in Wireless Medical Devices," *iMedicalApps*, June 6, 2012, at www.imedicalapps.com/2012/06/fcc-opens-chapter-wireless-medical-devices/. Accessed on May 10, 2015.

glossary

Anti-Virus Software product that protects systems by searching incoming e-mails and data files for "signatures" of known viruses and virus-like characteristics.

Client-Server Network common business network in which clients make requests for information or resources and servers provide the services.

Computer-Aided Design (CAD) IS with software that helps knowledge workers design products by simulating them and displaying them in three-dimensional graphics.

Computer-Aided Manufacturing (CAM) IS that uses computers to design and control equipment in a manufacturing process.

Computer Network group of two or more computers linked together by some form of cabling or by wireless technology to share data or resources, such as a printer.

Data raw facts and figures that, by themselves, may not have much meaning.

Data Mining the application of electronic technologies for searching, sifting, and reorganizing pools of data to uncover useful information.

Data Warehousing the collection, storage, and retrieval of data in electronic files.

Decision Support System (DSS) interactive system that creates virtual business models for a particular kind of decision and tests them with different data to see how they respond.

e-Commerce use of the Internet and other electronic means for retailing and business-to-business transactions.

Electronic Conferencing IT that allows groups of people to communicate simultaneously from various locations via e-mail, phone, or video.

Encryption System software that assigns an e-mail message to a unique code number (digital fingerprint) for each computer so only that computer, not others, can open and read the message.

Extranet system that allows outsiders limited access to a firm's internal information network.

Firewall security system with special software or hardware devices designed to keep computers safe from hackers.

Hacker cybercriminal who gains unauthorized access to a computer or network, either to steal information, money, or property or to tamper with data.

Hardware physical components of a computer network, such as keyboards, monitors, system units, and printers.

Hypertext Transfer Protocol (HTTP) communications protocol used for the World Wide Web, in which related pieces of information on separate Web pages are connected using hyperlinks.

Identity Theft unauthorized use of personal information (such as Social Security number and address) to get loans, credit cards, or other monetary benefits by impersonating the victim.

Information meaningful, useful interpretation of data.

Information System (IS) system that uses IT resources to convert data into information and to collect, process, and transmit that information for use in decision making.

Information Systems Managers managers who are responsible for the systems used for gathering, organizing, and distributing information.

Information Technology (IT) various appliances and devices for creating, storing, exchanging, and using information in diverse modes, including visual images, voice, multimedia, and business data.

Intellectual Property something produced by the intellect or mind that has commercial value.

Internet gigantic system of interconnected computer networks linked together by voice, electronic, and wireless technologies.

Intranet organization's private network of internally linked websites accessible only to employees.

Knowledge Information System information system that supports knowledge workers by providing resources to create, store, use, and transmit new knowledge for useful applications.

Local Area Network (LAN) computers that are linked in a small area, such as all of a firm's computers within a single building.

Management Information System (MIS) computer system that supports managers by providing information reports, schedules, plans, and budgets that can be used for making decisions.

Mass Customization principle in which companies produce in large volumes, but each item features the unique options the customer prefers.

Software programs that tell the computer how to function, what resources to use, how to use them, and application programs for specific activities.

Spam junk e-mail sent to a mailing list or a newsgroup.

Spyware program unknowingly downloaded by users that monitors their computer activities, gathering e-mail addresses, credit card numbers, and other information that it transmits to someone outside the host system.

"Super Wi-Fi" Network a powerful Wi-Fi network with extensive reach and strong signals that flow freely through physical objects such as walls.

VSAT Satellite Communications network of geographically dispersed transmitter-receivers (transceivers) that send signals to and receive signals from a satellite, exchanging voice, video, and data transmissions.

Wide Area Network (WAN) computers that are linked over long distances through telephone lines, microwave signals, or satellite communications.

Wi-Fi technology using a wireless local area network.

Wireless Local Area Network (Wireless LAN or WLAN) local area network with wireless access points for PC users.

Wireless Wide Area Network (WWAN) network that uses airborne electronic signals instead of wires to link computers and electronic devices over long distances.

World Wide Web branch of the Internet consisting of interlinked hypertext documents, or Web pages.

The Role of Accountants and Accounting Information

From Chapter 15 of *Business Essentials*, Eleventh Edition. Ronald J. Ebert, Ricky W. Griffin. Copyright © 2017 by Pearson Education, Inc.
All rights reserved.

"Crunching numbers" is not enough for today's accountants. They need to

communicate,

think critically, and lead.

After reading this chapter, you should be able to:

1 **Explain** the role of accountants and distinguish among the kinds of work done by public accountants, private accountants, management accountants, and forensic accountants.

2 **Explain** how the accounting equation is used.

3 **Describe** the three basic financial statements and show how they reflect the activity and financial condition of a business.

4 **Explain** the key standards and principles for reporting financial statements.

5 **Describe** how computing financial ratios can help users get more information from financial statements to determine the financial strengths of a business.

6 **Discuss** the role of ethics in accounting.

7 **Describe** the purpose of the International Accounting Standards Board and explain why it exists.

CSI: Wall Street

In the aftermath of a flurry of financial scandals, many companies are showing an urgent interest in the field of forensic accounting, the use of accounting for legal purposes. The expansion of the forensic accounting field—the Association of Certified Fraud Examiners (ACFE) has experienced a surging membership, with more than 55,000 professionals—is the result of increased vigilance against various kinds of financial scams, including a strong desire on the part of companies to protect themselves from accounting fraud.

Fraud examiners typically begin an investigation of a company by interviewing high-level executives. Team members pursue tips from employees or outsiders and then comb through e-mails, searching for suspicious words and phrases. The combination of interviews and e-mails may lead investigators to specific accounting files or ledger entries. According to Al Vondra, partner in Forensic Services and a Certified Fraud Examiner at PricewaterhouseCoopers, some of the most common fraudulent practices involve hiding revenues and expenses under phony categories, such as "Total Noncurrent Assets" or "Other Current Liabilities." At India's Satyam Computer Services Ltd., founder and former CEO Ramalinga Raju was arrested after admitting he falsified accounts that deceived investors for years. The Indian government's Serious Fraud Investigation Office is searching to identify collaborators who falsely reported more than $1 billion in cash and assets that didn't exist at India's fourth-largest software company.[1]

Although accounting scandals have always existed, they spike upward in economic downturns. Data from the ACFE indicate that corporate fraud cases began increasing significantly early in the 2008 recession, and worldwide fraud losses reached $3.5 trillion in 2012. At the same time, more than 3,000 fraud-related reports and whistle-blowing tips were reported from within U.S. firms. ACFE members believe the increase stems from heavier financial pressures: When employees feel less secure, they may falsify data to show better performance, or they may take greater risks that need to be covered up to show financial success. Forensic accounting professor Tommie Singleton states, "The cases of fraud will only climb as the country sinks into recession, and with that so will the demand for highly skilled, specialized forensic accountants to help prevent, detect, and prosecute those looking to cheat the system."[2]

Fraud exists also among the public at large. Fraudulent insurance claims are on the upswing: A private investigator films an injury victim throwing the neck brace into the back seat of his car after leaving the doctor's office, a homeowner inflates the cost of articles stolen in an alleged burglary, and victims of car

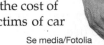

Se media/Fotolia

what's in it for me?

For most of us, the words and ideas in accounting can seem like a foreign language, and the specialized terminology can be used to mask fraud and corruption. However, accounting terminology is a necessary tool that allows professionals in every industry to analyze growth, understand risk, and communicate detailed ideas about a firm's financial health. This chapter will cover the fundamental concepts of accounting and apply them to familiar business situations. By grasping the basic accounting vocabulary you—as an employee, taxpayer, or owner—will be able to participate when the conversation turns to the financial matters that constitute so great a part of a firm's daily operations.

wrecks from years past suddenly submit injury claims. Employees, too, are a source of fraud; the U.S. Commerce Department estimates that one-third of business shutdowns are the result of employee theft. Inventory stolen from the firm's warehouse is resold; the company's strategic inside information is stolen and sold to a competitor; and employees receive reimbursement for falsely inflated business expenses.[3]

The broad scope of fraud—its costs, who commits it and how, and how it is detected—is revealed in *Global Fraud Studies* conducted by the ACFE.[4] Fraud typically costs organizations 5 percent of their annual revenues, but small businesses are especially vulnerable because they usually have fewer internal controls for protecting their resources. Global fraud loss is estimated at $3.5 trillion annually. Employees in the United States commit more cases of fraud than do managers, and top-level executives and owners are least involved. However, it comes as no surprise that financial losses by higher-level perpetrators are typically 10 times that of other employees. The most common kind of fraud is asset theft—stealing cash, falsifying business expenses, forging checks, and stealing noncash assets. The chief financial officer of a Florida tree farm, for example, falsified checks and misused company credit cards to embezzle $10 million, earning a 96-month prison sentence and a $14 million fine.[5] The least-common organizational fraud and the costliest by far, is financial statement manipulation. In 2012, for example, the financial officer of an energy company was convicted of lying to investors while raising funds for the company's energy projects. Instead, the funds were used for salaries for himself and others. Unsuspecting investors lost some $4.3 million in the scam. The culprit received a 97-month prison sentence.

How do these thieves get caught? Most commonly, detection starts from employee-supplied tips. Although internal audits are somewhat effective, external audits are less effective than commonly believed. The ACFE study concludes that any organization's number-one safeguard is employee education in recognizing, reporting, and preventing fraud. (After studying the content in this chapter, you should be able to answer a set of discussion questions found at the end of the chapter.)

What Is Accounting, and Who Uses Accounting Information?

OBJECTIVE 1
Explain
the role of accountants and
distinguish among the kinds
of work done by public
accountants, private accountants,
management accountants, and
forensic accountants.

Accounting *comprehensive system
for collecting, analyzing, and communicating financial information*

Bookkeeping *recording of accounting
transactions*

**Accounting Information System
(AIS)** *organized procedure for
identifying, measuring, recording,
and retaining financial information
for use in accounting statements and
management reports*

Accounting is a comprehensive system for collecting, analyzing, and communicating financial information to a firm's owners and employees, to the public, and to various regulatory agencies. To perform these functions, accountants keep records of taxes paid, income received, and expenses incurred, a process historically called **bookkeeping**, and they assess the effects of these transactions on business activities. By sorting and analyzing such transactions, accountants can determine how well a business is being managed and assess its financial strength.

Because businesses engage in thousands of transactions, ensuring consistent, dependable financial information is mandatory. This is the job of the **accounting information system (AIS)**, an organized procedure for identifying, measuring, recording, and retaining financial information so that it can be used in accounting statements and management reports. The system includes all of the people, reports, computers, procedures, and resources that are needed to compile financial transactions.[6]

Users of accounting information are numerous:

- *Business managers* use it to develop goals and plans, set budgets, and evaluate future prospects.

- *Employees and unions* use it to plan for and receive compensation and such benefits as health care, vacation time, and retirement pay.

- *Investors and creditors* use it to estimate returns to stockholders, determine growth prospects, and decide whether a firm is a good credit risk.

- **Tax authorities** use it to plan for tax inflows, determine the tax liabilities of individuals and businesses, and ensure that correct amounts are paid on time.

- **Government regulatory agencies** rely on it to fulfill their duties toward the public. The Securities and Exchange Commission (SEC), for example, requires firms to file financial disclosures so that potential investors have valid information about their financial status.

The **controller**, or chief accounting officer, manages a firm's accounting activities by ensuring that the AIS provides the reports and statements needed for planning, decision making, and other management activities. This range of activities requires different types of accounting specialists. In this section, we begin by distinguishing between the two main fields of accounting: *financial* and *managerial*. Then, we discuss the different functions and activities of *certified public accountants, private accountants, management accountants*, and *forensic accountants*.

Controller *person who manages all of a firm's accounting activities (chief accounting officer)*

Financial versus Managerial Accounting

In any company, the two fields of accounting—financial and managerial—can be distinguished by the users they serve: those outside the company and those within.[7]

Financial Accounting A firm's **financial accounting** system is concerned with external information users: consumer groups, unions, stockholders, suppliers, creditors, and government agencies. It prepares reports such as income statements and balance sheets that focus on the activities of the company as a whole rather than on individual departments or divisions.[8]

Financial Accounting *field of accounting concerned with external users of a company's financial information*

Managerial Accounting **Managerial accounting**, on the other hand, serves internal users. Managers at all levels need information to make departmental decisions, monitor projects, and plan future activities. Other employees also need accounting information. Engineers must know certain costs, for example, before making product or operations improvements, purchasing agents use information on materials costs to negotiate terms with suppliers, and to set performance goals, and salespeople need past sales data for each geographic region and for each of its products.

Mánagerial (Management) Accounting *field of accounting that serves internal users of a company's financial information*

Certified Public Accountants

Public accountants offer accounting services to the public and are distinguished by their independence from the clients they serve. That is to say, they typically work for an accounting firm providing services for outside client firms in which the public accountant has no vested interest, thus avoiding any potential biases in conducting their professional services. Among public accountants, **certified public accountants (CPAs)** are licensed by a state after passing an exam prepared by the American Institute of Certified Public Accountants (AICPA). Preparation for certification begins with majoring in a college program studying the theory, practices, and legal aspects of accounting. In addition to the CPA exam, certification in most states requires some practice, varying up to two years, in a private company or government entity under the direction of a CPA. Once certified, the CPA can perform services beyond those allowed by non-CPAs.[9] Whereas some CPAs work as individual practitioners, many form or join existing partnerships or professional corporations.

Certified Public Accountant (CPA) *accountant licensed by the state and offering services to the public*

The "Big Four" Public Accounting Firms Although thousands of CPA companies of various sizes, ranging from small local operations to large multinationals, are active in the United States, about one-half of their total revenues go to the four biggest CPA firms (listed with their headquarters):

- Deloitte Touche Tohmatsu (United States)

- Ernst & Young (United Kingdom)

Sometimes, companies ignore GAAP and accountants fail to disclose violations. Richard Causey (right) was Chief Account Executive at now-bankrupt Enron, and was responsible for the firm's public accounting statements. Pleading guilty to securities fraud, he was sentenced to seven years in prison and forfeited $1.25 million.

- PricewaterhouseCoopers, PwC (United Kingdom)
- KPMG (Netherlands)

In addition to prominence in the United States, international operations are important for all four of these companies. They have experienced especially rapid growth in recent years for CPA services in Asia and Latin America. Each of the Big Four firms has more than 150,000 employees worldwide.[10]

CPA Services Virtually all CPA firms, whether large or small, provide auditing, tax, and management services. Larger firms such as Deloitte Touche Tohmatsu and Ernst & Young earn much of their revenue from auditing services, though consulting (management advisory) services constitute a major growth area. Smaller firms earn most of their income from tax and management services.

Audit *systematic examination of a company's accounting system to determine whether its financial reports reliably represent its operations*

Generally Accepted Accounting Principles (GAAP) *accounting guidelines that govern the content and form of financial reports*

AUDITING An **audit** examines a company's AIS to determine whether financial reports reliably represent its operations.[11] Organizations must provide audit reports when applying for loans, selling stock, or when going through a major restructuring. Independent auditors who do not work for the company must ensure that clients' accounting systems follow **generally accepted accounting principles (GAAP)**, which are formulated by the Financial Accounting Standards Board (FASB) of the AICPA and govern the content and form of financial reports.[12] The auditing of a firm's financial statements is one of the services that can be performed only by a CPA. The SEC is the U.S. government agency that legally enforces accounting and auditing rules and procedures. Ultimately, the CPA performing the audit will certify whether the client's reports comply with GAAP.

Tax Services *assistance provided by CPAs for tax preparation and tax planning*

TAX SERVICES **Tax services** include assistance not only with tax-return preparation but also with tax planning. A CPA's advice can help a business structure (or restructure) operations and investments and perhaps save millions of dollars in taxes. Staying abreast of tax-law changes is no simple matter. Some critics charge that the changing of tax regulations has become a full-time vocation among some state and federal legislators who add increasingly complicated laws and technical corrections on taxation each year.

Management Advisory Services *assistance provided by CPA firms in areas such as financial planning, information systems design, and other areas of concern for client firms*

MANAGEMENT ADVISORY SERVICES As consultants, accounting firms provide **management advisory services** ranging from personal financial planning to planning corporate mergers. Other services include production scheduling, information systems studies, AIS design, and even executive recruitment. The staffs of the largest CPA firms sometimes include engineers, architects, mathematicians, and psychologists, all of whom are available for consulting.

Noncertified Public Accountants Many accountants don't take the CPA exam; others work in the field while getting ready for it or while meeting requirements for state certification. Many small businesses, individuals, and even larger firms rely on these non-CPAs for income-tax preparation, payroll accounting, and financial-planning services so long as they abide by local and state laws. Non-CPAs often put together financial statements that are used in the firm for internal purposes, based on information provided by management. These statements may include a notification that auditing methods were not used in their preparation.

The CPA Vision Project A continuing talent shortage in accounting, spanning years 2006–2012, has led the profession to rethink its culture and lifestyle.[13] With grassroots participation from CPAs, educators, and industry leaders, the AICPA, through its CPA Vision Project, is redefining the role of the accountant for today's world economy. The Vision Project identifies a unique combination of skills, technology, and knowledge, called **core competencies for accounting**, that will be necessary for the future CPA. The AICPA summarizes the project's core purpose as follows: "CPAs . . . Making sense of a changing and complex world."[14] As Table 1 shows, those skills, which include communication, critical thinking, and leadership, go far beyond the ability to "crunch numbers." They include certain communications skills, along with skills in critical thinking and leadership. Indeed, the CPA Vision Project foresees CPAs who combine specialty skills with a broad-based orientation to communicate more effectively with people in a wide range of business activities.

Core Competencies for Accounting *the combination of skills, technology, and knowledge that will be necessary for the future CPA*

Private Accountants and Management Accountants

To ensure integrity in reporting, CPAs are always independent of the firms they audit. However, many businesses also hire their own salaried employees, **private accountants**, to perform day-to-day activities.

Private Accountant *salaried accountant hired by a business to carry out its day-to-day financial activities*

Private accountants perform numerous jobs. An internal auditor at ConocoPhillips, for example, might fly to the North Sea to confirm the accuracy of oil-flow meters on offshore petroleum drilling platforms. A supervisor responsible for $2 billion in monthly payouts to vendors and employees may never leave the executive suite, with duties such as hiring and training, assigning projects, and evaluating performance of accounting personnel. Large businesses employ specialized accountants in such areas as budgeting, financial planning, internal auditing, payroll, and taxation. In small businesses, a single person may handle all accounting tasks.

Although private accountants may be either CPAs or non-CPAs, most are **management accountants** who provide services to support managers in various

Management Accountant *private accountant who provides financial services to support managers in various business activities within a firm*

table 1 Emerging Competencies for Success in Accounting

Skills in Strategic Thinking and Critical Problem Solving	The accountant can combine data with reasoning and professional knowledge to recognize and help solve critical problems for better strategic action.
Communications, Interpersonal Skills, and Effective Leadership	The accountant can communicate effectively in various business situations using meaningful communications skills that provide interpersonal effectiveness and leadership.
Dedication to Meeting Customer Needs	The accountant surpasses the competition in understanding each client's unique needs, in meeting those needs, and in visualizing the client's future needs.
Ability to Integrate Diverse Information	The accountant can combine financial and other kinds of information to gain new meaning that provides clients with useful insights and understanding for solving problems.
Proficiency with Information Technology	The accountant can use information technology (IT) in performing services for clients and can identify IT applications that the client can adopt for added value to the business.

Source: Based on "The CPA Vision Project and Beyond," *The American Institute of Certified Public Accountants*, at http://www .aicpa.org/RESEARCH/CPAHORIZONS2025/CPAVISIONPROJECT/Pages/CPAVisionProject.aspx, accessed on May 1, 2015.

activities (marketing, production, engineering, and so forth). Many hold the **certified management accountant (CMA)** designation, awarded by the Institute of Management Accountants (IMA), recognizing qualifications of professionals who have passed IMA's experience and examination requirements. With more than 65,000 worldwide members, IMA is dedicated to supporting accounting professionals to create quality internal controls and financial practices in their companies.

Certified Management Accountant (CMA) *professional designation awarded by the Institute of Management Accountants (IMA) in recognition of management accounting qualifications*

Forensic Accountants

Forensic Accounting *the practice of accounting for legal purposes*

One of the fastest-growing areas in accounting is **forensic accounting**, the use of accounting for legal purposes.[15] Sometimes known as "the private eyes of the corporate culture," forensic accountants must be good detectives. They look behind the corporate façade instead of accepting financial records at face value. In combining investigative skills with accounting, auditing, and the instincts of a bloodhound, they assist in the investigation of business and financial issues that may have application to a court of law. Forensic accountants may be called on by law enforcement agencies, insurance companies, law firms, private individuals, and business firms for both investigative accounting and litigation support in crimes against companies, crimes by companies, and civil disagreements. They may conduct criminal investigations of Internet scams and misuse of government funds. Civil cases often require investigating and quantifying claims of personal injury loss as a result of negligence and analyzing financial issues in matrimonial disputes. Forensic accountants also assist business firms in tracing and recovering lost assets from employee business fraud or theft.

Investigative Accounting Law enforcement officials may ask a forensic accountant to investigate a trail of financial transactions behind a suspected crime, as in a money-laundering scheme or an investment swindle. The forensic accountant, being familiar with the legal concepts and procedures of the case, would then identify and analyze pertinent financial evidence—documents, bank accounts, phone calls, computer records, and people—and present accounting conclusions and their legal implications. They also develop reports, exhibits, and documents to communicate their findings.

Litigation Support Forensic accountants assist in the application of accounting evidence for judicial proceedings by preparing and preserving evidence for these proceedings. They also assist by presenting visual aids to support trial evidence, by testifying as expert witnesses, and, especially, in determining economic damages in any case before the court. A divorce attorney, for example, may suspect that assets are being understated and request financial analysis by a forensic accountant. A movie producer may need help in determining damages for breach of contract by an actress who quits before the film is completed.

Certified Fraud Examiner (CFE) *professional designation administered by the ACFE in recognition of qualifications for a specialty area within forensic accounting*

CERTIFIED FRAUD EXAMINERS One specific area within forensic accounting, the **Certified Fraud Examiner (CFE)** designation, is administered by the ACFE. The CFE's activities focus specifically on fraud-related issues, such as fraud detection, evaluating accounting systems for weaknesses and fraud risks, investigating white-collar crime on behalf of law enforcement agencies, evaluating internal organizational controls for fraud prevention, and expert witnessing. Many CFEs, like Al Vondra from our opening story, find employment in corporations seeking to prevent fraud from within. The CFE examination covers four areas:

1 *Fraud prevention and deterrence*—Includes why people commit fraud, theories of fraud prevention, and professional code of ethics

2 *Financial transactions*—Examines types of fraudulent financial transactions incurred in accounting records

3 *Fraud investigation*—Pertains to tracing illicit transactions, evaluating deception, and interviewing and taking statements

4 *Legal elements of fraud*—Includes rules of evidence, criminal and civil law, and rights of the accused and accuser

Eligibility to take the exam includes both educational and experience requirements. Although a minimum of a bachelor's degree is required, it does not have to be in accounting or any other specific field of study. Candidates without a bachelor's degree, but with fraud-related professional experience, may substitute two years of experience for each year of academic study. Experience requirements for certification

managing in turbulent times

When Is Honesty the Best Policy?

In 2010, executives at Computer Sciences Corporation faced a difficult dilemma. The company was in the middle of a massive contract with the United Kingdom's National Health Service (NHS). Unfortunately, the profits that they once anticipated were never going to materialize—the company was unable to meet specified deadlines and the associated contract penalties would wipe out all the anticipated profits and more. A major loss would hurt the company's stock price and cut into executive bonuses, so CEO Michael Laphen, CFO Michael Mancuso, and others developed a "solution." Rather than following the GAAP rules concerning long-term contracts, the company developed a model that continued to show profits. The company also tried to convince NHS to agree to contract amendments that would restore some of the revenues, but these requests were denied.

Arnd Wiegmann/Reuters/Landov

The company's anticipated and realized losses should have been disclosed to investors (including shareholders). However, Mancuso and others disguised the situation, and their lack of cash flow, by essentially borrowing money at a high rate of interest from NHS in anticipation of future revenues. In a blatant act of deception, Mancuso reported to investors that the company was maintaining cash flow targets "the old-fashioned hard way." "When companies face significant difficulties, they and their top executives must truthfully disclose this information," according to Andrew J. Ceresney, Director of the SEC's Division of Enforcement. However, "CSC repeatedly based its financial results and disclosures on the NHS contract it was negotiating rather than the one that it actually had, and misled investors about the true status of the contract."

The company's deceptive accounting practices were not limited to the NHS contract. In an attempt to meet operating targets in 2009, regional CFO Wayne Banks overstated their earnings in Australia by artificially increasing revenues and failing to report all expenses. Similarly, in the company's Nordic region, the company incorrectly recorded expenses as prepaid assets, which resulted in an increase in net income on the income statement and an increase in assets on the balance sheet. CSC's finance director of the Nordic region Paul Wakefield and finance manager Claus Zimmer ultimately ended up settling charges with the SEC, although others in the area are still in litigation. As a part of the settlement, Wakefield assisted the SEC in its investigation of the culture of deception at Computer Sciences Corporation.

In 2012, the company made major changes to its top-level leadership and revised several years of financial statements. They also implemented a variety of programs to strengthen their internal control over their financial statements and worked to enhance compliance and disclosure. In addition, the company agreed to pay a penalty of $190 million in a settlement with the SEC for securities fraud. What happened to those who captained the ship during this period? Well, in 2015, former CEO Michael Laphen agreed to repay $3.7 million in compensation to CSC under provisions of the Sarbanes-Oxley Act of 2002. Laphen also paid a $750,000 penalty to the SEC. Similarly, CFO Michael Mancuso was required to repay $369,100 in compensation and pay a penalty of $175,000. Several others involved in the fraud failed to reach a settlement with the SEC, including Robert Sutcliffe, CSC's finance director for the NHS contract. By failing to reach a settlement, Sutcliffe and others face penalties of substantial fines as well as imprisonment under the terms of Sarbox. Sometimes, honesty really is the best policy.[16]

include at least two years in any of several fraud-related areas, such as auditing, criminology, fraud investigation, or law.

Federal Restrictions on CPA Services and Financial Reporting: Sarbox

Sarbanes-Oxley Act of 2002 (Sarbox or SOX) *enactment of federal regulations to restore public trust in accounting practices by imposing new requirements on financial activities in publicly traded corporations*

The financial wrongdoings associated with firms such as ImClone Systems, Tyco, WorldCom, Enron, Arthur Andersen, and others have not gone unnoticed in legislative circles. Federal regulations, in particular the **Sarbanes-Oxley Act of 2002 (Sarbox or SOX)**, have been enacted to restore and maintain public trust in corporate accounting practices.

Sarbox restricts the kinds of nonaudit services that CPAs can provide. Under the Sarbox law, for example, a CPA firm can help design a client's financial information system, but not if it also does the client's auditing. Hypothetically, an unscrupulous accounting firm's audit might intentionally overlook a client's false financial statements if, in return, the client rewards the accounting firm with a contract for lucrative nonaccounting services, such as management consulting. This was a core allegation in the Enron-Arthur Andersen scandal. Arthur Andersen, one of the world's largest accounting firms, filed audits that failed to disclose Enron's shaky financial condition that eventually led to the massive energy company's bankruptcy and to Anderson's dissolution. Andersen's auditor gained more money from consulting at Enron than it got for auditing.[17] By prohibiting auditing and nonauditing services to the same client, Sarbox encourages audits that are independent and unbiased.

Sarbox imposes new requirements on virtually every financial activity in publicly traded corporations, as well as severe criminal penalties for persons committing or concealing fraud or destroying financial records. CFOs and CEOs, for example, have to pledge that the company's finances are correct and must vouch for the methods and internal controls used to get those numbers. Companies have to provide a system that is safe for all employees to anonymously report unethical accounting practices and illegal activities without fear of retaliation. Table 2 provides brief descriptions of several of Sarbox's many provisions.

table 2 Selected Provisions of the Sarbanes-Oxley Act[18]

- Creates a national Accounting Oversight Board that, among other activities, must establish the ethics standards used by CPA firms in preparing audits
- Requires that auditors retain audit working papers for specified periods of time
- Requires auditor rotation by prohibiting the same person from being the lead auditor for more than 5 consecutive years
- Requires that the CEO and CFO certify that the company's financial statements are true, fair, and accurate
- Prohibits corporations from extending personal loans to executives and directors
- Requires that the audited company disclose whether it has adopted a code of ethics for its senior financial officers
- Requires that the SEC regularly review each corporation's financial statements
- Prevents employers from retaliating against research analysts who write negative reports
- Imposes criminal penalties on auditors and clients for falsifying, destroying, altering, or concealing records (10 years in prison)
- Imposes a fine or imprisonment (up to 25 years) on any person who defrauds shareholders
- Increases penalties for mail and wire fraud from 5 to 20 years in prison
- Establishes criminal liability for failure of corporate officers to certify financial reports

Source: Multi-source.

The Accounting Equation

All accountants rely on record keeping to enter and track transactions. Underlying all record-keeping procedures is the most basic tool of accounting, the **accounting equation**:

$$\text{Assets} = \text{Liabilities} + \text{Owners' Equity}$$

After each financial transaction (e.g., payments to suppliers, sales to customers, wages to employees), the accounting equation must be in balance. If it isn't, then an accounting error has occurred. To better understand the importance of this equation, we must understand the terms *assets, liabilities,* and *owners' equity.*

Accounting Equation *Assets = Liabilities + Owners' Equity; used by accountants to balance data for the firm's financial transactions at various points in the year*

Assets and Liabilities

An **asset** is any economic resource that is expected to benefit a firm or an individual who owns it. Assets for accounting purposes include land, buildings, equipment, inventories, and payments due the company (accounts receivable). Google, the Internet search and information provider, for example, held total assets amounting to $131,133 million at year end 2014.[19] A **liability**, on the other hand, is a debt that a firm owes to an outside party. The total of Google's liabilities—all the debt owed to others—was $26,633 million at the end of 2014.

Asset *any economic resource expected to benefit a firm or an individual who owns it*

Liability *debt owed by a firm to an outside organization or individual*

Owners' Equity

You may have heard of the *equity* that a homeowner has in a house, the amount of money that could be made (or lost) by selling the house and paying off the mortgage. Similarly, **owners' equity** is the amount of money that owners would theoretically receive if they sold all of a company's assets at their presumed value and paid all of its liabilities. Google's financial reports for 2014 declared shareholders' equity of $104,500 million. For the Google example, we see that the accounting equation is in balance, as it should be.

Owners' Equity *amount of money that owners would receive if they sold all of a firm's assets and paid all of its liabilities*

$$\text{Assets} = \text{Liabilities} + \text{Owners' Equity}$$

$$\$93.798 = \$22.083 + \$71.715 \text{ billion}$$

We can rewrite the equation to highlight how owners' equity relates to assets and liabilities.

$$\text{Assets} - \text{Liabilities} = \text{Owners' Equity}$$

Tim de Voogt/Alamy

The inventory at this auto dealership is among the company's assets: The cars constitute an economic resource because the firm will benefit financially as it sells them.

Another term for this is *net worth*: the difference between what a firm owns (assets) minus what it owes (liabilities) is its net worth, or owners' equity. If a company's assets exceed its liabilities, owners' equity is *positive*. At Google, owners' equity is $104,500 million (= $131,133 million − $26,633 million). If the company goes out of business, the owners will receive some cash (a gain) after selling assets and paying off liabilities. If liabilities outweigh assets, owners' equity is *negative*; assets are insufficient to pay off all debts, and the firm is bankrupt. If the company goes out of business, the owners will get no cash, and some creditors won't be paid.

Owners' equity is meaningful for both investors and lenders. Before lending money to owners, for example, lenders want to know the amount of owners' equity

entrepreneurship and new ventures

Working with the Accounting Equation

Etsy is the website at the center of a worldwide network of creative entrepreneurs, who, according to the company's website, "use Etsy to sell what they make or curate, the shoppers looking for things they can't find anywhere else, the manufacturers who partner with Etsy to help them grow, and the Etsy employees who maintain and nurture our marketplace." Whether you're in the market for a farmer's cheese kit or a graduation gift or a felt cat house, you can find it on Etsy. Sellers on Etsy run the gamut from very small to large, established retailers looking for a new outlet for their products. Perhaps your passion for woodworking has outgrown its status as a hobby and you'd like to venture into small business. The accounting equation,

Assets = Liabilities + Owners' Equity,

can be used to evaluate your business as it grows.

Bridgendboy/Fotolia

Generally, the first step in creating a business is to establish the business entity, often by setting up a business bank account. Suppose that you start your woodworking business by depositing $10,000 into a business bank account. Your business now has $10,000 in assets, the cash that you deposited, no liabilities, and $10,000 in equity. You'll remember that equity is the value of the business to the owner—what you would receive if you discontinued operations.

Perhaps you've decided that your best opportunity to make money is to make custom wooden shutters for the windows of historic homes. But, to be able to do this work efficiently, you'll need to buy an expensive piece of equipment costing $20,000. This greatly exceeds your cash, so you take out a loan to purchase the equipment. After this transaction, your business now has two assets—$10,000 in cash and a $20,000 piece of equipment—making your total assets $30,000. On the other side of the accounting equation, you have liabilities of $20,000 and your owners' equity is $10,000, making the total liabilities and owner's equity $30,000, just the same as your total assets.

Imagine that you're lucky enough to receive an order for 10 sets of custom shutters and your profit on this sale is the $20,000 sales price less your cost of $5,000 for wood and other supplies. Once the shutters have been delivered and the bill has been paid, you will have $15,000 in cash, which will be added to your beginning cash balance of $10,000. Your total assets are $45,000, consisting of $25,000 in cash and $20,000 in equipment. On the other side of the equation, your liabilities have remained the same, but your equity has now increased by your profit on your first sale, increasing from $10,000 to $25,000. As a result, your total liabilities and owners' equity are $20,000 in liabilities and $25,000 in equity or $45,000—exactly the same as your total assets.

Finally, after all your hard work, you'd like to treat yourself to a great vacation. You withdraw $8,000 cash from the business, which reduces both your cash and your equity by this amount. As a result, the accounting equation remains in balance, with total assets of $37,000 ($17,000 in cash and $20,000 in equipment) and total liabilities and owner's equity of $40,000 ($20,000 in liabilities and $17,000 in equity). As you can see, the accounting equation provides the framework around which financial information is organized.

in a business. A larger owners' equity indicates greater security for lenders. Owners' equity consists of two sources of capital:

1 The amount that the owners originally invested

2 Profits (also owned by the owners) earned by and reinvested in the company

When a company operates profitably, its assets increase faster than its liabilities. Owners' equity, therefore, will increase if profits are retained in the business instead of paid out as dividends to stockholders. Owners' equity also increases if owners invest more of their own money to increase assets. However, owners' equity can shrink if the company operates at a loss or if owners withdraw assets.

Financial Statements

OBJECTIVE 3
Describe
the three basic financial statements and show how they reflect the activity and financial condition of a business.

As noted previously, accountants summarize the results of a firm's transactions and issue reports to help managers make informed decisions. Among the most important reports are **financial statements**, which fall into three broad categories: *balance sheets*, *income statements*, and *statements of cash flows*. Together, these reports indicate the firm's financial health and what affected it. In this section, we discuss these three financial statements as well as the function of the budget as an internal financial statement.

Financial Statement *any of several types of reports summarizing a company's financial status to stakeholders and to aid in managerial decision making*

Balance Sheets

Balance sheets supply detailed information about the accounting equation items: *assets*, *liabilities*, and *owners' equity*. Because they also show a firm's financial condition at one point in time, they are sometimes called *statements of financial position*. Figure 1 is a simplified presentation of the balance sheet for Google, Inc. as of the end of 2014.

Balance Sheet *financial statement that supplies detailed information about a firm's assets, liabilities, and owners' equity*

Google, Inc.
Summary of Balance Sheet (condensed)
as of December 31, 2014
(in millions)

Assets		Liabilities and Shareholder's Equity	
Current Assets:		Current liabilities:	
Cash	$18,347	Accounts payable	$1,715
Marketable securities	46,048	Other	15,090
Other	16,290	**Total current liabilities**	**$16,805**
Total current assets	**$80,685**		
		Long-term liabilities:	
Fixed assets:		All long-term debts	$3,228
Property and equipment, net	$23,883	Other	6,600
Other	6,359	**Total long-term liabilities**	**$9,828**
Total fixed assets	**$30,242**		
		Total liabilities	**$22,083**
Intangible assets:			
Intangible assets	$4,607	Shareholder's equity:	
Goodwill	15,599	Paid-in capital	$28,794
Total intangible assets	**$20,206**	Retained earnings	75,706
		Total shareholder's equity	**$104,500**
Total assets	**$131,133**		
		Total liabilities and shareholder's equity	**$131,133**

Google's balance sheet for year ended December 31, 2014. The balance sheet shows clearly that the firm's total assets are equal to its total liabilities and owners' equity.

FIGURE 1 Google's Balance Sheet
Source: Google, Inc. (2015). 2014 Annual Report. Mountain View, California: Author.

Assets From an accounting standpoint, most companies have three types of assets: *current*, *fixed*, and *intangible*.

Current Asset *asset that can or will be converted into cash within a year*

Liquidity *ease with which an asset can be converted into cash*

CURRENT ASSETS **Current assets** include cash and assets that can be converted into cash within a year. The act of converting something into cash is called *liquidating*. Assets are normally listed in order of **liquidity**, the ease of converting them into cash. Debts, for example, are usually paid in cash. A company that needs but cannot generate cash—a company that's not "liquid"—may be forced to sell assets at reduced prices or even to go out of business.

By definition, cash is completely liquid. *Marketable securities* purchased as short-term investments are slightly less liquid but can be sold quickly. These include stocks or bonds of other companies, government securities, and money market certificates. Many companies hold other nonliquid assets such as *merchandise inventory*, the cost of merchandise that's been acquired for sale to customers and is still on hand. Google has no merchandise inventory because it sells services rather than physical goods.

Fixed Asset *asset with long-term use or value, such as land, buildings, and equipment*

Depreciation *accounting method for distributing the cost of an asset over its useful life*

FIXED ASSETS **Fixed assets** (such as land, buildings, and equipment) have long-term use or value, but as buildings and equipment wear out or become obsolete, their value decreases. Accountants use **depreciation** to spread the cost of an asset over the years of its useful life. To reflect decreasing value, accountants calculate an asset's useful life in years, divide its worth by that many years, and subtract the resulting amount each year. Every year, therefore, the remaining value (or net value) decreases on the books. In Figure 1, Google shows fixed assets of $30,242 million after depreciation.

Intangible Asset *nonphysical asset, such as a patent or trademark, that has economic value in the form of expected benefit*

Goodwill *amount paid for an existing business above the value of its other assets*

INTANGIBLE ASSETS Although their worth is hard to set, **intangible assets** have monetary value in the form of expected benefits, which may include fees paid by others for obtaining rights or privileges—including patents, trademarks, copyrights, and franchises—to your products. **Goodwill** is the amount paid for an existing business beyond the value of its other assets. A purchased firm, for example, may have a particularly good reputation or location. Google declares both intangible assets and goodwill in its balance sheet.

Current Liability *debt that must be paid within one year*

Accounts Payable (Payables) *current liability consisting of bills owed to suppliers, plus wages and taxes due within the coming year*

Long-Term Liability *debt that is not due for at least one year*

Liabilities Like assets, liabilities are often separated into different categories. **Current liabilities** are debts that must be paid within one year. These include **accounts payable (payables)**, unpaid bills to suppliers for materials as well as wages and taxes that must be paid in the coming year. Google has current liabilities of $16,805 million. **Long-term liabilities** are debts that are not due for at least a year. These normally represent borrowed funds on which the company must pay interest. The long-term liabilities of Google are $9,828 million.

Paid-In Capital *money that is invested in a company by its owners*

Owners' Equity The final section of the balance sheet in Figure 1 shows owners' equity (shareholders' equity) broken down into *paid-in capital* and *retained earnings*. When Google was first formed, it sold a small amount of common stock that provided its first *paid-in capital*. **Paid-in capital** is money invested by owners. Google's paid-in capital had grown to $28,794 million by year-end 2014, and includes proceeds from Google's initial public offering of stock in 2004 that created additional funds that were needed for expansion.

Retained Earnings *earnings retained by a firm for its use rather than paid out as dividends*

Retained earnings are net profits kept by a firm rather than paid out as dividend payments to stockholders. They accumulate when profits, which can be distributed to shareholders, are kept instead for the company's use. At the close of 2014, Google had retained earnings of $75,706 million. The total of stockholders' equity—paid-in capital plus retained earnings—had grown to $104,500 million.

The balance sheet for any company, then, is a barometer for its financial condition at one point in time. By comparing the current balance sheet with those of previous years, creditors and owners can better interpret the firm's financial progress and future prospects in terms of changes in its assets, liabilities, and owners' equity.

Income Statements

The **income statement** is sometimes called a **profit-and-loss statement** because its description of revenues and expenses results in a figure showing the firm's annual profit or loss. In other words,

$$\text{Profit (or Loss)} = \text{Revenues} - \text{Expenses}$$

Popularly known as the *bottom line*, profit or loss is probably the most important figure in any business enterprise. Figure 2 shows the 2014 income statement for Google, whose bottom line was $14,444 million. The income statement is divided into four major categories: (1) *revenues*, (2) *cost of revenues*, (3) *operating expenses*, and (4) *net income*. Unlike a balance sheet, which shows the financial condition at a specific *point in time*, an income statement shows the financial results that occurred during a *period of time*, such as a month, quarter, or year.

Revenues When a law firm receives $250 for preparing a will or a supermarket collects $65 from a grocery shopper, both are receiving **revenues**, the funds that flow into a business from the sale of goods or services. In 2014, Google reported revenues of $66,001 million from the sale of advertising and Web-search services to Google Network members, such as AOL.

Cost of Revenues (Cost of Goods Sold) In the Google income statement, the **cost of revenues** section shows the costs of obtaining the revenues from other companies during the year. These are fees Google must pay its network members—revenue sharing from advertising income—and also include expenses arising from the operation of Google's data centers, including labor, energy, and costs of processing customer transactions. The cost of revenues for Google in 2014 was $25,691 million.

Although cost of revenues is a relevant income statement category for service providers such as Google, goods producers do not use it. Instead, income statements for manufacturing firms such as Procter & Gamble use the corresponding category, **cost of goods sold**, which are the costs of obtaining materials to make physical products sold during the year.

Income Statement (Profit-and-Loss Statement) *financial statement listing a firm's annual revenues and expenses so that a bottom line shows annual profit or loss*

Revenues *funds that flow into a business from the sale of goods or services*

Cost of Revenues *costs that a company incurs to obtain revenues from other companies*

Cost of Goods Sold *costs of obtaining materials for making the products sold by a firm during the year*

Google, Inc.
Summary of Income Statement (condensed)
as of December 31, 2014
(in millions)

Revenues (gross sales)		**$66,001**
Cost of revenues	25,691	
Gross profit		**$40,310**
Operating expenses:		
Research development	9,832	
Selling, administrative and general	13,982	
Total operating expenses		**$23,814**
Operating income (before taxes)		$16,496
Income taxes*		2,052
Net income		**$14,444**
*approximated		

Google's income statement for year ended December 31, 2014. The final entry on the income statement, the bottom line, reports the firm's profit or loss.

FIGURE 2 Google's Income Statement
Source: Google, Inc. (2015). 2014 Annual Report. Mountain View, California: Author.

Gross Profit *preliminary, quick-to-calculate profit figure calculated from the firm's revenues minus its cost of revenues (the direct costs of getting the revenues)*

GROSS PROFIT Managers are often interested in **gross profit**, a preliminary, quick-to-calculate profit figure that considers just two pieces of data—revenues and cost of revenues (the direct costs of getting those revenues)—from the income statement. To calculate gross profit, subtract cost of revenues from revenues obtained by selling the firm's products.

OPERATING EXPENSES In addition to costs directly related to generating revenues, every company has general expenses ranging from pencils to the CEO's salary. Like cost of revenues and cost of goods sold, **operating expenses** are resources that must flow out of a company if it is to earn revenues. As shown in Figure 2, Google had operating expenses of $23,814 million.

Operating Expenses *costs, other than the cost of revenues, incurred in producing a good or service*

Research development expenses result from exploring new services and technologies for providing them to customers. *Selling expenses* result from activities related to selling goods or services, such as sales-force salaries and advertising expenses. *Administrative and general expenses*, such as management salaries and maintenance costs, are related to the general management of the company.

Operating Income *gross profit minus operating expenses*

Operating and Net Income

Operating income compares the gross profit from operations against operating expenses. This calculation for Google ($66,001 million − $23,814 million) reveals an operating income, or income before taxes, of $12.760 billion. Subtracting income taxes from operating income ($16,496 million − $2,052 million) reveals **net income (net profit** or **net earnings)**. Google's net income for the year was $14,444 million. The step-by-step information in an income statement shows how a company obtained its net income for the period, making it easier for shareholders and other stakeholders to evaluate the firm's financial health.

Net Income (Net Profit or Net Earnings) *gross profit minus operating expenses and income taxes*

Statements of Cash Flows

Some companies prepare only balance sheets and income statements. However, the SEC requires all firms whose stock is publicly traded to issue a third report, the **statement of cash flows**, which describes yearly cash receipts and cash payments. Because it provides the most detail about how the company generates and uses cash, some investors and creditors consider it one of the most important statements of all. It shows the effects on cash of three aspects of a business: *operating activities, investing activities*, and *financing activities*. Google's (simplified) 2012 statement of cash flows is reproduced in Figure 3.

Statement of Cash Flows *financial statement describing a firm's yearly cash receipts and cash payments*

- *Cash Flows from Operations.* This first section of the statement concerns main operating activities: cash transactions involved in buying and selling goods and services. For the Google example, it reveals how much of the year's cash balance results from the firm's main line of business, sales of advertising and Web-search services. Operating activities at Google contributed net cash inflows amounting to $22,476 million in 2014.

- *Cash Flows from Investing.* The second section reports net cash used in or provided by investing. It includes cash receipts and payments from buying and selling stocks, bonds, property, equipment, and other productive assets. These sources of cash are not the company's main line of business. Purchases of property, equipment, and investments made by Google, for example, consumed $21,055 million of net cash. A cash outflow is shown in parentheses.

- *Cash Flows from Financing.* The third section reports net cash from all financing activities. It includes cash inflows from borrowing or issuing stock, as well as outflows for payment of dividends and repayment of borrowed money. Google's financing activities provided a net cash out-flow of $1,439 million.

- The overall change in cash from these three sources is −$551 million for the year. The amount is added to the beginning cash (year-end cash from the 2013 balance sheet) to arrive at 2014's ending cash position of $18,347 million. When creditors

Google, Inc.
Summary of Statement of Cash Flows (condensed)
as of December 31, 2014
Increase (Decrease) in Cash
(in millions)

Net cash provided by operating activities		**$22,376**
Cash from investments:		
Purchases of property, equipment, and investments	(48,281.)	
Cash inflows from investment activities	35,225.	
Net cash used in investing activities		**($21,055.)**
Cash flows from financing activities:		
Repayment of debt	(11,643.)	
Borrowings	11,625 .	
Other	(1,421.)	
Net cash provided by financing activities		**($1,439.)**
Net increase in cash		(551.)
Cash at beginning of year		18,347.
Cash at end of year		**$18,347.**

Google's statement of cash flows for year ended December 31, 2014. The final entry shows year-end cash position resulting from operating activities, investing activities, and financing activities.

FIGURE 3 Google's Statement of Cash Flows
Source: Google, Inc. (2015). 2014 Annual Report. Mountain View, California: Author.

and stockholders know how a firm obtained and used funds during the course of a year, it's easier for them to interpret year-to-year changes in the balance sheet and income statement.

The Budget: An Internal Financial Statement

For planning, controlling, and decision making, the most important internal financial statement is the **budget**, a detailed report on estimated receipts and expenditures for a future period of time. Although that period is usually one year, some companies also prepare three- or five-year budgets, especially when considering major capital expenditures. The budget differs from the other statements we have discussed in that budgets are not shared outside the company; hence the "internal financial statement" title.

Budget *detailed statement of estimated receipts and expenditures for a future period of time*

Although the accounting staff coordinates the budget process, it needs input from many areas regarding proposed activities and required resources. Figure 4 is a sales budget for a hypothetical wholesaler, Perfect Posters. In preparing next year's budget, accounting must obtain from the sales group projections for units to be sold and expected expenses for the coming year. Then, accounting draws up the final budget and, throughout the year, compares the budget to actual expenditures and revenues. Discrepancies signal potential problems and spur action to improve financial performance.

Reporting Standards and Practices

OBJECTIVE 4
Explain

Accountants follow standard reporting practices and principles when they prepare external reports. The common language dictated by standard practices and spelled out in GAAP is designed to give external users confidence in the accuracy and meaning of financial information. GAAP covers a range of issues, such as when to

the key standards and principles for reporting financial statements.

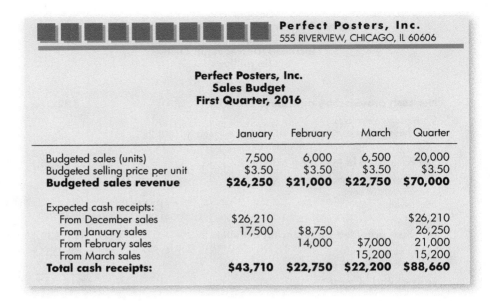

FIGURE 4 Perfect Posters' Sales Budget

recognize revenues from operations and how to make full public disclosure of financial information. Without such standards, users of financial statements wouldn't be able to compare information from different companies and would misunderstand—or be led to misconstrue—a company's true financial status. Forensic accountants, such as Al Vondra from the opening case, watch for deviations from GAAP as indicators of possible fraudulent practices.

Revenue Recognition and Activity Timing

The reporting of revenue inflows, and the timing of other transactions, must abide by accounting principles that govern financial statements. **Revenue recognition**, for example, is the formal recording and reporting of revenues at the appropriate time. Although a firm earns revenues continuously as it makes sales, earnings are not reported until the *earnings cycle* is completed. This cycle is complete under two conditions:

Revenue Recognition *formal recording and reporting of revenues at the appropriate time*

1 The sale is complete and the product delivered.

2 The sale price has been collected or is collectible (accounts receivable).

The end of the earnings cycle determines the timing for revenue recognition in a firm's financial statements. Suppose a toy company in January signs a sales contract to supply $1,000 of toys to a retail store with delivery scheduled in February. Although the sale is completed in January, the $1,000 revenue should not then be recognized (not be reported in the firm's financial statements) because the toys have not been delivered and the sale price is not yet collectible, so the earnings cycle is incomplete. Revenues are recorded in the accounting period—February—in which the product is delivered and collectible (or collected). This practice ensures that the statement gives a fair comparison of what was gained (revenues) in return for the resources that were given up (cost of materials, labor, and other production and delivery expenses) for the transaction.

Full Disclosure

To help users better understand the numbers in a firm's financial statements, GAAP requires that financial statements also include management's interpretations and explanations of those numbers. The idea of requiring input from the manager is known as the **full disclosure** principle. Because they know about events inside the company, managers prepare additional information to explain certain events or transactions or to disclose the circumstances behind certain results.

For example, previous annual reports and financial statements filed by Borders, once the second-largest bookseller in the United States, had discussed the competitive and economic risks facing the company before it eventually filed for bankruptcy in 2011. The disclosures noted that consumer spending trends were shifting to Internet retailers and eBooks, and away from in-store purchasing, thus posing risks for Borders' cash flows and overall financial condition. Management's discussion noted there could be no assurance that Borders would muster adequate financial resources to remain competitive and, indeed, it soon happened. On filing for bankruptcy, Borders' liabilities of $1.29 billion had surpassed its assets of $1.28 billion. This one-time book-industry giant closed its last U.S. store in September 2011.[20] The disclosure information helped investors and other stakeholders make informed decisions about risk associated with investing in or doing business with Borders. It would have been a far different story had Borders' managers offered deceptively optimistic assessments of the business's future.

Full Disclosure *guideline that financial statements should not include just numbers but should also furnish management's interpretations and explanations of those numbers*

Analyzing Financial Statements

OBJECTIVE 5
Describe
how computing financial ratios can help users get more information from financial statements to determine the financial strengths of a business.

Financial statements present a lot of information, but how can it be used? How, for example, can statements help investors decide what stock to buy or help lenders decide whether to extend credit? Answers to such questions for various stakeholders—employees, managers, unions, suppliers, the government, customers—can be answered as follows: Statements provide data, which can, in turn, reveal trends and be applied to create various *ratios* (comparative numbers). We can then use these trends and ratios to evaluate a firm's financial health, its progress, and its prospects for the future.

Ratios are normally grouped into three major classifications:

1 **Solvency ratios** for estimating short-term and long-term risk

2 **Profitability ratios** for measuring potential earnings

3 **Activity ratios** for evaluating management's use of assets

Depending on the decisions to be made, a user may apply none, some, or all of these ratios.

Solvency Ratio *financial ratio, either short or long term, for estimating the borrower's ability to repay debt*

Profitability Ratio *financial ratio for measuring a firm's potential earnings*

Activity Ratio *financial ratio for evaluating management's efficiency in using a firm's assets*

Solvency Ratios: Borrower's Ability to Repay Debt

What are the chances that a borrower will be able to repay a loan and the interest due? This question is first and foremost in the minds of bank lending officers, managers of pension funds and other investors, suppliers, and the borrowing company's own financial managers. Solvency ratios provide measures of a firm's ability to meet its debt obligations.

The Current Ratio and Short-Term Solvency
Short-term sol-vency ratios measure a company's liquidity and its ability to pay immediate debts. The most commonly used of these is the **current ratio** or "banker's ratio." This ratio measures a firm's ability to generate cash to meet current obligations through the normal, orderly process of selling inventories and collecting revenues from customers. It is calculated by dividing current assets by current liabilities. The higher a firm's current ratio, the lower the risk to investors.

As a rule, a current ratio is satisfactory at 2:1 or higher—that is, if current assets more than double current liabilities. A smaller ratio may indicate that a firm will have trouble paying its bills.

Short-Term Solvency Ratio *financial ratio for measuring a company's ability to pay immediate debts*

Current Ratio *financial ratio for measuring a company's ability to pay current debts out of current assets*

How does Google measure up? Look again at the balance sheet in Figure 1. Judging from current assets and current liabilities at the end of 2014, we see that

$$\frac{\text{Current assests}}{\text{Current liabilities}} = \frac{\$60.454 \text{ billion}}{\$14.337 \text{ billion}} = 4.2$$

The industry average for companies that provide business services is 1.4. Google's current ratio of 4.8 indicates the firm is a good short-run credit risk. That is, if necessary, Google could easily generate $4.80 for each $1.00 of its short-term debt.

Long-Term Solvency Stakeholders are also concerned about **long-term solvency.** Has the company been overextended by borrowing so much that it will be unable to repay debts in future years? A firm that can't meet its long-term debt obligations is in danger of collapse or takeover, a risk that makes creditors and investors quite cautious. To evaluate a company's risk of running into this problem, creditors turn to the balance sheet to see the extent to which a firm is financed through borrowed money. Long-term solvency is calculated by dividing **debt** (total liabilities) by owners' equity. The lower a firm's debt, the lower the risk to investors and creditors. Companies with more debt may find themselves owing so much that they lack the income needed to meet interest payments or to repay borrowed money.

Sometimes, high debt not only can be acceptable but also desirable. Borrowing funds gives a firm **leverage,** the ability to make otherwise unaffordable investments. In *leveraged buyouts,* firms have willingly taken on sometimes-huge debts to buy out other companies. If owning the purchased company generates profits above the cost of borrowing the purchase price, leveraging often makes sense. Unfortunately, many buyouts have caused problems because profits fell short of expected levels or because rising interest rates increased payments on the buyer's debt.

Debt *company's total liabilities*

Leverage *ability to finance an investment through borrowed funds*

Profitability Ratios: Earnings Power for Owners

It's important to know whether a company is solvent in both the long and the short term, but risk alone is not an adequate basis for investment decisions. Investors also want some indication of the returns they can expect. Evidence of earnings power is available from profitability ratios, such as *earnings per share.*

Defined as net income divided by the number of shares of common stock outstanding, **earnings per share** determines the size of the dividend that a firm can pay shareholders. As an indicator of a company's wealth potential, investors use this ratio to decide whether to buy or sell the firm's stock. As the ratio goes up, stock value increases because investors know that the firm can better afford to pay dividends. Naturally, stock loses market value if financial statements report a decline in earnings per share. For Google, we can use the net income total from the income statement in Figure 2, together with the number of outstanding shares of stock, to calculate earnings per share as follows:

Earnings Per Share *profitability ratio measuring the net profit that the company earns for each share of outstanding stock*

$$\frac{\text{Net income}}{\begin{array}{c}\text{Net of}\\\text{common shares}\\\text{outstanding}\end{array}} = \frac{\$10,737.0 \text{ million}}{\begin{array}{c}332.3 \text{ million}\\\text{shares of stock}\end{array}} = \frac{\$32.31}{\text{per share}}$$

This means that Google had net earnings of $43.47 (rounded) for each share of stock during 2014.

Activity Ratios: How Efficiently Is the Firm Using Its Resources?

The efficiency with which a firm uses resources is linked to profitability. As a potential investor, you want to know which company gets more mileage from its resources. Information obtained from financial statements can be used for *activity ratios* to measure this efficiency. For example, two firms use the same amount of resources or assets to

finding a better way

New Accounting Rules Aim to Save Sinking Pension Funds[21]

In the years since the 2008 recession, many state and local governments have been confronted with financial problems from underfunded employee pension funds; that is, employers have set aside less than they owe to employees and retirees. At year-end 2012, actual funding of the 100 largest public pensions in the United States was more than $860 billion short of their obligations; funds can't pay retirees what they are promised. Assets ($62.5 billion) in the Illinois fund cover only 45 percent of its total liability ($138.8 billion), whereas Wisconsin, in contrast, is fully funded. The shortfall, or unfunded liability, for all state and local governments is more than $2 trillion. If underfunded state and local governments borrow to meet their pension deficits, they face higher borrowing costs because their now-low credit ratings will fall even lower, reflecting the added risks from incurring more indebtedness that may not be repaid.

How (and why) did such massive funding discrepancies occur? First, tax revenues (income) fell during and after the recession, demands for public services increased, and costs of retiree medical coverage rose substantially, so funding for pensions suffered. Furthermore, the stock market decline and its slow recovery resulted in much lower returns, even losses, on pension-fund investments, driving pension assets well below anticipated amounts. The use of traditional methods for estimating investment returns in financial planning was critically damaging, as well. To estimate future financial inflows, some funds assumed investments would average as much as 8 percent annual returns for years ahead, based on healthy pre-recession investment success. Instead, many pension funds averaged a lean 1 percent for years 2008 to 2011, and far below the planned-for 8 percent into 2013.

Baki/Shutterstock

The resulting pension crisis was the impetus for new accounting rules from the Governmental Accounting Standards Board (GASB), the body responsible for setting accounting rules for state and local governments. In 2012, GASB announced two rules that will cause financial statements of pension funds to more accurately reflect each fund's true financial health: (1) The first rule requires that assets be valued and reported "at fair value" (market value), rather than as an average value over several years. The balance sheet must also report the "net pension liability," the difference between total pension liability and the fund's assets. (2) The second rule requires the use of a more realistic discount rate (or rate of return) that reflects the long-term return on investments.

Rules 1 and 2 became effective in 2014 and 2015, respectively. The new information will provide employees, retirees, and the public a clearer representation of each fund's financial obligations and incomes, so constituents have a better way to judge the fund's true overall financial health.

perform a particular activity. If Firm A generates greater profits or sales, it has used its resources more efficiently and so enjoys a better activity ratio. It may apply to any important activity, such as advertising, sales, or inventory management. Consider the activity of using the firm's resources to increase sales. As an example, suppose from its income statements we find that Google increases its annual sales revenues and does it without increasing its operating costs. Its sales activity has become more efficient. Investors like to see these year-to-year increases in efficiencies because it means the company is getting "more bang for the buck"—revenues are increasing faster than costs.

Bringing Ethics into the Accounting Equation

OBJECTIVE 6
Discuss
the role of ethics in accounting.

The purpose of ethics in accounting is to maintain public confidence in business institutions, financial markets, and the products and services of the accounting profession. Without ethics, all of accounting's tools and methods would be meaningless because their usefulness depends, ultimately, on veracity in their application.

In addition to the business world's many favorable opportunities and outcomes, there are also instances of misconduct. Amid public reports of unscrupulous activity, ethics remains an area in which one person who is willing to "do the right thing" can make a difference—and people do, every day. The role of ethics in the groundbreaking scandal from a decade ago remains a classic example: Refusing to turn a blind eye to unethical accounting around her at Enron, the now-failed giant energy corporation, Lynn Brewer tried to alert people inside about misstatements of the company's assets. When that failed, she, along with colleagues Sherron Watkins and Margaret Ceconi, talked with the U.S. Committee on Energy and Commerce to voice concerns about Enron's condition. To Brewer, maintaining personal and professional integrity was an overriding concern, and she acted accordingly.

AICPA's Code of Professional Conduct

Code of Professional Conduct
code of ethics for CPAs as maintained and enforced by the AICPA

The **code of professional conduct** for public accountants in the United States is maintained and enforced by the AICPA. The institute identifies six ethics-related areas—listed in Table 3—with which accountants must comply to maintain certification. Comprehensive details for compliance in each area are spelled out in the AICPA Code of Professional Conduct. The IMA maintains a similar code to provide ethical guidelines for the management accounting profession.

In reading the AICPA's code, you can see that it forbids misrepresentation and fraud in financial statements. Deception certainly violates the call for exercising moral judgments (in "Responsibilities"), is contrary to the public interest (by deceiving investors), and does not honor the public trust (in "The Public Interest"). Misleading statements destroy the public's confidence in the accounting profession and in business in general. Although the code prohibits such abuses, its success depends, ultimately, on its acceptance and use by the professionals it governs.

table 3 Highlights from the Code of Ethics for CPAs

By voluntarily accepting Certified Public Accountant membership, the accountant also accepts self-enforced obligations, listed here, beyond written regulations and laws.	
Responsibilities as a Professional	The CPA should exercise their duties with a high level of morality and in a manner that is sensitive to bringing credit to their profession.
Serving the Public Interest	The CPA should demonstrate commitment to the profession by respecting and maintaining the public trust and serving the public honorably.
Maintaining Integrity	The CPA should perform all professional activities with highest regards for integrity, including sincerity and honesty, so as to promote the public's confidence in the profession.
Being Objective and Independent	The CPA should avoid conflicts of interest, and the appearance of conflicts of interest, in performing their professional responsibilities. They should be independent from clients when certifying to the public that the client's statements are true and genuine.
Maintaining Technical and Ethical Standards Through Due Care	The CPA should exercise "due care," through professional improvement, abiding by ethical standards, updating personal competence through continuing accounting education, and improving the quality of services.
Professional Conduct in Providing Services	The CPA in public practice should abide by the meaning and intent of the Code of Professional Conduct when deciding on the kinds of services and the range of actions to be supplied competently and diligently for clients.

Source: Based on "Code of Professional Conduct," *AICPA*, at www.aicpa.org/Research/Standards/CodeofConduct/Pages/sec50.aspx, accessed on May 1, 2015.

table 4 Examples of Unethical and Illegal Accounting Actions[22]

Corporation	Accounting Violation
AOL Time Warner	America Online (AOL) inflated ad revenues to keep stock prices high before and after merging with Time Warner.
Freddie Mac	This U.S. government corporation fraudulently misstated $5 billion in earnings.
HCA, Columbia/HCA	Healthcare association and hospital defrauded Medicare, Medicaid, and TRICARE through false cost claims and unlawful billings (paid $1.7 billion in civil penalties, damages, criminal fines, and penalties).
Tyco	CEO Dennis Kozlowski illegally used company funds to buy expensive art for personal possession (he received an 8- to 25-year prison sentence).
Waste Management	Overstated income in financial statements (false and misleading reports) by improperly calculating depreciation and salvage value for equipment.
WorldCom	Hid $3.8 billion in expenses to show an inflated (false) profit instead of loss in an annual income statement.

Violations of Accounting Ethics and GAAP

Unethical and illegal accounting violations have dominated the popular press in recent years. Some of the more notorious cases, listed in Table 4, violated the public's trust, ruined retirement plans for thousands of employees, and caused shutdowns and lost jobs. As you read each case, you should be able to see how its violation relates to the presentation of balance sheets and income statements in this chapter. In each case, adversity would have been prevented if employees had followed the code of professional conduct. In each case, nearly all of the code's six ethics-related areas were violated, and "professionals" willingly participated in unethical behavior. Such unscrupulous behavior was the impetus for Sarbox.

Internationalizing Accounting

OBJECTIVE 7
Describe
the purpose of the International Accounting Standards Board and explain why it exists.

Accounting in its earliest forms is known to have existed more than 7,000 years ago in Mesopotamia and Egypt for recording trade transactions and keeping track of resources. With the passage of time, each country or region's accounting practices were refined to meet its needs in commerce while also accommodating local cultural traditions and developments in its laws. Although unique practices served each region well, they later posed problems as international business became prominent. By the late twentieth century, it was apparent that the upsurge in multinational organizations and the global economy demanded more uniformity among accounting practices. The development of "universal" procedures would allow governments and investors in, say, China, Brazil, and Italy to read, interpret, and compare financial statements from all those countries, whereas such comparisons even today are difficult if not sometimes impossible.

International Accounting Standards Board

Established in 2001 and housed at London, England, the **International Accounting Standards Board (IASB)** is an independent, nonprofit organization responsible for developing a set of global accounting standards and for gaining the support and cooperation of the world's various accounting organizations to implement those standards.

International Accounting Standards Board (IASB) *organization responsible for developing a set of global accounting standards and for gaining implementation of those standards*

finding a better way

Is a Big Tax Refund Really Worth Jail?

Tax preparation is big business in the United States. With complex rules around reporting income and claiming tax credits, many people have a CPA or other accounting practitioner prepare their tax return, often with the promise of a big refund. For example, consider the case of Ramona Johnson and her daughter-in-law, Nekia Everson, who operated a tax preparation business in Fort Worth, Texas, that collected $1.9 million in tax preparation fees over a four-year period. Johnson and Everson were able to charge high fees, attract new customers, and sustain a loyal client base by filing falsified tax returns. Returns prepared by Johnson, Everson, and their associates included deductions not allowed by law, inappropriate use of personal and dependency exemptions, and unwarranted claims for tax credits. When the false claims were discovered, unsuspecting taxpayers were required to repay portions of larger-than-legal refunds and Johnson and Everson were sentenced to 170 months and 95 months in prison, respectively.

While many in the accounting profession have pointed fingers at underqualified preparers, this type of abuse has occurred even with CPAs, who are expected to maintain the highest code of conduct. For example, in November 2014, Jeffrey Applewhite, operator of Applewhite and Company, CPA, in Inglewood, California, was sentenced to 36 months in prison and ordered to pay $9,249 as a result of 20 counts of filing false and fraudulent tax returns. In an attempt to get larger refunds for his clients, Applewhite, a CPA, prepared tax returns that overstated deductions, such as charitable donations, and improperly claimed credits to which his clients were not entitled.

As with many other fraudulent business operations, dishonest tax preparers often prey on those who lack sophisticated knowledge about money and taxes. Cathy Vinnett, operator of River Parish Tax Professionals, used recruiters to attract local potential clients, reporting that the government was offering stimulus funds that could be claimed by visiting their offices and filing a return. When these unsuspecting clients came to the office, Vinnett and others collected their personal information, although the clients never received the promised cash. However, the information collected by River Parish was used to prepare more than 300 fraudulent returns, using stolen identities to generate additional dependents and credits. As a result, Vinnett was sentenced to 41 months in prison and ordered to repay more than $1 million in restitution. As the old saying goes, "If it's too good to be true—it probably isn't."[23]

IASB's 14 board members from various countries are full-time accounting experts with technical and international business experience.[24] Because the board cannot command sovereign nations to accept its recommended standards, its commitment to gaining cooperation around the world is a continuing task. Yet, international acceptance is essential for success. Accordingly, the board's task is a long-term process that requires working with various countries to design proposed standards. As an example, for any IASB proposal to be accepted in the United States, it must first be approved by the U.S.-based FASB and by the U.S. SEC. However, IASB's efforts extend beyond the United States, to all nations. The expected timeline reaches beyond 2015 for convergence of the many local GAAP into one global set of practices.

Why One Set of Global Practices?

Although more than 138 countries have adopted IASB's accounting practices, over 50 others continue to use their national GAAP.[25] U.S.-based global companies such as Google, Caterpillar, and Microsoft may prepare different financial reports using local accounting practices for each country in which they conduct business. They also report the company's overall performance in a set of consolidated statements that combines the financial results of all its global affiliates, using U.S. GAAP. Using different accounting standards, however, can result in vastly different pictures of a firm's financial health. Income statements, balance sheets, and statements of cash flows using local GAAPs versus IASB practices, for example, may contain conflicting information with inconsistencies leading to confusion and misunderstandings among investors and other constituents. To emphasize this point, Hans Hoogervorst, Chairman of the IASB, notes that a company using IASB standards can report balance sheet figures that are twice the size of those using U.S. GAAP accounting standards.[26] Which of the reports tells how well the company is doing? Such inconsistencies in reporting are unacceptable in a global economy and, accordingly, protection against them is a goal of IASB.

Example Areas Targeted for Aligning U.S. GAAP and IASB

Among the many differences between the practices of U.S. GAAP and IASB—some reports identify more than 400 such discrepancies—the following examples illustrate some discrepancies and proposals for convergence toward universal standards in financial reporting.

- *In valuing assets* (reported on the balance sheet), U.S. GAAP allows an asset to be written down if for some reason its value decreases. However, the value cannot later be rewritten up, even if it its actual value has increased. IASB standards, in contrast, do allow such write-ups reflecting increased market value, so the reported value of a company's assets can be quite different, depending on the chosen accounting system.[27]

- *In revenue recognition*, when revenues from customers should be recognized (reported), and in what amounts on the income statement, the U.S. GAAP and IASB procedures differ from each other. A current joint proposal, if approved, would remove existing inconsistencies and provide a single standard that recognizes revenue at the time the goods and services are transferred to the customer, and in the amounts that are expected to be received (or are received) from the customer.[28]

- *In devaluing of financial assets*, such as writing down bad loans in the financial crisis, both U.S. GAAP and IASB currently use the same procedure: After a loss occurs (but not until after the fact), the loan's value can be written down in the firm's financial statements, reflecting its lower value. Both groups, however, believe an "expected loss model" that recognizes (and reports) likely loan losses *ahead of time* will provide more timely information for investors and financial planners. A joint proposal for such a procedure has been presented.[29]

- *In fair value disclosure*, the FASB and IASB jointly propose new standards for improving the comparability of fair value disclosures in financial statements. Unlike dissimilar disclosure practices among many local GAAP, both groups want the reported "fair value" for an asset, a liability, and an item in shareholders' equity to have the same meaning under both FASB and IASB procedures. The disclosure should identify the techniques and inputs used to measure fair value so that users can more clearly assess and compare financial statements.[30]

Timetable for Implementation

The U.S. SEC targeted 2015 as the earliest date that U.S. companies will be required to use IASB procedures for financial reporting. To meet the 2015 target, however, IASB must first demonstrate that its standards are developed adequately for use in the U.S. financial reporting system. Doing so would include assuring that investors have developed an understanding of and education in using IASB standards. Accounting education, too, must be updated to prepare U.S. accounting students for IASB, as well as updating practitioners in CPA firms. In 2011, the AICPA began a gradual process of introducing international standards in the CPA examinations. Most of the exam's new questions addressed some of the areas of difference between U.S. GAAP and International Financial Reporting Standards. Finally, the SEC must make a decision to phase in IASB all at once or, instead, to sequence its adoption beginning with a limited number of companies before final phase-in. The SEC's final report was delayed, however, so the U.S. wait continues while the challenges of switching to IFRS are resolved.[31]

summary of learning objectives

Explain the role of accountants and distinguish among the kinds of work done by public accountants, private accountants, management accountants, and forensic accountants.

The role of accountants is to maintain a comprehensive system for collecting, analyzing, and communicating financial information for use by external constituents and within firms for planning, controlling, and decision making. It measures business performance and translates the results into information for management decisions. The users of accounting information include business managers, employees and unions, investors and creditors, tax authorities, and government regulatory agencies.

The *controller*, or chief accounting officer, manages a firm's accounting activities by ensuring that the *accounting information system* provides the reports and statements needed for planning, decision making, and other management activities. Accounting activities may be either financial or managerial. *Financial accounting* is concerned with external users of information, such as consumer groups, unions, stockholders, and government agencies, and focuses on the entity as a whole. *Managerial accounting*'s focus is internal users, such as managers, engineers, purchasing agents, and salespeople. Managerial accounting focuses on the detailed information needed to make decisions within the organization.

Public accountants offer accounting services to individuals and businesses outside their organization and are distinguished by their independence from the clients they serve. *Certified public accountants (CPAs)* are licensed professionals who provide auditing, tax, and management advisory services for other firms and individuals. Only CPAs can audit a firm's financial statements, and CPAs are always independent of the firms they audit. Many businesses hire their own salaried employees—*private accountants*—to perform internal accounting activities, such as internal auditing, taxation, cost analysis, and budgeting. Among private accountants, *certified management accountants* have passed the profession's experience and examination requirements for proficiency to provide internal accounting services that support managers in various activities (such as marketing, production, and engineering). *Forensic accountants* use accounting for legal purposes by providing investigative and litigation support in crimes against companies, crimes by companies, and civil cases.

Explain how the accounting equation is used.

Accountants use the following equation to balance the data pertaining to financial transactions:

$$\text{Assets} - \text{Liabilities} = \text{Owners' Equity}$$

After each financial transaction (e.g., payments to suppliers, sales to customers, wages to employees), the accounting equation must be in balance. If it isn't, then an accounting error has occurred. An *asset* is any economic resource that is expected to benefit a firm or an individual who owns it. Assets include land, buildings, equipment, inventory, and payments due the company (accounts receivable). A liability is a debt that the firm owes to an outside party. Owners' equity consists of capital from two sources: (1) The amount that the owners originally invested; and (2) Profits (also owned by the owners) earned by and reinvested in the company. Owners' equity is meaningful for both investors and lenders. Before lending money to owners, lenders want to know the amount of owners' equity in a business. A larger owners' equity indicates greater security for lenders. As shown from the accounting equation, if assets exceed liabilities, owners' equity is positive; if the firm goes out of business, owners will receive some cash (a gain) after selling assets and paying off liabilities. If liabilities outweigh assets, owners' equity is negative; assets aren't enough to pay off debts. If the company goes under, owners will get no cash and some creditors won't be paid, thus losing their remaining investments in the company.

Describe the three basic financial statements and show how they reflect the activity and financial condition of a business.

Accounting summarizes the results of a firm's transactions and issues reports—including *financial statements*—to help managers and other stakeholders make informed decisions. The *balance sheet* (sometimes called the *statement of financial position*) supplies detailed information about the accounting equation items—assets, liabilities, and owners' equity—that together are a barometer of the firm's financial condition at a point in time. By comparing the current balance sheet with those of previous years, creditors and owners can better interpret the firm's financial progress and future prospects in terms of changes in assets, liabilities, and owners' equity.

The *income statement* (sometimes called a *profit-and-loss statement*) describes revenues and expenses to show a firm's annual profit or loss during a period of time, such as a year. The information in an income statement shows how a company obtained its net income for the accounting period, making it easier for shareholders and other stakeholders to evaluate the firm's financial health.

A publicly traded firm must issue a *statement of cash flows*, which describes its yearly cash receipts (inflows) and payments (outflows). It shows the effects on cash during the year from three kinds of business activities: (a) cash flows from operations, (b) cash flows from investing, and (c) cash flows from financing. The statement of cash flows then reports the overall change in the company's cash position at the end of the accounting period. When creditors and stockholders know how a firm obtained and used funds during the course of a year, it's easier for them to interpret year-to-year changes in the balance sheet and income statement.

For planning, controlling, and decision making, the most important internal financial statement is the *budget*, a detailed report on estimated receipts and expenditures for a future period of time. Budgets are internal documents and not usually shared outside the company.

Explain the key standards and principles for reporting financial statements.

Accountants follow standard reporting practices and principles when they prepare financial statements. The common language dictated by standard practices and spelled out in generally accepted accounting principles (GAAP) is designed to give external users confidence in the accuracy and meaning of financial information. Without these standards, users wouldn't be able to compare information from different companies, and they might misunderstand—or be led to misconstrue—a company's true financial status.

Two of the most important standard reporting practices and principles are revenue recognition and full disclosure. *Revenue recognition* refers to the rules associated with the recording and reporting of revenues in financial statements. All firms earn revenues continuously as they make sales, but earnings are not reported until the earnings cycle is completed. This cycle is complete under two conditions: (a) The sale is complete and the product delivered; (b) the sale price has been collected or is collectible (accounts receivable). This practice assures interested parties that the statement gives a fair comparison of what was gained (revenues) for the resources that were given up (cost of materials, labor, and other expenses) for the transaction.

Full disclosure recognizes that a firm's managers have inside knowledge—beyond just the numbers reported in its financial statements—that can explain certain events, transactions, or otherwise disclose the circumstances behind certain results. Full disclosure means that financial statements include management interpretations and explanations to help external users understand the financial information contained in statements.

Describe how computing financial ratios can help users get more information from financial statements to determine the financial strengths of a business.

Financial statements contain data that can be used in *ratios* (comparative numbers) to analyze the financial health of a company in terms of solvency, profitability, and efficiency in performing activities. Ratios can help creditors, investors, and managers assess a firm's current status and check its progress by comparing current with past statements. *Solvency ratios* use balance sheet data to measure the firm's ability to meet (repay) its debts. The most commonly used solvency ratio is known as the current ratio. The *current ratio* measures the ability to meet current (short-term) liabilities out of current assets. It is calculated by dividing current assets by current liabilities. The higher a firm's current ratio, the lower the risk to investors. A smaller ratio may indicate that a firm will have trouble paying its bills. Stakeholders are also concerned about long-term solvency. *Long-term solvency ratios* compare the firm's total liabilities (including long-term debt) against the owners' equity. High indebtedness (a high ratio) can be risky because it requires payment of interest and repayment of borrowed funds that may not be available.

Profitability ratios, such as earnings per share, measure current and potential earnings. Investors are interested in this ratio because it indicates the firm's earnings power and the returns they can expect from their investments. *Activity ratios* reflect management's use of assets by measuring the efficiency with which a firm uses its resources for a particular activity, such as sales, advertising, or inventory management. Sales efficiency, for example, can be measured from income statement data for annual sales revenues as compared with sales expenses. Sales efficiency has increased if the year-to-year growth in sales revenues is larger than the growth in sales expenses.

OBJECTIVE 6

Discuss the role of ethics in accounting.

The purpose of ethics in accounting is to maintain public confidence in business institutions, financial markets, and the products and services of the accounting profession. Without ethics, all of accounting's tools and methods would be meaningless because their usefulness depends, ultimately, on truthfulness in their application. Accordingly, professional accounting associations such as the AICPA and IMA enforce codes of professional conduct that include ethics-related areas, such as the accountant's responsibilities, the public interest, integrity, and due care. The codes prohibit, among other areas, misrepresentation and fraud in financial statements because misleading statements destroy the public's confidence in the accounting profession and in business in general. Although the code prohibits such abuses, its success depends ultimately on its acceptance and use by the professionals it governs.

OBJECTIVE 7

Describe the purpose of the International Accounting Standards Board and explain why it exists.

The International Accounting Standards Board (IASB) is an independent, nonprofit organization established for the purpose of developing a set of global accounting standards and for gaining the support and cooperation of the world's various accounting organizations to implement those standards. It exists because the upsurge in multinational organizations and the global economy demand more uniformity among accounting practices, so that accounting reports become more understandable across nations and regions. Because the board cannot command sovereign nations to accept its recommended standards, its commitment to gaining cooperation around the world is a continuing task that requires working with various countries to design proposed international standards. Although more than 100 countries have adopted IASB's accounting practices, nearly 40 others, including China, Canada, and the United States, continue to use their national accounting standards that are often not comparable and can result in vastly different pictures of a firm's financial health. The development of "universal" procedures would allow governments and investors everywhere to read, interpret, and compare financial statements from every country, whereas such comparisons even today are difficult if not sometimes impossible. Different accounting standards, such as how assets are valued and how revenues should be recognized, can result in vastly different pictures of a firm's financial health. Income statements, balance sheets, and statements of cash flows using U.S. GAAP versus IASB practices may contain conflicting information with inconsistencies leading to confusion and misunderstandings among investors and other constituents. The U.S. SEC has targeted 2015 as the earliest date that U.S. companies will be required to use IASB procedures for financial reporting. To meet the 2015 target, however, IASB must first demonstrate that its standards are developed adequately for use in the U.S. financial reporting system.

key terms

accounting
accounting equation
accounting information system (AIS)
accounts payable (payables)
activity ratio
asset
audit
balance sheet
bookkeeping
budget
Certified Fraud Examiner (CFE)
certified management accountant (CMA)
certified public accountant (CPA)
code of professional conduct
controller
core competencies for accounting
cost of goods sold
cost of revenues
current asset
current liability

current ratio
debt
depreciation
earnings per share
financial accounting
financial statement
fixed asset
forensic accounting
full disclosure
generally accepted accounting principles (GAAP)
goodwill
gross profit
income statement (profit-and-loss statement)
intangible asset
International Accounting Standards Board (IASB)
leverage
liability
liquidity
long-term liability

management accountant
management advisory services
managerial (management) accounting
net income (net profit, net earnings)
operating expenses
operating income
owners' equity
paid-in capital
private accountant
profitability ratio
retained earnings
revenue recognition
revenues
Sarbanes-Oxley Act of 2002 (Sarbox or SOX)
short-term solvency ratio
solvency ratio
statement of cash flows
tax services

To complete the problems with the ✪, go to EOC Discussion Questions in the MyLab.

questions & exercises

QUESTIONS FOR REVIEW

✪ 1. Who are the users of accounting information and for what purposes do they use it?

2. Identify the three types of services performed by CPAs.

3. Explain the ways in which financial accounting differs from managerial accounting.

4. Discuss the activities and services performed by forensic accountants.

5. What are the three basic financial statements, and what major information does each contain?

QUESTIONS FOR ANALYSIS

✪ 6. If you were planning to invest in a company, which of the three types of financial statements would you most want to see? Why?

✪ 7. Use the accounting equation to determine your net worth. Identify your assets and liabilities. With this information, how would you increase your net worth in the future?

8. Consider some possible reasons it is taking so long for IASB's accounting standards to become fully adopted for use in the United States. Using the Internet as your source for information, identify three or more barriers that have deterred implementation of the standards, and explain how (or why) each has (or is) causing implementation delays.

APPLICATION EXERCISES

9. Interview an accountant at a local business, nonprofit organization, or government entity. How does the firm use budgets? How does budgeting help managers plan business activities? How does budgeting help them control activities? Give examples.

10. Interview the manager of a local retailer, wholesale business, or manufacturing firm about the role of ethics in that company's accounting practices. Is ethics in accounting an important issue to the manager? If the firm has its own private accountants, what measures are taken for ensuring ethical practices internally? What steps, if any, does the company take to maintain ethical relationships in its dealings with CPA firms?

building a business: continuing team exercise

Assignment

Meet with your team members to consider your new business venture and how it relates to the accounting topics in this chapter. Develop specific responses to the following:

11. In your first year of operation, who will perform accounting functions inside your company? Will you contract some or all of the work to a public accounting firm?

12. Create a list of the types of transactions that your accountant will record, including the purchase and sale of assets as well as revenues and expenses.

13. Based on the development of your business to date, create a preliminary or pro forma income statement for your firm's first year of operation. Be sure it includes listings of relevant terms from the accounting equation. See if you can estimate anticipated data for each element in the income statement.

14. Based on the development of your business to date, create a preliminary or pro forma balance sheet for your firm's first year of operation. Be sure it includes listings of relevant terms from the accounting equation. See if you can estimate anticipated data for each element in the balance sheet.

15. Consider the sources for start-up funds you will need to finance your business. What financial ratios (ratio analysis), if any, are likely to be of interest to lending institutions, personal investors (including yourselves), or other providers of funds? Explain why ratio analysis will be of interest to them, or why it will not be of interest.

team exercise

AN AMERICAN LEGEND

Ford Motor Company is an iconic American company that has faced many challenges. For this exercise, you and your team need to find the company's most recent financial statements, including the income statement and balance sheet. There are many sources of this data, but one quick source is finance.yahoo.com. If you enter the company's ticket symbol, F, you will find a report on the company's stock price as well as other information. At the bottom of the document list on the left, you will see the company's financial statements. You may wish to print a copy of the income statement and balance sheet for each of your team members.

QUESTIONS FOR DISCUSSION

16. Looking at Ford's income statement, what has been the trend in sales (total revenue) as well as net income over the past three years?

17. As you have learned, gross profit is the difference between sales (or total revenues) and cost of sales (or cost of revenues). Gross profit percentage is calculated by dividing gross profit by sales (or total revenues). What is Ford's gross profit percentage for the last three years? What does this data tell you about Ford's pricing strategy and costs?

18. Looking at the balance sheet, what is Ford's current ratio for the three most recent years? What is the significance of these numbers?

19. How could a managerial accountant help Ford to improve its profitability?

exercising your ethics

GIVE AND TAKE WITH ACCOUNTING CLIENTS

The Situation

CPAs provide valuable services for their clients, both businesses and individuals. Although it's important to make clients happy, accountants have additional considerations when preparing financial statements and tax returns.

The Dilemma

Aaron Ault is the owner of a small contracting business. In late January 2016, he delivered original expense and income records so that his CPA, Katrina Belinski, could prepare 2015 financial statements and tax returns for Ault's small business firm.

Several weeks later, Katrina delivered the completed financial statements and tax return to Ault. Aaron was pleased with the financial statements but realized that he was going to owe a lot of money in taxes. His business is just recovering from tough times during the recession and he can't afford to pay such a large tax bill. One particularly large job was completed at the end of the year, and Ault has decided that he'd like to record this during the current year. This would result in a much lower taxable income for 2015. However, Ault is disappointed with Belinski, who tells him that she's not able to make this change. Now he's threatening to take his business elsewhere. Belinski is torn because Ault has been a long-time client and she doesn't want to lose his business.

QUESTIONS TO ADDRESS

20. What are the ethical issues in this situation?

21. What are the basic arguments for and against Aaron Ault's position in this situation? For and against Katrina Belinski's position?

22. What do you think that Ault and Belinski should do in this situation?

cases

CSI: Wall Street

At the beginning of this chapter, you read about CFEs and their role in fighting various kinds of fraudulent accounting practices, especially during troubled economic times. Also discussed were examples of fraud by the public at large, along with the resulting financial losses to U.S. businesses. Using the information presented in this chapter, you should now be able to answer the following questions.

QUESTIONS FOR DISCUSSION

23. What factors do you think are most important in choosing among various methods to protect against fraud in a firm?

24. Suppose you are hoping for a career as a CFE. How do recent trends in fraud provide new opportunities for such a career?

25. An external auditor, such as a CPA firm's accountant, may suspect some irregularities in a client firm's accounting practices. In what ways might a CFE be of assistance?

26. Consider the anti-fraud training for a company's employees. Which four (or more) topics should be included in that training?

27. What ethical issues, if any, are involved in a decision to investigate a suspected case of fraud in a firm's accounting activities?

Future Directions for the Modern Accountant

In the future, while an accountant's knowledge of business aided by analytical and technical skills will be essential, a wider skillset will be necessary to meet market demands in this changing profession. The traditional accountant's role was centered on analyzing historical financial data, creating financial statements, and providing interpretations of financial data and documents to facilitate business decisions. The expectations for the modern CPAs, increasingly, call for the more intimate role of leadership in demonstrating financial implications for many additional facets of the business, including its overall operations, strategy, data management, human resources, and technical resources. In consulting roles, accountants are being asked for guidance on broad issues, including business development, evaluating strategic opportunities, assessments of risks and threats, and strategies for using massive databases to identify promising directions for developing new products, improving customer service, and evaluating new lines of business to gain competitive advantage. Beyond just technical expertise, these kinds of participation require thorough knowledge of the client's business and the markets in which they operate.

The following trends have emerged and are contributing to the additional roles of the modern accountant:

- **Fewer restrictions from physical and geographic boundaries**—With increasing globalization, many foreign-based firms are interacting with firms based elsewhere around the world. Coupled with modern technology, accountants and clients in other countries are working together remotely. An accountant based at a company office, or at an office-in-the-home, in Omaha, Nebraska, can provide services to a client located in Singapore.

- **Social media have changed relationships and the way business is conducted**—Modern accountants establish professional relationships through active participation through social media. No longer do CPAs rely on face-to-face interactions at occasional professional meetings. Social media such as LinkedIn provide platforms for at-your-fingertips remote interactions allowing exchanges of information, professional advice, and temporary collaborations among accountants to serve clients in need of particular skill sets. New business opportunities arise, too, when accountants use a social networking presence to establish their business reputations.

- **Effectiveness as a communicator is a must for the accountant**—Communication skills are vital in the modern accountant's role in advising clients on global business trends and strategic perspectives. The accountant's thorough knowledge, to be leveraged into meaningful advice, must be communicated to clients on time, clearly and convincingly, both verbally and in writing. Effectiveness can be critical in a variety of communications contexts, ranging from formal presentations, to ad hoc interactive group meetings, to one-to-one informal conversations, either face to face or remotely.

- **Project management in the accountant's expanded role**—Serving as project manager is becoming commonplace for accountants because they provide guidance on the client's strategy, overall operations, and business development. These broad-based issues typically involve large-scale teams of specialists requiring long-term participation in activities such as financial forecasting, product and process engineering, financial interpretations, cost estimation, and human resources analysis. Success depends on the project manager's ability to decompose the project into manageable tasks, gain acceptance of task assignments, encourage timely reporting by task groups, and merge the project's many steps into coherent conclusions.

It is evident, then, that tomorrow's accountants need to be prepared with more than just traditional skills. They need to know the nature of the client's business and its competitive environment so that they can assist the client in gaining greater competitive advantage.[32]

QUESTIONS FOR DISCUSSION

28. In what ways, if any, does the discussion in this case apply to managerial accountants rather than to CPAs? Explain your response.

29. In what ways, if any, does the discussion in this case apply to forensic accountants rather than to CPAs? Explain your response.

30. Consider the restrictions on CPA services by provisions of the Sarbanes-Oxley Act (Sarbox). In what ways, if any, does this case's description of the modern accountant's activities conflict with Sarbox? Explain your response.

31. Ethics has a long-standing role in the accounting profession. Will the emerging role of the modern accountant bring with it a greater emphasis on ethics (as compared with traditional accounting)? Explain.

crafting a business plan

MANAGING INFORMATION

Goal of the Exercise

A business plan asks you to think about your business in terms of *information technology needs* and *costs*.

Exercise Background

This part of the business plan asks you to assess how you will use technology to improve your business. Will you, for example, use a database to keep track of your customers? How will you protect your business from hackers and other IT security risks?

This part of the business plan also asks you to consider the costs of doing business, such as salaries, rent, and utilities. You'll also be asked to complete the following financial statements:

- **Balance Sheet**—The balance sheet is a foundation for financial reporting. This report identifies the valued items of the business (its *assets*) as well as the debts that it owes (its *liabilities*). This information gives the owner and potential investors a "snapshot" into the health of the business.
- **Income Statement (or Profit-and-Loss Statement)**—This is the focus of the financial plan. This document will show you what it takes to be profitable and successful as a business owner for your first year.

Your Assignment

For the purposes of this assignment, you need to answer the following questions:

32. What kinds of IT resources will your business require?

Hint: Think about the employees in your business and what they will need to do their jobs. What computer hardware and software will they need? Will your business need a network and an Internet connection? What type of network?

33. How will you use IT to keep track of your customers and potential customers?

Hint: Many businesses—even small businesses—use databases to keep track of their customers. Will your business require a database? What about other information systems?

34. What are the *costs* of doing business? Equipment, supplies, salaries, rent, utilities, and insurance are just some of these expenses. Estimate what it will cost to do business for one year.

Hint: Try your best to include accurate costs for the expenses you think will be a part of doing business.

35. How much will you charge for your product? How many products do you believe that you can sell in one year (or how many customers do you think your business can attract)? Multiply the price that you will charge by the number of products that you hope to sell or the amount you hope each customer will spend. This will give you an estimate of your *revenues* for one year.

Hint: Be as realistic as you can.

36. Create a balance sheet and an income statement (profit-and-loss statement) for your business.

MyBizLab

Go to the Assignments section of your MyLab to complete these writing exercises.

37. The stakeholders of every business—employees, managers, owners, governments, the public—want information about the firm's financial health. Accordingly, companies maintain three basic financial statements reflecting that firm's activity and financial condition. (a) What are those three statements and what information do they contain? (b) In addition, discuss the kinds of accounting specialists that participate, and those that may not participate, in preparing those statements.

38. Suppose that you are a loan officer at a bank. A small, but growing company has approached your bank about obtaining a loan and has brought copies of three years of financial statements. How would you evaluate the information contained in each financial statement? What ratios would you use and why?

end notes

[1] Lison, Joseph, Sukumar, C. R., and Raghu, K. "Ramalinga Raju Admits to Accounting Fraud, Resigns," *livemint .com*, January 31, 2012, at http://www.livemint.com/Companies/ldmclvNdW3Z6dNayVfZSPI/Ramalinga-Raju-admits-to-accounting-fraud-resigns.html; Piore, Adam. "Fraud Scene Investigator," *Portfolio*, March 10, 2008, at http://www.portfolio.com/careers/job-of-the-week/2008/03/10/Forensic-Accountant-Al-Vondra; Vondra, Albert A. *LinkedIn*, December 12, 2012, at www .linkedin.com/pub/albert-a-vondra/1a/57b/459, accessed on February 14, 2013; Goyal, Kartik, and Sharma, Subramanian. "India Orders Fraud Office Probe into Satyam Computer Accounts," *Bloomberg.com*, January 13, 2009, at http://www.bloomberg.com/apps/news?pid=20601091&refer=india&sid=ayhBmRJs7nh0

[2] Smith, Adam. "The Reasons Fraud Spikes in a Recession," *Time*, May 20, 2009, at http://www.time.com/time/business/article/0,8599,1899798,00.html; "Recession-Proof Career: Forensic Accounting and IT Auditing Financial Fraud Increases in Economic Recessions," *UAB Media Relations*, November 6, 2008, at http://main.uab.edu/Sites/MediaRelations/articles/54133/. See https://www.uab .edu/newsarchive/54133-recession-proof-career-forensic-accounting-and-it-auditing-financial-fraud-increases-in-economic-recessions; Kenyon, Will. "Five Tips for Combating Fraud in the Recession," *Finance Week*, March 23, 2009, at http://www.financeweek.co.uk/risk/five-tips-combating-fraud-recession; "2012 Report to the Nations," *Association of Certified Fraud Examiners*, ACFE, Austin, Texas, 2012, accessed at http://www.acfe.com/rttn-Highlights.aspx; "U.S. Securities and Exchange Commission Annual Report on the Dodd-Frank Whistleblower Program, Fiscal Year 2012," at http://www.sec.gov/about/offices/owb/annual-report-2012.pdf. All accessed on May 11, 2015.

[3] Schreiber, Russ. "Fighting Fraud: Predictive Analytics & Business Rules Make a Powerful Combination," *Insurance & Technology*, March 19, 2012, at http://www .insurancetech.com/security/fighting-fraud-predictive-analytics-bus/232602826; Stech, Katy. "Fighting Fraud: Link Between Bogus Insurance Claims, Recession is Murky," *The Post and Courier*, August 9, 2010, at http://www.postandcourier.com/news/2010/aug/09/fighting-fraud/; Southerland, Randy. "Recession Pressures May Boost Employee Fraud," *Atlanta Business Chronicle*, August 19, 2010, at http://www.bizjournals.com/atlanta/stories/2010/08/23/focus9.html; "Fraud to Thrive Beyond the Economic Downturn," *Lloyd's*, January 18, 2010, at http://www.lloyds.com/News-and-Insight/News-and-Features/Business-Risk/Business-2010/Fraud_to_thrive_beyond_the_economic_downturn. All accessed on May 11, 2015.

[4] "2012 Report to the Nations," *Association of Certified Fraud Examiners*, ACFE, Austin, Texas, 2012, accessed at http://www.acfe.com/rttn.aspx. Accessed on May 11, 2015.

[5] "Examples of Corporate Fraud Investigations—Fiscal Year 2010," *IRS.gov*, at http://www.irs.gov/compliance/enforcement/article/0,,id=213768,00.html; "Examples of Corporate Fraud Investigations—Fiscal Year 2012," IRS.gov, all accessed on May 11, 2015; http://www.irs.gov/uac/Examples-of-Corporate-Fraud-Investigations-Fiscal-Year-2012

[6] See Marshall B. Romney and Paul John Steinbart, *Accounting Information Systems*, 13th ed. (Upper Saddle River, NJ: Prentice Hall, 2015), Chapter 1.

[7] See Anthony A. Atkinson, Robert S. Kaplan, Ella Mae Matsumura, and S. Mark Young, *Management Accounting*, 5th ed. (Upper Saddle River, NJ: Prentice Hall, 2007), Chapter 1.

[8] See Walter T. Harrison and Charles T. Horngren, *Financial Accounting and Financial Tips*, 7th ed. (Upper Saddle River, NJ: Prentice Hall, 2007), Chapter 1.

[9] "Public Accounting Tips," *LifeTips.com*, at http://account-ingjobs.lifetips.com/cat/64430/public-accounting/index.html, accessed on September 13, 2010; "Business Glossary," *AllBusiness.com*, at http://www.allbusiness.com/glossaries/review/4954577-1.html, accessed on March 20, 2011.

[10]Cohn, Michael. "Big Four Firms Saw Big Revenue Increase in 2012," *accountingTODAY for the WebCPA*," January 10, 2013, at http://www.accountingtoday.com/news/Big-Four-Firms-Saw-Big-Revenue-Increase-2012-65309-1.html. All accessed on May 11, 2015.

[11]See Alvin A. Arens, Randal J. Elder, and Mark S. Beasley, *Auditing and Assurance Services: An Integrated Approach*, 13th ed. (Upper Saddle River, NJ: Prentice Hall, 2010), Chapter 1.

[12]See Meg Pollard, Sherry T. Mills, and Walter T. Harrison, *Financial and Managerial Accounting* Ch. 1–14 (Upper Saddle River, NJ: Prentice Hall, 2008), Chapter 1.

[13]"2012 Talent Shortage Survey," *ManpowerGroup*, at http://www.manpowergroup.us/campaigns/talent-shortage-2012/, accessed February 11, 2013.

[14]"The CPA Vision Project and Beyond," *The American Institute of Certified Public Accountants*, at http://www.aicpa.org/RESEARCH/CPAHORIZONS2025/CPAVISIONPROJECT/Pages/CPAVisionProject.aspx, accessed on February 11, 2013.

[15]Crumbley, D. Larry, Heitger, Lester E., and Smith, G. Stevenson. *Forensic and Investigative Accounting*, 5th ed. (Chicago: CCH, 2011), Chapter 1.

[16]Gordon, Marcy. "Computer Sciences paying $190M to settle SEC fraud charges." *Yahoo Finance*, June 5, 2015. Accessed June 16, 2015. http://finance.yahoo.com/news/computer-sciences-paying-190m-settle-150213031.html: "SEC Charges CSC and Former Executives With Accounting Fraud." sec.gov. Last modified June 5, 2015. Accessed June 16, 2015. http://www.sec.gov/news/pressrelease/2015-111.html

[17]Rapoport, Michael. "Eyebrows Go Up as Auditors Branch Out," *Wall Street Journal*, December 7, 2012, pages C1, C2.

[18]"Executive Summary of the Sarbanes-Oxley Act of 2002 P.L. 107–204," Conference of State Bank Supervisors, at http://www.csbs.org/legislative/leg-updates/Documents/ExecSummary-SarbanesOxley-2002.pdf; "Sarbanes-Oxley Executive Summary," *Securities Law Update* (Orrick, Herrington & Sutcliffe LLP), August 2002, at http://www.orrick.com/fileupload/144.pdf. All accessed on May 11, 2015.

[19]"Consolidated Balance Sheets," *United States Securities Exchange Commission*, at http://www.sec.gov/Archives/edgar/data/1288776/000119312513028362/d452134d10k.htm#tx452134_23, accessed on May 10, 2015.

[20]"Borders Files for Bankruptcy, to Close 200 Stores," *Reuters*, February 16, 2011 at http://www.reuters.com/article/2011/02/17/us-borders-idUSTRE71F2P220110217

[21]King, Bill. "New Accounting Rules Put City's Net Assets at Risk," *Houston Chronicle*, February 15, 2013, at http://www.google.com/#hl=en&gs_rn=12&gs_ri=psy-ab&cp=50&gs_id=7&xhr=t&q=New+Accounting+Rules+Put+City%E2%80%99s+net+Assets+at+Risk&es_nrs=true&pf=p&output=search&sclient=psy-ab&oq=New+Accounting+Rules+Put+City%E2%80%99s+net+Assets+at+Risk&gs_l=&pbx=1&bav=on.2,or.r_qf.&bvm=bv.46471029,d.dmg&fp=ad0f34889e457013&biw=1242&bih=830; Rick Moran, "New Accounting Rules to Expose Pension Funding Gaps," *American Thinker*, August 17, 2012, at http://www.americanthinker.com/blog/2012/08/new_accounting_rules_to_expose_

pension_funding_gaps.html; Sauter, Michael B., Hess, Alexander E. M., and Weigley, Samuel. "Nine States with Sinking Pensions," *Yahoo Finance*, November 8, 2012, at http://finance.yahoo.com/news/nine-states-with-sinking-pensions.html?page=all; Quintero, James. "New GASB Rules Set to Burst the Bubble on Pensions," *TexasPolicy.com*, December 6, 2012, at http://www.texaspolicy.com/center/fiscal-policy/blog/new-gasb-rules-set-burst-bubble-pensions; "GASB Improves Pension Accounting and Financial Reporting Standards," *GASB (News Release)*, June 25, 2012, at http://www.gasb.org/cs/ContentServer?pagename=GASB/GASBContent_C/GASBNewsPage&cid=1176160126951. All accessed on May 11, 2015.

[22]Cantoria, Ciel S., Edited by Linda Richter, "Unraveling the Details of 10 High-Profile Accounting Scandals," *Bright Hub*, December 30, 2010, at http://www.brighthub.com/office/finance/articles/101200.aspx; "The Biggest Accounting Scandals of All Time (Photos)," *Huffington Post*, May 17, 2010 at http://www.huffingtonpost.com/2010/03/17/biggest-accounting-scanda_n_502181.html#s74418&title=Madoff_Scandal_; "The Corporate Scandal Sheet," *Citizen Works* (August 2004), at http://www.citizenworks.org/enron/corp-scandal.php; "Largest Health Care Fraud Case in U.S. History Settled," *Department of Justice* (June 26, 2003), at http://www.usdoj.gov/opa/pr/2003/June/03_civ_386.htm; "Kozlowski Is Found Guilty," *TheStreet.com*, June 17, 2005, at http://www.thestreet.com/story/10228619/1/kozlowski-is-found-guilty.html. All accessed on May 11, 2015.

[23]Internal Revenue Service, United States Department of the Treasury. "Examples of Abusive Return Preparer Investigations - Fiscal Year 2015." www.irs.gov. Last modified June 10, 2015. http://www.irs.gov/uac/Examples-of-Abusive-Return-Preparer-Investigations-Fiscal-Year-2015.

[24]"IASB and FASB Propose a New Joint Standard for Revenue Recognition," *Financial Accounting Standards Board*, June 24, 2010, at http://www.fasb.org/cs/ContentServer?c=FASBContent_C&pagename=FASB%2FFASBContent_C%2FNewsPage&cid=1176156953088

[25]"IFRS Overview," *NYSSCPA.ORG*, at http://www.nysscpa.org/ifrs/overview.htm, accessed on March 10, 2011.

[26]"IASB and FASB Propose to Align Balance Sheet Netting Requirements Differences in IFRS and US GAAP Offsetting Requirements to be Eliminated," *FASB: Financial Accounting Standards Board*," (news release) January 28, 2011, at http://www.fasb.org/cs/ContentServer?c=FASBContent_C&pagename=FASB/FASBContent_C/NewsPage&cid=1176158186333. All accessed on May 11, 2015.

[27]Briginshaw, John. "What Will the International Financial Reporting Standards (IFRS) Mean to Businesses and Investors?" *Graziadio Business Review*, 2008, Volume 11, Issue 4, at http://gbr.pepperdine.edu/2010/08/what-will-the-international-financial-reporting-standards-ifrs-mean-to-businesses-and-investors/

[28]"IASB and FASB Propose a New Joint Standard for Revenue Recognition," *Financial Accounting Standards Board*, June 24, 2010, at http://www.fasb.org/cs/ContentServer?c=FASBContent_C&pagename=FASB%2FFASBContent_C%2FNewsPage&cid=1176156953088

[29]"IASB and FASB Propose Common Solution for Impairment Accounting," *FASB: Financial Accounting Standards Board*," (news release) January 31, 2011, at http://www.fasb .org/cs/ContentServer?c=FASBContent_C&pagename= FASB/FASBContent_C/NewsPage&cid=1176158192211

[30]"FASB, IASB Propose Changes in Fair Value Standards," *Insurance Networking News*, June 29, 2010, at http:// www.insurancenetworking.com/news/insurance_fair_ value_standards_accounting_IASB_FASB_GAAP_IFRS- 25136-1.html; "Measurement Uncertainty Analysis Disclosure for Fair Value Measurements," *International Accounting Standards Board*, June 2010, at http://www .iasb.org/NR/rdonlyres/07855A41-D0A9-4197-ADF9- 15A1088E466A/0/EDMeasurementUncertainty Analysis0610.pdf. All accessed on May 11, 2015.

[31]Defelice, Alexandra, and Lamoreaux, Matthew G. "No IFRS Requirement Until 2015 or Later Under New SEC Timeline," *Journal of Accountancy*, February 24, 2010, at http://www.journalofaccountancy.com/Web/20102656 .htm; Rapoport, Michael. "Delay Seen (Again) for New Rules on Accounting," *Wall Street Journal*, July 6, 2012, pp. C1, C2; Rapoport, Michael. "Accounting Panel Expresses 'Regret' Over U.S. Stance," *Wall Street Journal*, July 16, 2012, p. C5; Gastecki, Shane. "CPA Candidates Are Confronted by Significant Changes to Exam," *accounting WEB*, June 14, 2011, at http://www.accountingweb.com/ topic/education-careers/cpa-candidates-are-confronted- significant-changes-exam, accessed on February 18, 2013.

[32]Tokc-Wilde, Iwona. "#AAYP 2013: Modern Accountants— People Who Think Differently," *AccountancyAge*, May 1, 2013, at http://www.accountancyage.com/aa/feature/ 2265153/-aayp-2013-modern-accountants-people- who-think-differently; "Intuit 2020 Report Depicts Future of the Accounting Profession: A New Mindset and Model Required to Thrive in a Connected World," *Intuit Inc.*, February 2, 2011, at http://about.intuit.com/ about_intuit/press_room/press_release/articles/2011/ Intuit2020ReportDepictsFuture.html; Walker, Rich. "Intuit 2020 Report Depicts Future of the Accounting Profession," *Intuit Accountants News Central*, February 2, 2011, at https://blog.accountants.intuit.com/intuit- news/intuit%C2%AE-2020-report-depicts-future-of-the- accounting-profession/; "Accountants—the Old and the New," *CA Saga*, August 15, 2012, at http://contract accountants.wordpress.com/2012/08/15/accountants- the-old-and-the-new/; "The Many Hats of a Modern Accountant," *Jobs.net*, May 14, 2013, at http://www .jobs.net/Article/CB-6-Talent-Network-Finance-Ins-The- Many-Hats-of-a-Modern-Accountant/

glossary

Accounting (or accountancy) comprehensive system for collecting, analyzing, and communicating financial information.

Accounting Equation Assets = Liabilities + Owner's Equity; used by accountants to balance data for the firm's financial transactions at various points in the year.

Accounting Information System (AIS) organized procedure for identifying, measuring, recording, and retaining financial information for use in accounting statements and management reports.

Accounts Payable (Payables) current liability consisting of bills owed to suppliers, plus wages and taxes due within the coming year.

Activity Ratio financial ratio for evaluating management's efficiency in using a firm's assets.

Asset any economic resource expected to benefit a firm or an individual who owns it.

Audit systematic examination of a company's accounting system to determine whether its financial reports reliably represent its operations.

Balance Sheet financial statement that supplies detailed information about a firm's assets, liabilities, and owner's equity.

Bookkeeping recording of accounting transactions.

Budget detailed statement of estimated receipts and expenditures for a future period of time.

Certified Fraud Examiner (CFE) professional designation administered by the ACFE in recognition of qualifications for a specialty area within forensic accounting.

Certified Management Accountant (CMA) professional designation awarded by the Institute of Management Accountants (IMA) in recognition of management accounting qualifications.

Certified Public Accountant (CPA) accountant licensed by the state and offering services to the public.

Code of Professional Conduct code of ethics for CPAs as maintained and enforced by the AICPA.

Controller person who manages all of a firm's accounting activities (chief accounting officer).

Core Competencies for Accounting the combination of skills, technology, and knowledge that will be necessary for the future CPA.

Cost of Goods Sold costs of obtaining materials for making the products sold by a firm during the year.

Cost of Revenues costs that a company incurs to obtain revenues from other companies.

Current Asset asset that can or will be converted into cash within a year.

Current Liability debt that must be paid within one year.

Current Ratio financial ratio for measuring a company's ability to pay current debts out of current assets.

Debt company's total liabilities.

Depreciation accounting method for distributing the cost of an asset over its useful life.

Earnings Per Share profitability ratio measuring the net profit that the company earns for each share of outstanding stock.

Financial Accounting field of accounting concerned with external users of a company's financial information.

Financial Statement any of several types of reports summarizing a company's financial status to stakeholders and to aid in managerial decision making.

Fixed Asset asset with long-term use or value, such as land, buildings, and equipment.

Forensic Accounting the practice of accounting for legal purposes.

Full Disclosure guideline that financial statements should not include just numbers but should also furnish management's interpretations and explanations of those numbers.

Generally Accepted Accounting Principles (GAAP) accounting guidelines that govern the content and form of financial reports.

Goodwill amount paid for an existing business above the value of its other assets.

Gross Profit preliminary, quick-to-calculate profit figure calculated from the firm's revenues minus its cost of revenues (the direct costs of getting the revenues).

Income Statement (Profit-and-Loss Statement) financial statement listing a firm's annual revenues and expenses so that a bottom line shows annual profit or loss.

Intangible Asset nonphysical asset, such as a patent or trademark, that has economic value in the form of expected benefit.

International Accounting Standards Board (IASB) organization responsible for developing a set of global accounting standards and for gaining implementation of those standards.

Leverage ability to finance an investment through borrowed funds.

Liability debt owed by a firm to an outside organization or individual.

Liquidity ease with which an asset can be converted into cash.

Long-Term Liability debt that is not due for at least one year.

Management Accountant private accountant who provides financial services to support managers in various business activities within a firm.

Management Advisory Services assistance provided by CPA firms in areas such as financial planning, information systems design, and other areas of concern for client firms.

Managerial (Management) Accounting field of accounting that serves internal users of a company's financial information.

Net Income (Net Profit or Net Earnings) gross profit minus operating expenses and income taxes.

Operating Expenses costs, other than the cost of revenues, incurred in producing a good or service.

Operating Income gross profit minus operating expenses.

Owner's equity amount of money that owners would receive if they sold all of a firm's assets and paid all of its liabilities.

Paid-In Capital money that is invested in a company by its owners.

Private Accountant salaried accountant hired by a business to carry out its day-to-day financial activities.

Profitability Ratio financial ratio for measuring a firm's potential earnings.

Retained Earnings earnings retained by a firm for its use rather than paid out as dividends.

Revenue Recognition formal recording and reporting of revenues at the appropriate time.

Revenues funds that flow into a business from the sale of goods or services.

Sarbanes-Oxley Act of 2002 (Sarbox or SOX) enactment of federal regulations to restore public trust in accounting practices by imposing new requirements on financial activities in publicly traded corporations.

Short-Term Solvency Ratio financial ratio for measuring a company's ability to pay immediate debts.

Solvency Ratio financial ratio, either short or long term, for estimating the borrower's ability to repay debt.

Statement of Cash Flows financial statement describing a firm's yearly cash receipts and cash payments.

Tax Services assistance provided by CPAs for tax preparation and tax planning.

Managing Business Finances

From Chapter 17 of *Business Essentials*, Eleventh Edition. Ronald J. Ebert, Ricky W. Griffin. Copyright © 2017 by Pearson Education, Inc.
All rights reserved.

Are you lucky enough to make it in the business world? What if luck has nothing to

do with it? How

many wealth-seekers actually find what

they want, and

what are their secrets?

After reading this chapter, you should be able to:

1   **Explain** the concept of the time value of money and the principle of compound growth, and discuss the characteristics of common stock.

2   **Identify** reasons for investing and the investment opportunities offered by mutual funds and exchange-traded funds.

3   **Describe** the role of securities markets and identify the major stock exchanges and stock markets.

4   **Describe** the risk–return relationship and discuss the use of diversification and asset allocation for investments.

5   **Describe** the various ways that firms raise capital and identify the pros and cons of each method.

6   **Identify** the reasons a company might make an initial public offering of its stock, explain how stock value is determined, and discuss the significance of market capitalization.

7   **Explain** how securities markets are regulated.

An Appetite for
Beef

Perhaps you've visited a Fogo de Chao restaurant—the company has 26 locations in the United States, one in Mexico, and ten in Brazil. Fogo de Chao is a Brazilian-style steakhouse or churrascaria, serving a variety of fire-roasted meats, carved at the table by gaucho chefs who have been trained in this southern Brazilian cooking style. Certainly, the roaming chefs serving custom cuts of meat is part of the charm of a Fogo de Chao visit, but it's also part of a unique delivery model that allows the restaurant to control costs by reducing the number of waitstaff required. To complement the assortment of meats, diners can visit the extensive buffet, which includes self-service salads, side dishes, and desserts.

This high-end restaurant, which competes head-to-head with Ruth's Chris and Capital Grill, has humble beginnings. In 1981, two sets of brothers, Jair and Arri Coser and Jorge and Aleixo Ongaratto, opened a churrascaria in a shed with a grass roof in Porto Alegre, Brazil.

The restaurant had a rustic flair, as is suggested in the name Fogo de Chao (for *fire on the ground*). Over the next six years, the company prospered and two additional locations were opened in Sao Paulo. But, a chance encounter with a former president, George H. W. Bush, launched their expansion into the United States. Dining at one of the Sao Paulo locations in 1995, the former president was so delighted with the food and service that he suggested the brothers expand their operations to the United States. Two weeks later, Jair and Jorge were headed to Texas. "I think about why I came to the United States all the time," says Jair Coser. "I cannot explain it. I had a good life at that time in Brazil. I have my house. I have my family. I have my business. And it was, 'Let's go.'"

Over the next 20 years, the restaurant chain grew, but there were changes in management and ownership. In 2005, the Ongaratto brothers sold their interests in the company to the Cosers, who became equal coowners. To allow for continued expansion, the Cosers brought in GP Investments, one of the largest investment funds in Brazil, the following year, but maintained a controlling interest. Although the recession took a big cut out of their business, by 2011, there were 16 U.S. restaurants and seven locations in Brazil. In 2012, the Coser brothers decided to liquidate their investments, reportedly selling the company for $426 million to Thomas H. Lee Partners L. P.

The new ownership team successfully continued the expansion of the restaurant chain, retaining many of the upper-level managers and bringing in new talent and expertise to shore up accounting and management practices. In order to repay some of the debt associated with the acquisition and to fund additional expansion, the company made an initial public offering of stock in 2015. While

Duckman76/Fotolia

what's in it for me?

Businesses from all over the world, representing every industry, converge in global financial markets every day, seeking funds that can be used to finance their activities and pay off their debts. Individual investors gather as well, in person or—more often—online, looking to make their money "work" for them by profitably trading commodities, stocks, and bonds. The history of Fogo de Chao illustrates each of these very points. This chapter will help you understand the various ways this is possible, whether your goals are short or long term, whether you are motivated by the desire for profit or security, or simply because you enjoy the challenges inherent in the successful raising and investing of capital.

Thomas H. Lee Partners have retained 80 percent ownership, the company's IPO in June 2015 brought in over $100,000,000. With this infusion of cash, the company will pay down some of the debt as well as expand. They have a goal of eventually operating more than 100 restaurants in both medium- and large-sized markets. The company notes in their registration statement with the Securities and Exchange Commission that they don't plan to pay dividends at any time in the foreseeable future, but will plow all earnings into maintaining and growing the business. As you can see, careful management of debt as well as the use of equity financing have allowed Fogo de Chao to expand from its operation in a shed with a grass roof to a successful international chain of high-end restaurants.[1] (After studying the content in this chapter, you should be able to answer a set of discussion questions found at the end of the chapter.)

OBJECTIVE 1
Explain
the concept of the time value of money and the principle of compound growth, and discuss the characteristics of common stock.

Maximizing Capital Growth

Wise investments are the key to growing your money, especially if you are seeking to accumulate capital to start your own business or simply as a cushion for a sound financial future. In searching for investment opportunities, a number of concepts come into play for evaluating alternative investments and sorting out the good from the bad.

The Time Value of Money and Compound Growth

The most-proven "road to wealth" lies in a strategy of saving and investing over a period of years. Only rarely does a "one-in-a-million" opportunity provide a quick fortune. Although the popular "I want it all, and I want it now!" mentality sounds good, it becomes a reality for very few wealth-seekers.

Time Value of Money *principle that invested money grows, over time, by earning interest or some other form of return*

Compound Growth *compounding of interest over time—with each additional time period, interest returns accumulate and earn more interest*

The **time value of money**, perhaps the single most important concept in business finance, recognizes the basic fact that, when it's invested over time, money grows by earning interest or yielding some other form of return. Time value stems from the principle of **compound growth**, the cumulative growth from interest paid to the investor over given time periods. With each additional time period, an investment grows as interest payments accumulate and earn more interest, thus multiplying the earning capacity of the investment.

The Rule of 72 We can better appreciate the concept of the "time value of money" with a practical example: How long does it take to double an investment? A handy rule of thumb is called the "Rule of 72." You can find the number of years needed to double your money by dividing the annual interest rate (in percent) into 72. If, for example, you reinvest annually at 8 percent, you'll double your money in about 9 years:

$$\frac{72}{8} = 9 \text{ years to double the money}$$

By the same reasoning, if you reinvest annually at 4 percent, your money will double in about 18 years.

The Rule of 72 can also calculate how much interest you must get if you want to double your money in a given number of years: Simply divide 72 by the desired number of years. If you want to double your money in 10 years, you need to get 7.2 percent:

$$\frac{72}{10} = 7.2 \text{ percent interest needed to double the money}$$

The lesson for the investor is clear: seek *higher* interest rates because money will double more frequently.

Making Better Use of Your Time Value What if you invested $10,000 at 7 percent interest for one year? You would earn $700 on your $10,000 investment. If you reinvested the principal amount plus the interest you earned during the first year, and reinvested interest annually for another four years, you'd end up with $14,025. Now, if you were planning for retirement and reinvested that money at the same interest rate for another 25 years, you could retire with $76,122—almost eight times the amount you started with!

Figure 1 illustrates how the returns from an initial investment of $10,000 accumulate substantially over longer periods of time. Notice that the gains for the last 10 years are much greater than for the first 10 years, illustrating the power of compound growth. Each year, the interest rate is applied to a larger sum. Notice also the larger gains from higher interest rates. Even a seemingly small increase in interest rates, from 7 to 8 percent, results in much larger accumulations.

As you can see from Figure 1, the best way to take advantage of the time value of money is to obtain a high rate of return on your investment. However, various kinds of investments offer opportunities for fulfilling different financial objectives, such as aggressive growth, financial safety, and others, which we discuss later.

Common Stock Investments

History has shown that one way to achieve a high rate of return, compared with many other ways, is to invest in the stock market. Consider the average rate of return on the U.S. stock market, as of the beginning of 2012. The 100-year average (1912–2012) was more than 9 percent annually, and the most recent 25-year average return was more than 11.29 percent.[2] A **stock** is a portion of the ownership of a corporation. The company's total ownership is divided into small parts called *shares* that can be bought and sold to determine how much of the company (how many shares of stock) is owned by each shareholder. This widespread ownership has become possible because of the availability of different types of stocks and because markets have been established that enable individuals to conveniently buy and sell them.

Stock *portion of ownership of a corporation*

Although several types of stock exist, common stock is the most prominent. A share of **common stock** is the most basic form of ownership in a company. Individuals and other companies purchase a firm's common stock in the hope that it will increase in value and provide dividend income; in addition, each common share has a vote on major issues that are brought before the shareholders.

Common Stock *most basic form of ownership, including voting rights on major issues, in a company*

Stock values are usually expressed in two different ways: as (1) *market value* and (2) *book value*.

1   A stock's real value is its **market value**, the current price of a share in the stock market. Market value reflects the amount that buyers are willing to pay for a share of the company's stock.

Market Value *current price of a share of stock in the stock market*

2   The **book value** for a share of common stock is determined as the firm's owners' equity (from the balance sheet) divided by the number of common shares owned by all shareholders. Book value is used as a comparison indicator because the

Book Value *value of a common stock expressed as the firm's owners' equity divided by the number of common shares*

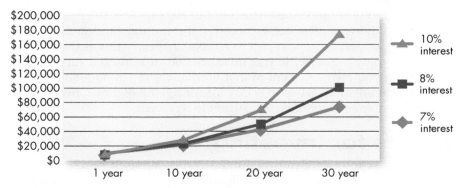

FIGURE 1 Amount to Which an Initial $10,000 Investment Grows

market value for successful companies is usually greater than its book value. Thus, when market price falls to near book value, some profit-seeking investors buy the stock on the principle that it is underpriced and will increase in the future.

Investment Traits of Common Stock Common stocks are among the riskiest of all investments. Uncertainties about the stock market itself can quickly change a given stock's value. Furthermore, when companies have unprofitable years, or when economic conditions go sour, they often cannot pay dividends, and potential investors become wary of future stock values, so share price drops. U.S. stocks, for example, lost more than half their value in the recession years 2008 and early 2009. On the positive side, however, common stocks offer high growth potential; when a company's performance brightens, because of public acceptance of a hot new product, for example, share price can sharply increase. Historically, stock values generally rise with the passage of time. By mid-2013, most U.S. common stocks had recovered the values they lost in 2008–09, and many had moved on to new record levels.

Dividends A **dividend** is a payment to shareholders, on a per-share basis, from the company's earnings. Dividend payments are optional and variable; the corporation's board of directors decides whether and when a dividend will be paid, as well as the amount that is best for the future of the company and its shareholders. Many companies distribute between 30 and 70 percent of their profits to shareholders. The so-called **blue-chip stocks**, those issued by the strongest, well-established, financially sound and respected firms, such as Coca-Cola and ExxonMobil, have historically provided investors steady income through consistent dividend payouts. However, some firms, especially fast-growing companies, do not pay dividends. Instead, they use cash earnings for expanding the company so that future earnings can grow even faster. What's more, any company can have a bad year and decide to reduce or omit dividend payments to stockholders.

We see, then, that success in accumulating capital depends significantly on exploiting the time value of money because compound growth from interest payments across several time periods multiplies the earning capacity of the firm's investments. Investments in common stocks, too, offer the potential for increasing capital growth, but only if the stock provides dividend income and its market value increases.

Dividend *payment to shareholders, on a per-share basis, out of the company's earnings*

Blue-Chip Stock *common stock issued by a well-established and respected company with a sound financial history and a stable pattern of dividend payouts*

Identify

reasons for investing and the investment opportunities offered by mutual funds and exchange-traded funds.

Mutual Fund *company that pools cash investments from individuals and organizations to purchase a portfolio of stocks, bonds, and other securities*

No-Load Fund *mutual fund in which investors pay no commissions when they buy in or sell out*

Load Fund *mutual fund in which investors are charged sales commissions when they buy in or sell out*

Investing to Fulfill Financial Objectives

Mutual funds and exchange-traded funds are popular alternatives to stocks because they offer attractive investment opportunities for various financial objectives and often do not require large sums of money for entry. In addition, the simple and easy transaction process makes them accessible to the public.

Mutual funds are created by companies such as T. Rowe Price and Vanguard that pool cash investments from individuals and organizations to purchase bundles of stocks, bonds, and other securities. The bundles are expected to appreciate in market value and otherwise produce income for the mutual fund and its investors. Thus, investors, as part owners, expect to receive financial gains as the fund's assets become increasingly valuable. If you invest $1,000 in a mutual fund with assets worth $100,000, you own 1 percent of that fund. Investors in **no-load funds** are not charged sales commissions when they buy into or sell out of funds. Investors in **load funds** generally pay commissions of 2 percent to 8 percent.

Reasons for Investing

It's relatively easy to open a mutual fund account online or by phone. There are numerous funds that meet any chosen financial objective. The funds vary in their investment goals; different funds are designed to appeal to the different motives and goals of investors. Three of the most common objectives are (1) financial stability, (2) conservative growth, and (3) aggressive growth.

- **Stability and Safety.** Funds stressing safety seek only modest growth with little fluctuation in principal value regardless of economic conditions. They include *money market mutual funds* and other funds that preserve the fund holders' capital and reliably pay current income. Typical assets of these funds include lower-risk U.S. corporate bonds, U.S. government bonds, and other similarly safe short-term securities that provide stable income from interest and dividends.

- **Conservative Capital Growth.** Mutual funds that stress preservation of capital and current income but also seek some capital appreciation are called *balanced funds*. Typically, these funds hold a mixture of long-term municipal bonds, corporate bonds, and common stocks with good dividend-paying records for steady income. The common stocks offer potential for market appreciation (higher market value), though there is always the risk of price declines if the general stock market falls.

- **Aggressive Growth.** *Aggressive growth funds* seek maximum long-term capital growth. They sacrifice current income and safety by investing in stocks of new (and even troubled) companies, firms developing new products and technologies, and other higher-risk securities. They are designed for investors who can accept the risk of loss inherent in common stock investing with severe price fluctuations but also the potential for superior returns over time.

Most Mutual Funds Don't Match the Market

Many, but not all, mutual funds are managed by "experts" who select the fund's stocks and other securities that provide the fund's income. Unfortunately, some estimates indicate that up to 80 percent of these managed funds do not perform as well as the average return of the overall stock market as a result of costly management expenses and underperforming stocks.[3] This underperformance disadvantage has resulted in the emergence of passively managed funds, in which the fund manager invests by using a fixed, predetermined strategy that replaces judgmental choices for buying and selling its stock holdings. Those choices are predefined by the strategy, not by the fund manager. The most widespread use of passively managed funds is with index mutual funds, which seek to mimic the holdings and performance of a particular market index. As an example, the widely watched S&P 500 market index, which is discussed later, consists of 500 specific common stocks. Any mutual fund company can establish its own index fund by purchasing shares of those same 500 companies, thus matching the market performance of the S&P 500. The selection of which stocks to purchase in an index fund is relatively automatic—it holds many of the same stocks as the market it tracks—and requires little human input, thus reducing management expenses.

Exchange-Traded Funds

As with an index mutual fund, an **exchange-traded fund (ETF)** is a bundle of stocks (or bonds) that are in an index that tracks the overall movement of a market. Unlike a mutual fund, however, an ETF can be traded like a stock. Each share of an ETF rises and falls as market prices change continuously for the market being tracked.

Exchange-Traded Fund (ETF) *bundle of stocks or bonds that are in an index that tracks the overall movement of a market, but unlike a mutual fund can be traded like a stock*

ETFs offer three areas of advantage over mutual funds. First, they can be traded throughout the day like a stock, they have low operating expenses, and they do not require high initial investments. Because they are traded on stock exchanges (hence, "exchange traded"), ETFs can be bought and sold—priced continuously—any time throughout the day. This *intraday trading* means you can time your transaction during the day to buy or sell when (or if) the market reaches a desired price. Mutual fund shares, in contrast, are priced once daily, at the end of the day. Thus, when you buy or sell during the day, you don't find out the share price until after the day has ended.

entrepreneurship and new ventures

An Entrepreneurship of Evil

Bernard Madoff's scheme was not a new idea; it dates back to 1899, when a New Yorker, William Miller, cheated investors out of $1 million. Miller's method was popularized by Boston businessman Charles Ponzi, who, in 1919 to 1920, swindled millions of dollars from unsuspecting investors; he expected to net a 50 percent profit in 90 days. Madoff's contribution to Ponzi-scheme history is the enormity of its size and duration: It reached more than $50 billion, perhaps up to $65 billion, and lasted at least 10 years. So convincing was his sales pitch that the minimum investment, reportedly ranging anywhere from $100,000 to $1 million, was paid willingly by a star-studded list, including the Wilpon family (owner of the New York Jets), actor Kevin Bacon, Baseball Hall of Famer Sandy Koufax, and Steven Spielberg, along with a host of banks, universities, churches, and charities.

Ponzi-scheme victims fit a certain pattern. Many are unsophisticated investors, do not rely on a professional representative, believe that unusually high returns are realistic, and place unfounded faith in personal relationships and tips that lure them into making bad decisions. Ponzi connivers operate by offering abnormally large returns, deflecting prying questions and doubts with personal reassurances and high dividends, and bolstering the scheme's allure by paying high returns to early investors by using new money raised from new clients. As word of high payoffs spreads, more new investors are attracted; otherwise, the scheme falls apart, and the investments disappear. Without an ever-growing pool of new clients, the payoff money runs dry.

Madoff's scheme collapsed when nervous investors, worried about the economic downturn in 2008, asked to withdraw their money. These investors believed that their $17.5 billion in investments had grown to more than $65 billion, although only a small fraction of this amount was on deposit with Madoff's firm. The Ponzi scheme was gradually revealed—not only were the exceptionally high returns fictional, but their deposits also had been used to pay off early investors in the scheme. At best, they realized that they were getting only a fraction of their inflated account balances back. A federal judge, calling the scheme especially evil, ordered that Bernard Madoff Investment Securities LLC be liquidated, and sentenced Madoff to a 150-year prison term. Meanwhile, victims have filed more

Steven Hirsch/Splash News/Newscom

than 15,000 claims against the fraud. Investor claims may be eligible for up to $500,000 each from the Securities Investment Protection Corporation (SIPC), a private fund authorized by Congress to protect securities investors. Some of the massive losses, but certainly not all, may be recovered from the liquidated company's assets. About $10.6 billion of lost funds had been recovered as of 2015. Meanwhile, the end question from Madoff's evil remains unanswered: What percentage of losses will eventually be recovered?[4]

Second, whereas many mutual funds pass the costs of expensive active management onto shareholders, an ETF is bound by a rule that specifies what stocks will be purchased and when; once the rule is established, little or no active human decisions are involved. The *lower annual operating expenses* mean that, for the buy-and-hold investor, annual fees for ETFs are as low as 0.04 percent of assets; annual fees for mutual funds average 1.4 percent.[5]

Finally, unlike mutual funds, ETFs require no minimum investment, meaning they offer *ease of entry* for investors getting started without much money.[6] On the other hand, because ETFs must be bought and sold through a broker, they require payment of a brokerage commission (transaction fees). Traders who buy and sell frequently can end up paying more in transactions fees, even surpassing a mutual fund's high management expenses.[7]

We see, then, because firms have different financial objectives for investing, they often consider other alternatives, in addition to common stocks, such as mutual funds with varying degrees of safety and stability, funds that seek conservative capital growth, and riskier aggressive growth funds. ETFs are available to those firms that have the time to track moment-to-moment stock market movements for intraday trading. By allowing low minimum investments, ETFs offer ease of entry in addition to low annual operating expenses.

The Business of Trading Securities

Stocks, bonds, and mutual funds are known as **securities** because they represent *secured*, or financially valuable claims on the part of investors. The markets in which stocks and bonds are sold are called **securities markets**. By facilitating the buying and selling of securities, the securities markets provide the capital that companies rely on for survival. Mutual funds, on the other hand, are not bought and sold on securities markets but are managed by financial professionals in the investment companies that create, buy, and sell the funds.

Securities *stocks, bonds, and mutual funds representing secured, or asset-based, claims by investors against issuers*

Securities Markets *markets in which stocks and bonds are sold*

Primary and Secondary Securities Markets

In **primary securities markets**, new stocks and bonds are bought and sold by firms and governments. Sometimes, new securities are sold to single buyers or small groups of buyers. These *private placements* are desirable because they allow issuers to keep their plans confidential.

Most new stocks and some bonds are sold on the wider public market. To bring a new security to market, the issuing firm must get approval from the U.S. **Securities and Exchange Commission (SEC)**, the government agency that regulates U.S. securities markets. The firm also relied, traditionally, on the services of an **investment bank**, a financial institution that specialized in issuing and reselling new securities. All that changed, however, in the financial collapse of 2008, when the fall of Lehman Brothers became the largest bankruptcy in U.S. history, Bear Stearns was purchased by JPMorgan Chase, and the two remaining large U.S. investment banks—Morgan Stanley and Goldman Sachs—were allowed to become bank holding companies (much like a commercial bank).[8] Although the companies' structures have changed, they still provide three important investment banking services:

Primary Securities Market *market in which new stocks and bonds are bought and sold by firms and governments*

Securities and Exchange Commission (SEC) *government agency that regulates U.S. securities markets*

Investment Bank *financial institution that specializes in issuing and reselling new securities*

1 Advise companies on the timing and financial terms of new issues.

2 *Underwrite*—buy and assume liability for—new securities, thus providing the issuing firms with 100 percent of the money (less commission). The inability to resell the securities is a risk that the banks must bear.

3 Create distribution networks for moving new securities through groups of other banks and brokers into the hands of individual investors.

New securities, however, represent only a small portion of traded securities. *Existing* stocks and bonds are sold in the much larger **secondary securities market**, which is handled by such familiar bodies as the New York Stock Exchange and by online trading with electronic communication networks.

Secondary Securities Market *market in which existing (not new) stocks and bonds are sold to the public*

Stock Exchanges

Most of the buying and selling of stocks, historically, has been handled by organized *stock exchanges*. A **stock exchange** is an organization of individuals coordinated to provide an institutional auction setting in which stocks can be bought and sold.

Stock Exchange *an organization of individuals to provide an institutional auction setting in which stocks can be bought and sold*

Founded in 1792 and located at the corner of Wall and Broad Streets in New York City, the New York Stock Exchange sees billions of shares change hands each day.

The Trading Floor Each exchange regulates the places and times at which trading may occur. The most important difference between traditional exchanges and the electronic market is the geographic location of the trading activity. Brokers at an exchange trade face-to-face on the *trading floor* (also referred to as an *outcry market*). The electronic market, on the other hand, conducts trades electronically among thousands of dealers in remote locations around the world.

Trading floors today are equipped with vast arrays of electronic communications equipment for displaying buy and sell orders or confirming completed trades. A variety of news services furnish up-to-the-minute information about world events and business developments. Any change in these factors, then, may be swiftly reflected in share prices.

The Major Stock Exchanges Among the stock exchanges that operate on trading floors in the United States, the New York Stock Exchange is the largest. Today, it faces stiff competition from both the electronic market in the United States and large foreign exchanges, such as those in London and Tokyo.

THE NEW YORK STOCK EXCHANGE For many people, "the stock market" means the *New York Stock Exchange (NYSE)*. Founded in 1792, the NYSE is the model for exchanges worldwide. The merger with Euronext in 2007 formed NYSE Euronext, bringing together marketplaces across Europe and the United States, representing one-third of stock trading worldwide. Only firms meeting certain minimum requirements—earning power, total value of outstanding stock, and number of shareholders—are eligible for listing on the NYSE.[9]

Today's NYSE is a *hybrid market* that uses both floor and electronic trading. When a client places an order through a brokerage house or online, it is transmitted to a broker on the NYSE floor. Floor brokers who want to trade that stock meet together to agree on a trading price based on supply and demand, and the order is executed. Alternatively, buyers can use the NYSE's Direct+ service to automatically execute trades electronically.

GLOBAL STOCK EXCHANGES As recently as 1980, the U.S. market accounted for more than half the value of the world market in traded stocks. Market activities, however, have shifted as the value of shares listed on foreign exchanges continues to grow. Table 1 identifies several stock exchanges, among hundreds of exchanges around the world, and the annual dollar volume of shares traded at each exchange.

table 1 Selected Global Stock Exchanges and Markets

Country/Region	Stock Exchange	Total Value of Trades, Year Ended 31 December 2014 (millions of U.S. dollars)
Australia	Australian Securities Exchange	64,289.4
Brazil	Sao Paulo (BM&F) Stock Exchange	58,198.8
Canada	Toronto Stock Exchange	148,900.8
China	Shanghai Stock Exchange	185,359.5
Hong Kong	Hong Kong Stock Exchange	171,830.6
Japan	Tokyo Stock Exchange	446,191.7
Germany	Deutsche Borse	142,125.2
United States/Europe	NYSE/Euronext	1,704,283.9

Source: "List of Stock Exchanges," based on www.world-stock-exchanges.net/top10.html, accessed on May 25, 2015.

While new exchanges are emerging in Vietnam, Laos, and Rwanda, earlier start-ups are flourishing in cities from Shanghai to Warsaw, and others are merging or partnering in different regions. NYSE Euronext, for example, gained a valuable presence in the Middle East by joining with Qatar Exchange, which enabled Qatar to become a stronger international exchange.[10]

THE NASDAQ MARKET The National Association of Securities Dealers Automated Quotation (NASDAQ) System, the world's oldest electronic stock market, was established in 1971. Whereas buy and sell orders to the NYSE are gathered on the trading floor, NASDAQ orders are gathered and executed on a computer network connecting 500,000 terminals worldwide. Currently, NASDAQ is working with officials in an increasing number of countries in replacing the trading floors of traditional exchanges with electronic networks like NASDAQ's.

The stocks of some 3,100 companies, both emerging and well known, are traded by NASDAQ. Examples include Marvell, Apple, Microsoft, Intel, and Staples. Although the volume of shares traded surpasses that of the NYSE, the total market value of NASDAQ's U.S. stocks is less than that of the NYSE.

National Association of Securities Dealers Automated Quotation (NASDAQ) System *world's oldest electronic stock market consisting of dealers who buy and sell securities over a network of electronic communications*

International Consolidation and Cross-Border Ownership

A wave of technological advances, along with regulatory and competitive factors, has propelled the consolidation of stock exchanges and the changeover from physical to electronic trading floors across international borders. Electronic communication networks have opened the door to around-the-clock and around-the-globe trading. Every major European stock exchange had gone electronic by the end of the twentieth century, and by 2010 the United States had caught up. Stock exchanges that didn't have enough savvy with electronic technologies to stay competitive have merged or partnered with those having more advanced trading systems. The intensified competition among stock exchanges has brought speedier transactions and lower transaction fees for investors.

Nonexchange Trading: Electronic Communication Networks

In 1998, the SEC authorized the creation of **electronic communication networks (ECNs)**, electronic trading systems that bring buyers and sellers together outside traditional stock exchanges by automatically matching buy and sell orders at specified

Electronic Communication Network (ECN) *electronic trading system that brings buyers and sellers together outside traditional stock exchanges*

prices. ECNs gained rapid popularity because the trading procedures are fast and efficient, often lowering transaction costs per share to mere pennies. They also allow after-hours trading (after traditional markets have closed for the day) and protect traders' anonymity.[11]

ECNs must register with the SEC as broker-dealers. The ECN then provides service to subscribers—that is, other broker-dealers and institutional investors. Subscribers can view all orders at any time on the system's website to see information on what trades have taken place and at what times. Individual investors must open an account with a subscriber (a broker-dealer) before they can send buy or sell orders to the ECN system.

Individual Investor Trading

While more than half of all U.S. citizens have some form of ownership in stocks, bonds, or mutual funds, more than half of the adults have holdings worth $5,000 or more.[12] Many of these investors are novices who seek the advice of experienced professionals, or brokers. Investors who are well informed and experienced, however, often prefer to invest independently without outside guidance.

Stock Broker *individual or organization that receives and executes buy and sell orders on behalf of outside customers in return for commissions*

Stock Brokers Some of the people on the trading floor are employed by the stock exchange. Others are trading stocks for themselves. Many, however, are **stock brokers** who earn commissions by executing buy and sell orders for outside customers. Although they match buyers with sellers, brokers do not own the securities. They earn commissions from the individuals and organizations for whom they place orders.

Discount Brokers As with many other products, brokerage assistance can be purchased at either discount or at full-service prices. Discount brokers, such as E*TRADE and Scottrade, offer well-informed individual investors who know what they want to buy or sell a fast, low-cost way to participate in the market. Buying 200 shares of a $20 stock in 2015 cost the investor a service fee of $7 at Scottrade, and $7.99 to $9.99 at E*Trade. Price differences are obvious even among the discount brokers, but the highest discount price is well below the price of a full-service broker. Sales personnel receive fees or salaries, not commissions. Unlike many full-service brokers, many discount brokers do not offer in-depth investment advice or person-to-person sales consultations. They do, however, offer automated online services, such as stock research, industry analysis, and screening for specific types of stocks.

Full-Service Brokers Despite the growth in online investing, full-service brokers remain an important resource, both for new, uninformed investors and for experienced investors who don't have time to keep up with all the latest developments. Full-service brokers, such as Merrill Lynch Wealth Management, offer clients consulting advice in personal financial planning, estate planning, and tax strategies, along with a wider range of investment products. In addition to delivering and interpreting information, financial advisors can point clients toward investments that might otherwise be lost in an avalanche of online financial data.

Online Investing The popularity of online trading stems from convenient access to the Internet, fast, no-nonsense transactions, and the opportunity for self-directed investors to manage their own investments while paying low fees for trading.

Book-Entry Ownership *procedure that holds investors' shares in book-entry form, rather than issuing a physical paper certificate of ownership*

Online investors buy into and sell out of the stocks of thousands of companies daily. Consequently, keeping track of who owns what at any given time has become a monumental burden. Relief has come from **book-entry ownership**. Historically, shares of stock have been issued as physical paper certificates; now they are simply recorded in the companies' books, thereby eliminating the costs of storing, exchanging, and replacing certificates.

finding a better way

Mass Communications with IT Puts Stock Trading Within Easy Reach

Just a decade or two ago, trading stocks was a somewhat cumbersome chore, delayed by time lags before the general public could access trade information, such as market trends, daily high and low prices for each stock, and current trading prices. Moment-to-moment information was available only by calling a stockbroker or by visiting a brokerage where New York Stock Exchange (NYSE) data were visible to visitors for each transaction flowing on an overhead screen. Many investors relied on newspaper reports summarizing the most recent day's market transactions before deciding if the time was right to buy or sell stocks.

Today's trading environment is a new and different world. Instead of reading the *Wall Street Journal* to see what happened yesterday, cable news outlets, such as CNBC, MSNBC, Bloomberg Television, and Fox Business provide real-time information and analysis, displaying transactions and market conditions as they occur on the NYSE and NASDAQ exchanges, along with continuous reports on the Dow, S&P 500, and NASDAQ indexes. Investors and traders seeking financial opportunities abroad have access to developments in global financial markets, including those in China, Australia, Europe, and elsewhere, including information on currency exchange rates.

With access to the Web, investors have access to even more detailed information. Investors seeking market information on specific stocks can visit any of the online sources, such as *Yahoo! Finance, Bloomberg.com, money.msn.com*, and *marketwatch.com*, for market quotes and financial information, including historical trade data, at any time. A number of highly respected sites, such as Investor Guide, Seeking Alpha, and Motley Fool, provide detailed analysis. Going beyond mere information gathering, Web trading has become a popular tool for investors. Logging on through your favorite Web browser, you can place trades—buying and selling stocks, bonds, and commodities—by establishing an account with one of the many online brokers. With mobile access, Web traders using a broker such as *TradeStation* can check prices, place trades, create charts, manage their account balances, and get access to additional market research and education resources, along with portfolio analysis and reports. Users can keep track of trading opportunities 24/7 from anywhere using a smartphone, tablet,

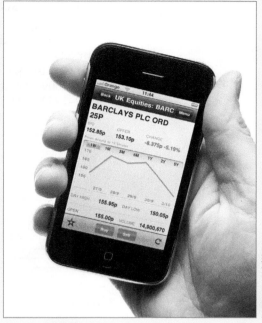

incamerastock/Alamy

or mobile device. Many Web brokers, both large and small, are luring customers with offerings of new stock-trading apps, including free ones, such as *Stockwits, TD Ameritrade Mobile, E-Trade Mobile, Bloomberg+, Yahoo! stocks*, and *DailyFinance*. With the growing availability of investment-related applications for mobile devices, some Web-trading firms report that mobile apps account for more than 15 percent of their customer activity.

The availability of large amounts of highly timely information has increased the popularity of day trading. As contrasted with investing, in which a buyer intends to hold the stock (or other financial instrument) into the future before selling for a long-term profit, a stock trader intends to hold a stock for only a brief period of time before selling to capture a short-term profit. Day trading is an even more specialized form of trading because the buying and selling is accomplished within one day, without holding the stock overnight. Day traders rely on speedy transactions to profit from the difference between buying and selling prices during the day, sometimes holding a stock for only a few seconds or minutes before selling. Unlike the previous era, when only financial companies had access to stock exchanges and market information, today's technology puts trading within easy reach of individual investors.[13]

Tracking the Market Using Stock Indexes

For decades, investors have used stock indexes to measure market performance and to predict future movements of stock markets. Although not indicative of the status of individual securities, **market indexes** provide useful summaries of overall price

Market Index *statistical indicator designed to measure the performance of a large group of stocks or track the price changes of a stock market*

Bull Market *period of rising stock prices, lasting 12 months or longer, featuring investor confidence for future gains and motivation to buy*

Bear Market *period of falling stock prices marked by negative investor sentiments with motivation to sell ahead of anticipated losses*

trends, both in specific industries and in the stock market as a whole. Market indexes, for example, reveal *bull* and *bear market* trends. **Bull markets** are periods of rising stock prices, generally lasting 12 months or longer; investors are motivated to buy, confident they will realize capital gains. Periods of falling stock prices, usually 20 percent off peak prices, are called **bear markets**; investors are motivated to sell, anticipating further falling prices.

As Figure 2 shows, the past 35 years have been characterized primarily by bull markets, including the longest in history, from 1981 to the beginning of 2000. In contrast, the period 2000 to 2003 was characterized by a bear market. The period 2007–2009 was the second-worst bear market of all time, exceeded only by that of 1929–1932.[14] The data that characterize such periods are drawn from four leading market indexes: the Dow Jones, Standard & Poor's, NASDAQ Composite, and the Russell 2000 (not shown in Figure 2).

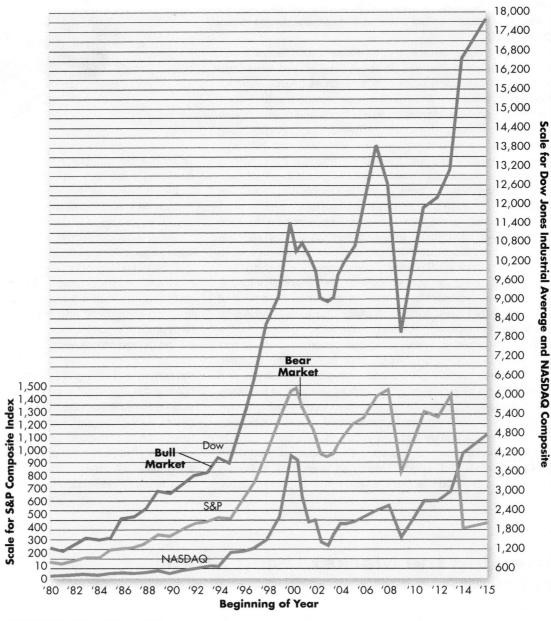

FIGURE 2 Bull and Bear Markets
Source: Yahoo! Finance, at http://finance.yahoo.com.

The Dow The **Dow Jones Industrial Average (DJIA)** is the oldest and most widely cited U.S. market index. It measures the performance of the industrial sector of the U.S. stock markets by focusing on just 30 blue-chip, large-cap companies as reflectors of the economic health of the many similar U.S. firms. The Dow is an average of the stock prices for these 30 large firms, and traders and investors use it as a traditional barometer of the market's overall movement. Because it includes only 30 of the thousands of companies on the market, the Dow is only an approximation of the overall market's price movements.

Over the last several decades, the Dow has been revised and updated to reflect the changing composition of U.S. companies and industries. Recent modifications occurred in 2008–2009, when three companies were added—Kraft Foods, insurance giant Travelers Companies, and technology titan Cisco Systems—replacing insurance company American International Group, banker Citigroup, and auto icon General Motors. Replacing the three outgoing firms, all facing substantial financial and restructuring upheavals, the new additions better represent today's food- and technology-based economy and the prominence of the financials industry.[15]

Dow Jones Industrial Average (DJIA) oldest and most widely cited market index based on the prices of 30 blue-chip, large-cap industrial firms on the NYSE

The S&P 500 Because it considers very few firms, the Dow is a limited gauge of the overall U.S. stock market. The **S&P 500**, the Standard and Poor's Composite Index, is a broader report, considered by many to be the best single indicator of the U.S. equities market. It consists of 500 large-cap stocks, including companies from various sectors—such as information technology, energy, industrials, financials, health care, consumer staples, and telecommunications—for a balanced representation of the overall large-cap equities market.

S&P 500 market index of U.S. equities based on the performance of 500 large-cap stocks representing various sectors of the overall equities market

The NASDAQ Composite Because it considers more stocks, some Wall Street observers regard the **NASDAQ Composite Index** as one of the most useful of all market indexes. Unlike the Dow and the S&P 500, all NASDAQ-listed companies, not just a selected few, are included in the index for a total of approximately 3,100 firms, mostly in the United States but in other countries as well. However, it includes a high proportion of technology companies, including small-company stocks, and a smaller representation of other sectors—financial, consumer products, and industrials.

NASDAQ Composite Index market index that includes all NASDAQ-listed companies, both domestic and foreign, with a high proportion of technology companies and small-cap stocks

The Russell 2000 Investors in the U.S. small-cap market are interested in the **Russell 2000 Index**, a specialty index that measures the performance of the smallest U.S. companies based on market capitalization. As the most quoted index focusing on the small-cap portion of the U.S. economy, its stocks represent a range of sectors such as financials, consumer discretionary, health care, technology, materials, and utilities.

Russell 2000 Index specialty index that uses 2,000 stocks to measure the performance of the smallest U.S. companies

Index-Matching ETFs Countless other specialty indexes exist for specific industries, countries, and economic sectors to meet investors' diverse needs. In addition, many ETFs are available to investors for duplicating (or nearly duplicating) the market performance of popular stock-market indexes. For example, one ETF, Standard & Poor's Depository Receipts (SPDRS, known as *Spiders*), owns a portfolio of stocks that matches the composition of the S&P 500 index. Similarly, the Fidelity® NASDAQ Composite Index® Tracking Stock holds a portfolio of equities for tracking the NASDAQ Composite Index.

We have seen that the securities markets, the markets in which stocks and bonds are bought and sold, provide the capital that companies rely on for survival. These markets also provide investment opportunities by which companies trade securities to increase the firm's wealth. Firms issuing new securities raise capital with the assistance of investment banking services. Existing securities are traded throughout the day in the secondary securities market (where buyers and sellers make transactions at the major stock exchanges) and through ECNs. For trading securities, many individuals and companies rely on the services of securities brokers, and other self-directed traders use online trading to self-manage their investments. Investors often use stock indexes to measure market performance and to predict future market movements of stock markets. Market indexes reveal bull and bear markets, revealing the risks and opportunities for gaining and losing wealth that are inherent in securities investments.

the risk–return relationship and discuss the use of diversification and asset allocation for investments.

The Risk–Return Relationship

Individual investors have different motivations and personal preferences for safety versus risk. That is why, for example, some individuals and firms invest in stocks whereas others invest only in bonds. Although all investors anticipate receiving future cash flows, some cash flows are more certain than others. Investors generally expect to receive higher returns for higher uncertainty. They do not generally expect large returns for secure, stable investments such as government-insured bonds. The investment's time commitment, too, contains an element of risk. While short-term investments are generally considered to be less risky, longer-term investments are subject to future uncertainties in the economy and financial markets. As of mid-2015, the average rate of return on a 1-year U.S. Treasury bill was 0.25 percent, versus 1.51 percent on a 5-year bill, and 2.10 percent on a 10-year bill. Each type of investment, then, has a **risk–return (risk–reward) relationship**: Safer investments tend to offer lower returns; riskier investments tend to offer higher returns (rewards).

Figure 3 shows the general risk–return relationship for various financial instruments, along with the types of investors they attract. Thus, conservative investors, who have a low tolerance for risk, will opt for no-risk U.S. Treasury Bills (fully insured by the U.S. government), or even intermediate-term high-grade corporate bonds that rate low in terms of risk on future returns, but also low on the size of expected returns. The reverse is true of aggressive investors who prefer the higher risks and potential returns from long-term junk bonds and common stocks.[16]

Risk–Return (Risk–Reward) relationship *principle that safer investments tend to offer lower returns, whereas riskier investments tend to offer higher returns (rewards)*

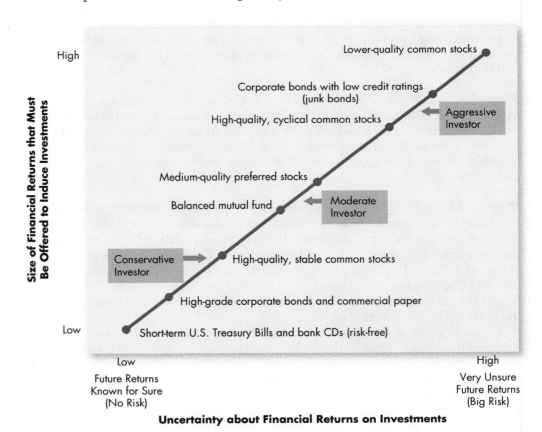

FIGURE 3 Potential Financial Returns Rise with Riskier Investments.
Source: Multi-Source.

Investment Dividends (or Interest), Appreciation, and Total Return

In evaluating potential investments, investors look at returns from dividends (or from interest), returns from price appreciation, and total return.

Dividends The rate of return from dividends paid to shareholders is commonly referred to as the **current dividend yield** (or, in the case of interest from a loan, the **current interest yield**) and is calculated by dividing the yearly dollar amount of dividend income by the investment's current market value. For example, during one recent time period, each share of AT&T stock was receiving annual dividends payments of $1.80. Now, if the share price was $35.67 on a particular day, the current yield would be 5.05 percent or ($1.80/$35.67 × 100). This dividend can then be compared against current yields from other investments. Larger dividend yields, of course, are preferred to smaller returns.

Current Dividend Yield and Current Interest Yield *yearly dollar amount of income divided by the investment's current market value, expressed as a percentage*

Price Appreciation Another source of returns depends on whether the investment is increasing or decreasing in dollar value. **Price appreciation** is an increase in the dollar value of an investment. Suppose, for example, you purchased a share of AT&T stock for $35.67 and then sold it one year later for $37.45. The price appreciation is $1.78 or ($37.45 − 35.67). This profit, realized from the increased market value of an investment, is known as a **capital gain**.

Price Appreciation *increase in the dollar value of an investment at two points in time (the amount by which the price of a security increases)*

Capital Gain *profit realized from the increased value of an investment*

Total Return The sum of an investment's current dividend (interest) yield and capital gain is referred to as its total return. Total return cannot be accurately evaluated until it's compared to the investment that was required to get that return. Total return as a percentage of investment is calculated as follows:

$$\text{Total return}(\%) = (\text{Current dividend payment} + \text{Capital gain}) / \text{Original investment} \times 100.$$

To complete our AT&T example, the total return as a percentage of our one-year investment would be 10.04 percent or [($1.80 + $1.78)/$35.67 × 100]. Again, obviously, larger total returns are preferred to smaller ones.

Fantasy Stock Markets

Enthusiasts of baseball, football, and hockey aren't the only fans energized by fantasy games. Fantasy stock markets are all the rage for learning how securities markets work, for trying your hand at various investment strategies, and earning a fantasy fortune (or going broke!). Internet-based games, including free ones such as *Wall Street Survivor* and *How the Market Works*, provide an investment experience that is educational, challenging, and entertaining. Starting with an initial sum in virtual cash with which to manage their own fantasy portfolio of real companies, participants must live with real market results. It's a learn-by-doing experience—using Web-based symbol lookups to enter stock ticker symbols, searching various information sources for research on companies of interest, making buy and sell decisions, and then discovering the financial results as real market prices change for the portfolio holdings. Many students and business practitioners are finding these "games" to be a valuable resource for learning the "how to" of online investing.

Managing Risk with Diversification and Asset Allocation

Investors seldom take an extreme approach—total risk or total risk avoidance—in selecting their investments. Extreme positions attract extreme results; instead, most investors select a mixed portfolio of investments—some riskier and some more conservative—that, collectively, provides the overall level of risk and financial returns that feels comfortable. After determining the desired *risk–return* balance, they then achieve it in two ways: through (1) *diversification* and (2) *asset allocation*.

Diversification purchase of several different kinds of investments rather than just one

Diversification **Diversification** means buying several different kinds of investments rather than just one. For example, diversification as applied to common stocks means that you invest in stocks of several different companies, companies in different industries, and companies in various countries. The risk of loss is reduced by spreading the total investment across different kinds of stocks because although any one stock may tumble, the chances are less that all of them will fall at the same time. More diversification is gained when assets are spread across a variety of investment alternatives—stocks, bonds, mutual funds, precious metals, real estate, and so on. Employees who did not have diversified investments and, instead, had all their retirement funds invested in their firm's stock can lose everything if their company goes bankrupt or invests poorly. The collapse of Enron Corporation in 2001, one of the 10 largest U.S. firms, was a financial disaster for its thousands of its employees because Enron's retirement program was invested solely in Enron common stock. The stock price dropped from near $90 per share to nearly $5, effectively wiping out employees' retirement savings. Putting all their eggs in one basket was an extremely risky position, as they sorrowfully learned. When their firm's stock took a free fall as a result of a market collapse and scandal, the retirement funds disappeared.

Asset Allocation relative amount of funds invested in (or allocated to) each of several investment alternatives

Asset Allocation **Asset allocation** is the proportion (the relative amounts) of funds invested in (or allocated to) each of the investment alternatives. You may decide, for example, to allocate 50 percent of your funds to common stocks, 25 percent to a money market mutual fund, and 25 percent to a U.S. Treasury bond mutual fund. Ten years later, with more concern for financial safety, you may decide on a less risky asset allocation of 20 percent, 40 percent, and 40 percent in the same investment categories, respectively. In this example, the portfolio has been changed from moderate-risk to lower-risk investments for the purpose of preserving the investor's accumulated capital. The asset allocation was changed accordingly.

Portfolio combined holdings of all the financial investments of any company or individual

Performance Differences for Different Portfolios Once an investor has chosen an investment objective with an acceptable risk level, he or she can put the tools of diversification and asset allocation to use in their investor's *portfolio*. A **portfolio** is the combined holdings of all the financial investments—stocks, bonds, mutual funds, real estate—of any company or individual.

Just like investors, investment funds have different investment objectives—ranging from aggressive growth/high risk to stable income/low volatility—and their holdings are diversified accordingly among hundreds of company stocks, corporate bonds, or government bonds that provide the desired orientation. The money in a diversified portfolio is allocated in different proportions among a variety of funds; if all goes according to plan, most of these funds will meet their desired investment objectives and the overall portfolio will increase in value.

A risk–return relationship is inherent in every business investment. Whereas safer investments tend to offer lower returns, riskier investments tend to offer higher returns (rewards). Different types of investments vary along the risk–reward continuum, and most firms strive for a mixture of investments that, overall, provide that firm's desired risk–return posture. Each investment's total financial return is the sum of its capital gain and dividend (interest) yield. After determining the desired risk–return balance, investors use two methods for achieving it: (1) diversification and (2) asset allocation. Diversification means buying several different kinds of investments rather than just one. Asset allocation is the proportion of funds invested in each of the investment alternatives. Diversification and asset allocation, together, are essential to protect against the uncertainties (risks) inherent in any single investment.

Financing the Business Firm

If you invest wisely, you may earn enough money to start your own firm; but that's only the first step in the complicated process of financing a business. Every company needs cash to function. Although a business owner's savings may be enough to get a firm up and running, businesses depend on sales revenues to survive. When current sales revenues are insufficient to pay for expenses, firms tap into various other sources of funds, typically starting with the owners' savings, owners contribute funds, or paid-in capital, from their own pockets). If a firm needs more money, they can turn to borrowing from banks, soliciting cash from private outside investors, or selling bonds to the public.

Secured Loans for Equipment

Money to purchase new equipment often comes in the form of loans from commercial banks. In a **secured loan (asset-backed loan)**, the borrower guarantees repayment of the loan by pledging the asset as **collateral** to the lender. Suppose a local trucking company gets a $320,000 bank loan to purchase eight dump trucks. The borrower pledges the trucks and the company's office building as collateral to the bank. That is, if the borrower defaults, or fails to repay the loan, the bank can take possession of the borrower's pledged assets and sell them to recover the outstanding debt. However, as we learned in the 2008 recession, assets from loans defaulted by businesses and home buyers may have little or no value.

The amount of money that is loaned and must be repaid is the **loan principal**. However, borrowers also pay the lender an additional fee, **interest**, for the use of the borrowed funds. The amount of interest owed depends on an **annual percentage rate (APR)** that is agreed on between the lender and borrower. The interest amount is found by multiplying the APR by the loan principal.

Secured Loan (Asset-Backed Loan) *loan to finance an asset, backed by the borrower pledging the asset as collateral to the lender*

Collateral *asset pledged for the fulfillment of repaying a loan*

Loan Principal *amount of money that is loaned and must be repaid*

Interest *fee paid to a lender for the use of borrowed funds; like a rental fee*

Annual Percentage Rate (APR) *one-year rate that is charged for borrowing, expressed as a percentage of the borrowed principal*

Working Capital and Unsecured Loans from Banks

Firms need more than just fixed assets for daily operations; they need current, liquid assets available to meet short-term operating expenses such as employee wages and marketing expenses. The firm's ability to meet these expenses is measured by its working capital:

$$\text{Working capital} = \text{Current assets} - \text{Current liabilities}$$

Positive working capital means the firm's current assets are large enough to pay off current liabilities. Negative working capital means the firm's current liabilities are greater than current assets, so it may need to borrow money from a commercial bank. With an **unsecured loan**, the borrower does not have to put up collateral. In many cases, however, the bank requires the borrower to maintain a *compensating balance*; the borrower must keep a portion of the loan amount on deposit with the bank in a non-interest-bearing account.

Unsecured Loan *loan for which collateral is not required*

Firms with bad credit scores typically cannot get unsecured loans. Because access to such loans requires a good credit history, many firms establish a relationship with a commercial bank and, over time, build a good credit record by repaying loan principal and interest on time.

In extreme conditions, however, even a good credit history may not be enough. During the deepening recession, the cash shortages at most banks prevented loans of nearly any kind to business customers, thereby slowing down the economy even more. Even after vast injections of cash from TARP and other government sources, banks lagged far behind in supplying loans to meet working-capital needs of cash-strapped business borrowers.

Small business entrepreneurs, especially, often underestimate the value of establishing bank credit as a source of funds. Some banks offer financial analysis, cash flow planning, and suggestions based on experiences with other local firms. Some provide loans to small businesses in bad times and work to keep them going. Obtaining credit, therefore, begins with finding a bank that can—and will—support a small firm's financial needs. Once a line of credit is obtained, the small business can seek more liberal credit policies from other businesses. Sometimes, for instance, suppliers give customers longer credit periods—say, 45 or 60 days rather than 30 days—to make payments. Liberal trade credit terms with their suppliers let firms increase short-term funds and avoid additional borrowing from banks.

Obtaining longer-term loans is more difficult for new businesses than for established companies. With unproven repayment ability, start-up firms can expect to pay higher interest rates than older firms. If a new enterprise displays evidence of sound financial planning, however, the U.S. Small Business Administration may support a guaranteed loan. The presentation of a business plan demonstrates to any lender that the borrower is a good credit risk. The business plan is a document that tells potential lenders why the money is needed, the amount, how the money will be used to improve the company, and when it will be paid back.

Planning for *cash flow requirements* is especially valuable for meeting the small business's financial needs. It also demonstrates to lenders the borrower's prudent use of financial resources. The firm's success or failure may hinge on anticipating those times when either cash will be short or excess cash can be expected. Consider how the owner would compare the expected cash inflows, cash outflows, and net cash position (inflows minus outflows) month by month for Slippery Fish Bait Supply Co., a highly seasonal business. Bait stores (Slippery's customers) buy heavily from Slippery during the spring and summer months. Revenues outpace expenses, leaving surplus funds that can be invested. During the fall and winter, however, expenses exceed revenues. Slippery must borrow funds to keep going until revenues pick up again in the spring. Comparing predicted cash inflows from sales with outflows for expenses will show the firm's expected monthly cash-flow position. Such information can be invaluable for the small-business manager. By anticipating shortfalls, managers can seek funds in advance and minimize their costs. By anticipating excess cash, a manager can plan to put the funds to work in short-term, interest-earning investments.

Angel Investors and Venture Capital

Once a business has been successfully launched, it needs additional capital for growth. Outside individuals who provide such capital are called **angel investors**. Angel investors help many firms grow rapidly by providing what is known as **venture capital**, private funds from wealthy individuals or companies that seek investment opportunities in new growth companies. In most cases, the growth firm turns to venture capital sources because they have not yet built enough credit history to get a loan from commercial banks or other lending institutions. Peter Thiel supplied an initial $500,000 angel investment in Facebook's early years.

In 2014 experts estimated that $24.8 billion was invested in around 70,700 entrepreneurial ventures. Estimates also suggested that there were just under 300,000 such investors in the United States. In return for their investment, angel investors typically expect a sizable piece of ownership in the company (up to 50 percent of its equity). They may also want a formal say in how the company is run. If the firm is bought by a larger company or if it sells its stock in a public offering, the angel may receive additional payments.

Sale of Corporate Bonds

Corporations can raise capital by issuing bonds. A **corporate bond** is a formal pledge (an IOU) obligating the issuer to pay interest periodically and repay the principal at maturity (a preset future date) to the lender. The federal government also issues bonds to finance projects and meet obligations, as do state and local governments (called *municipal bonds*) for financing the building of schools, roads, and sewage disposal systems.

Characteristics of Corporate Bonds

The bondholder (the lender) has no claim to ownership of the company and does not receive dividends. However, interest payments and repayment of principal are financial obligations; payments to bondholders have priority over dividend payments to stockholders in cases of financial distress.

Each new bond issue has specific terms and conditions spelled out in a **bond indenture**, a legal document identifying the borrower's obligations and the financial returns to lenders. One of the most important details is the **maturity date** (or due date), when the firm must repay the bond's **face value** (also called **par value**, or the amount purchased) to the lender.

Corporate bonds have been traditionally issued to fund outstanding debts and major projects for various lengths of time. Short-term bonds mature in fewer than 5 years after they are issued. Bonds with 5- to 10-year lives are considered intermediate term, and anything longer than 10 years is considered long term. Longer-term corporate bonds are somewhat riskier than shorter-term bonds because they are exposed to greater unforeseen economic conditions that may lead to default.

Bond Indenture *legal document containing complete details of a bond issue*

Maturity Date *future date when repayment of a bond is due from the bond issuer (borrower)*

Face Value (Par Value) *amount of money that the bond buyer (lender) lent the issuer and that the lender will receive on repayment*

Default and Bondholders' Claim

A bond is said to be in **default** if the borrower fails to make payment when due to lenders. Bondholders may then file a **bondholders' claim**, a request for court enforcement of the bond's terms of payment. When a financially distressed company cannot pay bondholders, it may seek relief by filing for **bankruptcy**, the court-granted permission not to pay some or all debts. After a restructured General Motors emerged from bankruptcy in 2009, the holders of the old General Motors Corporation's $24 billion in bonds wondered how much payment, if any, they would recover from the financially strapped company. In the 2011 settlement, investors holding bonds in the old GM received stock shares in the new GM that provided a recovery rate of about 40 percent on the dollar of the original bond investment.[17]

Default *failure of a borrower to make payment when due to a lender*

Bondholders' Claim *request for court enforcement of a bond's terms of payment*

Bankruptcy *court-granted permission for a company to not pay some or all debts*

Risk Ratings

To aid investors in making purchase decisions, several services measure the default risk of bonds. Table 2, for example, shows the rating systems of two well-known services, Moody's and Standard & Poor's. The highest (safest) grades are AAA and Aaa, and the lowest are C and D, representing speculative and highly risky bonds. Low-grade bonds are usually called *junk bonds*. Negative ratings do not necessarily keep issues from being successful. Rather, they raise the interest rates that issuers must offer to attract lenders.

Flawed Ratings Misread Recession Risks

The financial meltdown of 2008 has raised questions about whether any good purpose is being served by credit-rating agencies. Among many other investors, California Public Employees Retirement Fund (Calpers), the nation's largest public pension fund, has filed a suit against the three top agencies—Moody's, Standard & Poor's, and Fitch—charging losses caused by "wildly inaccurate and unreasonably high" credit ratings. Calpers officials relied on ratings for investments that turned sour—many failing altogether. Skepticism of agencies' ratings has soared following the collapse of highly rated giants such as Lehman Brothers, Goldman Sachs, and Citigroup, along with high ratings on billions of dollars of mortgage-backed securities that eventually became

table 2 Bond Rating Systems

Rating System	High Grades	Medium Grades (Investment Grades)	Speculative	Poor Grades
Moody's	Aaa, Aa	A, Baa	Ba, B	Caa to C
Standard & Poor's	AAA, AA	A, BBB	BB, B	CCC to D

toxic. Recent lawsuits, including those by the states of Ohio and Connecticut, accuse credit rating agencies of reckless assessments that misled investors.[18]

Mortgage-Backed Security (MBS) *mortgages pooled together to form a debt obligation—a bond—that entitles the holder (investor) to cash that flows in from the bundled mortgages*

Mortgage-backed securities (MBS) became a trillion-dollar investment industry during the pre-2007 housing market boom. Financial institutions bundled home mortgages into packages and resold them as securities to eager investors who trusted in the securities' risk ratings given by Moody's, Standard & Poor's, and Fitch. Each MBS is a group of mortgages bundled together to form a debt obligation (a bond) that entitles the holder (the investor) to the cash that flows in from the mortgages. Unknown to investors, some $3 trillion of MBSs contained subprime mortgages—high-risk loans to applicants with bad credit, low income, and low down payments—most of which had received high ratings (AAA) by credit-rating agencies. Misled by flawed risk assessments, investors were left with little or nothing when the highly rated securities turned toxic, causing the collapse of the housing and financial markets.[19]

OBJECTIVE 6
Identify
the reasons a company might make an initial public offering of its stock, explain how stock value is determined, and discuss the significance of market capitalization.

Becoming a Public Corporation

Initial public offerings (IPOs), the first sale of a company's stock to the general public, are a major source of funds that fuel continued growth for many firms and introduce numerous considerations inherent in running a public company. In one of the biggest IPOs in history, Facebook's public offering of common stock in 2012, with an opening price of $38 per share, raised more than $100 billion. In this section, we discuss many of the issues public companies face, such as potential loss of control, fluctuating share prices, how businesses use market capitalization, and how they choose capital sources.

Initial Public Offering (IPO) *first sale of a company's stock to the general public*

Going Public Means Selling Off Part of the Company

Private owners lose some control of the company when shares are sold to the public. Common shareholders usually have voting rights in corporate governance, so they elect the board of directors and vote on major issues put forth at the company's annual shareholders' meeting. Anyone owning a large proportion of the company's shares gains a powerful position in determining who runs the corporation and how.

When firms go public they sell part of their ownership to other investors through a public offering of stock. Monitors such as this one show current prices and overall stock price indicators such as the Dow, S&P and Nasdaq. Investors then use this information to decide when to buy or sell stock.

managing in turbulent times

Winners and Losers

The year 2014 was a banner one for IPOs. The U.S. IPO market was the biggest since 2000, both in terms of size and number. The largest of these was the Chinese e-commerce firm Alibaba, which raised $22 billion, but there were hundreds of others on both the New York Stock Exchange and NASDAQ. And, the trend was not limited to the United States. Globally, more than 1,200 IPOs raised $256.5 billion in 2014, according to a report by Ernst & Young, with the greatest activity in health care, technology, and industrials.

In general, a company enters into an initial public offering with the hopes of raising a large amount of capital with which to pay off debt and expand operations. For the company, the value of the IPO is primarily measured by the amount of money that they raise by selling stock at the issue price. For example, Citizens Financial was able to raise $3 billion and JD.com, Inc. raised $2.4 billion. The issue price is influenced by the company's past performance and expected results in the future, as well as market conditions. Companies issuing an IPO hope to have as high an issue price as possible so that they can raise a lot of capital.

For investors, they hope to buy low and sell high. Once a security purchased through an IPO is resold, the gain or loss goes to the owner of the security, not the company. While executives at the company who receive stock as part of their compensation package have a vested interest in the stock price, most of the risk after the IPO is on the investor side. There's a good

E.J. Baumeister Jr./Alamy

amount of uncertainty when purchasing an IPO and there are winners and losers. For example, Citizens Financial Group was issued at a price of $21.50 on September 24, 2015, and was trading at more than $28 nine months later. In less than a year, investors had seen a 30 percent increase in the value of their investment. However, North Atlantic Drilling Ltd. was not so lucky. They issued 13 million shares at $9.25 in January 2014, only to see the per share price fall to below $2 by the end of the same year, with limited prospects for recovery. While the company was able to raise more than $100 million, investors are wondering what went wrong.[20]

At an extreme, a **corporate raider**, an investor conducting a type of hostile (unwanted) takeover, buys shares on the open market, attempting to seize control of the company and its assets. The raider then sells off those assets at a profit, resulting in the company's disappearance.

A company is ripe for raiding when its stock price falls so shares can be cheaply bought, although its assets still have high value.

Corporate Raider *investor conducting a type of hostile corporate takeover against the wishes of the company*

Stock Valuation

What determines a stock's value after it is offered to the general public? Investors' assessments of the company's management record in past ventures, expectations for competing in the industry, and belief in the public's acceptance of the company's products are among many factors that affect a stock's value, which in turn affect the value of the business. In addition, different investors measure value differently, and their measurements may change according to circumstances. Because of the uncertainties involved in stock prices, investment professionals believe day-to-day prices to be a generally poor indicator of any stock's real value. Instead, a long-run perspective considers the company's financial health, past history of results and future forecasts, its record for managerial performance, and overall prospects for competing successfully in the coming years. Accordingly, any stock's value today looks beyond the current price and is based on expectations of the financial returns it will provide to shareholders during the long run.

Why Shares Are Different Prices

On one specific day in early 2015, the price of Google Inc. was about $567 per share on the NYSE, GE shares traded at about $25.43, Delta Airlines shares were priced at about $43.78, and Berkshire Hathaway shares traded for $214,748.36.

Why such differences? One reason is supply and demand for each company's shares; another is because some corporations want the shares to sell within a particular price range, say between $20 and $80, believing it will attract a larger pool of investors. If the price gets too high, many investors can't afford to buy shares. A company can restore shares to the desired lower range by a **stock split**, a stock dividend paid in additional shares to shareholders. Here's how it works. Suppose company X has 100,000 common shares outstanding that are trading at $100 per share, but the company wants it priced in the $20 to $80 range. X can declare a 2-for-1 stock split, meaning the company gives shareholders one additional share for each share they own. Now X has 200,000 shares outstanding but its financial performance has not changed, so the stock price immediately falls to $50 per share. Every shareholder's investment value, however, is unchanged: they previously owned one share at $100, and now they own two shares at $50 each.

Stock Split *stock dividend paid in additional shares to shareholders, thus increasing the number of outstanding shares*

Comparing Prices of Different Stocks

Consider a trading day when PepsiCo's share price was $81.04, and Coca-Cola was $40.74 per share. Does the price difference mean that PepsiCo is a better company than Coca-Cola because its shares are more expensive? Or does it mean that Coke shares are a better value because they can be bought at a lower price than PepsiCo's? In fact, neither of these two reasons is correct. Share prices alone do not provide enough information to determine which is the better investment. Table 3 can help us make a better comparison with further information.

First, earnings per share (EPS) are greater for PepsiCo ($3.90 versus $1.91 per share). Although you pay more to own a PepsiCo share, earnings per dollar of investment are slightly higher than for Coke ($3.90 earnings/$81.04 investment = $0.048 Pepsi; versus $1.91 earnings/$40.74 investment = $0.047 Coke): PepsiCo's earnings were about 4.8 cents for each dollar of its share price, whereas Coca-Cola earned almost the same at 4.7 cents. Both companies generated about the same earnings power for each dollar of shareholder investment.

Now consider annual dividends paid to shareholders. The dividend yield from Coca-Cola was 2.75 percent. That is, the dividend payment amounted to a 2.75 percent return on the shareholder's $40.74 investment, or $1.12 = ($40.74 × 2.75%). PepsiCo's dividend payment was about $2.27 or ($81.03 × 2.80%), representing a slightly larger return (yield) on shareholder investment than Coca-Cola (2.80% versus 2.75%).

Based on this limited information, it's not clear which of the two companies is the better investment. A more complete evaluation would compare historical performance consistency over a period of several years, along with indicators of each firm's prospects for the future.

Market Capitalization

A widely used measure of corporate size and value is known as **market capitalization (market cap)**, the total dollar value of all the company's outstanding shares, calculated as the current stock price multiplied by the number of shares outstanding.

Market Capitalization (Market Cap) *total dollar value of all the company's outstanding shares*

table 3 Financial Comparison: Coca-Cola and PepsiCo

	Coca-Cola	PepsiCo
Recent price	$40.74	$81.04
EPS	$ 1.91	$ 3.90
Dividend yield	2.75%	2.80%

table 4 Corporation Sizes Based on Capitalization

Capitalization Category	Range of Capitalization
Micro-Cap	Below $250 million
Small-Cap	$250 million–$2 billion
Mid-Cap	$2 billion–$10 billion
Large-Cap	Over $10 billion

As indicated in Table 4, the investment industry categorizes firms according to size of capitalization. Investors typically regard larger market caps as less risky, and firms with small market caps (small-cap firms) as being particularly risky investments. In November 2014, Apple hit a market cap of $700 billion, making it the largest among U.S. companies.

Choosing Equity versus Debt Capital

Firms can meet their capital needs through two sources: (1) *debt financing* (from outside the firm) or (2) *equity financing* (putting the owners' capital to work).

Pros and Cons for Debt Financing Long-term borrowing from sources outside the company, **debt financing**, via loans or the sale of corporate bonds is a major component in most U.S. firms' financial planning.

Debt Financing *long-term borrowing from sources outside a company*

LONG-TERM LOANS Long-term loans are attractive for several reasons:

- Because the number of parties involved is limited, loans can often be arranged quickly.

- The firm need not make public disclosure of its business plans or the purpose for which it is acquiring the loan. (In contrast, the issuance of corporate bonds requires such disclosure.)

Tripplaar Kristoffer/SIPA/Newscom

A firm's market capitalization (or market cap) is the number of outstanding shares of stock multiplied by the current price of that stock. General Electric is consistently one of the world's most valuable businesses (that it, it has one of the largest market caps). In 2015 GE's market cap ranged from a high of $274.09 billion to a low of $250.39 billion, with the changes due to fluctuations in its stock price.

Long-term loans also have some disadvantages. Borrowers, for example, may have trouble finding lenders to supply large sums. Long-term borrowers may also face restrictions as conditions of the loan. For example, they may have to pledge long-term assets as collateral or agree to take on no more debt until the loan is paid.

CORPORATE BONDS Bonds are attractive when firms need large amounts for long periods of time. The issuing company gains access to large numbers of lenders through nationwide bond markets. On the other hand, bonds entail high administrative and selling costs. They may also require stiff interest payments, especially if the issuing company has a poor credit rating. Bonds also impose binding obligations on the firm, in many cases for up to 30 years, to pay bondholders a stipulated sum of annual or semiannual interest, even in times of financial distress. If the company fails to make a bond payment, it goes into default. A classic example is WorldCom, which filed for bankruptcy in 2002 when it was the nation's number-two long-distance phone company. With $102 billion in assets, WorldCom's bankruptcy at the time was the largest in U.S. history. Even with those massive assets, however, the firm was crushed by its $41 billion debt, $24 billion of which was in bonds. Facing prospects that the firm would default on upcoming interest payments, many of its creditors began withholding additional money unless loans were secured with WorldCom assets. With more than 1,000 creditors—including Citibank, JPMorgan Chase, and Credit Suisse First Boston—the firm was allowed to operate while in bankruptcy. In 2003, WorldCom changed its name to MCI, before emerging from bankruptcy status in 2004.

Pros and Cons for Equity Financing

Although debt financing often has strong appeal, **equity financing**, looking inside the company for long-term funding, is sometimes preferable. Equity financing includes either issuing common stock or retaining the firm's earnings.

Equity Financing *using the owners' funds from inside the company as the source for long-term funding*

THE EXPENSE OF COMMON STOCK The use of equity financing by means of common stock can be expensive because paying dividends is more expensive than paying bond interest. Interest paid to bondholders is a business expense and therefore a tax deduction for the firm. Payments of cash dividends to shareholders are not tax deductible.

RETAINED EARNINGS AS A SOURCE OF CAPITAL *Retained earnings* are net profits retained for the firm's use rather than paid out in dividends to stockholders. If a company uses retained earnings as capital, it will not have to borrow money and pay interest. If a firm has a history of reaping profits by reinvesting retained earnings, it may be attractive to some investors. Retained earnings, however, mean smaller dividends for shareholders. This practice may decrease the demand for—and the price of—the company's stock.

We have seen, then, that becoming a public corporation means selling off part of the ownership through an initial public offering. Several factors determine the stock's value after that stock is available to the general public. The day-to-day price is a weak indicator of the stock's value, whereas prospects for the firm's future financial health, the performance record of its management, and prospects for competing in the future are considerations that determine the stock's value. Market capitalization, the current stock price multiplied by the number of shares outstanding, is a widely used measure of company size and overall value. A public corporation's continued growth is accompanied by the need for more capital that can be met through two sources: debt financing or equity financing. Borrowing via long-term loans and the issuance of corporate bonds can provide a large supply of funds but also imposes binding obligations on the firm. Likewise, funds can be raised by issuing additional common stock or by increasing retained earnings, but doing so means smaller dividends for shareholders. These practices may decrease the demand for—and the price of—the company's stock.

Regulating Securities Markets

OBJECTIVE 7
Explain
how securities markets are regulated.

The U.S. government, along with various state agencies, plays a key role in monitoring and regulating the securities industry. Businesses cannot exist in the United States without the public's trust and the public's willingness to participate in business ownership and everyday transactions with companies. Regulation of the U.S. securities markets plays a vital role in maintaining the public's trust in fair and open business ownership.

The Securities and Exchange Commission

The U.S. SEC is the regulation and enforcement agency that oversees the markets' activities, including the ways securities are issued. The SEC was created in 1934 to prevent the kinds of abuses that led to the stock market crash of 1929. The SEC regulates the public offering of new securities by requiring that all companies file prospectuses before proposed offerings commence. To protect investors from fraudulent issues, a **prospectus** contains pertinent information about both the offered security and the issuing company. False statements are subject to criminal penalties.

Prospectus *registration statement filed with the SEC, containing information for prospective investors about a security to be offered and the issuing company*

The SEC also enforces laws against **insider trading**, the use of special knowledge about a firm for profit or gain. It is illegal, for example, for an employee of a firm to tell others about an anticipated event that may affect the value of that firm's stock, such as an acquisition or a merger, before news of that event is made public. Those in possession of such insider knowledge would have an unfair advantage over other investors.

Insider Trading *illegal practice of using special knowledge about a firm for profit or gain*

Regulations Against Insider Trading

In March 2011, the U.S. Attorney began a criminal trial in New York against Raj Rajaratnam, founder of Galleon Group, on charges that the billionaire fund manager profited from illegal stock tips with a network of financial insiders. Reports indicate the accused gained profits of up to $60 million by using illicit information, confidential company information not available to the public, revealing that stock prices of various companies would be increasing or falling. In conjunction with his arrest in 2009, charges were leveled against 26 others in the case—executives and securities

ZUMA Press, Inc./Alamy

54-year old Raj Rajaratnam was sentenced to 11 years in federal prison after being convicted for insider trading.

traders—19 of whom pleaded guilty. In May 2011, Rajaratnam was convicted on 14 charges and faced possible maximum prison sentences totaling up to 205 years. He was finally sentenced to serve 11 years in prison, the longest ever for an insider-trading violation. In addition to the criminal trial, he faces additional civil charges brought by the SEC. As a U.S. Attorney stated some years previously, "Insider trading is a crime. Corporate executives are prohibited from enriching themselves while the public remains in the dark about the true financial condition of their companies."[21]

The SEC offers a reward to any person who provides information leading to a civil penalty for illegal insider trading. The courts can render such a penalty of up to three times the illegal profit that was gained, and the reward can, at most, be 10 percent of that penalty.

Along with the SEC's enforcement efforts, the stock exchanges and securities firms have adopted self-regulation by participating with the Financial Industry Regulatory Authority (FINRA) in detecting and stopping insider action, and violations of other industry regulations. Established in 2003, FINRA's mission is to protect U.S. investors by overseeing the nation's brokerage firms and securities representatives. The major U.S. stock markets are under contract that allows FINRA to regulate those markets by writing rules, examining securities firms, enforcing the rules, and enforcing federal securities laws as well.

summary of learning objectives

Explain the concept of the time value of money and the principle of compound growth, and discuss the characteristics of common stock

The time value of money, perhaps the single most important concept in business finance, recognizes the basic fact that, when it's invested over time, money grows by earning interest or yielding some other form of return. Time value stems from the principle of *compound growth*—the cumulative growth from interest paid to the investor over given time periods. With each additional time period, the investment grows as interest payments accumulate and earn more interest, thus multiplying the earning capacity of the investment.

The "Rule of 72" is a practical example that illustrates the concept of the time value of money. The rule shows the number of years required for an initial investment to double in value, depending on the interest rate received in return for the investment. The rule demonstrates that higher rates of return (interest) result in fewer years required to double the original investment.

A share of *common stock* is the most basic form of ownership in a company. Individuals and organizations purchase a firm's common stock in the hope that it will increase in value and provide dividend income. Each common share has a vote on major issues that are brought before the shareholders. A stock's real value is its *market value*—the current price of a share in the stock market—reflecting the amount buyers are willing to pay for a share of the company's stock. Common stocks are among the riskiest of all investments because uncertainties about the stock market can quickly change the stock's value. *Blue-chip stocks* are issued by the strongest and most well established, financially sound, and respected firms. They have historically provided investors steady income through consistent dividend payouts.

Identify reasons for investing and the investment opportunities offered by mutual funds and exchange-traded funds.

Mutual funds are attractive investments because different funds are designed to appeal to different financial motives and goals of investors. Three of the most common alternative objectives for investing in mutual funds are stability and safety, conservative capital growth, and aggressive growth. Funds stressing stability and safety seek only modest growth while preserving the fund holders' capital and reliably paying modest current income. Conservative capital growth funds stress preservation of capital and current income but also seek some capital appreciation. Aggressive growth funds seek maximum long-term capital growth.

Unfortunately, many mutual funds do not perform as well as the average return of the overall stock market as a result of costly management expense and underperforming stocks. Index mutual funds, however, closely match the performance of a particular market. An exchange-traded fund (ETF), as with an index mutual fund, is a bundle of stocks (or bonds) that are an index that tracks the overall movement of a market. However, ETFs offer three areas of advantage over mutual funds: They can be traded throughout the day like a stock (whereas a mutual fund cannot be traded like a stock), they have low operating expenses, and they require low initial investments resulting in ease of entry for investors getting started without much money. Because they are traded on stock exchanges (hence, "exchange traded"), ETFs can be bought and sold—priced continuously—any time throughout the day. Mutual fund shares, in contrast, are priced once daily, at the end of the day.

Describe the role of securities markets and identify the major stock exchanges and stock markets.

The markets in which stocks and bonds are sold are called *securities markets*. By facilitating the buying and selling of securities, the securities markets provide the capital that companies rely on for survival. In *primary securities markets*, new stocks and bonds are bought and sold by firms and governments. Sometimes, new securities are sold to single buyers or small groups of buyers. These private placements are desirable because they allow issuers to keep their business plans confidential. Firms issuing new securities must get approval from the SEC. Issuing firms also usually rely on investment banking services to issue and resell new securities. Investment banks provide several important services. (1) They advise companies on the timing and financial terms of the new issue. (2) The investment bank buys and assumes liability for the new securities, a process referred to *underwriting*. (3) Investment banks create distribution networks for moving new securities through groups of other financial institutions into the hands of individual investors. In contrast with new securities issues, *existing* stocks and bonds are sold in the much larger *secondary securities market*, consisting largely of *stock exchanges*. A stock exchange is an organization of individuals coordinated to provide an institutional auction setting in which stocks can be bought and sold. Major stock exchanges include the New York Stock Exchange, the NASDAQ market in the United States, NYSE Euronext, along with various other foreign exchanges such as the London Stock Exchange and the Tokyo Exchange, and by online trading with other stock exchanges around the globe.

In 1998, the SEC authorized the creation of *electronic communication networks (ECNs)*, electronic trading systems that bring buyers and sellers together outside traditional stock exchanges by automatically matching buy and sell orders at specified prices. ECNs gained rapid popularity because the trading procedures are fast and efficient, often lowering transaction costs per share to mere pennies. They also allow after-hours trading (after traditional markets have closed for the day) and protect traders' anonymity.

Stock brokers are financial services professionals who earn commissions by executing buy and sell orders for outside customers. As with many other products, brokerage assistance can be purchased at either discount or at full-service prices. Discount brokers, such as E*TRADE and Scottrade, offer well-informed individual investors who know what they want to buy or sell a fast, low-cost way to participate in the market. Full-service brokers, such as Merrill Lynch Wealth Management, offer clients consulting advice in personal financial planning, estate planning, and tax strategies, along with a wider range of investment products.

Although not indicative of the status of individual securities, *market indexes*, such as the Dow Jones Industrial Average and S&P 500, provide useful summaries of overall price trends, both in specific industries and in the stock market as a whole. Market indexes, for example, reveal *bull* and *bear market* trends. *Bull markets* are periods of rising stock prices, generally lasting 12 months or longer; investors are motivated to buy, confident they will realize capital gains. Periods of falling stock prices, usually 20 percent off peak prices, are called *bear markets*; investors are motivated to sell, anticipating further falling prices.

OBJECTIVE 4

Describe the risk–return relationship and discuss the use of diversification and asset allocation for investments.

Individual investors have different motivations and personal preferences for safety versus risk. While all investors anticipate receiving future cash flows, some cash flows are more certain than other riskier returns. Investors generally expect to receive higher financial returns for investments having higher uncertainty. They do not expect large returns from secure, stable investments. Each type of investment, then, has a risk–return (risk–reward) relationship. The risk–return relationship is the principle that investors expect to receive higher returns for riskier investments and lower returns for safer investments. Conservative investors who have a low tolerance for risk will seek safer investments with low expected returns. The reverse is true for aggressive investors who prefer taking higher risks with the potential for higher returns.

When evaluating potential investments, investors look at returns from dividends or interest, returns from price appreciation, and total return. The rate of return from dividends paid to shareholders is commonly referred to as the *current dividend* yield. In the case of interest from a loan, the term *interest yield* is used. *Price appreciation* is an increase in the value of an investment over time. *Total* return is the sum of the investment's dividend or interest yields and the *capital gain* from price appreciation.

Diversification and asset allocation are tools for helping investors achieve the desired risk–return balance for an investment portfolio. *Diversification* means buying several different kinds of investments—stocks of different companies, securities of companies in different industries, investments in different countries, combinations of stocks/bonds/real estate/precious metals—to reduce the risk of loss if the value of any one investment should fall. *Asset allocation* is the proportion of overall money invested in each of various investment alternatives so that the overall risks for the portfolio are low, moderate, or high, depending on the investor's objectives and preferences.

OBJECTIVE 5

Describe the various ways that firms raise capital and identify the pros and cons of each method.

Every company needs cash to function. Firms often begin with the owner's personal savings. As more money is needed, it is obtained from sales revenues, borrowing from banks, cash from private investors, by issuing bonds, or selling stock. Money to purchase new equipment often comes in the form of loans from commercial banks. In a *secured loan (asset-backed loan)* the borrower guarantees repayment of the loan by pledging the asset as *collateral* to the lender. The amount of money that is loaned and must be repaid is the *loan principal*. However, borrowers also pay the lender an additional fee, *interest*, for the use of the borrowed funds. The amount of interest owed depends on an *annual percentage rate (APR)* that is agreed on between the lender and borrower. The interest amount is found by multiplying the APR by the loan principal. With an *unsecured loan*, the borrower does not have to put up collateral. In many cases, however, the bank requires the borrower to maintain a *compensating balance*; the borrower must keep a portion of the loan amount on deposit with the bank in a non-interest-bearing account.

Once a business has been successfully launched, it needs additional capital for growth. Outside individuals who provide such capital are called *angel investors*. Angel investors help many firms grow rapidly by providing what is known as *venture capital*, private funds from wealthy individuals or companies that seek investment opportunities in new growth companies. In most cases, the growth firm turns to venture capital sources because they have not yet built enough credit history to get a loan from commercial banks or other lending institutions.

Corporations can raise capital by issuing bonds. A *corporate bond* is a formal pledge (an IOU) obligating the issuer to pay interest periodically and repay the principal at maturity (a preset future date) to the lender. The federal government also issues bonds to finance projects and meet obligations, as do state and local governments (called *municipal bonds*) for financing the building of schools, roads, and sewage disposal systems.

OBJECTIVE 6

Identify the reasons a company might make an initial public offering of its stock, explain how stock value is determined, and discuss the significance of market capitalization.

The initial public offering (IPO)—the first sale of a company's stock to the general public—is a major source of funds for fueling the growth of many firms. IPOs reach far more potential investors, thereby providing access to a larger pool of funds than is available from the owner's personal funds and other private sources. A stock's real value is its market value—the current price of a share in the stock market. Market value reflects the amount that buyers are willing to pay for a share of the company's stock at any given time. However, the valuing of any stock today looks beyond the current price and is based on expectations of the financial returns it will provide to shareholders during the long run. A long-run perspective considers the company's financial health, past history of results and future forecasts, its record for managerial performance, and overall prospects for competing successfully in the coming years. Although supply and demand are a major determiner of a stock's price, another factor is a company's desire that its shares sell within a particular price range, believing it will attract a larger pool of investors. If the stock's market price gets too high, many investors cannot afford to buy shares. A company can restore shares to the desired lower price range by using a stock split in which the company gives shareholders an additional stock holding for each share they own.

The market price per share falls immediately after the split, but with a larger number of shares, every shareholder's investment value is unchanged.

Market capitalization, the total market value of all the company's outstanding shares, is a widely used measure of corporate size and value. Investors leaning toward risk avoidance typically regard larger market-cap firms as less risky, and firms with small market-caps (small-cap firms) as being particularly risky investments. Thus, the persistent demand for large-cap stocks tends to sustain or increase their market values.

Although debt financing often has strong appeal, *equity financing*, looking inside the company for long-term funding, is sometimes preferable. Equity financing includes either issuing common stock or retaining the firm's earnings. The use of equity financing by means of common stock can be expensive because paying dividends is more expensive than paying bond interest. Interest paid to bondholders is a business expense and therefore a tax deduction for the firm. Payments of cash dividends to shareholders are not tax deductible. *Retained earnings* are net profits retained for the firm's use rather than paid out in dividends to stockholders. If a company uses retained earnings as capital, it will not have to borrow money and pay interest. If a firm has a history of reaping profits by reinvesting retained earnings, it may be attractive to some investors. Retained earnings, however, mean smaller dividends for shareholders. This practice may decrease the demand for—and the price of—the company's stock.

OBJECTIVE 7

Explain how securities markets are regulated.

The U.S. government, along with various state agencies, plays a key role in monitoring and regulating the securities industry. The U.S. Securities and Exchange Commission (SEC) is the regulation and enforcement agency that oversees the markets' activities. The SEC regulates the public offering of new securities by requiring companies to file *prospectuses* before proposed offerings commence. To protect investors from fraudulent securities issues, the prospectus contains information about the offered security and the issuing company. False statements are subject to criminal penalties.

The SEC also enforces laws against *insider trading*—the use of special knowledge about a firm for profit or gain. An example of illegal insider trading includes an employee of a firm telling others about an anticipated event that may affect the value of that firm's stock, such as an acquisition or a merger, before news of that event is made public. Those in possession of such insider knowledge would have an unfair advantage over other investors. The SEC offers a reward to any person who provides information leading to a civil penalty for illegal insider trading.

Along with the SEC's enforcement, the stock exchanges and securities firms have adopted self-regulation by participating with the Financial Industry Regulatory Authority (FINRA) in detecting and stopping violations of industry regulations. FINRA's mission is to protect U.S. investors by overseeing the nation's brokerage firms and securities representatives. FINRA regulates the U.S. stock markets by writing rules, examining securities firms, enforcing the rules, and enforcing federal securities laws.

key terms

angel investors	capital gain	dividend
annual percentage rate (APR)	collateral	Dow Jones Industrial Average (DJIA)
asset allocation	common stock	electronic communication network (ECN)
bankruptcy	compound growth	equity financing
bear market	corporate bond	exchange-traded fund (ETF)
blue-chip stock	corporate raider	face value (par value)
bond indenture	current dividend yield and current	initial public offering (IPO)
bondholders' claim	interest yield	insider trading
book value	debt financing	interest
book-entry ownership	default	investment bank
bull market	diversification	load fund

loan principal
market capitalization (market cap)
market index
market value
maturity date (due date)
mortgage-backed security (MBS)
mutual fund
NASDAQ Composite Index
National Association of Securities
  Dealers Automated Quotation
  (NASDAQ) system

no-load fund
portfolio
price appreciation
primary securities market
prospectus
risk–return (risk–reward) relationship
Russell 2000 Index
S&P 500
secondary securities market
secured loan (asset-backed loan)
securities

Securities and Exchange Commission
  (SEC)
securities markets
stock
stock broker
stock exchange
stock split
time value of money
unsecured loan
venture capital

MyBizLab

To complete the problems with the ✪, go to EOC Discussion Questions in the MyLab.

questions & exercises

QUESTIONS FOR REVIEW

1. Explain the concept of the *time value of money*.
2. What do mutual funds and exchange-traded funds offer, and how do they work?
✪ 3. What is a corporate bond? Why would a company use bonds as a source of financing?
4. How does the market value of a stock differ from the book value of a stock?
5. How do firms meet their needs through debt financing and equity financing?

QUESTIONS FOR ANALYSIS

6. After researching several stocks online, you notice that they have continually fluctuated in price. What might be the reason for this? Is a higher-priced stock a better investment than a lower-priced stock? What factors would you consider in purchasing stocks?
✪ 7. In which type of fund do you think you would invest, a mutual fund or an exchange-traded fund? What is the difference, and why would you favor one over the other?

✪ 8. Suppose that you are a business owner and you need new equipment and immediate funds to meet short-term operating expenses. From what sources could you gain the capital you need, and what are some of the characteristics of these sources?

APPLICATION EXERCISES

9. Go to http://www.sec.gov to research how a new security is approved by the Securities and Exchange Commission. What is the process involved and how long would it take? Next, contact a financial institution such as Merrill Lynch and request information about their procedures for issuing or reselling new securities. Share this information with your classmates.
10. There have been a number of high-profile cases in recent years concerning insider trading. Do an online search to find a case involving insider trading. Who was accused of insider trading and what was their relationship to the company? Were they convicted of insider trading, and, if so, what was the penalty? Finally, how could the person accused of insider trading have avoided the charges?

building a business: continuing team exercise

Assignment

Meet with your team members to consider your new business venture and how it relates to the finance topics in this chapter. Develop specific responses to the following:

11. What role will debt financing play in your business's financial plan? What types of debt financing will you use? Why?
12. As your business grows, will you consider bringing in angel investors or venture capital? Why or why not?

13. Would you consider selling stock to the general public? What advantages would a public sale of stock bring? Are there any downsides to this decision?
14. If you decide to sell stock through an initial public offering, what factors will be most important in the valuation of your stock?
15. How will the financing of your business change over time?

team exercise

MARKET UPS AND DOWNS

Background Information

Investing in stocks requires an understanding of the various factors that affect stock prices. These factors may be intrinsic to the company itself or part of the external environment.

- Internal factors relate to the company itself, such as an announcement of poor or favorable earnings, earnings that are more or less than expected, major layoffs, labor problems, new products, management issues, and mergers.
- External factors relate to world or national events, such as wars, recessions, weather conditions that affect sales, the Fed's adjustment of interest rates, and employment figures that are higher or lower than expected.

By analyzing these factors, you will often learn a lot about why a stock did well or why it did poorly. Being aware of these influences will help you anticipate future stock movements.

QUESTIONS FOR ANALYSIS

16. Choose a company with publicly traded stock that has experienced considerable price fluctuations in the past few years. You may wish to consider companies such as IBM, JPMorgan Chase, AT&T, Amazon.com, United Healthcare, and Apple. Information about stock prices can be found on many websites, including finance.yahoo.com. For example, on the Yahoo! site, you can search for data on a company and then click on Historical Prices to download prices for the past three years.

17. Create a graph of the company's stock price over the past three years using Microsoft Excel or other graphing software. Identify dates associated with sharp peaks or valleys in the stock price.

18. Use a search engine or your library's online databases to search for articles that might discuss internal or external factors that explain the change in stock price. Write a brief summary explaining why the stock increased or decreased in price during the periods that you have identified.

19. Based on your research, what internal and external factors will have the most significant impact on the price of the company's stock in the future?

exercising your ethics

ARE YOU ENDOWED WITH GOOD JUDGMENT?

The Situation

Every organization faces decisions about whether to make conservative or risky investments. Let's assume that you have been asked to evaluate the advantages and drawbacks of conservative versus risky investments, including all relevant ethical considerations, by Youth Dreams Charities (YDC), a local organization that assists low-income families in gaining access to educational opportunities. YDC is a not-for-profit firm that employs a full-time professional manager to run daily operations. Overall, governance and policy making reside with a board of directors—10 part-time, community-minded volunteers who are entrusted with carrying out YDC's mission.

For the current year, 23 students receive tuition totaling $92,000 paid by YDC. Tuition comes from annual fund-raising activities (a white-tie dance and a seafood carnival) and from financial returns from YDC's $2.1 million endowment, amassed from charitable donations during the past 12 years. The board's goal is to increase the endowment to $4 million in five years, hoping to increase the amount of scholarships that the organization can provide.

The Dilemma

Based on the finance committee's suggestions, the board is considering a change in YDC's investment policies. The current conservative approach invests the endowment in low-risk instruments, such as bonds and public utility stocks, which have consistently yielded a 5 percent annual return. This practice has allowed the endowment to grow modestly (less than 1 percent per year), with the remaining investment proceeds (4 percent) flowing out for tuition. The proposed plan is move the organization's investment to blue-chip stocks, which generally have a higher yield. For example, the average return on the S&P 500 over the past 5 years has been 16 percent. If the organization is able to generate at least 17.5 percent on their investment over the next 5 years, as well as maintain the current level of financial assistance, the endowment will reach its $4 million goal. Although some board members like the prospects of faster growth, others think the proposal is too risky. What happens if, instead of increasing, the stock market collapses and the endowment shrinks? What will happen to YDC's programs then?

QUESTIONS TO ADDRESS

20. Why might a conservative versus risky choice be different at a not-for-profit organization than at a for-profit organization?
21. What are the main ethical issues in this situation?
22. What action should the board take?

cases

An Appetite for Beef

At the beginning of this chapter, you read about Fogo de Chao and how the restaurant chain has grown from a single location in Brazil to an international operation. Using the information presented in this chapter, you should be able to answer the following questions:

23. When the Coser and Ongaratto brothers started Fogo de Chao, what were their primary sources of financing?

24. After the Coser brothers acquired the Ongaratto brothers' shares of the company, they brought in GP Investments, a Brazilian venture capital firm. What are the advantages and disadvantages of using venture capital to build a business venture?

25. After the sale of Fogo de Chao to Thomas H. Lee Partners, the board and management team decided to issue an IPO of common stock. What were the goals of the IPO?

26. What are the benefits of an IPO as a source of financing? What other options did the company have?

27. Would you consider investing in Fogo de Chao? Why or why not?

28. If an investor had bought stock during the IPO, what would that investment be worth today?

Time to Gogo?

If you've flown lately, you may be familiar with the in-flight Internet service Gogo. The company's roots go back to 1991, when the company, then called Aircell, developed technology for in-flight phone services. In 2006, the company made a major change in strategy when it secured a 10-year license through the Federal Communications Commission for in-flight Internet services. Industry leaders, including Virgin, America, Delta, United, and Frontier, have been offering Gogo in-flight services since 2008. The company uses a network of cell towers to provide Internet access to passengers on more than 1,900 planes. Southwest is the only major airline in the United States not aligned with Gogo, having signed an agreement with a competitor, Row 44.[22]

Over the years, the company has grown through attention to innovation, as well as debt and equity financing. However, the enormous technology costs associated with expanding their network have resulted in losses each year. As of March 31, 2013, the company had $419 million dollars in assets, but $264 million in debt financing. The company's common and preferred stock was held by company executives and a number of venture capital firms.[23]

Gogo realized that international expansion is critical to their long-term plan. Though they can achieve greater saturation of the domestic market by having their equipment installed on more planes, international expansion is the key to turning a profit. The company has begun this effort, signing an agreement with Delta to install their equipment on all 170 planes in their international fleet.

To raise the money needed for a major expansion, Gogo planned to offer its stock to the public in December 2011. However, an extremely sluggish economy and disappointing results for other 2011 IPOs convinced Gogo to wait. In June 2013, Gogo's IPO resulted in the sale of 11 million shares at $17 each.[24] As a result, the company raised $187 million to fund their international expansion. The IPO was underwritten by Wall Street heavy hitters such as Morgan Stanley, JPMorgan, and UBS.[25] However, the price of the stock fell quickly over the following month, down to just more than $12 within weeks of the IPO. Two years later, the company's stock is trading above $22 per share, although this is considerably lower than its peak of $32 per share in December 2013. The company has made a major investment in improving the speed of its service with the Gogo 2Ku systems that are expected to begin installation in 2016. Should Gogo successfully penetrate the international market, investors in Gogo stock could see a huge return on investment. However, there's certainly considerable uncertainty about the future, and only time will tell if this risky investment will pay off.[26]

QUESTIONS FOR DISCUSSION

29. Given the risk, what would motivate an investor to purchase stock in Gogo?

30. Why would Gogo sell stock rather than taking on additional debt financing? Do you think that this was a good decision?

31. What role did underwriters, such as Morgan Stanley, JPMorgan, and UBS, play in the IPO?

32. Use a Web source, such as Yahoo! Finance or www.nasdaq.com to obtain the current price of Gogo stock. What has happened to the price of the stock over the last 6 months? What about the last 2 years?

33. Using the data provided from the web source in the previous step, is Gogo a small or large cap stock? How would this affect the risk associated with this investment?

crafting a business plan

FINANCIAL ISSUES

Goal of the Exercise

Here you'll consider how you'll finance your business as well as create an executive summary for your plan.

Exercise Background

You must know the costs of doing business, as well as how much revenue you expect to earn in one year. Then, you have to think about how to finance the business. To get a "great idea" off the ground requires money. But how will you get these funds?

You'll then conclude by creating an *executive summary*. The purpose of the executive summary is to give the reader a quick snapshot into your proposed business. Once you're done writing it, you'll end up placing the executive summary at the *beginning* of your completed business plan.

Your Assignment

For the purposes of this assignment, you need to answer the following questions:

34. How much money will you need to get your business started?

    Hint: Analyze the costs involved in running your business. Approximately how much will you need to get your business started?

35. How will you finance your business? For example, will you seek out a bank loan? Borrow from friends? Sell stocks or bonds initially or as your business grows?

    Hint: Find out information on securities, such as stocks and bonds.

36. Now, create an executive summary for your business plan. The executive summary should be brief—no more than two pages long—and should cover the following points:

    - The name of your business
    - Where your business will be located
    - The mission of your business
    - The product or service you are selling
    - Who your ideal customers are
    - How your product or business will stand out in the crowd
    - Who the owners of the business are and what experience they have
    - An overview of the future prospects for your business and industry

    Hint: The executive summary is really a sales pitch—it's the investor's first impression of your idea. Therefore, as with all parts of the plan, write in a clear and professional way.

MyBizLab

Go to the Assignments section of your MyLab to complete these writing exercises.

37. Suppose you are managing the securities investments for the firm where you work. Several employees have heard hallway conversations about something called a "risk–return relationship" that sounds important, but they are unsure what it means. (a) Write an essay that explains the risk–return relationship and its importance. (b) Discuss the meanings of *diversification* and *asset allocation*. Be sure to explain how they relate to managing investment risk.

38. A recent college graduate has come to you looking for advice. He has just landed a great job and his grandmother has stressed the importance of starting to save for retirement right away. He's wondering if this is really good advice, so he's looking to you for guidance. What would be the advantage of starting to save right away rather than waiting a few years? If he did start to save immediately, would you recommend that he invest in common stock? Why or why not?

end notes

[1] Hall, Cheryl. "Fogo de Chão founder finds success as Texas transplant," *Dallas Morning News*, July 23, 2011. Accessed June 28, 2015. http://Fogo de Chão founder finds success as Texas transplant; Linnane, Ciara. "6 things to know about Fogo de Chao ahead of its IPO." *MarketWatch*, June 18, 2015. Accessed June 28, 2015. http://www.marketwatch.com/story/ 6-things-to-know-about-fogo-de-chao-ahead-of-its-ipo-2015-06-16

[2] Whitfield, Craig. "What Returns Should We Expect from the Stock Market?" *Whitfield & Company*, May 22, 2015, at http://www.whitfieldco.com/blog/?p=39

[3] "Advantages and Disadvantages of Mutual Funds," *The Motley Fool*, at http://www.fool.com, accessed on May 23, 2015; "Who Pays for Cap and Trade?" *Wall Street Journal*, March 9, 2009, at http://online.wsj.com/article/SB123655590609066021.html

[4] Sharma, Rahul. "Second Circuit Rules that SIPA Customer Protections Are for Customers Only," *Weil: The Bankruptcy Blog*, March 25, 2013, at http://business-finance-restructuring.weil.com/sipa-proceedings/second-circuit-rules-that-sipa-customer-protections-are-for-customers-only/; Altman, Alex. "A Brief History of: Ponzi Schemes," *Time*, January 8, 2009, at http://www.time.com/time/magazine/article/0,9171,1870510,00.html; "How Much Did Madoff Scheme Cost?" *CNNMoney.com*, January 5, 2009, at http://money.cnn

.com/2009/01/02/news/companies/madoff/index
.htm; "The Man Who Figured Out Madoff's Scheme,"
CBS News, June 14, 2009, at http://www.cbsnews.com/
stories/2009/02/27/60minutes/main4833667.shtml;
Associated Press, "Investors Named in Madoff List,"
Columbia Daily Tribune, February 5, 2009, p. 7B;
Henriques, Diana B. "Claims Over 15,400 in Fraud
by Madoff," *New York Times*, July 9, 2009, at http://
www.nytimes.com/2009/07/10/business/10madoff
.html?ref=nyregion; "Bernie Madoff Victim's Fund
Breaches $10.6 Billion After Feeder Firm Settlement,"
Time, March 24, 2015, at http://time.com/3755676/
bernard-madoff-feeder-fund-10-6-billion/

[5]"Why Exchange-Traded Funds?" *Yahoo! Finance Exchange-Traded
Funds Center*, at http://finance.yahoo.com/etf/education/
02, accessed on May 23, 2015; Coombes, Andrea.
"Calculating the Costs of an ETF," *Wall Street Journal*,
October 23, 2012, at http://online.wsj.com/article/SB10
0008723963904440242045780442093008576204.html

[6]Bary, Andrew. "Embracing ETFs," *Barron's*, November 15,
2010, pp. 29–34.

[7] Ibid.

[8]"U.S. Investment Banking Era Ends," *UPI.com*, September 22,
2008, at http://www.upi.com/Business_News/2008/09/
22/US-Investment-banking-era-ends/UPI-96221222086983/

[9] New York Stock Exchange, at http://www.nyse.com, accessed
on May 26, 2015.

[10]"The State of Qatar Launches 'Qatar Exchange' as it Signs
Today Formal Terms of Strategic Partnership with NYSE
Euronext," *NYSE News Release*, June 19, 2009, at http://
www.nyse.com/press/1245406656784.html

[11]"Electronic Communication Network (ECN)," *Investing Answers*,
accessed on June 4, 2013 at http://www.investing
answers.com/financial-dictionary/stock-market/electronic-
communication-network-ecn-757

[12]"Just 25% Recognize That Most Americans Are Investors,"
Rasmussen Reports, February 11, 2011, at http://www
.rasmussenreports.com/public_content/business/
general_business/february_2011/just_25_recognize_
that_most_americans_are_investors

[13]Carey, Theresa W. "Cut the Cord," *Barrons.com*, March 12,
2012, at http://online.barrons.com/article/SB50001424
052748704759704577267660673833538.html#articleTabs_
article%3D0; "Stock Market: Why Is Stock Market Data
Delayed by 20 Minutes (NYSE, NASDAQ) to the General
Public?," *Quora*, August 25, 2010, at http://www.quora.
com/Stock-Market/Why-is-stock-market-data-delayed-
by-20-minutes-NYSE-NASDAQ-to-the-general-public;
"Online Trading Software," *TradeStation*, at http://www
.tradestation.com/, accessed on June 7, 2013; "Where Can
I Find Information About Pre-and After-Hours Trading
on the NYSE and the Nasdaq?" *Investopedia*, February
26, 2009, at http://www.investopedia.com/ask/
answers/06/preaftermarket.asp; Adam Milton, "What
Is Day Trading?" *About.com*, at http://daytrading.about
.com/od/daytradingbasics/a/WhatIsDayTradin.htm,
accessed on June 8, 2013.

[14]Norwitz, Steven E., ed., "A Bear Market of Historic
Proportions," *T. Rowe Price Report*, Spring 2009, p. 1.

[15]"Dow Jones to Change Composition of the Dow Jones Industrial
Average," *Dow Jones (Press Release)*, June 1, 2009, at http://
www.djindexes.com/mdsidx/html/pressrelease/
press-release-archive.html#20090601

[16]Beidelman, Carl. *The Handbook of International Investing*
(Chicago, 1987), p. 133.

[17]Welch, David. "Old GM Bondholders Getting Shares in
New General Motors May Depress Price," *Bloomberg
.com*, April 6, 2011, at http://www.bloomberg.com/
news/2011-04-06/old-gm-bondholders-getting-shares-
in-new-general-motors-may-depress-price.html

[18]Kumar, Ajay. "Can We Trust Moody's, Fitch, Standard &
Poor's?" *CommodityOnline*, at http://www.commodity
online.com/printnews.php?news_id=15888, accessed on
July 22, 2009; Evans, David, and Salas, Caroline. "Flawed
Credit Ratings Reap Profits as Regulators Fail (Update
1)," *Bloomberg.com*, April 29, 2009, at http://www.bloom
berg.com/apps/news?pid=20670001&sid=au4oIx.judz4;
Wayne, Leslie. "Calpers Sues over Ratings of Securities,"
New York Times, July 15, 2009, at http://www.nytimes
.com/2009/07/15/business/15calpers.html; Segal,
David. "Ohio Sues Rating Firms for Losses in Funds,"
New York Times, November 20, 2009, at http://www
.nytimes.com/2009/11/21/business/21ratings.html;
Hume, Lynn. "Connecticut AG Sues All Three Rating
Agencies, *The Bond Buyer*, July 31, 2008, at http://www
.bondbuyer.com/issues/117_145/-292250-1.html

[19]"Mortgage-Backed Securities," *U.S. Securities and Exchange
Commission*, June 25, 2007, at http://www.sec.gov/
answers/mortgagesecurities.htm; "Mortgage-Backed
Security," *riskglossary.com*, at http://www.riskglossary
.com/link/mortgage_backed_security.htm, accessed on
July 24, 2009.

[20]"Worst Performing IPOs of 2014." *Zacks* (blog). Entry
posted December 31, 2014. Accessed June 28, 2015.
http://www.zacks.com/stock/news/158997/worst-
performing-ipos-of-2014

[21]Reuters, "Rajaratnam Insider Trading Trial Begins," March
9, 2011, *Huffington Post*, at http://www.huffingtonpost.
com/2011/03/09/rajaratnam-trial_n_833326.html; U.S.
Department of Justice, "Joseph P. Nacchio Indicted by
Federal Grand Jury: Former Chief Executive Officer of
Qwest Communications Charged with Insider Trading,
Selling Over $100 Million Stock," (December 20, 2005), at
http://lawprofessors.typepad.com/whitecollarcrime_
blog/files/nacchio_indictment.pdf

[22]Koenig, David. "IPO Shares of Flight Web Service Gogo Fall."
USA Today. June 22, 2013, http://www.usatoday.com/
story/money/business/2013/06/22/gogo-nasdaq-
airlines-wifi/2448083/, accessed on July 16, 2013.

[23]"GOGO: Summary for Gogo Inc.—Yahoo! Finance." *Yahoo!
Finance* July 16, 2013.

[24]Matherson, Nathaniel. "A Few Recent IPO Misses May Offer
Value, or Not." *The Motley Fool*. July 9, 2013, at http://
beta.fool.com/natematherson/2013/07/09/poor-
performing-ipo-draft/39274/, accessed on July 16, 2013.

[25]"Gogo—This Recent Public Offering Is Not Going Yet."
Seeking Alpha. June 28, 2013, http://seekingalpha.com/
article/1526942-gogo-this-recent-public-offering-is-not-
going-yet, accessed on July 16, 2013.

[26]Martin, Grant. "Delta Doubles Down on Gogo Inflight Internet
With Faster and Broader Service." *Forbes*. February 25,
2015, http://www.forbes.com/sites/grantmartin/2015/
02/25/delta-doubles-down-on-gogo-inflight-internet-
with-faster-and-broader-service/, accessed on June 24,
2015.

glossary

Angel Investors outside investors who provide new capital for firms in return for a share of equity ownership.

Annual Percentage Rate (APR) one-year rate that is charged for borrowing, expressed as a percentage of the borrowed principal.

Asset Allocation relative amount of funds invested in (or allocated to) each of several investment alternatives.

Bankruptcy court-granted permission for a company to not pay some or all debts.

Bear Market period of falling stock prices marked by negative investor sentiments with motivation to sell ahead of anticipated losses.

Blue-Chip Stock common stock issued by a well-established and respected company with a sound financial history and a stable pattern of dividend payouts.

Bond Indenture legal document containing complete details of a bond issue.

Bondholder's Claim request for court enforcement of a bond's terms of payment.

Book Value value of a common stock expressed as the firm's owners equity divided by the number of common shares.

Book-Entry Ownership procedure that holds investor's shares in book-entry form, rather than issuing a physical paper certificate of ownership.

Bull Market period of rising stock prices, lasting 12 months or longer, featuring investor confidence for future gains and motivation to buy.

Capital Gain profit realized from the increased value of an investment.

Collateral asset pledged for the fulfillment of repaying a loan.

Common Stock most basic form of ownership, including voting rights on major issues, in a company.

Compound Growth compounding of interest over time. With each additional time period, interest returns accumulate and earn more interest.

Corporate Bond formal pledge obligating the issuer (the company) to pay interest periodically and repay the principal at maturity.

Corporate Raider investor conducting a type of hostile corporate takeover against the wishes of the company.

Current Dividend Yield and Current Interest Yield yearly dollar amount of income divided by the investment's current market value, expressed as a percentage.

Debt Financing long-term borrowing from sources outside a company.

Default failure of a borrower to make payment when due to a lender.

Diversification purchase of several different kinds of investments rather than just one.

Dividend payment to shareholders, on a per-share basis, out of the company's earnings.

Dow Jones Industrial Average (DJIA) oldest and most widely cited market index based on the prices of 30 blue-chip, large-cap industrial firms on the NYSE.

Electronic Communication Network (ECN) electronic trading system that brings buyers and sellers together outside traditional stock exchanges.

Equity Financing using the owner's funds from inside the company as the source for long-term funding.

Exchange-Traded Fund (ETF) bundle of stocks or bonds that are in an index that tracks the overall movement of a market, but unlike a mutual fund can be traded like a stock.

Face Value (Par Value) amount of money that the bond buyer (lender) lent the issuer and that the lender will receive on repayment.

Initial Public Offering (IPO) first sale of a company's stock to the general public.

Insider Trading illegal practice of using special knowledge about a firm for profit or gain.

Interest fee paid to a lender for the use of borrowed funds; like a rental fee.

Investment Bank financial institution that specializes in issuing and reselling new securities.

Load Fund mutual fund in which investors are charged sales commissions when they buy in or sell out.

Loan Principal amount of money that is loaned and must be repaid.

Market Capitalization (Market Cap) total dollar value of all the company's outstanding shares.

Market Index statistical indicator designed to measure the performance of a large group of stocks or track the price changes of a stock market.

Market Value current price of a share of stock in the stock market.

Maturity Date (Due Date) future date when repayment of a bond is due from the bond issuer (borrower).

Mortgage-Backed Security (MBS) mortgages pooled together to form a debt obligation—a bond—that entitles the holder (investor) to cash that flows in from the bundled mortgages.

Mutual Fund company that pools cash investments from individuals and organizations to purchase a portfolio of stocks, bonds, and other securities.

NASDAQ Composite Index market index that includes all NASDAQ-listed companies, both domestic and foreign, with a high proportion of technology companies and small-cap stocks.

National Association of Securities Dealers Automated Quotation (NASDAQ) System world's oldest electronic stock market consisting of dealers who buy and sell securities over a network of electronic communications.

No-Load Fund mutual fund in which investors pay no commissions when they buy in or sell out.

Portfolio combined holdings of all the financial investments of any company or individual.

Price Appreciation increase in the dollar value of an investment at two points in time (the amount by which the price of a security increases).

Primary Securities Market market in which new stocks and bonds are bought and sold by firms and governments.

Prospectus registration statement filed with the SEC, containing information for prospective investors about a security to be offered and the issuing company.

Risk Return (Risk Reward) Relationship principle that safer investments tend to offer lower returns whereas riskier investments tend to offer higher returns (rewards).

Russell 2000 Index specialty index that uses 2,000 stocks to measure the performance of the smallest U.S. companies.

S&P 500 market index of U.S. equities based on the performance of 500 large-cap stocks representing various sectors of the overall equities market.

Secondary Securities Market market in which existing (not new) stocks and bonds are sold to the public.

Secured Loan (Asset-Backed Loan) loan to finance an asset, backed by the borrower pledging the asset as collateral to the lender.

Securities stocks, bonds, and mutual funds representing secured, or asset-based, claims by investors against issuers.

Securities and Exchange Commission (SEC) government agency that regulates U.S. securities markets.

Securities Markets markets in which stocks and bonds are sold.

Stock portion of ownership of a corporation.

Stock Broker individual or organization that receives and executes buy and sell orders on behalf of outside customers in return for commissions.

Stock Exchange an organization of individuals to provide an institutional auction setting in which stocks can be bought and sold.

Stock Split stock dividend paid in additional shares to shareholders, thus increasing the number of outstanding shares.

Time Value of Money principle that invested money grows, over time, by earning interest or some other form of return.

Unsecured Loan loan for which collateral is not required.

Venture Capital private funds from wealthy individuals seeking investment opportunities in new growth companies.

Attitude, Goal Setting, and Life Management

future • dreams • happiness

After studying these topics, you will benefit by:

- Discovering the influence professionalism and positive human relations have on personal, academic, and career success
- Knowing how individual personality, attitude, and values affect the workplace
- Recognizing how self-efficacy and personal branding affect your confidence
- Developing a strategy to deal with past negative experiences and other barriers to success
- Examining the impact goal setting has on creating a life plan in today's economy
- Choosing priorities to support your goals

HOW DO YOU RATE?

Are you self-centered?	Yes	No
1. Do you rarely use the word I in conversations?	☐	☐
2. When in line with coworkers, do you let coworkers go ahead of you?	☐	☐
3. Do you keep personal work accomplishments private?	☐	☐
4. Do you rarely interrupt conversations?	☐	☐
5. Do you celebrate special events (e.g., birthdays, holidays) with your coworkers by sending them a card, a note, or small gift?	☐	☐

▶ If you answered "yes" to two or more of these questions, well done. Your actions are more focused on the needs of others and you are most likely not self-centered.

From Chapter 1 of *Professionalism, Skills for Workplace Success*, Fourth Edition. Lydia E. Anderson, Sandra B. Bolt. Copyright © 2016 by Pearson Education, Inc. All rights reserved.

All About You

Congratulations! You are about to embark on a self-discovery to identify how to become and remain productive and successful in the workplace. The first step in this self-discovery is to perform a simple exercise. Look in a mirror and identify the first three words that immediately come to mind.

These three words are your mirror words. **Mirror words** describe how you view yourself and how you believe others view you. Your perception of yourself influences your relationship with coworkers and your workplace performance.

The goal of both your instructor and the authors is to not only assist you in securing the job of your dreams, but to keep that great job and advance your career based on healthy, quality, and productive work habits that benefit you, your coworkers, and your organization. **Professionalism** is defined as workplace behaviors that result in positive business relationships. The secret to healthy relationships at work is to first understand yourself. Once you understand your personal needs, motivators, and irritants, it becomes easier to understand and successfully work with others. This is why the first part of this chapter focuses on your personality, your values, and your self-concept.

An individual's personality and attitude dictate how he or she responds to conflict, crisis, and other typical workplace situations. Each of these typical workplace situations involves working with and through people. Understanding your own personality and attitude makes it much easier to understand your reaction to others' personalities and attitudes.

Human relations are the interactions that occur with and through people. These interactions create relationships. Therefore, you theoretically have relationships with everyone you come into contact with at work. For an organization to be profitable, its employees must be productive. It is difficult to be productive if you cannot work with your colleagues, bosses, vendors, and/or customers. Workplace productivity is a result of positive workplace interactions and relationships.

Personality is a result of influences, and there are many outside influences that affect workplace relationships. These influences may include immediate family, friends, extended family, religious affiliation, and even society as a whole. Conversely, experiences and influences at work affect your personal life. Therefore, to understand workplace relationships, you must first understand yourself.

Personality and Values

Behavior is a reflection of personality. **Personality** is a stable set of traits that assist in explaining and predicting an individual's behavior. Personality traits can be positive, such as being caring, considerate, organized, enthusiastic, or reliable. However, personality traits can also be negative, such as being rude, unfocused, lazy, or immature. For example, if you are typically organized at work and suddenly you become disorganized, others may believe something is wrong because your disorganized behavior is not in sync with your stable set of organized traits. An individual's personality is shaped by many variables, including past experience, family, friends, religion, and societal influences. Perhaps a family member was incredibly organized and passed this trait on to you. Maybe someone in your sphere of influence was incredibly disorganized, which influenced you to be very organized. These experiences (positive or not) shape your values. **Values** are things that are important to you as an individual based on your personal experiences and influences. These influences include religion, family, and societal issues such as sexual preference, political affiliation, and materialism. Note that you may have good or bad values. You may value achievement, family, money, security, or freedom. For example, one individual may not value money because he or she has been told that "money is the root of all evil." Contrast this with an individual who values money because he or she has been taught that money is a valuable resource used to ensure a safe, secure future. Because values are things that are important to you, they will directly affect your personality. If you have been taught that money is a valuable resource, you may be very careful in your spending. Your personality trait will be that of a diligent, hardworking person who spends cautiously.

Topic Situation

While in school, Charley worked hard to secure a new job as an assistant at his college bookstore. Charley's parents are both college graduates with successful careers, which influences Charley's values and beliefs in the ability to perform successfully at school and work. However, many of Charley's friends are not attending college, and have a hard time securing and/or maintaining employment. For this reason, Charley gets no support from these friends regarding earning a degree and holding a job.

TOPIC RESPONSE

If Charley continues to associate with his non-supportive friends, how could these friendships influence Charley's performance at school and work?

Attitude

An **attitude** is a strong belief about people, things, and situations. For example, you either care or do not care how your classmates feel about you. Your attitude is related to your values and personality and affected by past success and failures. Using the previous example, if you value money, your attitude will be positive toward work because you value what you get in return for your work effort—a paycheck. Attitude affects performance: An individual's performance significantly influences a group's performance, and a group's performance, in turn, affects an organization's performance. Think about a barrel of juicy red apples. Place one bad apple in the barrel of good apples, and, over time, the entire barrel will be spoiled. That is why it is so important to evaluate personal influences. The barrel reflects your personal goals and your workplace behavior. Your attitude affects not only your performance, but also the performance of those with whom you come in contact.

Does this mean you avoid anyone you believe is a bad influence? Not necessarily. You cannot avoid certain individuals, such as relatives and coworkers. However, you should be aware of the impact individuals have on your life. If certain individuals have a negative influence, avoid or limit your exposure to them (bad apple). If you continue to expose yourself to negative influences, you can lose sight of your goals, which may result in a poor attitude and poor performance. Choose your friendships wisely and surround yourself with positive people. Positive people are truthful, faithful, loving, and supportive. Negative people interfere with you reaching your goals by making you uncomfortable or by distracting you.

Think About It

Identify one friend that you believe is a positive influence on you and a friend that is a negative influence. How should you handle these relationships?

Talk It Out

What cartoon character best reflects your personality and why?

Self-Efficacy and Its Influences

Review your "mirror words" from the beginning of this chapter. Were your words positive or negative? Whatever you are feeling is a result of your **self-concept**. Self-concept is how you view yourself. Thinking you are intelligent or believing you are attractive are examples of self-concept. **Self-image** is your belief of how others view you. If your self-concept is positive and strong, you will display confidence and not worry about how others view you and your actions. If you are insecure, you will rely heavily on what others think of you. Although it is important to show concern for what others think of you, it is more important to have a positive self-concept. Note that there is a difference between being conceited and self-confident. Those who behave in a conceited manner have too high an opinion of themselves as compared to others. People are drawn to individuals who are humble, display a good attitude, are confident, and are consistently positive. It is easy to see the tremendous impact both personality and attitude have in the development of your self-esteem and self-concept. One final factor that influences self-concept and performance is that of self-efficacy. **Self-efficacy** is your belief in your ability to perform a task. For example, if you are confident in your math abilities, you will most likely score high on a math exam because you believe you are strong in that subject. However, if you are required to take a math placement exam for a job and are not confident in your math abilities, you will most likely not perform well. The way you feel about yourself and your environment is reflected in how you treat others. This is called **projection**. A positive self-concept will be projected toward others.

Envision a hand mirror. The handle of the mirror (the foundation) is your personality. The frame of the mirror represents your personal values. The mirror itself is your attitude, which is reflected for you and the world to see. The way you view yourself is your self-concept; the way you believe others see you is your self-image. As you begin networking with others, interviewing for a new job, or embarking on a new career, create a **personal brand**. A personal brand reflects traits you want others to think of when they think of you. These personal traits may include your appearance, your values, or specific knowledge or skills that make you unique, interesting, and of value to others.

Exercise 1

Define your personal brand. Identify desired appearance, personality, knowledge and skills, personal values, and attitude.

_____

_____

_____

Dealing with Negative Baggage

Many of us have experienced people who appear to have a chip on their shoulder that negatively influences their behavior. The negativity is reflected in an individual's personality. More often than not, the "chip" is a reflection of a painful past experience. What many do not realize is that negative past experiences sometimes turn into personal baggage that creates barriers to career success. Examples of negative past experiences may include traumatic issues such as an unplanned pregnancy or a criminal offense. Other times, the negative experience involved a poor choice or a failure at something that had great meaning. These experiences are the ones that most heavily influence one's personality, values, and self-concept, and in turn, may affect workplace attitude and performance.

Topic Situation

When starting high school, Keira made a poor choice and got in minor trouble with the law. Keira paid her dues, yet is still embarrassed and sometimes feels unworthy of a successful future. Keira is trying to climb the mountain of success carrying a hundred-pound suitcase. The suitcase is filled with the thoughts of a previous poor choice and embarrassment. Because of Keira's motivation to complete college, most friends and acquaintances are unaware of her past mistake. However, if Keira continues to carry this negative baggage, she may lose sight of her goals.

TOPIC RESPONSE

What steps should Keira take to help her achieve her goals?

If you have had a negative experience that is hindering your ability to succeed, recognize the impact your past has on your future. Although you cannot change yesterday, you can most certainly improve your today and your future. Take these steps toward a more productive future:

1. *Confront your past.* Whatever skeleton is in your past, admit that the negative event occurred. Do not try to hide or deny that it happened. There is no need to share the episode with everyone, but it may help to confidentially share the experience with someone you trust (friend or trained professional) who had no involvement with the negative experience. Acknowledgement of the negative event is the first step toward healing.

2. *Practice forgiveness.* Past negative experiences hurt. A process in healing is to forgive whoever hurt you. Forgiveness does not justify that what occurred was acceptable, but reconciles in your heart that you are dealing with the experience and are beginning to heal. Identify who needs forgiveness. The act of forgiveness may involve a conversation with someone, or it may just involve you deciding to no longer carry this burden.

3. *Move forward.* Let go of hurt, guilt, and/or embarrassment. Do not keep dwelling on the past and using it as an excuse or barrier toward achieving your goals. If you are caught in this step, physically write the experience down on a piece of paper and the words "I forgive Joe" (replace the name with the individual who harmed you). Then take the paper and destroy it. This physical act puts you in control and allows you to visualize the negative experience being diminished. As you become more confident in yourself, your negative experience becomes enveloped with the rest of your past and frees you to create a positive future.

This sometimes painful process is necessary if your goal is to become the best individual you can be. Dealing with negative baggage is not something that happens overnight. As mentioned previously, some individuals may need professional assistance to help them through the process. There is no shame in seeking help. In fact, there is great freedom when you have finally let go of the baggage and are able to climb to the top of the mountain unencumbered.

Locus of Control

The reality is that you will not always be surrounded by positive influences and you cannot control everything that happens in your life. Your attitude is affected by who you believe has control over situations that occur in your life, both personally and professionally. The **locus of control** identifies who you believe controls your future. An individual with an *internal* locus of control believes that he or she controls his or her own future. An individual with an *external* locus of control believes that others control his or her future.

Extremes on either end of the locus of control are not healthy. Realize that individual effort and a belief in the ability to perform well translate to individual success. External factors also influence your ability to achieve personal goals. You cannot totally control the environment and future. Power, politics, and other factors play an important part in the attainment of goals. Successful individuals take personal responsibility and avoid blaming others.

Learning Styles

Another element of personality is one's **learning style.** Learning styles define the method of how you best take in information and/or learn new ideas. There are three primary learning styles: visual, auditory, and tactile/kinesthetic.

To determine what your dominant learning style is, perform this simple exercise. Imagine you are lost and need directions. Do you:

a. Want to see a map
b. Want someone to tell you the directions
c. Want to draw or write down the directions yourself

If you prefer answer *a,* you are a visual learner. You prefer learning by seeing. If you selected *b,* you are an auditory learner. You learn best by hearing. If you selected *c,* you are a tactile/kinesthetic learner, which means you learn best by feeling, touching, or holding. No one learning style is better than the other. However, it is important to recognize your primary and secondary learning styles so that you can get the most out of your world (in and out of the classroom or on the job). As a visual learner, you may digest material best by reading and researching. Auditory learners pay close attention to course lectures and class discussions. Tactile/kinesthetic learners will learn best by performing application exercises and physically writing course notes. Recognize what works best for you and implement that method to maximize your learning experience. Also recognize that not everyone learns the same way you do and not all information is presented in your preferred method. With that recognition, you can become a better classmate, team member, coworker, and boss.

Exercise 2

Exercise 2

Apply the learning styles discussed and complete the following statements.

In the classroom, I learn best by _____

In the classroom, I have difficulty learning when _____

How will I use this information to perform better? _____

Importance and Influences of Personal Goal Setting

Everyone has dreams. These dreams may be for a college degree, a better life for loved ones, financial security, or the acquisition of material items such as a new car or home. Goal setting is the first step toward turning a dream into a reality. This important process provides focus and identifies specific steps that need to be accomplished. It is also a common practice used by successful individuals and organizations. A **goal** is a target. Think of a goal as a reward at the top of a ladder. To reach a goal, you need to progress up each step of the ladder. Each step contributes to the achievement of a goal and supports your personal values. Goals help you decide what you want in your future, increase self-concept, and help overcome procrastination, fear, and failure.

When you set goals, career plans become more clear and meaningful. They motivate you to continue working to improve yourself and help you achieve—not just hope for—what you want in life.

Topic Situation

At 22 years of age, Austin had only a high-school education. After working odd jobs at minimum wage since graduating from high school, Austin decided to attend college to become a Certified Public Accountant (CPA). Austin set a long-term goal to finish college in five years. Self-supporting and having to work, he set a realistic goal to obtain an associate degree in accounting within three years. After achieving that goal, Austin plans to find a job as an account clerk while finishing school. This goal will increase his income and self-confidence. Still committed to becoming a CPA, he plans to earn a bachelor's degree in accounting within two years after receiving the associate degree.

TOPIC RESPONSE

What are specific steps Austin can take to ensure he reaches his goal of becoming a CPA?

Goals can and should be set in all major areas of your life, including personal, career, financial, educational, and physical. Goals help maintain a positive outlook. They also contribute to creating a more positive perception of yourself and result in improved human relations with others.

Example of Austin's goals:

Talk It Out

Share one goal you have set for this class.

Five-year long-term goal	Obtain a bachelor's degree in accounting
Three-year long-term goal	Obtain an associate degree in accounting and secure a job as an account clerk
One-year short-term goal	Successfully pass the appropriate courses toward the associate degree and identify an internship
Now	Apply for school and find a part-time job to obtain work experience

How to Set Goals

As explained earlier, achieving goals is like climbing a ladder. Imagine that there is a major prize (what you value most) at the top of the ladder. The prize can be considered your long-term goal, and each step on the ladder is a progressive short-term goal that helps you reach the major prize.

Set short-term and long-term goals and put them in writing. **Long-term goals** are goals that take longer than a year to accomplish, with a realistic window of up to 10 years.

To set a goal, first identify what you want to accomplish in life. Write down everything you can think of, including personal, career, and educational dreams. Next, review the list and choose which items you most value. In reviewing your list, ask yourself where you want to be in one year, five years, and 10 years. The items you identified are your long-term goals. Keep each goal realistic and something you truly want. Each goal should be attainable, yet challenging enough to work toward. Identify why each goal is important to you. This is a key step toward setting yourself up for success. Next, identify opportunities and potential barriers toward reaching these goals. Remember Austin's goal to be a CPA? Austin believes becoming a CPA represents success. It is important to him, and it is a realistic goal that can be reached.

Exercise 3

Identify educational, personal, and professional accomplishments you would like to achieve in 5–10 years.

_____

_____

_____

Short-term goals are goals that can be reached within a year's time. They are commonly set to help reach long-term goals. Businesses often refer to short-term goals as objectives because they are measurable and have a one year or less time line. Short-term goals can be achieved in one day, a week, a month, or even several months. As short-term goals are met, long-term goals should be updated. Just like long-term goals, short-term goals (objectives) must be realistic, achievable, and important to you. They need to be measurable so you know when you have actually reached them.

An additional long-term goal for Austin is to buy a car one year after graduation. Austin has set several short-term goals, one being to save a specific amount of money each month. To do this, he needs to work a certain number of hours each week. He also needs to be specific about the type of car, whether to buy used or new, and whether he needs to take out a loan. The answers to these questions will determine how much money Austin will need to save each month and if the one-year time frame is realistic.

Exercise 4

Using the goals you identified in Exercise 3, identify how you can turn each dream into a reality.

_____

_____

_____

A popular and easy goal-setting tool is the SMART method. **SMART** is an acronym for writing goals to ensure they are specific, measurable, achievable, relevant, and time based.

			Example
S	Specific	Clearly identify what exactly you want to accomplish and, if possible, make your goal quantifiable. This makes your goal specific.	Become a manager for a top accounting firm
M	Measurable	Make your goal measurable. Identify how you will know when you have achieved your goal.	Having the job as a manager
A	Achievable	Keep your goal achievable but not too easily attainable or too far out of reach. A good achievable goal is challenging, yet attainable and realistic.	Getting good grades in college and gaining work experience along the way
R	Relevant	Relevant personal goals have meaning to its owner. The goal should belong to you, and you should have (or have access to) the appropriate resources to accomplish the goal.	I want to do this
T	Time Based	Attach a specific date or time period to provide a time frame for achieving the goal.	By 2021

For example, instead of writing, "I will become a manager in the future," write, "After attending college and getting work experience, I will become a manager with a top accounting firm by the beginning of the year 2021." After you have written a goal, give it the SMART test to increase its probability for success.

After you have written positive and detailed goals, there are a few additional aspects of goal setting to consider. These include owning and taking control of your goals.

Owning the goal ensures that the goal belongs to you. You are the one who should decide your goals, not your parents, spouse, significant other, friends, relatives, or anyone else. For example, if Austin goes to college because it is his personal dream to be a CPA, that goal will be accomplished. However, if Austin becomes a CPA because his parents want him to be a CPA, this will not be Austin's goal and it will be harder to accomplish.

Take control of your goal by securing information necessary to accomplish it. Know what resources and constraints are involved, including how you will use resources and/or get around constraints. If your goal is related to a specific career, identify what is required to attain that career in regard to education, finances, and other matters. Clarify the time needed to reach your goals by writing them as short-term or long-term goals. Applying the concept of locus of control, remember that not every factor is within your control. Therefore, be flexible and realistic with your goals and the time you take to achieve them.

Creating a Life Plan

Identifying goals contribute to the creation of a **life plan**. A life plan is a written document that identifies goals for all areas of your life, including career, family/social, spiritual, and financial.

Consider what you want in the following areas of your life:

- *Education and career:* Degree attainment, advanced degrees, respectable job titles, specific employers
- *Social and spiritual:* Marriage, family, friends, religion
- *Financial:* Home ownership, car ownership, investments
- *Activities:* Travel, hobbies, life experiences

Create goals for each of these major life areas and establish goals that reflect your values. Note that some goals may blend into two or more areas. Remember that goals can change over time; stay focused but flexible.

It is common for younger students to be uncertain of their career goals. Others may feel overwhelmed that they have a life goal but lack the necessary resources to accomplish one or more goals. Education is an important key to achieving personal and career goals and no one can take your knowledge from you. When writing your life goals, consider the degrees/certificates, the time frame, the financial resources, and the support network you will require for educational success. Make college course choices based on your desired educational goals. Choose courses that will benefit you, help you explore new concepts, and challenge you. To be successful in your career, it is important to enjoy what you do. Select a career that supports your short-term and long-term goals. When planning your career consider:

- Why your target career is important to you
- What resources are needed to achieve your career goal
- How you will know you have achieved career success

People choose careers for different reasons, including earning power, status, intellect, values, and self-satisfaction. If there is a career center available at your college, take time to visit and explore the various resources it offers. There are also several personality and career interest tests that will help you determine career options. Career assessments are offered at many college career centers and online. These useful assessments assist in identifying interests, abilities, and personality traits to determine which career will suit you best. Take advantage of all available resources and gather information to assist you in making the optimal career decision. Conduct an Internet search, perform an internship, volunteer, interview, or job shadow someone working in the field that interests you. Doing so will help clarify your goals and life plan.

Web Search

Discover your personality: Take one of the personality and career assessments available on MyStudent-SuccessLab, or conduct a web search to identify an online quiz that will help you discover your personality and career interests.

Consider the type of personal relationships you want in the future. Goals should reflect your choice of marriage, family, friends, and religion. Identify where you want to be financially. Many people dream of becoming a millionaire, but you need to be realistic. Think about what kind of house you want to live in and what type of car you want to drive. If a spouse and children are in your future, account for their financial needs as well. Also identify what outside activities you enjoy, including hobbies and travel. The personal financial plan you create will be a part of achieving these goals. Think about what results and rewards will come from achieving your goals.

Intrinsic and extrinsic rewards motivate individuals to achieve their goals. **Intrinsic rewards** come from within you and reflect what you value, including such things as self-satisfaction and pride of accomplishment. **Extrinsic rewards** come from external sources and include such things as money and praise. Identify what type of intrinsic and extrinsic rewards motivate you, and then use them to help you maintain a positive outlook while working toward your goals.

Talk It Out

Share common rewards that are important to you. Identify these rewards as intrinsic or extrinsic.

Priorities

Priorities determine what needs to be done and in what order. Properly managing priorities is a valuable tool for reaching goals. Not only is prioritizing important in your personal life, but it will be necessary at work.

As you work toward your goals, priorities may change. There may be a period when your first priority is not necessarily what is most important in life; it is just that a particular activity demands the most attention at that specific point in time. For example, if Amelia has a young child, that child is important in Amelia's life. However, if Amelia is attending college and needs an evening to study for a big exam, the priority is to study for the exam. That does not mean the exam is more important than the child. However, passing the exam is a step toward a better future for Amelia and her child.

Amelia's decision is called a **trade-off**. A trade-off is giving up one thing to do something else. Another example involving Amelia is her decision to purchase a car in one year; she needs to save a certain amount of money each month. In order to do this, she may have to give up buying coffee each morning and instead make her coffee at home in order to save enough money to purchase the car.

Life plans require flexibility. When working toward goals, be flexible. Times change, technology changes, and priorities may change, all of which affect your goals. Reevaluate goals at least once a year. You may need to update or revise your goals and/or time lines more frequently than once a year because a situation changed. Do not abandon a goal because a situation changed—simply modify the goal and move forward.

Talk It Out

Identify priorities and trade-offs for successfully completing this course.

Workplace Dos and Don'ts

Do realize the impact your personality has on overall workplace performance	*Don't* assume that everyone thinks and behaves like you
Do believe that you are a talented, capable human being	*Don't* become obsessed with how others view you
Do let go of past baggage	*Don't* keep telling everyone about a past negative experience
Do set goals in writing	*Don't* set goals that are too difficult to reach
Do set long-term and short-term goals	*Don't* give up on goals
Do make your goals attainable	*Don't* wait to create goals
Do have measurable goals	*Don't* create unrealistic goals
Do set priorities and include trade-offs and flexibility when setting goals	*Don't* give up when working to reach your goals

Concept Review and Application

You are a Successful Student if you:

- Explain the importance of professionalism
- Create a strategy to enhance your personal brand
- Write a life plan

Summary of Key Concepts

- How you view yourself dictates how you treat others and what type of employee you will be.
- Your views of yourself, your environment, and your past experiences comprise your personality, values, attitude, and self-efficacy.
- Negative past experiences create unnecessary baggage that either delays or prevents you from reaching your goals. Acknowledge and begin dealing with these negative experiences.
- There are three primary learning styles: visual, auditory, and tactile/kinesthetic (sight, sound, and touch). Individuals must recognize how they best learn and also be aware that others may or may not share their same learning style.
- Goal setting is important in helping you keep focused. It will enhance your self-concept and help you become more successful in all areas of your life.
- As goals are reached, motivation and self-confidence will increase.
- Goals need to be put into writing. They need to be realistic and measurable. Know who owns the goals and who controls the goals. A time frame is needed to know when you plan on reaching these goals.
- Long-term goals are set to be achieved in five to 10 years.
- Short-term goals are achieved within a year's time and are needed to reach long-term goals.
- When creating a life plan, consider all aspects of your life, including personal, career, and education.
- Flexibility and properly managing priorities are needed to successfully achieve goals.

Self-Quiz MATCHING KEY TERMS

Match the key term to the definition using the identifying number.

Key Terms	Answer	Definitions
Attitude		1. Your belief in your ability to perform a task
Extrinsic rewards		2. Identifies who you believe controls your future
Goal		3. An individual's perception of himself or herself
Human relations		4. A strong belief about people, things, and situations
Intrinsic rewards		5. Giving up one thing to do something else
Learning style		6. An individual's perception of how others view him or her
Life plan		7. A target in your life plan
Locus of control		8. How you best take in new information and/or learn new ideas
Long-term goals		9. Describe how you view yourself and how you believe others view you
Mirror words		10. Rewards that come from within and may include self-satisfaction and pride of accomplishment
Personal brand		11. Determine what needs to be done and in what order
Personality		12. Things that are important to an individual
Priorities		13. Rewards from external sources such as money and praise
Professionalism		14. Workplace behaviors that result in positive business relationships
Projection		15. Interactions occurring with and through people
Self-concept		16. A target that takes longer than one year to accomplish
Self-efficacy		17. The way you feel about yourself is reflected in how you treat others
Self-image		18. Set of traits that assist in explaining and predicting an individual's behavior
Short-term goals		19. Reflects traits you want others to think of when they think of you
Smart		20. Goals that can be reached within a year's time
Trade-off		21. Acronym for goal setting method
Values		22. A written document that identifies goals in all areas of your life

Think Like a Boss

1. How would you deal with an employee who displays poor self-efficacy?

2. How would recognizing different learning styles help you be a better boss?

3. Why is it important that an employer ensure that employees set personal and career goals?

Activities

Activity 1

Write four words to describe your ideal self-concept (personal brand).

1	3
2	4

What steps are necessary to make your desired personal brand a reality?

_____

_____

Activity 2

What factors affect your attitude toward educational success?

Positive Factors	Negative Factors

Activity 3

Identify and write your long-term personal, educational, and career goals, giving each the SMART test.

Personal	Education	Career

Activity 4

Write three short-term goals to support each long-term goal identified in Activity 3, giving each the SMART test.

	Personal	Education	Career
Long-term goal			
Short-term goal 1			
Short-term goal 2			
Short-term goal 3			

Glossary

attitude: a strong belief about people, things, and situations

extrinsic rewards: rewards that come from external sources including such things as money and praise

goal: a target

human relations: interactions occurring with and through people

intrinsic rewards: internal rewards that include such things as self-satisfaction and pride of accomplishment

learning style: the method of how you best take in information and/or learn new ideas

life plan: a written document that identifies goals in all areas of your life

locus of control: identifies who you believe controls your future

long-term goal: a target that takes longer than one year to accomplish

mirror words: words that describe the foundation of how you view yourself, how you view others, and how you will most likely perform in the workplace

personal brand: reflects trains you want others to think of when they think of you

personality: a stable set of traits that assist in explaining and predicting an individual's behavior

priorities: determine what needs to be done and in what order

professionalism: workplace behaviors that result in positive business relationships

projection: the way you feel about yourself is reflected in how you treat others

self-concept: how you view yourself

self-efficacy: your belief in your ability to perform a task

self-image: your belief of how others view you

short-term goals: goals that can be reached within a year's time (also called *objectives*)

SMART goal: a goal that is specific, measurable, achievable, relevant, and time-based

trade-off: giving up one thing to do something else

values: things that are important to an individual

Suggested Readings

Rotter, J. B. "Generalized Expectancies for Internal versus External Control of Reinforcement." *Psychological Monographs*, Vol. 80, No. 1 (1966): 1–28.

Taylor, M. "Does Locus of Control Predict Young Adult Conflict Strategies with Superiors? An Examination of Control Orientation and the Organizational Communication Conflict Instrument." *North American Journal of Psychology*, Vol. 12, No. 3 (2010): 445–458.

Bandura, A. (1994). Self-efficacy. In V. S. Ramachaudran (Ed.), *Encyclopedia of Human Behavior*, Vol. 4. New York: Academic Press, pp. 71–81.

Bandura, A. "Human Agency in Social Cognitive Theory." *American Psychologist*, Vol. 44, No. 9 (1989): 1175–1184.

"Work-Family Conflicts Affect Employees at All Income Levels," *HR Focus* 87 (April 2010): 9.

Golden, E. Organizational Renewal Associates. 1971. Golden LLC, May 2011, www.goldenllc.com

http://www.forbes.com/sites/actiontrumpseverything/2013/01/13/how-to-plan-your-life-when-you-cant-plan-your-life/

Hoel, H., Glasco, L., Hetland, J., Cooper, C. L., and Einarsen, S. "Leadership Styles as Predictors of Self-reported and Observed Workplace Bullying." *British Journal of Management*, Vol. 21, No. 2 (2010): 453–468.

Newhouse, N. "Implications of Attitude and Behavior Research for Environmental Conservation." *Journal of Environmental Education*, Vol. 22, No. 1 (Fall 1990): 26–32.

Savickas, Mark L. "Career Studies as Self-Making and Life Designing." *Career Research and Development* 23 (2010): 15-18.

Robins, E.M. (2014, April 24). An Instructional Approach to Writing SMART Goals. PowerPoint presented at the 19th Annual Technology, Colleges, and Community Worldwide Online Conference.

Platt, G. "SMART Objectives: What They Mean and How to Set Them." *Training Journal* (August 2002): 23.

Credit

Credits are listed in order of appearance.

Time and Stress Management and Organization Skills

resourceful • calm • efficient

After studying these topics, you will benefit by:

- Recognizing how stress affects performance
- Examining the types, causes, and methods of dealing with stress
- Identifying and utilizing time management tools
- Dealing with procrastination to improve personal productivity
- Stating how organization affects time and stress management
- Naming and applying organizational techniques to academic and workplace success

HOW DO YOU RATE?

Is your life in order?	Yes	No
1. The inside of my car is usually clean.	☐	☐
2. My personal workspace is free of clutter.	☐	☐
3. My computer files are in order and it is easy to find documents.	☐	☐
4. I maintain an address book (electronic or traditional) to manage my professional network.	☐	☐
5. I make my bed every day.	☐	☐

▶ If you answered "yes" to three or more of these questions, you are on the path to optimal organization. Organization in all areas of your life decreases stress and improves time management—two factors that will contribute to workplace success.

From Chapter 3 of *Professionalism, Skills for Workplace Success*, Fourth Edition. Lydia E. Anderson, Sandra B. Bolt. Copyright © 2016 by Pearson Education, Inc. All rights reserved.

The Impact of Stress on Performance

Walk into a workplace and you'll quickly form an impression of the work environment. Your first impression will most likely be based on the demeanor of the employees and their interactions with each other. You will also notice if the work area is messy and disorganized or if it is clean and orderly. This chapter examines the influences that stress management, time management, and organization have on workplace productivity. Items arranged in an organized manner make our jobs easier and save us time. When we fail to plan appropriately and do not have enough time to complete our work, we get stressed. Of course, there are other factors that contribute to a productive workplace, but time, stress, and organization are certainly major contributing forces. Stress management, time management, and organizational ability are personal skills that must be developed and consistently practiced. Positive personal habits spill into the workplace and become positive workplace behaviors. Employers need employees who are healthy, relaxed, and well organized. Healthy employees are able to perform at their highest levels, have decreased absenteeism, and have fewer health claims than their unhealthy counterparts.

Stress is the body's reaction to tense situations. Stress also affects workplace productivity and is influenced by self-care matters such as diet and exercise and organizational issues like time management. Stress can cause more than just a bad day. Constant stress can result in permanent mental and/or physical harm.

Although some stress keeps you mentally challenged, long-term (chronic) stress will eventually harm you in one way or another. It may start to affect both your work performance and personal life. While not all stress is within your control, try to maintain a low stress level. Stress-related losses are high and, according to the World Health Organization, costs U.S. businesses an estimated $300 billion dollars a year.

Types of Stress

Think About It

How can stress from school affect other areas of your life?

You arrive in class and your teacher announces that today students are to give impromptu presentations on the lecture material. The students who are prepared and confident may be quite excited about the activity, whereas those who are not prepared or not confident presenting in public may suddenly flush and feel their hearts racing. As a result, they will be stressed. This illustration demonstrates that stressful situations vary from individual to individual. Stress is a normal part of life. What is important is that you recognize when you are stressed and deal with the stress appropriately. You will experience stress at school, at work, and at home. There is no avoiding it. However, how you react to and deal with stress determines how it will affect you. Some stress is minor and affects you at a specific time. This can be **positive stress**. Positive stress is a productive stress that provides strength to accomplish a task. However, even positive stress can become negative if it continues and becomes problematic. For example, if you have a rushed deadline for a special project, your adrenaline will increase, giving you the mental and/or physical strength to finish the project on time. However, if you consistently have rushed deadlines, your stress level can increase and will eventually start working negatively on your mind and body.

Negative stress causes you to become emotional or illogical. This type of stress may affect your mental and/or physical health. Negative stress commonly results in anger, depression, and/or distrust. Other signs of negative stress may include frequent headaches, fatigue, diminished or increased appetite, a poor immune system, or other physical weakness. Continuous negative stress can ultimately result in ulcers, heart disease, or mental disturbances.

Talk It Out

What are common negative stressors students face and possible positive responses to these stressors?

Topic Situation

Dylan has started experiencing headaches and fatigue. After thinking about recent activities, he realizes the headaches and fatigue may be a symptom of stress. With college and a job, there seems to be no time for relaxation. Dylan decides that his situation needs to change or his physical symptoms may get worse. He makes time to reevaluate his goals, write a plan, and identify stress management techniques to help him through this challenging period. Soon after, Dylan feels more control in balancing school and work, and has found free time to relax.

TOPIC RESPONSE
What other symptoms of stress might Dylan experience?

Exercise 1

List at least three significant stresses that you have experienced in the last year. Write the result of the stressor, including how you responded mentally and/or physically.

_____

_____

_____

Dealing with Stress

The first step in dealing with stress is to identify key stressors in your life. Learning to both identify and deal with these stressors will reduce their negative effects. Be aware of them and how they affect your attitude and behavior. Life is not stress free. The following steps will assist you in not allowing stressful situations to get the best of you:

1. Find out what is causing you to be stressed.
2. Recognize why and how you are reacting to the stressor.
3. Take steps to better deal with the stress by visualizing and setting a goal for responding in a positive manner.
4. Practice positive stress relief.

Topic Situation

Grace has been noticing that a coworker, Zoey, has been short-tempered and moody lately. Because Zoey is normally very pleasant to work with, Grace decides to ask her if something is wrong. Visiting with Zoey, Grace finds that Zoey is being harassed by someone at work. Zoey tells Grace how stressful this has been and that it is affecting her work and personal life. Grace encourages Zoey to take steps to stop this harassment. Grace also gives her tips to help deal with the stress. After a few weeks, Grace notices a positive change in Zoey. Dealing with the problem, along with using stress relievers, is helping Zoey get back to her pleasant self.

TOPIC RESPONSE
What advice would you give a friend who has noticeable stress?

Ignoring stress does not make it go away. Being aware of what causes your stress helps you change how it will affect you.

There are common strategies to help relieve stress, including diet and exercise. A healthy body leads to a healthy mind. Consistently eat a balanced diet, including breakfast, lunch, and dinner. At these meals, balance protein, carbohydrates, vegetables, and fruit. Do not skip meals, especially breakfast.

Along with a balanced diet, exercise is essential. When you exercise, your body produces endorphins, which are chemicals that make you feel good. These endorphins help improve your mood, increase sleep, and reduce depression and anxiety. Exercise is also a good way to clear your mind of troubles and increase creativity. You do not have to join a gym or lift weights; you only need a consistent exercise plan that keeps your body moving. There are simple ways to increase physical activity, including using the stairs instead of taking the elevator or parking your car a little farther away from a building to increase your walking distance. Exercising for 10 minutes several times a day will increase energy and improve your health. Diminish—or ideally, eliminate—the use of alcohol and/or drugs. These stimulants may cause mood swings that typically make matters worse. Though common among college students, lack of sleep is also a contributor to stress. Sleep deprivation contributes to obesity, depression, and other chronic diseases. The Center for Disease Control recommends adults receive 7–9 hours of sleep per night. If you are not consistently waking up refreshed, you most likely are sleep deprived. Take small steps to gradually change your sleep pattern. Begin going to bed earlier; limit caffeine intake prior to bedtime; and sleep in a quiet, dark space (even if it includes ear plugs and a sleep mask). When you are able to consistently wake up on time, without an alarm clock, you body is most likely getting the amount of sleep it needs. When your body gets enough sleep, you will see a noticable improvement in your energy level, your attitude, and your productivity.

There are other simple physical activities that relieve stress that you probably do without realizing their benefits. These include enjoying leisure time, listening to music, meditating, deep breathing exercises, and using positive visualization.

Recognizing what situations cause stress allows you to better control them. The more organized you are, the better prepared you will be, thus reducing stress.

Keep your emotions in check. Becoming emotional means you are losing control and risk becoming illogical in your response to the stress. When at work, if you cannot surround yourself with positive people, create a positive personal space where you can take a few minutes for yourself. Realize that people are not always going to agree with you at the workplace. There may be annoying people, and there may be people with whom you may not have a positive relationship.

You may find yourself in situations that become very stressful. Use the stress relief methods mentioned earlier in this chapter and make the best of the situation. Only you can control your attitude and your response to challenging situations.

Take time outside of work to relax. Do not bring work troubles home with you, nor take home troubles to work. When you recognize personal stressors and take care of yourself, you can reduce and/or eliminate the impact stress may have both at home and at work. Create and maintain a support network. Identify a few close friends and family members in whom you can confide and share concerns. Develop realistic goals.

If your company offers an employee assistance program (EAP), use it to get professional help. Typical employee assistance programs offer help with financial, legal, and psychological issues.

Job burnout is a form of extreme stress where you lack motivation and no longer have the desire to work. Factors that lead to job burnout include not being able to control decisions that affect your job; being unclear of your job duties; working with bullies, negative colleagues, or a bad boss; and not enjoying your job or career.

Signs of job burnout include:

- Frequent tardiness or absenteeism
- Continually complaining or gossiping
- Exhibiting poor physical and emotional health
- Lacking concern for quality
- Clock-watching and being easily distracted
- Lack of satisfaction in your work
- Demonstrating a desire to cause harm to the company (theft of or damage to property)

Determine the source of job burnout and take steps to deal with or eliminate the issue before it causes significant damage. If you have seriously tried to improve the current work situation and still find yourself at a dead end, you may need to consider a job change. Continuing in a job in which you have not been motivated in for a long period of time is destructive not only to you, but also to your company and coworkers.

Web Search

Conduct a web search for an online quiz that will help you measure your stress level.

Exercise 2

What can you do if you begin feeling job burnout?

_____

_____

_____

Time Management

Recall the earlier scenario in which the teacher assigned impromptu presentations on the lecture material. Perhaps some students were stressed because they did not study and therefore were not prepared. There is a clear link between stress and time management. There is also a link between time management and success. **Time management** is how you manage your time. In business, time is money. The ability to use time wisely is a skill in itself—one that is necessary in the workplace. When you use your time efficiently, your tasks will be completed on time or even early. Without proper time management skills, you may forget, lose, or spend more time than needed on an important project. Proper time management at work frees up more time for other activities, both at work and at home. If you are being efficient and paying attention, your employer sees that you care about your job and are organized. In turn, this may lead to higher pay and/or a promotion.

You may get stressed at work because you do not have enough time to complete a project. However, many work projects are similar in nature and can therefore be managed easily. Prior to starting a project, make a plan. Set priorities and get organized. Do not wait until the last minute. If you have similar projects, create a template so you are not starting over with each project. Focus on completing a job right the first time; rushing through a job typically results in errors that will only take more time to correct.

A common workplace interruption is that of individuals who visit your work area and stay longer than necessary. When dealing with these individuals, always be professional and polite. Inform the individual that although you would like to visit, you have work that must be completed. If you are in an office environment, do not sit down or invite your office visitor to sit. Standing by the door or entry to your workspace, politely tell your visitor that you are busy and unable to visit. Avoid having items on your desk that attract unwanted guests such as a candy dish.

Break larger tasks into simpler, smaller ones. When you break down tasks, you can space out projects. This enables you to organize the time needed to complete each task before starting the next. Again, the exception to this rule is if you have a priority task that needs to be completed immediately.

At the end of the chapter, Activity 1 provides the opportunity to identify how you are currently spending your time.

The following tips will help you organize and control your time:

1. Make a list of tasks for each day and prioritize that list; this is commonly referred to as a *to-do list*. Many PCs and smartphones offer task applications to make electronic lists.

2. Keep a calendar accessible at all times. List all appointments, meetings, and tasks on your personal electronic or traditional calendar.

3. Organize your work area. Use file folders and in-boxes to organize and prioritize projects, including your computer desktop and files.

4. Practice a one-touch policy. After you have looked at a project, letter, memo, or other item, either file it, place it in a priority folder, forward it to the appropriate individual, or throw it away. Do not pile papers on your desk.

5. Answer memos that only require a short response by writing the response directly on the original memo and keeping a copy for your records.

6. Avoid time wasters. Time wasters are small activities that take up only a small amount of time but are done more frequently than you may realize. These include unnecessary visiting or inappropriate activities such as personal texting or participating in social networking.

7. If possible, set aside time each day to address all communication at once during a certain time of the day, as opposed to handling messages as they arrive (e.g., e-mail and phone messages).

8. If needed, ask for help. Asking for help is not a sign of weakness or inefficiency if you are practicing sound time management techniques.

Exercise 3

List time wasters you have experienced in the past few weeks. How do these time wasters affect productivity? What change should be made?

_____

_____

_____

Procrastination is putting off tasks until a later time. This poor habit severely impedes time management and contributes to stress. People procrastinate for many reasons, including fear of failure, perfectionism, disorganization, or simply not wanting to perform the task because it is not pleasant. Procrastination can lead to the loss of opportunities. As a result of a late project, you may lose money, lose respect from coworkers and/or your boss, or not be as successful as possible. To overcome procrastination, first visualize the completed task. Knowing your end result and how you will feel when it is completed will motivate you to get started. The next step is to make a plan for completion by identifying what information and resources are required for the end result you envisioned. List every activity and piece of information you will need. After you have made your plan, get to work. If the task appears overwhelming, break it down into smaller tasks and complete each task in priority order. Breaks and celebrations are not only essential, but encouraged when you are working on a big project.

Think About It

List a recent time when you procrastinated on a project. What was the reason for procrastination? What was the result?

Topic Situation

Jonelle was taking a chemistry class in which the instructor assigned a semester-long research project. When the project was assigned at the start of the semester, the instructor encouraged the students to make a plan and schedule dates to complete sections of the research throughout the semester so as to produce a quality project. Jonelle struggled with the class material and procrastinated working on the assignment. Unfortunately, as the semester wore on, Jonelle became immersed with other courses, a job, and personal issues and kept delaying the research project. The more Jonelle thought about the project, the more stressed she became. Finally, two weeks before the end of the semester, the instructor reminded the class that all research projects were due the day before the final. Jonelle realized there was no time to properly study for exams and also complete the research project. The procrastination resulted in her being stressed and receiving a failing grade in the chemistry course because she gave up and did not even attempt to write the paper or take the final exam.

TOPIC RESPONSE

What steps could Jonelle have taken to avoid procrastination in this situation?

One final issue that contributes to both stress and poor time management is the inability for individuals to say no to coworkers, bosses, or others. At work, our goal is to be as productive as possible by prioritizing our current workload. Overcommitting ourselves risks compromising quality for quantity.

When you are pressed for time and someone asks you to assist with a project, first evaluate if the project is part of your primary work duties. If it is not your job and it does not conflict with your priority projects, agree to take on the new project if you have the time. If you do not have time and you have greater priorities, decline the project. If it is your boss that is making the request, politely inform your boss that you want to help wherever and whenever possible, but you are currently working on another priority project and ask him or her which project should take precedent. Many bosses are unaware of an individual's workload at any given time, so your goal is to communicate your current priorities.

Talk It Out

What other school-related activities do students procrastinate getting completed?

Organizing and Performance

Individuals who are organized operate around goals and have learned that being surrounded by clutter deters focus. Organized individuals arrange their belongings in their homes and work environments in a manner that reflects their goals.

Getting organized for optimal performance is not difficult and will result in your using your time more efficiently and reducing stress.

Although it may take time to organize, the time you invest in cleaning and organizing your space will release much more time for you to accomplish your goals. An organized and clutter-free area is calming and allows you to focus.

Tools for getting organized in the workplace can also be used at home. Technology has made it easier to get organized with electronic devices. However, there are other common organization tools to use, including shredders, files, and desk space organizers.

One of the easiest ways to get organized is to use a calendar. There are many options, including a computerized calendar, a mobile calendar, and a traditional paper calendar. For efficiency, businesses prefer an electronic calendar for computer networking purposes. It is common to have access to a computerized information manager on the web, a computer, and/or a mobile device. Determine which type of calendar works best for your work situation; sometimes the solution is to use more than one calendar and sync them. Once you have determined which option is best for you, make a commitment to record all work-related and personal meetings and important deadlines. If your personal information manager and communications program is electronic, store telephone numbers, e-mail addresses, and other important messaging data in the program for easy access. Tasks, to-do lists, and notes can also be monitored and updated. Keep data current by immediately recording changes. If you use multiple organization tools, make a habit of transferring information on a daily basis, or connect with web programs that automatically sync and update all your electronic devices. For maximum efficiency, customize applications to suit your needs.

Other ways to keep organized and improve performance is to check and answer your phone messages and e-mails at specific intervals. It is inefficient to return each phone message or e-mail as it comes in. The only exception is when there is an important message or e-mail that needs to be sent or answered immediately.

If you are assigned a personal workspace, keep your work environment and desk clean and clutter free. Maintain a professional look by having only a minimal number of personal items on your desk. Take inventory of your workspace; if you don't need an item, remove it from your work area. If an item is necessary but not used often, store it. Keep frequently used work tools easily accessible, including a stapler, tape, a notepad, pens, pencils, paperclips, scissors, a ruler, a calculator, highlighters, and a computer storage device. Place items where they are required (i.e., printer paper by the printer, notepad near the phone). Return items to their appropriate area after use. In addition, the use of a small bulletin/whiteboard for posting important reminders will help you keep track of important tasks and appointments. Have a trash can close to your desk, and throw away supplies that have been used or do not work anymore. Shred confidential materials at least once a day.

When managing paper files, maintain these files properly in a file cabinet and keep files neatly arranged in clearly labeled file folders. Avoid miscellaneous piles and folders. File dated documents in chronological order (most recent first). Other files can be arranged by subject or alphabetically. Be consistent in your filing method. Routinely used files should be easily accessible. Files should be updated and old files disposed of properly. Any unnecessary files with personal information or identification numbers are considered confidential and should be shredded. If files are not important and do not have identification, they may be thrown in the trash.

For efficiency and security purposes, keep electronic files organized. Your computer desktop should contain only shortcuts to frequently used programs and files that you are currently working with. Routinely clean your computer desktop to ensure it is clutter free. Just as with paper files, electronic files should be well organized and labeled. Establish folders for major projects, committees, and other items related to your job. Place appropriate documents inside the respective major project folder. Whenever possible, create subfolders for large projects so that you can properly file and quickly retrieve documents when necessary. Keep both folder and file names simple and easily identifiable. Also remember to routinely back up and/or secure your files to protect confidential information.

Effective organization includes the proper handling of both electronic and paper mail. Your job may include sorting and/or opening mail. Use a letter opener to open all paper mail at one time. After opening the paper mail, sort it into piles. Throw away or shred junk mail immediately after opening. Respond to the sender of the mail if needed, file the document, or forward the mail to the appropriate party within the company. Do not open mail that is marked confidential unless instructed to do so. Mail should be kept private and not shared with coworkers. If you encounter a piece of mail that should be confidential, place it in a separate envelope and mark it confidential. Company letterhead or postage is not for personal mail.

MyStudentSuccessLab | Please visit **MyStudentSuccessLab**: Anderson|Bolt, Professionalism Skills for Workplace Success, 4/e for additional activities, resources, and outcomes assessments.

Workplace Dos and Don'ts

Do recognize your stressors	*Don't* let stress go until you get mentally or physically sick
Do deal with stress appropriately	*Don't* think that stress will just go away
Do eat a balanced diet and have an exercise plan	*Don't* skip breakfast
Do manage your time by setting priorities	*Don't* be afraid of asking for help when getting behind
Do take time to get organized	*Don't* give in to time wasters

Concept Review and Application

You are a Successful Student if you:

- Apply the tools in this chapter to create a stress management plan
- Create and utilize a calendar system
- Summarize ideas for organizing your work area

Summary of Key Concepts

- Stress is a physical, chemical, or emotional factor that causes bodily or mental tension.
- Stress can be positive or negative.
- Signs of stress include becoming emotional or illogical or losing control of your temper.
- The first step in dealing with stress is to identify the stressor.
- A balanced diet along with exercise will help you to better manage stress.
- There are many ways to reduce stress, such as setting goals, relaxing, and getting enough sleep.
- Good time management comes from being organized.
- Avoid procrastination.
- Being organized will optimize your performance and reduce stress.

Self-Quiz MATCHING KEY TERMS

Match the key term to the definition using the identifying number.

Key Terms	Answer	Definitions
Job burnout		1. Putting off tasks until a later time
Negative stress		2. How you manage your time
Positive stress		3. A body's reaction to tense situations
Procrastination		4. A form of extreme stress where you lack motivation and no longer have the desire to work
Stress		5. Productive stress that provides strength to accomplish a task
Time management		6. Unproductive stress that affects your mental and/or physical health

Think Like a Boss

1. You have noticed that an employee is frequently calling in sick and appears agitated when at work. What do you do?

2. You have just become the supervisor for a new department. What can you do to make the department and its employees more organized? Discuss appointment tools, necessary equipment, and software.

Activities

Activity 1

Your instructor will distribute a time log or you may create your own. For the next 24 hours, use this log to track how you spend your time. Account for every minute. When you are finished, identify specific time wasters.

List three time wasters from your time log
1.
2.
3.

Activity 2

In addition to those mentioned in this chapter, research physical responses generated by prolonged stress. List your findings.

1.	4.
2.	5.
3.	6.

Activity 3

List five time management tools commonly used in your target career.

Tools
1.
2.
3.
4.
5.

Activity 4

A nutritious diet can make a difference in how you perform throughout the day and how you react to stressful situations. List what you have eaten in the last 24 hours, recording the time of day, your mood or situation, and if the item was nutritious. Evaluate if changes need to be made to your diet.

Time of Day	Food	Mood/Situation	Was It Nutritious?

Activity 5

Identify one space at home you need to organize. Create a plan to overcome your procrastination of dealing with this issue.

Space	Plan

Glossary

job burnout: a form of extreme stress where you lack motivation and no longer have the desire to work

negative stress: an unproductive stress that affects your mental and/or physical health including becoming emotional or illogical or losing your temper

positive stress: productive stress that provides strength to accomplish a task

procrastination: putting off tasks until a later time

stress: a body's reaction to tense situations

time management: how you manage your time

Suggested Readings

http://www.stress.org/workplace-stress/

http://www.forbes.com/sites/work-in-progress/2012/08/02/stress-at-work-is-bunk-for-business/

http://www.cdc.gov/features/dssleep/

Glynn, Anthony. *Is absenteeism related to perceived stress, burnout levels and job satisfaction?*. Diss. Dublin Business School, 2014.

Page, Matthew, and Matthew Page. *Agent-Based Modelling of Stress and Productivity Performance in the Workplace*. Diss. 2013.

Rhoade, Collin, and Shawn M. Carraher. "Strategic Knowledge Worker Productivity and Leisure Time." *Allied Academies International Internet Conference*. Vol. 14. 2012.

Gallagher, Vickie Coleman. "Managing Resources and Need for Cognition: Impact on Depressed Mood at Work." *Personality and Individual Differences* 53.4 (2012): 534–537.

Cole, Michael S., et al. "Job Burnout and Employee Engagement A Meta-Analytic Examination of Construct Proliferation." *Journal of management* 38.5 (2012): 1550–1581.

Rosekind, M. R., and Gregory, K. B., et. al. "The Cost of Poor Sleep: Workplace Productivity Loss and Associated Costs." *Journal of Occupational & Environmental Medicine*. Vol. 52, No. 1 (2010): 91–98, doi: 10.1097/ JOM.0b013e3181c78c30

Finkelstein, E.A., et al. "The Costs of Obesity in the Workplace." *Journal of Occupational and Environmental Medicine* 52.10 (2010): 971–976.

Leeds, R. One Year to an Organized Work Life. (Cambridge, MA: Da Capo Press, 2008).

Knight, C. and Haslam, S.A. "The Relative Merits of Lean, Enriched, and Empowered Offices: An Experimental Examination of the Impact of Workspace Management Strategies on Well-Being and Productivity." *Journal of Experimental Psychology: Applied* 16.2 (2010): 158.

DeVries, G. "Innovations in Workplace Wellness: Six New Tools to Enhance Programs and Maximize Employee Health and Productivity." *Compensation Benefits Review*, Vol. 42, No. 1 (January/February 2010): 46–51.

http://www.smartceo.com/3-ways-entrepreneurs-can-reduce-stress/ (March, 2013)

Centers for Disease Control and Prevention/National Institute for Occupational Safety and Health, www.cdc.gov/niosh/

Forbes, "Stress at Work is Bunk for Business" by Judy Martin, http://www.forbes.com/sites/work-in-progress/2012/08/02/stress-at-work-is-bunk-for-business

Mayo Clinic, exercise and stress: "Get moving to manage stress," http://www.mayoclinic.com/health/exercise-and-stress/SR00036

Credit

Credits are listed in order of appearance.

WavebreakMediaMicro/Fotolia

Communication

trust • honesty • information

- Demonstrating knowledge of the communication process and the impact effective communication has on workplace and career success
- Stating the primary communication media and their appropriate uses
- Considering the importance word choice and effective listening have in verbal communication
- Describing the primary methods of non-verbal communication
- Identifying the appropriate written communication to use in various workplace situations
- Explaining the purpose and process of effective documentation
- Developing the elements of effective presentations

HOW DO YOU RATE?

Have you mastered workplace communication?	Yes	No
1. I do not use foul language.	☐	☐
2. I respect people's personal space.	☐	☐
3. I do not allow emotions to influence my communication.	☐	☐
4. I believe I am a good listener.	☐	☐
5. When appropriate, I send handwritten notes to coworkers.	☐	☐

If you answered "yes" to four or more of these questions, you are well on your way to mastering workplace communication. Communication success begins by presenting your message in a professional manner and focusing on the needs of the receiver.

From Chapter 9 of *Professionalism, Skills for Workplace Success*, Fourth Edition. Lydia E. Anderson, Sandra B. Bolt. Copyright © 2016 by Pearson Education, Inc. All rights reserved.

Communication at Work

Meetings, e-mails, phone calls, texts, presentations, and formal and informal discussions play an important role in business and require proper attention and protocol. Employees who have a basic understanding of how to effectively and appropriately communicate in the workplace are at a significant advantage. Knowing what, when, and how to communicate creates a positive impression on others and helps you achieve your objective. Effective professional and electronic communication is vital to workplace success. This chapter presents the fundamentals of professional communication.

Workplace Communication and its Channels

Imagine going to work, sitting at your desk, and for one day sending and receiving no communication. If there were no face-to-face contact, no phones, no e-mails, no text messages, no meetings, and no memos to receive or write, business would come to a complete standstill. Even if you are talented at your job, if you cannot communicate with others, you will not keep a job, much less succeed. This chapter discusses the process and importance of effective communication in the workplace and provides information on how to improve workplace communication skills. **Communication** is the process of a sender transmitting a message to a receiver with the purpose of creating mutual understanding.

Improving communication skills is an ongoing process. Information is power. Therefore, your goal at work is to share appropriate, timely, and accurate information with your boss, your coworkers, and your customers.

Topic Situation

TOPIC RESPONSE

What type of information do employees need to know?

While eating lunch with employees from other departments, Sarah listened to others complain about how their bosses did such a poor job communicating with them. The employees complained that they never knew what was going on within the company. Sarah had no reason to complain, because she has a manager who makes every effort to share whatever information he knows within the department. After each manager's meeting, Sarah receives an e-mail outlining major topics that were discussed. During Sarah's department meeting, her manager reviews the information a second time and asks his employees if there are any additional questions. Sarah appreciates the fact that the manager enjoys and values communicating important information with his employees.

You have a professional obligation to share timely and relevant information with the appropriate people at work. In the workplace, there are two primary communication channels: formal and informal. **Formal communication** occurs through the formal (official) lines of authority. This includes communication within your immediate department, division, or throughout the company. Formal communication occurs either vertically or horizontally within an organization. Vertical communication either flows down an organizational structure (via written correspondence, policies/procedures, and directives and announcements from management) or up (most commonly through reports, budgets, and requests). Horizontal communication occurs among individuals or departments at the same or close organizational levels.

The second type of communication channel is informal. **Informal communication** occurs among individuals without regard to the formal lines of authority. For example, while eating lunch with friends, you may learn of a new policy. A major element of the informal communication network is called the **grapevine**. The grapevine is an informal network where employees discuss workplace issues of importance. However, it rarely is 100 percent accurate. Although it is important to know about current events at work, do not contribute negative or inaccurate information to the grapevine. Avoid making assumptions if the information is incomplete. When you are aware of the facts, clarify the information. If someone shares information that is harmful to the company or is particularly disturbing to you, you have a responsibility to approach your boss and ask him or her to verify the rumor.

When the grapevine is targeting individuals and their personal lives, it is called **gossip**. Gossip is personal information about individuals that is hurtful and inappropriate. Spreading gossip reflects immaturity and unprofessional behavior and you risk losing credibility with others. Should someone begin sharing gossip with you, politely interrupt and clarify the misinformation when necessary. Respectfully tell the individual that you do not want to hear gossip and/or transition the conversation to a more positive subject. You have a right to defend your coworkers from slander (individuals bad-mouthing others), just as you would expect coworkers to defend you. After a while, your colleagues will learn that you do not tolerate gossip at work and they will reconsider approaching you with gossip.

Refrain from speaking poorly of your coworkers and boss. As a result of human nature, you may not enjoy working with all of your colleagues and bosses. You do not have to like everyone at work, but everyone needs to be treated with respect. Even if someone speaks poorly of you, do not reciprocate the bad behavior. It only displays immaturity on your part and communicates distrust to your colleagues.

The Communication Process

The purpose of communication is to create mutual understanding. Communication is important for maintaining good human relations. Without basic communication skills, processes break down and an organization may collapse.

The communication process (illustrated in Figure 1) involves a sender and a receiver. Communication begins with a **sender**, the individual conveying a message. The sender must identify what message needs to be sent and how best to transmit this message. The sender has several options for sending the message. The message can be sent verbally, in written form, or non-verbally. Identifying the specific message and how it will be sent is called **encoding**.

Once the sender encodes the message, the message is sent to a receiver. The **receiver** is an individual that receives and decodes a message. **Decoding** is how the receiver interprets the message. The receiver then sends feedback to

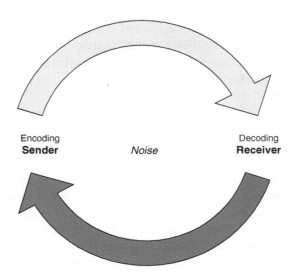

Encoding
Sender

Noise

Decoding
Receiver

Figure 1

Communication Process

the sender. **Feedback** is a response to a sender based on the receiver's interpretation of the original message.

Many barriers can hinder the process of creating mutual understanding and successful communication, causing a breakdown in the communication process. The first barrier to overcome is clearly identifying the specific message to be sent. Once the message is identified, the sender needs to determine how best to send (encode) the message in a manner that will be properly interpreted (decoded) by the receiver. If the sender is not a strong communicator, his or her verbal, written, or non-verbal communication may be misinterpreted by the receiver because the message was at risk of being misinterpreted before it was even sent. The receiver contributes to the communication breakdown if he or she incorrectly interprets the message.

Another barrier to effective communication is **noise**. Noise is anything that interrupts or interferes with the communication process. The noise can be audible (you can actually hear it with your ears), or the noise can occur through other senses, such as visual, mental, touch, or smell. Noise may also include emotions such as hurt, anger, joy, sadness, or surprise.

Talk It Out

Identify the noise you experience during class.

Topic Situation

TOPIC RESPONSE

How could Keira have been more open to the speaker?

A supervisor in another department really irritates Keira. Keira has never shared this annoyance with anyone. One day, Keira was asked to attend a meeting led by the irritating supervisor. As Keira sat in the meeting, she had a hard time focusing on the message. Her mind was wandering through mental noise. At the end of the meeting, Keira was embarrassed that there were no notes to share. Dislike for the irritating supervisor affected her ability to listen and be a good receiver. Keira learned a tough lesson that day and made a commitment to be open to every communication, regardless of liking or disliking the sender.

Communication is complete only when all the components of the communication process work together to effectively send the message as they are intended to be sent. In order for this to occur, the sender must select the right medium and overcome noise. The receiver must then be willing to accept the message and provide feedback to acknowledge that the message has been received correctly.

A key element of effective communication is the communication medium (how the message will be sent). Communication media include verbal, non-verbal, and written communication. Let us further explore these three types of communication media.

Verbal Communication and Listening

Verbal communication is the process of using words to send a message. The words you select are extremely important. When you use only basic words in your communications, you risk appearing uneducated or inexperienced. In contrast, when you use a highly developed vocabulary, you may appear intimidating or arrogant. If others do not know the definitions of the words you are using, they will most likely not ask for clarification for fear of appearing ignorant. Therefore, your intended message will fail. When selecting words for your message, identify whether these words are appropriate or if the words can be misinterpreted. Use proper English and grammar. Be as clear as possible in your intent and how you verbally convey your message. When people are nervous or excited, they frequently speak at a rapid pace, increasing the probability that the message will be misinterpreted. Your tone of voice also conveys or creates images. It adds to others' perception of you, which either enforces or detracts from your message.

Successful verbal communication involves **listening**, the act of hearing attentively. Listening occurs not only with our ears, but also through our non-verbal responses. The three primary levels of listening are active listening, passive listening, and not listening at all. **Active listening** is when the receiver provides full attention to the sender without distraction. An active listener will provide frequent positive feedback to the sender through non-verbal gestures such as nodding, eye contact, or other favorable body language. Favorable verbal feedback may also include rephrasing the message to ensure or clarify understanding. With **passive listening**, the receiver is selectively hearing parts of the message and is more focused on responding to what is being said instead of truly listening to the entire message being sent. Passive listening is sometimes called conversational listening. In today's society, we have so many inputs trying to attract our attention that we often get anxious to share our point of view in a conversation and interrupt the sender. Interrupting is rude and disrespectful. Show others respect by not interrupting conversations. If you accidentally interrupt someone, immediately apologize and ask him or her to continue his or her statement. When a receiver fails to make any effort to hear or understand the sender's message, he or she is in **non-listening mode** and is allowing emotions, noise, or preconceptions to impede communication. Sometimes it is obvious the listener is not listening, because he or she either responds inappropriately or does not respond at all.

While the ideal is to consistently be an active listener, we know this is not always possible. However, every effort should be made to strive toward active listening. When you are talking, stop and listen for feedback. Too frequently, a person will have so much to say that he or she does not stop talking long enough to provide the receiver time to respond. The receiver's response is the only way a sender can verify that a message has been properly received.

Web Search

Are you a good communicator? Search the Internet to identify and take an online quiz related to effective communication.

Talk It Out

Name situations where it is easy to be in non-listening mode. What can an individual do to improve his or her listening skills in such situations?

Non-Verbal Communication

Non-verbal communication is what you communicate through body language. Even without uttering a word, you can send a very strong message. Body language includes eye contact, facial expressions, tone of voice, and the positioning of your body. Non-verbal communication also includes the use of silence and space.

An obvious form of body language is eye contact. It is common to look someone in the eye to communicate honesty and sincerity. At other times, looking someone in the eye coupled with a harsh tone of voice and an unfriendly facial expression may imply intimidation. In the United States, those who fail to look someone in the eye risk conveying to their receiver that they are not confident or, worse, are being dishonest. Make eye contact with your audience (individual or group), but do not stare. Staring is considered rude and intimidating. If your direct eye contact is making the receiver uncomfortable, he or she will look away. Be aware of his or her response and adapt your behavior appropriately.

Eye contact is part of the larger communication package of a facial expression. A receiver will find it difficult to interpret your eye contact as sincere and friendly when your message is accompanied by a frown. A smile has immense power and value. On the other hand, make sure you don't smile when listening to someone who is angry or upset. He or she may misinterpret your smile as condescending or as pleased by the distress. When actively listening, a nod implies that you are listening or agreeing with a sender's message. Even the positioning of your head can convey disagreement, confusion, or attentiveness.

Another element of non-verbal communication is the use and positioning of your body. Having your arms crossed in front of your body may be interpreted in several ways. You could be physically cold, angry, or uninterested. When you are not physically cold, having your arms crossed implies that you are creating a barrier between yourself and the other person. To eliminate any miscommunication, it is best to have your arms at your side. Do not hide your hands in your pockets. In speaking with others, be aware of the positioning of your arms and those of your audience. Also, be aware of the positioning of your entire body. Turn your body toward those to whom you are speaking. It is considered rude to turn your back to or ignore someone when he or she is speaking. In this case, you are using your entire body to create a barrier. Avoid this type of rude behavior. This only communicates immaturity on your part.

Exercise 1

With a partner, take turns identifying and noting the physical cues for the following emotions: concern, distrust, eagerness, boredom, and self-importance.

_____

_____

_____

The use of your hands is extremely important in effective communication. Through varied positioning, you can use your hands to nonverbally ask someone to stop a behavior, be quiet, or reprimand him or her. Be aware of the positioning of your hands and fingers. In the United States, it is considered rude to point at someone with one finger. Many finger and hand gestures commonly used in the United States are quite offensive in other countries. If you have nervous gestures such as popping your knuckles, biting your nails, or continually tapping your fingers, take steps to eliminate these habits.

Apart from a professional handshake, touching another person at work is not acceptable. People in our society frequently place a hand on another's shoulder as a show of support; however, some interpret that gesture as a threat or sexual advance. Therefore, when at work, keep your hands to yourself.

Proxemics is the study of distance (space) between individuals and is also an important factor in body language. An individual's personal space is about one-and-a-half feet around him or her. The appropriate social space is four feet from an individual. Standing too close may be interpreted as intimidation or may imply intimacy. Neither is appropriate for the workplace. However, distancing yourself too far from someone may imply your unwillingness to communicate. Be aware of the space you allow between you and your receiver. Many variables are involved in effective nonverbal communication. Interpret body language within its entire context. For example, if you are communicating with a colleague with whom you have a positive working relationship and your coworker crosses his or her arms, your coworker is most likely cold. Consider the entire package: environment, relationship, and situation.

Silence is also an effective and powerful communication tool. Silence communicates to your audience that you are listening and are allowing the other party consideration. Not immediately responding to a message provides the sender time to clarify or rephrase a message and provides you time to control your response.

Silence sometimes makes individuals uncomfortable because our society is used to filling up silence with noise. Active listeners take time to digest what is being said and formulate a thoughtful response. An active listener will wait at least three to five seconds before responding. When first using silence, it may feel awkward, but you will quickly discover that you are becoming a better communicator because you are taking time to respond thoughtfully and appropriately. Recognize that there are times when it is appropriate to not speak. In stressful situations, silence is perhaps one of the most important communication tools you possess. Silence can also be a powerful tool when dealing with both conflict and negotiation.

Emotion is another element that affects non-verbal communication. Although reality may cause you to express emotions that are difficult to control, try to control your emotions in public. If you feel you are beginning to cry or have an outburst of anger, excuse yourself. Find a private area and deal with your emotion. When you are crying or distraught, splash water on your face and regain control of your emotions. If you are getting angry, assess why you are angry, control your anger, and then create a strategy to regain control of how best to handle the situation in a professional manner. Any overt display of anger in the workplace is inappropriate, can damage workplace relationships, and could potentially jeopardize your job. When you become emotional at work, you lose your ability to logically deal with situations and risk losing credibility and the trust of others. Practice effective stress management and think before you respond.

Written Communication

Professional writing is a necessary skill for effective workplace communication. **Written communication** is a form of business communication that is printed, handwritten, or sent electronically. Because the receiver of your message will not have verbal and non-verbal assistance in interpreting your written message, take great care to ensure that the correct message is being communicated. You are normally not present when a written message is received; therefore, the receiver will be drawing additional conclusions about you based on the grammar, vocabulary, and presentation used in the written communication.

As you advance in responsibility within an organization, you will be required to conduct an increasing amount of written communication, including formal business letters, memos, and e-mail messages. You may also have the opportunity to communicate through instant messaging, texts, blogs, or wikis. Written business correspondence represents not only your professionalism and intelligence, but also your organizational abilities. Consistently present written correspondence in a professional manner. Ensure all written communication is error-free by proofreading the message prior to sending. Choose words that clearly and concisely communicate your message. The three most common forms of written communication in the workplace are letters, memos, and electronic messages. Written communication in a professional workplace should be typed and not handwritten. An exception to this rule is when you are sending a handwritten note conveying a personal message.

Plan your message for successful written communication. Identify what you want to communicate, to whom you need to communicate, and what desired action you want the reader to take after reading your message. After you have determined what you want to communicate, write a draft that is free of emotion and negativity. Written communication should begin with a professional greeting and end with a complimentary closing. If the purpose of your correspondence is to address a negative situation (e.g., complaint), begin with a positive note and then factually address the situation, but do not attack an individual. Do not send or write any message conveying anger. A good rule of thumb is to always put good news in writing and place negative information in writing only when necessary.

After you have drafted your message and eliminated emotions and negativity, review your correspondence and delete unnecessary words. Keep written correspondence short and simple. Do not be wordy, and minimize personalization words (*I, my*) as much as possible. Well-written correspondence not only communicates a core message, but also clearly communicates how the sender wants the reader to respond to the communication. Include contact information and a deadline in your written communication if relevant.

Keep the correspondence simple. Identify and insert words that project a professional image. Know the definitions of the words you are using, and use these words appropriately. A thesaurus is an excellent tool to expand one's vocabulary, but do not overdo it, and be sure to use words in the correct context.

After you have finished writing your message, identify who should receive the message. Share your correspondence only with individuals who need to know the information and, when appropriate, with individuals whom the correspondence affects.

The remainder of this chapter focuses on common written business correspondence, including a business letter, a memo, and a handwritten note.

Business Letters

A **business letter** is a formal, written form of communication used when your message is being sent to an individual outside of your organization. External audiences may include customers, vendors, suppliers, or members of the community. Although it is still common for formal business letters to be sent through traditional mail, many businesses now send formal business letters as attachments to e-mails. Letters are to be written in proper business format and on company letterhead. Clearly communicate your message and expected follow-up activity to the receiver in a professional and concise manner. Letters sent should be error-free. Proofread, sign, and date the letter before mailing.

Company **letterhead** is quality paper that has the company logo and contact information imprinted on it. Letters sent as attachments in an e-mail should be typed on company letterhead. Figure 2 shows the correct business

(Do not type QS and DS, these are shown for correct spacing.)	
Since most business letters will be on letterhead (preprinted business address), you need about a two-inch top margin before entering the current *date*.	August 1, 2018 *QS (4 enters or returns)*
The *inside address* should include the title, first, and last name of receiver.	Ms. Suzie Student Word Processing Fun 42 Learn Avenue Fresno, CA 93225 *DS (2 enters or returns)*
The *salutation* should have title and last name only.	Dear Ms. Student: *DS* The first paragraph of a letter should state the reason for the letter. If you had any previous contact with the receiver, mention it in this paragraph. *DS*
For the *body,* all lines begin at the left margin. Use a colon after the salutation and a comma after the complementary closing.	The second (and possibly a third) paragraph should contain details. All information needing to be communicated should be included here. *DS* The last paragraph is used to close the letter. Add information that is needed to clarify anything you said in the letter. Also, add any follow-up or contact information. *DS*
Keep the *closing* simple.	Sincerely, *QS*
The writer's first and last name should be four enters or returns after the closing to give the *writer* room to sign (remember to have the writer sign).	*Sarah S. Quirrel* Sarah S. Quirrel Instructor *DS*
Typist's initials *Enclosure* is used only if you add something in the envelope with the letter.	bt Enclosure

Figure 2

Letter Format

419

August 1, 2018

Ms. Suzie Student
Word Processing Fun
42 Learn Avenue
Fresno, CA 93225

Dear Ms. Student:

It was a pleasure speaking with you over the telephone earlier today. I am delighted that you have agreed to serve as a guest speaker in my Communications class. The purpose of this letter is to confirm the details of the upcoming speaking engagement.

As I mentioned in our conversation, the date for your scheduled lecture is Wednesday, October 14, 2018. The class meets from 6:00 p.m.–8:30 p.m. You may take as much time as you need, but if possible please allow a student question and answer period. There are approximately 60 students, and the classroom contains state-of-the-art technology. If you have specific technology requests, do not hesitate to contact me. Enclosed is a parking permit and map of the campus directing you to the appropriate classroom.

Once again, thank you for continued support of our students. I and my students are looking forward to you sharing your communications insight and expertise with us on October 14. If you have any additional questions, please do not hesitate to contact me via e-mail at S.Quirrel@teaching.com or call me at 123-456-7890.

Sincerely,

Sarah S. Quirrel

Sarah S. Quirrel
Instructor

bt
Enclosure

Figure 3

Letter Example

letter format. Figure 3 provides an example of a business letter. Please note that a business letter can have various styles; employees should follow the company-preferred style.

When a business letter is not being sent electronically, most companies utilize matching number 10 envelopes (Figure 4). Address the envelope with the

Exercise 2

Practice folding a letter to fit into a number 10 envelope.

_____

_____

_____

```
S&L Professionalism Corp.
222 Student Success Lane
Kahului, HI  93732


                    Ms. Suzie Student
                    Word Processing Fun
                    42 Learn Avenue
                    Fresno, CA 93225
```

Figure 4

Envelope Example

same information that is in the inside address. Fold the letter in thirds, starting at the bottom and folding up one-third of the way and then fold the top over the bottom, and place it in the envelope with the opening on top.

Business Memos

Business memos (sometimes called interoffice memorandums) are used internally—that is, when the written communication is being sent to a receiver within an organization. Although e-mail is the most common form of internal communication, a traditional business memorandum is still used for internal formal documentation and announcements and is sometimes attached to an e-mail message. A memo includes the receiver's name, sender's name, date, and subject. As with a business letter, include all facts needed to properly communicate the message, but be brief and to the point. Ideally, memos should be no longer than one page. Most word processing software has templates for creating memos.

Figures 5 and 6 illustrate common business memo formats. As with business letters, many companies have a preferred memo style. Check with your employer to ensure you are utilizing the proper format.

Handwritten Notes

A handwritten note is a personal form of communication. In a professional workplace, it is appropriate to send a handwritten note to acknowledge special events in careers or personal lives (e.g., promotion, birthday, or birth of a child). It is also acceptable to send a handwritten note to encourage a colleague, offer condolences for the loss of a loved one, or to thank someone. Handwritten notes are written in pen on a note card. However, it is also acceptable to acknowledge an occasion with an appropriate greeting card. In some situations it is acceptable to send an electronic thank-you or personal message. Handwritten notes do not need to be lengthy; generally, just a few sentences are sufficient. Acknowledge or encourage coworkers, bosses, and others with whom you work by sending handwritten notes when appropriate.

A thank-you note is a powerful tool for building relationships. When you express thanks, individuals are more likely to continue assisting and supporting you. Send a thank-you note when someone does something for you that takes

Talk It Out

Share a recent situation where it would have been appropriate to send a handwritten note.

(Do not type DS, these are shown for correct spacing.)	
Start the memo two inches from the top of the page.	**MEMO TO:** Loretta Howerton, Office Manager *DS* **FROM:** Lawrence Schmidt, OA/CIS Trainer
Double-space after each *heading.* Bold and capitalize only headings, not the information. Use initial caps in the *subject line.*	*DS* **DATE:** January 6, 2018 *DS* **SUBJECT:** Memo Format for Internal Correspondence

Body—single-space, no tabs, left align. Double-space between paragraphs.	*DS*
	A memorandum is an internal communication that is sent within the organization. It is often the means by which managers correspond with employees and vice versa. Memos provide written records of announcements, requests for action, and policies and procedures. Use first and last names and include the job title.
	       DS
	Templates, or preformatted forms, often are used for creating memos. Templates provide a uniform look for company correspondence and save the employee the time of having to design a memo. Word processing software has memo templates that can be customized. Customize the template so it has the company name and your department name at the top. Make sure you change the date format (month, day, year). It should be as it is seen at the beginning of this memo.
	       DS

Reference initials (typist's initials) *Attachment notation*, only if needed (if you attach something)	bt Attachment

Figure 5

Memo Format

MEMO TO: Loretta Howerton, Office Manager

FROM: Lawrence Schmidt, OA/CIS Trainer

DATE: January 6, 2018

SUBJECT: Accounting Department Computer Training

This memo is to confirm that the computer training for the accounting department will occur on February 1, 2018, in the large conference room. Although the training is scheduled from 9:00 a.m.–11:30 a.m., I have reserved the room for the entire morning, beginning at 7:00 a.m.

As we discussed last week, this may be a good opportunity to offer breakfast to the department prior to the training. If this is something you would like to pursue, please let me know by next Tuesday, and I will make the proper arrangements. Thank you again for the opportunity to provide computer training to your team.

bt

Figure 6

Memo Example

Include the date.	*June 3, 2018*
Start your note with a salutation and the receiver's name.	*Dear Ms. McCombs,*
Be brief but specific about why you are thanking the person. Include how you benefited from the person's kindness. Do not begin every sentence with *I*.	*Thank you for loaning me your book on business etiquette. I especially liked the chapter on social events and dining. Your constant encouragement and mentoring mean so much to me.* *Sincerely,*
Use a complimentary closing, and do not forget to sign your name.	*Mason Yang*

Figure 7

Thank-You Note

more than five minutes or when someone gives you a gift. Deliver the note as soon as possible. Handwritten thank-you notes are commonly sent to an interviewer after an interview. Figure 7 displays the correct format and key elements of a handwritten note.

Documentation

Documentation is a formal record of events or activities. Some industries require documentation to track a project's progress or an employee's time for client billing. Documentation may be necessary for an employee evaluation, for advancement, in an instance in which a policy is not enforced, or when an abnormal event has occurred that has the potential to evolve into conflict at a later date. These events may support performance issues, business relationships, and business operations. It is not necessary to record every event that occurs at work. Employees should maintain a file of positive feedback received from coworkers, supervisors, or customers. Employees should also document relevant negative business situations, such as a workplace injury, an angry customer, or an employee conflict, in order to protect themselves and/or the employer. Although there are numerous methods of documenting and retaining important information and events, the basic elements to be recorded remain the same.

Depending on the purpose of your documentation, effective documentation records the who, what, when, where, and why of a situation. Effective documentation essentials include who was present when the event occurred and how witnesses to the event behaved or responded. When describing what happened, keep the documentation factual and do not allow feelings and assumptions to distort the facts. Include the date, time, and location of the event. Documentation can be kept electronically, in a journal, or through minimal notations on a calendar. If the documentation is for billing or client purposes, your employer will provide the documentation format. Whatever system you choose, keep your documentation in a secure, private location along with copies of supporting memos, letters, or other communications. If you are ever called on to defend your actions, you will have the ability to easily gather pertinent information.

Presentations

Formal and informal presentations are normal workplace events, and sometime in your career you may be asked to give a presentation. Being prepared and professional will help increase audience interest and reception. Presentations are rich in media and may include written, verbal, visual, and/or non-verbal communication. A successful presentation begins with a goal. Identify the purpose of your presentation and ensure that every word, visual aid, activity, and/or handout will support the overall goal of the presentation. After the purpose of the presentation has been identified, an outline of key points should be identified to reinforce the message you want individuals to respond to or remember.

Formal presentations include three elements: the verbal content, the visual content, and support content. Verbal content provides the primary message, visual content summarizes the message, and support content reinforces the message. Verbal content includes the detailed information you wish to share with the audience. When presenting, do not read directly from the visual content. Speak clearly and at a normal pace using professional and appropriate language. Face your audience. If you are using a screen, keep your back toward the screen. Do not block the audience's view of your visual. Beware of both verbal and non-verbal gestures. Nothing will distract an audience quicker than an overuse of "um," "like," and "you know." Hands in pockets, crossed arms, or tapping feet are examples of distracting physical gestures. Dress professionally, and do not wear anything that may distract from your message.

Visual content includes anything the audience will view or any activity the audience will perform during your presentation. Often this involves some type of technology, including presentation software, videos, or music. When using presentation software, do not overdo the use of graphics, color, or animations. Test all equipment and software prior to the actual presentation to ensure the equipment is working and the software is compatible. Preparation and practice ensure that your visual content and/or activities are the appropriate length. If you are including your audience in an activity (e.g., game), make directions simple and the activity brief. Keep your audience focused, and do not allow the activity to distract from your message.

Support content normally comes in the form of a handout. This is an excellent way to reinforce your verbal and visual message in writing. A popular format for a handout allows the audience to fill in the blanks as you present your message. Add non-distracting professional and visual appeal to your handout. As you create your handout, follow the same order as the presentation outline. Check your visual presentation and support materials for clarity, spelling, and grammatical errors. When you are certain your support content is error-free and professional, make enough copies for each member of your audience.

Formal presentations are an excellent way to increase workplace credibility and individual confidence. Successful presentations are a result of planning. Remember, practice makes perfect.

Slang and Foul Language

Slang is an informal language used among a particular group. Although different generations, cultures, and technology use slang, avoid using slang in the workplace to ensure your message is not misinterpreted by others. Become a more effective communicator in the workplace by eliminating the use of slang.

Your words reflect what is going on in your heart and mind. There is no appropriate time to use profane and offensive language at work. Even in times of stress or at social functions, you are representing your company and must do so in a professional manner. Practice self-control. Attempt to eliminate foul or offensive language from your personal and professional vocabulary. If you utilize inappropriate language at work, immediately apologize. Make a mental note of what situation caused you to behave poorly and learn from the experience. Ask yourself how you could have better handled the situation, and mentally rehearse a proper, more acceptable method of verbally handling a challenging situation.

Think About It

What slang terms do you use in text messages that may be offensive to others?

Potentially Offensive Names

Names that could be considered sexist and offensive are inappropriate in a business setting. These include names such as honey, sweetie, and sexy. Using inappropriate names toward coworkers could expose you and your company to a potential sexual harassment lawsuit. Even if the individual being called these names acts as if he or she is not offended, the person may actually be offended or insulted but is afraid to tell you. Eliminate these words from your workplace vocabulary. In addition, do not use gender-specific titles when referring to certain jobs. For example:

Instead of	Use
Postman	Postal Carrier
Policeman	Police Officer
Waitress	Server
Stewardess	Flight Attendant
Maid	Housekeeper

Not Always About You

There is one word that often dominates written and verbal communication but frequently turns receivers off. Unfortunately, too often, the sender is unaware of its overuse. The word is *I*. Be cautious with the use of this word. Self-centered people use it to draw attention; whereas those who lack self-confidence may subconsciously use the word to protect themselves. Many individuals who overuse this word may not know how to turn the conversation to others, so they choose to stay in a safety zone. When you are using verbal communication, think before you speak. When writing, if your initial sentence includes *I*, try to rephrase your message. Prior to sending written correspondence, review your message and reduce the number of sentences that begin with the word *I*.

Exercise 3

Take five minutes and interview a classmate about college and his or her career choice. While you are getting to know each other, keep track of how many times your new friend says the word *I*.

_____

_____

_____

MyStudentSuccessLab   Please visit **MyStudentSuccessLab**: Anderson|Bolt, Professionalism Skills for Workplace Success, 4/e for additional activities, resources, and outcomes assessments.

Workplace Dos and Don'ts

Do carefully think through your message and the appropriate medium	*Don't* be in such a hurry to send your message that an incorrect message is sent
Do demonstrate professionalism in the formatting, word choice, and grammar in your written communication	*Don't* write and send messages when you are angry
Do express kindness to others with both your words and body language	*Don't* utilize foul language at work or at home

Concept Review and Application

You are a Successful Student if you:

- Demonstrate proper formatting for a business letter and memo
- Write a handwritten thank-you note
- Create a documentation record
- Explain the difference between gossip and the grapevine

Summary of Key Concepts

- Effective communication is necessary for workplace success.

- The goal of communication is to create a mutual understanding between the sender and the receiver.

- There are appropriate times to utilize both the formal and informal communication channels.

- The communication process involves a sender, a receiver, noise, and feedback.

- Listening and silence are effective tools for effective communication.

- Thoughtfully consider the right words to increase the chance of successful written and verbal communication.

- Because the receiver of your message will not have verbal and non-verbal assistance in interpreting your message, take great care with all written messages.

Self-Quiz MATCHING KEY TERMS

Match the key term to the definition using the identifying number.

Key Terms	Answer	Definitions
Active listening		1. Communication that occurs through formal lines of authority
Business letter		2. The process of using words to send a message
Business memos		3. When a receiver is selectively hearing parts of a message and is more focused on responding
Communication		4. A formal record of events or activities
Decoding		5. The process of a sender transmitting a message to a receiver with the purpose of creating mutual understanding
Documentation		6. An informal network where employees discuss workplace issues of importance
Encoding		7. Quality paper that has the company logo and contact information printed on it
Feedback		8. Communicating through body language
Formal communication		9. How the receiver interprets a message
Gossip		10. When the grapevine is targeting individuals and their personal lives
Grapevine		11. The study of distance (space) between individuals

Key Terms	Answer	Definitions
Informal communication		12. Written communication sent within an organization
Letterhead		13. Communication that occurs among individuals without regard to formal lines of authority
Listening		14. A form of business communication that is printed, handwritten, or sent electronically
Noise		15. An informal language used among a particular group
Non-listening mode		16. The act of hearing attentively
Non-verbal communication		17. A response to a sender's message
Passive listening		18. The individual conveying a message
Proxemics		19. A formal, written form of communication sent to individuals outside of an organization
Receiver		20. When a receiver fails to make any effort to hear or understand the sender's message
Sender		21. Anything that interrupts or interferes with the communication process
Slang		22. An individual that receives and decodes a message
Verbal communication		23. When the receiver provides full attention to the sender without distraction
Written communication		24. Identifying a specific message and how it will be sent

Think Like a Boss

1. One of your employees uses bad grammar that is reflecting poorly on your department's performance. How can you get a handle on this problem?

2. Employees keep saying they do not know what is going on at work. What steps would you take to increase workplace communication?

Activities

Activity 1

Without infringing on someone's privacy, discreetly observe a stranger's body language for approximately five minutes. Stay far enough away to not hear him or her speak. Name at least two assumptions you can make by simply watching the person's gestures, movements, and expressions.

Gesture, Movement, or Expression	Assumption

Activity 2

Watch a television news show for a half hour. Document at least two facial expressions of an individual being interviewed. Did the individual's facial expressions match his or her statements?

Facial Expression	Statements

Activity 3

Review the following letter. Identify five formatting errors and correct those errors.

April

Sandra Wong, Vice President
Human Resource Department
Robinson Enterprises
55123 W. Robinson Lane
Prosperity, CA 99923

Dear Sandra Wong

It was a pleasure speaking with you this afternoon regarding the average salary you pay your receptionists. This data will be useful as our company begins creating a new receptionist position for our California site.

I am most appreciative of your offer to mail me a copy of your most recent salary guide for all production positions. I look forward to receiving that guide in the mail. As a thank you for your kindness, I am enclosing coupons for our company product.

If there is any information I can provide to assist you, please let me know. Thank you again for your cooperation.

Sincerely,

Cory Kringle

List Errors	Correction
1.	
2.	
3.	
4.	
5.	

Activity 4

Review the following memo. Identify five errors (not including spacing) and make the appropriate corrections.

MEMORANDUM

Re: Budget Meeting

To: Mason Jared

From: Cory Kringle

Date: May 1

Hey Mason. I wanted to remind you that we have a meeting next week to talk about next year's budget. Bring some numbers and we'll work through them. Bye.

-Cory

List Errors	Correction
1.	
2.	
3.	
4.	
5.	

Activity 5

You received a letter of recommendation from a teacher. Write a thank-you note.

_____

_____

_____

Glossary

active listening: when a receiver provides a sender full attention without distraction

business letter: a formal written form of communication used when a message is being sent to an individual outside of an organization

business memo: written communication sent within an organization (also called *interoffice memorandum*)

communication: the process of a sender transmitting a message to an individual (receiver) with the purpose of creating mutual understanding

decoding: how a receiver interprets a message

documentation: a formal record of events or activities

encoding: identifying how a message will be sent (verbally, written, or nonverbally)

feedback: when a receiver responds to a sender's message based upon the receiver's interpretation of the original message

formal communication: workplace communication that occurs through memos, meetings, or lines of authority

gossip: personal information about another individual that is hurtful and inappropriate

grapevine: an informal communication network where employees talk about workplace issues of importance

informal communication: workplace communication that occurs among individuals without regard to the formal lines of authority

letterhead: quality paper that has the company logo, mailing address, and telephone numbers imprinted on it

listening: the act of hearing attentively

noise: anything that interrupts or interferes with the communication process

non-listening: When a receiver fails to make any effort to hear or understand the sender's message

nonverbal communication: what is communicated through body language

passive listening: the receiver is selectively hearing parts of a message

proxemics: the study of distance (space) between individuals

sender: an individual wanting to convey a message

slang: an informal language used among a particular group

verbal communication: the process of using words to send a message

written communication: a form of business communication that is printed, handwritten, or sent electronically

Suggested Readings

Gallo C. "Why Leadership Means Listening," *Businessweek* (January 31, 2007), http://www.businessweek.com/smallbiz/content/jan2007/sb20070131_192848.htm

http://articles.economictimes.indiatimes.com/2010-12-10/news/27591286_1_
leadership-responsibility-authority. Sangeeth Varghese, Dec 10, 2010,
03.13am IST www.economic times.Com

Dan, R. J. (2010). In the Company of Others: An Introduction to Communication. (New York: Oxford University Press), pp. 157–166.

Susan, Y. "The New Trend in Communication: Silent Listening," *Salesopedia.*
Retrieved May 31, 2011, www.salesopedia.com/index.php/component/
content/1863?task=view&Itemid=10479.

Paul, P. "Proxemics in Clinical and Administrative Settings." *Journal of Healthcare Management.* Vol. 50, No. 3 (May–June 2005): 151–154.

Carter, L. Ideas for adding soft skills education to service learning and cap-
stone courses for computer science students. ACM Technical Symposium
on Computer Science Education Proceedings. Dallas, TX. March 9–12,
2011, pp. 517–522.

Credits

Credits are listed in order of appearance.

Andresr/Shutterstock; Shutterstock; Figure 2–5 and Activities 3–4: Sandra
Bolt/Author Owned Sandra Bolt; Sandra Bolt; Sandra Bolt; Sandra Bolt;
Author Owned; Sandra Bolt; Sandra Bolt

Job Search Skills

target • research • network

After studying these topics, you will benefit by:

- Conducting a job search in a targeted career, industry, and location
- Ensuring a professional online identity and protection of privacy
- Collecting items to be included in a job search portfolio
- Identifying references to be used in a job search
- Discovering sources for job leads
- Describing how networking is a powerful job search tool
- Explaining appropriate behaviors to utilize during the job search process
- Summarizing the importance of maintaining the right attitude during a job search

HOW DO YOU RATE?

Are you job search savvy?	True	False
1. It is best to attend a job fair prepared as if it is an interview.	☐	☐
2. It is acceptable to distribute personal business cards at social functions.	☐	☐
3. It is not necessary to share personal information such as a birthdate and Social Security number during a job search.	☐	☐
4. A job search portfolio is a foundation for the interview portfolio.	☐	☐
5. Most realistic job leads are found through networking.	☐	☐

▸ If you answered "true" to four or more of these questions, congratulations—you are well on your way to finding the job of your dreams. Knowing how the job search process works, creating a job search plan, and properly utilizing job search tools pave the way to job search success.

The Job Search

An effective job search is the key to finding a great job. A successful job search involves creating a plan, conducting research, and taking action. Doing so takes time, organization, communication, and professionalism. This chapter is designed to help you create a job search strategy. A successful job search strategy identifies what type of job you will be looking for, what tools and resources you will need, and how these tools and resources are best used. The job search is an integral part of your life plan as it brings life to your career goals. The ultimate goal of a job search is to secure an interview that paves the way toward obtaining the job of your dreams.

Choosing the Right Career

Creating a job search plan begins with choosing the right career. This involves **self-discovery**. Self-discovery is the process of identifying key interests and skills built on your career goals. Knowing your key knowledge, skills, and abilities and linking these with your career goals will assist you in landing a job you will enjoy. This process includes identifying key interests and accomplishments from your work, educational, and personal experiences. A method for identifying key interests is creating an accomplishments worksheet, shown in Activity 1. The worksheet inventories skills you have acquired from work or non-work experience and serves as a tool to assist you in identifying the right career. Utilize power words when completing the accomplishments worksheet. **Power words** are action verbs that describe your accomplishments in a lively and specific way. These power words provide an excellent foundation when you create your personal commercial and build your résumé. Table 1 lists power words that will assist you in identifying your accomplishments.

Table 1 Power Words			
Adapted	Communicated	Instructed	Projected
Addressed	Coordinated	Installed	Recommended
Analyzed	Created	Introduced	Risked
Arranged	Determined	Investigated	Saved
Assisted	Developed	Learned	Staffed
Built	Earned	Located	Taught
Calculated	Established	Managed	Typed
Chaired	Financed	Motivated	Updated
Cleaned	Implemented	Organized	Won
Coached	Increased	Planned	Wrote

After you have completed your accomplishments worksheet, reread your responses. They will most likely reveal a targeted career of interest to you.

A second means of identifying key skills and jobs of interest is to take a formal career assessment to identify what careers best match your interests and abilities. Common career assessment tools include the Golden Personality Type Indicator, the Myers-Briggs Type Indicator, and the Strong Interest Inventory. Many college career centers offer these assessments, as do various online sources. Sponsored by the U.S. Department of Labor, an excellent online resource is the ONET Interest Profiler.

Once you have identified careers and specific jobs that are of interest to you, conduct a realistic job preview. A realistic job preview identifies day-to-day activities and common tasks that are performed and required for a specific job and also makes you fully aware of both the positive and negative aspects of a specific job. Identify standard qualifications and education requirements. For example, if you are a felon, you may not be allowed to work in some areas of health care and education. There are other careers that require a clean DMV record or credit history. Thoughtfully researching and understanding what is required to secure and succeed in a desired job early in the career exploration process will save time and money.

After identifying a target career, make your job search personal by creating a career summary statement. This statement provides focus for your job search by summarizing your career objective, knowledge, skills, abilities, and accomplishments. Your career summary statement will be used for networking purposes and will be a vital element of your personal commercial. Complete Activity 3 to create your career summary statement.

Industry Research

One step in a successful job search is research. When a job fits your personality and skills, you are more likely to succeed. A satisfying career comes from performing a job you enjoy and working at a company that reflects your values. Conducting industry research will provide career information to reinforce that you have made the right career decision to support your life plan. Identify industries that require the key skills you possess.

Your research will most likely reveal that there are more industries that require your key skills than you thought. The easiest way to conduct industry research is by using the ONET Database. This database of occupational information was developed for the U.S. Department of Labor and provides key information by job title. Match the key knowledge, skills, and abilities required for your target job with the knowledge, skills, and abilities you possess.

Once you have identified industries requiring your skills, begin identifying specific jobs in these industries. Note the different job opportunities and various job titles that exist within each industry. Being aware of the various job titles for which you qualify allows increased job search flexibility. After determining industries and job titles that fit your skills, identify the various environments available, including where the jobs are located and the specific work setting desired.

For example, if you finished college with a business degree, conduct research on industries that need employees with a business background, such as health

Web Search

Search and take the ONET Interest Profiler.

Talk It Out

What career area do you believe suits your skills and experiences?

Talk It Out

Discuss the difference between a job and an industry.

care, retailing, and manufacturing. Once an industry is identified, begin reviewing job titles that match the skills you have acquired in college, such as a financial analyst, general accountant, marketing assistant, or human resource generalist. After identifying specific job titles that match your skill sets, decide what type of work environment you desire. If you select health care, you may have the choice of working in a hospital, a clinic, or a private physician's office.

Conducting industry and work environment research will provide you information that will simplify your job search. Instead of sending out hundreds of résumés in hopes of securing any job, target companies that are a good match with your life plan, your skills, and your desired work environment.

The Targeted Job Search

After you have a clearly defined career summary and have identified jobs that suit your personal and career goals, it is time to begin a targeted job search. A **targeted job search** leads you through the process of discovering open positions for which you are qualified, in addition to identifying specific companies for which you would like to work.

Part of a job search is to determine in what city you want to work. If your job search is limited to your local area, you will be restricted to local employers. If you are willing to commute outside of your area, determine how far you are willing to commute (both directions) on a daily basis. If you wish to move out of the area, identify what locations are most appealing. Should you desire to move to a new location, consider the cost of living in your desired location. The **cost of living** is the average cost of basic necessities such as housing, food, and clothing. For example, it is much more expensive to live in Manhattan, New York, than it is to live in Cheyenne, Wyoming. Although a job in Manhattan may pay a lot more than a job in Cheyenne, living expenses typically justify the higher salary.

Exercise 1

Identify three companies/employers in your target location that may be of interest to you.

_____

_____

_____

Online Identity

Web Search

Conduct an Internet search on yourself.

With the popularity of social networking sites, your personal life has a greater chance of being exposed in the job search process. Ensure you have a favorable online identity. An online identity is the image formed when someone is communicating with you and/or researching you through electronic venues.

Because the majority of information on the Internet is public information, an increasing number of employers are conducting web searches on potential employees to gain a better perspective of the applicant's values and lifestyle.

With today's overabundance of electronic social networking and information sites, personal blogs, and other file-sharing services, ensure that defamatory photos, writings, or other material will not be a barrier in your job search. When conducting an Internet search on yourself, remove any information that portrays you in a negative light. If you are actively involved in social networking sites, carefully evaluate any personal information such as photos and/or statements about you on these sites. If negative information is on your personal site, immediately remove it. If it is contained on sites of your friends, explain your job search plans and politely ask them to remove the potentially harmful information.

An additional step toward ensuring a clean online identify is to maintain a professional e-mail address. Sending a potential employer an e-mail from the address "prty2nite" is not the image you want to project. If necessary, establish a new e-mail address that utilizes some form of your name or initials to maintain a clean and professional online identity. Two final considerations in maintaining a professional online identity are the maintenance of a professional voice mail message and the avoidance of text slang in all written communication. Your job search strategy will involve extensive communication with employers and other individuals who will assist you with your job search. Interaction with these individuals needs to be professional.

Think About It

Does your social network site contain information that may hinder a friend's job search?

Talk It Out

What type of photos, writings, or materials do you think are inappropriate for a potential employer to see?

Job Search Portfolio

A **job search portfolio** is a collection of paperwork used to keep you organized and prepared while searching for a job. These items and their purpose will be discussed here.

When creating and managing your job search portfolio, it is best to have a binder with tabs to keep all paperwork organized and protected. When you begin collecting items for your portfolio, have the original and at least two copies of each item available at all times. Copies will be transferred to your interview portfolio when needed. Original documents should not be removed from your job search portfolio. Place original documents in plastic notebook protectors; do not punch holes in original documents.

Because many of today's job searches occur over the Internet, it is also recommended you create an electronic job search portfolio. An **electronic job search portfolio (e-portfolio)** is a computerized folder that contains electronic copies of all job search documents. For your electronic job search file, scan copies of all documents you will be keeping in your hard-copy portfolio. Save these scanned files in portable document format (.pdf) to ensure the documents are able to be easily retrieved by the receiver. Keep your electronic job search portfolio in an electronic folder that is both easy to retrieve and access. When sharing job search files with potential employers and others, these electronic documents will be sent as attachments. The electronic job search portfolio may be very useful in your job search should an employer request documentation, as you will have immediate access to this information through a mobile electronic device.

You may be sharing some of these items with employers, so when creating documents, proofread and ensure they are professional and error-free. Table 2 is a list of items to include in your job search portfolio.

Table 2 Job Search Portfolio

Item	Description
Awards	Documents that demonstrate proficiency in specific skills
Certificates	Documents that demonstrate proficiency in specific skills
Completed generic application	Generic job application that makes information readily available
Copy of ID and/or driver's license	A valid ID and proof of ability to drive (if driving is a job requirement)
Copy of recent DMV record (if relevant to your career)	Used to ensure a safe driving record
Cover letter	Introduces a résumé
Current state licenses (if relevant to your career)	Documents that verify the ability to practice certain professions
Job search notebook	Three ring binder to store all job search documents secure in one place
Letters of recommendation	A written professional reference to verify work experience and character
Network list	A list of professional relationships used for job contacts
Pen	Used for tracking and keeping notes
Performance appraisals from previous jobs	Proof of positive work performance
Personal business cards	Cards with personal contact information used to share for job leads
Personal commercial	Statement that assists with interview
Plastic inserts	Use for originals (do not place holes in originals)
Reference list	A list of individuals who will provide a professional reference
Résumé	A formal profile that is presented to potential employers
Small calendar	Used to track dates
Small note pad	Use for notes
Thank you notes with a draft message	Use for post-interview follow up
Transcripts	Documents that verify education (have both official and copies available; sealed transcripts may be required)
Work samples	Documents that demonstrate proficiency in specific skills

Many careers that involve driving require a copy of your driving history. This information is secured by contacting your local Department of Motor Vehicles (DMV). If you have a poor driving record, check with your local DMV to identify how long this history stays on your record. Those with a blemished driving history may have a tougher time securing a job in a field that involves driving. When sharing your DMV record, as with all other portfolio items, provide only a copy (unless otherwise required) and maintain the original in your job search portfolio.

Employment Applications

Keep a completed generic employment application in your job search portfolio so you have required information readily available. If you have a smartphone, simply take a photo of the completed application and store this information on your device for quick and easy retrieval. To protect yourself from potential identity theft, do not list your Social Security number or birthdate on any employment application, if possible. On some electronic applications, this information is a required field. If such is the case, ensure you are utilizing a secured site.

An employment application is a legal document. When completing the application, read the fine print prior to signing the document. Commonly, at the end of the application, there will be a statement that grants the potential employer permission to conduct reference and various background checks, including a credit check, if the information is relevant to the job for which you are applying. Fully understand why this background information is necessary and how it will be used in the hiring process. If you do not fully understand the statements on the application, get clarification prior to signing the application.

It is common for employers to request that the applicant complete an employment application and submit this document along with the résumé package. If you submitted only a cover letter and résumé, you may be asked to complete an application after you have been interviewed. Many employment applications can now only be completed and submitted through a kiosk located at a worksite or downloaded, completed, and submitted directly through a company website. A typed employment application is best. If typing is not possible, complete the application by printing neatly in black ink. In some instances, after you have completed an online application, you may be asked to take a pre-employment test as part of the application process.

Personal References and Recommendations

Create a list of professional references that a potential employer can contact to verify your work experience and personal character. While a professional reference list is part of your résumé package, references are not to be included on your résumé; list them on a separate page. Do not send your reference list with your résumé unless it is requested by the employer. However, have a copy available to share if the employer requests references during the interview. References can be from past or present employers and supervisors, coworkers, instructors, or from a representative of an organization with which you have volunteered. Do not use relatives, friends, or religious leaders unless you have worked or volunteered with or for them.

Prior to including individuals on your reference list, ask each person if he or she is willing to provide a reference. When asking someone to serve as a reference, share with them details on your job search, including your career goal, target employers/job, and the status of your search. Make certain each person on this list will provide a positive reference. Have at least three names to submit as references. Include each reference's name, relationship, contact phone number, e-mail address, and business mailing address.

In addition to reputable references, it is wise to have at least three **letters of recommendation**. A letter of recommendation is a written testimony from another person that states that you are credible. Begin collecting letters of recommendation before you actively engage in a job search. Strong letters of recommendation reflect current job skills, accomplishments, and positive human relations skills and should be no older than one year. Letters of recommendation can be from past or present employers, coworkers, instructors, or someone you worked for as an intern or volunteer. It is common and acceptable to have someone write a formal letter of recommendation and serve as a personal reference. When asking for a letter of recommendation, provide details about the job skills, accomplishments, or human relations skills you feel they observed. This information will be valuable when they write your letter. Provide your reference a minimum of two weeks to write your letter. If possible, have the letter written on company or personal letterhead. Also ensure the letter is dated and signed. After receiving your letter, immediately send your reference a note or small gift of thanks for their effort.

Ask your reference to include the following information in the reference letter:

- Connection to you, why he or she knows you are qualified, and why he or she is providing a reference letter
- Information about your skills and how they would benefit the company (provide information and/or a copy of the job qualifications if applicable)
- A summary of why he or she is recommending you
- Reference contact information

In addition to routinely updating your résumé, keep your reference list updated. References listed should be relevant to your career goal. Occasionally contact your references to verify that they are still willing to serve as references. Keep these individuals current on your job search status and career goals.

Think About It

Other than an instructor, identify someone from whom you can secure a personal letter of recommendation.

Sources of Job Leads

Your search for job leads is a job in itself. Potential employers will not seek you. You must actively seek them. Fortunately, there are many available sources for job leads. The most obvious job lead is directly from a targeted company. View the company website or personally visit the target company's human resource department for current job announcements. It is also common for employers to post job announcements on social networking and job search websites. If you do not have a targeted company but have a location where you would like to work, conduct an Internet search using the target city and position as key search words. Search associations in your targeted industry to view industry-specific online job banks. Check online message boards and popular job search sites. Maintain a record of the sites you are utilizing for your job search and monitor activity. Many larger cities and counties offer one-stop centers for job seekers. These government-funded agencies provide job-seeker assistance and serve as a link between job seekers and local employers. Other job sources include job fairs, newspaper advertisements, industry journals, and current employees who work in your targeted industry and/or company.

Do not rely solely on posted job positions. Many jobs are unsolicited (not advertised to the general public). The way to become aware of these unsolicited jobs is to use your professional network. A professional network is a group of relationships that are established primarily for business purposes. Use your network to identify individuals who either are or know current employees who work in your targeted industry and/or company. Inform network members of your desire for a job and ask for potential job leads. The larger your professional network, the more you will become aware of unannounced job leads. A discussion on how to create and utilize a professional network is presented in the next section.

Treat all face-to-face job search situations—including distributing your résumé, meeting a potential network contact, attending a job fair, or visiting a company to identify open positions—as if you are going to an interview. Dress professionally, go alone, display confidence, keep easy access to your online portfolio, and bring your interview portfolio. In networking situations where there are many job seekers, such as a job fair, be polite and professional in your interactions with everyone. Do not interrupt or be rude to other job seekers. Take the lead in introducing yourself to company representatives. Sell your skills and confidently ask the company representative if he or she has an open position requiring your skills. The goal in such a situation is to favorably stand out from the crowd, share your résumé, and arrange an interview. There are situations where applicants are invited to "on the spot" interviews. Your professional appearance, preparation, and interview portfolio will demonstrate that you are a serious candidate for the job. Dressing casually and/or having a child or friend in tow will communicate unprofessionalism to a potential employer.

If you are unable to identify a job lead, send an unsolicited cover letter and résumé to your target company either electronically or through traditional mail. When sending an unsolicited résumé, send two copies: one to the human resource manager, and the other to the manager of your target job. Prior to sending your résumé, call or research the company to ensure you have identified the correct spelling and gender for the individuals to whom you will be sending your résumé. Sending two résumés to the same company increases the opportunity of securing an interview. The targeted department manager will most likely read and file your résumé for future reference. The human resource manager will also review your résumé and may identify other jobs for which you are qualified.

An internship is an excellent method of enhancing your job skills and a venue to expand your professional network. An internship is a paid or unpaid method of on-the-job training and can prove to a potential employer that you can handle the demands of the job. Many colleges provide assistance in securing an intern position. Approach an internship as an ongoing interview, as your manager and the individual with whom you will be working are evaluating you on your performance and professional behavior. Throughout your internship, demonstrate value to the company by being responsible. Also, use your internship as a means of increasing your professional network. At the end of a successful internship, it is appropriate to request a letter of recommendation from the employer and/or coworkers.

Professional Networking

According to the Bureau of Labor Statistics, over 70 percent of jobs are found through networking, although many estimate that number to be higher. Therefore, establishing and maintaining a professional network is important for career success. A **professional network** is a group of relationships that are established primarily for business purposes. A professional network is created through **networking**, the act of creating professional relationships. Think of networking as a connection device. The purpose of creating a professional network is to have a resource of individuals whom you can call on for professional

Talk It Out

What job fair behaviors demonstrate to a recruiter that you are professional?

Talk It Out

How can you specifically use an internship to increase your professional network?

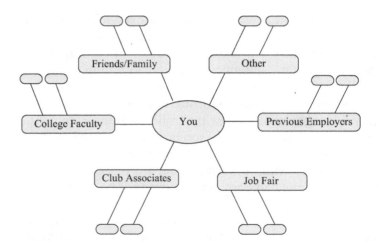

Figure 1

Professional Network

assistance and/or advice. The intent of this discussion is to utilize a professional network for job search purposes; however, a professional network is also a useful tool for collaborating and assisting others.

Creating a professional network involves meeting individuals and communicating a need. In the case of a job search, you inform one person that you are looking for a job. Ideally, that individual will inform others, then those people inform others, and soon you have many people who know that you are searching for a job. Should any of these individuals know of a potential job, they will feed the information back to you. Figure 1 provides a visual of a professional network.

Professional networking is necessary throughout a job search. There are two primary forms of networking. The first form is the traditional method, which involves face-to-face interaction. The second method utilizes social media. Traditional networking involves interacting with and meeting as many people as possible who work or know someone who works in your targeted industry. There are many formal networking opportunities for job seekers, including attending association meetings, service clubs, and conferences. Additionally, many college career centers provide networking events for students to interact with local employers. Job fairs, volunteer fairs, and trade shows are also excellent venues for professional networking. The key to successful networking is to create a network before you need one. Doing so provides time to develop networking skills, increase your confidence, and identify which networking venues work best. Many college recruiters enjoy meeting students a year prior to graduation. Students who network early in their job search convey organization, planning, and strategic skills, which are behaviors highly desired by employers.

Create and maintain a **network list**, an easily accessible list of all network contacts' names, industries, e-mail and traditional addresses, and phone numbers. Provide contacts that are actively assisting with your job search a copy of your most current résumé and keep them updated on your search. When communicating with members of your network, be sensitive to their time. Do not annoy them or be inconsiderate in your interactions. Ensure that your network contact list is current. Find and consistently utilize a database system that is convenient for you. Most individuals use an electronic database, although some still prefer a traditional address book. When you secure a job, immediately remove job search postings and inform members of your network who were actively assisting you with your job search.

Has Tran created a professional network? Why or why not? How can Tran enhance this network?

Almost every person you know may be a part of your network, including coworkers, supervisors, instructors, family, and friends.

Topic Situation

Tran has been working as a mechanic for a year. During this time, Tran has acquired new skills, learned the latest technologies related to auto mechanics, and earned a degree. He begins telling supervisors and coworkers what skills, education and technologies he has learned over the last year and shares career goals. Tran then tells family members and friends the same information.

When engaging in traditional networking, remember that the success of one's networking attempts begin with a positive attitude. First and foremost, believe in yourself and know what key skills and abilities you have to offer. Be confident and willing to approach and initiate an introduction with strangers. People are drawn to positive people. When engaging in face-to-face networking, dress professionally—first impressions matter. A useful networking and introduction tool is a personal business card. This small card contains contact information, including your name, mailing and e-mail addresses, and phone number. It is a good practice to share your personal business card with anyone you meet, especially in networking, informational interview, and mentoring encounters. Doing so makes it easier for a new acquaintance to remember and contact you in the future. Personal business cards are inexpensive and valuable networking tools. When designing a personal business card, ensure it contains all relevant contact information and reflects a professional image. Use an easy-to-read font style and avoid fancy graphics, pictures, or too many words. Simple is better.

Have your personal business card and a career summary statement of your key skills and abilities to informally share with anyone you meet. When you share a business card, ask for one in return so you can follow up and add these individuals to your network list. Practice the art of introducing yourself in a positive and mature manner, beginning with a professional handshake. Listen carefully to the name of the individual you are meeting. After the handshake, exchange business cards. Focus the conversation on the other person. Prior to telling your new contact about you and your job search, get the individual to talk about where he or she works, what he or she does, and what he or she enjoys about the job. Use this time to build rapport. At the appropriate time, tell the individual about you and your job search. As your conversation continues, watch for body-language cues. If the person is engaged, he or she will make direct eye contact and turn his or her body toward you. When the individual no longer wishes to visit, he or she will most likely look away and/or turn his or her body away from you. Utilize these cues to either continue the visit or politely thank him or her for their time and end the conversation.

Though it is common to have food and beverages available at formal networking events, it is best to refrain from eating and drinking until you have met your desired network contacts. Practice proper etiquette by not overindulging in food. You are in attendance to meet people, not to eat. Refrain from drinking alcohol.

Within 24 hours of creating a new contact, follow up with a brief message sharing with the individual that it was a pleasure meeting him or her.

Exercise 2

Write a brief message to someone you have recently met and would like to include in your network list.

_____

_____

_____

Additional network opportunities include volunteering for community organization, performing internships, and participating in work experience programs. A U.S. Census study found that volunteers have a 27 percent better chance of finding a job than those who do not volunteer. Volunteering provides opportunities to meet people in different organizations and learn about new positions. Volunteering is an excellent venue to develop leadership and team-building skills, network, and, most importantly, give back to your community. In addition to contacting a company directly for an internship or work experience opportunity, utilize your campus career resource center. Join clubs and professional organizations and actively participate. Attend professional workshops, conferences, and seminars to meet people from corporations that are in your targeted industry. Use the opportunity as a means of enhancing your skills and job search network. When performing these jobs, treat them as if you are in a paid job. Dress appropriately, use proper communication, perform all work in a quality manner, don't complain, and consistently behave in a professional manner. Be social, but avoid becoming personally involved with others. Get to know the employees and the company/organizational culture. Show your willingness to help solve problems and learn new skills.

Current technologies now provide ample social media outlets to not only post your résumé to targeted industries, but also to create an electronic network. Popular online professional networking venues include LinkedIn and Facebook. These venues offer special support services for job seekers, as do many industry-specific online networking sites. When utilizing a social networking site for your job search, ensure that your career information is current and consistent with your résumé. When there is an opportunity to post a professional photo of yourself, do so, as social media is a visual venue. It is also becoming increasingly popular to create and post a job video. The purpose of a job video is to utilize visual media to sell your skills. Dress professionally, practice and review what you will communicate (including body language), and make your video unique. After completing your video, solicit input from a trusted friend, and only post the video when you are certain it represents you in a positive and professional manner. If you are not comfortable on video, consider a blog or podcast as a means of utilizing social media tools. Be cautious when sharing personal information over social media venues by only posting on respected sites.

Earlier in this section, college career centers were suggested as a means of creating and/or expanding a professional network. Today's college career centers provide a tremendous amount of contemporary job search resources that reach beyond a traditional job fair. They provide job counseling services that include practice interviews, career assessments, workshops, networking events, and online job and interview information specific to your school and geographic location. It is common for these centers to tweet or text job postings to qualified students.

Talk It Out

What is appropriate and inappropriate information to share with an online network?

Think About It

Do you know where your career center is located? Have you taken advantage of the resources they have to offer?

Another means of expanding your professional network is to conduct an informational interview. An **informational interview** is when a job seeker meets with a business professional to learn about a specific career, company, or industry, not to ask for a job. Politely request an appointment, but do not attach your résumé. During an informational interview, ask the business professional questions about targeted careers, hiring, and the culture of the company. The process of meeting and talking with business professionals increases your professional network. When conducting an informational interview, explain who you are and the purpose of the interview. Inform the contact that the interview is only for career information gathering. Ask if you can have a few minutes of their time, usually about 20 minutes, to discuss their career and organization and to answer career-specific questions. Prior to the interview, research the company and prepare questions. During the interview use only the questions you prepared and respect time limits. If you conduct your informational interview in person, dress professionally and bring your career portfolio in case the interviewee requests a copy of your résumé. After the informational interview, promptly send a thank-you note.

Exercise 3

Identify appropriate questions to ask during an informational interview.

_____

_____

_____

Networking for both business and job search purposes is work, but the effort reaps tremendous benefits if done appropriately. Every few months, review your professional network list. If there is someone with whom you have not recently connected, contact him or her to say hello, share industry-specific information you think may be of value to them, or simply keep him or her updated on your career and growth plans. When networking, do not be afraid to ask your contact for additional contacts that might be able to assist you. Networking involves giving and taking. If you read an industry-related article, attend a conference, or are working on a project that may interest someone in your network, share the information and demonstrate how you can be of value to them.

Protecting Your Privacy

The job search process involves sharing personal information. Be cautious and share only personal information with reputable sources or you may become a target for identify theft. If you are applying for a job and have never heard of the employer, conduct research to verify that the employer is legitimate. Whenever possible, do not share your birth date or Social Security number with anyone, including employers, until after you are a finalist for a job.

TOPIC RESPONSE
What should Ravyn do?

Gene's friend Ravyn was looking for a job. Ravyn found a job on an online classified job site that sounded legitimate. The employer asked that Ravyn submit a résumé online. Within a few days after sharing her résumé, Ravyn received an e-mail telling her that she was a finalist for the job. The only step left in the process was for her to forward a copy of her credit report. Although Ravyn was desperate for a job, she thought this was a little strange, so she asked Gene what he thought of the situation. Gene helped Ravyn conduct an Internet search on the company, but could not find any evidence that the company even existed.

Keeping the Right Attitude

Throughout this text, you have learned how to be successful in the workplace. The importance of maintaining a positive attitude throughout your career cannot be stressed enough. This also holds true during your job search. The job search process is a lot of work and is often stressful and frustrating. Do not be discouraged if you do not get an interview or job offer on your first try. In tight job markets, it may take many interviews before receiving a job offer. Follow these tips to maintain a healthy attitude during this time of transition:

1. *Stay positive.* Start each day with a positive affirmation. Speaking aloud, tell yourself that you are a talented and great person who deserves a good job (and believe what you say). Your attitude is reflected in your actions. If you allow negativity to influence your job search, you will be at a disadvantage.

2. *Stay active.* Create a daily and weekly "to do" list. Every day, check the websites of targeted industries, associations, and companies in addition to relevant job sites. Schedule time for industry and company research. A job search is a job in itself. You do not want to be an unproductive employee in the workplace, so begin creating good work habits now by making the most of your time in a job search.

3. *Keep learning.* Use job search down time to learn or develop a skill. Identify a skill that will assist you when you are offered a job. Finances do not have to be a barrier to learning new skills. There are many free tutorials available on the Internet. Topics to consider include computer skills, writing skills, or any skill specific to your target industry.

4. *Stay connected.* Participate in networking on a weekly basis. Although it is natural to not want to socialize with others when discouraged, the job search period is the time when you most need to be in the presence of others. Keep your current network updated on your job search; identify valid reasons to communicate with your network. Consistently work on expanding your network by attending association meetings and events, volunteering, and scheduling informational interviews. Plan at least one meeting and/or activity each day. As opposed to sitting around the house waiting for the phone to ring, dressing professionally and networking every day will contribute to maintaining a positive outlook.

5. *Stay focused.* During this time of transition, manage your professional job search, your personal health, and your environment. Maintain an up-to-date calendar with scheduled follow-up activities relating to your job search. Because a job search is a stressful experience, practice healthy stress management techniques, including a proper diet, regular exercise, and positive self-talk. Invest a portion of your time in something of interest other than your job search. Consider volunteering for an organization of special interest to you. Doing so will provide a mental break, provide possible new network contacts, and provide you the satisfaction of helping others. Make wise choices regarding personal finances. Be cautious and conservative with your money. Make thoughtful purchases and avoid emotional spending. Finally, surround yourself with individuals who are positive and supportive of you and your efforts.

If you are currently working and are looking for a new job, keep your job search confidential unless you have completed training or education that will qualify you for an internal promotion. When in good standing with your supervisor, let him or her know you are looking for a new job and briefly explain why. Do not quit your current job before accepting a new job. Also, do not bad-mouth your company or anyone who works for your current or former employer(s).

MyStudentSuccessLab Please visit **MyStudentSuccessLab**: Anderson|Bolt, Professionalism Skills for Workplace Success, 4/e for additional activities, resources, and outcomes assessments.

Workplace Dos and Don'ts

Do keep your original job search documents in a portfolio	*Don't* give employers your original documents and expect them to be returned to you
Do keep a network list and keep the people on your list updated	*Don't* be annoying or inconsiderate of your network contacts' time
Do realize that a targeted job search takes time	*Don't* get discouraged if you do not get an interview or job offer on your first try
Do explore various sources of job leads, including your personal network, the Internet, and industry journals	*Don't* limit your job leads to one source

Concept Review and Application

You are a Successful Student if you:

- Conduct a self-discovery assessment to identify the right career
- Create a formal network list
- Create a professional reference list

Summary of Key Concepts

- The career objective or personal profile is a brief statement that sells your key skills and relates to your self-discovery.
- A targeted job search leads you through the process of identifying open positions for which you are qualified, in addition to identifying companies for which you would like to work.
- Ensure you have a professional electronic image while job searching.
- Professional networking is the act of creating professional relationships.
- In addition to people you already know, develop additional network contacts through various sources of job leads.
- Creating and maintaining a job search portfolio will keep you organized and prepared during the job search process.
- Create a list of professional references for employers.

Self-Quiz MATCHING KEY TERMS

Match the key term to the definition using the identifying number.

Key Terms	Answer	Definitions
Cost of living		1. When a job seeker meets with a business professional to learn about a specific career, company, or industry
Electronic job search portfolio		2. The process of identifying key interests and skills built on career goals
Informational interviews		3. Average cost of basic necessities such as housing, food, and clothing for a specific geographic area
Job search portfolio		4. A written testimony from another person that states that a job candidate is credible
Letter of recommendation		5. The act of creating professional relationships
Network list		6. Action verbs that describe your accomplishments in a lively and specific way
Networking		7. Process of discovering positions for which you are qualified, in addition to identifying specific companies for which you would like to work

Key Terms	Answer	Definitions
Power words		8. A computerized folder that contains electronic copies of all job search documents
Professional network		9. An easily accessible list of all professional network contacts' names, industries, addresses, and phone numbers
Self-discovery		10. A collection of paperwork needed for a job search
Targeted job search		11. A group of relationships that are established primarily for business purposes

Think Like a Boss

1. What information would you supply to a job seeker during an informational interview with you?

2. If you discovered that one of your top interview candidates had an unprofessional website, what would you do?

Activities

Activity 1

Complete the following accomplishments worksheet. Use power words to answer each question. Whenever possible, quantify your answers by documenting how many, how often, and how much. Include education as well as non-work experience such as volunteerism.

Question	Response
1. Of what career-related activity are you most proud?	
2. Name a work- or school-related achievement.	
3. List major work and career-building tasks you have performed.	
4. What results have you produced from the tasks performed? (Include samples for your job search portfolio.)	
5. List three completed projects that demonstrate your ability to produce results.	
6. Provide a specific example of how you have successfully worked with others.	
7. What other life accomplishments make you proud?	

8. List extracurricular activities and volunteer work you have been involved with.	
9. List special skills or foreign languages you speak or write.	
10. What areas of interest do you have?	

Activity 2

Using ONET or other Internet resources, identify three specific job titles that match your career goals and current qualifications.

1. _____

2. _____

3. _____

Activity 3

Utilizing information from your accomplishments worksheet, career assessment, and realistic job preview, complete the following table to create a career summary statement.

	Example	**Key Message**
Target Job	Entry-level event planner	
Primary Skills	Organized, creative, attention to detail	
Qualifications	Marketing and business courses; customer service experience; bilingual (Spanish)	
Career Summary Statement	Organized, creative individual seeking entry-level event planner position. Bilingual (Spanish) with experience in customer service and successful completion of courses in marketing and general business.	

Based on the information from your accomplishments worksheet and your interest profiler results, assess whether your target job supports your life plan. If not, what modifications need to be made to your personal, educational, and/or career goals?

_____

_____

_____

Activity 4

Create a job search portfolio by compiling the items from Table 2 and placing them in a binder.

Activity 5

Secure and complete a blank job application, with the exception of your signature. Add this document to your job search portfolio.

Activity 6

Name three issues to consider when identifying appropriate references.

_____

_____

_____

Activity 7

Complete the following reference list. This information will become part of your job search portfolio and the résumé package.

	Your Name: **Address:** **City, Zip:** **Contact Phone:** **E-mail:**
Name	
Employer/Relationship	
Phone	
E-mail	
Address	
Name	
Employer/Relationship	
Phone	
E-mail	
Address	
Name	
Employer/Relationship	
Phone	
E-mail	
Address	

Activity 8

Use the following table to create a networking list (this document will become part of your job search portfolio).

Network List				
Name	**Address**	**Phone No.**	**E-Mail Address**	**Last Date of Contact**

Activity 9

Design a personal business card (this card will become part of your job search portfolio).

Activity 10

Create a five question informational interview sheet

1.
2.
3.
4.
5.

Glossary

cost of living: average cost of basic necessities such as housing, food, and clothing for a specific geographic area

electronic job search portfolio (e-portfolio) is a computerized folder that contains electronic copies of all job search documents

informational interview: when a job seeker meets with a business professional to learn about a specific career, company, or industry

job search portfolio: a collection of paperwork needed for job searches and interview

letter of recommendation: a written testimony from another person that states that a job candidate is credible

network list: an easily accessible list of all professional network contacts' names, industries, addresses, and phone numbers

networking: meeting and developing relationships with individuals outside one's immediate work area; the act of creating professional relationships

power words: action verbs that describe your accomplishments in a lively and specific way

professional network: a group of relationships that are established primarily for business purposes. A professional network is created through networking.

self-discovery: the process of identifying key interests and skills built upon career goals

targeted job search: job search process of discovering positions for which you are qualified in addition to identifying specific companies for which you would like to work

Suggested Readings

Volunteering as a Pathway to Employment Report. (2013 June).

Rothberg, S. (2013 March 28). "80% of Job Openings Are Unadvertised," http://www.CollegeRecruiter.com

Lytle, T. (2013 May 1). Education and Training College Career Centers Create a Vital Link. SHRM. Vol. 58 No.5. http://www.shrm.org

Clay, K. (2014 May 18). "This Service Cleans Up your Social media Profiles for Job Hunting, College Admissions, and Dating." http://payscale.com

Erwin, M. (2013 June 26)."Employers Finding Reasons Not to Hire Candidates on Social Media," http://www.prnewswire.com

Running Background Checks on Job Applicants (May 2014). http://www.nolo.com/employmentlaw/

http://www.onetonline.org/

Golden, J.P. (2014 May 25). Golden Personality Type Profiler. http://www.goldenllc.com

www.myersbriggs.org

UC Santa Cruz Career Center, (2012)."Information interviewing," http://www
.careersucsc.edu

The Riley Guide (2014 May). "References & Recommendations," http://www
.rileyguide.com

Credits

Credits are listed in order of appearance.

Syda Productions/Shutterstock; Sandra Bolt

Résumé Package

accurate • appealing • effective

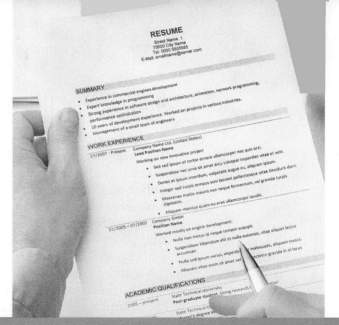

- Building a powerful résumé package
- Communicating a clear career objective/personal profile
- Utilizing power words and quantifiable outcomes to reflect personal accomplishments and experiences
- Identifying methods for effectively sharing a résumé
- Developing a cover letter
- Integrating methods to tailor the résumé package for target industries and employers
- Addressing special circumstances and time gaps

HOW DO YOU RATE?

Do you have résumé expertise?	True	False
1. Paper résumés are no longer necessary in today's electronic age.	☐	☐
2. Career objectives are used on all résumés.	☐	☐
3. Unique skills such as being bilingual or serving in the military can lead to discrimination and should not be listed on résumés.	☐	☐
4. Using a word processing résumé template is best when creating a résumé.	☐	☐
5. Those with a job gap on their résumé should make up a job to fill in the gap.	☐	☐

▶ If you answered "true" to at least two questions, use the information and tools in this chapter to improve your chances of creating and utilizing a winning résumé.

Building Your Résumé Package

Before employers decide to meet you, they first view your application materials. Traditionally, the set of application materials is referred to as a résumé package, which includes a résumé and a cover letter. Although many employers only allow online applications, which may not require a résumé and/or cover letter, every job seeker needs to create a formal résumé and cover letter. This information is used as a foundation for information an employer will require in the application process. The creation of a quality résumé package provides a job seeker with personalized, concise, and accurate information that can be used in any job search situation.

Your résumé package needs to efficiently and effectively sell your skills and communicate how your attributes are unique compared to all other candidates vying for your target job. A **résumé** is a formal written profile that presents a person's knowledge, skills, and abilities to potential employers. Your résumé is an important job search tool that should be created in advance of a job search and continually updated throughout your career. Even if you are not currently searching for a new job, a time will come when a current résumé is needed. Do not wait until that time to create or update your résumé. Continually add new job skills, accomplishments, and experiences to your résumé.

When you begin to create your résumé, you will quickly discover that there are various types of résumés and résumé formats. You may also receive conflicting advice as to how the perfect résumé should look and what it should include. The appropriate type of résumé used depends on your work experience, education, and other factors. A well-written résumé makes it easy for potential employers to quickly and easily identify your skills and qualifications that make you the right choice for the job.

This chapter will present the tools for creating a professional résumé and cover letter. As you go through the process of constructing your résumé package, make every word sell your skills and career accomplishments. Your résumé package represents you. Therefore, be honest with the information you provide and display character by not lying or embellishing the truth. There are five steps toward building a winning résumé:

1. Gathering Information
2. Creating an Information Heading and Utilizing Proper Layout
3. Writing a Skills Summary or Personal Profile
4. Inserting Skills, Accomplishments, and Experience
5. Reviewing the Completed Résumé

Step One: Gathering Information

The first step in building a résumé is to create a draft document with key headings. This involves collecting and merging all relevant information into one document. Begin identifying and listing the following information into an electronic document:

1. *Education.* List schools, degrees, certificates, credentials, GPA, licenses, and other relevant education-related information, including military experience. Include dates with each entry.

2. *Skills.* List all relevant skills and accomplishments.
3. *Employment.* Starting with the most recent job, list the employer, start and end dates of employment (month and year), job title, and responsibilities.
4. *Languages.* List foreign languages, fluency levels, and if you can read, speak, and/or write the foreign language.
5. *Honors and awards.* List any honors and awards you have received at school, work, or from the community.
6. *Professional/community involvement.* List volunteer work and community service projects. Include any leadership role you took in these activities.

Note that when compiling information to include in your résumé, there is no personal information listed. Personal information such as birthdate, Social Security number, marital/child status, ethnicity, or religion should not be included on a résumé. It is also inappropriate to list hobbies or include photographs. There are laws that protect employees from discrimination in hiring and advancement in the workplace, and employers should not be aware of personal information unless it is relevant to the job for which you are applying. Older job seekers should not list the date of graduation on a résumé, as it could be used for age discrimination.

Step Two: Creating an Information Heading and Utilizing Proper Layout

The second step in developing a successful résumé is to begin your electronic document. This includes listing personal contact information and identifying and arranging your information in the proper résumé layout. The top of your résumé is called the **information heading**. An information heading contains relevant contact information, including name, mailing address (city, state, ZIP code), contact phone, and e-mail address. Use your complete and formal name, including a middle initial if you have one. When listing your e-mail address, remove the hyperlink. If your current e-mail address is unprofessional, secure an address that is professional. Include only one contact phone number that is active with a professional voice mail message. Review the information heading for completeness, proper grammar and spelling, and accuracy. Spell out the names of streets. When using abbreviations, check for appropriate format, capitalization, and punctuation.

Once you have created your information heading, lay out your résumé. If you are at the start of your career and/or do not have extensive work experience, create a résumé using the **functional résumé layout**. This layout is used to emphasize relevant skills when you lack related work experience. A functional résumé focuses on skills and education. When writing a functional résumé, the first section contains the skills summary statement that you will create in step three. Immediately below the skills summary you will list relevant skills and education. Include your high school in the education section only if you have not yet graduated from college. Finally, list your work experience. Most functional

Talk It Out

Which résumé layout is best for your situation? Why?

résumés are only one page in length. Refer to Figure 1 for the functional résumé layout and Figures 2 and 3 for examples of a functional résumé with and without career-related work experience.

Those with extensive career experience should use an advanced skill set résumé layout. An **advanced skill set layout** best highlights, communicates, and sells specific job skills and work accomplishments. In the advanced skill set layout, the skills summary is replaced with a personal profile, which you will write in step three. Your personal profile will emphasize key skill sets. These skill sets will be used as subheadings in the professional experience heading, which will be the section listed immediately after the personal profile. When writing a personal profile, include key general skills and qualities desired by your target employer. Related work experience, specific skills, important activities, and significant accomplishments will be detailed under each respective subheading. Share major accomplishments and responsibilities from each position listed in your work history. Education and then work history are listed after professional experience. If necessary, add a second page to your résumé. Refer to Figure 4 for the advanced skill set résumé layout and Figure 5 for an example of an advanced skill set résumé.

For both résumé layouts, present employment history and education in reverse chronological order (most recent job first). When listing work history, bold the job title, not the place of employment. Only the month and year should be used when listing dates of employment. Be consistent in how dates are listed on the résumé.

Once you have determined which résumé layout is best for your current situation, in your electronic document, arrange the information gathered in step one into the correct résumé layout. Avoid résumé templates; these can be difficult to update, modify, and personalize.

Step Three: Writing a Skills Summary or Personal Profile

A foundation for both your job search strategy and building a winning résumé is to write a skills summary statement or personal profile. A **skills summary** is an introductory written statement for individuals with little or no work experience and is used on a functional résumé. The summary statement replaces the traditional one-sentence career objective. A skills summary statement encapsulates a job seeker's knowledge and skills in a brief statement that communicates his or her career objective while highlighting the value an individual brings to a prospective employer. A **personal profile** is an introductory written statement for individuals with professional experience related to their target career and is used on an advanced skill set résumé. The skills summary or personal profile will be the first item listed on your résumé following the information heading.

Employers spend little time looking at the entire résumé, and most of that time is spent looking at the top of the résumé. A good summary or profile is a way to make your résumé personalized and powerful. Depending on the layout of your résumé, this information will either have the heading "Skills Summary" or "Personal Profile." Make your skills summary or personal profile specific to the employer and job for which you are applying to increase your chances of being considered for the job. The skills summary or personal profile is the only place on a résumé where it is acceptable to use the words "I" and "my."

Those with little or no work experience in a targeted career will utilize the skills summary. In creating a skills summary, include your target job, employer, and key skills and experience into a one- to two-sentence statement.

Skills Summary Examples

- **Skills Summary:** Highly motivated and positive person seeking to obtain a position as an Office Professional with Roxy's Clothing Company that will enable me to utilize my current customer service skills and office assistant education.
- **Skills Summary:** To obtain a Medical Assistant Clinician position at Healthcorp, where I can demonstrate and increase my current medical assisting skills such as pharmacology, laboratory, and diagnostic procedures.

Those with extensive work experience will utilize a personal profile. In creating a personal profile, review your key skills and accomplishments and group these items into general categories. Also identify key qualities you possess that are required for your target job. Take this information and turn it into a two- to three-sentence statement that provides a snapshot of your professional qualifications in a manner that sells your knowledge, skills, and abilities.

Personal Profile Example

- **Personal Profile:** Highly professional and detail-oriented accounting professional with demonstrated leadership and success in the areas of payroll, collections, and project management. Possess excellent analytical, communication, computer, and organizational skills. Bilingual English/Spanish (read, write, and speak).

Exercise 1

Write a draft of your skills summary or personal profile.

_____

_____

_____

Step Four: Insert Skills, Accomplishments, and Experience

After arranging your information into the correct layout and inserting your career summary or profile, it is time to detail the information listed in your skills, work experience, and professional accomplishments. List skills relevant to your target job first. Be specific when referring to common workplace skills. For example, computer skills are too general and typically include many different areas such as networking, programming, applications, data processing, and/or repair. An employer needs to know what specific computer skills you possess and the proficiency level (e.g. basic, intermediate, or advanced) with specific software. Work experience includes learned skills, job duties, and accomplishments from paid, unpaid, and volunteer work. When presenting work experience, list the job title, company name, city, state, and duties of the position. Make every effort to not state "responsible for . . ." Instead, list specific accomplishments. Accomplishments are activities you achieved beyond your job duties. Do not assume the reader will know what you have done. Whenever possible, quantify outcomes related to your skills, responsibilities, and professional accomplishments. For example, if your duties included working with others, phrase your duties to read "Worked with team of 12 to assist over 350 customers daily."

As you insert professional accomplishments and responsibilities into your electronic file, include job-specific, transferable, and soft skills. **Job-specific skills** are those that are directly related to a specific job or industry. If you were to change careers, job-specific skills would probably not be useful. For example, if you are a medical billing clerk who knows how to use a specific software program such as Medical Manager, you will not use this skill if you become an elementary school teacher.

Transferable skills are skills that are transferred from one job to the next. Should you change careers, you will still be able to use these skills. For example, you learned how to input data into a computer for billing purposes. If you then become an elementary school teacher, you will use these keyboarding skills when you report student data. Speaking a foreign language is an excellent transferable skill. If you are bilingual (speak or write a second language), include this information in your résumé. Inform the employer if you read, write, or only speak that second language.

The term **soft skills** refers to the people skills necessary when working with others. Employers want employees that are reliable, team players, good communicators, and able to get along well with others. Employers need employees with job-specific, transferable, and soft skills; therefore, list all these skills on your résumé.

Résumés do not normally contain complete sentences. They contain statements that sell your skills, qualifications, and work experience. Except for the skills summary or personal profile, the words "I" and "my" should not appear.

Exercise 2

List as many job-specific, transferable, and soft skills as possible. If you have not yet held a job, list job skills you have developed from academic studies or volunteer work.

_____

_____

_____

Organize your skills and work experience by first listing the key skills required for your target job. When communicating your skills, experiences, and accomplishments, write with energy. Use action verbs. Action verbs are also referred to as power words and are used to describe your accomplishments in a lively and specific way. For example:

Instead of: "I started a new accounts receivable system."

Write: "Developed a new accounts receivable system that reduced turnaround time by 20 percent."

Or

Instead of: "Updated electronic medical records."

Write: "Converted paper to electronic medical files for a five-member physician office."

Refer to Table 1 for sample power statements. When using power statements, quantify your accomplishments whenever possible.

Exercise 3

Review these accomplishments and turn them into powerful statements. Quantify whenever possible.

_____

_____

_____

Table 1   Power Statements

Assisted in preparing, cooking, garnishing, and presenting food for _____

Inspected quality of incoming supplies and maintained inventory for _____

Established and maintained positive and effective working relationships with _____

Ordered, maintained, and trained in the use of _____

Knowledgeable of _____ software

Recorded patient history and vitals for _____

Cleaned and sterilized instruments and disposed of contaminated supplies for _____

Built website for _____

Developed technology protocols for _____

Wrote copy that was utilized in _____

Designed new brand identity for _____

Evaluated code to update existing site for _____

Analyzed, planned, and repaired _____

Prepared and processed _____

Organized and maintained records for _____

Drafted and typed business correspondence for _____

Scheduled and distributed _____

Step Five: Review the Completed Résumé

Prior to finalizing your résumé, ensure you have added all information identified in steps one through four to your electronic document. As you finalize your résumé, check for information that is frequently forgotten or not presented appropriately. Confirm your information heading contains complete contact information.

Carefully evaluate the skills summary or personal profile to ensure it introduces the reader to who you are and motivates him or her to learn more about your specific knowledge, skills, abilities, and key accomplishments.

In step two, you determined whether a functional or advanced skills set résumé layout was appropriate for your situation. Review the respective layout for proper heading order and refer to the sample résumés. Confirm that your experience and education are listed in reverse chronological order (most recent first). Keep your résumé consistent in its presentation, including all periods or no periods at the end of each line, line spacing, alignment of dates, date format, bold/italics, upper- and lowercase words, underlines, and other formatting. Also, review for consistency with the use of tense in each section (e.g., -ing and -ed) and with the use of the postal abbreviation for your state (e.g., the state is CA, not Ca., not Ca, not C.A.). When your draft résumé is complete, spell-check and proofread the document to ensure it is free of typographical errors and inconsistencies.

Underlines, bold, and italic print are acceptable for emphasis but should not be overdone. Avoid using bullets throughout your résumé; use bullets only to emphasize key areas. Only use small round or square bullets. Fonts and sizes should be easy to read. Times New Roman or Arial are most common. Apart from your name on the information heading, do not use more than two different font sizes (no smaller than 11 point and no larger than 14 point). Unless you are in the graphic design industry, avoid using different color fonts, highlights, or graphics on your résumé; use only black ink. It is not appropriate to state, "References Available Upon Request" at the close of your résumé. Professional references are to be listed on a separate sheet and provided only when requested.

Once you have made sure your résumé is presented professionally, is free of errors, and does not contain unnecessary or inappropriate information, print the résumé in black ink on 8½ × 11–inch, letter-sized paper. Double-sided résumés are not appropriate. If your résumé is more than one page, place your name at the top of each page after page one. Proper résumé paper is cotton-fiber, 24-pound white or off-white (not bond) paper of good quality. Colored paper, especially if dark, is both difficult to read and does not photocopy well. Do not use fancy paper stocks or binders. Also, avoid stapling your résumé or other job search documents. Since résumés are frequently photocopied, stapled résumés and other job search documents may be torn in the process.

When you have completed your résumé and believe it is ready for distribution, have several individuals whom you trust review it for clarity, consistency, punctuation, grammar, typographical errors, and other potential mistakes. Remember that complete sentences are not necessary and, with the exception of your career objective, the words "I" or "my" should not be used. Your résumé must create a positive, professional visual image and be easy to read.

Sharing Your Résumé

As you prepare to share your completed résumé with both potential employers and members of your professional network, you may have the option of presenting your résumé on résumé paper (traditional hard copy) or electronically (online). Your traditional résumé contains key information necessary for sharing with all potential employers. When sharing your résumé online, ensure it contains key words relevant to your target job. Employers and job boards commonly drop résumés into a database or résumé tracking system that allows recruiters to search for potential applicants based on key words and phrases that match the position they are trying to fill. When posting an online résumé, you may be required to cut and paste sections from your traditionally formatted résumé. During this process, you may lose the formatting. Do not worry. Visual appeal is not an issue in this process. You are merely dropping your information into a database. Your focus should be on utilizing key words and phrases related to the target job that concisely sell your skills and quantify your accomplishments.

Exercise 4

Circle the inconsistencies and errors on the following résumé.

1100 EAST FAVOR AVENUE • POSTVILLE, PA 16722
PHONE (555) 698-2222 - E-MAIL AERIE@PBCC.COM

AMANDA J. ERIE

OBJECTIVE

Seeking a position as an Administrative Assistant where I can utilize my office skills to better my career

SUMMARY OF QUALIFICATIONS

- Computer software skills include Microsoft Word, Excel, Outlook, Access, and Power point
- Knowledge of Multi-line telephone system, filing, data entry, formatting of documents and reports, and operation of office equipment.
- Excellent interpersonal skills and polished office etiquette.
- written and oral communication skills
- Typing skills
- Bilingual

EDUCATION

Reese Community College, Postville, PA Currently pursuing AA Degree in Office Occupations.

Calvin Institute of Technology, Cambridge, OH Office Technology Certificate Spring 2010

WORK AND VOLUNTEER EXPERIENCE

| 01/11 – Present | *Rigal Entertainment Group* | Postville, CA |

Usher – Responsible for ensuring payment of services. Answer customer inquiries. Collect and count ticket stubs.

| 11/07 – 02/09 | Lablaws | Cambridge, OH |

Cashier – Operated cash register, stocking, assisting customers

| Jan/07 – 04/07 | Jolene's Diner | Cambridge, OH |

Server – Provided customer service by waiting tables, cleaned, and operated cash register

The second consideration when converting a traditional résumé to an online version is sending it as an attachment to preserve formatting. If you are sending your résumé as an attachment, it is best to send it as a portable document file (.pdf). Doing so ensures that the résumé layout is properly maintained through the file transfer, and also ensures that those who do not use the same word processing software are able to read the file.

Most colleges and career centers host electronic job boards that allow students to upload their résumés for recruiters and employers who are seeking to hire students. Make use of this valuable resource. There are also many job boards specific to industries. Another popular means of sharing an electronic résumé is through social media sites. Make certain you are posting your information on valid business and industry sites and not personal sites. As with a traditional job search, track and monitor all activity related to your online search.

Résumés that are posted online are frequently dropped into databases and scanned for key words that match qualifications/skills required for current job openings. Therefore, ensure you thoroughly research and include key words on your résumé for targeted positions. Doing so will increase the probability that your résumé will match the target job posting.

When posting a résumé online, date your résumé and update it every two to three months. Most employers won't view online résumés that are more than six months old. Just as with a hard-copy résumé, protect your identity and do not share personal information of any kind, including marital status, birthdates, or your Social Security Number.

Cover Letters

A **cover letter** serves as an introduction to your résumé and is often the first impression a potential employer will have of you. Employers frequently use cover letters as screening tools. Even when limiting your job search to online venues, create a cover letter and use the body of the letter as the primary content of your e-mail message. Whenever possible, tailor your cover letter by including information found when researching the company and position for which you are applying.

When writing a cover letter, convey a friendly yet professional tone using complete sentences and proper grammar. The goal of a cover letter is to communicate how your key skills, experience, and accomplishments can meet the employer's needs. A basic cover letter contains three paragraphs. The first paragraph contains the purpose of the letter, the specific position for which you are applying, and how you learned of the position. If you have a contact within your target company, share the name of this individual and refer to how that individual informed you of the open position. In one sentence, summarize why you are interested and/or qualified for the position. Finally, share why you are interested in the organization, indicating any research you have conducted on the position and/or employer.

The second paragraph refers to the attached résumé and highlights the skills and qualifications you possess that the employer is requesting for the target job. Summarize how your key skills and qualifications match the employer's needs. Communicate what you can offer the company, not what you want from the company. Do not duplicate what is already listed on your résumé; instead, emphasize your experience and key skills.

Although it is acceptable to use the words "I" and "my" in a cover letter, be cautious to not begin most of your sentences with the word "I." Instead, focus the attention toward the employer by placing the company first and making its needs the priority. For example:

Instead of writing, "I am proficient in the most recent version of Word." Write, "Your company will benefit from my proficiency in the most recent version of Word."

The purpose of the final paragraph is to request an interview (not the job). Do not state that you look forward to the employer contacting you; instead display initiative by stating that you will follow up on your request for an interview within a week. Include your phone number and e-mail contact information, even though it is already included in your information heading. Close courteously and include an enclosure notation for your résumé.

Do not address your cover letter to a department, the company name, or "to whom it may concern." Address the cover letter to a specific person, ideally to the person who will be making the hiring decision. This is typically the individual who directly supervises the target position. Research or call the company to identify a specific name and title, including the appropriate spelling and gender. If you still cannot secure a specific name, use a subject line instead of a salutation. Instead of "To Whom It May Concern," write "Subject: Account Clerk Position." Use the proper business letter format for your cover letter. Each word and paragraph in your cover letter must have a purpose. Your goal is to communicate how your knowledge, skills, abilities, and accomplishments fill a targeted company's needs and make the reader want to review your résumé. The cover letter setup and sample cover letter in Figure 6 will assist you in creating a winning cover letter.

Cover Letter Setup and Example, see Figure 6

Print the cover letter on the same paper used for your résumé. Use the same information heading you created for your résumé to create a consistent and professional visual appeal for your résumé package. Avoid common mistakes such as typographical or grammatical errors, forgetting to include a date, or forgetting to sign the cover letter. When sharing your résumé package via the Internet, utilize an electronic signature on your cover letter. As with your résumé, have someone you trust proofread your letter before you send it to a potential employer. Any error communicates a lack of attention to detail and has the potential to disqualify you from securing an interview.

To complete your résumé portfolio, use the same information heading from your résumé and cover letter and add it to your reference list. Refer to Figure 7 for an example of a professional reference list.

Reference Page Example, see Figure 7

Tailoring Your Résumé and Cover Letter

Tailor both your résumé and cover letter specifically to each job and company for which you are applying. Carefully review the target job announcement and identify key job skills that the position requires. If possible, secure a copy of the job description from the company's human resource department. In addition, conduct an occupational quick search on the ONET database. This database was developed for the U.S. Department of Labor and provides key information by job title. Add the key knowledge, skills, and abilities from your ONET research to those the employer desires and then emphasize this information on your résumé. If necessary, rearrange the order of the information presented on your résumé so the key skills required for your target position are presented first. Also, emphasize your specific qualifications that match those required for the open position on your cover letter.

List a daytime phone number and e-mail address on both the cover letter and résumé. Because most invitations for job interviews occur over the phone, your voice mail message needs to be professional. Do not include musical introductions or any other greeting that does not make a positive first impression to a potential employer. Maintain a professional e-mail address to use in your job search.

Topic Situation

TOPIC RESPONSE

What would be an appropriate voice mail message for Rebecca? Should Rebecca acknowledge the interviewer's voice mail recommendation when she goes into the interview?

Emily's friend Rebecca was a practical joker. Emily enjoyed calling Rebecca because her voice mail message started with a joke or had some strange voice and/or music. However, the last time she called Rebecca, she noticed that her message was normal. The next time Emily saw Rebecca, she asked her why her voice message was suddenly so serious. Rebecca explained that she had recently applied for a job and had been selected to interview. However, she was embarrassed because when the interviewer called to arrange the appointment, he left a message suggesting that Rebecca change her voice mail to be more professional.

Tips for Special Circumstances

Gaps in work experience on your résumé will sometimes be a red flag for an employer. It is common for an individual to have time gaps in a résumé as a result of staying at home to raise a young child, care for an elderly relative, or continue his or her education. Many have time gaps simply from seeking employment. If the time gap is less than a year, list only years instead of the months and years. If the gap is longer than a year, individuals should use the advanced skill set résumé format. Identify a key skill you sharpened during the time gap and relate this experience to a key skill necessary for your target job and industry. For example, if you stayed at home to care for an elderly relative, the experience most likely improved your time management and organizational skills. You also most likely improved your awareness of diverse populations, including the elderly and disabled. Without revealing personal information, list your activity as you would any other job on your résumé. You need to be prepared to answer questions about gaps in the interview.

If you are an ex-offender and have served time in prison and are now attempting to reenter the workforce, you are to be congratulated for wanting to move forward with your life. By succeeding in college you have shown you made restitution for your past choices. Be honest with the potential employer.

On your résumé, include all jobs you have held and skills you learned while incarcerated. For the jobs you held while incarcerated, list the correctional facility in place of the employer. Also, list all education, including degrees and courses you received while making restitution along with the educational institution that provided the courses.

The employment application is a legal document. At the bottom of this document, applicants sign a statement affirming that all information provided on the application is true. Therefore, you must not lie. If, after being hired, your employer discovers that you have lied on the application, you may face immediate termination. The majority of applications ask if you have been convicted of a felony. Please note that arrests are not convictions. If you have been convicted of a felony, check "Yes." The application should also provide a space to write a statement after the felony question. Do not leave this space blank. In this space, write, "Will explain in detail during interview."

| MyStudentSuccessLab | Please visit **MyStudentSuccessLab**: Anderson\|Bolt, Professionalism Skills for Workplace Success, 4/e for additional activities, resources, and outcomes assessments. |

Workplace Dos and Don'ts

Do keep your résumé updated with skills and accomplishments	*Don't* wait until the last minute to update your résumé
Do change your résumé layout after you have advanced skill sets	*Don't* lie on your résumé or cover letter
Do pay attention to formatting details on your résumé and cover letter	*Don't* distribute a résumé or cover letter that has not been proofread by someone you can trust
Do ensure your résumé and cover letter are free of errors prior to sharing them to employers	*Don't* forget to sign your cover letter

YOUR NAME (16 point, bold)

Your Address (12 or 14 point, bold) ■ **City, State, Zip**
■ **Phone Number** (Give only one number and include area code)
Email Address (Remove hyperlink)

Horizontal line optional, weight varies

> Section headings can be left or centered, 12- or 14-point font, and uppercase or initial cap. Format headings consistently throughout the résumé. Keep spacing equal between each section.

SKILLS SUMMARY

Headings can be on the left or centered, 12- or 14-point font, and uppercase or initial cap, but should be formatted consistently throughout the résumé. Keep spacing equal between each section

QUALIFICATIONS (OR SKILLS)

- Relate to target job, use job-related skills and transferable skills
- Most relative to the job are listed first
- Bullet (small round or small square only) these items to stand out

> Emphasize skills and education before work experience.

EDUCATION

You may list before qualifications

List schools in chronological order, most recent attended first

Do not list high school if you graduated from college (if listed, do not include dates)

Include the years attended college or pending graduation date

WORK EXPERIENCE

Name of Company and City, State—No Addresses

Job title, dates employed (month, year)

List the jobs in chronological order with most recent first

List the duties, responsibilities, and achievements and be consistent in your setup by using same tense throughout (*-ed* or *-ing*)

OTHER CAPABILITIES

Optional items in this section such as honors or awards may not be directly related to the job but may interest the employer.

> - Watch periods, punctuation, and spelling
> - Align all dates and format them consistently
> - Keep to one page
> - Use a regular 12-point font (except heading), no color
> - Use résumé paper, no dark or bright colors
> - Do not use full sentences or *I, me,* or *my*
> - References are not necessary; you will list these on a separate sheet

Figure 1

Functional Résumé Layout

Cory S. Kringle
4 Success Lane, Fresno, CA 93702
555-123-4567
ckringle15@careersuccess.job

SKILLS SUMMARY

Highly motivated and positive person seeking to obtain a position as an Office Professional with Roxy's Clothing Company that will enable me to utilize my current customer service skills and office assistant education.

QUALIFICATIONS

- Type 50 wpm with 97% accuracy
- Intermediate skills using Microsoft Word, Excel, Access, PowerPoint, and Outlook
- Accurately proofread and edit documents
- Knowledge in records management; traditional and computerized
- Positive telephone skills
- Excellent oral and written communications skills
- Positive attitude, motivated, and organized
- Excellent and positive customer service skills

EDUCATION

2013–2015   Fresno Community College   Fresno, CA
Associate of Art Degree, Business & Technology
Office Professional Certificate
GPA 3.9, Dean's list

Courses

- Working Relations
- Business English
- Records Management (traditional and computerized)
- Today's Office
- Document Processing using Microsoft Word
- Computer Applications using Microsoft Office

EXPERIENCE

06/2013–present   Fine Linens by Jen   Fresno, CA

Cashier

Provide customer service including cashiering and returns in a busy setting, serving an average of 200 customers a day. Assist team of 7 with inventory, processing and placing merchandise on the floor, helping return go backs, stocking of merchandise in back/ stockroom, and training new hires.

Figure 2

Functional Résumé
Example without Career
Work Experience

CORY S. KRINGLE
4 Success Lane ▼ Fresno, CA 93702 ▲ 555-123-4567 ▼
ckringle15@careersuccess.job

SKILLS SUMMARY

Newly licensed and motivated utility technician professional seeking an entry-level gas utility position. With training in mechanical aptitude and schematic reading I am ready to be a part of the success at Great Utility Company.

KEY SKILLS AND QUALIFICATIONS

- Computer literacy and applications including MS Word and Excel
- Knowledge and practice in mapping and schematic reading
- Certification in gas theory, principles, and technical skills
- Practice using occupational safety, health, and environmental concerns
- Introduction to electronics and industrial mechanics
- Highly ethical
- Responsible
- Detail oriented
- Excellent communication skills
- Knowledgeable of governmental regulations and safety standards

EDUCATION AND CERTIFICATIONS

Yu Technical College, Meadville, CA   12/15
Associate of Science Degree — Utility Technician

WORK HISTORY

Gas Apprentice — residential wiring   8/15–12/15
Pennsylvania Local #7777, Meadville, CA
Under the direction of a journeyman, worked indoors and outdoors with gas lines. Checked for gas leaks, repaired gas lines, and installed and connected gas lines for both residential and industrial sites. Read meters, installed meters, and adjusted meters. Tested electrical systems and continuity of wiring, equipment, and fixtures utilizing current technologies.

Grocery Clerk/Assistant Butcher
Great Foods, Meadville, CA   5/13–8/15
Assisted three butchers in meat department weighing, pricing, and wrapping products. Cut and prepared product for cases. Applied excellent customer service in taking and filling orders. Served as cashier and front duties when necessary. Cleaning and secured area for store closing.

Figure 3

Functional Résumé
Example with Career
Work Experience

YOUR NAME (16 point, bold—include middle initial)

Address (12 or 14 point, bold) ■ **City, State Zip** ■ **Phone Number** (Give only one number and include area code)
E-Mail Address (Remove hyperlink)

> Section headings can be left or centered, 12- or 14-point font, and uppercase or initial cap. Format headings consistent throughout the résumé. Keep spacing equal between each section.

PERSONAL PROFILE:

In a three- to four-sentence statement, insert key skills and accomplishments related to the target job. Group key skill sets into categories that will be used as skill set subheadings in the Professional Experience section. Include key qualities you possess required for the target job.

PROFESSIONAL EXPERIENCE:

> Use the skill set categories listed in the Personal Profile as subheadings. Under each skill set subheading, elaborate on key skills, experience, and accomplishments related to each category. On an advanced skill set résumé, Professional Experience is listed before Education and Employment History.

First Skill Set Subheading

- Communicate experience and key accomplishments relating to your first skill set subheading
- Using power words, quantify as much as possible
- Include duties, responsibilities, and achievements

Second Skill Set Subheading

- Communicate experience and key accomplishments related to your second skill set subheading
- Accomplishments and experience most relative to target job are listed first
- Communicate both job-related and transferable skills

Third Skill Set Subheading

- Communicate experience and key accomplishments related to your third skill set subheading
- Use consistent tense for statements (-ing for present tense, -ed for past tense)
- Do not use *I, me,* or *my*
- Complete sentences are not necessary

WORK HISTORY:

Name of Company, City, State (do not include address)   Dates Employed (month & year)
Job Title (bold the job title, NOT the employer)
List jobs in reverse chronological order

> Proofread for proper punctuation and spelling. Advanced skill set résumés can be one or two pages. If more than one page, place name at the top of second page. Avoid color and graphics. Utilize consistent alignment of bullets and dates.

EDUCATION AND LICENSES:

Degree
College, City, State (do not include address)   Date Degree Awarded (month & year)
License, State, or Organization Awarding Certification   Date of Award (month & year)
Degree College, City, State (do not include address)   Date Degree Awarded (month & year)

PROFESSIONAL AFFILIATIONS/CERTIFICATIONS:

Name of Organization, status (member, officer, etc.)   Dates of Membership
Certification, Certifying Organization   Date of Certification
Volunteer or Service Activities   Dates of Service (month & year)

Figure 4

Advanced Skill Set
Résumé Layout

CORY S. KRINGLE

4 Success Lane ■ Fresno, CA 93702 ■ 555-123-4567 ■ ckringle15@careersuccess.job

PERSONAL PROFILE

Results- and efficiency-focused professional with experience in sales/vendor relations, inventory/warehousing, and management/supervision. Proven ability in relationship management with demonstrated and consistent increase in sales over a five-year period. Inventory expertise includes streamlined operations, improved productivity, and favorable inventory ratio utilization for wholesale food supplier. Management ability to create goal-driven teams, groom leaders, and facilitate the creation of a learning organization.

PROFESSIONAL EXPERIENCE

Customer Service Orientation ■ Innovative Risk Taker ■ Excellent Quantitative Skills Purchasing, Inventory Planning, & Control ■ Supply Chain Management ■ Warehouse Operations ■ Process Improvement ■ Cost Containment ■ Hiring, Staffing & Scheduling Safety Training ■ Excellent Computer Knowledge

Sales/Vendor Relations

- Through the establishment of vendor relationships, schedule product installations, exchanges, buy-backs or removals of equipment or other assets including supplier networks and agent contacts in order to meet customer expectations for private soda company, have grown sales territory from a two-county area to (highly profitable) tri-state contract area over four-year period.
- Source and facilitate delivery of product (e.g., beverage equipment, parts, point of sale material, return of assets) for retail suppliers. Sales complaints are consistently under 5% per year, while sales volume and customer satisfaction rates are the highest of all national sales teams and consistently continue to grow.
- Research and resolve issues for customers, business partners, and company associates in order to expedite service, installations, and/or orders utilizing information systems and working with 12 regional supply chain partners.
- Create and maintain partnerships with customers, clients, or third-party service providers (e.g., contract service/installation agents, distributors) by establishing common goals, objectives, and performance target requirements in order to improve customer service and satisfaction (which is currently 98.7%) for clients that are my direct responsibility.
- Developed troubleshooting equipment process which allows retail suppliers to receive immediate response on service issues (e.g., beverage vending, dispensing) via telephone or Internet to minimize customer down time and service cost.

Figure 5

Advanced Skill Set
Résumé Example

Cory S. Kringle

Inventory/Warehousing

- Maintain customer contact to confirm service or orders and to ensure accuracy with equipment repairs, product deliveries, and routine service scheduling for regional food service broker who was responsible for 65% of annual company revenue.
- Receive, record, and respond to customer inquiries using specially designed database which documents best practices from nationwide food service association to provide improved service, order accuracy, and optimized supply chain efficiency.
- Process daily orders for goods and services with over 20 food service business partners, customers, suppliers, and company associates, either through direct telephone contact or electronic means, to increase speed and accuracy of order transactions and improve loss prevention systems.

Management/Supervision

- Developed and trained team of 20 on inventory control, customer service, and safety for local food service provider. Program was so successful customers within the company supply chain requested and received training. To date, over 500 individuals have received custom training.
- Supervised cross-functional team of 100 including order technicians, outside repair personnel, transportation associates, warehouse attendants, and loss prevention specialists.
- As assistant manager for college-town restaurant, assisted in the hiring, training, scheduling, and performance evaluation of staff for small soda company and local food service supplier.

WORK HISTORY

Connor Cola Company, Susanville, CA **Vendor Relations Associate**	2012–present
Elizabeth Food Service, Pocatoe, NE **Warehouse Manager**	2009–2012
Mango and Carolyn Ribs'N Stuff, Pocatoe, NE **Assistant Restaurant Manager**	2006–2009

EDUCATION/PROFESSIONAL DEVELOPMENT

University of Nebraska, Lincoln, NE Bachelor of Science, Business Management/Marketing	2012

Figure 5

(*continued*)

Utilize the same heading as your résumé to create a consistent, professional presentation.

Utilize the business letter format.

Tailor cover letter and address to a specific individual. Ensure correct spelling and title.

Personalize the salutation.

First paragraph includes the purpose of the letter, position applying for, and how you learned of the position. Summarize why you are interested and qualified, and indicate any research conducted.

Second paragraph refers to résumé and highlights skills and qualifications you possess for the target job. Summarize how your key skills and qualifications match the employer's needs. Limit the use of *I* and *my*. Communicate what you can offer the company, not what you want from the company. Do not duplicate what is already listed on the résumé; emphasize experience and key skills.

The closing paragraph requests an interview. Display initiative by stating that you will follow up on a request to interview within a week. Include your phone number and e-mail.

Use a courteous closing. Sign your name (if appropriate, use an electronic signature). Utilize proper business-letter formatting.

CORY S. KRINGLE

4 Success Lane, Fresno, CA 93702
555-123-4567 ckringle15@careersuccess.job

September 22, 2015

Anita Stephens, HR Manager
Clay Office Supplies
435 East Chesny Street
Fresno, CA 91188

Dear Ms. Stephens:

I recently spoke with Terry Moody, a production manager for Clay Office Supplies, and he recommended that I forward you a copy of my résumé. Knowing the requirements for the position and that I recently received my degree in office occupations, Mr. Moody felt that I would be an ideal candidate for your Office Assistant position.

I would welcome the opportunity to be employed at Clay's Office Supplies since this is the largest and best-known office supply company in the city. Your company has a reputation of providing excellent products and service, which is why Clay's Office Supplies would benefit from my knowledge and skills. I am accustomed to and thrive in a fast-paced environment where deadlines are a priority and handling multiple jobs simultaneously is the norm. As you can see on the attached résumé, my previous job required me to be well organized, accurate, and friendly. My educational courses taught me how to utilize current skills and technologies and sharpened my attention to detail. I enjoy a challenge and want to contribute to the success of your company.

Nothing would please me more than to be a part of your team. I would like very much to discuss with you how I can benefit Clay Office Supplies. I will contact you next week to arrange an interview. In the interim, I can be reached at 555-123-4567 or at ckringle15@careersuccess.job.

Sincerely,
Cory S. Kringle

Cory S. Kringle
Enclosure

Figure 6

Cover Letter Setup
and Example

CORY S. KRINGLE

4 Success Lane, Fresno, CA 93702

555-123-4567 ckringle15@careersuccess.job

PROFESSIONAL REFERENCE LIST

Name	Relationship	Phone	E-mail	Mailing Address
Autumn Hart	Former Instructor, Yu Technical College	555.555-1111	atmnhrt@yutc.scl	123 Hillvalley Meadville, CA
Gloria Montes	Owner, Fine Linens by Jen	555.555-1112	gloria@linens.sleep	5432 Food Ct. Fresno, CA
Gary Solis	Manager, Conner Cola	555.555-1113	solisg@conner.cola	2220 Tulare Susanville, CA
Patty Negoro	Owner, Mango Ribs	444.555-1114	pattyn@eatribs.com	444 Adoline Pocatoe, NE

Figure 7

Reference Page Example

Concept Review and Application

You are a Successful Student if you:

- Write a career objective/personal profile
- Write a résumé
- Write a cover letter

Summary of Key Concepts

- A winning résumé makes it easy for potential employers to quickly and easily identify your skills and experience.
- Update your résumé with new skills and accomplishments at least once a year.

- Include both job-specific skills and transferable skills on your résumé.

- Use the correct résumé layout for your career work experience.

- A cover letter is most often an employer's first impression of you.

- Check that your résumé and cover letter are free of typographical and grammatical errors.

- Share your résumé electronically as a .pdf file to ensure the résumé layout is maintained.

Self-Quiz MATCHING KEY TERMS

Match the key term to the definition using the identifying number.

Key Terms	Answer	Definitions
Advanced skills set résumé layout		1. An introductory written statement used on a functional résumé for individuals with little or no work experience
Cover letter		2. An introductory written statement used on an advanced skill set résumé for individuals with professional experience related to their target career
Functional résumé layout		3. A formal written profile that presents a person's knowledge, skills, and abilities to potential employers
Information heading		4. A letter that introduces your résumé
Job-specific skills		5. Skills that can be transferred from one job to another
Personal profile		6. A résumé layout that emphasizes relevant skills when related work experience is lacking
Résumé		7. People skills that are necessary when working with others
Skills summary		8. Skills that are directly related to a specific job or industry
Soft skills		9. A résumé heading that contains relevant contact information including name, mailing address, city, state, ZIP code, contact phone, and e-mail address
Transferable skills		10. A résumé layout used by those with extensive career experience that emphasizes related work experience, skills, and significant accomplishments

Think Like a Boss

1. What would you look for first when reviewing a résumé?

2. What would your reaction be if you were reading a cover letter that had several spelling and grammar errors?

Activities

Activity 1

Complete the following table.

Education (list most recent first)				
School Name	City, State	Dates	Degree, Certificate, Credential, License	GPA

Skills

Employment (list most recent first)			
Employer	Employment Dates	Job Title	Duties

Languages	Fluency (Read, Write, and/or Speak)

Honors and Awards	Dates	Place

Professional/Community Involvement		

Activity 2

Conduct an Internet search to identify résumé power words/phrases. List at least five new words that are not in the text.

1. _____

2. _____

3. _____

4. _____

5. _____

Activity 3

Search for a specific job you would like to have when you graduate and then complete the following table. This information will be used to tailor your résumé and cover letter.

Position for which you are applying	
How you learned about the job	
Any contact you have had with the employer or others about the job	
Why are you interested in this job?	
Why are you interested in this company?	
What products or services are provided?	
List relevant skills related to the job description	
List reasons this company should hire you	
Indicate your desire for an interview	
Indicate your flexibility for an interview (time and place)	

Activity 4

Using a word processing program and the steps and/or exercises from this chapter, create a résumé for the job you found in Activity 3.

Activity 5

Using a word processing program and the information from this chapter, create a cover letter for the job you found in Activity 3.

Glossary

advanced skill set résumé layout: a résumé layout used by those with extensive career experience that emphasizes related work experience, skills, and significant accomplishments

cover letter: a letter that introduces your résumé

functional résumé layout: a résumé layout that emphasizes relevant skills when related work experience is lacking

information heading: a résumé heading that contains relevant contact information including name, mailing address, city, state, ZIP code, contact phone, and e-mail address

job-specific skills: skills that are directly related to a specific job or industry

personal profile: an introductory written statement used on a résumé for individuals with professional experience related to their target career

résumé: a formal written profile that presents a person's knowledge, skills, and abilities to potential employers

soft skills: people skills that are necessary when working with others in the workplace

transferable skills: skills that can be transferred from one job to another

Suggested Readings

SHRM Survey Findings: Resumes, Cover Letters and Interviews (2014 April 28). http://www.shrm.org

Bowers, T. (2013 September 16). "10 Mistakes That Could Ruin Your Resume," http://techrepublic.com

"Making Your Résumé E-Friendly: 10 Steps," *The Quick Résumé and Cover Letter Book,* Farr. July 2013, www.careerbuilder.com/Article

"Advanced Résumé Concepts, Electronic Resumes" Kendall, July 2013, www.reslady.com/electronic.html

"How to Write a Resume Profile," Clark-salaam, March 2014, www.ehow.com

"How to Explain Employment Gaps, Sabbaticals, and Negatives on Your Resume" Vaas, May 2014, www.theladders.com

"Resume Dilemma: Employment Gaps and Job-Hopping, Isaacs, July 2013, www.career-advice.monster.com/resumes-coverletters

Susan Ireland's Resume Site, "How to Explain Unemployment," www.susanireland.com/resume/how-to-write

Credit

Interview Techniques

prepared • poised • present

After studying these topics, you will benefit by:

- Implementing pre-interview strategies and activities
- Conducting company- and job-specific research for interview preparation
- Creating a powerful and unique personal commercial
- Compiling an interview portfolio and e-portfolio
- Practicing interview techniques and appropriate responses to common interview questions
- Implementing pre-interview preparation activities
- Demonstrating winning behavior during face-to-face and technology-based interviews
- Naming and describing common interview methods and types of interview questions
- Explaining key areas of employee rights and knowing how to respond to discriminatory questions
- Formulating appropriate responses to special circumstances and tough questions
- Preparing for post-interview activities including salary negotiation, employment screenings, tests, and medical exams

HOW DO YOU RATE?

Do you know proper interview techniques?	True	False
1. It is unprofessional to arrive more than 10 minutes early to the office where your interview is to take place.	☐	☐
2. It is best to have a draft of a post-interview thank-you note written prior to an interview.	☐	☐
3. The same amount of pre-interview preparation should be made for an Internet and/or telephone interview as is made for a traditional face-to-face interview.	☐	☐
4. Employers expect a job candidate to ask relevant questions during interviews.	☐	☐
5. When offered a job, it is acceptable to negotiate a salary.	☐	☐

▶ If you answered "true" to the majority of these questions, congratulations. You are already aware of effective interview techniques and are ready to successfully interview.

From Chapter 15 of *Professionalism, Skills for Workplace Success*, Fourth Edition. Lydia E. Anderson, Sandra B. Bolt. Copyright © 2016 by Pearson Education, Inc. All rights reserved.

The Interview

You've conducted a targeted job search and created and distributed your résumé, and now it is time to interview. A successful interview involves more than dressing sharp. It includes advance preparation, confidence, and a strategy to be used before, during, and after this important meeting. During an interview, an employer is looking to hire the best person to represent his or her company. Your goal is to communicate visually and verbally that you are the right person for the job. A job search takes work, takes time, and can sometimes be frustrating. Do not be discouraged if you do not get an interview or job offer on your first try. The purpose of this chapter is to provide you the skills and confidence to secure a good job in a reasonable time.

The Invitation to Interview

There is a strategy to successful interviews, and it starts as soon as you receive an invitation to interview. Most interview invitations are extended by phone or e-mail. Therefore, regularly check and immediately respond to both phone and electronic messages. This is a good reminder to maintain a professional voice mail message and e-mail address. When you are invited to interview, attempt to identify with whom you will be interviewing. You may be meeting with one person or a group of individuals. Your first interview may be a pre-screening interview where a human resource representative or some other representative from the company briefly meets with you to ensure you are qualified and are the right fit for the job.

During the invitation to interview, ask how much time the company has scheduled for the interview. If possible, also identify how many applicants are being asked to interview. If you are friendly, respectful, and professional, most companies will share this information. Attempt to arrange your interview at a time that puts you at an advantage over the other candidates. The first and last interviews are the most memorable, so try to secure one of these slots. If you are given a choice of times to interview, schedule your interview in the morning. People are much more alert at that time, and you will have a greater advantage of making a favorable and memorable impression. If this is not possible, try to be the last person interviewed prior to the lunch break or the first person interviewed immediately after the lunch break. Be aware that sometimes you will have no say in when your interview is scheduled so do not make demands. Politely ask the scheduler if it is possible for him or her to tell you who will be conducting the interview. Finally, note the name of the individual who is assisting you in arranging the interview. This will allow you to contact him or her should you need additional information and will also allow you to personally thank him or her should you meet on the day of the interview. The goal is to secure as much information as possible prior to the interview so you are prepared.

Exercise 1

Role-play an invitation to interview with another student.

_____

_____

_____

Company-Specific Research

There is no question that pre-interview research will assist you during a job interview. Unfortunately, many candidates ignore this step, thinking it is unnecessary or takes too much time. Prior to an interview, conduct research and identify as much as you can about the organization and the department of your target job. Not only will you have an advantage in the interview, but you will know if the company is the right fit for you and your career goals. Learn as much as you can about the company's leadership team, strategy, and any current event that may have affected the company. Review the company web and social network sites if available, or conduct a general Internet search to read blogs and other posts related to the company. Note products the company produces, identify the company's key competitors, and note any recent community activities or recognized accomplishments the company has been involved with.

In addition to the Internet, other sources for securing company information include company-produced brochures and literature, industry journals, and interviews with current employees and business leaders. Job-specific information is easily gathered by conducting a quick search on the ONET database using the position title as your keyword. This database of occupational information provides key information by job title.

Use your research during the interview by mentioning specific information about the company. For example, a popular interview question is, "Why do you want to work for this company?" Be specific in your answer and respond with information that reflects your research. For example, say, "Your company has been green-conscious in the last two years, which is an area I believe is important," instead of saying, "I have heard it is a great company."

Topic Situation

Anita's friend Tomasz was excited about an interview he would be having in a week. When Tomasz was sharing his excitement with Anita, she asked him if he had conducted research on the company. Tomasz said he really didn't need to conduct research because the company was pretty well known. Anita explained that it is important to conduct research beyond general knowledge to make sure Tomasz stood out from the other candidates. They conducted an extensive Internet search on the target company and discovered useful information that Tomasz was able to use throughout his interview. After a successful interview, Tomasz thanked Anita and told her that the research prior to his interview gave him a lot of confidence that ultimately helped him secure the job.

TOPIC RESPONSE

What specific details should you identify when researching a company?

The Personal Commercial

Prepare a personal commercial that sells your skills and ties these skills to the specific job for which you are interviewing. A **personal commercial** is a brief career biography that conveys your career choice, knowledge, skills, strengths, abilities, and experiences that make you uniquely qualified for the position for which you are applying and your interest in the targeted position. Use the personal commercial at the beginning or end of an interview. Your goal is to sell yourself by communicating how your skills support the company and target job throughout the interview. Your personal commercial is essentially your "sales pitch" that communicates how you are the right candidate for the job.

Exercise 2

If you were alone in an elevator with the hiring manager of your target job, what key pieces of information about yourself would you communicate as you rode from the fifth floor to the first floor?

_____

_____

_____

Think About It

What hobby or unique skill unrelated to your target job is appropriate to use in your personal commercial?

Use information from your résumé that highlights your personal accomplishments in your personal commercial. When writing your personal commercial, make it reflect your personality. Include your interest in your chosen career, activities related to the career, the skills you have acquired, and why you have enjoyed learning these skills. Also, when possible, share something unique about yourself that makes you stand out from other candidates and serves as a conversation starter for the employer.

In this one instance, a hobby or unique skill unrelated to your target job can be used. Do not include marital status or other potential discriminatory information. Your personal commercial should take no more than one minute to deliver. The following are examples of a personal commercial:

Medical Assistant Clinician	I just received my Medical Assistant Clinician Certificate from Success College. I enjoyed my courses and would like to ultimately become a nurse. As part of my training, I performed my required work experience at Community Hospital, where I was able to polish my clinical, medical terminology, and patient care skills. I especially enjoyed assisting the medical professionals in sometimes highly stressful situations and helping patients and their family. I would enjoy contributing to Dr. Bewell's success serving as a medical assistant.
Culinary	For the past five years, I worked in the food service industry, where I learned the importance of accuracy, quality, and customer service. I actually started as a fast food cook at a local grill and decided I wanted to expand my culinary skills. I am working toward a degree in culinary arts and am quickly discovering that I particularly enjoy the baking/pastry activities. I've gained extensive experience in food safety, inventory control, and creating decorative food displays. I am hardworking, creative, and resourceful, and I play the tuba in my spare time. Thank you for this opportunity to meet with you. I promise, you won't regret hiring me.

Use your personal commercial at the start of your interview when asked, "Tell me about yourself." If you are not given this instruction during the interview, include it at the end. Memorize your personal commercial and, in front of a mirror, practice delivering it until it is communicated naturally and confidently.

The Interview Portfolio

An **interview portfolio** contains relevant documents that are taken to an interview. Use a professional business portfolio or a high-quality paper folder with pockets. The portfolio should be a color that will not draw attention. Include copies of items pertinent to the position for which you are applying. Original documents (unless required) should not be given to the employer, only photocopies. Have the following items in your interview portfolio: copies of your résumé, cover letter, reference list, generic application, and a copy of your personal commercial. Also include a calendar, note paper, a pen, and personal business cards. Print copies of your résumé, cover letter, and references on résumé paper. Copies of other items such as skill or education certificates, recent performance evaluations, job samples, or other documents you have in your job search portfolio may be included if the information is relevant to the job. During the interview keep your interview portfolio on your lap. Place your personal commercial on the top of your portfolio for easy access. Do not read the commercial. Use the copy for reference or to merely glance at, should you become nervous and forget what to say. Use the checklist in Table 1 to ensure the items are included in your interview portfolio.

Table 1 Interview Portfolio		
Item	**Description**	**Included**
Copies Necessary for Each Interview		
Awards	Educational, professional, and personal	
Calendar (electronic or small traditional)	To track dates	
Completed generic application	Available information if asked to fill out an application on site	
Cover letter	Signed and on résumé paper	
Letters of recommendation	No older than one year	
Note pad	To document names and notes from interview	
Pen	For note taking	
Performance appraisals from previous jobs	Proof of positive work performance	
Personal business cards	Share with the interviewer	
Personal commercial	Use to glance for reference	
Reference list	On résumé paper	
Résumé	On résumé paper	
Transcripts	A copy of official school transcripts	
Copies if Relevant for the Job		
Certificates	To prove official relevant certification	
Copy of ID and/or driver's license	If driving is a job requirement	
Copy of recent DMV record (if relevant to your career)	If driving is a job requirement	
Current state licenses	To prove current relevant licensing	
Work samples	Examples to demonstrate proficiency in specific skills	

Practice Interview Questions

Another activity to perform when preparing for an interview is to practice interview questions. Table 2 identifies common interview questions, appropriate answers, and topics to avoid. Review this list and begin creating appropriate responses to each question. When answering an interview question, avoid simply answering "yes" or "no" or providing a generic answer. Elaborate your response by providing examples of specific skills and experiences that support your answers and meet the key requirements of the target job. These experiences do not have to be based on work experience; you may use examples from school or volunteer work. The more real-life examples you provide, the more you demonstrate your experience and skill level to the employer. Anyone can say, "I can handle stress." However, providing a specific example of how you handled stress on a busy day clearly communicates how you handle stress.

With each answer you are being judged on your qualifications and how you will fit into the culture of the company. Interviewers look for what value you will bring to the company. Listen to each question carefully and determine what the employer is trying to identify about you. If you are asked a question you do not understand, do not ask the interviewer to repeat the question, as the interviewer may think you were not listening. Ask for clarification. Although some questions can be answered with a simple yes or no or a basic statement, fully answer the question being asked by presenting your related skill and/or experience. For example, if the interview asks, "How many years of experience do you have working in a law office?" do not simply respond with a number. Elaborate by sharing what type of legal environments you have worked in and what type of activities you performed.

With any question asked, be prepared to provide at least two specific examples. Use personal experiences from a previous job, an internship, classwork, or a school-related activity. If the question involves sharing a challenge or hardship you have faced, avoid providing personal details and use examples that demonstrate your ability to overcome a challenge. For example, if you are asked how you handle stressful situations and you have no work experience, share a time you worked on a team project in school and you had a member not performing his portion of the project. Although the team member was making you angry and causing you stress, mention how you used stress methods and state how you took control of the situation by displaying leadership and constantly communicated with the team member to hold him accountable.

Table 2	Common Interview Questions	
Question	**Response**	**Avoid**
Tell me about yourself.	Use your personal commercial modified to the job description.	Do not divulge where you were born, your age, if you are married, if you have children, or other personal information.
What are your strengths?	Include how your strengths meet the job requirements and how they will be an asset to the company.	Do not include strengths that are not related to the job. Do not include personal information (e.g., "I'm a good mother").

Tell me about a time you failed.	Use an example that is not too damaging. Turn it into a positive by including the lesson learned from the experience.	Do not place blame for why the failure occurred.
Tell me about a time you were successful.	Use an example that relates to the job for which you are applying.	Avoid coming across as arrogant. Do not take full credit if the success was a team effort.
How do you handle conflict?	Use an example that is not damaging and discuss how the conflict was positively resolved.	Avoid examples that place you in a negative light. Do not provide specifics on how the conflict occurred, and do not place blame on others.
Would you rather work individually or in a team? Why?	State why you prefer one or the other, but relate your answer to the job requirements.	Do not state that you will not work one way or the other.
Why do you want this job?	Convey career goals and how the specific job/company supports your current skills. Include company information learned through research.	Do not include money or benefits in your response.
How do you deal with stress?	Share positive stress reducers.	Do not state that stress does not affect you. Do not use negative examples.
What is your greatest weakness?	Use a weakness that will not damage your chance of getting the job. Explain how you are minimizing your weakness or are turning it into strength (e.g., "I have not been particularly organized in the past; but since going to school I have used my lessons in time management and improved").	Do not state, "I don't have any." Do not just state a weakness; instead, show how you are turning it into a strength.
Where do you want to be in five years?	Share your career goals.	Do not say you want the interviewer's job.
Tell me about a time you displayed leadership.	Use a specific example and try to relate it to the needed job skills.	Do not appear arrogant.
If you are currently employed, why do you want to leave your job?	Be positive and specific. Relate back to education and career goals. Be honest if you are losing your job based on a change in company strategy.	Do not speak poorly of a company or its employees.
Why do you want to work for us?	Share the company information from your research and relate it to your career goals.	Do not include money or benefits in your response.
What motivates you?	Identify tasks you have completed that motivated you to finish a project.	Do not include money or benefits in your response.
What was your favorite subject in school?	Identify a subject that is related to the target job and add why you enjoyed the course. If you have a secondary subject that is unique (e.g., athletics or music), share that as well.	Do not say "all of them" or "none of them."
What are your salary expectations?	Based on your research, provide a salary range. Avoid discussing specific compensation issues until the final stages of the hiring process.	Do not provide a specific number. When it comes time to discuss salary, identify the lowest and ideal salary so you have room to negotiate.

Talk It Out

Identify difficult interview questions you would not want to be asked and formulate appropriate responses.

Practice answering interview questions in front of a mirror, and, if possible, create a video of yourself answering common interview questions. Critically analyze your responses to see if you are appropriately answering the questions, selling your key skills, and projecting a professional image. You should appear honest, confident, and sincere. If you display nervous gestures, work on eliminating the distracting gestures. This exercise will better prepare you for an interview and will increase your self-confidence.

Pre-Interview Preparation

Prior to the day of your interview, conduct a "practice day" interview. If possible, travel to the interview location, ideally during the same hour as your scheduled interview to identify potential transportation problems such as traffic and parking. Once you arrive at the site, walk to the specific location where the interview will be held. This will enable you to become comfortable and familiar with your surroundings and let you know how much time you will need to arrive on time the day of the interview. Do not go into the specific office, just the general area. Make note of the nearest public restroom so you can use it the day of the interview to freshen up prior to your meeting.

Prior to the day of the interview, also ensure that your interview attire is clean and you have a professional appearance. Dress at a level above the position for which you are interviewing. For example, if you are interviewing for an entry-level position, dress like you are interviewing for a supervisor position. Clothes should fit appropriately and shoes should be clean. Cleanliness is important. Ensure that your hair and fingernails are professional and appropriate for an interview. If necessary, get a haircut prior to your interview. Use little or no perfume/aftershave and keep jewelry to a minimum. When conducting research, identify the company's dress code policy. Depending on the job and industry, you may need to cover tattoos and remove extra piercings (if you have them).

Customize your interview portfolio by including copies of any documents related to the target job. Place your portfolio where you will not forget it when you leave your home. With the common use of smartphones and other portable electronic devices, it is a good idea to have your e-portfolio items ready for use in the interview. If you decide to utilize your e-portfolio, inform the interviewer that you would like to use your device during the interview to show him or her items from your e-portfolio.

Purchase a package of simple but professional thank-you notes. The evening before your interview, write a draft post-interview thank-you note on a blank piece of paper. Keep the thank-you note brief, only three to four sentences. In the note, thank the interviewer for his or her time. State that you enjoyed learning more about the position, are very interested in the job, and look forward to hearing from the interviewer soon. The draft note will be used as a foundation for notes (traditional or electronic) you will be writing and sending immediately after your interview. Place the draft note, the package of thank-you notes, several personal business cards, and a black pen alongside your interview portfolio to take with you.

Exercise 3

Write a draft post-interview thank-you note.

_____

_____

_____

The Interview Process

The interview process varies from employer to employer. One position may only require a one-on-one interview and then a job offer, whereas another position may involve pre-employment testing, a phone interview with the human resource department, then a panel interview with potential coworkers, and then a face-to-face interview with the department manager. Some hiring processes will occur rather quickly; other employer hiring processes may take months. The following sections will explain in greater detail the various venues, methods, and types of interviews.

Interview Day

On the day of the interview be well rested and have food in your stomach prior to the interview. Look in the mirror to ensure a professional appearance. Clothes should fit properly and project a professional image. If you smoke, refrain from smoking prior to the interview. The smell may be a distraction to the interviewer.

Be on time and plan to arrive at your destination 15 minutes early. This provides time to deal with unforeseen transportation issues. If there is a public restroom available, visit the restroom and freshen up. Check your hair, clothing, and makeup, if applicable. Turn off your communication device, and if you are chewing gum, throw it away. Enter the specific meeting location 5 but no more than 10 minutes prior to your scheduled interview.

This is where your interview unofficially begins. First impressions matter and any interaction with representatives of the organization must be professional.

Immediately upon entering the interview location, introduce yourself to the receptionist. Offer a smile and a handshake, and then clearly and slowly state your name. For example, "Hi, I'm Cory Kringle, and I am here for a 9:00 A.M. interview with Ms. Dancey for the accounting clerk position." If you recognize the receptionist as the same individual who arranged your interview appointment, make an additional statement thanking the individual for his or her assistance. For example, "Mrs. Wong, were you the one that I spoke with on the phone? Thank you for your help in arranging my interview." Be sincere in your conversation, and convey to the receptionist that you truly appreciate his or her efforts. The receptionist will most likely ask you to have a seat and wait to be called into the interview. Take a seat and relax. Avoid using your mobile device during this time. While you are waiting, use **positive self-talk**. Positive self-talk is a mental form of positive self-reinforcement. It helps remind you that you are

Talk It Out

Why should you not arrive too early to the meeting location?

qualified and deserve both the interview and the job. Mentally tell yourself that you are prepared, qualified, and ready for a successful interview. Review your personal commercial, your qualifications, and the key skills you want to convey in the interview.

Topic Situation

TOPIC RESPONSE
What more could Shelby and Johnelle have done to prepare for the interview?

Johnelle's friend Shelby had been asked to interview with one of her target companies. Shelby really wanted the job but was afraid she was not going to do well during her interview. Johnelle worked with Shelby a few days before the interview by role-playing interview questions and reviewing Shelby's company research. Johnelle had Shelby dress in her interview attire. They then videotaped a mock interview and critiqued the video. Finally, they traveled to the interview site and made sure Shelby knew the exact interview location. The next day, when Shelby arrived for the interview, she arrived early, thanked the receptionist, and took a seat. As she waited to be called in to the interview, she began getting extremely nervous. Remembering Johnelle's tips, Shelby briefly closed her eyes and used positive self-talk to improve her attitude, increase her confidence, and calm her nerves. After doing this, she felt more confident when called in to the office to begin the interview.

Traditional Face-to-Face Interviews

A traditional interview involves a face-to-face meeting between an applicant and the employer. As with any type of interview, convey confidence. Your primary message during the interview will be how your knowledge, skills, and abilities will be assets to the company and make you the best candidate for the job. When you are called to interview, stand up straight and approach the individual who called your name. If it is not the receptionist who called you, extend a smile and a handshake, and then (speaking clearly and slowly) introduce yourself. For example, "Hi, I'm Cory Kringle. It's nice to meet you." Listen carefully to the interviewer's name so you will remember it and use it during the interview. He or she will escort you to an office or conference room where the interview will take place. If you enter a room and there is someone in the room that you have not met, smile, walk to the individual, extend a handshake, and introduce yourself. Once in the room, do not be seated until you are invited to do so. When seated, write down the names of the individuals you have just met. Whenever possible, interject the interviewer's name(s) during the interview. Although you may be offered something to drink, it is best to decline the offer so there is nothing to distract you from the interview. If you are sitting in a chair that swivels, place your feet flat on the floor to remind yourself not to swivel. If you forgot to turn off your communication device and it rings during the interview, do not answer it. Immediately apologize to the employer and turn it off. Do not take time to see who called.

If the interview is taking place in an office, look around the room to get a sense of the person who is conducting the interview, assuming it is his or her office. Doing so provides useful information for conversation, should it be necessary. Depending on the time available and the skills of the interviewer(s), you may first be asked general questions, such as, "Did you have trouble finding our office?" The interviewer is trying to get you to relax. During the interview, pay attention to body language—both yours and that of the individual conducting the interview. Sit up straight, sit back in your chair, and try to relax. Be calm and confident, but alert. Keep your hands folded on your lap or ready to take notes, depending on the situation. If you are seated near a desk or table, do not lean on the furniture. Make eye contact, but do not stare at the interviewer. Your job is to connect with the interviewer by being sincere and personable.

If you are given the opportunity to provide an opening statement, share your personal commercial. If you are not able to open with your personal commercial, include it in an appropriate response or use it at the end of the interview. Do not talk over the interviewer or interrupt when he or she is speaking. When asked a question, listen carefully. Take a few seconds to think about what information the interviewer truly wants to know. Formulate an answer and relate your response back to the job qualifications and/or job duties. Avoid cliché or general answers. As covered in a previous section, your goal is to favorably stand out from other candidates while conveying how your skills will assist the company in achieving success. Provide a complete response without rambling. Sell your skills and expertise by including a specific example, and whenever possible, interject information you learned about the company during your research.

Employer interviewer styles and questions differ. In every situation, demonstrate how you are the best match for the target job. If you are asked questions that appear completely irrelevant to the interview (e.g., "If you were invited to a department potluck, what item would you bring and why?"), do not get defensive. Remain professional and be sincere in your response. When interviewers utilize silence, they are most likely gaining an understanding of how you handle stressful situations. Throughout the interview, be aware of and avoid nervous gestures. Remain relaxed, poised, and confident.

Interview Methods and Types of Interview Questions

There are several common interview methods, including one-on-one interviews, group interviews, and panel interviews. **One-on-one interviews** involve a one-on-one meeting between the applicant and a company representative. The company representative is typically either someone from the human resource department or the immediate supervisor of the department with the open position. **Group interviews** involve several applicants interviewing at the same time while being observed by company representatives. The purpose of a group interview is to gauge how an individual behaves in a competitive and stressful environment. In a group interview, practice positive human relation and communication skills toward other applicants. Listening and communicating that you are the best candidate is critical to a successful group interview. If another applicant is first asked a question and you are immediately asked the same question, do not repeat what the other applicant said. If you agree with the first applicant's response, state, "I agree with Ms. Bell's response and would like to add that it is also important to . . . ," and then elaborate or expand on the first applicant's response. If you do not agree with the first applicant's response, state, "I believe . . . ," and then confidently provide your response. Show respect by not demeaning other applicants. Be professional, do not interrupt, and behave like a leader by being assertive, not aggressive.

Panel interviews involve the applicant meeting with several company representatives at the same time. During a panel interview, make initial eye contact with the person asking the question. While answering the question, connect with all members of the interview panel. Whenever possible, call individuals by name. As with a one-on-one interview, your job is to appear personable and attempt to create a favorable impression that makes each panelist want to hire you.

The three general types of interview questions are structured, unstructured, and behavioral. **Structured interview questions** address job-related issues where each applicant is asked the same question(s). The purpose of a structured interview question is to secure information related to a specific job. An example of a structured question is, "How long have you worked in the retail industry?" Although the sample question appears to be closed-ended, a skilled candidate will elaborate on his or her response. For example, avoid simply answering, "I have worked in retail for two years." Add additional information to your response; for example, "I have two years of retail experience. One year I worked in a small family business and the other for a large retail chain. During this time I have increased my general knowledge of business and my customer service skills. I liked the family business best because I enjoyed getting to know our loyal customers."

An **unstructured interview question** is a probing, open-ended question. The purpose of an unstructured interview question is to identify if a candidate can appropriately sell his or her skills. An example of an unstructured interview question is, "Tell me about yourself." When you are asked to talk about yourself, start with your personal commercial and, if appropriate, show job samples from your interview portfolio when referring to a specific skill. Make every attempt to provide specific examples without rambling and relate answers back to the target job.

Behavioral interview questions are questions that ask candidates to share a past experience related to a workplace situation. The purpose of a behavior interview is to identify what a candidate has done in the past, including how the candidate behaves under a specific circumstance. An example of a behavioral question is, "Describe a time you motivated others." Prior to answering the question, take a moment to formulate your answer. Attempt to have the interviewer view the situation from your perspective by briefly providing the background to your experience. Describe how you used specific skills to solve a problem or improve a situation. For example, "Our department had just gone through a series of layoffs and employees were working hard but feeling unappreciated. Although I was not the team leader, I thought we needed something to help us deal with the stress, so for one week, and with my direct report's permission, I planned brief, fun activities for our daily morning meetings. The first day, we played a game I made up called 'Name That Stress.' At first glance, it seemed silly, but it actually started a conversation about how stressed we all were and how we could collectively deal with the stress in a challenging situation."

Phone and Other Technology-Based Interviews

In some situations, your first interview may take place over the phone. Phone interviews may or may not be prearranged. During your job search, consistently answer your phone in a professional manner and keep your interview portfolio in an accessible place. If a company calls and asks if it is a good time to speak with you and it is not, politely respond that it is not a convenient time and ask if you can reschedule the call. Try to be as accommodating as possible to the interviewer.

Those being interviewed by phone should follow these tips:

- *Be professional and prepared.* Conduct the interview in a quiet room and focus solely on the conversation. Unless an electronic device (e.g., computer) is necessary for part of the interview, turn it off. Remove any additional distractions, including music, pets, television, and other individuals from your quiet area. Company research, personal examples, and the use of your personal commercial are just as important to interject into the phone conversation as during a face-to-face interview. Take notes and ask questions.
- *Be concise with your communication.* Those conducting the phone interview are not able to see you; therefore, they are forming an impression of you by what you say and how it is stated. Speak clearly, at a normal pace, and do not interrupt. When responding, count to three in your head to allow time for telecommunications overlap. Speak naturally, but loud enough for the interviewer to hear and understand you. Smile and speak with enthusiasm throughout the interview. Use proper grammar and beware of "ums" and other nervous verbal phrases. If you stand while conducting your phone interview, you will stay alert, focused, and more aware of your responses.
- *Be polite.* Exercise good manners. Do not eat or chew gum during your interview. It is not appropriate to use a speaker phone when being interviewed, nor is it polite to take another call or tend to personal matters. Your attention should be completely focused on the interview. When the conversation is over, ask for the job, and thank the interviewer for his or her time.

It is becoming increasingly common for interviews to take place through video chat venues such as Skype, WebEx, and Google Talk. An individual participating in a video chat interview needs a computer, a web cam, and a reliable Internet connection. When taking part in a video chat interview, the participant will receive a designated time and specific instructions on where and how to establish the connection. In addition to following the phone interview tips, the interviewer needs to prepare and treat the video chat interview as if it were a face-to-face interview. Therefore, use the following tips:

- *Plan ahead.* Research the venue you will be using to address any unforeseen issues. Identify where you will conduct the interview and what technology is required. If possible, arrange a pre-interview trial to ensure all equipment works properly and you know how to use it (including the volume and microphone).
- *Dress professionally.* Attire should be the same as a face-to-face interview. You will be in plain view of the interviewer, so visual impressions matter.
- *Maintain a professional environment.* Conduct your interview in a quiet and appropriate location void of distractions. Ensure the background is appropriate. A bedroom, public place, or outside location is not appropriate.
- *Speak to the camera.* Focus on the web cam as if it were the interviewer's face. Feel free to ask questions, take notes, and use hand gestures. Although it may be more difficult to communicate, make every effort to not only project your personality, but, more importantly, sell your knowledge, skills, abilities, and unique qualifications. As with a traditional face-to-face interview, your job is to connect with the interviewer.

Discrimination and Employee Rights

Title VII of the Civil Rights Act was created to protect the rights of employees. It prohibits employment discrimination based on race, color, religion, sex, or national origin. Other federal laws prohibit pay inequity and discrimination against individuals 40 years or older, individuals with disabilities, and individuals who are pregnant. This does not mean that an employer must hire you if you are a minority, pregnant, 40 or older, or have a disability. Employers have a legal obligation to provide every qualified candidate equal opportunity to interview. Their job is to hire the most qualified candidate. Although discriminatory questions are illegal, unfortunately, some employers may ask them in an interview. Table 3 was taken from the California Department of Fair Employment and Housing to provide examples of acceptable and unacceptable employment inquiries.

If an interviewer asks you a question that is illegal or could be discriminatory, do not directly answer the question. Instead, answer the question in

Table 3 Illegal Interview Questions

Subject	Acceptable	Unacceptable
Name	Name	Maiden name
Residence	Place of residence	Questions regarding owning or renting
Age	Statements that employment is subject to verification if applicant meets legal age requirement	Age Birthdate Date of attendance/completion of school Questions that tend to identify applicants over 40
Birthplace, citizenship	Statements/inquiries regarding verification of legal right to work in the United States	Birthplace of applicant or applicant's parents, spouse, or other relatives Requirements that applicant produce naturalization or alien card prior to employment
National origin	Languages applicant reads, speaks, or writes, if use of language other than English is relevant to the job for which applicant is applying	Questions as to nationality, lineage, ancestry, national origin, descent, or parentage of applicant or applicant's spouse, parent, or relative
Religion	Statement by employer of regular days, hours, or shifts to be worked	Questions regarding applicant's religion Religious days observed
Sex, marital status, family	Name and address of parent or guardian, if applicant is a minor Statement of company policy regarding work assignment of employees who are related	Questions to indicate applicant's sex, marital status, number/ages of children or dependents Questions regarding pregnancy, child birth, or birth control Name/address of relative, spouse, or children of adult applicant
Arrest, criminal record	Job-related questions about convictions, except those convictions that have been sealed, expunged, or statutorily eradicated	General questions regarding arrest record

Source: California Department of Fair Employment and Housing Fact Sheet. DFEH-161 (8/01)

an indirect manner by addressing the employment issue and stating how your qualifications are well-suited for the job. For example, if the interviewer says, "You look Hispanic. Are you?" your response should not be "Yes" or "No." Politely smile and say, "People wonder about my ethnicity. What can I tell you about my qualifications for this job?" Do not accuse the interviewer of asking an illegal question or say, "I will not answer that question because it is illegal." Most employers do not realize they are asking illegal questions. However, some employers purposely ask inappropriate questions. If you are asked several illegal questions, you need to decide if you want to work for an employer who either does not properly train its interviewers or intentionally asks illegal questions.

Know and protect your rights. It is inappropriate to disclose personal information about yourself during an interview. Avoid making any comment referring to your marital status, children, religion, age, or any other private issue protected by law.

Talk It Out

Role-play an interview. During the interview, ask one legal question and one illegal question. Practice answering the illegal question with confidence but in a non-offensive manner.

Special Circumstances and Tough Questions

Life is unpredictable and sometimes results in situations that can be embarrassing or difficult to explain during a job interview. These situations may include a negative work experience with a previous employer, time gaps in a résumé, or a prior felony conviction. The following information provides the proper response to interview questions related to these difficult situations.

Some job seekers have had negative work-related experiences that they do not want to disclose during an interview. Disclosing such information could be potentially devastating to a job interview if it is not handled properly. Some of these experiences include being fired, quitting due to poor working conditions, having a poor performance evaluation, or knowing that a former manager or teacher will not provide a positive reference if called. Perhaps you behaved in a negative manner prior to leaving your old job.

If you had a negative work experience and are not asked about the situation, there is no need to disclose the unpleasant event. The only exception to this rule is if your current or former boss has the potential to provide a negative reference. If this is the situation, tell the interviewer that you know you will not receive a positive reference from him or her and request that the interviewer contact another manager or coworker who will provide a fair assessment of your performance.

Being honest and factual is the best answer to any difficult question. If you were fired, performed poorly, or left in a negative manner, state the facts, but do not go into great detail. Tell the interviewer that you have matured and realize that you did not handle the situation appropriately. Add what lesson you have learned. Do not speak poorly of your current or previous employer, boss, or coworker. Also avoid placing blame by stating who you feel was right or wrong in the negative workplace situation.

It is common for an individual to have time gaps in a résumé as a result of an extended job search, staying home to raise a young child, caring for an elderly relative, or continuing his or her education. Those who have gaps in their résumé may need to be prepared to explain what they did during the time gap. Identify a key skill you sharpened during your time gap and relate this experience to a key skill necessary for your target job and industry. If you volunteered for projects, include this information. For example, if you stayed at home to care for an elderly relative and are asked about the time gap, explain the situation without providing specific details, and then share how the experience improved your time management and organizational skills in addition to improving your awareness of diverse populations, including the elderly and disabled.

If you have a felony record, you may be asked about your conviction. As with other difficult interview questions, be honest and factual in your response. Explain the situation and tell the interviewer that you have made restitution, are making every attempt to start anew, and are committed to doing your very best. Sell your strengths and remember to communicate how your skills will help the company achieve its goals. Your self-confidence and honesty will be revealed through your body language and eye contact. Be sincere. Depending on the type and severity of your offense, it may take more attempts to secure a job than during a typical job search. You may also need to start at a lower level and/or lower pay than desired. The goal is to begin to reestablish credibility. Do not give up. Each experience, be it positive or negative, is a learning experience.

Closing the Interview

After the interviewer has completed his or her questioning, you may be asked if you have any questions. Having a question or closing statement prepared for the close of your interview demonstrates to the prospective employer that you have properly prepared for the interview. A good question refers to a current event that has occurred within the company. For example, "Ms. Dancey, I read about how your company employees donated time to clean up the ABC school yard. Is this an annual event?" A statement such as this provides you one last opportunity to personalize the interview and demonstrate that you researched the company. This is also a good time to share additional relevant information you have in your portfolio that you were not able to present during the interview.

Do not ask questions that imply you did not research the company or that you care only about your needs. Inappropriate questions include questions regarding salary, benefits, or vacations. These questions imply that you care more about what the company can do for you than what you can do for the company. However, it is appropriate and important to ask what the next steps will be in the interview process, including when a hiring decision will be made. Table 4 contains questions that may and may not be asked.

Table 4 Closing Interview Questions	
Questions You May Ask	**Questions You Should Not Ask**
What is the next step in the interview process?	How much does this job pay?
What do you enjoy about working for this company?	What benefits will I get?
What type of formal training does your company provide?	How many vacation days do I get?
What are you looking for in an employee?	How many sick days do I get?
Does your company have any plans for expansion?	What does your company do?
What is the greatest challenge your industry is currently facing?	How long does it take to get a raise?

After the interviewer answers your general questions, make a closing statement. Summarize your personal commercial and ask for the job. An example of a strong closing statement is: "Once again, thank you for providing me the opportunity to interview, Ms. Dancey. As I stated at the beginning of our meeting, I feel I am qualified for this job based on my two years of retail experience, business knowledge, and demonstrated leadership. I would like this job and believe I will be an asset to XYZ Company." The purpose of a job interview is to sell yourself and your skills. A sale is useless if you do not close the sale by asking for the job.

Exercise 4

Write a closing interview statement.

_____

_____

_____

After you make your closing statement, the interviewer will signal that the interview is over. He or she will do this either through conversation or through body language, such as standing up and walking toward the door. Prior to leaving the interview, hand the interviewer your personal business card and ask the interviewer for a business card. You will use this business card for the interview follow-up. Look your interviewer in the eye, shake the interviewer's hand, thank him or her, and state that you look forward to hearing from him or her soon. Continue communicating confidence, friendliness, and professionalism to every employee you encounter on your way out of the building.

After you have left the building, retrieve your draft thank-you note. If appropriate, modify the draft thank-you note to include information that was shared during your interview. Handwrite a personalized thank-you note to each individual who interviewed you. Use your finest handwriting and double-check spelling and grammar. Refer to the business card(s) you collected for correct name spelling. Do not forget to sign the thank-you note and include a personal business card if you have one. After you have written your note, immediately hand deliver it to the reception area and ask the receptionist to deliver the notes. Your goal is to make a positive last impression and stand out from the other candidates. If you are unable to provide a handwritten note immediately after the interview, send an e-mail thanking the company representatives the same day as the interview. As with a handwritten thank-you note, ensure your communication is professional, error-free, and includes identifying contact information.

After the Interview

After sending or delivering your thank-you notes, congratulate yourself. If you did your best, you should have no regrets. When you are able, make notes regarding specific information you learned about your prospective job and questions you were asked during the interview. In the excitement of an interview, you may forget parts of your meeting if you do not immediately make notes. Write down what you did right and areas in which you would like to improve. This is a good time for you to evaluate your impressions of the company and determine if it is a company where you will want to work. This information will be helpful in future interviews.

Salary Negotiation

Soon after your initial interview, you should hear back from the company. At that point, you may be called in for a second interview or may receive a job offer. A job offer may be contingent upon reference and background checks. This will be a good time to contact the individuals on your reference list to provide them an update on your job search and ensure they are prepared to respond appropriately to the individual conducting your reference check.

If you are a final candidate for the job, the interviewer may ask you about your salary requirements. In order to negotiate an acceptable salary, first conduct online research and compare your research to the salary range that was included in the job announcement. Determine local and regional salaries and attempt to match the job description as closely as possible to that of the job for which you are applying. Depending on your experience, start a few thousand dollars higher than your desired starting salary and do not forget to consider your experience or lack thereof. Some companies do not offer many benefits but offer higher salaries. Other companies offer lower salaries but better benefits. Weigh these factors when determining your desired salary. Prior to stating your salary requirement, sell your skills. For example, "Ms. Dancey, as I mentioned in my initial interview, I have over five years' experience working in a professional accounting office and an accounting degree; therefore, I feel I should earn between $35,000 and $45,000." If you are offered a salary that is not acceptable, use silence and wait for the interviewer to respond. This minute of silence may encourage the employer to offer a higher salary.

Topic Situation

TOPIC RESPONSE

Why is it important to research, know, and state a desired salary when asked during an interview?

Isaac had a successful interview because he did his research and practiced questions. Isaac received a call from the employer and was invited to a second interview. Prior to the interview, Isaac reviewed notes from his first interview and again prepared for potential questions and situations that he might encounter. Isaac had his friend Bret help him practice for the second interview. In their practice, Bret asked Isaac about his starting salary. Isaac said he did not care; he would just be happy to get a job. Bret reminded Isaac that he needed to sell his skills and have a desired target salary. They then conducted an Internet search of both local and statewide jobs that were similar to the one Isaac wanted.

Pre-Employment Tests, Screenings, and Medical Exams

Pre-employment tests are assessments that are given to potential employees as a means of determining if the applicant possesses the desired knowledge, skills, or abilities required for a job. Pre-employment tests can be giving during the application process, during the interview process, or prior to receiving a job offer. Some employers require applicants to take online pre-employment tests. Some tests may require lifting, others are skills-based, and others measure listening or logic. Legally, pre-employment tests must be job-related. Depending on the type of test, you may be given the results immediately. In other cases, you may need to wait for the results. If you pass the employment test(s), you will be invited to proceed with the interview process. It is common for employers to have applicants who did not pass a pre-employment test to wait a predetermined period prior to reapplying.

Employers may also conduct pre-employment screenings and medical exams. Pre-employment screenings include criminal checks, education verification, driver's license history, security checks, previous employment checks, credit checks, reference checks, and drug tests. The number and type of pre-employment screenings performed will be based on how relevant the check is to the job you will be performing. Legally, employers can require medical exams only after a job offer is made, but they may require pre-employment drug tests. The exam must be required for all applicants for the same job, and the exam must be job-related. Employers are not allowed to ask disability questions related to pre-employment screenings and medical exams. Common medical exams include vision and strength testing.

An employer legally cannot conduct these checks without your permission. Most employers will secure your permission in writing when you complete an employment application or when you are a finalist for the position.

When You are Not Offered the Job

A job search is a full-time job and can sometimes be discouraging. When you are not invited to interview, reevaluate your job search approach and tools. First consider your target companies. Ensure you are applying for jobs that fit your current knowledge, skills, and abilities. Continuous networking increases the chances your résumé package will receive the proper attention. Pay attention to application instructions and deadlines. Only submit complete application materials and submit them on time. Most companies require a completed application, cover letter, and résumé. Some companies require all submissions be made online, whereas others prefer a traditional approach with a simple paper résumé package. Evaluate your résumé and cover letter. Your cover letter should spark curiosity in the reader by emphasizing select details of your qualifications and make them want to read the attached résumé. Review both for typographical or grammatical errors. Ensure you have referenced key words directly from the job description and that your résumé lists important skills that reflect the needs of your target job. Have someone who knows you and your skills, and whom you trust, review your cover letter and résumé. Many times, a fresh perspective will catch obvious errors or opportunities for improvement. Although many job applicants state they will follow up in their cover letter, many do not. If you indicated you would follow up, do so within two weeks of submitting your application package. This provides you an additional opportunity to communicate your interest and qualifications for the target position.

If you are invited to interview but do not receive a job offer, do not be discouraged. Remember to make every experience a learning experience. Review your personal commercial to ensure it is personal, powerful, and unique. With notes you took from past interviews, carefully review each step in the interview process and grade yourself. Consider your preparation, your appearance, your responses, your ability to interject company research into each answer, and your overall attitude. Any area that did not receive an "A" grade is an area poised for improvement.

There are several steps you can take to increase the probability for success in your next interview. Consider your overall appearance. Make sure you convey professionalism from head to toe. Ensure that your clothes are clean and fit properly. Have a hairstyle that is flattering and well-kempt. Check that your fingernails and jewelry are appropriate and do not distract from your personality and job skills.

Mentally review job interview questions that were asked and the responses you provided. Every answer should communicate how your knowledge, skills, and abilities will assist the target company in achieving success. Review the amount of company research you conducted. Did you feel amply prepared, or did you simply research the bare minimum? If you felt you did conduct the appropriate amount of research, evaluate whether you fully communicated your research to the interviewer.

Assess your body language and attitude. Stand in front of a mirror and practice your answers to difficult and/or illegal questions. If possible, have a friend videotape you and provide an honest evaluation of your appearance, attitude, and body language. Check for nervous gestures, and keep practicing until you are able to control nervous habits.

Be honest about your overall performance before, during, and after the interview. Review your activities after the interview, including immediately sending a thank-you note. Prior to your next interview, identify at least two areas of the interview process you would like to improve and begin working on those areas. Improving these areas will make you a stronger interviewee so that you stand out above all other candidates and receive a coveted job offer.

Workplace Dos and Don'ts

Do tailor your résumé and personal commercial to the needs of your targeted employer	*Don't* have unprofessional introductions on your voice mail message
Do try to schedule your interview at a time that puts you at an advantage over the other candidates and secure information that better prepares you for the interview	*Don't* make demands from the individual scheduling the interview
Do learn as much as you can about the company, its strategy, and its competition	*Don't* arrive late or too early
Do practice interview questions and formulate answers that highlight your skills and experience	*Don't* forget to include company and industry research information in your interview responses
Do remember that your interview begins the minute you step onto company property	*Don't* show up to an interview unprepared and empty handed
Do know how to handle inappropriate questions that may be discriminatory	*Don't* let your nerves get the better of you in a job interview
Do prepare questions to ask the interviewer	*Don't* answer an illegal question; instead address the issue

Concept Review and Application

You are a Successful Student if you:

- Create an interview portfolio
- Videotape yourself in a practice interview
- Identify and create responses to difficult interview questions specific to you and your situation

Summary of Key Concepts

- Create and modify your personal commercial and adapt it to the requirements of your target job.

- Review common interview questions and formulate answers as part of your interview preparation.

- Conduct a pre-interview rehearsal to ensure you are prepared the day of the interview.

- During your interview, communicate how your knowledge, skills, and abilities will be assets to the company.

- Understand the laws that protect employees from discrimination in the interviewing and hiring process.

- Be prepared to confidently handle gaps in employment and other difficult interview questions.

- Know how to sell yourself and professionally ask for the job at the close of an interview.

Self-Quiz MATCHING KEY TERMS

Match the key term to the definition using the identifying number.

Key Terms	Answer	Definitions
Behavioral interview question		1. An interview that involves a one-on-one meeting between the applicant and a company representative
Group interview		2. A type of interview question that addresses job-related issues where each applicant is asked the same question
Interview portfolio		3. A mental form of positive self-reinforcement that helps remind you that you are qualified and deserve both the interview and the job
One-on-one interview		4. An interview that involves several applicants interviewing at the same time while being observed by company representatives
Panel interview		5. A brief career biography that conveys one's career choice, knowledge, skills, strengths, abilities, and experiences
Personal commercial		6. An interview that involves the applicant meeting with several company employees at the same time
Positive self-talk		7. A probing, open-ended interview question intended to identify if the candidate can appropriately sell his or her skills
Structured interview question		8. Interview question that asks candidates to share a past experience related to a specific workplace situation
Unstructured interview question		9. A folder to be taken on an interview that contains photocopies of documents and items pertinent to a position

Think Like a Boss

1. What kind of information should you share with your current staff members as they prepare to interview a new employee?

2. How would you handle a prospective employee who disclosed inappropriate information during the job interview?

Activities

Activity 1

Identify a local company for which you would like to interview. Using the following table, conduct a thorough targeted job search on this company. Answer as many of the questions as possible.

Company name	
Company address	
Job title	
To whom should the cover letter be addressed?	
What are the job requirements?	
Is this a full-time or part-time job?	
What are the hours/days of work?	
What are the working conditions?	
Is there room for advancement?	
What kind of training is offered?	
What other positions at this company match my qualifications?	
What are the average starting salaries (benefits)?	
Is traveling or relocation required?	
Where is the business located (home office, other offices)?	
What are the products or services that the employer provides or manufactures?	
What is the mission statement?	

(Continued)

What kind of reputation does this organization have?	
What is the size of the employer's organization relative to the industry?	
What is the growth history of the organization for the past 5, 10, or 15 years?	
How long has the employer been in business?	
Who is the employer's competition?	

Activity 2

Using information from Exercise 2, write a personal commercial.

_____

_____

_____

_____

_____

Activity 3

Write a statement to use during an invitation to an interview that will help you secure all relevant interview information.

_____

_____

Activity 4

Using information obtained in your target company research (Activity 1), write three common interview questions and answers. Integrate relevant company information and examples in your answers.

Question	Answer
1.	
2.	
3.	

Activity 5

Conduct a salary search for a target job. Identify the salary range. Using your research data, write out a statement you could use to negotiate a higher salary.

Lowest Salary	Highest Salary
$	$

Salary Negotiation Statement:

_____

_____

Activity 6

Without using an example provided in this chapter, write one question that you can ask at the end of an interview.

_____

_____

Glossary

behavioral interview question: interview question that asks candidates to share a past experience related to a specific workplace situation

group interview: an interview that involves several applicants interviewing at the same time while being observed by company representatives

interview portfolio: a folder to be taken on an interview that contains photocopies of documents and items pertinent to a position

one-on-one interview: an interview that involves a one-on-one meeting between the applicant and a company representative

panel interview: an interview that involves the applicant meeting with several company employees at the same time

personal commercial: a brief career biography that conveys one's career choice, knowledge, skills, strengths, abilities, and experiences

positive self-talk: a mental form of positive self-reinforcement that helps remind you that you are qualified and deserve both the interview and the job

structured interview question: a type of interview question that addresses job-related issues where each applicant is asked the same question

unstructured interview question: a probing, open-ended interview question intended to identify if the candidate can appropriately sell his or her skills

Suggested Readings

"How to Stand Out from the Crowd and Kick-Start Your Own Recovery," *U.S. News & World Report* 147 (May 2010): 14–16.

National Association of Colleges and Employers, Bethlehem, PA, www.Jobweb .com

Smith, J. (2013 July 2). "7 Things You Can Do After A Really Bad Job Interview," http://forbes.com

Skorkin, A. The Main Reason Why You Suck at Interviews: Lack of Preparation. *Lifehacker.com*, http://lifehacker.com/5710712/the-main-reason-why-you-suck-at-interviews-lack-of-preparation December 10, 2010.

Credit

appendix

Managing Your Personal Finances

Dealing with personal finances is a lifelong job involving a crucial choice between two options:

1 Committing to the rational management of your personal finances by controlling them, helping them grow, and therefore enjoying greater personal satisfaction and financial stability.

2 Letting the financial chips fall where they may and hoping for the best (which seldom happens) and therefore inviting frustration, disappointment, and financial distress.

Personal finance management requires consideration of cash management, financial planning and control, investment alternatives, and risk. Let's start by looking at one key factor in success: the personal financial plan. We'll then discuss the steps in the planning process and show how you can make better decisions to manage your personal finances.

Building Your Financial Plan

Financial planning is the process of looking at your current financial condition, identifying your goals, and anticipating steps toward meeting those goals. Because your goals and finances will change as you get older, your plan should always allow for revision. Figure 1 summarizes a step-by-step approach to personal financial planning.

Financial Planning *process of looking at one's current financial condition, identifying one's goals, and anticipating requirements for meeting those goals*

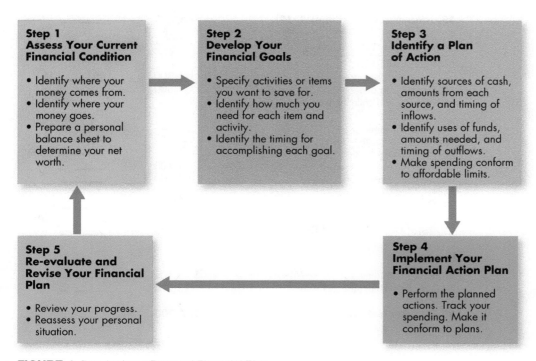

Step 1
Assess Your Current Financial Condition

• Identify where your money comes from.
• Identify where your money goes.
• Prepare a personal balance sheet to determine your net worth.

Step 2
Develop Your Financial Goals

• Specify activities or items you want to save for.
• Identify how much you need for each item and activity.
• Identify the timing for accomplishing each goal.

Step 3
Identify a Plan of Action

• Identify sources of cash, amounts from each source, and timing of inflows.
• Identify uses of funds, amounts needed, and timing of outflows.
• Make spending conform to affordable limits.

Step 5
Re-evaluate and Revise Your Financial Plan

• Review your progress.
• Reassess your personal situation.

Step 4
Implement Your Financial Action Plan

• Perform the planned actions. Track your spending. Make it conform to plans.

FIGURE 1 Developing a Personal Financial Plan

From Appendix III of *Business Essentials*, Eleventh Edition. Ronald J. Ebert, Ricky W. Griffin. Copyright © 2017 by Pearson Education, Inc. All rights reserved.

509

Assessing Your Current Financial Condition

Personal Net Worth *value of one's total assets minus one's total liabilities (debts)*

The first step in developing a personal financial plan is assessing your current financial position. Your **personal net worth** is the value of all your assets minus all your liabilities (debts) *at the present time.* The worksheet in Figure 2 provides some sample calculations for developing your own personal "balance sheet." Because assets and liabilities change over time, updating your balance sheet not only allows you to monitor changes but also provides more accurate information for realistic budgeting and planning.

Assets: What You Own	Example Numbers	Your Numbers
LIQUID ASSETS:		
1. Cash $	300	
2. Savings +	3,700	
3. Checking +	1,200	
INVESTMENTS:		
4. IRAs +	12,400	
5. Securities +	500	
6. Retirement Plan +	—	
7. Real Estate (other than primary residence) +	—	
HOUSEHOLD:		
8. Cars (market value) +	18,000	
9. House (market value) +	—	
10. Furniture +	3,400	
11. Personal Property +	6,600	
12. Other assets	—	
13. Total Assets (add lines 1–12)	**= $46,100**	
Liabilities (Dept): What You Owe		
CURRENT LIABILITIES:		
14. Credit-card balance $	1,300	
15. Unpaid bills due +	1,800	
16. Alimony and child support +	—	
LONG-TERM LIABILITIES:		
17. Home mortgage +	—	
18. Home equity loan +	—	
19. Car loan +	4,100	
20. Student loan +	3,600	
21. Other liabilities +	2,400	
22. Total Liabilities (add lines 14–21)	**= $13,200**	
Net Worth		
23. Total Assets (line 13)	$ 46,100	
24. Less: Total Debt (line 22) –	13,200	
25. Results: Net Worth	**= $32,900**	

FIGURE 2 Worksheet for Calculating Net Worth

Develop Your Financial Goals

Step 2 involves setting three different types of future goals: *immediate* (within one year), *intermediate* (within five years), and *long-term* (more than five years). The worksheet in Figure 3 will help you establish these goals. By thinking about your finances in three different time frames, you'll be better able to set measurable goals and completion times, or to set priorities for rationing your resources if, at some point, you're not able to pursue all your goals.

Because Step 3 (identifying a plan of action) and Step 4 (implementing your plan) will affect your assets and liabilities, your balance sheet will change over time. As a result, Step 5 (re-evaluating and revising your plan) needs periodic updating.

Name the Goal	Financial Requirement (Amount) for This Goal	Time Frame for Accomplishing Goal	Importance (1= Highest, 5 = Lowest)
Immediate Goals:			
Live in a better apartment			
Establish an emergency cash fund			
Pay off credit-card debt			
Other			
Intermediate Goals:			
Obtain adequate health, life, disability, liability, property insurance			
Save for wedding			
Save to buy new car			
Establish regular savings program (5% of gross income)			
Save for college for self			
Pay off major outstanding debt			
Make major purchase			
Save for home remodeling			
Save for down payment on a home			
Other			
Long-Term Goals:			
Pay off home mortgage			
Save for college for children			
Save for vacation home			
Increase personal net worth to $___ in ___ years.			
Achieve retirement nest egg of $ __ in ___ years.			
Accumulate fund for travel in retirement			
Save for long-term care needs			
Other			

FIGURE 3 Worksheet for Setting Financial Goals

Making Better Use of the Time Value of Money

The value of time with any investment stems from the principle of compound growth, the compounding of interest received over several time periods. With each additional time period, interest receipts accumulate and earn even more interest, thus, multiplying the earning capacity of the investment. Whenever you make everyday purchases, you're giving up interest that you could have earned with the same money if you'd invested it instead. From a financial standpoint, "idle" or uninvested money, which could be put to work earning more money, is a wasted resource.

Planning for the Golden Years

The sooner you start saving, the greater your financial power will be—you will have taken advantage of the time value of money for a longer period of time. Consider coworkers Ellen and Barbara, who are both planning to retire in 25 years, as can be seen in Figure 4.

Over that period, assume that each can expect a 10 percent annual return on investment (the U.S. stock market averaged more than 10 percent for the 75 years before the 2008 recession). Their savings strategies, however, are different: Barbara begins saving immediately, whereas Ellen plans to start later but invest larger sums. Barbara will invest $2,000 annually for each of the next 5 years (years 1 through 5), for a total investment of $10,000. Ellen, meanwhile, wants to live a little larger by spending rather than saving for the next 10 years. Then, for years 11 through 20, she'll start saving $2,000 annually, for a total investment of $20,000. They will both allow annual

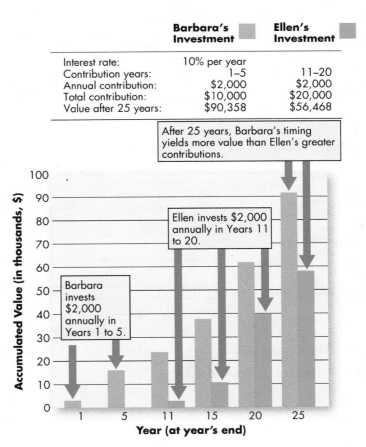

	Barbara's Investment	Ellen's Investment
Interest rate:	10% per year	
Contribution years:	1–5	11–20
Annual contribution:	$2,000	$2,000
Total contribution:	$10,000	$20,000
Value after 25 years:	$90,358	$56,468

After 25 years, Barbara's timing yields more value than Ellen's greater contributions.

Ellen invests $2,000 annually in Years 11 to 20.

Barbara invests $2,000 annually in Years 1 to 5.

FIGURE 4 Compounding Money over Time

n	1%	2%	4%	6%	8%	10%
1	1.010	1.020	1.040	1.060	1.080	1.100
2	1.020	1.040	1.082	1.124	1.166	1.210
3	1.030	1.061	1.125	1.191	1.260	1.331
4	1.041	1.082	1.170	1.262	1.360	1.464
5	1.051	1.104	1.217	1.338	1.469	1.611
6	1.062	1.126	1.265	1.419	1.587	1.772
7	1.072	1.149	1.316	1.504	1.714	1.949
8	1.083	1.172	1.369	1.594	1.851	2.144
9	1.094	1.195	1.423	1.689	1.999	2.358
10	1.105	1.219	1.480	1.791	2.159	2.594
15	1.161	1.346	1.801	2.397	3.172	4.177
20	1.220	1.486	2.191	3.207	4.661	6.727
25	1.282	1.641	2.666	4.292	6.848	10.834
30	1.348	1.811	3.243	5.743	10.062	17.449

Note: n = number of time periods; % = various interest rates

FIGURE 5 Timetable for Growing $1.00

returns to accumulate until they retire in year 25. Ellen expects to have a larger retirement fund than Barbara because she has contributed twice as much, but she is in for a surprise. Barbara's retirement wealth will be much larger—$90,364 versus Ellen's $56,468—even though she invested only half as much. Barbara's advantage lies in the length of her savings program. Her money is invested longer—over a period of 21 to 25 years—with interest compounding over that range of time. Ellen's earnings are compounded over a shorter period—6 to 15 years. Granted, Ellen may have had more fun in years 1 to 10, but Barbara's retirement prospects look brighter.

Time Value as a Financial-Planning Tool

A good financial plan takes into account future needs, the sources of funds for meeting those needs, and the time needed to develop those funds. When you begin your financial plan, you can use various time-based tables to take into account the time value of money. Figure 5 shows how much a $1.00 investment will grow over different lengths of time and at different interest rates.

A timetable like this can determine the factor at which your money will multiply over a given period of time and at a given interest rate. It can also help you determine how long and at what interest rate you will need to invest to meet your financial goals. For example, if you wanted to double your money in fewer than 10 years, you would have to find an interest rate of return of at least 8 percent. The catch is that to obtain a high interest rate, you will have to make riskier investments, such as buying stocks. Because higher interest rates carry greater risks, it is unwise to "put all your eggs in one basket." A sound financial plan will include more conservative investments, such as a bank savings account, to mitigate the risks of more speculative investments.

Conserving Money by Controlling It

A major pitfall in any financial plan is the temptation to spend too much, especially when credit is so easy to get. Because many credit-card issuers target college students and recent graduates with tempting offers appealing to the desire for financial independence, it is important that you arm yourself with a solid understanding of the financial costs entailed by credit cards. The same lessons apply equally to other loans, such as home mortgages, cars, and student financial aid.

Credit Cards: Keys to Satisfaction or Financial Handcuffs?

Although some credit cards don't charge annual fees, all of them charge interest on unpaid (outstanding) balances. Figure 6 reprints part of a page from Bankrate.com's credit-card calculator at www.bankrate.com/brm/calc/MinPayment.asp. Using the table as a guide, suppose you owe $5,000 for credit-card purchases, and your card company requires a minimum monthly payment (minimum payment due [MPD]) of 5 percent of the unpaid balance. The interest rate is 18 percent APR (annual percentage rate) on the outstanding balance.

If you pay only the monthly minimum, it will take you 115 months—more than 9½ years—to pay off your credit-card debt. During this time, you will pay $2,096.70 in interest, almost half again the principal balance! Repayment takes so long because you are making only the MPD, which decreases with each monthly payment.

Save Your Money: Lower Interest Rates and Faster Payments

Figure 6 confirms two principles for saving money that you can apply when borrowing from any source, not just credit cards: Look for lower interest rates and make faster repayments.

Seeking Lower Interest Rates Look again at Figure 6 and compare the cost of borrowing $5,000 at 18 percent with the cost of borrowing it at 9 percent. If you assume the same 5 percent minimum monthly payment, a 9 percent APR will save you $1,232.14 in interest during the repayment period—a nearly 59 percent savings.

Making Faster Payments Because money has a time value, lenders charge borrowers according to the length of time for which they borrow it. In general, longer lending periods increase the cost, and shorter periods are cheaper. Using Figure 6, compare the costs of the 5 percent MPD with the faster 10 percent MPD. The faster schedule cuts the repayment period from 115 to 55 months and, at 18 percent APR, reduces interest costs by $1,222.84.

Combining both faster repayment and the lower interest rate cuts your total interest cost to $450.30—a savings of $1,695.07 over the amount you'd pay if you made slower repayments at the higher rate.

Declining Asset Value: A Borrower's Regret Financially speaking, nothing's more disappointing than buying an expensive item and then discovering that it's not worth what you paid. For example, if you buy a $5,000 used car with a credit card at 18 percent APR and make only the MPD, as in the preceding example, you'll end up spending a total of $7,407.50 over 9½ years. By that time, however, the

Balance = $5,000	MPD 3%		MPD 5%		MPD 10%	
APR	Months	Costs	Months	Costs	Months	Costs
6%	144	$5,965.56	92	$5,544.58	50	$5,260.74
9%	158	$6,607.24	96	$5,864.56	51	$5,401.63
12%	175	$7,407.50	102	$6,224.26	53	$5,550.32
18%	226	$9,798.89	115	$7,096.70	55	$5,873.86
21%	266	$11,704.63	123	$7,632.92	57	$6,050.28

Note: APR, annual percentage rate; MPD, minimum payment due

FIGURE 6 Paying off Credit Card Debt

Renting	Buying
• No down payment to get started	• Must make payments for mortgage, property taxes, and insurance
• Flexibility to leave	• Equity builds up over time
• No obligation for upkeep or improvements	• More privacy
• No groundskeeping	• Value of property may increase
• Easy cash-flow planning (a single monthly payment)	• Lower income taxes: mortgage-interest and property tax payments reduce taxable income
• May provide access to recreation and social facilities	• Financial gains from selling house can be exempt from taxes
• Rental conditions may be changed by owner	• Greater control over use of property and improvements
• Timing for repairs controlled by owner	• The home can become a source of cash by refinancing with another mortgage loan or a home-equity loan

FIGURE 7 To Buy or Not to Buy

car you bought will be worth less than $1,000. Some of this loss in asset value can be avoided through realistic planning and spending—by knowing and staying within your financial means.

Financial Commitments of Home Ownership

Deciding whether to rent or buy a home involves a variety of considerations, including life stage, family needs, career, financial situation, and preferred lifestyle. If you decide to buy, you have to ask yourself what you can afford, and that requires asking yourself questions about your personal financial condition and your capacity for borrowing. Figure 7 summarizes the key considerations in deciding whether to rent or buy.

How Much House Can You Afford?

Buying a home is the biggest investment in most people's lives. Unfortunately, many make the mistake of buying a house that they can't afford, resulting in unnecessary stress and even devastating financial loss. This happened on a massive scale in the housing downfall that began in 2007 and has not fully ended. The seeds for destruction sprouted during the years 2000–2007 when millions of optimistic home buyers borrowed beyond their means by getting larger loans than they could afford. With the rising demand for home ownership, housing prices became inflated and borrowers responded by seeking unrealistically larger loans. They expected market prices would continue to rise indefinitely, thereby providing a profitable investment. Borrowers were aided by lenders using loose credit standards, unlike the time-proven standards that will be presented here, leading to unrealistic repayment requirements. By 2007, the housing market was oversold and the U.S. economy entered a severe recession. With rising unemployment, borrowers were unable to meet monthly payments, especially when interest rates (and thus payments) on loans increased; housing vacancies increased and property values plummeted. Borrowers lost their homes and the equity they had built up in them. The depressed housing market did not begin to revive until 2014.

In addition to loan payments, the typical demands of ownership, time and other resources for maintaining and improving a home, tend to cut into the money left over for recreation, eating out, taking vacations, and so on. You can reduce the financial pressure by calculating in advance a realistic price range—one that not only lets you buy a house but also lets you live a reasonably pleasant life once you're in it.

Most people need a loan to buy a house, apartment, or condominium. A **mortgage loan** is secured by the property—the home—being purchased. Because the size of a loan depends on the cost of the property, both borrowers and lenders want to know whether the buyer can afford the house he or she wants. To determine how much you can afford, one time-tested (though somewhat conservative) rule recommends

Mortgage Loan *loan secured by property (the home) being purchased*

Interest Rate (%)	Length of Loan				
	3 Years	5 Years	10 Years	20 Years	30 Years
5.0	$299.71	$188.71	$106.07	$66.00	$53.68
6.0	304.22	193.33	111.02	71.64	59.96
6.5	306.49	195.66	113.55	74.56	63.21
7.0	308.77	198.01	116.11	77.53	66.53
8.0	313.36	202.76	121.33	83.65	73.38
9.0	318.00	207.58	126.68	89.98	80.47
10.0	322.67	212.47	132.16	96.51	87.76
11.0	327.39	217.42	137.76	103.22	95.24
12.0	332.14	222.44	143.48	110.11	102.86

FIGURE 8 Monthly Payments on a $10,000 Loan

keeping the price below 2½ times your annual income. If your income is $48,000, look for a house priced below $120,000.

Any such calculation, however, will give you just a rough estimate of what you can afford. You should also consider how much money you have for a down payment and how much you can borrow. Lending institutions want to determine a buyer's borrowing capacity, the borrower's ability to meet the *recurring costs* of buying and owning.

PITI Every month, the homeowner must pay principal (pay back some of the borrowed money), along with interest, taxes, and homeowner's insurance, or PITI, for short. As Figure 8 shows, the size of principal and interest payments depends on (1) the mortgage amount, (2) the length of the mortgage loan, and (3) the interest rate.

In evaluating loan applications, lenders use PITI calculations to estimate the buyer's ability to meet monthly payments. To determine how much someone is likely to lend you, calculate 28 percent of your gross monthly income (that is, before taxes and other deductions). If your PITI costs don't exceed that figure, your loan application probably will receive favorable consideration. With a monthly gross income of $4,000, for example, your PITI costs shouldn't exceed $1,120 (28 percent of $4,000). Additional calculations show a house price of $162,382 is the most this borrower can afford. Figure 9 gives a sample calculation, and you should be able to make step-by-step computations by plugging your own numbers into the worksheet.

Other Debt In evaluating financial capacity, lenders also look at any additional outstanding debt, such as loans and credit-card bills. They will generally accept indebtedness (including PITI) up to 36 percent of gross income. Because PITI itself can be up to 28 percent, you might be allowed as little as 8 percent in other long-term debt. With your $4,000 monthly gross income, your total debt should be less than $1,440 ($1,120 for PITI and $320 for other debt). If your total debt exceeds $1,440, you may have to settle for a smaller loan than the one you calculated with the PITI method. Websites such as http://mortgages.interest.com provide mortgage calculators for testing interest rates, lengths of loans, and other personal financial information.

Cashing Out from Tax Avoidance (Legally)

Personal expenditures always require cash outflows; some also reduce your tax bill and save you some cash. Individual retirement accounts (IRAs) and some education savings accounts have this effect. (Before you commit any money to these instruments or activities, check with an expert on tax regulations; they change from time to time.)

ASSUMPTIONS:

30-year mortgage
Closing costs (fees for property, survey, credit report, title search,
     title insurance, attorney, interest advance, loan origination) = $5,000
Funds available for closing costs and down payment = $25,000
Interest rate on mortgage = 6½% per year
Estimated real estate taxes = $200 per month
Estimated homeowner's insurance = $20 month

Example Numbers   Your Numbers

1. Monthly income, gross (before taxes or deductions)........$4,000   _____
2. Apply PITI ratio (0.28 x amount on line 1) to determine
    borrower's payment capacity:
    0.28 x $4,000 = ...$1,120   _____
3. Determine mortgage payment (principal and interest)
    by subtracting taxes and insurance from
    PITI (line 2)...–$ 220   _____
4. Result: Maximum mortgage payment
    (principal and interest)................................. $900   _____

5. Using Table Figure 11, find the monthly mortgage payment
    on a $10,000 loan at 6½% interest for
    30 years.. $63.21   _____
6. Since each $10,000 loan requires a $63.21 monthly payment,
    how many $10,000 loans can the borrower afford
    with the $900 payment capacity? The answer is
    determined as follows:
        $900.00/$63.21 =
        14.2382 loans of $10,000 each   _____

7. Result: Maximum allowable mortgage loan [calculated
    as follows]:
        14.2382 loans (from line 6 above)
        x $10,000 per loan] = ...**$142,382**   _____

8. Result: Maximum house price borrower can afford
    using PITI (amount of house that can be bought with
    available funds):

        From loan...........................$142,382   _____
        From down payment............$ 25,000   _____
        Less closing cost.................–$ 5,000   _____

               ....**$162,382**   _____

FIGURE 9 Worksheet for PITI Calculations

The IRA Tax Break

With a **traditional individual retirement account (IRA)**, you can make an annual tax-deductible savings deposit of up to $5,000, depending on your income level. IRAs are long-term investments, intended to provide income after age 59½. For distant future savings, an IRA boasts immediate cash advantages over a typical savings account because it reduces your current taxable income by the amount of your contribution.

Here's how it works: You're a qualified employee with a federal income tax rate of 20 percent in year 2009. If you contribute $4,000 to an IRA, you avoid $800 in income taxes (0.20 × $4,000 = $800). Your untaxed contributions and their accumulated earnings will be taxed later when you withdraw money from your IRA. The tax break is based on the assumption that, after you retire, you're likely to have less total income and will have to pay less tax on the money withdrawn as income from your IRA.

Traditional Individual Retirement Account (IRA) *provision allowing individual tax-deferred retirement savings*

Assumptions:
    Initial contribution and earnings average 10 percent growth annually.
    Initial contribution and earnings remain invested for 40 years.
    Income tax rate is 30 percent.
	Traditional IRA	Roth IRA

Initial cash contribution to IRA	$3,000	$3,000
Income tax paid initially: $4,285 income x 30% tax rate = $1,285 tax	0	1,285
Total initial cash outlay	**$3,000**	**$4,285**
Accumulated earnings (40 years)	$132,774	$132,774
Initial contribution	+ 3,000	+ 3,000
Total available for distribution after 40 years	= $135,774	= $135,774
Income tax at time of distribution	− $40,732	0
After-tax distribution (cash)	**= $95,042**	**= $135,774**

FIGURE 10   Cash Flows: Roth IRA versus Traditional IRA

IRA Risks If you underestimate your future cash requirements and have to withdraw money before you reach 59½, you'll probably get hit with a 10 percent penalty. You can, however, make penalty-free withdrawals under certain circumstances: buying a first home, paying college expenses, and paying large medical bills.

The unpredictability of future income tax rates also poses a financial risk. If tax rates increase substantially, future IRA withdrawals may be taxed at higher rates, which may offset your original tax savings.

Roth IRA *provision allowing individual retirement savings with tax-free accumulated earnings*

Roth IRA versus Traditional IRA The **Roth IRA** is the reverse of the traditional IRA in that contributions are not tax deductible, withdrawals on initial contribution are not penalized, and withdrawals on accumulated earnings after the age of 59½ are not taxed.

Figure 10 shows the significant advantage of this last feature. Accumulated earnings typically far outweigh the initial contribution, so although you pay an extra $1,285 in front-end taxes, you get $40,732 in additional cash at retirement—and even more if income-tax rates have increased.

IRAs and Education Depending on your income level, you can contribute up to $2,000 annually to a Coverdell Education Savings Account (also known as an *Education IRA*) for each child under age 18. As with the Roth IRA, your initial contribution is not tax deductible, your earnings are tax-free, and you pay no tax on withdrawals to pay for qualified education expenses. However, the Education IRA requires that you use the money by the time your child reaches age 30. Funds that you withdraw but don't use for stipulated education expense are subject to taxation plus a 10-percent penalty.

Protecting Your Net Worth

With careful attention, thoughtful saving and spending, and skillful financial planning (and a little luck), you can build up your net worth over time. Every financial plan should also consider steps for preserving it. One approach involves the risk–return relationship. Do you prefer to protect your current assets, or are you willing to risk them in return for greater financial growth? At various life stages and levels of wealth, you should adjust your asset portfolio to conform to your risk and return preferences: conservative, moderate, or aggressive.

Why Buy Life Insurance?

You can think of life insurance as a tool for financial preservation. A life insurance policy is a promise to pay beneficiaries after the death of the insured party who paid the insurance company premiums during his or her lifetime.

What Does Life Insurance Do?

Upon the death of the policyholder, life insurance replaces income on which someone else is dependent. The amount of insurance you need depends on how many other people rely on your income. For example, while insurance makes sense for a married parent who is a family's sole source of income, a single college student with no financial dependents needs little or no insurance.

How Much Should I Buy?

The more insurance you buy, the more it's going to cost you. To estimate the amount of coverage you need, begin by adding up all your annual expenses—rent, food, clothing, transportation, schooling, debts to be paid—that you pay for the dependents who would survive you. Then multiply the total by the number of years that you want the insurance to cover them. Typically, this sum will amount to several times—even 10 to 20 times—your current annual income.

Why Consider Term Insurance?

Term insurance pays a predetermined benefit when death occurs during the stipulated policy term. If the insured outlives the term, the policy loses its value and simply ceases. Term-life premiums are significantly lower than premiums for whole-life insurance.

Unlike term life, *whole-life insurance*, also known as *cash-value insurance*, remains in force as long as premiums are paid. In addition to paying a death benefit, whole life accumulates cash value over time—a form of savings. Paid-in money can be withdrawn; however, whole-life savings earn less interest than most alternative forms of investment.

How Much Does It Cost?

The cost of insurance depends on how much you buy, your life expectancy, and other statistical risk factors. To get the best match between your policy and your personal situation, you should evaluate the terms and conditions of a variety of policies. You can get convenient comparisons on websites such as www.intelliquote.com.

glossary

Financial Planning process of looking at one's current financial condition, identifying one's goals, and anticipating requirements for meeting those goals.

Mortgage Loan loan secured by property (the home) being purchased.

Personal Net Worth value of one's total assets minus one's total liabilities (debts).

Roth IRA provision allowing individual retirement savings with tax-free accumulated earnings.

Traditional Individual Retirement Account (IRA) provision allowing individual tax-deferred retirement savings.

Index